SUSE
LINUX

Other Linux resources from O'Reilly

Related titles
Fedora Linux
Knoppix Hacks™
Linux Annoyances for Geeks
Linux Cookbook™
Linux Desktop Hacks™
Linux in a Nutshell
Linux Network Administrator's Guide
Linux Multimedia Hacks™
Linux Security Cookbook™
Linux Server Hacks™
Linux Server Security
Running Linux
Ubuntu Hacks™

Linux Books Resource Center
linux.oreilly.com is a complete catalog of O'Reilly's books on Linux and Unix and related technologies, including sample chapters and code examples.

ONLamp.com is the premier site for the open source web platform: Linux, Apache, MySQL, and either Perl, Python, or PHP.

Conferences
O'Reilly brings diverse innovators together to nurture the ideas that spark revolutionary industries. We specialize in documenting the latest tools and systems, translating the innovator's knowledge into useful skills for those in the trenches. Visit *conferences.oreilly.com* for our upcoming events.

Safari Bookshelf (*safari.oreilly.com*) is the premier online reference library for programmers and IT professionals. Conduct searches across more than 1,000 books. Subscribers can zero in on answers to time-critical questions in a matter of seconds. Read the books on your Bookshelf from cover to cover or simply flip to the page you need. Try it today for free.

SUSE LINUX

Chris Brown

O'REILLY®
Beijing · Cambridge · Farnham · Köln · Paris · Sebastopol · Taipei · Tokyo

SUSE Linux
by Chris Brown
Contributor: Simon Crute

Copyright © 2006 O'Reilly Media, Inc. All rights reserved.
Printed in the United States of America.

Published by O'Reilly Media, Inc., 1005 Gravenstein Highway North, Sebastopol, CA 95472.

O'Reilly books may be purchased for educational, business, or sales promotional use. Online editions are also available for most titles (*safari.oreilly.com*). For more information, contact our corporate/institutional sales department: (800) 998-9938 or *corporate@oreilly.com*.

Editor: Brian Jepson
Production Editor: Darren Kelly
Copyeditor: Nancy Kotary
Proofreaders: Genevieve d'Entremont, Colleen Gorman, and Darren Kelly

Indexer: John Bickelhaupt
Cover Designer: Marcia Friedman
Interior Designer: David Futato
Illustrators: Robert Romano and Jessamyn Reed

Printing History:

July 2006: First Edition.

Nutshell Handbook, the Nutshell Handbook logo, and the O'Reilly logo are registered trademarks of O'Reilly Media, Inc. The *Linux* series designations, *SUSE Linux*, images of the American West, and related trade dress are trademarks of O'Reilly Media, Inc.

Many of the designations used by manufacturers and sellers to distinguish their products are claimed as trademarks. Where those designations appear in this book, and O'Reilly Media, Inc. was aware of a trademark claim, the designations have been printed in caps or initial caps.

While every precaution has been taken in the preparation of this book, the publisher and author assume no responsibility for errors or omissions, or for damages resulting from the use of the information contained herein.

RepKover. This book uses RepKover™, a durable and flexible lay-flat binding.

ISBN: 0-596-10183-X
[M]

Table of Contents

Preface ix

1. Quick Start 1
    1.1 Installing SUSE Linux from Local Media   1
    1.2 Set Up a Local Printer   12
    1.3 Get Started with Email   16
    1.4 Configure a Network Card   21
    1.5 Access Documentation   27

2. Basic System Administration 33
    2.1 View and Edit Text Files   34
    2.2 Explore the Filesystem   40
    2.3 Manage Files and Directories   47
    2.4 Set File Access Permissions and Ownership   52
    2.5 Access a Remote Printer   57
    2.6 Create User Accounts   60
    2.7 Rescue a System That Won't Boot   66
    2.8 Finding Files   72
    2.9 Mounting Filesystems   78
    2.10 Access Your Desktop Remotely   84

3. Using SUSE Linux on Your Desktop 89
    3.1 Configure Your Graphics Card and Monitor   90
    3.2 Configure Your Keyboard and Mouse   97
    3.3 Configure the KDE Menus and Panel   104
    3.4 Configure the KDE Desktop   109
    3.5 Lock Down the Desktop for Kiosk Mode   115
    3.6 Configure the GNOME Desktop   119

		3.7 Play Audio and Video	123
		3.8 Burn Your Own CDs and DVDs	128
		3.9 Capture Screenshots	132
		3.10 Use Command-Line Tools	136
		3.11 Configure Multiheaded Displays	143
		3.12 Animate the Desktop with Xgl and Compiz	148
	4.	**Using Linux on Your Laptop**	**155**
		4.1 Configure Laptop Power Management	155
		4.2 Configure Wireless Networking	159
		4.3 Configure Bluetooth Devices	165
		4.4 Synchronize Files with Your Desktop	172
	5.	**Package Management**	**180**
		5.1 Find Out What's Installed	180
		5.2 Finding the Packages You Need	188
		5.3 Install and Upgrade RPMs	191
		5.4 Remove Software Packages	198
		5.5 Perform an Online Update	199
		5.6 Manage Software Packages Using ZENWorks	202
		5.7 Manage Software Packages Using YUM	209
		5.8 Compile and Install Source Code	212
	6.	**System Administration for Servers**	**224**
		6.1 Control Boot-Time Service Startup	224
		6.2 Start Services on Demand	232
		6.3 Create and Mount Disk Partitions	237
		6.4 Create Logical Volumes	248
		6.5 Monitor and Manage Processes	255
		6.6 Examine and Manage Log Files	264
		6.7 Monitor System Load and Performance	270
		6.8 Backup and Restore Filesystems	275
		6.9 Configure and Debug Network Interfaces	283
		6.10 Configure Name Resolution	292
	7.	**Network Services**	**297**
		7.1 Set Up Disk Quotas	297
		7.2 Configure a DNS Server	301
		7.3 Share Files Using NFS	308
		7.4 Serve Filesystems to Windows with Samba	314

		7.5	Configure a DHCP Server	321
		7.6	Configure a Web Server with Apache	327
		7.7	Configure a Mail Server	334

8. Security 342

8.1	Set a Boot-Time Password	343
8.2	Provide Secure Remote Login with SSH	344
8.3	Set Up a Firewall	356
8.4	Define a Security Level	363
8.5	Provide Role-Based Access Control with sudo	368
8.6	Assess Vulnerabilities Using Nessus	373
8.7	Detect Intrusion	380
8.8	Protect Your Applications with AppArmor	386

9. Alternative Installations 393

9.1	Configure a Dual-Boot System	393
9.2	Install from an Installation Server	399
9.3	Automate Installations with AutoYaST	403
9.4	Run Multiple Operating Systems with Xen	411

Index 421

Preface

Welcome to SUSE Linux: A Complete Guide to Novell's Community Distribution. I have tried to make this an intensely accessible book: its lab-based structure focuses on real, practical activities. Each lab is largely self-contained; there is no underlying plot or thematic development requiring you to start at page 1. No prior knowledge of Linux is needed, but I do assume some level of computer literacy. My ideal reader, I suppose, is the enthusiastic pilgrim journeying from the Land of Windows, or from a commercial version of Unix, or from some other flavor of Linux, or from Mac OS X (though the fierce brand loyalty of Mac users makes such pilgrimages unusual).

I have tried to strike a balance between using the desktop and using the command line. If a job can be done both using YaST (SUSE's configuration tool) and at the command line, I have in many cases covered both methods. If you need a primer on using Linux at the command line, start with Lab 3.10, "Use Command-Line Tools."

Brown's law states that things always take longer than you expect. It didn't state that yesterday, because I only just made it up. But it does today. Brown's law is recursive. That is, it still applies even after you've applied it. A more complete statement might be, "Things always take longer than you would expect even after allowing for the fact that they will take longer than you expect." (I have always wanted to have a law named after me. Trouble is, all the really good laws have been claimed already by eminent physicists such as Newton, Einstein, and, of course, Murphy. But I think that Brown's law is every bit as fundamental as gravity and relativity.)

By all of which I am trying to get around to the confession that I started writing this book around February 2005. At the time, SUSE Linux 9.3 was the latest version. About halfway through writing, SUSE Linux 10.0 came out. And as I wrap up the final round of revisions and we put the book into production, SUSE 10.1 is with us. Fortunately, each release of SUSE Linux represents an evolution, rather than a revolution, of what has gone before. Much of what I discuss in this book is relevant to all versions of SUSE Linux. (Actually, much of it is relevant to other Linux distributions, too.) I trust that you won't be too much dismayed by any cosmetic differences between the screenshots in the book and the ones you'll see in whatever distribution of SUSE Linux you happen to be using, or if a menu selection has been reorganized or renamed, or if a URL listed in the book has gone away.

SUSE 10.1 introduces a few new features, including new package management tools intended to support multiple repository types, a new Network Manager, a version of the Beagle search tool that actually works, and the new and incredibly cool compositing window manager, compiz, along with the OpenGL X server, xgl. You'll find coverage of all of these in the book. There's also been a slimming-down of the desktop menus. Whilst this is undoubtedly less confusing for newcomers, it does mean—even more than before—that there are far more applications on the distribution media than a walk through the menus would suggest. In 10.1 Novell continues to promote Mono, the open-source implementation of the CLI (Common Language Infrastructure—the underpinning of Microsoft's .NET Framework) with a growing number of Mono-based applications, including f-spot for photo management, the zen-updater and zen-installer package management tools, the music player Banshee, the afore-mentioned Beagle search tool, and Blam!, a tool for managing RSS news feeds. Mono is a very interesting development, but it still seems to have a solution-looking-for-a-problem feel to it.

How This Book Is Organized

Each chapter consists of a series of labs, each of which introduces a new feature or capability, shows how it's used, and then walks you through an example, explaining the details you need to understand along the way. You'll also find "What About…" sections that attempt to anticipate and answer follow-up questions, as well as "Where to Learn More" sections that tell you where you can learn more about each topic.

Chapter 1, *Quick Start*
: Introduces SUSE Linux, and gets you up and running quickly, with labs that show you how to install SUSE and get all your essentials connected and configured.

Chapter 2, *Basic System Administration*
: Covers basic system administration for desktop machines, but much of this will apply to notebook users as well. You'll learn how to work with text files, find your way around the filesystem, and more.

Chapter 3, *Using SUSE Linux on Your Desktop*
: Describes how to start putting SUSE Linux to work. You'll find help for getting the X Window System working just right, and find your way around the KDE and GNOME desktop environments.

Chapter 4, *Using Linux on Your Laptop*
: Shows laptop users how to get everything set up just right with SUSE Linux, including laptop power management and wireless networking.

Chapter 5, *Package Management*
> Describes all about package management. You'll learn how to install new software from local media and from the Internet, and to use package management tools to avoid conflicts and version discrepancies during upgrades, and you'll discover how easy it is to build software from source.

Chapter 6, *System Administration for Servers*
> Focuses on the server capabilities of SUSE. Even if you are primarily a desktop user, there might be something in here for you. You'll learn how to specify which services start up when your computer starts up, how to work with disk partitions, and more.

Chapter 7, *Network Services*
> Dives into network services such as email, file sharing, and more.

Chapter 8, *Security*
> Gives you a comprehensive collection of labs that explain how to keep your system secure. You'll learn how to set up a firewall, restrict access, and monitor attempts to break into your server.

Chapter 9, *Alternative Installations*
> Explains other ways you can install SUSE, from dual-boot configurations to virtual machine installations with Xen.

What You Need to Use This Book

If you already have a computer running SUSE Linux 10.1, you've got everything you need. If you're running an older version of SUSE, a lot of these labs will make sense to you, but you will come across some differences.

If you don't yet have SUSE Linux running, be sure to check out the first lab in this book, Lab 1.1, "Installing SUSE Linux from Local Media," before doing anything else!

Conventions Used in This Book

The following typographical conventions are used in this book:

Italic
> Indicates new terms, URLs, email addresses, filenames, file extensions, pathnames, and directories.

`Constant width`
> Indicates commands, options, switches, the contents of files, or the output from commands.

`Constant width bold`
> Shows commands or other text that should be typed literally by the user.

`Constant width italic`
> Shows text that should be replaced with user-supplied values.

~
: This is a shortcut for the current user's home directory. If you use it at a Linux command prompt, it will be interpreted as such.

$
: This is the shell prompt that you'll see at the Linux command prompt. This is used to indicate that a command should be typed in by a normal user.

#
: This is the shell prompt for root, also known as the super-user. You can get this prompt by running the command su or sudo -s at the normal Linux command prompt. You'll be prompted to provide the root user password that you chose when you installed SUSE.

This icon signifies a tip, suggestion, or general note.

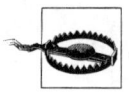
This icon indicates a warning or caution.

Using Code Examples

This book is here to help you get your job done. In general, you may use the code in this book in your programs and documentation. You do not need to contact O'Reilly for permission unless you're reproducing a significant portion of the code. For example, writing a program that uses several chunks of code from this book does not require permission. Selling or distributing a CD-ROM of examples from O'Reilly books *does* require permission. Answering a question by citing this book and quoting example code does not require permission. Incorporating a significant amount of example code from this book into your product's documentation *does* require permission.

We appreciate, but do not require, attribution. An attribution usually includes the title, author, publisher, and ISBN. For example: "*SUSE Linux,* by Chris Brown. Copyright 2006 O'Reilly Media, Inc., 0-596-10183-X."

We'd Like to Hear From You

Please address comments and questions concerning this book to the publisher:

O'Reilly Media, Inc.
1005 Gravenstein Highway North
Sebastopol, CA 95472
800-998-9938 (in the United States or Canada)
707-829-0515 (international or local)
707-829-0104 (fax)

There is a web page for this book, which lists errata, examples, and any additional information. You can access this page at:

> http://www.oreilly.com/catalog/suselinux

To comment on or ask technical questions about this book, send email to:

> bookquestions@oreilly.com

For more information about books, conferences, software, Resource Centers, and the O'Reilly Network, see the O'Reilly web site at:

> http://www.oreilly.com

Safari® Enabled

When you see a Safari® Enabled icon on the cover of your favorite technology book, that means the book is available online through the O'Reilly Network Safari Bookshelf.

Safari offers a solution that's better than e-books. It's a virtual library that lets you easily search thousands of top tech books, cut and paste code samples, download chapters, and find quick answers when you need the most accurate, current information. Try it free at *http://safari.oreilly.com*.

Acknowledgments

I'd like to thank my editor, Brian Jepson, for succeeding at the delicate task of refining my prose without damaging my ego, and for his technical insight and suggestions in a significant number of the labs. Special thanks, also, to Simon Crute, my mole within Novell, who has patiently provided answers to many dumb questions, and who contributed the material for several of the labs in Chapter 4 and Chapter 9. My gratitude also goes, as always, to my dear wife Lynne, who endured many husbandless days as I worked on this book, in the full knowledge that she wouldn't understand a word of it. Finally, my thanks to the open source developer community, without whom I would have nothing to write about.

CHAPTER 1
Quick Start

I have never liked delayed gratification. I don't buy self-assembly furniture or bake cakes from scratch—there's too much waiting involved. Bonsai? You must be joking! With software products and operating systems especially, I want to start putting them to use the instant I have them in hand. Hopefully, this book will help you do that with SUSE Linux. In particular, this first chapter is intended to get you started quickly—to get the system installed; to get your printer, email, and network set up; and to take a step on the road to self-sufficiency through reading the documentation. Changing your operating system is like moving to a new home. You need to figure out how to turn on the electricity, water, and heating. You need to make a hot drink. You need to get the bed assembled before nightfall. Unpacking your CD collection can wait.

Once the system is installed, I suggest you spend some time exploring the menus. From web browsers to HTML editors, from databases to CD players, from image editors to chess programs—there's just so much stuff! And that's just the graphical tools. A whole new world of command-line utilities also awaits you. As the SUSE folks say, "Have a lot of fun."

1.1 Installing SUSE Linux from Local Media

Not too long ago—five years, maybe—installing Linux required a great deal of patience and technical know-how. Getting it to work properly on a laptop was especially tricky, rather like teaching chickens to fly. Anyone found in possession of a flying chicken would be besieged by questions from others anxious to see their pet hen airborne. Since then, the device support in Linux has improved beyond recognition; the installation tools in a modern Linux distribution auto-detect most hardware, install the right drivers, and deliver a default installation that is almost certainly going to work.

In this lab I walk through a typical installation of SUSE Linux from local media (in this case, a DVD or set of CDs). Everyone's installation is different, of course. You may be installing onto a completely "empty" machine, or you may wish to preserve existing partitions and operating systems. You may have specific requirements for the selection of software you want to install. You almost certainly have different hardware than I do. For this walk-through, I use a desktop machine of dubious breeding (I built it myself), which has an existing installation of Windows 2000 (which I will keep) and an existing installation of an earlier version of Linux (that I will replace). Depending on which version of SUSE Linux you're installing, there may be some minor differences between the screens you'll see and the screenshots in this book.

How Do I Do That?

Start by booting from the DVD included with your SUSE Linux distribution. (If your machine won't boot from DVD, or if you've created the CDs by downloading ISO images from the OpenSUSE web site [*http://www.opensuse.org*], boot from CD1.) You will be presented with an initial boot menu that will (if you let it time out) boot from the hard drive. This isn't what you want, so select "Installation" from the menu. A Linux kernel and a RAM-disk image will now be loaded from the DVD or CD. The RAM-disk image is a small filesystem, held in memory, that Linux uses during the installation. You'll be asked to select the language you want to use for the installation.

Next, you'll be invited to perform a media check on the discs you plan to install from. This check verifies the MD5 checksums of the media (CDs or DVDs) that you will install from. My experience (particularly if you are installing from purchased media) is that media errors are relatively rare, and that it is quicker to cancel this check and proceed with the installation. You'll be informed by the installer if there are read errors on specific packages. You may also be asked to agree to Novell's license agreement.

After probing the hard drive, my installer detected the existing Linux installation and asked whether I want to perform a new installation, or update the existing one. (Clicking Other also allows you to repair an existing installed system.) I chose to perform a new installation. Note that it's the existing Linux partitions that I'm replacing here, not the Windows installation. Whichever option I choose, the existing Windows partition will not be touched. (In fact, the installer will automatically include an option to boot Windows in the boot loader configuration and will automatically arrange for the Windows partition to be mounted into the Linux filesystem when I boot Linux.)

Next, you're asked to enter your geographic region and time zone. SUSE 10.1 then asks if you want a KDE or Gnome desktop. You can also choose a text-mode installation (appropriate for servers) by selecting Other. This selection will likely catch Windows users off-balance. On a Windows system, you get the desktop that Microsoft provided, and there are no alternatives. For Linux there are a dozen or so window managers and desktop toolsets you might choose to use. The mainstream choices presented by the installer are Gnome and KDE. Both are fine. KDE is, if anything, better supported by SUSE, and is the desktop I'm most familiar with, so that's what I chose.

After further probing of your system, the installer will present a proposal for the new installation. Figures 1-1 and 1-2 show the top and bottom halves of this screen. This is a screen where you'll probably spend some time, as most of the installation decisions are made from here. SUSE Linux 10.1 adds Overview and Expert tabs to this screen. The figures correspond to the expert view.

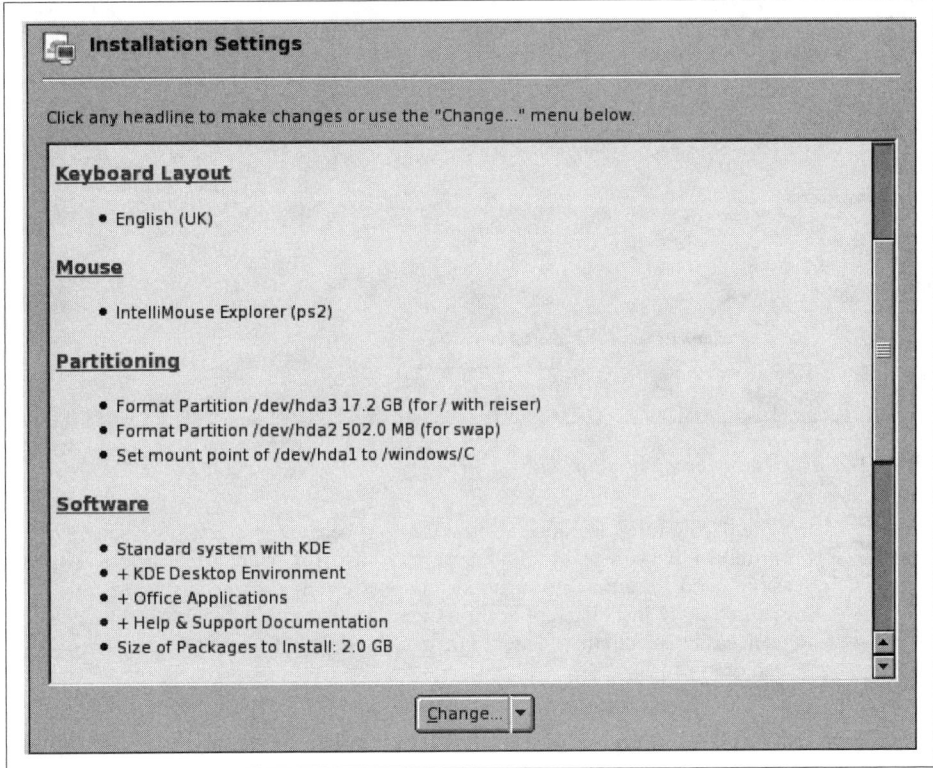

Figure 1-1. Installation settings (top half)

If you're totally new to Linux, and you simply don't understand the choices presented to you here, just accept the proposed installation. It will work well enough, and will be fine to get started with. Later on, when you're more experienced, you can always reinstall. In my experience, the categories you're most likely to want to change are Partitioning and Software. To change these, click on the underlined blue links, or use the Change button at the bottom of the screen.

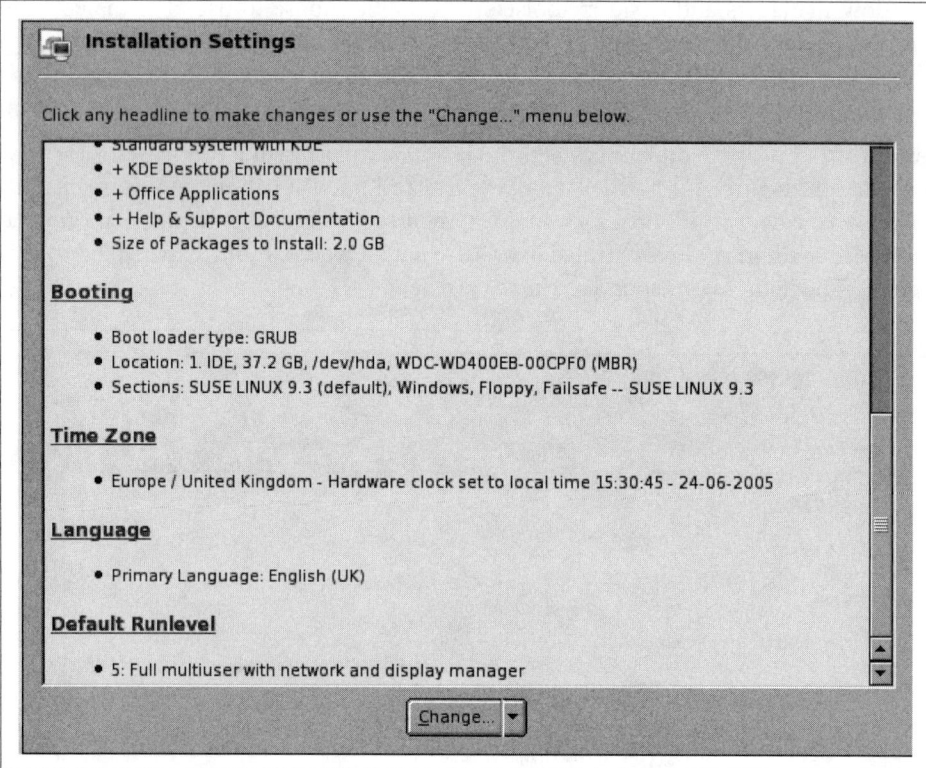

Figure 1-2. Installation settings (bottom half)

 The partitioning decisions are the hardest, because the first time you install Linux you really don't have any basis for making good decisions, and because they're almost impossible to change afterwards. Forgetting to install an application or two isn't a problem, because you can easily install them later, but getting the partitioning wrong is tedious to fix.

A *partition* is a fixed-sized region of a hard drive. It could be the whole disk or just a part of it. A partition is what Windows calls a "drive." For Linux, you need at least two partitions, one for *swap space* (temporary disk storage used as an overflow area for main memory) and one for the filesystem. This is the simplest possible scheme and is the one you'll see proposed in Figure 1-1 where the installer is simply proposing to take over the existing Linux partitions (*hda2* and *hda3*) for the swap space and the file system, respectively. But it's not set in stone. Suppose that you need to make a change to this (in my case, I wanted *hda3* to be smaller, to leave some unpartitioned space on the drive for later use) Click the Change button, then select Partitioning from the menu. This brings you to the Suggested Partitioning screen where you need to select "Base Partition setup on this proposal."

Next you'll see the Expert Partitioner screen. Here you can add, edit, or delete partitions to your exact requirements. I'm planning to resize the *hda3* partition from 17.2 GB to 10 GB, but the only way to do this is to delete it and create it again, so I selected it from the list and clicked Delete, followed by Create. After you click Create, you're asked if you want a primary partition or an extended partition. I discuss this whole issue of partitioning in detail in Chapter 9, but for now, on my system, I selected a Primary Partition.

The next screen allows you to specify the size and type of the filesystem to put on the partition (Figure 1-3).

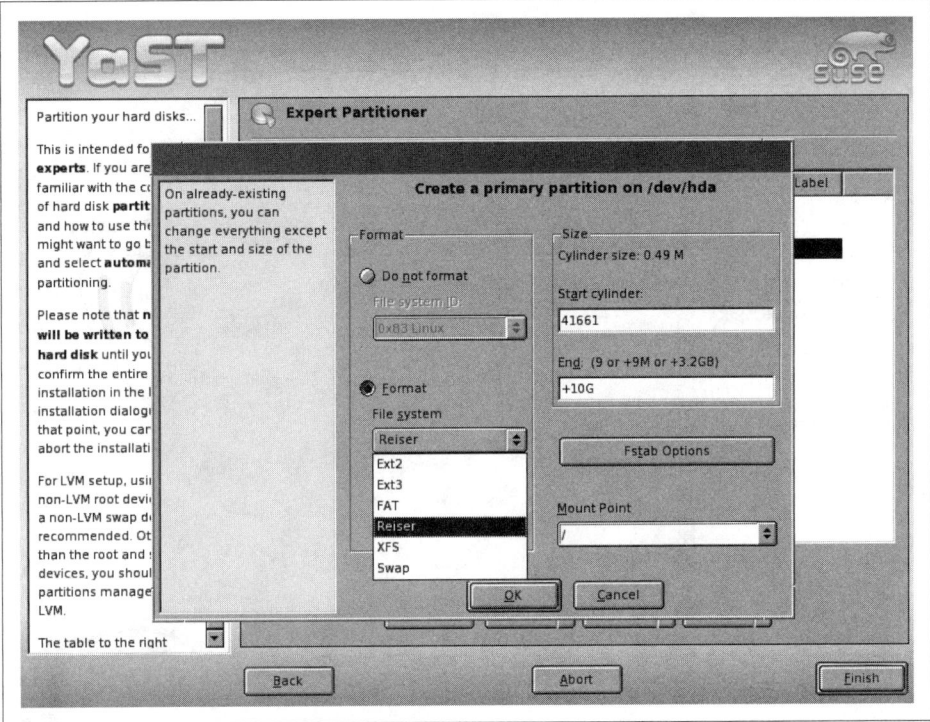

Figure 1-3. Creating a new partition

There are two mainstream filesystem types used by Linux, called *ext3* and *Reiser*. These names refer to the layout of the actual data structures on the disk, in the same way that FAT32 and NTFS refer to file system formats used by Windows. Although you will find people who will argue strongly in favor of one file system or the other, the reality is that either ext3 or Reiser will serve perfectly well in most cases. Here I have chosen a Reiser filesystem and set its size to 10 GB.

 Each partition always begins and ends on a cylinder boundary, so the actual partition size will be rounded to a whole number of cylinders. If you prefer to deal directly in terms of the drive geometry, you can specify the partition size in terms of a starting and ending cylinder number, though there's little point in doing it that way.

With the *hda3* partition now set to 10 GB, the partitioning proposal looks like Figure 1-4. At this point, you can click Finish on the Expert Partitioner screen. Note that no changes have actually been made to the partitions on the hard drive yet. That won't happen until you actually commit to the installation.

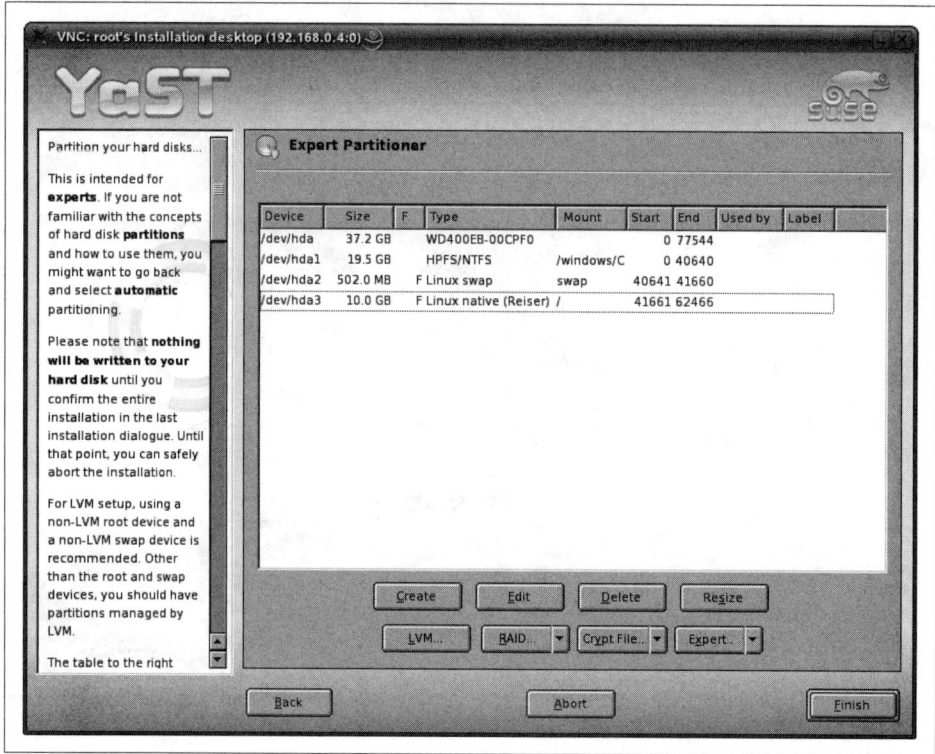

Figure 1-4. The final partitioning scheme

Now you're back at the main Installation Settings screen, which has been updated to reflect your partitioning changes.

You may also want to add your own choice of software packages to the default selection proposed by the installer, so click on the Change button and select Software from the menu, which brings you to the main Software Selection screen shown in Figure 1-5.

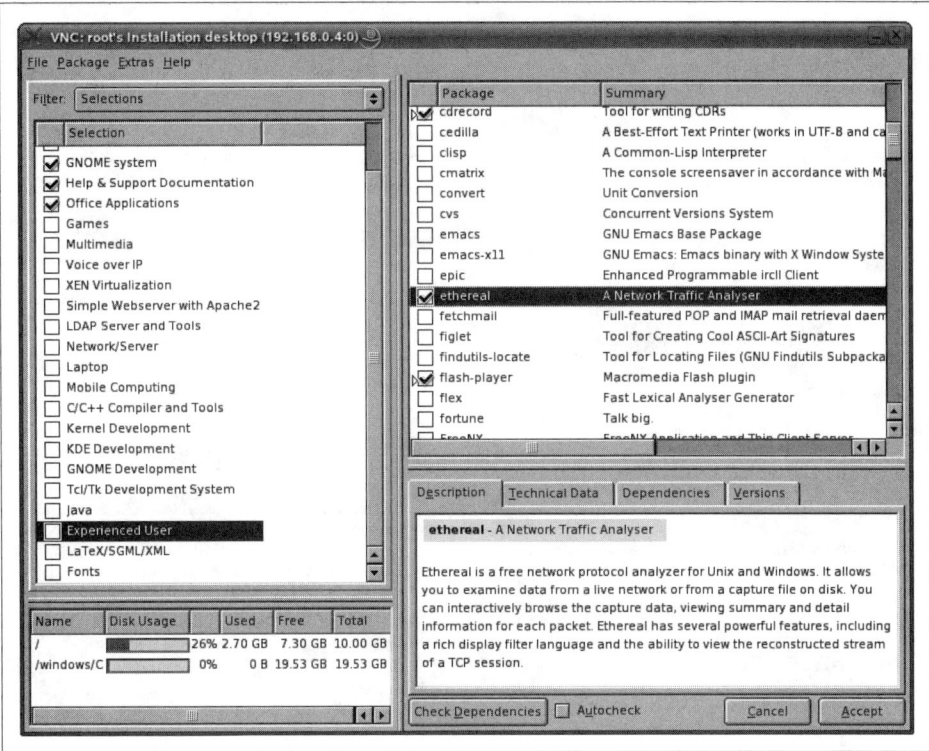

Figure 1-5. Selecting package categories for installation

This is quite a complicated screen, but its purpose is simply to allow you to select software packages to install. The drop-down list box labeled "Filter" near the top-left corner provides various views for software selection. The Selections view allows you to select whether to include or exclude about 25 package categories. Unless you're a Linux expert or are very short on disk space, don't try to make a selection at a more detailed level than these categories. I chose to add the Gnome system and OpenOffice, so I checked those boxes. I also wanted to add a tool called Ethereal, which is a network traffic monitor that I find really useful. So, I needed to drill down to that more detailed level.

Because I want just a single package here, and I know its name, it's simplest to select the Search filter and type "ether" into the box (or however many letters you need to find what you're after). This will bring up a list of matching package names in the top-right pane. I just checked "ethereal," as shown in Figure 1-6.

Once you're happy with the software selection, click Accept to go back yet again to the main Installation Settings screen (shown in Figure 1-2). There are, potentially, other things you could change here. For example, right at the bottom is an entry labeled Default Run Level. Leave this at 5 if you want the system to boot directly into

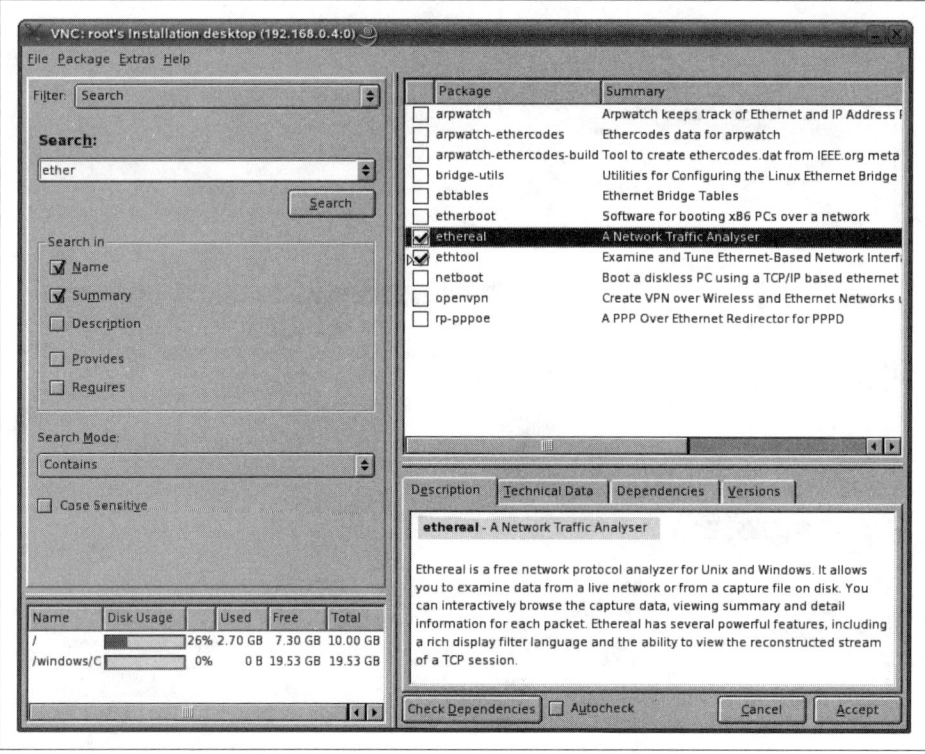

Figure 1-6. Selecting an individual package for installation

a graphical desktop. Set it to 3 if you want the system to boot to a command-prompt login with no graphical desktop. You can also configure the boot loader, which is called GRUB (The GRand Unified Boot loader), but I suggest that you leave it alone. If you already have a Windows installation, you will notice that the installer automatically includes an entry in the boot menu to allow you to boot from your old Windows partition.

Once you're satisfied with your installation choices, click Accept, which will bring you to the Confirm Installation screen, your last possible chance to change your mind. Once you confirm the install, the installer will repartition your disk, which is the point of no return.

Now begins the long haul of package installation. If you're installing from CD, you'll be asked to insert CD2, CD3, and so on at appropriate times. This is not necessary for DVD installations as everything is on one disc. The length of time taken to complete the installation is difficult to predict, as it depends on how many packages you're installing and the speed of your hardware, but an hour is not unusual. When all the packages have been loaded, the system performs some further installation and then reboots. This reboot is necessary so that the system can discard the kernel it had loaded from CD1 and start running the kernel it has now installed on the hard drive. If installing from CDs, the reboot occurs after loading the packages from CD1, then installation continues from CD2 onward. How many of the CDs you'll need depends on which packages you're installing.

One of the first things you're asked to do after package installation is complete is to choose a hostname and domain name for the machine. Your domain name may be determined for you by your network administrator. If your machine does not have an entry in DNS, the domain name you assign here is largely irrelevant; example.com is a safe choice. Next, you need to enter a password for the super-user account. Traditionally, the login name for this account is root. This account is roughly equivalent to the Administrator account in Windows. Every Linux installation must have a super-user account. Some password strength-checking is applied to your choice of the super-user password. This password is important, so don't forget it, and don't write it down on a sticky note on the screen. It's worth spending a moment to choose a strong password; that means (at minimum) not a word you'll find in a dictionary. (If you really do forget the root password, read Lab 2.7, "Rescue a System That Won't Boot," in Chapter 2). At this screen, if you click on Expert Options, you can specify the algorithm that will be used to encrypt the passwords (technically, passwords are *hashed*, not encrypted, but we'll not worry about the difference here). The default algorithm (Blowfish) is probably the most secure; there is little reason to not use it.

Next comes the network configuration screen (Figure 1-7). I chose to leave the settings as they are; in particular, I chose to use a DHCP server to establish my network settings, because the ADSL modem that provides me with my Internet connectivity includes a DHCP server. Dial-up modems (if you have one) are also detected and configured at this stage. In SUSE 10.1 there is an important additional setting on this screen called Network Mode. There are two options: "User Controlled Interface via NetworkManager Applet" and "Traditional Method without NetworkManager Applet." The Network Manager applet is recommended if you have a laptop that roams between, say, a wired network connection and one of several wireless connections. NetworkManager will automatically select the "best available" connection without manual intervention. For a machine with a static wired network connection—particularly one that has a fixed IP address—the "traditional method" may be preferable.

You can do detailed firewall setup here, as well. For more information on security, see Chapter 8.

Next, you'll be offered the opportunity to test connectivity to the Internet, download the latest release notes, and check for any updates. For security, I recommend installing the most recent updates available from SUSE. However, if you choose not to update at this stage, you can easily do so later. You'll see how in Chapter 5.

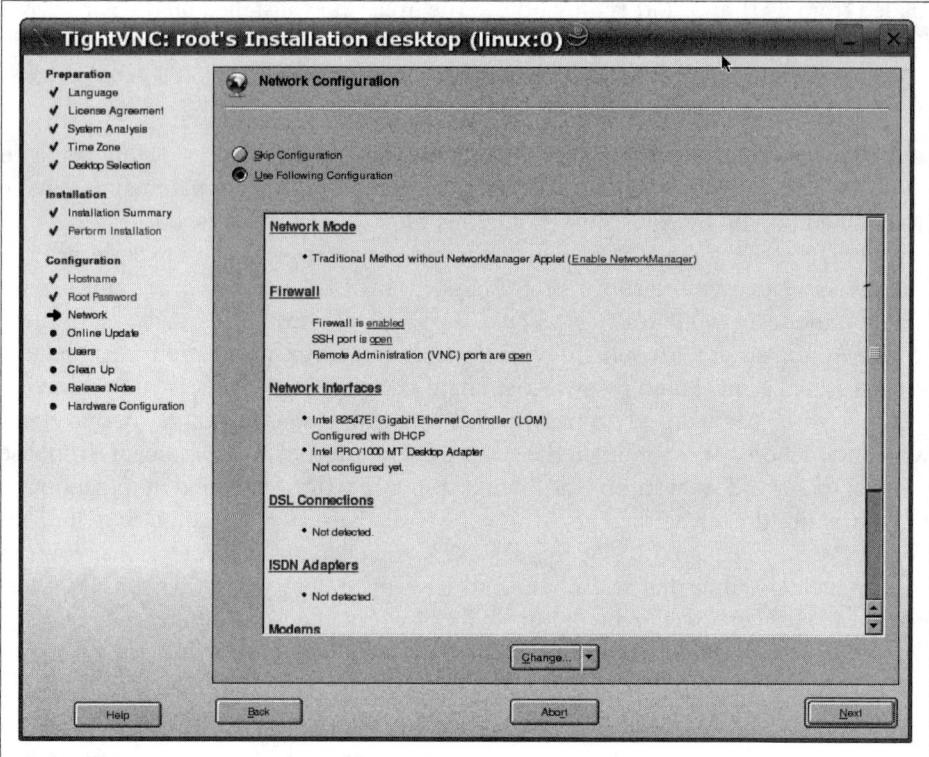

Figure 1-7. Network configuration

Next, you will be asked to choose a User Authentication Method; that is, to specify where the system looks for its user accounts. There are four choices:

- Local (/etc/passwd)
- LDAP
- NIS
- Samba

If you are installing the system for use on a corporate network that runs a centralized account database using—for example, LDAP or NIS—you may need to set that up at this point. Samba authentication might be appropriate if you're trying to integrate your accounts with those on a Windows domain controller. Otherwise, I would recommend that you keep things simple by keeping accounts locally (in the */etc/passwd* file).

Next you'll be asked to create at least one regular user account (see Figure 1-8). If you click the User Management button on this screen, you'll be taken to the main user management screen, where you can add further accounts. You'll learn more about account creation in Chapter 2.

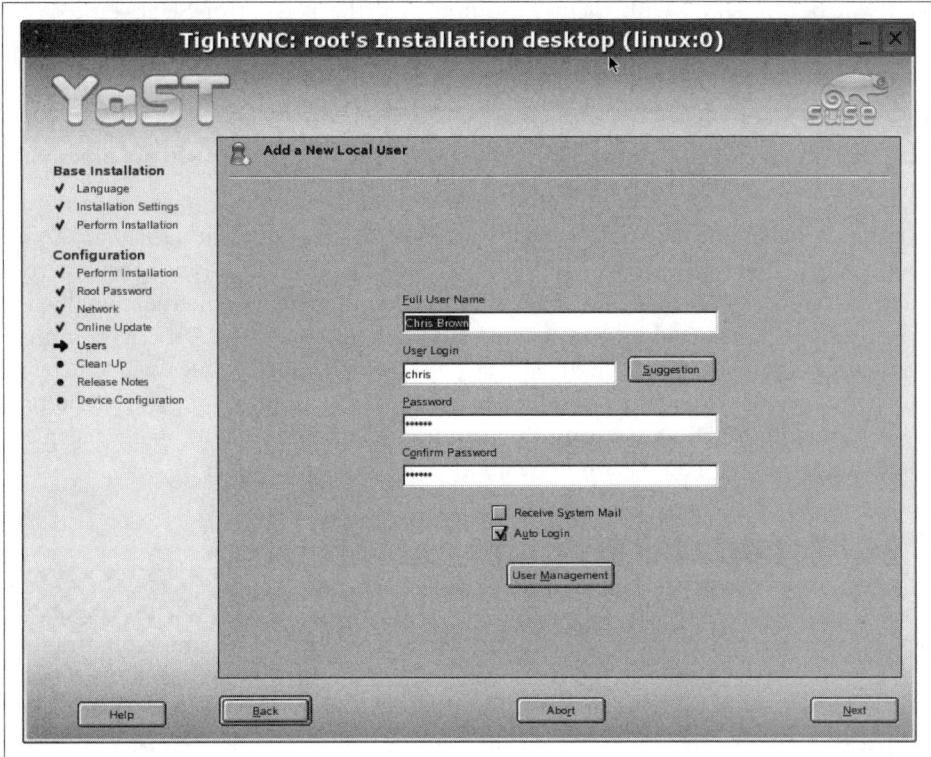

Figure 1-8. Adding a user account

One popular Linux distribution suggests that you should not bother creating a regular user account and should log in as root all the time. Even for single-user systems intended for use in a home environment, I do not recommend this way of working, because root is all-powerful and it's just too easy to do a lot of accidental damage by fumbling a command or a menu selection. For a machine in a corporate environment, it's a *really* bad idea.

I would also advise against checking the box marked "Auto Login" on this screen and I'm disappointed to see that this is checked by default. Yes, it's marginally more convenient to be able to just power up your PC and move directly to the point of being logged in to a graphical desktop without supplying your username and password, but it means that anyone who can press the reset button on your computer has access to your account. (Actually, any really knowledgeable user who has physical access to your machine can do this anyway...but that's another story.)

Now you're almost done. The system will run a number of scripts to propagate the configuration selections that you've made into the various system configuration files.

You will be presented with the release notes for the version of SUSE Linux that you're installing. You will, of course, be much too excited about the prospect of logging in to your new system and exploring it to actually read these!

You will see the hardware configuration screen next. From this screen you can (for example) install a local printer, configure your sound card, or set up Bluetooth. You'll see how to do all of these in later labs.

With the installation complete, you will be invited to log in to SUSE Linux and "have a lot of fun…" There is no need to reboot a second time—in fact, in theory, there is no need to reboot ever again—at least not until you upgrade your kernel. Finally, it's worth pointing out the checkbox labeled "Clone this System for AutoYaST" on the Installation Completed screen. If you check this box, the installer will create an AutoYaST profile corresponding to the installation you've just completed. The profile is written to */root/autoinst.xml*. You can use this profile to automate subsequent similar installations. You'll learn more about AutoYaST in Chapter 9.

1.2 Set Up a Local Printer

Moving to a new computer, or to a new operating system, is a bit like moving into a new house. It takes a while to feel comfortable in it, and to get all your stuff arranged just how you want it. And if you're moving, one of the first things you'll want to do in your new home is make a cup of tea. So, it's particularly important to clearly label the packing case in which you packed the tea bags and the kettle. Similarly, if you're migrating to a new desktop operating system, one of the first things you'll want to get working is your printer.

If you're living in a country, such as the United States, where it is almost impossible to buy anything that the British would regard as even remotely resembling tea, feel free to think of coffee and coffeepots.

How Do I Do That?

In this lab you'll see how to set up a locally connected printer. In Chapter 2 you'll see how to connect to a print server across the network.

You will configure the printer using YaST (Yet another Setup Tool). YaST is an integrated collection of modules that perform a wide variety of system administration tasks from a graphical user interface. It is a key component of SUSE Linux and you will meet it many times in this book.

If your printer was plugged in when you installed SUSE Linux, you'll probably have been offered the opportunity to configure it at that stage. If not, it is easy to add a locally connected printer. In fact, if you simply plug in a printer to a USB port, SUSE should automatically detect it and display a New Hardware Found dialog box asking whether you want to configure it. Answering Yes in this dialog box will start the YaST printer module. As always, when YaST starts up, it will display the Run as Root screen to ask you for the root password. YaST should auto-detect the printer and include it in the list of available printers in the main printer configuration screen, as shown in Figure 1-9.

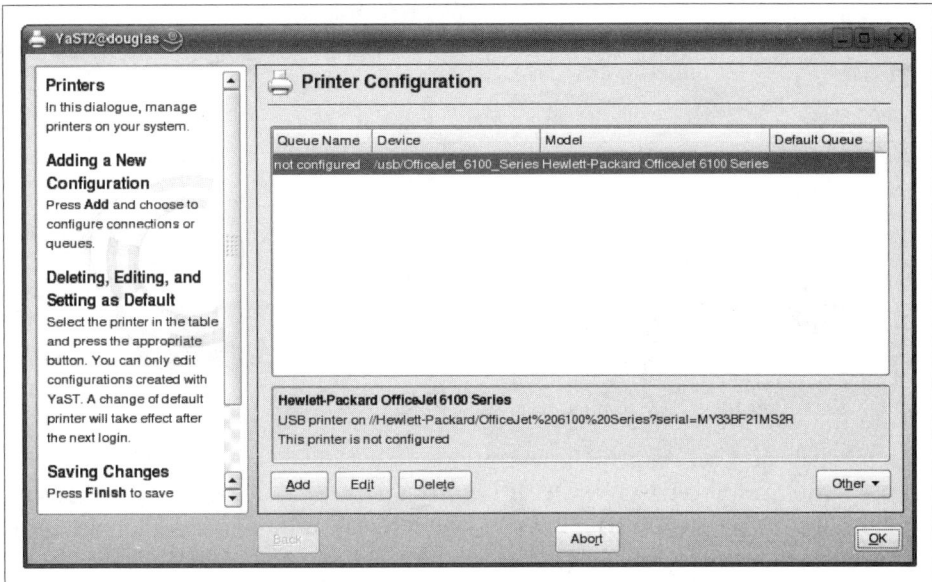

Figure 1-9. YaST main printer configuration screen

Select the printer from the available printers list and click Edit. This will take you to the Edit Configuration screen shown in Figure 1-10.

You can adjust the settings in any of the option areas by selecting the option area and clicking Edit. The one you're most likely to edit is "Name and basic settings," where you can set the name for the printer. This is the name that will show up in the printer list in any print-aware applications such as OpenOffice.

Back on the Edit Configuration screen, click Test to send a test page to the printer. Doing so verifies correct operation and provides you with a printout of your printer configuration. Assuming all is well, close the printer configuration screens, and you're done.

If the printer is not auto-detected when you plug it in, try starting YaST manually from Main Menu → System → Yast. From the panel on the left, select Hardware, then select Printer from the panel on the right. YaST will try to auto-detect your printer and bring you to the main printer configuration screen. YaST should auto-detect

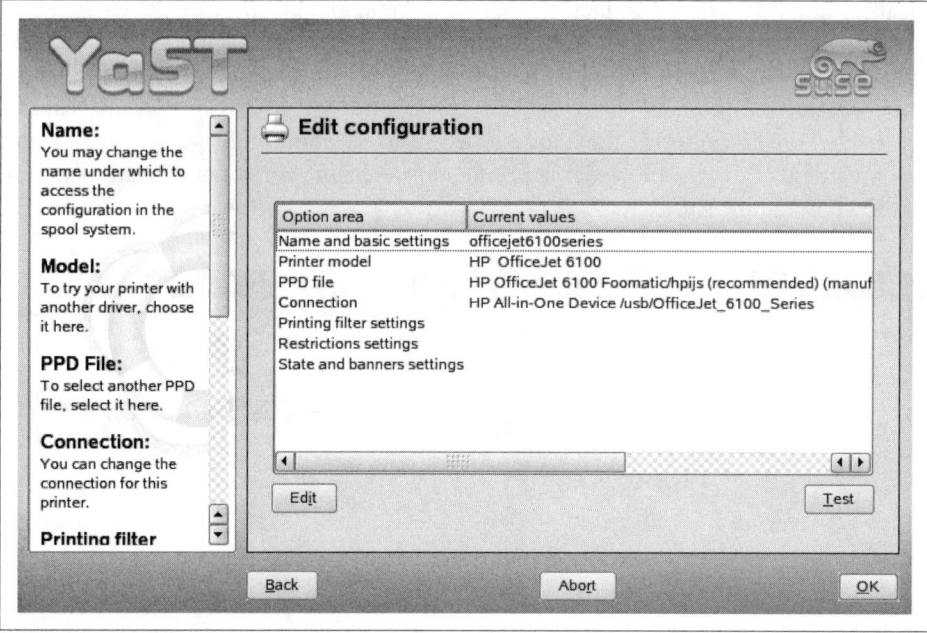

Figure 1-10. Editing the printer configuration

both parallel and USB printers. If your printer now shows up in the list of available printers, you can proceed as before. If not, try selecting Add from the main printer configuration screen. If you go this route, you'll be taken through additional screens and will need to specify how the printer is connected to your computer, its manufacturer, and model number.

Within KDE, there is an alternative tool for printer configuration and management called KDEPrint, accessible via Main Menu → Utilities → Printing → Printing Manager. From this tool you can view and modify settings for existing printers, add new printers, and manage the printer job queues, as shown in Figure 1-11.

What About...

...choosing a printer? If you are planning to buy a printer specifically to use with Linux, it is worth doing a little research to make sure that you get something that's fully supported. Support for printers under Linux is vastly better than it used to be, thanks to the (relatively) new print system called CUPS (Common Unix Print System), but you cannot rely 100% on all printers having drivers for Linux, and especially cannot rely on those drivers being shipped on a CD with the printer, like you can for Windows. The HPLIP (HP Linux Imaging and Printing) driver project from Hewlett-Packard is worthy of special mention here. The HPLIP drivers integrate with CUPS to provide high-quality printing on most HP InkJet and LaserJet printers, and also provide support for scan and fax functions (for more information, see *http://hpinkjet.sourceforge.net*).

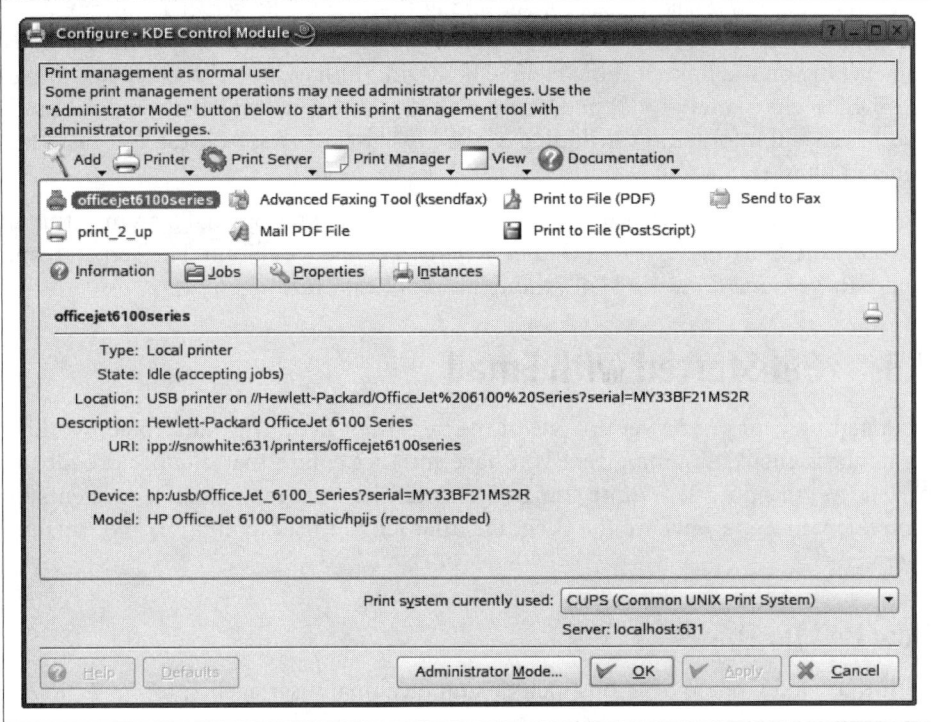

Figure 1-11. The KDE print manager

Printing in Linux is largely based on PostScript, and any printer that uses PostScript is likely to be 100% supported, though PostScript tends to be found only on the more expensive models. The print system includes filters for converting to other printer languages such as PCL (used by HP printers) or ESC/P (used by Epson), so printers that use these languages are also likely to work. The printers most likely to cause problems with Linux are the so-called "GDI" printers at the bottom end of the retail market. These printers are intended to work with the manufacturer's own drivers and to support Microsoft's proprietary GDI graphics API. They are really cheap, but quite apart from any compatibility issues, most of them have a very flimsy build standard and I recommend against buying them.

Where to Learn More

There's a detailed hardware compatibility database for SUSE Linux at *http://cdb.suse.de* that shows the support status of a huge number of printers, graphics cards, sound cards, modems, networks cards, scanners, and more, under the various versions of SUSE Linux. Another site to go for advice about choice of printer is *http://www.linuxprinting.org*. There is some good tutorial material on this site, too.

The underlying print system used by SUSE Linux is CUPS (Common Unix Print System). You'll find documentation on CUPS in */usr/share/doc/packages/cups*, and on their web site, *http://www.cups.org*. Assuming that the CUPS server is running, you can also access the documentation by pointing your browser to *http://localhost:631* and clicking on the link On-Line Help. The KDEPrint handbook (accessible through the SUSE Help Center or via the Documentation button on the KDEPrint tool itself) also has useful information including a good discussion about PostScript, rasterization and filtering.

I also discovered (somewhat to my surprise) a good chapter on CUPS architecture in *The Official SAMBA-3 HOWTO and Reference Guide* by John H. Terpstra and Jelmer R. Vernooij (Prentice Hall), though it is not easy reading.

1.3 Get Started with Email

After getting your printer set up, one of the next things you will want to get working on Linux is email. Assuming that you have Internet connectivity (either broadband or dial-up), this process is quite straightforward. There are many mail user agents for Linux. (Mail user agents are the programs that let you read, compose, and organize your mail.)

How Do I Do That?

Both KDE and Gnome desktops include graphical mail user agents; for KDE there's KMail and for Gnome there's Evolution. Mozilla Thunderbird is also available, but is not installed by default. If you're coming from a Windows background, think of these as roughly equivalent to Outlook Express.

Kmail

Start Kmail from the KDE desktop using Main Menu → Internet → KMail. (Later, you may want to add a launch icon for KMail onto the toolbar. You'll see how to do that in Chapter 3.) The very first time you launch Kmail, it will offer a wizard that guides you through a few screens to set up an initial account. I recommend that you cancel the wizard on its first screen, and proceed to the main KMail screen, from which you can set up your own accounts.

Before you can send and receive email with Kmail you will need, at minimum, to define an "identity" and specify your ISP's inbound and outbound mail servers.

Incoming mail is usually received from a POP3 or IMAP server. Outbound mail is usually sent to an SMTP server. The mail servers for incoming and outgoing mail are entirely separate and may not even be operated by the same service provider. In any case, they need to be configured separately in KMail.

16 | Chapter 1: Quick Start

From KMail's main menu, select Settings → Configure KMail. The configuration dialog has several sections that you can select via the pane on the left. Begin by selecting Identities. An identity is basically just a named collection of KMail configuration settings. You probably won't need to define more than one of these, so click Modify to edit the default identity. Complete the form by entering your name, organization and email address (as you would like them to appear on outbound mail) and click OK.

Next, you need to point KMail at your inbound mail server. In the main configuration screen, click Accounts and then the Receiving tab. Typically, you'll need to add only one mail server to the list, but you can configure KMail to retrieve mail from multiple mail boxes if you want. To add a new POP3 server, click Add, then specify an account type of POP3 (use IMAP if you have an IMAP server). Fill in the form (as in Figure 1-12), specifying the server name, login name, and password that your ISP or employer has (hopefully) given you. If you need to use a secure connection (recommended if available), click the Extras (POP3) or Security (IMAP) tab and specify the encryption scheme (SSL or TLS).

Next, you need to specify the SMTP server for outbound mail. Return to the main KDE configuration screen and select the Sending tab. Click Add and specify SMTP as the transport type, then fill in the form (see Figure 1-13) with the SMTP server name that your ISP or employer has given you. If your server requires a username and password, check the "Server requires authentication" checkbox and enter the login name and password there.

If your SMTP server uses a secure connection, visit the Security tab and specify the details. If you are using an external SMTP server (such as your employer's) via a broadband connection, or if you plan to use it in public hotspots, you may find that you can't reach it on port 25 (the default SMTP port). If this is the case, contact the system administrator in charge of the SMTP server, and ask whether an alternate port is available.

The reason you may be unable to access port 25 is that ISPs only allow you to connect to their SMTP servers from their own network, and will block you from accessing the server from other networks. This means that usually you'll have to use an SMTP server that belongs to the same ISP as provides your dial-up or broadband service. The ISP isn't just being deliberately difficult; SMTP servers that will relay mail from anywhere are known as "open relays" and are a really bad idea, because spammers can hide behind them. Not only that, but some worms need to make direct SMTP connections to other servers in order to propagate.

If you send mail from a single physical location, this isn't a problem, but if you regularly move your laptop to another location you may find that you have to reconfigure KMail to use a different SMTP service. This is where KMail's "Identities" are useful. For example, you could define one identity as "Me at home" and another as "Me in the office."

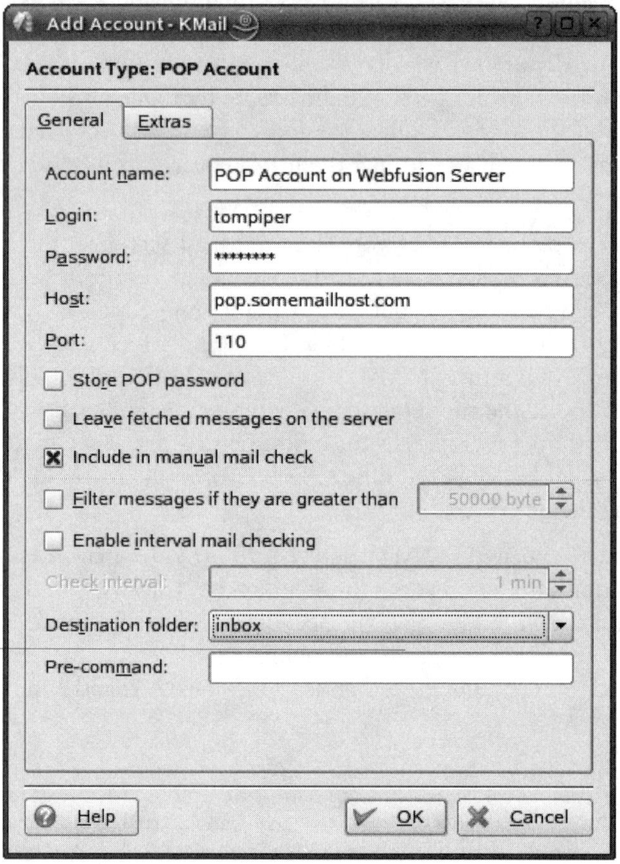

Figure 1-12. Adding a POP account to KMail

With your inbound and outbound servers specified, you should be able to send and receive mail. As a mail user agent, KMail presents a fairly conventional user interface, shown in Figure 1-14. It also provides an address book, accessible via Tools → Address Book on its main menu. (If you want to add a toolbar button for the address book, go to Settings → Configure Toolbars.)

Evolution

Evolution is a collaboration tool from Ximian. In addition to functioning as a mail user agent, it offers calendar and contact management tools. The first time you run Evolution, a setup wizard kicks in and guides you through the process of configuring your inbound and outbound mail servers. On the four screens of this wizard, you will need to supply essentially the same information as when configuring Kmail:

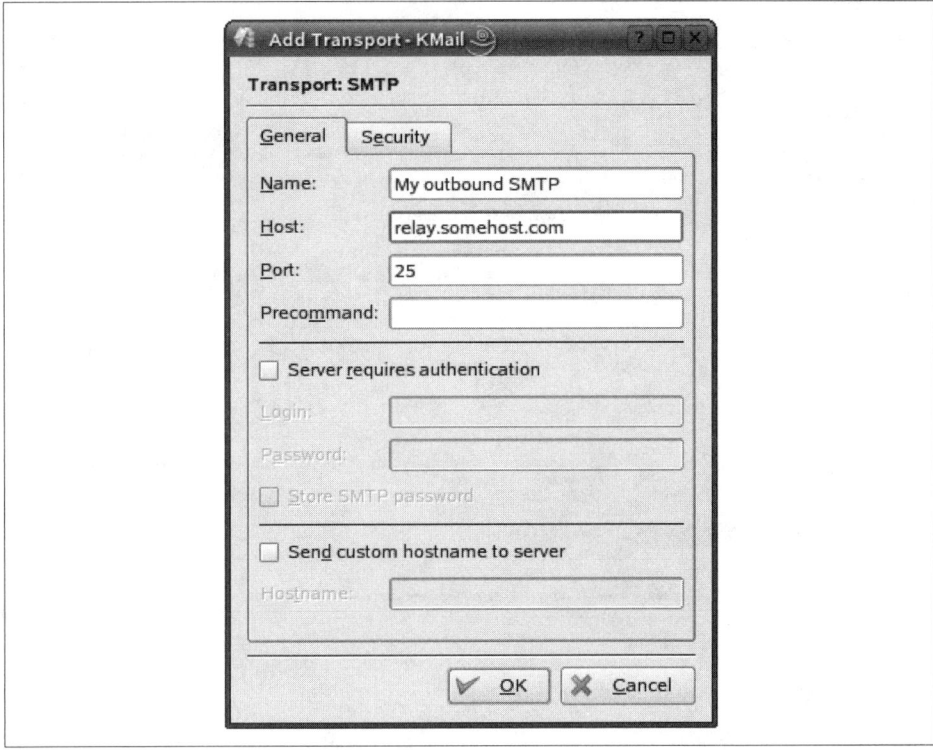

Figure 1-13. Adding an outbound SMTP server to KMail

- Identity screen
  — Full name
  — Email address
  — Reply-To address (optional)
  — Organization name (optional)
- Receiving email screen
  — Server type (interestingly, one of the mail servers supported by evolution is Novell's Groupwise)
  — Server host name
  — Account name on server
  — Authentication type
- Sending email screen
  — Server type (probably SMTP)
  — Server host name
  — Type of authentication (if any)

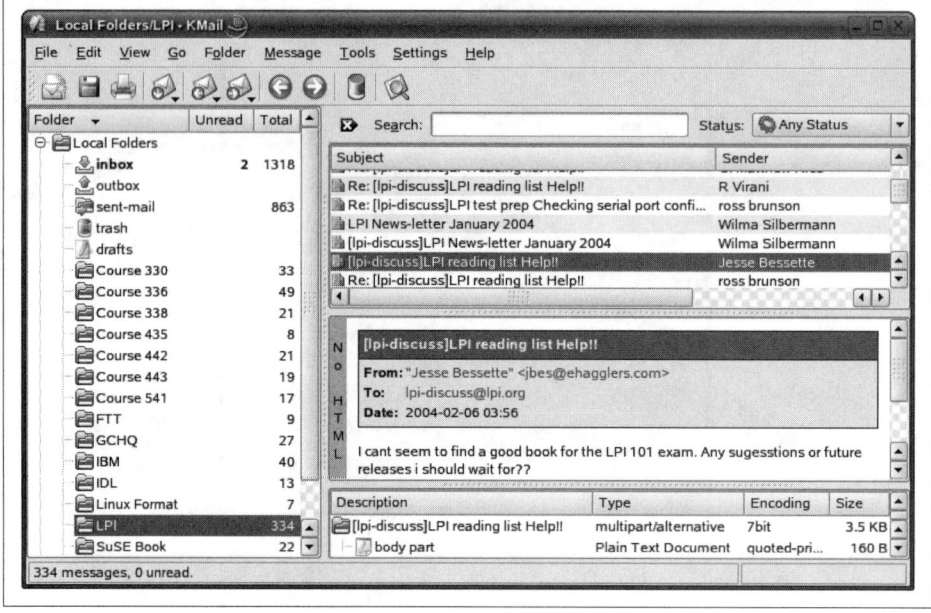

Figure 1-14. KMail main window

- Account Management screen
    — An account name of your choice (simply used to identify this configuration)

What About…

…importing mail from other mailers? If you are using an IMAP-based mail server, the responsibility for long-term storage and organization of your mail messages lies with the mail server. It is easy to migrate your mail between machines, because there is no locally held message store to migrate. That's the benefit of IMAP. However, if you are using a POP3-based mail server, the responsibility for long-term storage of mail messages lies with your machine. The message store is held locally. It's this case—of migrating local message stores—that I consider here.

If you're migrating to a new mail user agent, you'll almost certainly want to transfer your existing mail archive from the old user agent to the new one. It has always surprised me that there is no universally accepted format for storing mail messages on a computer, but the fact is that each mail user agent has its own way of doing things. In the Unix/Linux world, there is the traditional "mbox" format. Using this format, all the messages for each folder are stored in a single flat file named after the folder. This file contains all the messages in the folder, one after the other, with a From line marking the start of each. KMail can use the mbox format, but by default it uses the newer (or at least, less ancient) maildir format for its folders. In this format, each folder has its own directory and each message appears as a separate file in that directory. For example, I have a folder called "SUSE_Book." Each message in that folder is held in a file in the directory /home/chris/Mail/SUSE_Book/cur.

When it comes to migrating your mail folders from one mail user agent to another, the number of possible combinations of "from" and "to" is too large to handle them all here. I look at one common case: migrating mail folders from Microsoft's Outlook Express to KMail.

KMail provides a tool called KMailCVT, which can import mailboxes from a variety of user agents, including Outlook Express. The biggest challenge lies in finding the mailbox files on your Windows system, and physically copying them to the Linux system. On my old Windows 2000 system, for example, a user's mail folders are stored in files with the extension *.dbx*, and you can use the Search tool in Windows to find these files. Once found, the Outlook Express mailbox files need to be copied over to the Linux system. If you are running a dual-boot system, you can just boot into Linux and reach across into the Windows partition to find the files. (If you install SUSE Linux onto a machine that already has Windows installed, it will arrange to mount your Windows filesystems onto directories such as */windows/C* and */windows/D*.) If your Windows system is running on a different machine, you will need to find some other way to copy the files across. For example, you can use Samba on your Linux machine to make your home directory visible to Windows across the network and copy your *.dbx* files onto that. (You'll see how to do this in Lab 7.4, "Serve Filesystems to Windows with Samba.") Or, if your machines are not networked, you can copy the files onto a USB memory stick, external drive, or (failing all else) burn them onto a CD or DVD. You'll see how to access removable media in Chapter 3.

Once you have your *.dbx* files accessible on the Linux system, start KMail and select Tools → Import Messages from the main menu. The drop-down menu on this tool shows that there's a variety of mailer formats that KMail can import from. For a *.dbx*, select Import Outlook Express Emails. On the following screen, navigate to the file where you saved your exported Outlook Express mailbox. Folders will be imported with *OE-* prefixed to their name; for example, a folder named *quilting* in Outlook Express will be imported as *OE-quilting* in KMail. Once you have imported the folders, you can easily rename them within KMail by right-clicking on the folder and selecting Properties.

1.4 Configure a Network Card

It's perfectly possible to install and operate a completely standalone Linux system with no network connection at all, but it's rather unusual. Most systems need to connect to a local area network, either in the office or at home. In this lab you'll see how to configure a network card to connect to a local wired network (i.e., Ethernet). I'll begin by looking at the traditional YaST way (which requires the root password), then I'll look at a couple of more recent applets (netapplet and NetworkManager) that allow easy—though limited—management of network interfaces without root privilege. In Chapter 6, you'll see how to set up wireless networking.

How Do I Do That?

If your network card was auto detected during installation, you will have been offered the opportunity to configure it at that stage. If not, or if you need to configure it later, use YaST (K Menu → System → YaST).

On YaST's main screen, select Network Devices from the panel on the left, then Network Card from the panel on the right. On the main network card configuration screen, you will see a list of available (but unconfigured) cards. To configure one of these, select it from the list and click Configure.

A list of already-configured devices is shown at the bottom of the screen. To change one of these, click Change. On the next screen, titled Network Card Configuration Overview, you'll again see the list of configured cards. They will probably have names like "eth-id-00:01:02:8E:21:9." Select the card that you want to configure and click Edit. This will bring you to the Network Address Setup screen shown in Figure 1-15.

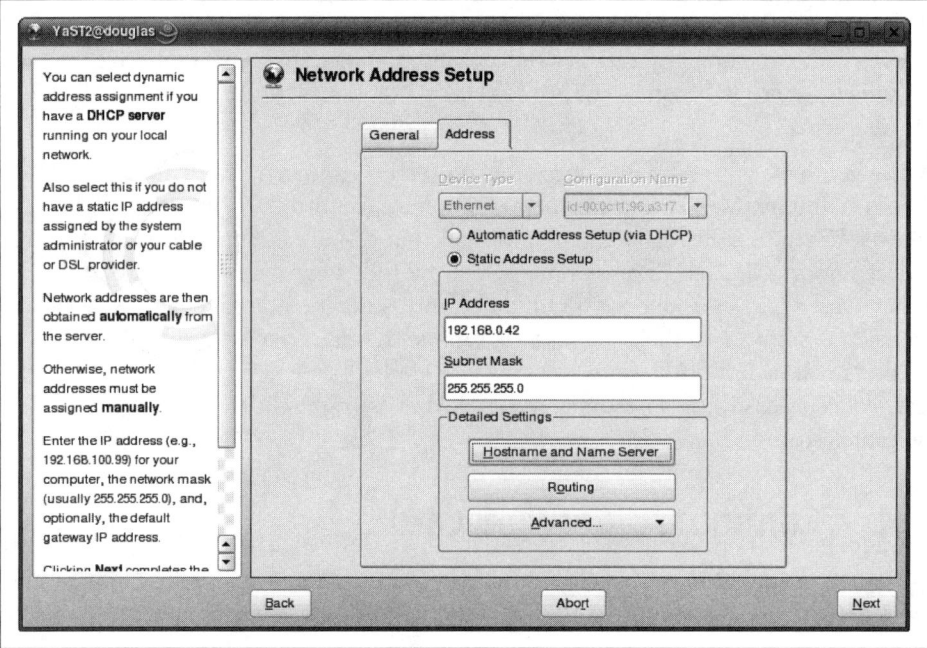

Figure 1-15. Assigning an IP address

The easiest way to configure a network card is to select Automatic Address Setup (via DHCP). Using this method, the machine will broadcast a request over the network when it starts up (or to be more accurate, whenever the interface is activated), hoping to find a DHCP server that will supply its IP address, subnet mask, default gateway, and other network settings. This choice is usually appropriate if you are putting your machine onto a corporate network, which probably operates a DHCP server. If you have a home network with an ADSL modem/router, it's likely that the router offers DHCP, so you can use this setting here also.

If you have no DHCP server, or if (for example) you are configuring a machine as a gateway, proxy, or firewall and need to explicitly set an IP address, then click on Static Address Setup and fill in the IP address and subnet mask. You may also wish to click the Host Name and Name Server button in the Detailed Settings panel. This will bring you to the Host Name and Name Server Configuration screen (see Figure 1-16).

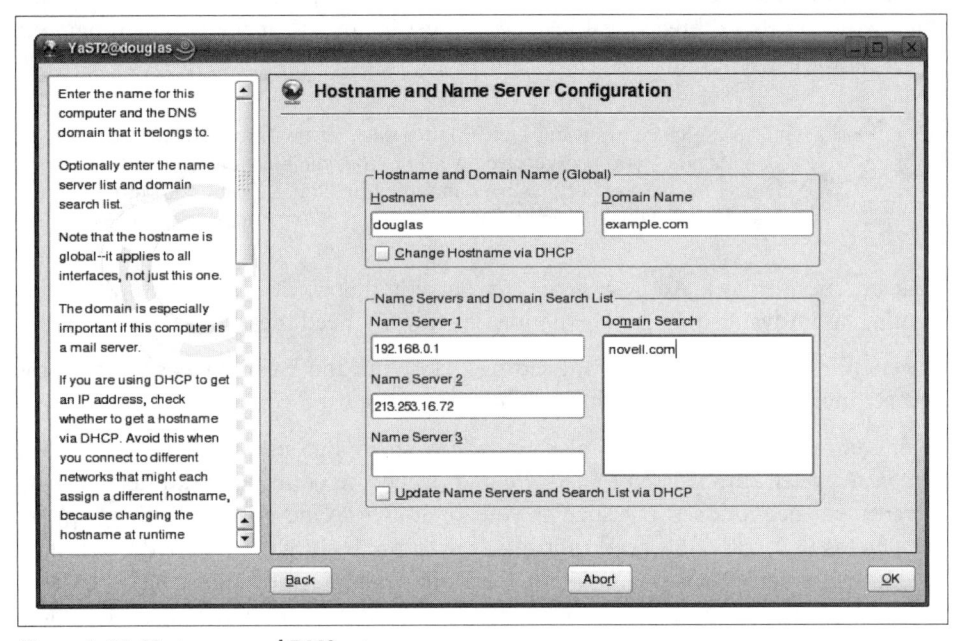

Figure 1-16. Host name and DNS setup

Here you can specify a hostname and domain name for your own machine, and the IP addresses of up to three DNS servers to use. Notice the checkboxes labeled "Change Host Name via DHCP" and "Update Name Servers and Search List via DHCP." By un-checking these boxes, you can still retain explicit control of things like your hostname and DNS servers even if you're using DHCP to get your basic network settings.

The boxes that allow you to specify a domain search order are, in my opinion, best left blank. The idea is that you can specify default domains in which DNS lookups can be performed. For example, if you specify a search domain of *novell.com* you can type `ping www` at the command line and you'd be pinging *www.novell.com*, or you can point your browser to *http://www* and see Novell's home page. This feature has been around a long time in Unix and Linux. It made some sort of sense back in the days when every machine on a corporate network had a fixed IP address and an entry in the DNS. By including your own domain name in the search list, you could, for example, telnet to a local machine just by typing:

```
$ telnet zaphod
```

rather than having to use a fully qualified name:

```
$ telnet zaphod.mycompany.co.uk
```

However, specifying a list of (external) search domains such as *novell.com* and *redhat.com* and *suse.com* is effectively saying "if I use the name www, I don't really mind which of these three sites I reach." So, just include your own domain name in the list and leave it at that.

> If you are currently using DHCP, after clicking on "Host Name and Name Server," you may receive a warning that the file you're about to change (*/etc/resolv.conf*) has been modified by DHCP. Just click Modify and YaST will allow you to edit the settings.

Back on the Network Address Setup screen, you'll see two more buttons labeled Routing and Advanced. In most situations, you won't need these.

Once you're finished entering your settings, close out the YaST screens to cause the new settings to be written and the interfaces to be restarted.

Some versions of SUSE Linux also include a small but useful application called *netapplet*, which can be used to activate and deactivate your network interfaces and to verify key network settings such as your IP address. One of the nice things about *netapplet* is that you don't need root privilege to run it. It may be started from Main Menu → Internet → Administration → Network Selector, and once it has started, it will place a small icon in the system tray near the righthand end of the KDE main panel. Clicking on this icon raises a menu that will allow you to activate or deactivate your network (Ethernet) interfaces, and your wireless network connections too, if your machine has a wireless card. The menu item labeled "Connection Information" will report your IP address, subnet mask and other settings. Figure 1-17 shows the menu, the Connection Information box, and the netapplet icon (just to the left of the clock).

SUSE Linux 10.1 ships with a new network management tool called NetworkManager. This tool substantially simplifies the management of network connections and is a replacement for netapplet. It's available for both Gnome and KDE, and like

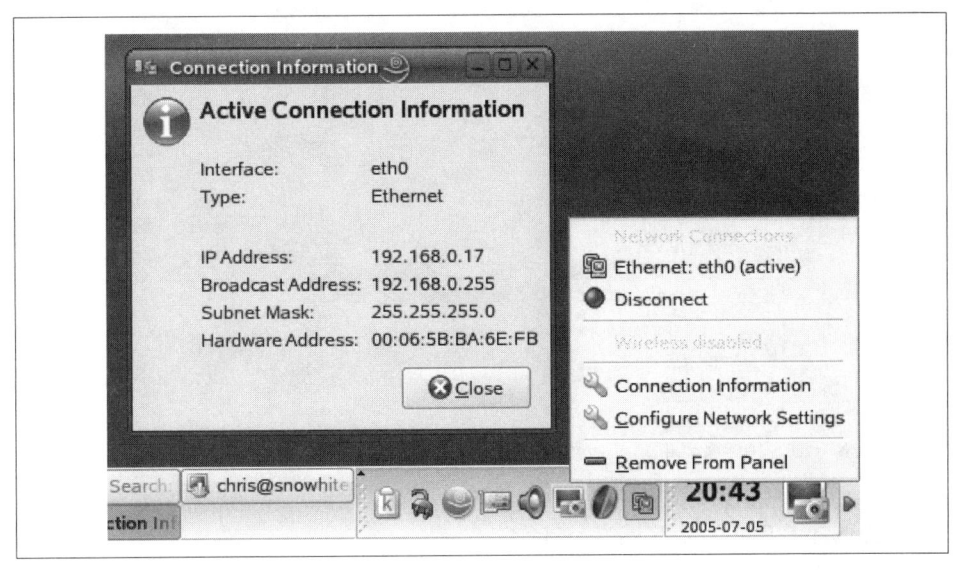

Figure 1-17. The netapplet

netapplet, it permits management of network connections without requiring root privileges. It is particularly useful on laptops which may, at different times, use wired network connections or connections via any one of several wireless networks. When moving into range of networks that you've connected to before, NetworkManager automatically connects to the last network you chose to connect to and will choose the network with the strongest signal, if appropriate. When back at the desk, NetworkManager will switch to the faster, more reliable wired connection. NetworkManager tries to implement an "always connected" policy.

When using KDE, the applet KNetworkManager places a small icon in the system tray. Hovering over this icon displays a tooltip showing the currently active network interface. Left-clicking brings up the KnetworkManager menu, shown in Figure 1-18. From here you can activate and deactivate interfaces and examine the settings of each interface. This screenshot comes from a machine that has two Ethernet cards but no wireless interface.

NetworkManager offers a number of benefits. It supports wired, wireless, and dial-up network connections, and has integrated VPN handling. NetworkManager is primarily intended to manage interfaces that are configured using DHCP, and does not provide a user interface for setting static IP addresses on interfaces. However, it does honor static settings established using YaST.

How It Works

Like most configuration changes you make using YaST, all you are really doing is editing the underlying configuration files, all of which are plain-text files and can be

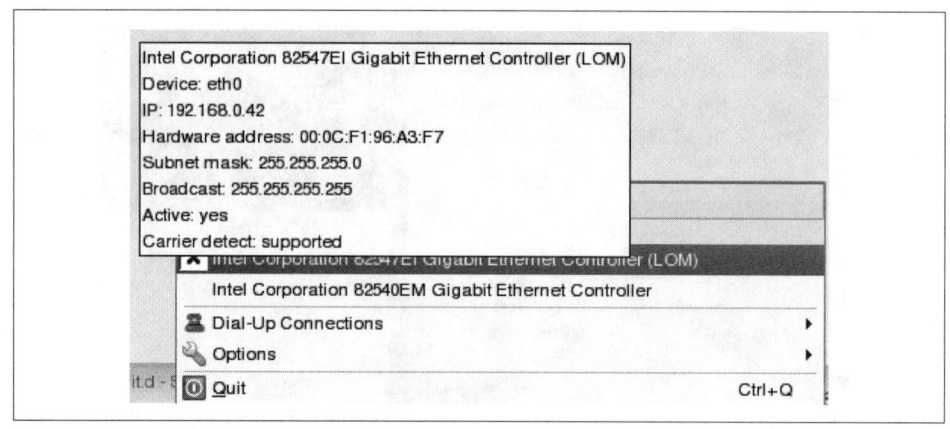

![Figure 1-18 screenshot showing NetworkManager applet with Intel Corporation 82547EI Gigabit Ethernet Controller (LOM), Device: eth0, IP: 192.168.0.42, Hardware address: 00:0C:F1:96:A3:F7, Subnet mask: 255.255.255.0, Broadcast: 255.255.255.255, Active: yes, Carrier detect: supported]

Figure 1-18. The NetworkManager applet

viewed with commands like *less* or edited directly with editors such as *vi*. (See Lab 2.1, "View and Edit Text Files" for details.)

Each named network device in SUSE Linux has a configuration file to hold settings such as its IP address. For example, the settings for a device named xyz are stored in the file */etc/sysconfig/network/ifcfg-xyz*. In this way, a specific group of settings is associated with a specific device name. In earlier versions of SUSE Linux, network devices had simple names like eth0 and eth1. The names were allocated in the order that the cards were detected as the system booted—the first was eth0, the second was eth1, and so on. Until the advent of hot-pluggable devices, this arrangement worked fine. The order that cards were detected in (and hence the name of the device and the name of its configuration file) was stable.

Hotplugging changes all that. We can no longer assume that the first device to be detected is always the same physical device. So, a smarter device naming scheme was introduced to ensure that the right configuration is associated with the right device. The scheme can use several ways to uniquely identify a device; two common ways are to use the MAC (Media Access Control) address of the card, or to use its position on the computer's bus. For example, the name:

    eth-id-00:01:02:8E:21:9

refers to an Ethernet device with the MAC address 00:01:02:8E:21:9, whereas the name:

    eth-bus-pci-0000:00:07.2

refers to any device in PCI slot 0000:00:07.2. Of course, this scheme is overkill for most machines, which have only one network interface.

Here is a sample configuration file for a statically configured card with the IP address 192.168.0.44. On my current system, the filename is */etc/sysconfig/network/ifcfg-eth-id-00:06:5b:ba:6e:fb*. Note in particular the settings for the parameters BOOTPROTO and IPADDR:

```
BOOTPROTO='static'
MTU=''
NAME='Dell 3c905C-TX/TX-M [Tornado]'
REMOTE_IPADDR=''
STARTMODE='auto'
UNIQUE='rBUF.oOfgbdRycVB'
USERCONTROL='no'
_nm_name='bus-pci-0000:02:01.0'
BROADCAST='192.168.0.255'
IPADDR='192.168.0.44'
NETMASK='255.255.255.0'
NETWORK='192.168.0.0'
```

DNS configuration is stored in the file */etc/resolv.conf*. A typical example looks like this:

```
nameserver 192.168.0.1
nameserver 213.253.16.72
search example.com
```

This example specifies two name servers (the second is tried only if the first fails) and a single search domain.

Where to Learn More

If you don't know what an IP address, a subnet mask, or a default gateway is, you might want to read an introductory text on TCP/IP, though you really don't need to know much of this to get a basic network connection going. There are guides available at The Linux Documentation Project (*http://www.tldp.org*); in particular, look for "The Linux Network Administrator's Guide Second Edition," which is available as a free download in PDF form. If you'd prefer a real paper book, try *Linux TCP/IP Network Administration* by Scott Mann (Prentice Hall). Both of these books are beginning to show their age, but they provide a good introduction.

For the gory details on the device naming scheme, look at the manual page for the command getcfg. (The following lab, Lab 1.5, "Access Documentation," shows how to read manual pages.)

For more detail on the entries in the *ifcfg-** files, try reading */usr/share/doc/packages/sysconfig/Network*. There is also a rather technical discussion of the design rationale in */usr/share/doc/packages/sysconfig/README*.

1.5   Access Documentation

It used to be said that Unix and Linux were short on documentation. Nowadays, if anything, there's too much. This lab will guide you to some of the sources of documentation.

I will deal first with the most traditional source of documentation for Unix and Linux systems, the so-called "manual" pages, often abbreviated to "manpages." The usage and format of these goes back many years. They were originally intended to document the command-line tools, and that is still their main purpose. You will, generally speaking, not find manpages for the graphical tools.

How Do I Do That?

From a command prompt, access the manpages with the man command; for example:

```
chris@snowhite:~> man gcc
```

will show the manual page for the GNU C compiler (the first screen of it is shown in Figure 1-19).

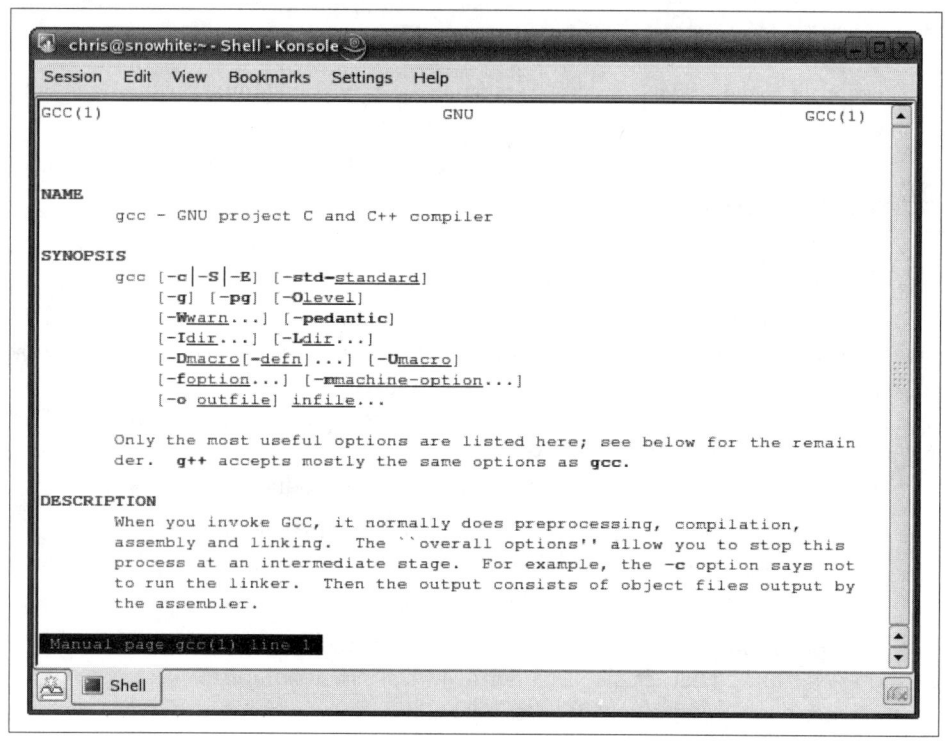

Figure 1-19. The manual page for gcc

As you'll see even from this small example, the manpages are very terse. The content is provided under various standard headings—NAME, SYNOPSIS, DESCRIPTION, OPTIONS, and so on. Most of them have a SEE ALSO section near the end, which provides a cross-reference to related commands. The manpages vary enormously in length and complexity. The page for the id command is just 64 lines. The page for gcc is over 9,000 lines. When viewed from a command prompt, manpages are piped through the program *less* to allow you to browse them. I discuss *less* in more detail in Chapter 2, but for now it is sufficient to know that you can press the up and down arrow keys to scroll through the material, and q to quit.

Of course, looking up a command by name works only if you already know the name of the command. If you don't, you can try using the `apropos` command to search the keyword-in-context index of the manpages and show matching entries. For example:

> chris@snowhite:~> **apropos compiler**

will show you all manpages with the word 'compiler' in their 'NAME' section.

There are other ways to access the manpages. From the Konqueror browser, for example, entering "man:gcc" into the location field will show you the manpage for gcc. It is formatted to look a little prettier than viewing it from the command prompt, but it's derived from exactly the same unformatted source, so the actual content is identical.

You can also access the manpages via the SUSE Help Center on the main menu. On the help center's home page, click Linux Documentation.

In addition to the manpages there's another command-line tool called *info*, which has its own database of documentation. The info system comes from the developers at the Free Software Foundation who were responsible for (re)writing many of the command-line tools in Linux (most of which are closely based on their earlier counterparts in Unix) and *info* is the preferred documentation system for these developers. Consequently you may find more complete or more up-to-date documentation in the info pages than in the manpages.

> In a way it's a shame that there are two "competing" command-line documentation tools, but that's the price you pay for the freedom of choice that open systems bring you.

From a command prompt, you can access the info page on a topic with the `info` command; for example:

> chris@snowhite:~> **info gcc**

will show you the top-level screen of the gcc documentation (Figure 1-20).

Each "page" within info is called a *node*, and the nodes are arranged in a hierarchy, allowing you to drill down to greater levels of detail, or up to broader coverage of a topic. From each node you can navigate to a neighboring node as follows:

- To move down to a more detailed topic, move the text cursor to any line beginning with an asterisk ('*') and press Enter.
- To move up in the hierarchy, press **u**.
- To move to the next topic at the same level in the hierarchy, press **n**.
- To move to the previous topic at the same level in the hierarchy, press **p**.

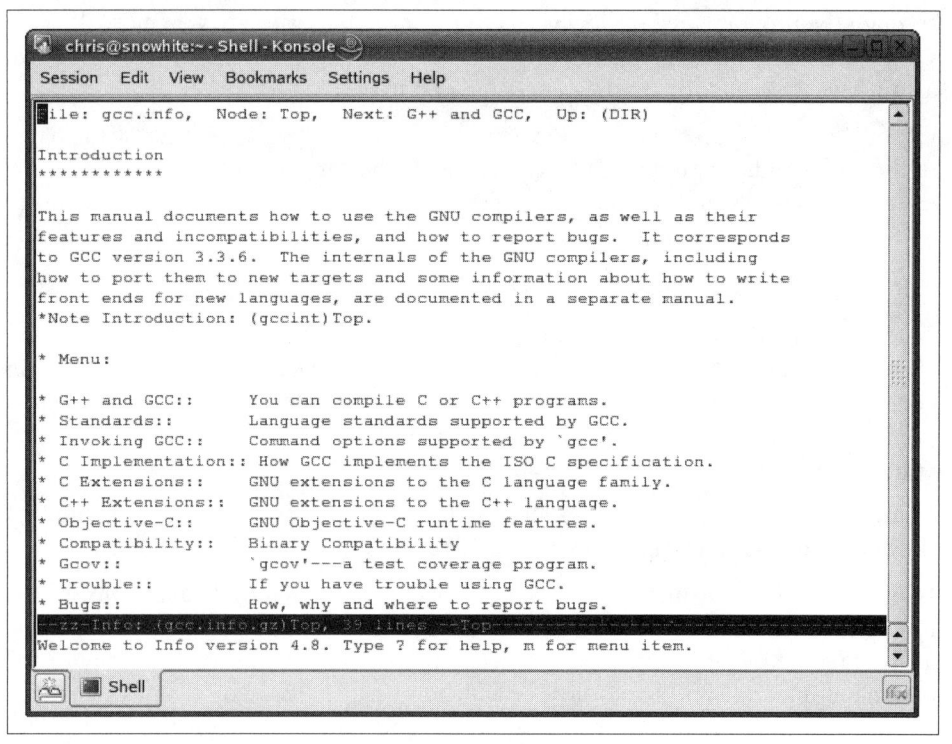

Figure 1-20. Top-level info page for gcc

If you keep pressing **u**, you'll end up at the very top-level node, which is where you would have started out if you ran the info command with no arguments.

Both man and info are designed for use in a command-line environment, and are designed to provide documentation for command-line tools. They both provide terse reference material, often with no actual examples of command usage and little or no tutorial content.

From the graphical desktop, the most obvious source of help is the SUSE Help Center, accessed via the life belt/preserver icon on the main menu. This tool brings together help from a number of sources. Perhaps the most important of these are the HTML versions of the printed User Guide and Administration Guide that you would have received if you bought the boxed product of SUSE Linux Professional. The content is identical to the printed manuals, but the HTML version has the benefit of hyperlinks for the cross-references. Also available through SUSE Help Center are the user manuals for many individual KDE applications. These are arranged in topics that correspond (approximately) to the main menu hierarchy on the KDE desktop. Handbooks are included for the KMail and Evolution mail clients, the Konqueror browser, the Kate and KWrite editors, the KDE Print manager, and much else. The help center includes a tree view which makes it easier to see the overall structure and makes navigation easy (see Figure 1-21).

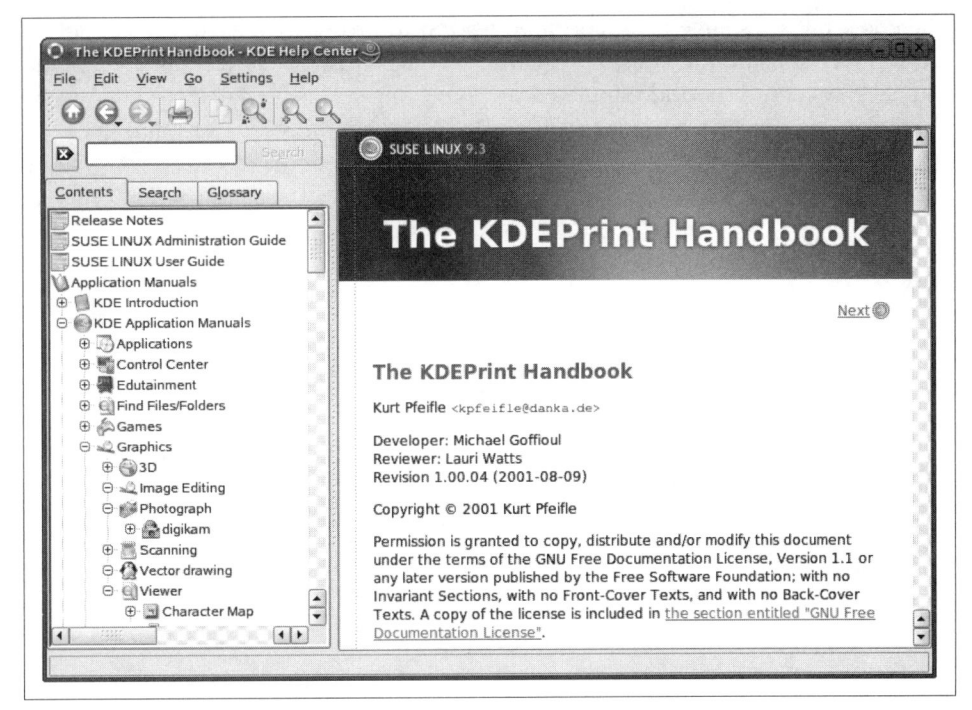

Figure 1-21. The SUSE Help Center

Many of the KDE applications include an item on their Help menu that will take you directly to the SUSE Help Center, opened up to the application's handbook.

Where to Learn More

Many of the packages installed on the system include documentation in subdirectories under */usr/share/doc/packages*. There are nearly a thousand of them. Be aware, though, that much of this is written by developers and some of it is fairly technical stuff aimed at system administrators and other developers.

On the web, several sites collect Linux documentation. For example, The Linux Documentation Project, at *http://www.tldp.org*, carries a huge number of guides and HOWTO documents.

> The HOWTO documents have long been an important source of information on a huge variety of topics ranging from Astronomy to Zip Drives. The HOWTO collection is the Linux equivalent of *The Hitchhiker's Guide to the Galaxy*—"a very unevenly edited book containing many passages that simply seemed to its editors like a good idea at the time."

There is a huge resource here, and if you begin to browse it, you will find yourself moving well outside the comfortable world of a preinstalled, preconfigured point-and-click system to a world populated by pioneering spirits prepared to spend many hours figuring out how to make stuff work on the bleeding edge of Linux technology. Do not believe everything you read in a HOWTO. Some of them are very old. Some apply to versions of Linux you don't have. A few are plain wrong, though doubtless they seemed like a good idea at the time.

CHAPTER 2
Basic System Administration

Once upon a time, Unix (the forerunner of Linux) had no graphical desktop at all. A command prompt was the only user interface. Of course, Linux now has a high-quality, modern, graphical desktop (indeed, it has more than one). Nowadays there are tools that let you perform most system administration through a graphical interface (in particular YaST, in SUSE Linux). Nonetheless, Linux retains its command-line interface (you'll also hear this referred to as a shell prompt, "shell" being the Linux name for a command interpreter), and you'll find plenty of Linux users (especially the hardcore geeks) who prefer this interface to the graphical tools. Throughout this book, I'll often discuss how to perform a particular task using graphical tools and how to do the same thing from the command line. It is not my intention to embark on a religious crusade in favor of either the graphical desktop or the command line. Both have their strengths and weaknesses. Which you prefer depends largely on your background and expectations.

It is easy to access a command prompt from a Linux desktop. In KDE, for example, select System → Terminal → Konsole from the main menu. There is also an icon on Kicker (the KDE main panel). Either method will bring up a *terminal window* and start a shell. For a really old-fashioned, authentic view of the command line, you can use the shortcut keys Ctrl-Alt-F1 through Ctrl-Alt-F6 to view up to six *virtual terminals* on which you can log in and enter commands. (From a virtual terminal, use Alt-F7 to return to the graphical desktop.) When comparing Linux to Windows, it's important to note that you don't have to install a window manager or any graphical applications if you don't want to. Indeed, Linux systems intended for use as, say, a mail server or a database server are usually set up this way.

When the shell is ready for another command, it prints a *prompt*. The prompt can be configured to be anything you want, but by default it is of the form:

   username@*hostname*:directory>

For example:

   chris@snowhite:~>

Note that the tilde (~) is a shorthand notation meaning "my home directory." For simplicity, in this book I show the prompt simply as $ (but I show the # prompt when you should enter commands as the root user).

Commands generally consist of a command name, possibly some options, and one or more arguments, which often specify the names of files or folders to operate on. For example, in the command:

    $ ls -l /etc

ls is the name of a command that lists the files in a directory, -l is an option (meaning "long"—i.e., detailed—listing), and /etc is the directory whose contents are to be listed.

2.1 View and Edit Text Files

Linux uses a lot of files that contain "plain old text," including (almost without exception) all system-wide and user-specific configuration files. Being able to view and edit such files is a key skill for driving Linux in anything beyond first gear. This lab looks at some of the tools for viewing and editing plain text files, and covers both graphical tools and command-line tools.

How Do I Do That?

If you're using a graphical desktop, clicking on a text file in either the Konqueror file browser (KDE) or in Nautilus (GNOME) displays the contents of a text file in the browser's window.

From the command line, a good tool for viewing a text file is less. It's easy to run: you just supply the filename as an argument:

    $ less /usr/share/doc/packages/sodipodi/README

> The name less is a reference to an earlier and simpler program called more, which let you browse through the file a screenful at a time. Each time you pressed the spacebar, you saw more of the file. The later program less is actually fancier; in particular, you can page up as well as down through the file. "Less is more" is the wisdom on the streets. You will discover that the names of many Linux commands are either (a) an historical accident, (b) an obscure reference to something that came earlier, or (c) a testimony to the somewhat limited sense of humor of people who give names to Linux commands.

When you run less, it will display the first screenful of the file, then pause, wondering what to do next. There are many single-character commands that you can enter at this stage; typing **h** will show you a command summary (the top part of which is shown in Figure 2-1), but you can drive less satisfactorily with rather few commands (see Table 2-1).

Table 2-1. Key commands for less

Command	Description
Spacebar or Page Down	Scroll forward one screen
b or Page Up	Scroll backward one screen
Down arrow	Scroll forward one line
Up arrow	Scroll backward one line
/string	Search forward for string
?string	Search backward for string
n	Repeat previous search
5G	Go to line 5
h	Display help screen
q	Quit (back to command prompt)

The searching commands (especially /) are worth memorizing.

If you need to edit a text file, as opposed to just looking at it, the options are more numerous.

> Every man and his dog seems to have written a text editor for Linux. The ones written by dogs tend to involve a lot of barking and sniffing around the connectors at the back of the computer, and are probably best ignored. But that still leaves quite a lot.

From the graphical desktop, use gedit or kwrite. Nominally, gedit is a GNOME application and kwrite is a KDE application, but both will run fine in either environment. If you know how to use an editor like Notepad in Windows, you can use gedit and kwrite. Both are a little fancier than Notepad, but not much. gedit supports multiple tabs, allowing you to switch between several files in the same window, and will show simple document statistics (line and word counts). kwrite has bookmarks and does color syntax highlighting. This means that it will try to figure out what kind of language is used in the file—a C program, a Perl program, an HTML file, and so on—and will display the various contextual elements of the file, such as keywords, comments, and text strings, in different colors.

For a more advanced graphical editor, consider using Kate (KDE Advanced Text Editor). Among other things, Kate does syntax highlighting and will also handle split views; that is, you can edit several files in different panes. Both of these features are shown in Figure 2-2.

From the command line, the classic editor is vi, but many others are available.

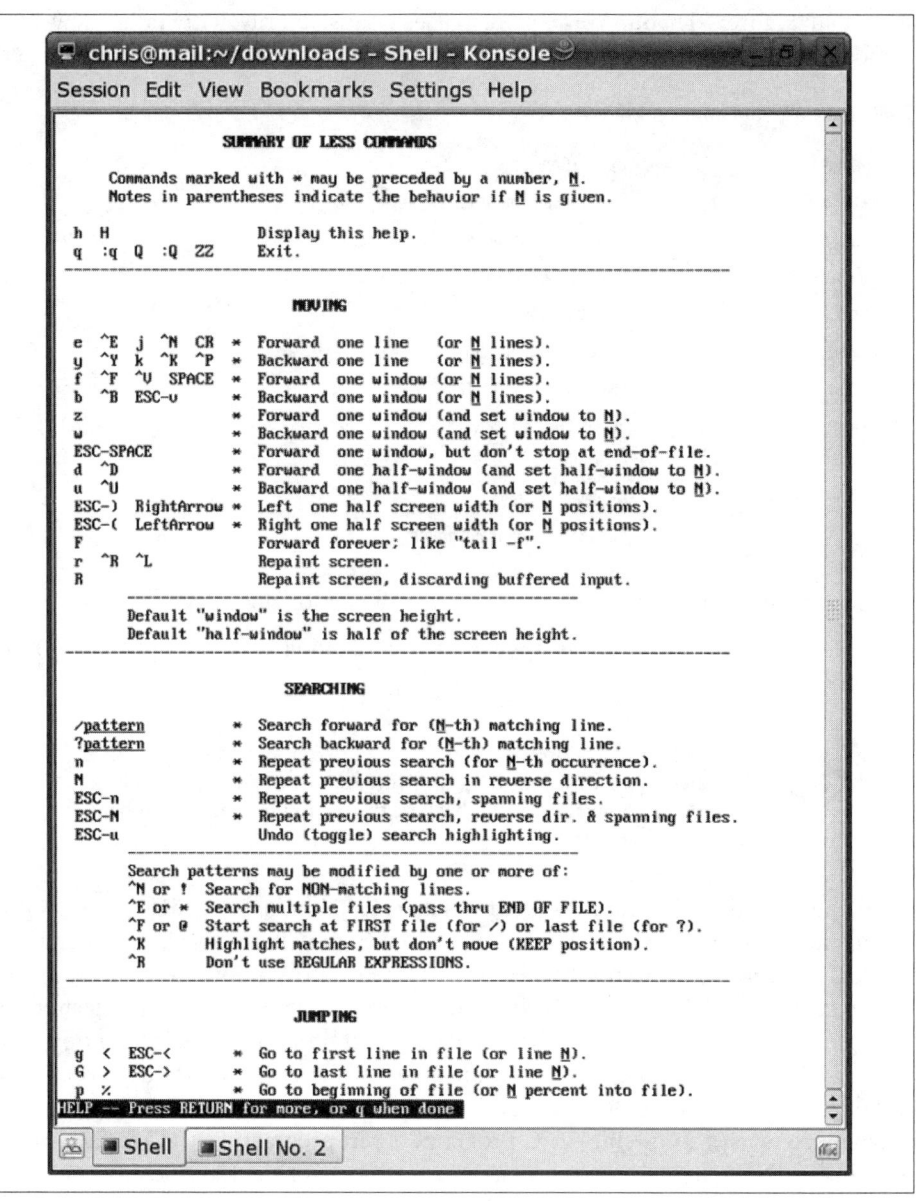

```
                    SUMMARY OF LESS COMMANDS

        Commands marked with * may be preceded by a number, N.
        Notes in parentheses indicate the behavior if N is given.

  h  H                   Display this help.
  q  :q  Q  :Q  ZZ       Exit.
---------------------------------------------------------------------
                              MOVING

  e  ^E  j  ^N  CR   *  Forward  one line   (or N lines).
  y  ^Y  k  ^K  ^P   *  Backward one line   (or N lines).
  f  ^F  ^V SPACE    *  Forward  one window (or N lines).
  b  ^B  ESC-v       *  Backward one window (or N lines).
  z                  *  Forward  one window (and set window to N).
  w                  *  Backward one window (and set window to N).
  ESC-SPACE          *  Forward  one window, but don't stop at end-of-file.
  d  ^D              *  Forward  one half-window (and set half-window to N).
  u  ^U              *  Backward one half-window (and set half-window to N).
  ESC-)  RightArrow  *  Left  one half screen width (or N positions).
  ESC-(  LeftArrow   *  Right one half screen width (or N positions).
  F                     Forward forever; like "tail -f".
  r  ^R  ^L             Repaint screen.
  R                     Repaint screen, discarding buffered input.
---------------------------------------------------------------------
        Default "window" is the screen height.
        Default "half-window" is half of the screen height.
---------------------------------------------------------------------
                             SEARCHING

  /pattern           *  Search forward for (N-th) matching line.
  ?pattern           *  Search backward for (N-th) matching line.
  n                  *  Repeat previous search (for N-th occurrence).
  N                  *  Repeat previous search in reverse direction.
  ESC-n              *  Repeat previous search, spanning files.
  ESC-N              *  Repeat previous search, reverse dir. & spanning files.
  ESC-u                 Undo (toggle) search highlighting.
---------------------------------------------------------------------
        Search patterns may be modified by one or more of:
        ^N or !    Search for NON-matching lines.
        ^E or *    Search multiple files (pass thru END OF FILE).
        ^F or @    Start search at FIRST file (for /) or last file (for ?).
        ^K         Highlight matches, but don't move (KEEP position).
        ^R         Don't use REGULAR EXPRESSIONS.
---------------------------------------------------------------------
                              JUMPING

  g  <  ESC-<        *  Go to first line in file (or line N).
  G  >  ESC->        *  Go to last line in file (or line N).
  p  %               *  Go to beginning of file (or N percent into file).
HELP -- Press RETURN for more, or q when done
```

Figure 2-1. Part of the help screen for less

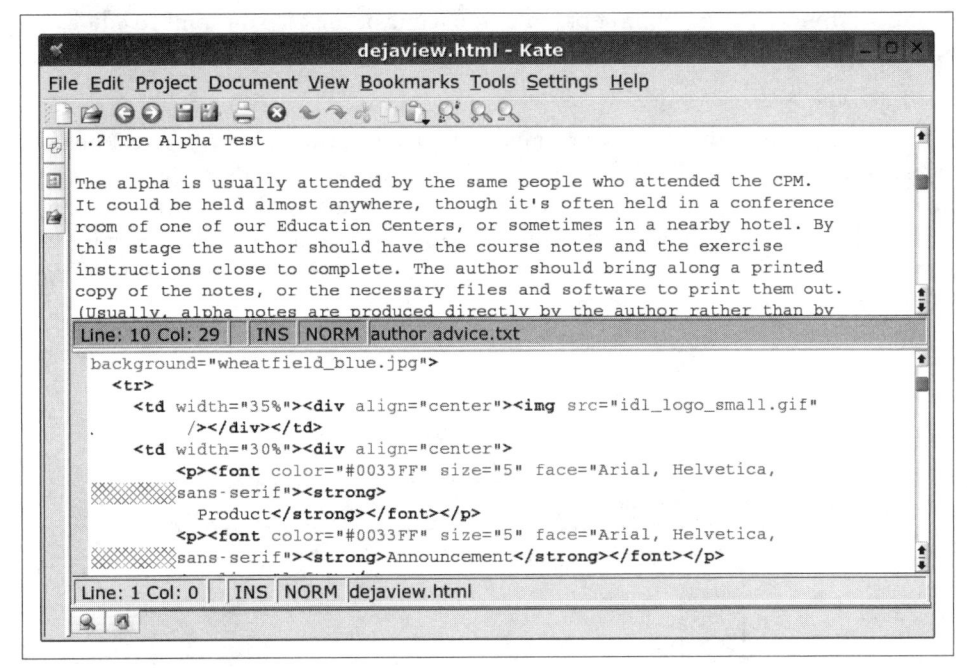

Figure 2-2. The Kate text editor

> Originally, vi was written by Bill Joy when he was at the University of California at Berkeley. He later went on to cofound Sun Microsystems. This was quite a long time ago. Many experienced Linux users prefer vi and would use nothing else; it is an extremely efficient editor once you get used to it. However, I will be the first to admit that it is not the easiest editor in the world to learn. Bill Joy is credited with saying that if he had known how popular vi would become, he would never have written it. By the way, if you want to avoid disgracing yourself amongst the Linux cognoscenti, you should pronounce vi "vee-eye." Do not call it "vie." (My esteemed contributor Simon Crute is unconvinced by this, and confesses to disgracing himself in this way on a daily basis.)

The vi editor is available on every Unix and Linux system. It is available on the SUSE Rescue disk. It works on character terminals, without a graphical user interface, and it is fast and powerful once you get to know it. Most of the difficulty in getting to grips with vi comes from the fact that it is a *modal* editor. In other words, the effect of the keys that you type depend on what mode you're in. For example, if you're in command mode, typing an x will delete the character under the cursor, but if you're in insert mode, typing an x will insert an x into the text you're editing.

To run vi from a command prompt, enter the name of the file you want to edit as an argument to the command; for example:

```
$ vi /etc/fstab
```

Figure 2-3 illustrates the three major modes of vi and shows a few of the commands available in each mode. Table 2-2 shows a few of the commands available in command mode, and Table 2-3 shows a few of the commands available in "bottom line" mode. The commands illustrated here will not make you a vi expert, nor will they make you appreciate the power and regularity of vi's command structure, but they will allow you to survive with it.

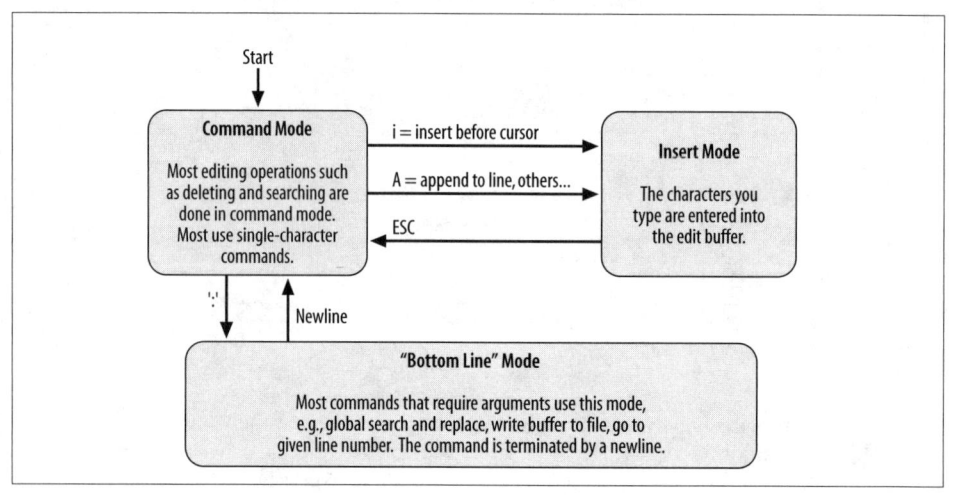

Figure 2-3. Operating modes in vi

Table 2-2. Some vi commands

Command	Description
i	Switch to insert mode, insert text before cursor position
A	Switch to insert mode, append to current line
x	Delete the character under the cursor
dd	Delete the current line (and put it in the paste buffer)
D	Delete to end of line
/*pattern*	Search for *pattern*, forward from current position
?*pattern*	Search for *pattern*, backward from current position
n	Repeat the search in the same direction
yy	"Yank" (copy) the current line into the paste buffer
p	Insert the paste buffer before the current cursor position
ZZ	Save the file and exit
.	Repeat the previous change at the new cursor position

Table 2-3. Some commands used on the bottom line of the screen

Command	Description
:q!	Quit the editor, abandoning any changes that have been made
:wq	Write out the file and exit (same as ZZ in command mode)
:w *file*	Write the edit buffer to the specified file
:41	Go to line 41

What About...

...exchanging text files with Windows? There is a minor issue that can arise if you're trading plain text files back and forth between Linux and Windows. In Windows, a text file usually has two characters to mark the end of a line—CR (carriage return) followed by LF (line feed). Linux uses just LF. The command-line tool dos2unix performs the conversion one way, and (predictably) unix2dos goes the other way.

...viewing binary files? The tools I discussed in this lab are really meant for viewing and editing plain text files. There are a few tools to help you peer inside other file types.

First, the file command will try to guess what kind of information is contained in a file. For example:

```
$ file /etc/fstab ./pics/sunset1.jpg /home/chris
/etc/fstab:        ASCII text
./pics/sunset1.jpg: JPEG image data, JFIF standard 1.02
/home/chris:       directory
```

The command uses a set of pattern-matching rules (read from the file */usr/share/misc/magic*) to determine the file type. It usually gets it right, but not always.

The strings command pulls out strings of ASCII text embedded in any file. It can be interesting to run strings on an executable file to see the text strings it contains—many of them are error messages. On one occasion I used the strings command to recover text from a Microsoft Word file (a *.doc* file) that a friend of mine had accidentally mangled. (You might be surprised to learn how much text you thought you'd deleted actually remains buried in a *.doc* file!)

Here is the (very heavily edited) result of running strings on the Linux kernel image, */boot/vmlinuz*:

```
$ strings -n 8 /boot/vmlinuz
Direct booting from floppy is no longer supported.
Please use a boot loader program instead.
Remove disk and press any key to reboot . . .
No setup signature found ...
Wrong loader, giving up...
linux: fatal error: A20 gate not responding!
2.6.11.4-20a-default (geeko@buildhost) #1 Wed Mar 23 21:52:37 UTC 2005
... lots more output deleted ...
```

Such output can be difficult to interpret, because you are seeing just the text in the file, without knowing the context. However, you'll notice that most of the messages in the kernel are error messages!

If all else fails, you can view any file byte by byte using the od command. The command supports a number of options that specify the output format. For example, -x shows the contents in hexadecimal, and -c shows the contents as printable ASCII characters wherever possible. Here's an example, again heavily edited, showing the contents of a backup of my Palm address book:

```
$ od -c address.dat
0000000  \0 001   B   A   O   C   :   \   P   r   o   g   r   a   m
0000020   F   i   l   e   s   \   P   a   l   m   \   B   r   o   w   n
0000040   C   \   a   d   d   r   e   s   s   \   a   d   d   r   e   s
0000060   s   .   d   a   t 304   C   u   s   t   o   m       1  \n   C
0000100   u   s   t   o   m       2  \n   C   u   s   t   o   m       3
0000120  \n   C   u   s   t   o   m       4  \n   0   1   2   7   4  \n
0000140   1  \n   1   6  \n   1   0   0   0   0   0   0   0   0   0
0000160   0   0   0   0   0   0   0   0   0   0   0   0   0   0
... lots more output deleted ...
```

You probably won't use od often. I have occasionally used it to examine program source code that looked fine but refused to compile due to (it turned out) the presence of a nonprinting ASCII character. There is also a graphical tool called ghex2 (from the GNOME desktop), which supports a similar byte-by-byte display of a file and even lets you edit the file at this level, though you'd have to be fairly desperate to do this! ghex2 even allows you to display the data in binary files that contain integer or floating-point data.

2.2 Explore the Filesystem

Linux, like Windows, has a hierarchical filesystem. That is, there is an organization of folders and subfolders arranged in a tree. In the Linux world, you are more likely to hear folders referred to as *directories*; the two terms are interchangeable. If you're coming from a Windows background, there are a few differences you'll need to get accustomed to.

First, a typical *pathname* for a file in Windows looks like this:

```
C:\Program Files\Adobe\Acrobat 6.0
```

Here's an example of a pathname in Linux:

```
/opt/mozilla/bin
```

First, notice that Linux uses forward slashes ("/") to separate the components of a path name, not backslashes ("\"). This is easy to get used to. Second, Linux does not use drive letters like C: and D:. I know that users coming from a Windows background have grown very attached to their drive letters and sometimes view their absence in Linux as an omission. I would prefer that you see it as progress. Even though a filesystem on Linux may be split across several drives (including hard disk partitions, removable media such as CDs, and filesystems on remote file servers), everything is assembled together into a single filesystem tree. When you make reference to a file, you do not need to know which drive it is on, or whether it is local or remote—you just need to know its name. You'll see how this works later.

The most significant differences between the Windows and Linux filesystems, however, lie in the actual organization—the actual names of the directories and the details of what goes where. This lab describes that organization and also examines the tools that will allow you to explore the filesystem.

How Do I Do That?

From the KDE desktop, use Konqueror to browse the filesystem. Konqueror is the Linux equivalent of Windows Explorer. To launch Konqueror, click on the blue "home" icon on the main panel. This will launch Konqueror in your home directory. Konqueror has several view modes, selectable from the View → View Mode menu. These include:

An icon view
    Each file or folder is represented by an icon with the name displayed underneath.

A tree view
    Each file or folder is represented by one line in the view. Folders have a + icon, which you can click to expand the view to include the contents of that folder.

A detailed list view
    Each file or folder is represented by one line in the view, which shows the file's name, size, type, last modified timestamp, access permissions, and ownership. This view is roughly equivalent to the output from `ls -l` at the command line.

Konqueror also includes a navigation panel, which shows (among other things) a tree view of the filesystem. If it's not showing up, select Show Navigation Panel from the Window menu. You should see a sidebar of icons appear on the left. Click on the little blue home icon to open the tree view in your home directory or on the red folder to open the tree view in the root directory. You may also need to drag the vertical divider bar to the right to open up some space for this view. There are other views that can be shown in the navigation panel, including a history of recently visited sites and folders, and your bookmarks.

Figure 2-4 shows Konqueror with the navigation panel displaying a tree view of the root directory and the main panel in icon view mode.

Konqueror works very much like Windows Explorer, and so Windows users should have little difficulty getting used to it.

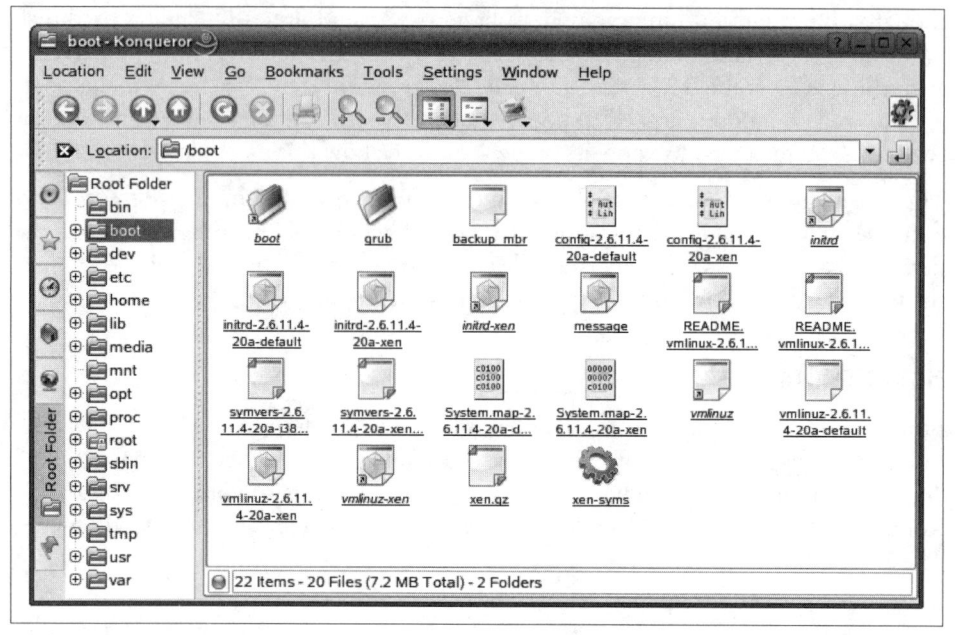

Figure 2-4. Konqueror in icon view mode

> You will quickly discover that Konqueror (indeed, most of the KDE desktop) responds to a single mouse click, whereas Windows and Mac OS X normally need two. If you don't want to actually open a file but merely to select it (for example to drag and drop it to another folder), Ctrl-click. In Lab 3.4, "Configure the KDE Desktop," you'll see how to change the behavior to the double-click style. The GNOME desktop, on the other hand, defaults to double-click behavior.

There are several ways to navigate within Konqueror. To go to a folder, you can:

- Single-click on the folder in the main view.
- Select the folder from the tree view in the navigation panel on the left.
- Type the pathname of the folder in the location bar.

The toolbar also includes the usual "back," "forward," "up," and "home" buttons.

If you have chosen to use the GNOME desktop instead of KDE, you will use Nautilus instead of Konqueror as your filesystem browser. Nautilus has a superbly modern, uncluttered appearance, as shown in Figure 2-5.

Nautilus has just two main views: an icon view and a list view, selectable from the View menu. Like Konqueror, it also has a side pane (use function key F9 to turn this on and off). A drop-down list at the top of the pane provides multiple view types, including a tree view of the filesystem (shown in the figure), a history list of recently

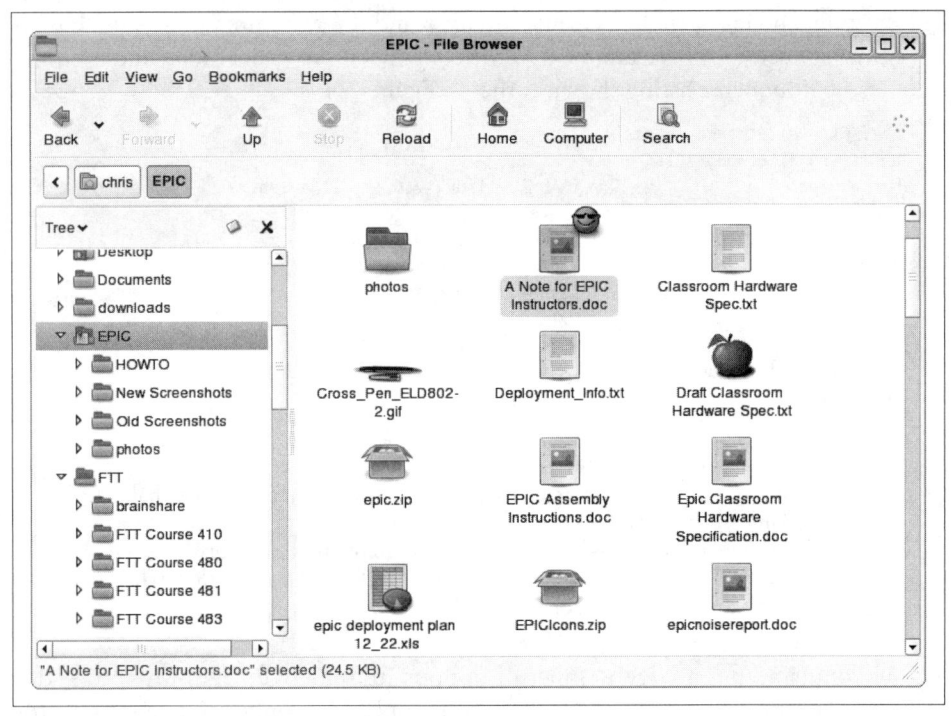

Figure 2-5. Nautilus in icon view mode

visited folders, a notes view (which allows you to attach written notes to a directory), and an emblems view. Emblems are icons that you can attach to a file; from the emblems view in the side panel, drag and drop the emblem of your choice onto the file of your choice. A file can have multiple emblems attached. You can see an example of an emblem (a smiley wearing shades) in the figure.

There are several ways to navigate within Nautilus. To go to a folder, you can:

- Double-click on the folder in the main view.
- Select the folder from the tree view in the side panel on the left.
- Type the pathname of the folder in the location bar (select Go → Location from the main menu, or type Ctrl-L to see the location bar).

The toolbar also includes the usual "back," "forward," "up," and "home" buttons.

Using the command line

From the command line, there are two key commands for navigating within the filesystem: `cd` and `ls`.

2.2 Explore the Filesystem | 43

The cd command changes the current directory, and the ls command lists the files in the current directory. This example lists the contents of the folder /boot, and is equivalent to the Konqueror listing shown earlier in Figure 2-4:

```
chris@snowhite:~> cd /boot
chris@snowhite:/boot> ls
backup_mbr                      README.vmlinux-2.6.11.4-20a-xen.gz
boot                            symvers-2.6.11.4-20a-i386-default.gz
config-2.6.11.4-20a-default     symvers-2.6.11.4-20a-xen-xen.gz
config-2.6.11.4-20a-xen         System.map-2.6.11.4-20a-default
grub                            System.map-2.6.11.4-20a-xen
initrd                          vmlinuz
initrd-2.6.11.4-20a-default     vmlinuz-2.6.11.4-20a-default
initrd-2.6.11.4-20a-xen         vmlinuz-2.6.11.4-20a-xen
initrd-xen                      vmlinuz-xen
message                         xen.gz
```

> When you enter filenames as arguments to commands, note that a name such as */home/chris/Documents* that begins with a slash is an absolute name and is interpreted relative to the root directory. A name that doesn't begin with a slash, such as *Documents/workshop.txt*, is interpreted relative to the current directory.

The ls command has a large number of options (too many for its own good—run the command man ls for the details). A commonly used option is -l, which produces a long listing that includes the file's attributes. For example:

```
chris@snowhite:~> ls -l /boot
total 7466
-rw-r--r--  1 root root      512 2005-05-30 21:46 backup_mbr
lrwxrwxrwx  1 root root        1 2005-05-30 21:36 boot -> .
-rw-r--r--  1 root root    60418 2005-03-24 00:31 config-2.6.11.4-20a-default
-rw-r--r--  1 root root    57383 2005-03-24 00:05 config-2.6.11.4-20a-xen
drwxr-xr-x  2 root root      480 2005-05-30 21:46 grub
```

This example also shows that you can enter a folder name (/boot, in this case) as an argument to ls. You'll learn what all the file attributes mean in Lab 2.4, "Set File Access Permissions and Ownership" later in this chapter. For the present, these commands are sufficient to allow you to browse the filesystem from the command line.

How It Works

Although the directory structure in Linux may look arbitrary at first meeting (it is certainly quite different from Windows), the organization is logical once you get used to it—although some of the actual directory names are a little quaint. The directories shown in the navigation panel on the left of Figure 2-3 show the directories at the top level of the filesystem, immediately under the root. Table 2-4 explains these.

Table 2-4. A brief tour of the root of the filesystem

Directory	Contents
/bin	"bin" is short for binary. A (relatively small) number of key system applications live here.
/boot	This folder contains the files needed during booting. This includes GRUB (the boot loader) and its configuration files, and the actual Linux kernel images.
/dev	The entries in this directory are not real files. They are "special device files" and serve to give filenames to hardware devices. For example, */dev/lp0* is the parallel port—the Linux equivalent of LPT1: in Windows.
/etc	"etc" is short for et cetera. This is where Linux stores most of its system-wide configuration (as opposed to per-user configuration). Most of these are plain text files and can be viewed using `less` and (if you know what you're doing and are logged in as root) edited with `vi`.
/home	*/home* is where users' home directories live. My home directory, for example, is */home/chris*.
/lib	"lib" is short for library. Most Linux applications use dynamic linking; that is, they attach to the libraries they need at runtime. In Windows these are called Dynamic Link Library (DLL) files; in Linux they are called "shared objects" and have names ending in *.so*. Some key libraries live in this directory.
/media	This directory contains the *mount points* for removable media. For example, if I insert a floppy disk, I can mount it on */media/floppy*. The filesystem on the floppy then shows up under that directory. (There is nothing special about */media/floppy*. It is just an empty directory waiting to be mounted on.)
/mnt	This directory is a sort of general-purpose mount point, sometimes used to temporarily attach other filesystems.
/opt	"opt" is short for optional. The idea is that each supplier of third-party software for Linux installs their applications into folders under here. The folders are named after the supplier. It is a bit like the *Program Files* folder in Windows or the *Applications* folder in Mac OS X.
/proc	"proc" is short for process. The things you'll see in here aren't real files; they're figments of the kernel's imagination. They provide a way for diagnostic applications to peer into the address space of a running process.
/root	This is the super-user's home directory. Do not confuse */root* with "the root directory" (/).
/sbin	This directory contains tools for booting, restoring, configuring, and repairing the filesystem. For the most part, only root can run these programs to make changes to the system.
/srv	If you are running a server that provides content over the network, that content should be placed here. For example, content for an FTP server would go in */srv/ftp*, and content for a web server would go in */srv/www*. This convention is often not followed.
/sys	Another virtual filesystem, similar to */proc*, that provides a way to peer into the kernel's view of the hardware devices present in the system. */sys* is updated dynamically as hot-pluggable devices are added to or removed from the system.
/tmp	"tmp" is short for temporary. Anyone can create files here. Some applications use it as a sort of "scratch pad" area.
/usr	Discussed in the following section.
/var	"var" is short for variable. Some programs record their runtime status in here. For example, a game might store its high-score league table here. Most servers and system services store their logs in */var/log*.

The /usr directory deserves special mention. You'll see some folders under here, such as *bin*, *lib*, and *sbin*, that have cousins in the root directory.

> Some writers claim that *usr* stands for "Unix System Resources" (which it unarguably does, just as it stands for "Universal Sand Reclamation"), but I think that it was originally short for "user." In some early versions of Unix, user directories were stored here, instead of in /home.

Newcomers to Linux are understandably puzzled why (for example) some libraries are in /lib and some (most, actually) are in /usr/lib. The answer has to do with partitioning. It's common for a Linux filesystem, particularly on larger production systems, to be split across several partitions, and quite possibly across several disks. One of these partitions is called the *root partition*. The root partition is special in that it is the only partition that is automatically mounted into the filesystem when the kernel boots. Consequently, everything that the kernel needs during the initial stages of booting must be on the root partition. (The really obvious candidate here is the mount command, which is used to attach additional partitions.) Actually, the root partition contains everything that is needed to boot to a command prompt. This is useful for repair and configuration work when all other partitions are offline (or maybe even corrupt). Consequently, directories such as /boot, /bin, /sbin, and /lib are always on the root partition.

It's quite common for /usr to be on a separate partition. One reason for this is that the contents of /usr should not change during normal system operation, allowing the partition to be mounted read-only to improve security. Applications and libraries that are not essential for minimal system operation (that is, most of them) are placed in /usr/bin, /usr/sbin, and /usr/lib.

/usr/local is conventionally used as a place to install software you've built from source. Most open source packages will (by default) install into here. Finally, /usr/share is intended for "read-only architecture independent data files" (I'm quoting from the official documentation here for want of a better description). "Architecture independent" means that the files are equally valid for a Pentium platform, or (say) for a Power PC, or an IBM Z-series mainframe. In practice this means that most of the stuff living under here is documentation. There is actually a huge amount of good stuff in here, especially under the directory /usr/share/doc/packages.

What About...

...accessing Windows partitions? Linux is able to access Windows filesystems. If you install SUSE Linux onto a machine that already had Windows partitions on the disk, to create a dual-boot system, the SUSE installer will automatically create mount points for those partitions and arrange for the partitions to be automatically mounted when Linux boots. The mount points are in the folder /windows and are called C, D, etc., according to the drive letters C: and D: that they would be known by in Windows. If you `cd` to the directory */windows/C* and list the files there, you are looking at the C: drive of your Windows installation.

Linux supports both read and write access to FAT32 filesystems, but it only supports read access to NTFS filesystems. Actually, recent versions of the driver do support writing, but only to existing files and only if the file size is not changed. Take a look at *http://www.linux-ntfs.org* for more detail on the status of this driver.

Where to Learn More

The SUSE Linux filesystem conforms quite closely to The Filesystem Hierarchy Standard (FHS)—a vendor-independent standard that describes what should go where in a Linux fileystem. The FHS is not really a formal standard but more a detailed set of guidelines and a rationale behind the organization. It is quite easy to read and is available at *http://www.pathname.com/fhs*.

There's a shorter (and slightly less up to date) description of the filesystem organization in the *hier* manual page. Try `man hier` for details.

2.3 Manage Files and Directories

There are some fundamental skills needed for any operating system—the ability to create, move, rename, and delete files and directories—that everyone needs. This lab shows how to do those things using both the graphical desktop and the command line.

How Do I Do That?

The previous lab discussed the use of Konqueror and the command-line tools to browse the filesystem. Table 2-5 compares some graphical and command-line operations.

Table 2-5. Comparing graphical and command-line operations

To do this	In Konqueror	From a command prompt
Delete a file	Right-click the file and select Move to Trash from the context menu.	`$ rm filename`
Rename a file	Right-click the file and select Rename from the context menu. Enter the new name.	`$ mv oldname newname`
Copy a file	Control-click to select the file, then type Control-C or select Edit → Copy from the menu. Navigate to the destination directory, and then type Control-V or select Edit → Paste from the menu. You can also copy files using drag-and-drop between two Konqueror windows.	`$ cp oldname newname`
Create a file	Right-click a whitespace area and select Create New from the menu that appears.	`$ touch filename`

There is rather more power and subtlety in the command-line tools than the table suggests. For one thing, all of the commands can operate on multiple files. So, for example:

```
$ rm tuna dory cod
```

will delete all three files. (By the way, note that rm really does delete the files. It does not place them in the trash, so it is not possible to recover from inadvertent use of rm.)

Similarly, if I have a directory called *fish* in my current directory, I could move multiple files into that directory with:

```
$ mv tuna dory cod fish
```

or copy them with:

```
$ cp tuna dory cod fish
```

Note that specifying multiple files in this way works only if the last argument is the name of an *existing* directory.

The shell also supports the use of wildcards to perform pattern matching on filenames. A complete treatment of wildcards deserves a lab of its own, but the most commonly used wildcard is *, which matches any sequence of zero or more characters. For example, to delete all filenames ending in *.wav* from the current directory:

```
$ rm *.wav
```

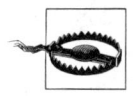

> Beware of the infamous **rm ***, which will delete all the files in the current directory. This is roughly equivalent to the old DOS command **erase *.***. DOS users may remember that erase used to ask for confirmation of this by asking "Are you sure?" Newcomers to Linux sometimes wonder why rm doesn't do the same. The answer is that it's the *shell* that expands the wildcards (substituting a list of matching names back into the command line); rm simply sees the expanded list. Users with a nervous disposition may prefer to use rm -i. This will ask you to confirm each deletion. It's possible to define an alias for the rm command, such that it always expands to rm -i.

As another example, if you had an existing directory called *sounds* you could move all your *.wav* files into it with:

```
$ mv *.wav sounds
```

The -r option of the rm command is very useful (and very dangerous). It can be used to delete entire subtrees of the filesystem by recursing down into the subdirectories For example:

```
$ rm -rf /tempbuild
```

will delete everything in (and below) the directory */tempbuild*. You need to be really careful with this, especially if you're logged in as root. Small typos can make a big difference. For example:

```
# rm -rf / tempbuild
```

(note the unintended space after the /) will attempt to recursively delete the entire filesystem.

> I have actually known someone who did this. He was the system administrator of our Sun workstations at Sheffield University. I was away teaching at the time and I received a phone call that started "I think I've just done something really bad...."

If you want to remove an empty directory, simply use **rmdir** *directoryname*.

Returning to the graphical desktop, you can move files and folders around using drag and drop. The mechanics work like this:

1. Position the cursor over the file you want to move.
2. Press and hold down the left mouse button.
3. Drag the file where you want it to go.
4. Release the mouse button.

For example, you can drag and drop files between the desktop and a folder that you have open in Konqueror.

You can also drag files between folders. One way to do this is simply to open two Konqueror windows, then navigate to the source folder in one and the destination folder in the other. Alternatively, if you have the navigation panel visible in Konqueror, you can drag files onto a directory shown in the tree view and drop them there. (This example ignores, for the moment, the issue of whether you have permission to put files in these directories.) A third way is to split the main window in Konqueror to view two different directories (use Window → Split View Left/Right or Window → Split View Top/Bottom). You can then drag and drop between the two views.

To select multiple files for moving, hold down the left mouse button and drag out a rectangle around the files you want to select, or you can Ctrl-click each file. Ctrl-A selects all the files. You can also use wildcards to select files matching a specified text pattern. To do this, go to Edit → Selection → Select, then type in the wildcard pattern (such as *.wav) you need.

Whenever you drag and drop files in KDE, you will see a pop-up menu asking if you want to Move Here, Copy Here, or Link Here. It's important that you understand the differences. If you select Move Here, you are moving the reference to the file to a different directory. (The data itself does not move anywhere, just the reference.) If you select Copy Here, you end up with two references to two completely separate copies of the file. If you were to edit one of the copies, it would not affect the other. If you select Link Here, you end up with two references to a single copy of the file. (This is similar to what Windows calls a "shortcut.") By the way, a reference to a file is called a *link* in Linux terminology. For an explanation of what I mean by data and references, read on.

How It Works

I have been teaching Unix and Linux for many years, and over time I have gradually reduced the amount of "behind the scenes" detail about the filesystem that I discuss. I still believe, however, that some knowledge of those details is useful in understanding the behavior of the filesystem.

There are really three aspects to a file. It contains *data*, it has *attributes* (access permissions, ownership, etc.), and it has one or more *names*. These three things are stored in different places in the filesystem. A file's data is stored within a pool of data blocks, that occupy the majority of the space within a disk partition. A file's attributes are stored in a data structure called an *inode* (originally short for "intermediate node"). Each file has exactly one inode, which contains:

- The file's type. (Is it a regular file? A directory? A device file? And so on.)
- The file's access permissions, owner, and group.
- The file's timestamps—time of last access, time of last modification, and time of last status change.
- Pointers to whereabouts this file's data blocks are.
- A count of the number of links to this inode. I discuss links shortly.

The inodes are stored on disk, and each one is identified by a number called (predictably) the *inode number*. The one thing that isn't in the inode is the file's name.

A file has a name (and hence a position within the directory tree) by virtue of having a link in a directory somewhere that points to its inode. Links are the things that associate names with inode numbers (and hence with the actual file), and a directory is essentially just a list of links. (See Figure 2-6.)

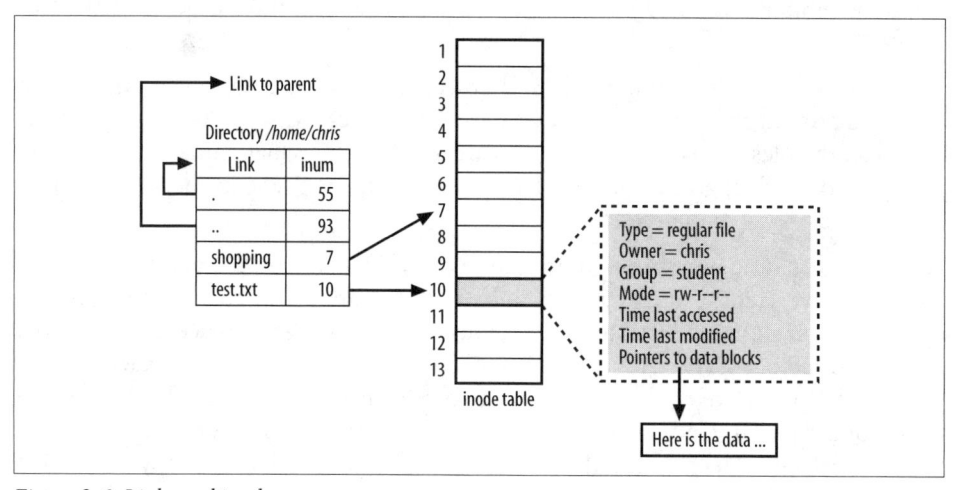

Figure 2-6. Links and inodes

The figure shows a simplified view of my home directory, which contains two files (actually, two links) called *shopping* and *test.txt* that refer to inode numbers 7 and 10 (these numbers are unrepresentatively small compared to a real-world filesystem). When I move a file to another directory, it is really only the link that moves. The inode and data blocks stay put. The figure also shows two links that exist in every directory. The link called . refers to the current directory, and the link called .. refers to the parent directory. You'll typically see this used in commands such as:

    $ cd ..

which moves up one level in the tree (from a subdirectory to its parent directory).

This design makes it easy for a file to have more than one name, simply by having more than one link pointing to the same inode. The links might be in the same directory or (perhaps more usefully) in different directories. The command `ln` creates a new link to an existing file. For example:

    $ ln shopping purchases

creates a second link called *purchases* that points to the same file as *shopping*. There is still only one copy of the file.

> It would be wrong to think of one link as pointing to the other link. It's not like that. You have two links (of exactly equal status) pointing to the same file—that is, the file has two names.

There is also a special file type called a symbolic link, also known as a *symlink*, or occasionally as a "soft link." A symlink is just a small file that contains the name of some other file. From the shell, you can create symlinks using `ln -s`. For example:

    $ ln -s test.txt mytext

creates a symlink called *mytext* that points to the link *test.txt* (as opposed to a real, or hard, link, which would point to the same inode that *test.txt* points to). If you open the file *mytext*, the system notices that it's a symlink and says to itself, "Aha...you don't really want to open *mytext*, you want to open *test.txt*," and starts looking up the filename all over again. A symlink is like a shortcut in Windows.

What About...

...recovering files deleted by accident? Files deleted using Konqueror are placed in a folder called *The Trash*. (I was amused to note that in Novell's internal version of the Novell Linux Desktop released in Europe, they had renamed this to *Wastebin*.) To access the trash folder, click the trashcan icon on the desktop or enter **trash:/** into the location bar in Konqueror. To restore a file to its original location, right-click the file and select Restore from the file menu. Alternatively, you can just drag a file out of the trash and drop it into any folder of your choice.

Files deleted from the command line with rm are not recoverable (without highly specialized tools)—unless, of course, you happen to have them backed up somewhere.

Where to Learn More

There are lots of books that discuss how to use Linux at the command prompt. For a terse, printed command reference, try O'Reilly's *Linux in a Nutshell* (Siever et al.). If you want to become a true "power user," try O'Reilly's *Unix Power Tools* by Powers et al. This book has been around a long time (since 1993) and is now in its third edition. It's one of the more interesting, challenging, and rewarding reads on the Linux bookshelf.

2.4 Set File Access Permissions and Ownership

So far, I have conveniently ignored the issue of access permissions (i.e., who can do what) on files. Traditionally, a full discussion of the Linux security model is part of any introductory Linux course or text. But in fact, if you have a basic Linux setup with just a few user accounts on it, you can get by without knowing much about the security model at all because Linux will, for the most part, just do the right thing.

"The right thing" basically means this:

- You will be able to view and modify any files that you yourself create.
- You will be able to view (but not modify) the contents of files created by other users who have accounts on the system. (This may be a more permissive arrangement than you'd like.)
- You will be able to view (but not modify) most system files.
- If you're logged in as root, you can do anything!

This lab explores the underlying security model in Linux and shows how to change a file's ownership and access permissions, both from a graphical interface and from the command prompt.

How Do I Do That?

To view or change a file's attributes using Konqueror, right-click the file and select Properties from the file menu. In the file properties dialog, the General tab shows the file's size and its timestamps. You cannot edit these. Click the Permissions tab to see and change a file's ownership and access permissions. This dialog provides drop-down lists to allow you to set the access rights on the file to be read/write, read-only, or forbidden (no access). You can set the permissions separately for the owner of the file, for members of the file's group, and for everyone else (Others).

These permission sets are actually a slight simplification of the real underlying permissions, which you can see if you click Advanced Permissions. Figure 2-7 shows the permissions dialog and the advanced permissions screen.

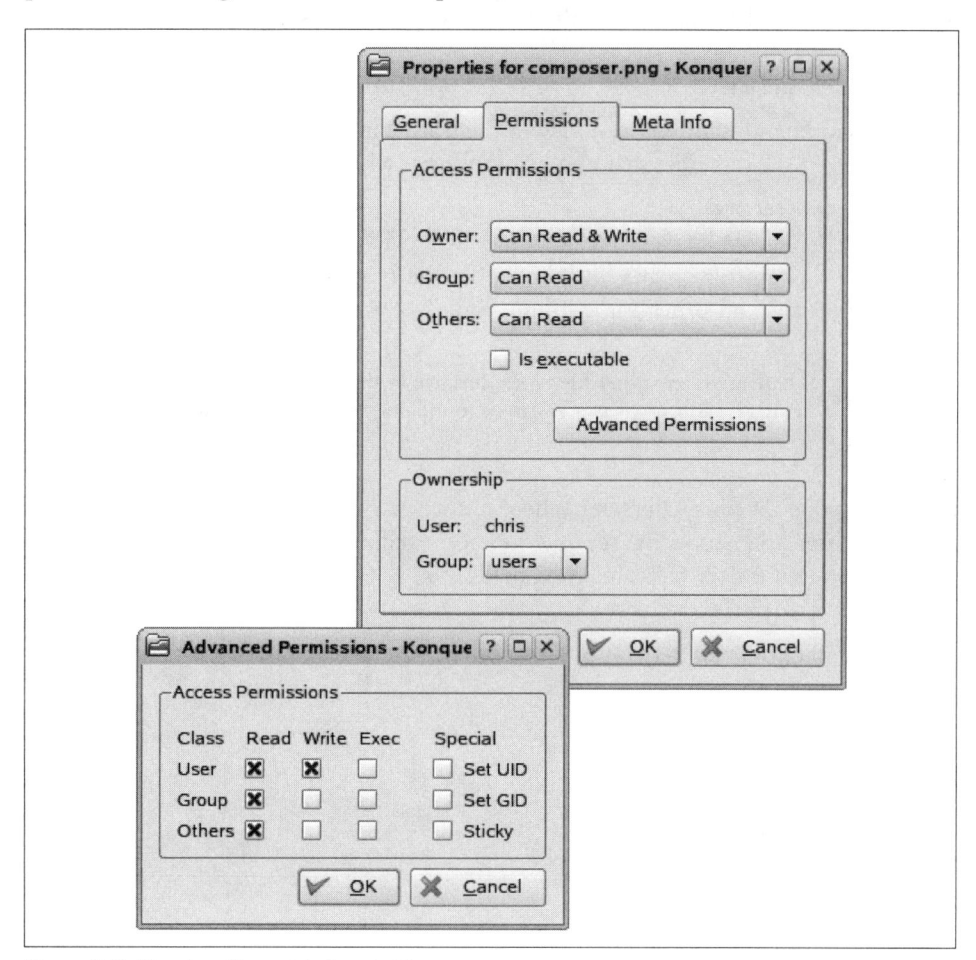

Figure 2-7. Showing file permissions in Konqueror

Ignoring, for the present, the Special permissions shown in Figure 2-7, you can see that each file carries read, write, and execute permission for its user (meaning the owner), members of the file's group, and everyone else. Read and write are hopefully self-explanatory. Execute permission allows the file to be executed as a command and is really only appropriate for fully compiled applications (what Windows would call an *.exe* file, though Linux does not use this extension) and for scripts written in interpreted languages such as the shell or Perl. You can change the permissions only on files you own. If you examine the properties on a file you don't own, the current settings will be shown, but they will be greyed out to prevent you from changing them.

The file's owner is also displayed in the properties dialog, but you cannot change this unless you are root. The file's group is also displayed; you have some freedom to change this, but you can only set it to be a group you're a member of. Konqueror automatically populates the Group drop-down box with a list of these groups.

Using the command line

From the command line, you can view a file's attributes with `ls -l`. The following example shows the same file that you just looked at with Konqueror:

```
$ ls -l composer.png
-rw-r--r--  1 chris users 92156 2004-02-09 15:02 composer.png
```

The very first character on the line shows the file type. `-` means an ordinary file, `d` means a directory, and `l` means a symbolic link.

> There are a few other file types that live in the filesystem, but they're quite rare and very shy and can be found only at night, with a torch.

The next group of nine characters, here shown as `-rw-r--r--`, divides into three groups of three and shows the read, write, and execute permissions for *user*, *group*, and *other*, in that order. The remaining fields are:

1
    The number of links to the file. This does not include symbolic links.

chris
    The file's owner.

users
    The file's group.

92156
    The file's size in bytes.

2004-02-09 15:02
    The date and time that the file was last modified.

composer.png
    The file's name.

If you're logged in as root, you can change a file's owner with chown:

```
# chown barbara composer.png
```

and you can change the group with chgrp:

```
# chgrp student composer.png
```

You can even change the user and the group in one go, like this:

```
# chown barbara:student composer.png
```

You can give more than one filename as argument to these commands:

```
# chown barbara composer.png artist.png sculptor.png
```

And don't forget the wonder of wildcards. For example:

```
# chown barbara *.png
```

will change the ownership of all *.png* files in the current directory.

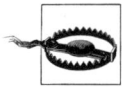

> The # here denotes the super-user prompt. I had someone on a course once who thought it was part of the command and was carefully including it in what she typed. This didn't help because in fact #, when seen as input by the shell, introduces the remainder of the line as a comment!

You can change the permissions on any file you own with chmod.

> chmod is short for "change mode." Originally, the set of permission flags were known as the "mode" of the file. Don't ask why. I don't know. By the way, don't think that any of this is specific to SUSE Linux. It isn't. The security model described here is common to all versions of Linux and was inherited from Unix. It hasn't really changed in years.

The syntax of chmod is tricky. Rather than attempt a formal description, here are a few examples that should give you the idea. *foo* is the filename in each case:

Turn on execute permission for the user (owner)
```
$ chmod u+x foo
```
Turn off write permission for the group
```
$ chmod g-w foo
```
Turn off read and write permission for others (everyone else)
```
$ chmod o-rw foo
```
Turn on execute permission for group and others
```
$ chmod go+x foo
```

Of course, you can specify more than one filename on the command line, and again, don't forget about wildcards. This example will tighten up access by removing all permissions for everyone except the user (owner) for all files in the current directory:

```
$ chmod go-rwx *
```

> A common mistake among beginners is to misremember o as standing for owner. Remember: *u*ser, *g*roup, *o*ther, and *r*ead, *w*rite, *e*xecute.

How It Works

There are two sides to the Linux security model, as there are to any security model: authentication and authorization. Authentication is the business of establishing who you are, and authorization is the business of establishing what you can do.

When your account is created on Linux a line is added to the file */etc/passwd*. This file contains (among other things) your account name and your numeric user ID, which is how the system knows you internally. Your password is encrypted and stored in a line in a separate file, */etc/shadow*.

> Okay—before anyone writes in to complain—technically, the passwords are hashed, not encrypted. But for the present purposes, you can think of hashing as a sort of "one way" encryption.

When you log into Linux (either to a graphical desktop or to a command line), the password you supply is encrypted again and the result compared against the encrypted version in */etc/shadow*. If they agree, the login is successful, and a process is created to run a shell, or to run a window manager. This process carries with it the user identity (actually, the numeric user ID) that you just established by logging in. This identity will be inherited by all processes you subsequently start, and is the identity against which all access control checks are made when an application tries to access a file or directory.

What About...

...permissions on directories? Directories carry the same set of nine permissions as ordinary files (that is, read/write/execute for user/group/other), but their meanings are a little different and not entirely intuitive (so pay attention!).

Read permission on a directory allows you to list the filenames (only) in that directory. Execute permission allows you to cd into a directory or to include it in a pathname. In reality, although read and execute permissions control different types of access to the directory, it almost never makes sense to grant one and not the other. If you want to give read access to a directory, give read and execute permission. If you don't, remove both permissions.

Write permission on a directory allows you to create or delete links in that directory. In effect, this means that you can create, delete, or rename files in that directory. This sounds very logical until you realize that write permission on a directory is the *only* thing that determines whether you're able to delete a file from that directory. I say that again: files do not have "you can delete me" permission flags. The only thing that determines whether you can delete a file is whether you have write permission on the directory you're trying to delete it from. You do not even have to have write permission on the file. (Though the rm command does in fact warn you if you ask it to delete a "write-protected" file.)

If you view the permissions on a directory in Konqueror, you will see that different names are used for the permissions to reflect their different meaning. See Figure 2-8.

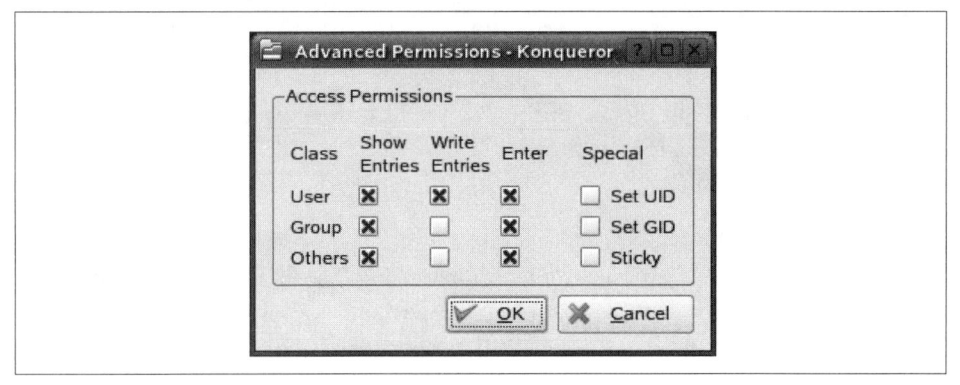

Figure 2-8. Showing directory permissions in Konqueror

What About...

...access control lists? Some of the more advanced users coming from a Windows background are familiar with the full glory of access control lists in the NTFS filesystem and find the Linux scheme rather primitive. They have a point, but the fact is that the Linux model, ancient though it may be, is sufficient for most needs and much easier to understand than NTFS ACLs.

In fact, ACLs have been added to the Linux filesystem, but in my experience they are not much used. They do not extend the permission set—you still have just r,w,x—but they allow you to apply these permission sets to an arbitrary number of users and groups. If you're interested, look up the manual pages for `getfacl` and `setfacl`. Be aware, also, that the filesystem needs to be mounted with the `acl` option set for this to work. (You'll learn more about mount options in Lab 6.3, "Create and Mount Disk Partitions.")

Where to Learn More

Look at the manual pages for `ls`, `chown`, and `chmod`. See also Lab 2.6, "Create User Accounts," later in this chapter.

2.5 Access a Remote Printer

I have a confession to make. I don't understand how printing works in Linux. Back in the days of the lpd printing daemon in Unix, I had a reasonable idea of what was going on. I could even get it to work. Nowadays, most Linux printing is done using CUPS (the Common Unix Print System). Although in some ways it's much easier to use (you just press the obvious buttons and—hey presto!—it works), the underlying architecture is something of a mystery. I put this lack of understanding down in part to my advancing years, but also in part to the lack of a really good description of the CUPS architecture. Also, it is difficult to disentangle the underlying CUPS system from the printer configuration tools that are supplied as part of the KDE desktop and as part of YaST.

Notwithstanding these problems, in this lab you'll learn how to set up your SUSE Linux system to print to a remote printer.

How Do I Do That?

You can configure access to a remote printer using YaST. From the main YaST screen, select Hardware from the panel on the left, and then Printer from the panel on the right. This will bring you to the top-level Printer Configuration screen. From this screen, click on Add. The next screen asks if your printer is local ("Directly Connected") or remote ("Network Printers"). Select Network Printers at this point. This will bring you to the Printer Type screen shown in Figure 2-9. (In versions of SUSE Linux prior to 10.1, selection of local and remote printers was combined into a single screen.)

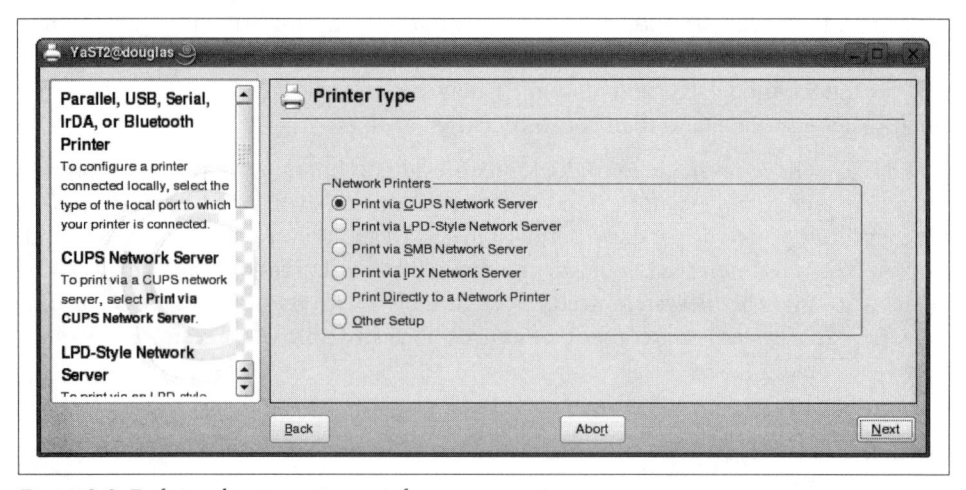

Figure 2-9. Defining the connection type for a remote printer

This screen is poorly named. It really refers to the type of the *connection*, rather than the type of the printer itself. As you will see from the figure, you can define queues to remote printers using a variety of protocols (CUPS, LPD, SMB, IPX, and network printers). In this lab, you need to select "Print via CUPS Network Server." On the next screen, labeled Connection Type, you have three choices:

CUPS client only
   This selection is appropriate if your network has a single CUPS server that has multiple printer queues. All the named print queues on this server will be made

available for use on your machine. "Client only" is a convenient and reliable way of working, and I would recommend it if your machine stays connected to a single network. Note, however, that it can cause problems if you take your machine off that network, as some applications (notably OpenOffice and Firefox) present very long start-up delays (several minutes) as they try to enumerate the printer queues on a nonexistent print server. I have even seen delays in restarting the YaST printer module if the print server is taken offline.

CUPS using broadcasting
This selection is appropriate if you have a large network with multiple print servers, or if you move your machine between networks and would like to pick up the printers on whichever network you're connected to. Potentially this configuration provides "zero-effort" printer configuration. Note, however, that this technique will pick up only print servers that are on the same network as you are (because broadcast traffic is usually ignored by routers) and that the broadcast traffic may be blocked by the firewall settings, either on your own machine or on the print server.

Remote IPP queue
This selection is appropriate if you wish to access a single print queue on a single CUPS server.

For a simple home network in which you have one Linux machine that physically hosts a printer and other machines that need to print to it, select "CUPS client only." If you select this option, on the screen labeled CUPS Server, you'll need to specify the name or IP address of the print server. (There is an option to scan for IPP servers automatically, but I have had limited success with this and prefer to enter an IP address explicitly.) Click on Test Remote IPP Access to verify that you can reach the print server; if this fails, you need to fix the problem before continuing. You can also specify which of that server's queues will be your default queue, or accept that server's default queue as your own default. (In simple scenarios, where you have only one printer, it really doesn't make much difference!) Click the Lookup button to query the print server and obtain a list of printer queues automatically. Once these settings are in place, exit from the YaST printer setup screens. You should now find that the printer will show up in any printer-aware applications, such as OpenOffice. (You will need to restart the applications if they were running before you added the printer.)

What About...

...using a shared Windows printer? It's also possible to print to a printer hosted by a Windows XP machine on your network. To do this, on the screen labeled Printer Type, select Print via SMB Network Server. Next, on the screen labeled Samba or Windows Printer, you'll need to specify:

- The workgroup of the machine that hosts the printer.
- The hostname or IP address of the machine that hosts the printer.

- The name of the printer queue as known on the remote machine. (The Lookup button, which promises to discover the queue names for you, does not seem to work.)
- A username and password that are valid on the XP machine.

Click on Test Remote SMB Access to verify that you can access the print server.

I have had mixed success with setting up printing to Windows-hosted print servers. I have seen it work fine. I have also seen it cause printing-aware applications to hang, and I have seen it fail to work altogether.

2.6 Create User Accounts

Creating user accounts is one of the most fundamental tasks of system administration. Even in the simplest case of a machine intended for use by a single person, you should create a proper user account for yourself. In Windows installations, it's not uncommon to create just one user account that has administrative privileges and to use that for everything. Doing this on Linux is a really bad idea (actually, it's a bad idea on Windows, too) because if you're permanently logged in as root, there are no underlying safeguards to stop you from inadvertently deleting or overwriting vital files, or to prevent malicious scripts or programs that you run from doing bad things to your system.

For a machine intended for home use, you should create accounts for everyone who wants to use your machine: your roommate, your spouse, each of your kids, and so on. That way, everyone can maintain their own preferences and settings and have a piece of the filesystem (their home directory) to call their own. For a machine intended for use as a company-wide server, you may find yourself maintaining hundreds or thousands of user accounts.

As with most things, there are graphical and command-line tools for creating and managing user accounts. All these tools manipulate the same underlying files and account information.

> Some people talk about "creating users" rather than "creating accounts," but to literal-minded folk like me, creating users is a biological activity well outside the scope of this book.

How Do I Do That?

There's a YaST module for managing user accounts. From YaST's main screen, select Security and Users in the panel on the left, and then choose User Management from the panel on the right. This will bring you to the main user management screen shown in Figure 2-10.

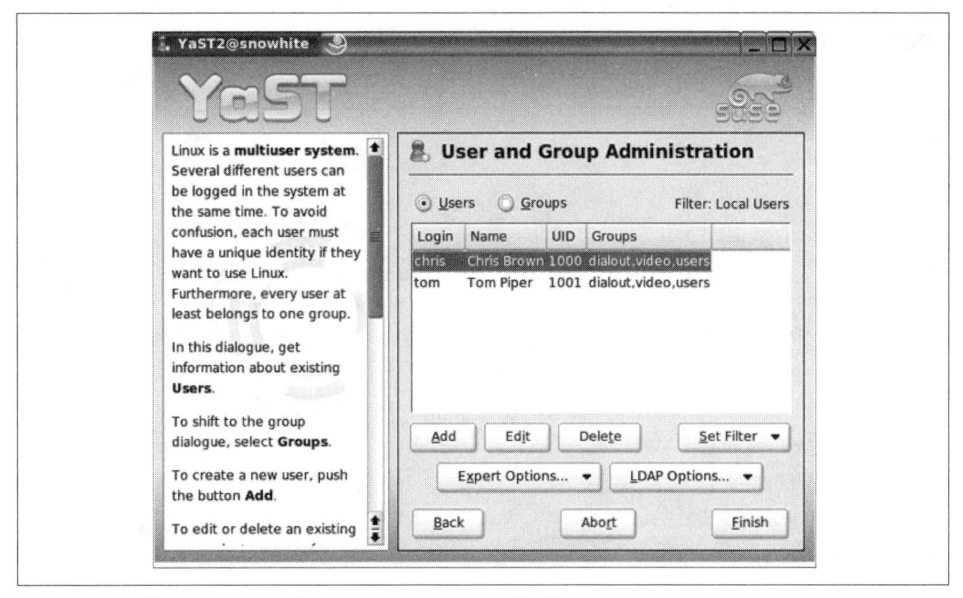

Figure 2-10. The main user administration screen in YaST

Click on the Set Filter button and select Local Users. This will allow you to manage user accounts that are stored in local files. From this screen you can add new accounts or edit and delete existing accounts.

To add a new local account, click Add. This will bring you to the New Local User screen shown in Figure 2-11.

The User's Full Name field on this form corresponds to the GECOS field of Table 2-6 (shown later in this lab); this field can be displayed, for example, by the KDE login manager to identify users in the user list. Putting the user's full name into this field is common practice. However, the only essential fields on this form are the username (this is the user's login name, which must be unique on this system) and the password. YaST will apply a password strength check and warn you if the password is too short, too simplistic, or based on a dictionary word. However, the warnings it issues are simply that—warnings—and if you persist, YaST will relent and allow you to choose a dumb password. In most cases these are the only fields you need to complete. Click Create and allow YaST to supply defaults for the other account settings.

If you need control over other account settings, select the Details tab, which brings you to the screen shown in Figure 2-12.

On this screen you can enter the account's numeric user ID. IDs must be unique. By default YaST will chose a value one bigger than the highest currently in use.

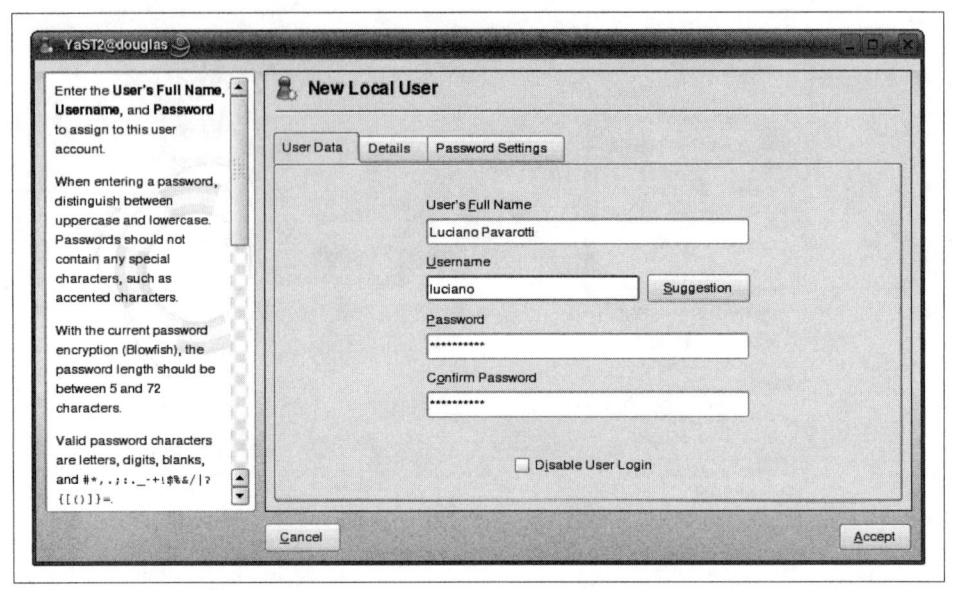

Figure 2-11. Adding a new account in YaST

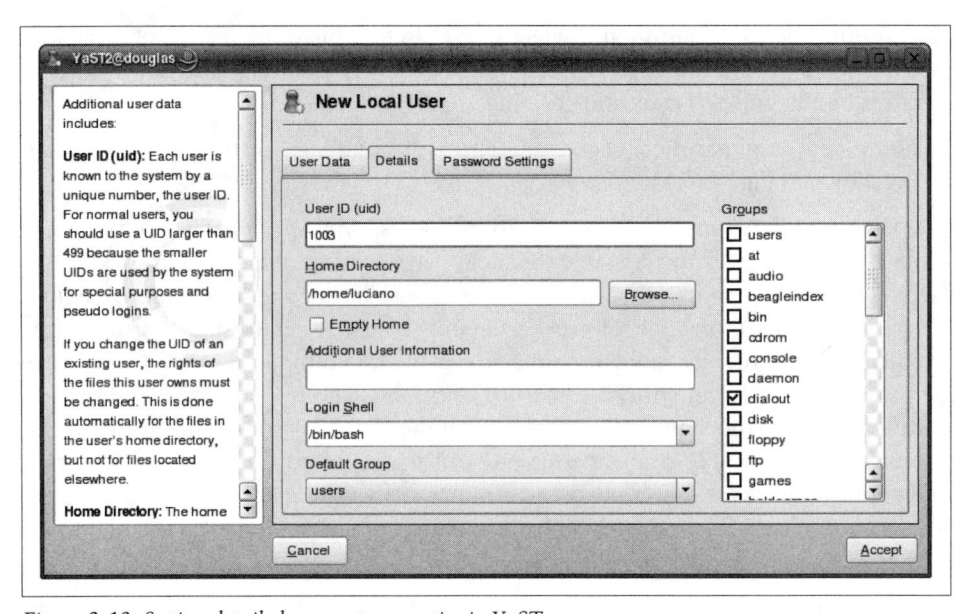

Figure 2-12. Setting detailed account properties in YaST

> There are a couple of reasons I can think of for specifying an account ID explicitly. The first is if you're creating an account that you want to inherit ownership of files from an account you've deleted. By reusing the previous account's ID, the new account will automatically assume ownership of the previous user's files. The second reason is to keep user IDs in sync across a small network that is sharing files using NFS. Otherwise, just let YaST choose the user ID for you.

Also in the Detail User Properties screen you can specify the account's home directory. By default, YaST will create a directory under */home* with the same name as the login name of the account. You might need to change this if your home directories are mounted from a file server or if you have a nonstandard partitioning scheme.

By default, a new account's home directory is initialized with a set of configuration files taken from the directory */etc/skel*. Checking the Empty Home box disables this.

The drop-down list box labeled Login Shell allows you to select which shell will be started when a user logs in. There are several general-purpose shells that you can use, including `bash`, `csh`, and `sh`. Now is not the time to conduct a comparative review of shells; `bash` is the default (and the most popular shell on Linux), and you should choose it unless you happen to be more experienced with some other shell. If you are manually creating a system account for a service to run under, you may want to specify */bin/false* here. This is a program that does absolutely nothing except exit; specifying it as the login shell prevents anyone from using the account as a regular login.

Also on this screen you can specify the user's primary group. On SUSE Linux, all new accounts are in the users group by default. This differs from the RedHat scheme, which puts each account into its own private group. Groups allow convenient assignment of file permissions to multiple users, but some thought is required to set up group memberships and file permissions to achieve the desired effect, and you'll probably want to ignore them, except perhaps on a corporate machine with many users and a more complex security policy.

Back at the New Local User screen, selecting the Password Settings tab brings up a screen where you can set the password aging parameters. You can use this mechanism, if you want, to force users to set a new password from time to time.

Once all the settings are correct, click on Accept. Then, back on the main User and Group Administration screen, click on Finish to update the system configuration.

From the command line, the `useradd` command adds accounts. At its simplest, you just specify a username, like this:

```
# useradd -m luciano
```

Note that the command must be run as root. The `-m` flag is important; it tells `useradd` to create the user's home directory. Without `-m` this doesn't happen. Be aware that useradd does not set a password for the account; you need to do that separately using passwd, like this:

```
# passwd luciano
Changing password for luciano.
New password:
Re-enter new password:
Password changed.
```

A password strength check will be made, but, just as when you add accounts using YaST, it will relent if you persist in your choice.

There are many options for useradd that allow specification of other account settings. Some of these are shown in Table 2-6.

Table 2-6. Options for the useradd command

Option	Description
-d *homedir*	Specifies the home directory
-u *1600*	Specifies the account ID
-g *120*	Specifies the group ID
-m	Specifies that the home directory should be created
-c *Full Name*	Specifies the full name (GECOS field)
-s *shell*	Specifies the login shell

For example:

```
# useradd -m -d /local/home/dave -u 2420 -s /bin/csh dave
```

will create an account called dave with a home directory of */local/home/dave*, an account ID of 2420, and a login shell of */bin/csh*.

How It Works

Table 2-7 lists the information associated with a user account. Most of these have default values and do not need to be set explicitly during account creation.

Table 2-7. Information associated with a user account

Item	Description	Example
Account name	This is the name you log in as. The processes you run and the files you create will be owned by this user.	chris
Account ID	This numeric ID is how the system represents your identity internally. There is usually a one-to-one correspondence between names and IDs. In SUSE Linux, account IDs are allocated from 1000 upwards.	1002
Password	The string you must enter to prove your identity. It is not stored on the system in clear text, but in a hashed (encrypted) form.	dogpainter
Home directory	The pathname of the directory that holds all your files and subdirectories.	/home/chris

Table 2-7. Information associated with a user account (continued)

Item	Description	Example
GECOS field	Commonly contains a number of comma-separated fields, the first of which is usually the user's full name.	Chris Brown, Tel 123-4567
Login shell	The shell (command-line interpreter) that will be started if you log in on a character terminal (i.e., not on a graphical desktop).	/bin/bash
Primary group	The group associated with the account. Any files you create will belong to this group. It's possible to associate additional groups with an account, but this is a property of the groups, not of the accounts.	users
Expiration date	An absolute date after which the account cannot be used.	2006-12-31
Max pw age	Maximum number of days you can use the same password for.	60
Min pw age	Minimum number of days you can use the same password for.	7
pw warning	Number of days before password must be changed at which you are warned.	7
Grace period	Number of days after password expires that you may log in.	3

For a locally defined account, Linux stores the information in two files, */etc/passwd* and */etc/shadow*. The use and format of these files was inherited from Unix and hasn't changed in many years. Each file has one line per account, and each line contains a number of colon-separated fields. Here is an entry from */etc/passwd*:

```
chris:x:1000:100:Chris Brown:/home/chris:/bin/bash
```

The fields are:

- The login name
- A field that used to hold encrypted passwords, now defunct
- The numeric user ID of the account
- The numeric ID of the user's primary group
- The GECOS field
- The home directory
- The login shell

It perhaps seems strange that the one thing that isn't in the *passwd* file is the password. Originally, encrypted passwords *were* stored in here, but they were removed into */etc/shadow* to improve security. Here is an entry from that file, split out onto three lines for legibility:

```
chris:
$2a$05$LoswiJ1Q1.bhBOcUMLGwkes7ICDeO4G/vCV8Ww0535TcESOESlj6i:
12886:1:99999:14::13148:
```

The first field is the login name. The second field is the encrypted (hashed) password. The remaining fields in */etc/shadow* are password-aging parameters.

What About...

...deleting an account? You can do this from the User and Group Administration screen of YaST by selecting the account and clicking Delete. You'll be asked to confirm whether you also want to delete the account's home directory.

From the command line, use a command such as:

    # userdel -r luciano

The -r flag causes removal of the account's home directory.

Where to Learn More

Look at the manual pages for useradd and userdel.

2.7 Rescue a System That Won't Boot

You don't usually expect problems at boot time. You expect to simply switch on and be greeted by a login prompt soon after. So it can come as a bit of a shock if the boot process comes to a screaming halt. This lab examines some techniques for recovering systems that won't boot, and, as a side effect of this, how to recover if you forget the root password.

How Do I Do That?

There is no "one size fits all" solution to the problem of fixing systems that won't boot, but I offer some general pieces of advice: first, you need some understanding of how the system is supposed to boot in the first place, and second, you need to read the boot-time messages very carefully and try to figure out how far the boot process actually got and what the first indication of trouble was (i.e., the first error message). I emphasize "first" here because the system may stagger on a ways and produce further messages or errors before actually stopping.

> SUSE Linux normally covers up the boot-time messages with a pretty splash screen. To view the boot process in detail, press Escape (or F2 in some versions).

My third piece of general advice is even more obvious. Most boot-time failures occur as a result of making some configuration change, so it helps if you can remember what you changed! (And as a rule, when you're changing something tricky, make one change at a time, reboot to make sure all is well, and move on to the next change.)

Assuming that the boot process gets as far as loading the boot loader GRUB (GRand Unified Bootloader), it will, left to its own devices, time out and boot using whatever commands are defined as the default in its configuration file */boot/grub/menu.lst*. You can interrupt the process by pressing Escape when you see GRUB's boot menu. This will drop you into a character-mode interface that will allow you to edit the GRUB commands that will be used to boot the system, or even to type new commands in from scratch. A common use of this technique is to append parameters to the settings used to boot the kernel. In particular, appending the word `single` to the `kernel` command in grub will make the kernel boot in single-user mode.

Actually, the version of GRUB supplied with SUSE Linux makes it especially easy to supply parameters to the kernel at boot time because there is a text-entry field labeled Boot Options on the initial GRUB splash screen. To boot single-user, interrupt the boot process by pressing any key (Shift is a good choice) when you see the splash screen, and then press F2. A text-entry field labeled Boot Options will appear. Type the word `single` into this field and press Enter.

If you boot single-user, none of the standard system services is started. You'll be prompted for the root password and will end up with a root shell running on the console. No filesystem partition (except the root partition) is mounted, and no other processes are running. This is a good state in which to verify the integrity of the other filesystems or to fix */etc/fstab* if it turns out that you have errors in this file that are preventing the other partitions from being mounted.

Once you're finished with single-user mode, I recommend that you enter the command `init 6`, which will reboot into your default runlevel.

> In theory, you should be able to enter `init 3` to enter runlevel 3 or `init 5` to enter runlevel 5 (this is the runlevel that provides a full graphical desktop login), but in practice I have found that not everything is initialized correctly if you do this.

To recover from a lost root password, interrupt the GRUB boot process as before, and enter the command `init=/bin/sh` in the Boot Options field. This instructs the kernel to run */bin/sh* (the shell) as process ID 1, instead of `init`. In this case, you will end up with the root filesystem mounted and a root shell running. From here you can run the `passwd` command to set a new root password. (Note that it is not possible to recover the old password.) Now run the command `reboot` to reboot the system. If this doesn't work, you might need to force a hardware reboot (or recycle the power) to reboot back into multiuser mode from here.

Adding boot-time kernel parameters is easy, thanks to GRUB's Boot Options field. If you want to edit any other aspects of the way GRUB boots (for example, if you want to change the name of the kernel image file or the ramdisk image file), you will need to interrupt the boot process by pressing Escape when you see GRUB's graphical boot menu. This will drop you into a character-based menu. From here you can edit any of the commands from the *menu.lst* file before using them to boot, or you can even type the GRUB boot commands in from scratch. The user interface is a little clunky; read the onscreen instructions that GRUB provides and follow them carefully.

It can be rather alarming to learn how easy it is to get a root shell without knowing the root password. You may feel a little more secure if you set a GRUB password. Doing this will have no effect on using GRUB to boot Linux using the commands defined in *menu.lst*, but it will prevent users from adding boot options or otherwise editing the GRUB commands at boot time unless they know the password. You'll see how to do this in Lab 8.1, "Set a Boot-Time Password," in Chapter 8.

With a password set, GRUB does not display its graphical splash screen at boot time but drops straight into the character-mode menu mentioned earlier. From here you can still boot Linux using any of the menu entries provided in *menu.lst,* but you cannot edit those entries (for example, to supply additional kernel parameters) without first entering the password.

> You might feel a little more secure if you do this, but there is little you can do to really protect your system against a would-be intruder who has physical access to the machine. Setting a GRUB password does not prevent users from booting from rescue media (also discussed in this lab) or (if all else fails) physically removing the hard disk from the machine and installing it elsewhere.

Booting single-user is helpful for some types of problems, but it still requires that the kernel can successfully mount the root partition. If it can't, it will not complete the boot process. Corruption of the root partition, or key files that have gone missing, will cause this problem. In this case, booting from *rescue media* may be the only solution. The basic idea is to boot a Linux kernel from CD, load and attach a filesystem from a ramdisk image (also on CD), and then use this to attach, probe, and hopefully fix the filesystems on the hard drive. You can, in principle, use the boot CD of almost any Linux distribution to do this (I used to carry around a Slackware boot CD for this purpose), but I'll tell you how to use the SUSE Linux distribution media.

Boot from the SUSE Linux CD1 (or DVD1), and select Rescue System from the initial install menu. The installer will load a Linux kernel and a ramdisk image from CD. You'll be asked to select a keyboard layout. At the Rescue login prompt, log in as root. No password is required, and you'll end up at a shell command prompt.

From here you can begin to explore the hard disk. For example:

```
# fdisk -l /dev/hda
```

will show you the partition table on the first hard drive. (use */dev/hdb* if you have a second IDE drive, */dev/sda* if you have a SCSI or SATA drive, and so on).

You can check whether a filesystem has become corrupt using `fsck`. For example:

```
# fsck /dev/hda3
```

checks the filesystem on hda3. (With no options supplied to the command, fsck reports any problems it finds. To have it repair them automatically, use fsck -a.)

You can try to mount one of the partitions. For example, for a system whose root partition is on */dev/hda2*, try:

```
# mount /dev/hda2 /mnt
```

Now you can cd into the */mnt* directory, look around at the root filesystem of the hard drive, view and edit the config files, and so on. Keep in mind that the root filesystem of your hard drive is mounted on */mnt*, not on */*. So, for example, if you wanted to fix an error in */etc/fstab*, edit */mnt/etc/fstab*. If you edit */etc/fstab*, you are merely changing the copy in the ramdisk filesystem.

You may find it convenient to run the command:

```
# chroot /mnt
```

which will change your shell's concept of the root directory such that all pathnames are resolved relative to the */mnt* directory rather than to the real root directory. (This is known as a *chroot jail*.) Be aware, however, that if you do this, any commands that you try to run will be taken from the root filesystem on the hard drive, rather than from the in-memory filesystem, so your root partition needs to be at least partially intact.

How Does It Work?

Figure 2-13 shows the overall sequence of events as Linux boots.

PCs have software in read-only memory, called the BIOS, which initially assumes control of the computer after it is powered on or reset. The BIOS performs a POST (power-on self-test) to check and initialize the hardware (hence the saying "the check's in the POST"), then looks around to find a device to boot from. Typically it will be configured to look first at removable media—CDs or floppies—before trying to boot from the hard disk. It may also have an option to do a PXE (Preboot Execution Environment) boot, which allows it to obtain network settings from a DHCP server and to download its kernel from a server on the network. The BIOS has configuration screens that let you determine the order in which these are tried. Incorrect BIOS settings, or leaving a nonbootable floppy or CD in the machine, is a fairly common cause of boot failures. Usually you have a short time window (a few seconds) in which to press a specific key (often F2 or Delete) to access the BIOS configuration screens.

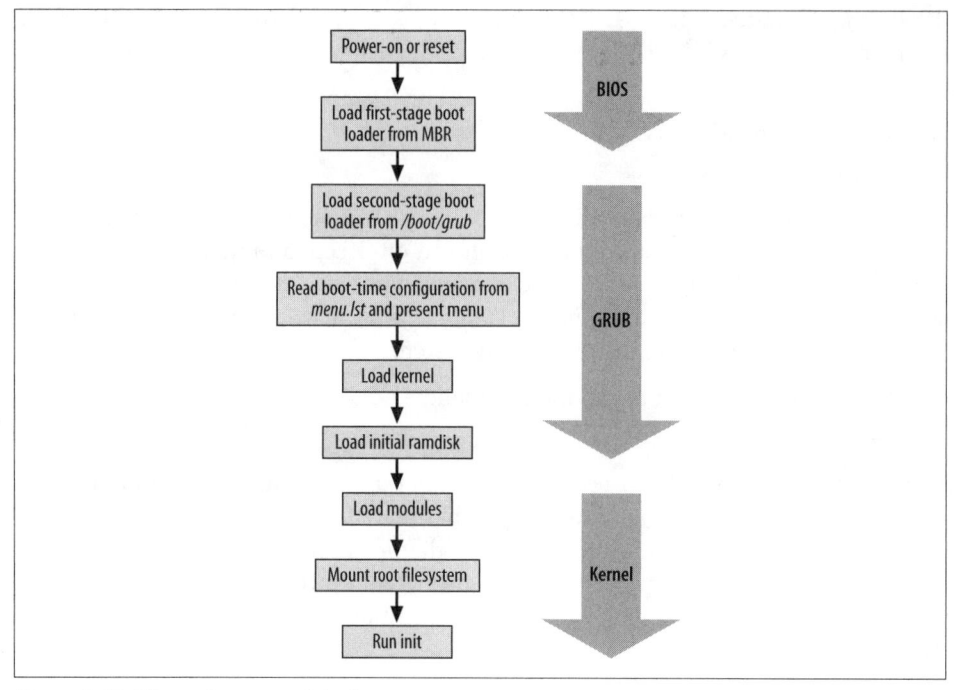

```
         Power-on or reset
                ↓
                              BIOS
       Load first-stage boot
        loader from MBR
                ↓
      Load second-stage boot
      loader from /boot/grub
                ↓
    Read boot-time configuration from
       menu.lst and present menu       GRUB
                ↓
           Load kernel
                ↓
         Load initial ramdisk
                ↓
           Load modules
                ↓
        Mount root filesystem          Kernel
                ↓
            Run init
```

Figure 2-13. The early stages of the boot process

> Before the advent of solid-state read-only memory, computers really did start from nothing when powered on. As a post-graduate student I used a PDP15, a minicomputer whose primary bootstrap (about a dozen instructions as I recall) had to be entered by hand, in binary, on the front-panel switches. Over time, I got really fast at this, and became rather proud of my short but virtuoso performance with the switches.

Assuming that the system is configured to boot from the hard drive, the BIOS loads the MBR (Master Boot Record) of the hard drive into memory and transfers control to the primary bootstrap loader contained within the MBR. The BIOS is then pretty much finished, although it continues to provide support for accessing the hard drive during early stages of the boot process.

There are several bootstrap loaders that might be found in the MBR. It's possible to boot Linux using the boot loaders from Windows or Solaris, for example, though you're only likely to want to do this on a dual-boot machine. On a Linux-only system, it's much more likely that you'll be using LILO or GRUB (during the installation of SUSE Linux, you get the choice of installing either). This discussion assumes that you're using GRUB, which is more modern than LILO and more flexible. Figure 2-13 shows the overall sequence of events when booting with GRUB.

Most of the pieces involved in the remainder of the boot process are files that live in the /boot and /boot/grub directories. In /boot/grub, for example, you'll find the files that make up the next stage of the boot loader. They have names like *e2fs_stage1_5*, *fat_stage1_5*, and *reiserfs_stage1_5*. These names might look vaguely familiar—e2fs, fat, and reiser refer to the filesystem formats supported by Linux. This stage of the boot loader, which we are obliged to call stage 1.5, is able to interpret the filesystem structure, and can locate files on the hard drive by name. (In contrast, the smaller and dumber first stage boot loader in the MBR needs an explicit list of block numbers to allow it to find the next stage.) The stage 1.5 loader loads the stage 2 loader, which reads the configuration file /boot/grub/menu.lst to figure out what operating systems are available to boot, and what GRUB commands are needed to boot them. Here's an example (the line numbers are for reference; they are not part of the file):

```
1   color white/blue black/light-gray
2   default 0
3   timeout 8
4   gfxmenu (hd0,2)/boot/message
5
6   ###Don't change this comment - YaST2 identifier: Original name: linux###
7   title SUSE LINUX 10.0
8       root (hd0,2)
9       kernel /boot/vmlinuz root=/dev/hda3 vga=0x314 selinux=0 \
10              resume=/dev/hda2  splash=silent showopts
11      initrd /boot/initrd
12
13    ###Don't change this comment - YaST2 identifier: Original name: SUSE 9.3###
14  title SUSE 9.3
15      kernel (hd0,0)/boot/vmlinuz root=/dev/hda1 vga=0x314 selinux=0 \
16             splash=silent resume=/dev/hda2   showopts
17      initrd (hd0,0)/boot/initrd
```

Line 1 defines the colors of the (text-based) menu screen. Line 2 says to boot the first choice of operating system if the user doesn't make a selection, and line 3 says to wait 8 seconds for user input. Line 4 specifies the filename of a cpio archive that contains the graphical elements and other components needed to build the graphical splash screen that GRUB normally presents. Line 7 defines a GRUB menu item that will be labeled "SUSE LINUX 10.0", and lines 8–11 specify the GRUB commands that will be executed if that item is selected. Lines 14–17 define a second menu entry and its associated commands.

For the present purposes, the important lines are the kernel and initrd commands. These commands tell GRUB to load two files into memory. The first is an image of the kernel and the second is an image of an *initial ramdisk*—an in-memory filesystem that the kernel uses to load the modules it needs to access the real root filesystem on the hard disk. These files live in /boot and have names like *vmlinuz-2.6.11.4-20a-default* and *initrd-2.6.11.4-20a-default*. GRUB loads both these files into memory and starts the kernel, telling the kernel where it has placed the ramdisk image in memory.

Once the kernel is running, it loads some modules from the ramdisk image, and mounts the real root filesystem from the hard disk. Then it's ready to roll. Successfully mounting the root filesystem is a key point in the boot process, and if you're troubleshooting boot failures, it's vital to figure out whether this succeeded. The kernel now creates a single process "by hand." This initial process has a process ID of 1, and runs the program */sbin/init*. (The */sbin* directory is one of those directories that must be on the root partition.) The init process is, directly or indirectly, the parent of every other process in the system. It reads the file */etc/inittab* to figure out what other services it should start. But that, as they say, is another story.

Where to Learn More

For a full list of the kernel parameters you can pass through the "Boot Options" field, see */usr/src/linux/Documentation/kernel-parameters.txt*. This file is part of the kernel source code package.

If you want all the gory details of GRUB, there's a 60-page manual online at *http://www.gnu.org/software/grub/manual/*.

2.8   Finding Files

It's not unusual to forget where you put a file that you've created or downloaded from the Internet. Or, you might have questions about what you've got installed—for example, do I have the `libdvdcss` library? Then you unexpectedly run out of space on a partition—is there some giant file filling it up that you don't know about? As another example, suppose you've just removed the account for the user dave. Presumably most of dave's files were in his home directory, */home/dave*, but are there any files anywhere else owned by dave?

SUSE Linux provides both graphical and command-line tools that will let you search the filesystem (or a specified part of it) for files that meet various criteria. You can search on the filename (either a complete or partial match) or on the file's attributes, (such as its size or ownership or time of last modification), or even on a string match on the file's contents.

How Do I Do That?

KDE includes a graphical tool called `kfind`. From the main KDE menu, select Find Files. This will display the file finder dialog, which has three tabs under which you can enter search criteria: Name/Location, Contents, and Properties. Simple name-based searches can be performed using only the Name/Location tab (Figure 2-14). Enter the name, check the Include subfolders box if you want the search to recurse down into directories below the one you start in, and click Find.

> The filename you enter in the Named text box can include the same *, ?, and [...] wildcard notations that the shell understands. For example, [A-Z]*.png will find files whose name begins with an uppercase letter and ends with *.png*.

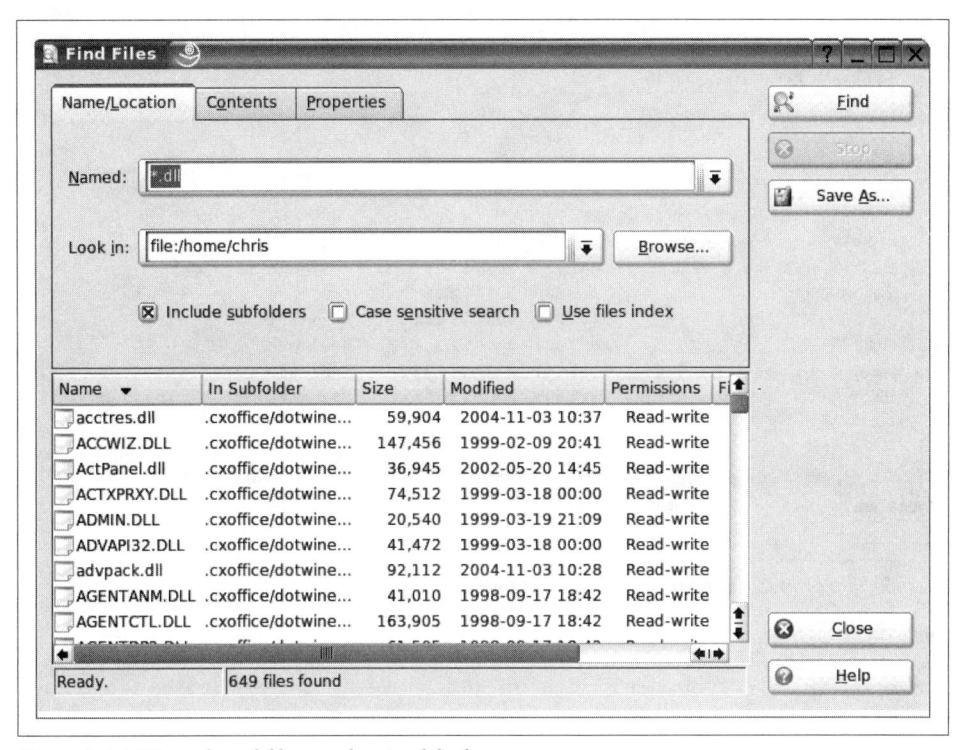

Figure 2-14. Name-based file search using kfind

You can combine name-based searches with searches based on the file's content using the Contents tab, and with searches based on file attributes such as ownership, size, or time of last modification using the Properties tab. (Figure 2-15 shows a search for files larger than 100 MB.) A list of all the files that were found will be shown in a scrollable window at the bottom of the tool. You can sort the files on any of the column headings displayed (name, size, and so on) by clicking on the column heading.

The command line offers even more options for finding files through the find command—one of the most powerful of all command-line tools. Unfortunately, it also has quite a complicated syntax that can take some getting used to. Table 2-8 shows some of the search criteria that you can use with find.

2.8 Finding Files | 73

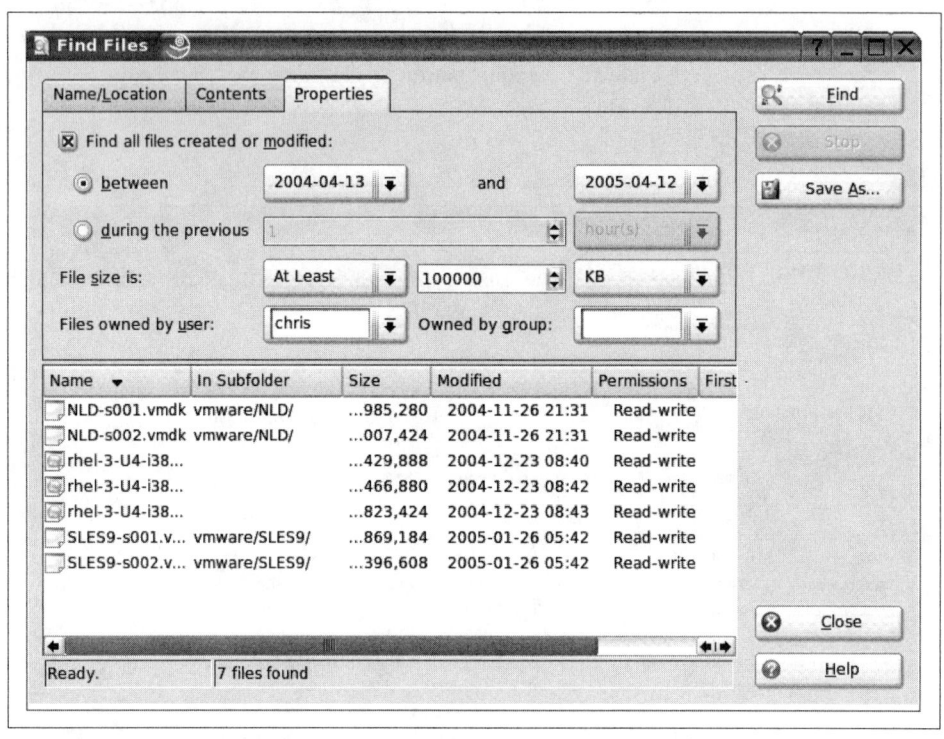

Figure 2-15. Attribute-based file search using kfind

Table 2-8. Search criteria for the find command

Syntax	Description	Example
`-name string`	Filename matches `string` (wildcards are allowed).	`-name '*.old'`
`-iname string`	Same as `-name` but not case-sensitive.	`-iname 'greet*'`
`-user username`	File owned by `username`.	`-user chris`
`-group groupname`	File has group `groupname`.	`-group users`
`-type d|f|l`	File is directory, regular file, or symbolic link.	`-type d`
`-size +N`	File is bigger than N blocks (suffix c = bytes, k = kilobytes).	`-size +1000k`
`-size -N`	File is smaller than N blocks.	`-size -50c`
`-mtime +N`	File last modified more than N days ago.	`-mtime +14`
`-mtime -N`	File last modified less than N days ago.	`-mtime -2`
`-atime +N`	File last accessed more than N days ago.	`-atime +7`
`-atime -N`	File last accessed less than N days ago.	`-atime -1`

The command syntax is typically of the form:

```
$ find <where to look> <search criteria> <action>
```

Here are some examples. The first one searches in (and below) the current directory for files called *letter.txt*.

    `$ find . -name letter.txt`

The filename can include wildcards: * to match zero or more characters, ? to match exactly one character, and [...] to match any one of the characters enclosed in the square brackets. These wildcards are the same as those that the shell understands, but in this case, you want find to interpret them, not the shell. So you need to enclose them in single quotes on the command line so that the shell doesn't try to expand them, but instead simply passes them through unaltered as arguments to find (otherwise, a command like **find . -name *** would see * expanded to the list of all files in the current directory).

This example searches the entire filesystem (starting from /) for all filenames ending in *.dll*. Note that if you do this as an ordinary (nonroot) user, you'll get lots of "permission denied" error messages as find tries to descend into directories that you don't have permission to read:

    `$ find / -name '*.dll'`

You can find files owned by a specific user. This command searches */home* for all files owned by dave:

    `$ find /home -user dave`

To eliminate the "permission denied" error messages, discard the standard error stream:

    `$ find / -name '*.dll' 2> /dev/null`

You can find files based on their timestamps. For example, to find all files in and below the current directory that have been accessed within the last 30 minutes, use this command:

    `$ find . -amin -30`

Notice the use of -30 to mean "less than 30 minutes." You can use +30 to mean "more than 30 minutes." If you use -amin 30, you would be looking for files that were last accessed exactly 30 minutes ago, which is probably not very useful. This + and - notation applies to most of the numeric arguments for find.

Here's another example of using find with a numeric argument—this time to find files that are bigger than 100 MB:

    `$ find /home/chris -size +100000k`

If you specify more than one search criterion, the implied combination is "and"; that is, you select files that satisfy all the criteria you specify. For example, to find files in */tmp* with names ending in *.bak* that have not been accessed for two weeks, you could use:

    `$ find /tmp -name '*.bak' -atime +14`

You can also use -o to combine search criteria using "or," though in practice I find this less useful. For example, the command:

```
$ find /tmp -name '*.bak' -o -atime +14
```

will find files that either have names ending in *.bak* or that have not been accessed in two weeks.

When find finds a file that matches the criteria you specify, its default action is to display the name of the file (that is, to write the filename to standard output). You can specify your own actions if you want, using the -exec option, but the syntax gets messy. This example extends the previous one by deleting the selected files rather than just listing them:

```
$ find /tmp -name '*.bak' -atime +14 -exec rm {} \;
```

The curly bracket notation {} is used by find to substitute the name of the file that was found into the command. The ; marks the end of the arguments to -exec, and it needs to be escaped with a preceding backslash (or by putting it into single or double quotes) to stop the shell from interpreting it as a command separator.

You can combine the power of find and grep to search for files that meet find's search criteria and also contain a specified string. For example, to find files in and below the current directory that have names beginning *invoice* and that contain the string "outstanding":

```
$ find . -name 'invoice*' -exec grep -l outstanding {} \;
```

How It Works

Both of these tools work by making a recursive descent into the filesystem tree. That is, they will examine each file in the directory they start in. If that file turns out to be a directory, they will descend into that and examine each file there, continuing down through the hierarchy of directories until all files beneath the starting directory have been visited. There are many command-line tools that can show this behavior, but typically it must be requested via a command-line option (often -R). The find command is recursive by default.

What About…

…making the search more efficient? The find command can take a while to run because it performs a recursive search though an entire subtree of the filesystem. Some other command-line tools are less general in scope than find, but are much faster.

The locate command queries a prebuilt database of filenames to perform lightning-fast searches. Like find, locate understands filename wildcards. To search for files with names containing the string libdvdcss, use:

```
$ locate libdvdcss
```

`locate` is not as flexible as `find`, because it searches only on the filename and it's only as up to date as the database it searches, but it's much faster and much easier to use. The database of filenames is built by the command `updatedb`. On SUSE Linux, this command is run every 24 hours using cron (see the file */etc/cron.daily/updatedb*). The `locate` and `updatedb` commands are included in the package `findutils-locate`; this may not be installed by default.

The `whereis` command is even more restricted in scope. It's designed specifically to find binaries (executables), source code, and manual page files for a command. Here is an example:

```
$ whereis chage
chage: /usr/bin/chage /usr/share/man/man1/chage.1.gz
```

which shows the binary and the manpage for the `chage` command.

The command `which` is even more restricted. It only looks for files in the directories that are in your search path. For example, the command:

```
$ which passwd
/usr/bin/passwd
```

effectively answers the question, "If I entered the command `passwd`, where would it be found?"

There are also notations for pruning the search tree in `find`. For example:

```
$ find . -maxdepth 1 -name 'foo*'
```

will find files beginning with *foo* but only in the current directory—it will not descend into subdirectories. Similarly:

```
$ find . -mount -name 'foo*'
```

will prevent `find` from traversing mount points; that is, it will restrict the search to the filesystem it started on.

What About...

...other search tools? There is a rather different and perhaps more intuitive search tool called Beagle. After struggling to get Beagle to work reliably on earlier versions of SUSE Linux, I am pleased to note that on SUSE Linux 10.1 it appears to work out of the box. Beagle "ransacks your personal information space" (their phrase, not mine) and builds an index so that keyword searches can be performed very quickly. Beagle is oriented toward finding documents based on content rather than on filenames and attributes. The work-horse of Beagle is the daemon, *beagled*, which runs in the background and is responsible for building and maintaining the index. Indexing is a resource-hungry process, and *beagled* automatically throttles back its activities to avoid placing too heavy a load on the system. You can expect it to take several hours to complete initial indexing. Beagle can look inside text files, OpenOffice documents, PDF files, KMail and Evolution mailboxes, browser history, and much else besides. You can to some extent control what gets indexed with the `beagle-settings` command, which invokes a graphical tool that allows you to specify which folders to include and exclude from the index. By default, everything under your home directory is indexed.

There are command-line tools for performing Beagle queries (see the manual pages for `beagle-query` and `beagle-status`, among others), but the nicest interface is the graphical version called Kerry Beagle, shown in Figure 2-16, which shows partial results for the keyword "deadline," including a mail attachment, a PDF file, a web page, and the body of a mail message.

> I was initially unsure whether this was a reference to John Kerry or Kerry Packer—both seemed unlikely. In fact, Google tells me that a Kerry Beagle is a variety of foxhound found in Ireland (in County Kerry, I presume).

Where to Learn More

Read the manpage for `find`, but try not to get bogged down with the formal syntax, which is confusing. There's an entire chapter on `find`, with some great examples, in *Unix Power Tools* (O'Reilly).

The online help for KDE has a user guide for `kfind`, but most of what it says is fairly obvious from the user interface.

For Beagle, try reading the manual pages for `beagled`, `beagle-query`, and `beagle-status`, although the Kerry Beagle search tool is intuitive and simple enough to need no documentation. The Beagle web site is *http://www.beagle.org*.

2.9 Mounting Filesystems

One of the key differences between Windows and Linux is that Windows uses *drive letters* such as C: and D: and Linux does not. I have met people who are transitioning from a Windows desktop to Linux, and who are so used to drive letters in Windows that they are seriously discomfited by their absence in Linux. "How do I know where to find my stuff if there are no drive letters?" is a question I've been asked more than once. It is tempting for an experienced Linux user to dismiss such questions as naïve, but the reality is that many people come to Linux with their expectations and prejudices set by the way Microsoft does things, and those people deserve a proper explanation of why things are different in Linux (and, perhaps, why the advocates of Linux would consider it superior).

> My own view (just as biased as anyone else's, in its own way) is that drive letters represent an implementation issue that should really be hidden from users. Why should I need to know which drive a file is on (or even whether it's on the local hard drive or on a network server)? Surely, I should just need to know the name of the file?

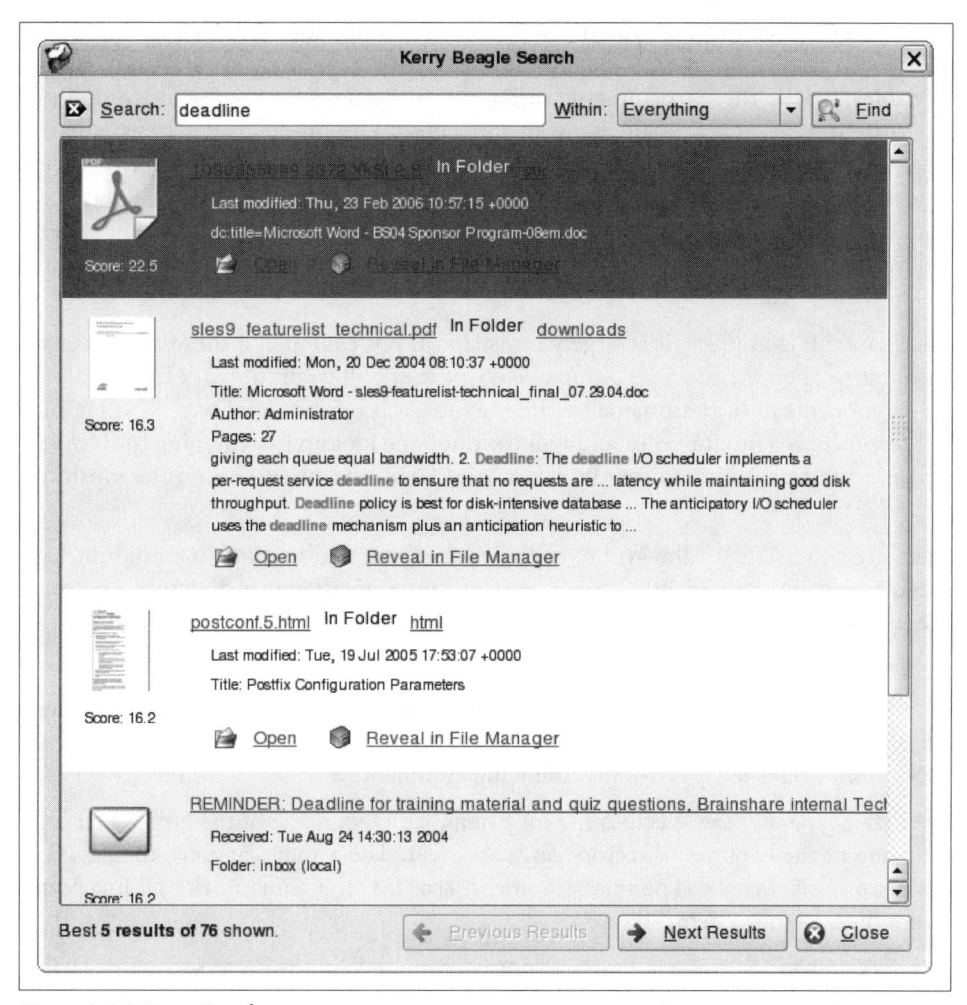

Figure 2-16. Kerry Beagle

Linux provides the illusion of a single filesystem tree (even though in reality that filesystem might be spread across multiple physical disks, removable media, and network file servers) by attaching pieces of the filesystem into the overall naming tree that starts at the root (/). The operation of attaching a filesystem in this way is known as *mounting*, and is the subject of the rest of this lab.

How Do I Do That?

A filesystem contained on a partition of a local disk drive can be mounted using a command something like this:

```
# mount -t ext3 /dev/hda5 /usr/local
```

Here, **-t ext3** specifies the type of the filesystem to be mounted. The mount command will usually figure this out for itself, so this argument is often not necessary. **/dev/hda5** is the partition containing the filesystem that you want to mount, and **/usr/local** is what's called the *mount point*. The mount point is usually an empty directory within the root partition created specifically for that purpose. (It is possible to mount onto a nonempty directory, and if you do, the original contents of the directory are "covered up" by the contents of the mounted filesystem and will reappear when the mount is removed, but it is not usual to do this, except by mistake.)

Once a mount is in place, it is largely transparent. For example, if the kernel receives a request to open the file */usr/local/include/xine.h*, it will begin to work its way along the components of the pathname to find the file. As it reaches */usr/local*, it will notice that */usr/local* is a mount point and will continue the lookup by searching for *include/xine.h* in the filesystem mounted on */usr/local*—i.e., the filesystem on the partition */dev/hda5*.

There are extensions to the syntax of the mount command to allow it to mount filesystems held on network file servers. For example, to mount a directory exported from an NFS file server, use a command something like this:

```
# mount -t nfs bambi.disney.com:/home /home
```

Here, **-t nfs** specifies that you're mounting an NFS filesystem. It is usually not necessary to include this syntax, because the mount command can recognize this as an NFS mount from the syntax of the following argument.

bambi.disney.com:/home specifies the fully qualified DNS name of the NFS server and the name of the exported directory on that server. The **:** that separates the two is a key piece of the syntax. The final argument, **/home**, is the name of the mount point within the local filesystem.

In a similar way, filesystem *shares* exported from a Windows file server using the SMB protocol can be mounted using a command something like this:

```
# mount -t smbfs -o username=mary //dopey/herring /mnt/dopey
```

Here, **-t smbfs** indicates that this is an SMB mount. **//dopey/herring** is the UNC (Universal Naming Convention) name of the share: **dopey** is the NetBios name of the server, and **herring** is the name of the share point on that server. The option **username=mary** specifies the name that mount will use to authenticate to the server.

> Microsoft's use of the term "Universal Naming Convention" seems a little pretentious to me. I am fairly sure that if we should ever make contact with a race of little green men living on a planet in orbit around Alpha Centauri, it will turn out that they are not, in fact, using this naming convention.

How It Works

The transparency of access to filesystems on a variety of local media (IDE drives, SCSI drives, USB drives, floppies, and so on) and to filesystems on network file servers is largely due to the virtual filesystem layer in the Linux kernel, illustrated in Figure 2-17. The virtual filesystem layer ensures that the same set of system calls can be used to open, close, read, and write files, regardless of the underlying filesystem type or the physical medium used to store them.

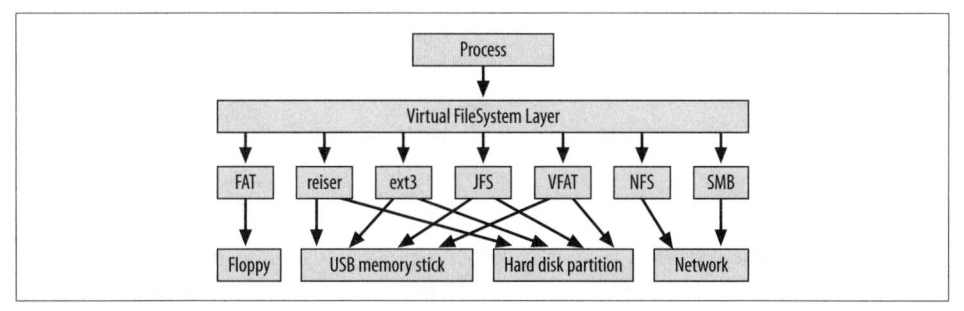

Figure 2-17. The virtual filesystem architecture

What About...

...making mounts "permanent"? Mounts put in place by the mount command are not permanent; that is, they will not persist across reboots. To make a mount permanent, you need to put an entry into the file */etc/fstab*.

> The distinction between making a configuration change temporarily at the command line and making it permanently via entries in a configuration file is a common distinction in Linux. There is often a way of configuring something temporarily by entering commands at a command prompt, and a way to configure something permanently by adding lines to a configuration file. Using mount versus using fstab is a classic example. Another good example is the use of the ifconfig command to set the parameters for a network interface, compared to the configuration files in */etc/sysconfig/network*, which control the settings that will be applied every time the system boots.

In fact, there are really three reasons for placing an entry in *fstab*:

- To define mounts that will be put in place automatically at boot time.
- To define mounts that can be put in place manually by ordinary users—i.e., not the super-user. These entries usually relate to removable media.
- To simplify the use of the mount command by specifying the partition name and mount options associated with a particular mount point.

Here are some sample entries from this file (some of the lines have been wrapped to fit the page):

LABEL=root	/	reiserfs	acl,user_xattr	1 1
/dev/cdrecorder	/media/cdrecorder	subfs	noauto,ro,fs=cdfss, user	0 0
/dev/fd0	/media/floppy	subfs	noauto,nodev,nosuid, fs=floppyfss,sync	0 0
/dev/hda3	/local	reiserfs	acl,user_xattr	1 2
bambi.disney.com:/home	/home	nfs	hard,intr	0 0
//dopey/herring	/mnt/dopey	smbfs	????	0 0

The fields in this file are:

- The name of the partition to be mounted. It's also possible to use a volume label here to specify the partition (see the first line), or the name of an exported NFS directory (see the next-to-last line), or the UNC name of an SMB share (see the last line).
- The pathname of the mount point in the local filesystem. Usually this lives in the root partition.
- The filesystem type. The type `subfs` means that the filesystem will be mounted automatically by the `submount` daemon; this is normally used only for removable media. The type `auto` means that `mount` will attempt to determine the type of the filesystem automatically by reading the filesystem's *superblock* (a portion of a disk partition that holds information about the filesystem on it).
- A list of mount options. The allowable options depend on the filesystem type.
- A field indicating whether this filesystem should be backed up by the `dump` utility. You are unlikely to use this and it should certainly be zero for remote filesystems.
- A field indicating the order in which the filesystem consistency check utility, `fsck`, should be run on the partitions. This is usually 1 for the root partition, 2 for all other local partitions, and 0 for remote filesystems or removable media.

When the system boots, it will automatically attempt to mount all the filesystems listed in *fstab* unless they have the `noauto` option set. So, why would you put a line in *fstab* with the noauto option? There are two reasons. First, an entry in *fstab* can simplify use of the `mount` command by automatically filling in options and arguments you don't supply. For example, the line:

```
/dev/hdb1    /docs    ext3    noauto,ro    0 0
```

would mean that you could mount */dev/hdb1* onto */docs* simply by typing:

```
# mount /docs
```

rather than the entire command:

```
# mount -t ext3 -o ro /dev/hdb1 /mnt
```

Second, entries in *fstab* with the user option set allow filesystems to be mounted by ordinary (nonroot) users. This is discussed in more detail in the following section.

What About...

...authentication and access control? First of all, you should note that filesystems normally can be mounted only by root. If the user option appears in the options field in *fstab*, the filesystem it refers to can be mounted by any user. This option is typically used to allow ordinary users to mount removable media. There are some significant security concerns in allowing users to introduce removable media into the machine. One concern is the use of files with the *set user ID* flag enabled. Such files run with the effective identity of their owner. Anyone with access to a root account on some other Linux machine could easily make a copy of a program (the bash shell, for example), set the owner to root, enable the set user ID flag, copy it to a CD, and mount it into the filesystem of some other machine. The nosuid mount option prevents this attack by telling Linux not to honor the set user ID flag on any files mounted from this device. Similarly, the mount option nodev stops users from introducing *device file* entries on removable media (which could otherwise be used to give an ordinary user read and write access to any raw disk partition), and the noexec options prevent the running of *any* executable program from the mounted device.

Assuming that the mount succeeds, for filesystems on local media (either fixed or removable), the usual file access permission checks are made. For filesystems mounted from network servers, the situation is more complicated. For NFS filesystems, when an attempt is made to open a file on an NFS server, the numeric user ID (not the login name) of the user making the request on the client is propagated to the server, and the server will apply access permission checks against that identity. This approach works well if the mappings from login names to numeric user IDs is consistent across the machine, but can give confusing (and usually undesirable) results if not. For example, if chris has the UID 1004 on the NFS client, and mary has UID 1004 on the NFS server, chris will appear to be the owner of mary's files on any filesystem mounted from that server. Often, NFS is deployed in conjunction with NIS, which centralizes the user account information and guarantees consistent name-to-UID mappings across all machines.

For SMB mounts, the SMB server will collect a username and password from the client and use that to authenticate the user on the server (which could be one of several things, such as a Windows 2003 machine acting as Primary Domain Controller, a desktop machine running Windows XP, or a Linux box running Samba). You can explicitly specify the username as an option to the mount command, like this:

```
# mount -t smbfs -o username=mary //dopey/herring /mnt/dopey
```

You'll be prompted for the password. You can even specify the password within the mount command like this:

```
# mount -t smbfs -o username=mary%terces //dopey/herring /mnt/dopey
```

to specify "terces" as the password. This trick is handy to use in scripts but has the disadvantage that the password appears in clear text on the command line. The password can also be passed in through the PASSWD environment variable. A better approach might be to use the credentials= option:

```
# mount -t smbfs -o credentials=/root/sambacreds //dopey/herring /mnt/dopey
```

then create the file */root/sambacreds* with content as follows:

```
username = mary
password = terces
```

Where to Learn More

Look at the manual pages for the mount command, and the fstab file. The manpage for the submount daemon describes the automatic mounting of removable media and the manpage for smbmount (don't confuse this with submount) details the options available for mounting SMB filesystems.

2.10 Access Your Desktop Remotely

Have you ever been in the position of trying to help someone perform some task with his or her computer, but not being physically in front of the machine? Trying to talk someone through a multistep process with a graphical user interface can be quite difficult and frustrating.

> Interestingly, it's actually easier to talk a remote user through using a command line than a graphical interface because you can explicitly specify the commands rather than engaging in vagaries such as "click the little button just under the penguin."

An application called VNC (Virtual Network Computing—not the best of names) lets you access a desktop session on a remote machine. The remote machine runs a VNC server, and the local machine runs a VNC viewer. This lab explores the use of VNC to start up and access a brand new desktop session, and how to use the tool Krfb to gain shared access to an existing desktop.

How Do I Do That?

VNC is a client/server application. The server (which runs on the "target" machine—that is, the machine whose desktop you want to control) is called Xvnc, and the client (which runs on the machine you're actually sitting at) is called vncviewer.

If you want to set up a desktop session that can be accessed remotely, begin by running `vncpasswd` on the target machine. This process will ask you for a password, encrypt it, and store it in *~/.vnc/passwd*. Optionally, you can specify a "view only" password which, if you use it to connect to the target machine, will allow you to passively observe a desktop, but not actively control it.

Next, start the server using `vncserver`. This is a Perl script in */usr/bin*. It is essentially a "wrapper" that starts the VNC server, `Xvnc`, with appropriate arguments.

`vncserver` will report the *desktop number* of the desktop session it has started. You will need this to connect to the session using `vncviewer`. In the following example, the desktop is ":1".

```
$ vncserver

New 'X' desktop is snowhite:1

Starting applications specified in /home/chris/.vnc/xstartup
Log file is /home/chris/.vnc/snowhite:1.log
```

As the preceding example shows, vncviewer reads the file *~/.vnc/xstartup* to determine which applications to start. By default, it starts a window manager called `twm` (Tab Window Manager, or Tom's Window Manager, depending on whom you ask). On SUSE Linux, TWM is unconfigured (and consequently unusable), so I suggest that you stop the VNC server with **vncserver -kill :1** (replace **:1** with whatever desktop number it used), edit (or create, if you haven't started vncserver yet) the file *~/.vnc/xstartup*, and replace its contents with the two lines:

```
#!/bin/sh
startkde &
```

which will start up a new KDE session the next time you launch the VNC server.

There are a number of options that you can supply to the `vncserver` command. You can explicitly specify which desktop number to use and the resolution of the display (the size of the desktop). For example:

```
$ vncserver :3 -geometry 800x600
```

will use desktop :3 with 800×600 resolution.

Now, on the client machine, you can start a VNC viewer, specifying the IP address or hostname of the target machine and the desktop number. For example:

```
$ vncviewer snowhite:1
```

Or, you can specify an IP address instead:

```
$ vncviewer 192.168.0.17:2
```

You'll be prompted for the password to connect to the target's VNC server; then, vncviewer will open a window showing the desktop session on the target machine.

You can stop the VNC server on desktop :1 with the command:

```
$ vncserver -kill :1
```

As an alternative to vncviewer, you can connect to a remote desktop with the KDE application krdc (System → Remote Access → Krdc).

Instead of starting vncserver yourself, you can also set up remote desktop access using YaST. From the main YaST screen, select Network Services from the panel on the left, then Remote Administration from the panel on the right. Here you can enable or disable remote administration. In SUSE 10.0 and later, it is also possible to enable VNC and set a password using the X server configuration utility sax2.

How It Works

The VNC server and client communicate using a protocol called RFB (Remote Frame Buffer). The basic idea of this protocol is to communicate changes to the screen contents from the server to the client in as efficient a manner as possible, and it uses a variety of encoding techniques to do this. RFB also allows mouse and keyboard input on the client to be transmitted to the server, so that the client can not only passively observe the server's desktop, but actively interact with it.

The Xvnc program acts as an X server. It accepts connections and X11 protocol messages from graphical applications just as any other X server would. The difference is that a "real" X server has a real frame buffer behind it (i.e., a real graphics display), whereas Xvnc has only an in-memory frame buffer. It accepts connections from VNC viewers and tells the viewer about any changes to its in-memory frame buffer. The viewer, in turn (assuming it's running on a Linux box), connects to its own X server to actually get the image drawn on its screen (on other operating systems, it would use the native display technology). This architecture is shown in Figure 2-18.

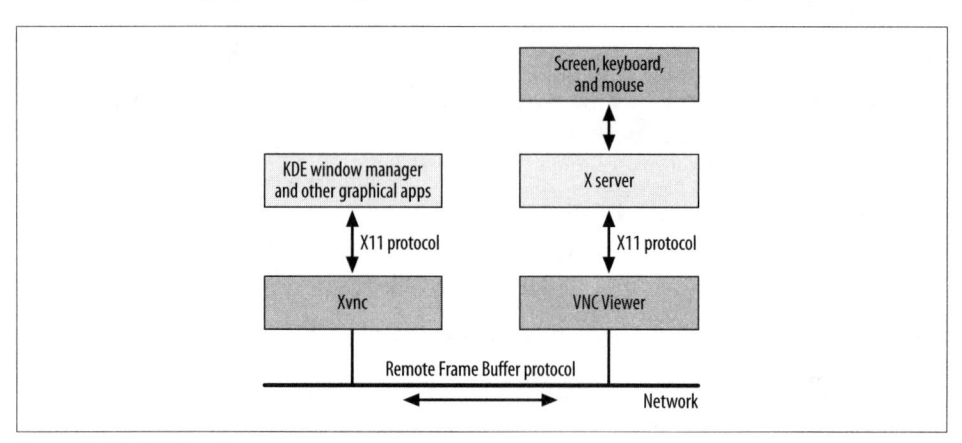

Figure 2-18. VNC architecture

The port number that the VNC server listens on is 5900 + the desktop number. For example, the VNC server for desktop :1 listens on port 5901. The VNC server also listens for HTTP requests on port 5801 (for desktop :1). If you connect to this port using a Java-enabled browser, the server will download to the browser a Java applet that acts as a VNC viewer and connects back to the server on port 5901. The class files for this Java applet are in the directory */usr/share/vnc/classes* and are part of the tightvnc package.

It's also possible to start the VNC server automatically using xinetd. The configuration file */etc/xinted.d/vnc* contains several entries that (if enabled) will listen on ports 5901, 5902, and 5903 and will start an Xvnc server and a graphical login manager. The configuration file is designed to start up the desktop at a different resolution for each port. In SUSE Linux 10.0, these entries are all disabled by default, but in 10.1 the entry for port 5901 is active. This means that you can connect to VNC desktop :1 of a SUSE 10.1 system without doing any configuration at all—it comes that way out of the box. If you are security-conscious, you might want to disable this. You'll learn about configuring xinetd-based services in Chapter 6.

What About ...

...firewall settings? If you have configured a firewall on your machine, by default it will not allow the VNC traffic through. If you are using YaST to configure your firewall, you need to enable the Remote Administration service. This opens up ports 5801 and 5901, which are used by the VNC server that serves desktop :1. It does *not* open up any of the other ports; in particular, it does not open port 5900, which is used to access a user's regular desktop session. If you are having problems connecting with vncviewer, try disabling the firewall on the target machine, using the command:

    # rcSuSEfirewall2 stop

If this fixes the problem, fine. Of course, this is a rather extreme and insecure solution, and you might want to come back and rethink the firewall settings so that you can use VNC without disabling the firewall altogether. If you use the YaST module to configure remote sharing, there is an option to automatically open up the relevant ports on the firewall if need be. For more details on controlling firewall settings, see Lab 8.3, "Set Up a Firewall."

...connecting from a computer that's not running Linux? There are many VNC viewer clients out there for Windows, Mac, and other devices, including cell phones and PDAs. See *http://www.realvnc.com* and *http://www.tightvnc.com* to find clients for Windows and other operating systems. Chicken of the VNC (*http://sourceforge.net/projects/cotvnc*) is an excellent VNC viewer for Mac OS X.

...connecting to an existing desktop session? Using VNC in the way you've seen so far allows a desktop to be accessed remotely, but it does not really provide desktop sharing. The new desktop session is quite separate from any other that might be running on the target machine.

By contrast, the program krfb (System → Remote Access → Krfb) allows remote access to the *existing* desktop session on the target machine. It does this by issuing invitations. An *invitation* basically just notifies the potential user of the machine name (or IP address) and display number that they should connect to, and provides a password that is valid for one hour. Krfb can generate a personal invitation that requires the user of the target machine to communicate it to the potential user somehow (by phone, perhaps), or it can generate an email invitation and automatically drop you into a mailer so that you can mail the invitation to the potential user. Once the invitation has been received, the remote user connects to the desktop using a VNC viewer in the normal way. The user of the target machine receives notification (via a pop-up window) when the connection is attempted, and can choose whether to allow or deny the connection.

Krfb provides true desktop sharing, in the sense that both the user of the target machine and the user of the remote machine can see, and interact with, the same desktop. This makes it an excellent vehicle for "let me show you how to do it" training, or for "let me fix your machine for you" activities by IT support staff.

Note that the config file for krfb is *~/.kde/share/config/krfbrc* and that this file can be edited by hand, if need be. I have seen this technique used to gain graphical access to a remote desktop, starting from (say) a root login via ssh. By editing the config file directly, you can effectively issue your own invitations. Then you can start krfb by running this:

```
# dcop --user FOO kinetd setEnabled krfb true
```

Where to Learn More

Read the manpages for vncviewer, vncserver, and Xvnc. You can even look at the vncserver Perl script (*/usr/bin/vncserver*). You might also want to visit the web sites *http://realvnc.com* and *http://www.tightvnc.com*.

CHAPTER 3
Using SUSE Linux on Your Desktop

This chapter looks at SUSE Linux through the eyes of an end user (whatever that is!) and examines how to do some of the everyday things that end users do—configure the desktop to look pretty, play multimedia files, burn CDs, and so on. The assumption is that you'll be using a graphical desktop interface to do most of these things, though you'll see how to do some of them from the command line, too.

It will probably help you make sense of what's going on in some of these labs if you know a little bit about the graphics architecture in Linux first. If you are coming from a Microsoft Windows or Mac OS background, you will find it's rather different.

The key point to understand is that the Linux windowing system uses a client/server architecture. The server component, which runs on the machine where the physical user interface resides (the screen, keyboard, and mouse), is called the *X server*. The client components (any applications that wish to present a graphical user interface) may run on the local machine, or may be remote, as shown in Figure 3-1. In a nutshell, any time a program (such as the Firefox web browser or OpenOffice word processor) wants to put a character up on the screen or draw a picture, it has to ask the X server to do the drawing on its behalf.

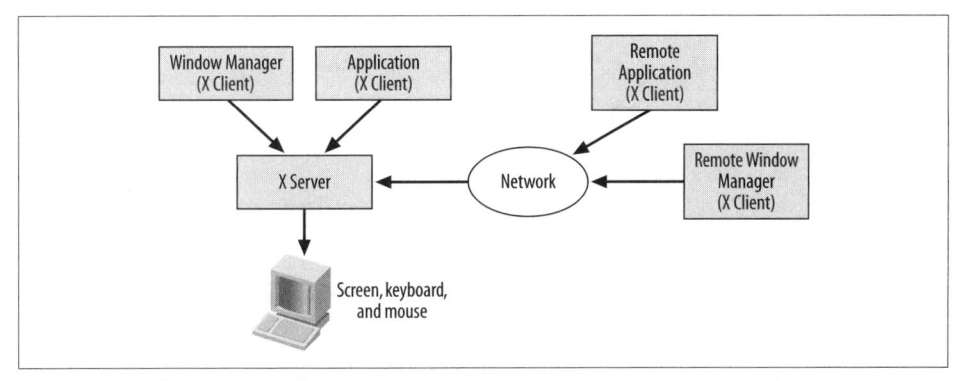

Figure 3-1. X client/server architecture

The X server provides the basic capability to render text and graphical elements onto the screen and to retrieve input from the keyboard and mouse (or other pointing device). The X server provides "mechanism, not policy"; that is, it does not define a look and feel for a graphical application—that's up to the application itself and the graphical toolkit that it uses. The X server does not even provide basic window management—those *decorations* around a window that allow it to be moved, resized, minimized, maximized, or closed. These features are provided by a window manager, which, in terms of the client/server architecture of X, is just another client of the X server.

Newcomers to this architecture sometimes puzzle over the client/server relationships here, thinking that they're the wrong way around. People are used to clients running locally, with the servers possibly being remote. Here, the X server always runs locally, and it's the clients that might be remote. If you think about the service that's being provided (essentially just access to the physical user interface), then it makes sense.

> If it helps, think of the X server as a sort of graphics driver, but one that you talk to through a network connection and a standard protocol called X11.

This architecture has some interesting features. In particular, it's possible to run a graphical application on a remote machine and present its user interface via the X server on the local machine. For example, a scientific application to render 3-D imagery of a skull from an X-ray tomography scan (something that takes a lot of computing power) could run on a big, fast machine down the hallway and display on your relatively modest desktop machine. Alternatively, you can run an entire graphical desktop (including the window manager) on a remote machine and have it present its entire user interface on the local machine. For example, one customer I know runs multiple KDE desktops on a single IBM mainframe and displays them on X servers running on desktop machines. (In that case, those X servers are actually running on Microsoft Windows—although X is thought of as a Linux or Unix environment, you can get excellent free X servers for Windows and Mac OS X.)

You should also be aware that Linux can be installed and operated perfectly well without any graphical desktop—no X server, no window manager, no graphical applications at all. Indeed, many Linux-based servers are configured and administered exactly this way. I look at server administration in Chapter 6.

3.1 Configure Your Graphics Card and Monitor

Getting the X server to properly drive your graphics card and your monitor used to be among the darkest magic involved with a Linux installation. Nowadays, thanks to vastly improved auto-probing of the hardware and much better configuration tools, in most cases it is a simple point-and-click process. Indeed, you were probably taken through the process by the YaST installer and already have a system working at the correct resolution. If you do, you can probably skip this lab!

How Do I Do That?

SUSE Linux includes an X server configuration tool called `sax2`. You can run this from the main YaST screen by selecting Hardware from the panel on the left, then Graphics Card and Monitor from the panel on the right. You can also run `sax2` directly from the command line; in fact, you can even run it from a terminal window without having a graphical desktop running at all. However, `sax2` requires a graphical user interface and will start its own X server if it needs to. The main screen of `sax2` is shown in Figure 3-2.

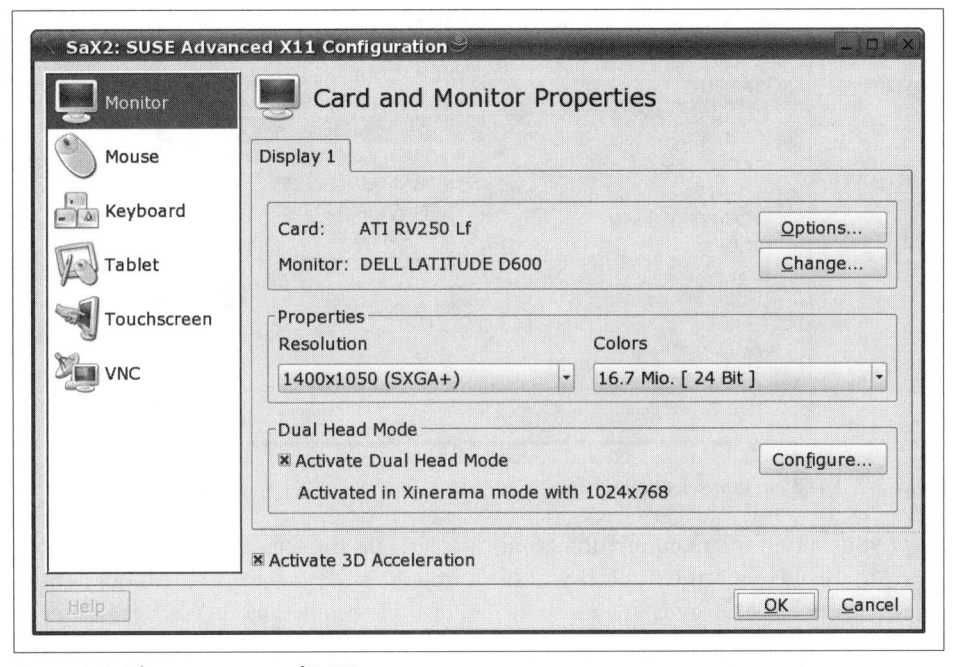

Figure 3-2. The main screen of SaX2

From this screen, you can set the resolution and color depth of the display. The color depth refers to the number of bits that are used to represent the color of each pixel on the display. Greater color depth gives more colors and hence greater color fidelity. A 16-bit color depth is adequate for older machines, and will often give better performance. However, if you have a recent mid-range to high-end video card, you won't take a performance hit by using 24-bit color (and you'll enjoy the full effect of the latest eye candy in GNOME or KDE). You will probably want to set the spatial resolution to the highest that your monitor is capable of (if you have an LCD monitor and you use a setting that's less than the maximum, your LCD monitor will have to scale the display, leading to unpleasant visual artifacts). Under some circumstances, if you set the resolution higher than this, you'll get a "window" (whose size is determined by the physical resolution of your screen) that you can pan and scroll around within a larger desktop (whose size is determined by the resolution you specify) using the mouse. I don't like this mode of operation.

To choose your monitor type, click Change. This will bring you to the monitor selection screen shown in Figure 3-3.

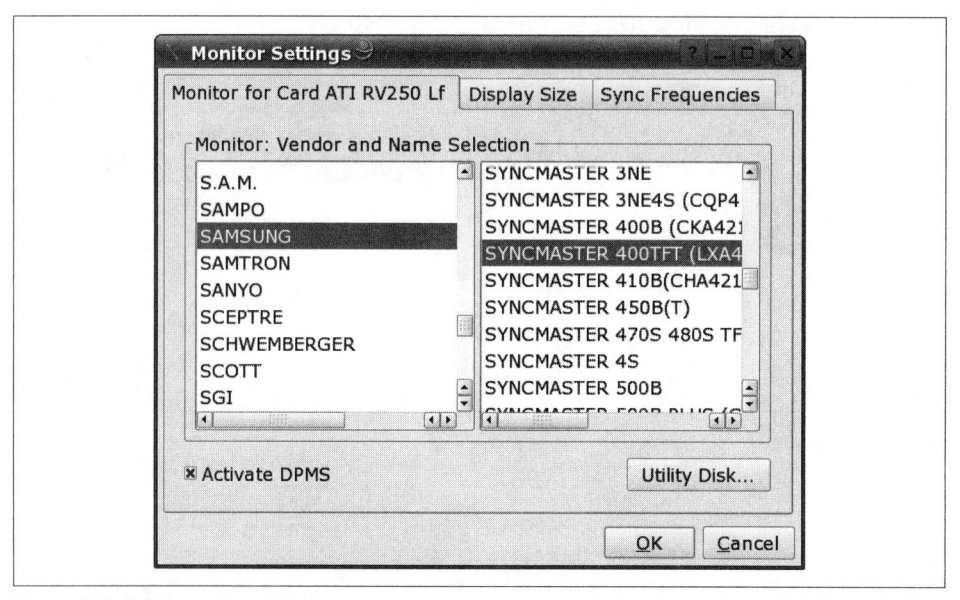

Figure 3-3. SaX2 monitor selection screen

Select your monitor's manufacturer from the panel on the left, then the model number from the panel on the right. If you can't find an exact match on the model number, a reasonable strategy is to choose the nearest one *below* the one you've got.

If you can't find a monitor model in the list that resembles yours, try selecting either VESA (for a traditional CRT monitor) or LCD (for an LCD or laptop screen) from the manufacturer list on the left. For these "manufacturers," you'll see a list of settings with names like 1024X768@75HZ, which show the resolution and the frame refresh rate. These represent standard settings that should work with a wide range of monitors. Your monitor's instruction manual should at least tell you the resolution and sync frequency ranges that your monitor supports. If you don't have the manual, many manufacturers' web sites carry this information.

If you select a resolution or sync frequencies for your monitor that are higher than it can handle, you might damage it. This warning really only applies to CRT monitors that will fail catastrophically if you ask them to push excessively high frequencies through the horizontal scan coils, but most modern CRT monitors have sufficient instinct for self-preservation to prevent you from damaging them in this way. The most likely result is simply that the monitor won't sync up properly and will instead display a message on the screen indicating that your settings are out of range. However, you have been warned!

The checkbox labeled Activate DPMS (Display Power Management Signaling) turns on the ability to put the monitor into standby, suspend, or power off mode to save the screen (and delay the onset of global warming). This works by shutting down the horizontal and/or vertical sync signals to the monitor.

The Monitor Settings screen also has tabs on which you can set the physical dimensions of the display (which are used to calculate optimal dots per inch when needed, such as for photo and graphics applications) and the range of vertical and horizontal sync frequencies. This will normally be set automatically from the choice of monitor model, and you're unlikely to need to change them.

The main SaX2 screen has an Options button for setting specific options for the graphics card. You're probably best leaving these alone. Some of them are boolean options and can be selected to turn them on; others require parameters to be specified. There are manual pages that describe these options. Try the command:

```
$ apropos 'video driver'
```

to list these. The trick is to find the right manpage for your card.

Once all your settings are complete, click OK on the main SaX2 screen. You will be offered the opportunity to test the new settings. I strongly recommend that you do this. If the settings won't work, it is easy to recover at this stage. However, if you save untested settings that turn out not to work, it is harder to recover. So click on Test. If all is well, you'll see a screen that allows you to fine-tune the position and size of the image. These adjustments really apply only to CRT monitors or LCD monitors used with analog input. If the settings are OK, click Save. If the settings don't work (for example, if you just see some sort of unsynchronized mess on the screen), you can terminate the test with Ctrl-Alt-Backspace. Alternatively, wait 30 seconds for the test to time out. (Don't waggle the mouse around during this 30 seconds; it will reset the timeout counter.)

Assuming that the test was successful, you'll be returned to the main SaX2 screen and a message box telling you that the new settings will kick in the next time the X server is restarted.

How It Works

SaX2 edits the main X server configuration file, */etc/X11/xorg.conf*. This is a plain text file, but you really don't want to edit it by hand. Trust me on this! However, if you're curious (or desperate!), here's a brief description of the major sections of this file.

Files section

This section is used to specify some path names required by the server, including FontPath entries, which tell the X server where to search for font databases, and ModulePath entries, which tell the server where to search for loadable modules.

ServerFlags section

This section specifies global server options. Options appearing here can be overridden by options appearing in ServerLayout sections, discussed shortly. Examples of options appearing here include:

AllowMouseOpenFail

Allows the server to start even if the mouse can't be initialized

DontZap

Disallows use of Ctrl-Alt-Backspace to terminate the server

DontZoom

Disallows use of Ctrl-Alt-Plus and Ctrl-Alt-Minus to switch resolution

Module section

This section is used to specify which X server modules should be loaded.

InputDevice section

This is where we begin to describe the hardware environment for the server. Each input device will have its own section here, so usually there are two: one for the keyboard and one for the mouse.

Monitor section

Here the monitors (physical screens) are described, including the valid ranges of vertical and horizontal synchronization frequencies. Also here you will find a specification of one or more video timing modes, either directly contained within this section, or via a UseModes directive that includes a named set of timing modes defined in a separate section of the file.

Modes section

In this section, a number of video timing modes are defined. Each mode, defined by a Modeline directive, has a name (typically of the form "1024×768") and a set of video timing parameters. Although these numbers are documented in the manpage for `xorg.conf`, you cannot reasonably be expected to figure these out for yourself, and if you ever find yourself needing to hack the config file at this level, I would recommend that you consider an alternative occupation. Delivering pizza, perhaps?

Device section
 A device section describes a video card, giving it a name and specifying the driver to be used.

Screen section
 The screen section associates a graphics card (defined in the Device section) with a monitor (defined in the Monitor section), resulting in a named screen.

ServerLayout section
 This is where it really all comes together. A ServerLayout section defines a complete configuration, associating one or more input devices (keyboards and mice) with a screen.

Although not immediately obvious from a quick reading of the *xorg.conf* file, there is a hierarchical relationship between the key components in the file, shown in Figure 3-4. A server layout binds together one or more input devices (typically a keyboard and a mouse) with a screen, which in turn associates a device (graphics card) with a monitor.

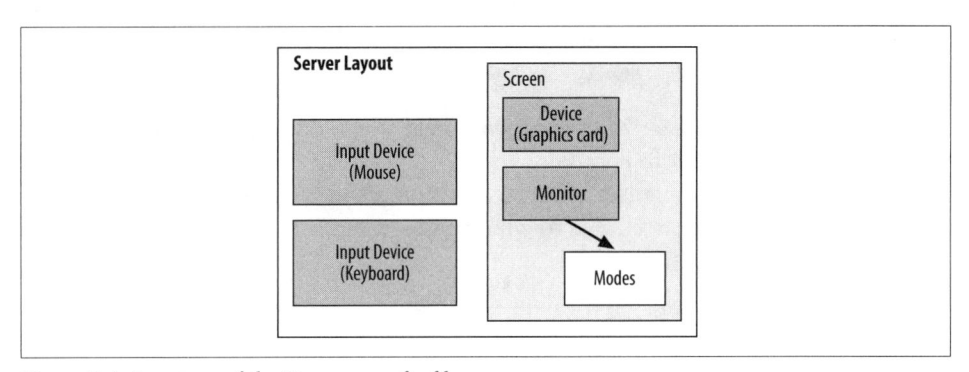

Figure 3-4. Structure of the X server config file

What About...

...the case where it just doesn't work? Occasionally, after you've completed your Linux installation, you can't bring up a graphical login. Perhaps the X server won't start, or maybe it starts but the screen display is garbled. This is a depressing scenario for a Linux newbie who is likely to despair and restart the entire installation from scratch. That should not be necessary.

First of all, if the screen is completely garbled, press Ctrl-Alt-Backspace to terminate the X server. If it insists on trying to restart, press Ctrl-Alt-F1. This should bring you to a command-line login on a virtual text terminal, which does not use X. Log in on this as root.

At this point, you might want to temporarily set the default run level to 3. I discuss run levels in detail in Lab 6.1, "Control Boot-Time Service Startup," in Chapter 6, but for the time being, edit the file */etc/inittab* and change the line:

```
id:5:initdefault:
```

to:

```
id:3:initdefault:
```

Now, when you reboot, the system will not attempt to start the X server but will provide you with a text login. You should change the default run level back to 5 once you have the X server working.

As an alternative to editing `inittab`, you may prefer to switch to run level 3 temporarily with the command:

```
# init 3
```

Whichever way you do it, the object is to get to the point where you have a text console login and no X server running.

Now you can try starting SaX2 from the text-based login:

```
# sax2
```

If this succeeds in starting an X server, it will present you with a graphical user interface, and you can proceed to configure your X server as described in the earlier part of this lab. If the X server fails to start, try looking in the log files */var/log/SaX2.log* and */var/log/Xorg.0.log* for a clue as to what went wrong. (In the *Xorg.0.log* file, look for lines tagged with the string '(EE)'.)

If SaX2 won't start, there are a few things you might try. First, try this command:

```
# sax2 -a
```

which will attempt to create a config file automatically without bringing up a graphical user interface. You might also try:

```
# sax2 -l
```

which will bring up the user interface in low resolution (800 × 600) mode. Note that this is the resolution that SaX2 will run at, not necessarily the resolution you ultimately *want* to configure.

You can force a specific resolution and refresh rate with a command of the form:

```
# sax2 -r -V 0:1024x768@75
```

Another thing to try is:

```
# sax2 -m 0=fbdev
```

which will force SaX2 to use the frame buffer driver, or:

```
# sax2 -r
```

which forces reinitialization of the hardware detection database.

Hopefully, one of these strategies will result in a working X server.

Where to Learn More

Read the manpage for `sax2`. If you really want the gory details on X, read the manpages for `X` and `xorg.conf`. There are manpages describing the individual driver modules for the various driver cards; try:

```
$ apropos 'video driver'
```

to see these.

The X.org Foundation web site is at *http://wiki.x.org*.

3.2   Configure Your Keyboard and Mouse

Living, as I do, in England, it is a constant source of wonder to me that I can get on a Eurostar train in London and arrive two hours later in a country where they make strange noises with their mouths that I cannot understand. That is, they speak French. There is no directly analogous experience in the United States, though a New Yorker might try getting on a plane to Birmingham, Alabama, and attempt to hold a conversation with a taxi driver there. In addition to TV programs like Big Brother, one of the penalties of being a highly evolved species is that we have no global standard for language, except for (in the case of the Brits) shouting slowly in English on the assumption that anyone who doesn't understand that isn't worth talking to.

It is hard to know the score for lower life forms but I am prepared to bet good money that English mice and French mice have no such barrier to communication, apart, perhaps, from a minor disagreement on the relative merits of Camembert and Wensleydale. We don't even agree with the French on how to write dates, whistle the National Anthem, or lay out the keys on our keyboards. Our qwerty is their azerty. We have no idea how to put a cedilla under our c's or a circumflex over our a's.

It's not just the French. The Spanish have their own ideas how to do things. Their qwerty is in the right place, but they have these weird upside-down question marks and twiddly things (I think they're called tildes) over their letter N. Even the Yanks and the Brits disagree over keyboard layouts. Americans looking for the @ sign or Brits looking for the quotation mark over the 2 on the wrong side of the pond will be well adrift. To the Brits, a pound sign is a currency symbol like this: £. To the Americans, a pound sign looks like this: #. I once tried to explain this to a class in San Francisco and came close to being lynched in disbelief. In desperation I circulated a British banknote around the class to show what a "proper" pound sign looks like. It didn't help, though I did get the note back. If this kind of thing interests you, I recommend that you visit Michael Quinion's wonderful web site at *http://www.worldwidewords.org* and look up the "octothorpe."

In this lab, you'll see how to set a keyboard layout and customize operation of the mouse.

How Do I Do That?

The most convenient way to set the keyboard layout is from the KDE control center, accessible directly from the main KDE menu. Make sure that you have the Index tab selected from the pane on the left, then select Regional and Accessibility → Keyboard Layout. From this screen (Figure 3-5) you can chose amongst the available layouts (the list on the left) and add them to the active layouts (the list on the right) by clicking Add. Also make sure that the "Enable keyboard layouts" checkbox is checked.

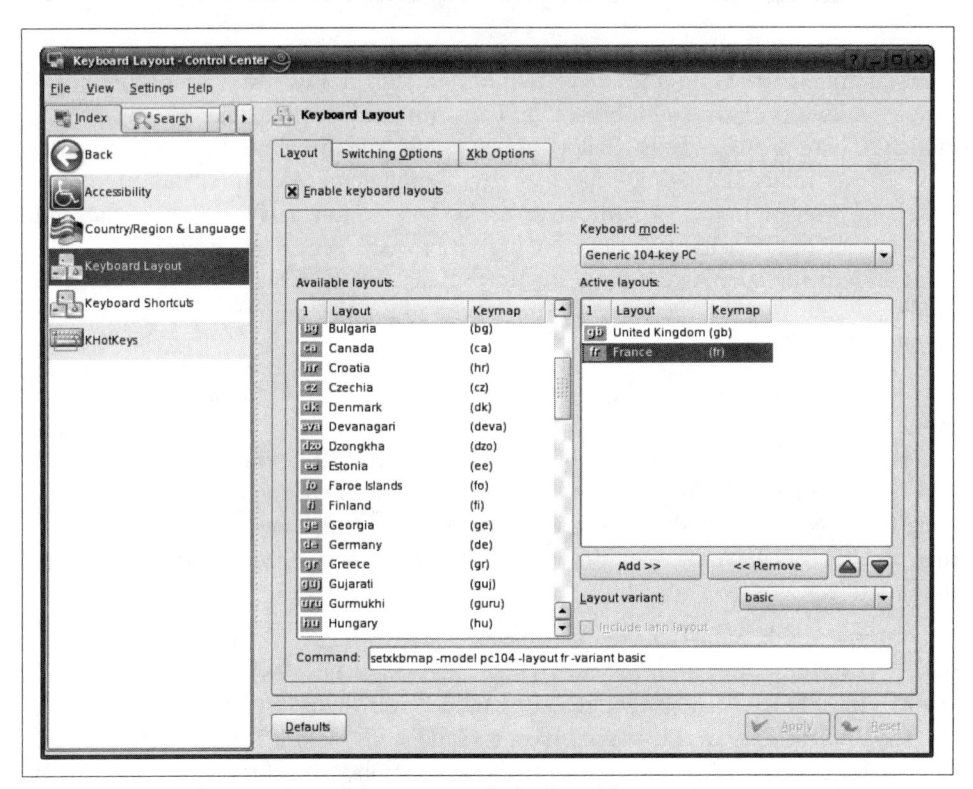

Figure 3-5. Using the KDE Control Center to set the keyboard layout

If you want more than one active layout, select the layout you want as the default from the list on the right and move it to the top of the list by clicking the up-arrow button. If you specify more than one active layout, KDE will automatically start the keyboard layout switching utility, called kxkb, which will place a small icon in the system tray. Left-clicking this icon will cycle through the active layouts. Alternatively, you can right-click on the icon and select the layout directly from the pop-up menu. (The only reason I can think of why you might want to do this is if you occasionally need to enter characters not in your usual character set. Apart from this, to my mind it only makes sense to change the keyboard map if you physically change the keyboard.) Changes made in this way affect only the user who made the change. They do not, for example, change the keyboard layout used by the login manager.

In SUSE 10.1, GNOME has a roughly equivalent tool. Select Utilities → Desktop → Gnome Control Center from the main menu. On the Desktop Preferences screen, select Keyboard. Then, on the Keyboard Preferences window, select the Layout tab. Here, click Add and select the required keyboard layout from the scroll list of available layouts.

It is also possible to set the keyboard layout in the underlying X server configuration using YaST. From the main YaST screen, select Hardware from the pane on the left, then Keyboard Layout from the pane on the right. This will launch SaX2, which is the configuration utility for the X server. (See Figure 3-6.) From here you can select your primary keyboard layout along with any additional layouts you'd like to be able to select. When you have made your selections, click OK. You'll be asked if you want to test your settings, but this test is mainly intended to verify that the X server display settings are correct, and you haven't changed those. So just click on Save, and then quit from SaX2.

If you set the keyboard layout this way, you will need to restart the X server before the changes will kick in. In practice, this means that you'll need to log out and then log back in again. Changes that you make in this way affect all users.

Neither of these methods of setting the keyboard layout is appropriate if you're not running a graphical desktop—in other words, if you're simply using a character-based console or one of the six virtual terminals that are supported by SUSE Linux. To set the keymap for the character terminals, use the command loadkeys. For example:

```
$ loadkeys uk
```

will load the British keymap, whereas:

```
$ loadkeys us
```

will load the American keymap. If you really want to know, the command:

```
$ dumpkeys
```

will show the currently loaded keymap.

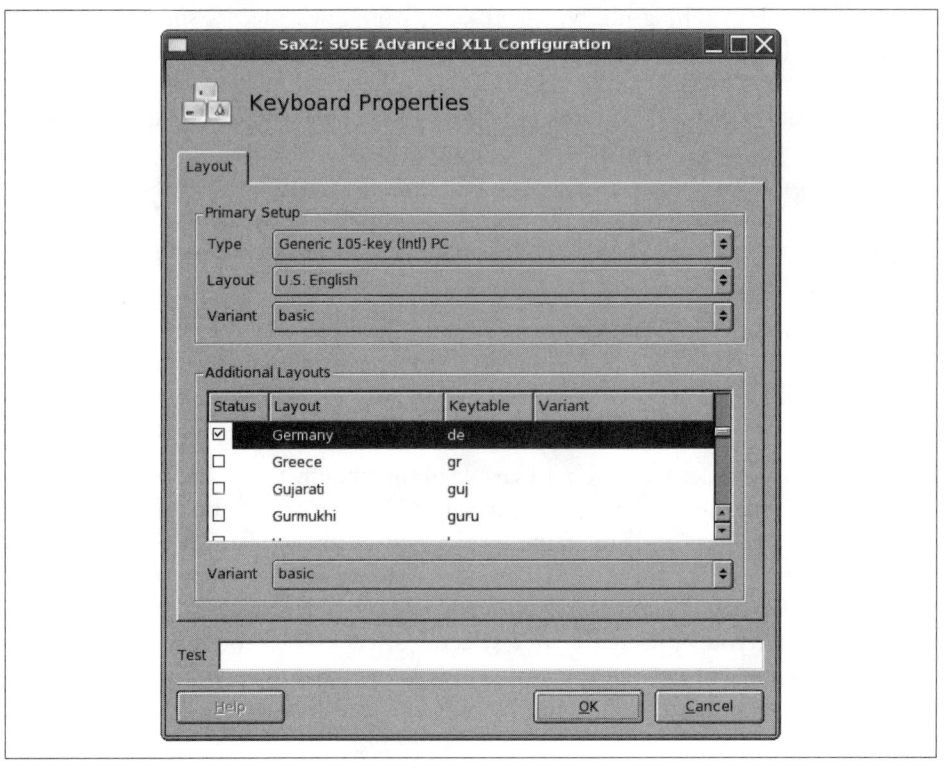

Figure 3-6. Using SaX2 to set the keyboard layout

What About...

...configuring the mouse?

> Before we move on, here's a little test. When was the computer mouse invented? No Googling—make a guess. The answer's right at the end of the chapter. If you didn't already know the answer, and you've been using computers long enough to remember when they didn't come with a mouse, you might marvel at how long it took this now-indispensable aspect of computing to trickle down to the masses.

You can configure various aspects of mouse behavior, including left/right-handedness, single- or double-click behavior, and the cursor appearance, using the KDE control center. Launch Personal Settings from the main KDE menu, then select Peripherals → Mouse from the pane on the left. (Versions of SUSE Linux prior to 10.1 labeled this menu item "KDE Control Center.") The mouse configuration screen has four tabs:

General
> Here you can set left-handed or right-handed behavior, reverse the operation of the scroll wheel, and set single-click or double-click behavior. (Double-click may suit users coming from Microsoft Windows and is also the default behavior in GNOME, but single-click is the default for KDE.) You can also turn on or off a change in the appearance of the cursor as you hover over a selectable item, and there is a mystery checkbox labeled Automatically Select Icons that (I eventually discovered) causes a file or folder icon to be selected if you hover over it, just as if you were to Ctrl-click on the icon.

Cursor Theme
> Here you can select amongst various sets of images that will be used as cursors. "Crystal White" is the default, and I see no good reason to change this unless you prefer the nonanimated version.

Advanced
> Here you can specify a number of mouse parameters:
>
> *Pointer acceleration*
> > Controls the overall sensitivity to mouse movement—that is, the "gear ratio" between the distance the mouse moves and the distance the cursor moves.
>
> *Pointer threshold*
> > The smallest distance that the mouse must move before the acceleration parameter has any effect.
>
> *Double-click interval*
> > The maximum time between mouse clicks for KDE to register a double-click. Old age and excess alcohol consumption might be cause to increase this value.
>
> *Drag time and drag start distance*
> > Determine when KDE recognizes mouse activity as a drag operation. The drag time specifies the maximum time that can elapse after selecting an item before starting the drag, and the drag start distance specifies the minimum movement that will be recognized as a drag.
>
> *Scroll wheel sensitivity*
> > Sets the gear ratio of the scroll wheel in terms of text lines per click.
>
> Unless you are having some particular difficulty in operating the mouse, it's probably best to leave all these settings alone.

Mouse Navigation
> Here you can enable the use of the numeric keypad to move the pointer, as an alternative to using the mouse.

What About…

…configuring a touchpad? If you have a laptop, you may find that your touchpad "just works" without any special configuration. For example, it may provide cursor movement and "left-button" mouse clicks by tapping the touchpad. However, you can get much finer control over the behavior of your touchpad by using the synaptics touchpad driver, which is included with the SUSE Linux distribution. This driver also works with ALPS touchpads. For example, you can arrange to generate mouse-wheel "scroll" events by stroking down the righthand edge of the touchpad. To configure this driver, you will need to edit the X server configuration file */etc/X11/xorg.conf*. (Elsewhere in this book, I caution against hand-editing this file. But sometimes, well, a man's gotta do what a man's gotta do. But be aware that any changes you make to *xorg.conf* will be overwritten if you run sax2.) You will need to be root to edit this file. First, in the ServerLayout section of the file, add the line:

```
InputDevice "TouchPad" "AlwaysCore"
```

Second, add an InputDevice section that loads the synaptics driver and specifies its parameters. You may need to experiment a little to establish settings that work well for you, but here's an entry to get you started:

```
Section "InputDevice"
    Driver          "synaptics"
    Identifier      "TouchPad"
    Option          "Device"            "/dev/psaux"
    Option          "Protocol"          "auto-dev"
    Option          "LeftEdge"          "200"
    Option          "RightEdge"         "800"
    Option          "TopEdge"           "150"
    Option          "BottomEdge"        "600"
    Option          "FingerLow"         "25"
    Option          "FingerHigh"        "30"
    Option          "MaxTapTime"        "180"
    Option          "MaxTapMove"        "220"
    Option          "VertScrollDelta"   "100"
    Option          "MinSpeed"          "0.09"
    Option          "MaxSpeed"          "0.18"
    Option          "AccelFactor"       "0.0015"
    Option          "SHMConfig"         "on"
EndSection
```

The option that enables SHMConfig is particularly important. It allows you to set the synaptics driver parameters on the fly, using the synclient program, which I'll discuss in a moment. With these entries in place in *xorg.conf*, log out from the desktop and log in again, to force a restart of the X server. Your touchpad should now be enabled using the synaptics driver.

There are many parameters that you can adjust to configure operation of this driver. For a detailed description, look at the manual page for "synaptics," using the command:

```
$ man synaptics
```

The program `synclient` lets you tweak the synaptics driver settings on the fly, without having to edit *xorg.conf* and restart the X server each time. However, changes you make with `synclient` affect only the currently running X server. Once you have established satisfactory settings using `synclient`, you should edit them into the *xorg.conf* file.

You can interrogate the current synaptics driver settings with the command:

```
$ synclient -l
```

You can change one specific parameter with a command such as:

```
$ synclient LeftEdge=150
```

You can obtain a readout of the coordinates and other parameters reported by the touchpad using a command such as:

```
$ synclient -m 100
```

For example, I have used this command to examine the range of X and Y coordinates reported by the touchpad in order to determine appropriate values for parameters such as `LeftEdge`, `RightEdge`, `TopEdge`, and `BottomEdge`.

A common requirement is to enable the touchpad for cursor movement but to disable it for simulated button presses via tapping. You can do this by setting the parameter `MaxTapTime` to zero, either by using the command:

```
$ synclient MaxTapTime = 0
```

or by editing the file *xorg.conf*.

Alternatively, you may wish to disable the touchpad altogether. This can usually be done in the laptop's BIOS setup screens. Usually there are settings to turn off the touchpad altogether, or to disable it if a mouse is plugged in.

How It Works

Be aware that keyboard input is handled in two entirely different ways depending on whether you're using the X server (i.e., running a graphical desktop). Setting the keyboard map used for the nongraphical virtual terminals does not affect the keyboard map used in X windows, and vice versa.

Dynamic switching of the keyboard layout under KDE is handled by the tool kxkb. In turn, this invokes the command-line tool `setxkbmap`, which uses the Xkeyboard (xkb) extensions to the X protocol to dynamically establish a keyboard map.

Where to Learn More

The KDE control center is extensively documented in the KDE Help Center. There are links to this documentation from within the control center itself. For behind-the-scenes information about key mappings in console terminals, read the manpages for loadkeys, dumpkeys, and keymaps. For information about the synaptics touchpad driver, see *http://web.telia.com/~u89404340/touchpad/index.html*.

3.3 Configure the KDE Menus and Panel

The KDE desktop is customizable in almost endless detail. You can change the background wallpaper, the screensaver, the color scheme, the icons, the menus, the panel, the shortcut keys, and much else. Some of these changes bring real improvements in productivity, but in my experience, extensive tinkering with the desktop is often used as a displacement activity to avoid doing any real work. In this lab, we'll see how to customize the menus and the panel.

How Do I Do That?

To customize the main menu, right-click on the main menu button at the left end of the main panel, and select Menu Editor from the pop-up menu. (You can also run kmenuedit from a command prompt.) The menu editor screen has a tree control in the panel on the left that allows you to navigate through the menu hierarchy. For the sake of a simple example, here's how to add a shortcut key to invoke the Konsole terminal window:

1. You already know that this application is on the menu under System → Terminal → Konsole, so navigate through the tree view control accordingly, expanding System, then Terminal, and finally selecting Konsole.

2. The menu editor will display the current settings for this menu entry as shown in Figure 3-7. There is probably no shortcut key currently allocated. To set one, click on the button labeled "Current shortcut key."

3. In the dialog labeled Configure Shortcut, make sure that the radio button labeled "Primary shortcut" is selected, then enter the key combination you want to use as the shortcut—for example, Alt-T. (Do not be tempted to use a printing character such as Shift-T. If you do, every time you try to type an uppercase T, you'll launch a terminal window!)

4. From the KDE Menu Editor's menu, select File → Save to save the new settings, then quit the application.

As another example, let's add a new menu item. There's a handy program called top that displays a useful summary of the system load and the most resource-hungry processes currently running. System administrators find it useful for monitoring the health of busy servers. Here's how to put it on the System → Monitor menu:

1. Begin by opening the KDE menu editor as before. Navigate to System using the tree view, but then, instead of opening the Monitor branch, right-click it and select New Item from the pop-up menu. (Notice that you also have the option to

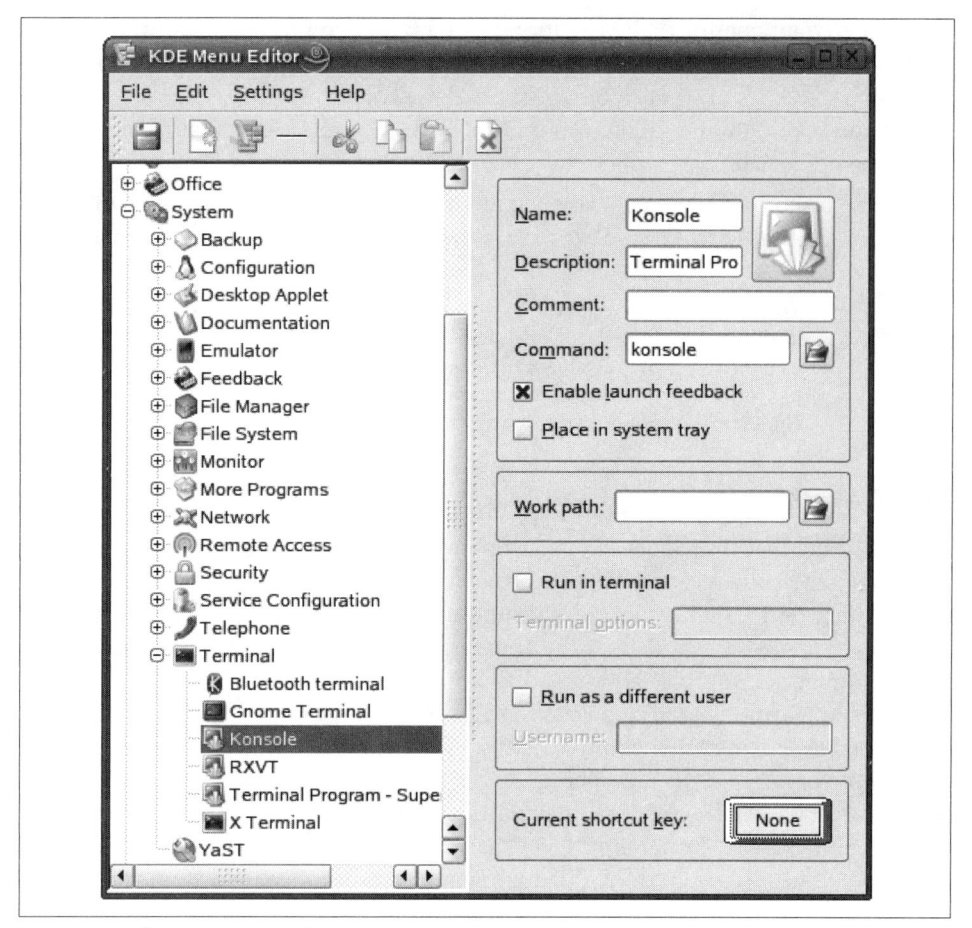

Figure 3-7. The KDE Menu Editor

create a new submenu at this point.) Input a name for the item (this is the label that will appear on the menu), then press Enter.

2. Fill in the remaining fields on the form. At a minimum, you'll need to enter the command that runs the application. This is the command you'd use to start the application from a command prompt. It can include options or arguments if necessary. If the command is on your *search path*, you can just enter the name (in this case, simply **top**). Otherwise, you'll have to enter the full path name here.

3. The field labeled Work Path sets the current directory in which the application will be started. Usually there is no need to enter anything here.

4. Because top is not a graphical application (it does not create its own window but expects to run inside a terminal window), you also need to check the box labeled "Run in terminal."

5. To select an icon for the application, click on the icon to the right of the Name field. You will be presented with a fairly large collection of system icons from which to choose. Just click on your selection. This icon will also show up on the menu. (You can also design your own icon, of course, but that's outside the scope of this lab.)

6. Define a shortcut key for the application if you want. Then, from the KDE Menu Editor's menu, select File → Save to save the new settings, and quit the application.

> You may notice that there are more items in the menu structure shown in the menu editor than appear on the actual menu. The rule appears to be that if a menu category is empty, it is not displayed. For example, on my own machine the entire Edutainment menu hierarchy is completely empty, so it doesn't show up.

How It Works

I used to think that the sequence of startup files read by the shell was about as much as I could handle, but comparing KDE's config files to the shell's is a bit like comparing the flight deck of a Boeing 767 with the dashboard of a Citroen Deux Chevaux. There is no single file that defines the contents of the KDE menus. They are built up from a number of sources, allowing menus to contain a combination of GNOME and KDE applications, and allowing both system-wide and per-user configuration. The principle system-wide definition of the KDE menus is a collection of *.menu* files in the directory */etc/xdg/menus*. These are XML files. If you customize the menu, the per-user settings will be stored in *.menu* files under *~/.config/menus*. Individual applications are described in *.desktop* files (discussed in Lab 3.4, "Configure the KDE Desktop"), and ultimately the individual menu entries are created from these files. The actual menu is maintained by a program called ksycoca, which caches the menu structure and information about all available applications. (I'm guessing the name stands for "KDE system configuration cache.") This structure is built by the program kbuildsycoca. The command:

```
$ kbuildsycoca --menutest
```

will show you exactly which *.desktop* files actually end up in the menus. It shows you where all the pieces have come from. Here's a fragment of the output, including the line for the "top" menu item that we just added:

```
$ kbuildsycoca --menutest
Graphics/Scanning/  kde-kooka.desktop   /opt/kde3/share/applications/kde/kooka.desktop
Graphics/Image Editing/ gimp.desktop    /opt/gnome/share/applications/gimp.desktop
Graphics/Vector Drawing/       draw.desktop    /usr/share/applications/draw.desktop
Internet/E-Mail/  kde-ktnef.desktop   /opt/kde3/share/applications/kde/ktnef.desktop
Internet/E-Mail/  kde-KMail.desktop   /opt/kde3/share/applications/kde/KMail.desktop
System/Monitor/ top.desktop   /home/chris/.local/share/applications/top.desktop
```

What About...

...the KDE panel (also known as "Kicker")? This panel can also be extensively customized.

One of the simplest things you can do with the panel is to move it. Just find some empty space on the panel (if there is any), press and hold down the left mouse button, and drag the panel to whichever edge of the screen you prefer. (Personally, I find that it doesn't work too well down the left and right edges.)

Other panel configuration options can be accessed by right-clicking on an empty space on the panel and selecting Configure Panel from the pop-up menu. This will start the Configure KDE Panel tool. This tool has several screens. If you click the Layout icon in the pane on the left, you will see a screen with four tabs.

On the Arrangement tab, you can:

- Set the position of the panel.
- Set the length of the panel (as a percentage of the length of the side it's displayed on).
- Set the size of the icons on the panel.

On the Hiding tab, you can:

- Turn on automatic hiding of the panel. (The panel will hide automatically a specified number of seconds after the cursor leaves it. Move the cursor to the bottom edge of the screen to get the panel back.)
- Turn on or off the panel hiding buttons (the little black triangles at the end of the panel that let you hide it manually).
- Control the speed of the panel-hiding animation. (Yes, there is animation! It won't impress you if you've ever seen the "Genie" effect on the Mac desktop, but it's a start.)

On the Menus tab, you can:

- Add extra items to the Actions section of the main KDE menu.
- Determine the number of items that will be shown in the Most Used Applications section of the main KDE menu, or turn this feature off completely by setting the number to zero.

On the Appearance tab, you can set a number of more cosmetic features:

- Enable icon zooming (a cute feature that makes the launch icons on the panel bigger as you mouse over them). Again, not done as well as on the Mac desktop (yet).
- Set the backgrounds for the launch icons on the panel.
- Make the panel's background transparent.

Finally, if you click on the Taskbar icon in the pane on the left, you will see one further screen of configuration options. The Taskbar is that region of the panel that shows all your currently open windows and allows you to easily navigate to any running application.

Don't forget to click OK when you're done configuring the panel to make your changes kick in, and quit the application.

You can add launch icons to the panel by dragging them off the main menus. This is useful for frequently used applications:

1. Left-click on the main menu button at the left end of the panel. (Don't hold down the mouse button—just click.)
2. Navigate to the item you want to add to the panel.
3. Press and hold down the left mouse button and drag the item onto the panel.

(You can do the same thing by right-clicking on the panel, then selecting Add Application to Panel, but I find it easier to just drag items off the menus.)

If you run out of space on the main panel, you can add a child panel. Right-click on the main panel, and then select Add New Panel → Panel. The new panel will be created immediately above the original, but you can drag it to whichever edge you prefer. This new panel is just "more space"—you can add launch icons and other items onto it just as you can for the main panel.

There are a few other useful applets you can add to the panel. Right-click on the panel and select "Add Applet to Panel." Three I've found especially useful are:

The Show Desktop button
    This minimizes all your windows so you can see the desktop.

The Quick File Browser button
    This handy tool gives you access to your files through a hierarchical collection of menus. If you just want to navigate to a file and open it, this is a fast way to do it.

The Recent Documents menu
    This application lets you easily reopen recently opened files.

Where to Learn More

I don't know of a good, modern book dealing specifically with KDE, though there are several that devote attention to it as part of a broader coverage of Linux. The complete user guide is available online at *http://docs.kde.org/development/en/kdebase/userguide*; in particular, there's a good description of the menu definition files at *http://docs.kde.org/development/en/kdebase/userguide/kde-menu.html*. Also take a look at *http://docs.kde.org/development/en/kdebase/userguide/customizing-kde.html#desktop-icons*.

3.4 Configure the KDE Desktop

KDE users fall broadly into one of two camps: there are those who are happy to leave the look and feel of their desktop entirely alone and get on with some work, and there are those to whom it is important to have their window borders exactly the right shade of pink, see a different picture of their pet tortoise behind each virtual desktop, and hear a drum roll each time they open a window. It is to this latter group that this lab is dedicated.

How Do I Do That?

Some of the most common desktop configuration options are available by right-clicking on the desktop and selecting Configure Desktop from the pop-up menu. In this tool, you can make changes in five categories, which are selected by clicking on the icons in the pane on the left.

On the Background settings screen, you can:

- Set a background image for the desktop. You can either set the same background for each virtual desktop or set a different one for each. There is quite an extensive collection to choose from, or you can import your own images and use those. You can even select a "slide show," which cycles around a specified collection of images at a specified rate.
- Select a color instead of a background image—either a simple solid color or a gradient between two colors.
- Select a blend between a background image and a color or color gradient.

On the Behavior settings screen, you can:

- Turn the desktop icons on or off.
- Turn the desktop menu bar on or off. (This menu bar mostly duplicates the functions available by right-clicking on the desktop.)
- Turn on a Mac OS–style menu bar. In this mode, a menu bar corresponding to the application that currently has input focus appears at the top of the desktop. This is the normal style for a Mac desktop, so if you're from a Mac background, you will probably like it; if you're not, you probably won't.
- Determine the behavior of the left, middle, and right mouse buttons when clicked on the desktop.

On the Multiple Desktops screen, you can:

- Set the number of virtual desktops (up to a maximum of 16, though I find 4 is the maximum I can keep track of).
- Give names to the virtual desktops.

On the Screensaver screen, you can:

- Select your screensaver. (Linux has lots of excellent screensavers; in fact, I sometimes wonder if it would sell better if it were marketed as a screensaver collection rather than as an operating system.)
- Select the time before the screensaver kicks in.
- Determine whether you need to enter your password to stop the screensaver and return to your desktop.

> It worries me these days how few of the people I meet know what screensavers are actually for. (It worries me only because it reminds me that I'm older than they are.) So, for the benefit of my younger readers: screensavers were originally invented to prevent a static image from remaining on the screen for hours on end and producing a burn in the phosphor coating of the CRT. You can sometimes see this effect on the display monitors in airports, where, dimly visible in negative behind the announcement that your flight to Copenhagen is three hours late, it says "No Smoking." Nowadays, screensavers have become more of an art form, and it wouldn't surprise me to find a computer with the image of a favorite screensaver burnt into the phosphor coating of the CRT.

On the Display screen, you can:

- Set the resolution and refresh rate of your display.
- Adjust the gamma settings for your display. You can tune the display to ensure that it shows a full range of brightness values and correct color balance. You are most likely to be interested in this if you do professional photographic work on the machine.
- Turn display power management on and off, and set the time delays before the various power-saving modes kick in.

There are many more configuration options available under Personal Settings (on the main menu). This launches the KDE Control Center; on earlier versions of SUSE Linux, the menu item was labeled Control Center. This tool takes quite a while to explore. Excluding the YaST screens, which are also linked from here, there are more than 70 screens of configuration options (and some of them have multiple tabs!), though a few duplicate those we've already seen under Configure Desktop. I find this tool much easier to navigate using its tree view than using its icon view, so I suggest the first thing you do is select View → Mode → Tree View from its main menu.

Many of the configurable settings under Personal Settings are per user settings that can be changed as an ordinary (nonroot) user. Other changes need root privilege, so you'll find some screens have some or all of the fields grayed out (disabled). These screens have an Administrator Mode button at the bottom that prompts you for the root password and promotes you to root privilege.

The number of configurable options in KDE is so large that an exhaustive treatment of them would take up the rest of the book. Here, I examine just a few of the options that may be of interest.

To set file associations

The Konqueror file browser maintains a set of file associations. That is, it associates specific filename extensions with a specific action to be taken if you click on a file of that type. In some cases, Konqueror will open the file in an embedded viewer (i.e., within the Konqueror window itself). In other cases, it will open the file in an external application. If it doesn't have a defined association for the file, it will bring up a dialog to let you choose which application to use. You can edit these file associations in Control Center. As an example, we'll change the behavior for plain text files. By default, Konqueror opens these in an embedded viewer. We'll change this so that they are opened in a separate window using the KDE editor, Kate.

Begin by selecting Personal Settings → KDE Components → File Associations. In the tree view list of known types, expand the Text node and select the file type *plain*. In the panel on the right labeled Filename Patterns, you will see that this file type is used for files with names ending in *.txt*. You can add other patterns to this list if you want. Now click on the Embedding tab and select the radio button "Show File in Separate Viewer." Now click on the General tab and examine the panel labeled Application Preference Order. Here, you will probably see a short list of text editors or viewers; hopefully, Kate is already on the list. (You can add it if it isn't.) Click Kate, then click "Move up" until Kate is at the top of the list. Finally, click Apply. Note that if Konqueror is already running, you will need to restart it for the change to kick in.

To associate sounds with desktop events

Sounds can be associated with a wide range of desktop events. As an example, I'll show you how to change the sound that's played when KDE starts up. Begin by selecting Personal Settings → Sound and Multimedia → System Notifications. In the drop-down list box labeled Event Source, select KDE System Notifications. In the event list, select "KDE is starting up. You can turn the sound for this event on or off by clicking in the sounds column (the one headed with a tiny loudspeaker icon), or by using the checkbox labeled "Play a sound." Now you can navigate to the sound file you want to associate with this event. KDE provides a modest collection of sounds in */opt/kde3/share/sounds*. Of course, you can add your own if you want. (If you don't want your fellow travelers on the train to realize that you're using Linux when you boot your laptop, you could even copy *The Microsoft Sound.wav* from your Windows box and use that, though I dare say it contravenes Microsoft's license agreement.) Figure 3-8 shows the Control Center's System Notifications screen.

To start applications automatically when you log in

When you log in, the KDE session manager will automatically restart any KDE applications that were open the last time you logged out. You can turn this

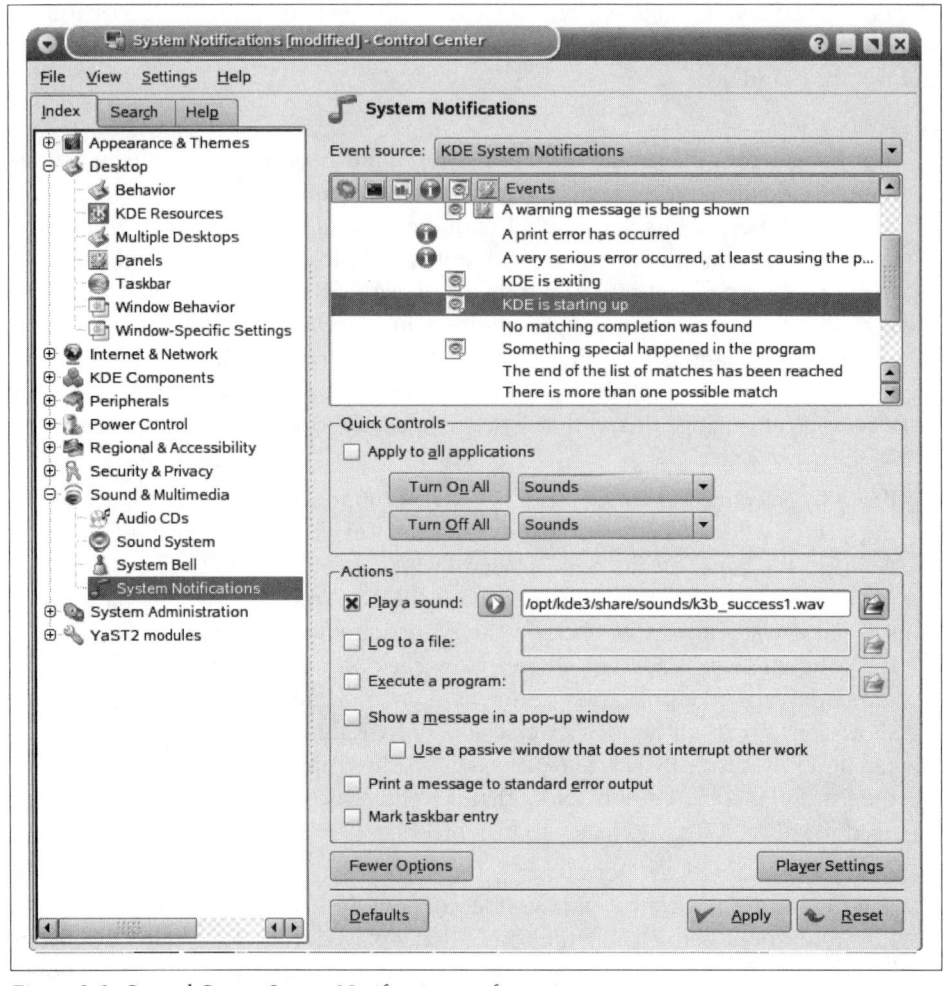

Figure 3-8. Control Center System Notification configuration

behavior off by going to Personal Settings → KDE Components → Session Manager and clicking the radio button labeled Start With an Empty Session. To start applications automatically when you log in, you need to put links to those applications into the folder *~/.kde/Autostart*. Here's how to arrange for the load monitoring tool xosview to start automatically when you log in:

a. Begin by opening Konqueror.

b. In the View menu, select Show Hidden Files (otherwise, you won't be able to see the *.kde* folder).

c. Navigate to the folder *.kde/Autostart*.

d. From the Window menu in Konqueror, select Split View Top/Bottom.

e. In the top view, navigate to the folder */usr/X11/bin*, locate the xosview application, and drag it into the Autostart folder in the bottom view. Select Link Here.

To change the mouse behavior to double-click

Select Personal Settings → Peripherals → Mouse → General tab. Select the radio button labeled "Double click to open files and folders." This affects mouse behavior when you click on an icon on the desktop or in Konqueror. Users coming from a Windows or Mac background may find this setting helpful.

To change the login theme

SUSE Linux provides its own "themed" login screen that, in the default configuration, replaces the KDE login screen. The SUSE theme is defined by the files in the directory */opt/kde3/share/apps/kdm/themes/SUSE*. You can replace some of the graphical elements in this theme if you wish (for example, the background image *Background.png*). Alternatively, you can turn off the SUSE theme altogether, and revert to the KDE login screen. To do this, edit the file */etc/opt/kde3/share/config/kdm/kdmrc* and change the line:

    UseTheme=true

to:

    UseTheme=false

To configure the KDE login screen, go to Personal Settings → System Administration → Login Manager and select Administrator mode, entering the root password when requested. From here you can change the look and behavior of the login screen in a number of ways, including:

- Change the background image (on the Background tab)
- Change the welcome message (on the Appearance tab)
- Specify whether to show a list of available accounts (on the Users tab)
- Enable automatic login, and select the user (on the Convenience tab)
- Specify who is allowed to shut the computer down (on the Shutdown tab)

How It Works

The KDE desktop and its associated applications store their configuration in plain text files.

There are three directory hierarchies for KDE configuration files, two of which are system-wide and one of which is per-user. On SUSE Linux, the system-wide hierarchies are rooted at */opt/kde3* and */etc/opt/kde3*, and the per-user hierarchy is rooted within the user's home directory at *~/.kde*. Additional hierarchies can be defined through use of the environment variable KDEDIRS. The per-user settings take precedence over the system-wide settings. Thus, the system-wide settings can be regarded as providing a default.

Each of these hierarchies follows the same structure, some of which is shown in Table 3-1 (this is not a complete list).

Table 3-1. Where the KDE config files live

Directory	Description
/share/applnk/	Contains .desktop files describing the KDE menu. These files provide legacy support for pre–KDE 3.2 systems.
/share/apps/	Contains application-specific data files. Each application has a subdirectory here for storing its files. For example, the amaroK sound player stores its configuration in files under /opt/kde3/share/apps/amarok.
/share/config/	Contains configuration files. Configuration files are normally named after the application they belong to, followed by rc. There are also files that are specific to a component and as such are referenced by all applications that use that component. A special case is kdeglobals; this file is read by all KDE applications.
/share/config/session/	This directory is used by session management and is normally available only under the per-user hierarchy. At the end of a session, KDE applications store their state here. The file names start with the name of the application, followed by a number. The session manager ksmserver stores references to these numbers when saving a session in ksmserverrc.
/share/icons/	Under this directory, icons are stored. Icons are categorized per theme, dimension, and usage category.
/share/services/	This directory contains .desktop files that describe services. Services and Applications are very similar; the major difference is that a Service is usually used by other Services or Applications, while an Application is in general started by the user. Services do not appear in the KDE menu.
/share/sounds/	This directory contains sound files.
/share/wallpapers/	This directory contains images that can be used as background pictures.

Not all of these directories are present in both the system and user hierarchies. For example, the directory /opt/kde3/share/wallpapers contains JPEG images for use as desktop background images, but there is no equivalent directory in the per-user hierarchy.

The .desktop files themselves all have the same basic structure. Each consists of one or more groups, and within each group are a number of parameter definitions. Each definition is of the form key=value. Here are a couple of fragments from the config file for the multimedia player amaroK, just to show the syntax:

```
[Desktop Entry]
X-SUSE-translate=true
Type=Application
Version=0.9.4
Encoding=UTF-8
Name=amaroK
... edited ...
Terminal=false
Categories=Qt;KDE;AudioVideo;Player;
Actions=Enqueue;
InitialPreference=7

[Desktop Action Enqueue]
Exec=amarok -e %U
Name=Enqueue in amaroK
... edited ...
```

Here, Version is a *parameter* (or key), 0.9.4 is its value, and it's in the group Desktop Entry.

Another interesting configuration file, this time from the per-user hierarchy, is *~/.kde/share/config/kdeglobals*. Here, KDE keyboard shortcuts are defined. This file was quite an eye-opener for me, as I discovered lots of shortcuts I never knew about before, such as Alt-Ctrl-Shift-Page Down to halt the system without confirmation. (No, I am not making this up!)

You can hand-edit these files with any text editor. If you would prefer a more structured way to edit them, try `kconfigeditor`, downloadable from *http://extragear.kde.org/apps/kconfigeditor/*.

Where to Learn More

Take a look at the KDE web site, in particular *http://www.kde.org/areas/sysadmin/config_file.php*.

3.5 Lock Down the Desktop for Kiosk Mode

The configurability of KDE is one of its great strengths. However, there are situations when you'd like to restrict the amount of configuration that end users can perform. Examples of this are Linux-based kiosk applications, such as an information terminal in a library or airport, computers in Internet cafés, the computer you set up for your aging (and technically inept) aunt and uncle, and even corporate desktop systems intended for nontechnical users. In this lab, you'll see how you can lock down the desktop (for example, you can prevent the user from logging out, stop them from changing the icons and files on the desktop, disable context menus, and much else besides) for these situations.

> As a (completely irrelevant) aside, a Linux-loving friend of mine called Bob tells the slightly tongue-in-cheek story about setting up a computer for his elderly parents so they could do email and surf the Web, or at least paddle in it. Of course, he chose to set up a Linux system. He spent some time explaining how to use it and went away, doubtful of how well they'd manage. Over the next few weeks Bob received a lot of phone calls asking for clarification on how to do this and that, but the calls tapered off and eventually stopped altogether. Suspecting that they'd simply given up, on his next visit home he made a point of asking how they were getting on. "Oh, we're doing fine," they assured him. "Is there anything you want to ask while I'm here?" he enquired. "Well," they said, "There is one thing. Since we got a computer, we've been talking to our other friends who have computers, and there's something they seem to do a lot of that we don't know how to do." "Oh, what's that?" asked Bob. "Well," they said, "We'd like to know how to reboot."

How Do I Do That?

First, you will need to install the kiosktool package (which is not installed by default). Once it's installed, launch kiosktool from the main KDE menu using System → Configuration → Kiosk Admin Tool. To use kiosktool, you begin by defining KDE *profiles* (a profile is basically a collection of KDE settings), and then you assign profiles to users. From the main menu of kiosktool, you can modify the existing profiles or add new ones. There are four predefined profiles:

- default
- redmond
- simplified
- ThinClient

To add a profile, click Add New Profile. You'll be asked to enter a name and a short description for the profile. To edit a profile (for example, the one you just created), select the profile from the list and click Setup Profile. This will bring you to the main profile editing screen shown in Figure 3-9.

As you'll see from this screen, you can define a profile under 12 headings as follows:

General
　On this screen you can disable a number of features, including the window manager context menu, bookmarks, access to a command shell, the ability to log out, the ability to lock the screen, the Run Command (Alt-F2) option, moving the toolbars, and starting a second X session.

Desktop Icons
　On this screen you can disable context menus (these are the menus you see if you right-click on a desktop item), lock down the desktop settings, and/or lock down all desktop items. This screen works in a way typical of how many of the other screens work. There's a button labeled Preview Desktop Icons that will show you how the desktop will look in the profile you're editing, and a button labeled Setup Desktop Icons that lets you edit the desktop as if it were your current desktop. See Figure 3-10.

Desktop Background
　On this screen you can set up, preview, and lock down the image or colors that will be used as the desktop background.

Screensaver
　On this screen you can setup, preview, and lock down the screensaver that will be used.

KDE Menu
　On this screen you can disable all menu items that would require the root password, and you can lock down the menus (i.e., disable menu editing).

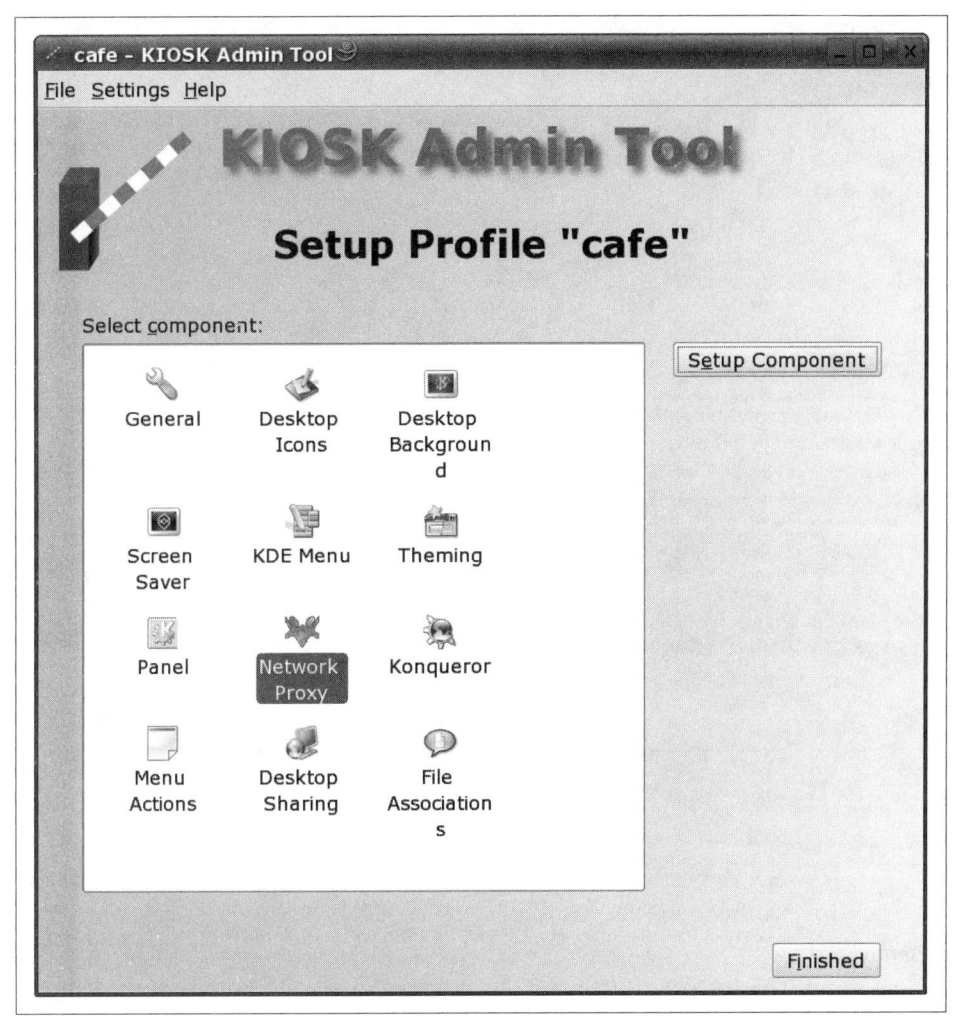

Figure 3-9. Kiosktool profile setup screen

Theming
On this screen you can disable the selection of style, color, font, and window decoration settings.

Panel
On this screen you can set up, preview, and lock down the main panel (Kicker) configuration. You can also disable context menus.

Network Proxy
On this screen you can set up and lock down the settings for network proxies.

Konqueror
On this screen you can disable various features of the Konqueror web browser.

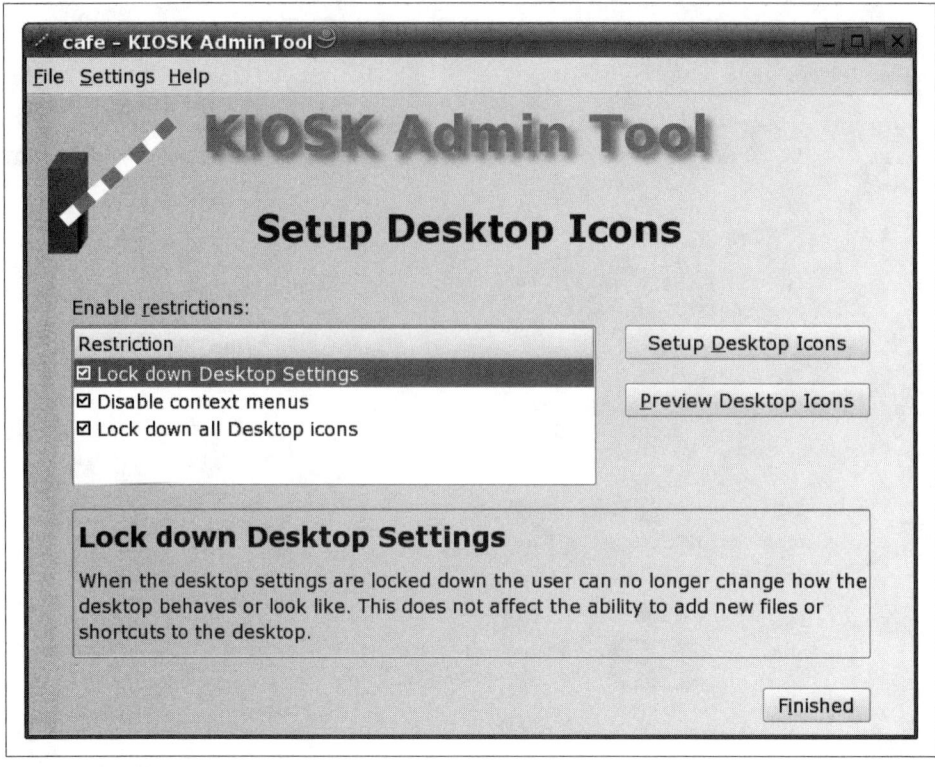

Figure 3-10. Kiosktool desktop icon setup screen

Menu Associations
    On this screen you can enable or disable the various menu items of KDE applications; for example, you can enable or disable the File → Save As menu item.

Desktop Sharing
    This screen allows you to set up desktop sharing options—i.e., are you willing to allow remote users to take over control of the desktop using a VNC viewer?

File Associations
    This screen allows you to establish file associations—i.e., the actions that will be taken if you click on files of specified types.

Once you have defined a profile, it remains to associate that profile with a user or a group. From the main menu in kiosktool, click on Assign Profiles. From this screen, you can assign the named profile you've just created to a specified user or to a specified group.

How Does It Work?

Locking down a KDE setting is done by by placing [$i] after the key name in the system-wide *.desktop* files (see Lab 3.4, "Configure the KDE Desktop"); for example:

    Exec[$i]=amarok -u %U

This prevents individual users from overriding this default setting.

3.6 Configure the GNOME Desktop

Of the dozen or more desktops available for Linux, KDE and GNOME are the most mature and are certainly the only two that are decently supported and configured in SUSE Linux. Some Linux distributions (or distros) are strongly biased in favor of one or the other; for example, Ubuntu Linux strongly favors GNOME. My impression is that SUSE favors KDE, but only by a small margin. There is little point in attempting a reasoned discussion about whether KDE or GNOME is better. They're both very good, both well styled, both highly customizable, and both will let you get the job done. I will confess a personal preference for KDE, but that's probably only because I know it better than GNOME.

Overall, GNOME perhaps has a cleaner and simpler look than KDE. By default, Gnome uses two panels (task bars) instead of KDE's one: one across the top edge of the screen and one across the bottom. (However, in SUSE 10.1, the default setup has no task bar along the top edge.) By default, the top panel carries the menus and the launch icons; the bottom panel carries the window list and the virtual workspace switcher. (I keep saying "by default" because, like KDE, GNOME is endlessly customizable, which is the purpose of this lab.)

Instead of the single main menu in KDE, there are (since GNOME version 2.10) three menus on the top panel: Applications, Places, and Desktop. Applications lists all the GNOME applications. Places has links to the user's home folder, the desktop, bookmarks, all removable devices (which are mounted), network servers, and the recently used files list. Places also lets you search for files and connect to remote servers. The Desktop menu consists of submenus for desktop configuration and entries for logging off, locking the screen, and so on. (If you prefer a single menu closer to the KDE style, you can add the main GNOME menu to the panel as described next.)

How Do I Do That?

To configure either the top or bottom panel, right-click on the panel and select Properties. From the panel properties dialog, you can:

- Change the size of the panel.
- Add hide buttons or turn on auto-hiding.

- Set the background and transparency of the panel. (Personally, I can't get too excited about transparency on the desktop. Maybe I'm getting old.)

There are a number of useful tools you can add to the panel. Right-click on the panel and select Add to Panel. A selection of the available tools is shown in Table 3-2.

Table 3-2. Tools that can be added to the GNOME panel

Tool	Description
Application Launcher	A launch icon for a program already on the GNOME menus. (You can also add an application launcher by dragging an item directly from the menus onto the panel.)
Custom Launcher	A launch icon for a program specified by name. This is discussed in the following text.
Mini-commander	A tool that provides a text entry field for entering single commands, as an alternative to using a terminal window.
Character Palette	This is a really useful tool that gives you access to all those hard-to-enter characters, such as Euro currency symbols and Ns with twiddly things on top and Cs with twiddly things underneath. It works by copying the characters onto the clipboard so that you can paste them into most applications.
Dictionary Lookup	This tools provides a text entry field right on the panel for entering words to look up in the dictionary (Websters).
Disk Mounter	A tool for mounting removable media (CDs, DVDs, floppy disks, USB memory sticks, etc.).
Drawer tool	A drawer provides additional drop-down panel space that appears when you click on the drawer icon. This is a neat idea and is similar to the pop-up panels in CDE (Common Desktop Environment), for those of you who remember CDE. You can add launch icons and other items to a drawer, just as you can for any other panel space.
Force Quit	A tool that forces some other application to terminate.
Lock Screen	Locks the screen to prevent unauthorized use of your computer until you enter a password.
Logout	An easy way to log out.
Main Menu	A single launch point for all the GNOME menus.
Show desktop	A tool that minimizes all your windows so you can see the desktop.
Window selector	A tool that presents a drop-down list of your current windows and allows you to select one. This provides an alternative to the window list that appears on the bottom panel, and takes up less space.

One of the items in the table perhaps needs further explanation. Adding a custom launcher icon to the panel lets you launch any application with a single click. To do this, right-click on the panel and select Add To Panel → Custom Application Launcher. In the Create Launcher dialog, you'll need to enter (at minimum) a name for the launcher and the command needed to invoke it, complete with any options, just like you would type it at the command line. You can also select an icon from a fairly large collection provided with the distribution, or browse to and select one of your own. (See Figure 3-11.)

In addition to configuring the panel, there are many other aspects of the desktop that can be customized. For example, to change the desktop background, right-click on

Figure 3-11. Adding a launch icon to the GNOME desktop

the desktop and select Change Desktop Background. In the Desktop Background Preferences dialog, you can select an image, or a solid color, or a color gradient. To use your own image as a background, click on Add Wallpaper and browse to your image file.

More extensive configuration options are available in the GNOME Control Center. (Select GNOME Control Center from the Desktop menu.) Here you can change settings under four main headings:

Under the hardware heading, you can:

- Set the screen resolution and refresh rate.
- Set the mouse to be left-handed or right-handed.
- Set the cursor size and the mouse speed parameters.
- Turn the keyboard repeat on or off, and set the repeat rate and delay.
- Set the keyboard layout (the region, plus some meta-key options).
- Enforce a typing break at specified intervals.

Under the Look and feel heading, you can:

- Determine the windows input focus behavior.
- Set the color and style of the window decorations (theme).

- Set the fonts used by various desktop components and applications.
- Set the desktop background (same as right-clicking on the desktop).

Under the Personal heading, you can:

- Define keyboard shortcuts for a specified list of desktop actions. (It is worth looking at this list just to see what shortcuts are currently defined, even if you don't intend to change them.)
- Change your password.
- Enable assistive technologies for the visually impaired: a suite of tools called Gnopernicus that provides a screen reader, magnifier, and onscreen keyboard. This tool can also be started directly under Applications → Utilities → Desktop → Screen Reader and Magnifier.
- Improve keyboard accessibility for the physically impaired by specifying a minimum hold-down time for keys and a minimum time between duplicate key presses.

Under the System heading, you can:

- Associate sounds with specific user interface events and system events, and also with events in some specific games and applications.
- Configure the behavior of the system bell (audible or visual).
- Specify applications to be started automatically at login.
- Enable power management and specify standby, suspend, and power-off timeouts.
- Select a screensaver and specify the time before it kicks in.
- Turn on automatic screen locking and specify the time before it kicks in.
- Specify network proxies for HTTP, FTP, and SOCKS services.

What About...

...editing the menus? GNOME's capability to edit menus is limited, and the subject of quite a bit of discussion (not all of it complimentary) on the mailing lists. There is a menu editor (right-click on the Application menu on the main menu bar and select Edit Menus). In GNOME 2.8, the tool appears to allow you to view the menu hierarchy but not to actually edit it. In GNOME 2-12 (shipped with SUSE Linux 10.1), the tool has checkboxes that let you specify which of a predefined list of items should appear on the menu, but there is no way to add items of your own. There is also a tool called SMEG (Simple Menu Editor for GNOME—nothing to do with *Red Dwarf*) that is available for Ubuntu Linux, but current traffic on the SUSE Linux forums suggests that it is a little too bleeding-edge for general use on SUSE Linux at the moment. It is certainly not a part of the SUSE Linux distribution.

Where to Learn More

There is an online magazine about GNOME at *http://www.gnomejournal.org*. This magazine has a good overview of the new features in GNOME 2.10 at *http://www.gnomejournal.org/article/17/gnome-210-desktop-and-development-platform*. You can download additional wallpaper images, desktop themes and icon sets from *http://art.gnome.org*.

To learn more about SMEG, see *http://www.realistanew.com/projects/smeg*.

3.7 Play Audio and Video

Because I've grown up in an environment of "scientific" computing (and in an era when CPU cycles were always in short supply), the idea of using a computer for anything so frivolous as playing music or movies would never have occurred to me. Times have changed. In this lab, you'll learn how you can use SUSE Linux to play and manipulate digital audio and video content.

Not all of the software you'll need to turn SUSE Linux into a capable multimedia player is included in the standard distribution. If you are running SUSE Linux 9.3, there's a multimedia option pack that you should install. It is available via YOU (YaST Online Update). There is no multimedia option pack for 10.0 or 10.1. However, you might want to visit the Packman site (for SUSE 10.0, the URL is *http://packman.iu-bremen.de/suse/10.0*), where you will find a number of multimedia packages. You'll learn about installing packages with YOU in Chapter 5.

How Do I Do That?

Playing audio CDs on SUSE Linux is a bit of a no-brainer. If you insert an audio CD, SUSE Linux should auto-detect it and offer to start the player KsCD. If it doesn't, you can start the player manually by selecting Multimedia → CD Player → KsCD from the main KDE menu.

This player is easy to use; to describe its user interface would be to insult your intelligence. The only slightly nonobvious feature is a drop-down list at the top of the KsCD screen that gives access to the track list. If you have an Internet connection, the player will automatically contact a CDDB server to obtain a track list for your CD. (Go to Extras → Configure KsCD → CDDB to select a server; the default is *freedb.freedb.org*.) Track lists are cached in the *~/.cddb* folder.

The GNOME CD player, gnome-cd, is also available, and has, if anything, an even cleaner user interface. (Select Multimedia → CD Player → CD Player from the main KDE menu.)

To rip an audio CD

For "ripping" CDs (i.e., converting the tracks into encoded audio files), use Grip. (Select Multimedia → CD/DVD tools → Grip from the main KDE menu.) Actually, Grip also functions fine as a CD player, but ripping is its main purpose. If you do not see it on the menu, try installing the Grip RPM. Grip uses a hierarchical organization of screens with a row of tabs at each level, which makes it difficult to navigate until you get used to it. I would have preferred a tree view control.

When Grip rips a CD, it initially writes each track as a *.wav* file. Optionally, it can then encode it. To select the encoder you want to use, click the Encode tab, then click the Encoder tab. There you will find a drop-down list offering a choice of encoders. Although Grip offers a list of potential encoders, the ones that are actually available depends upon the encoders that are installed, and here you begin to get into messy issues of licenses and patents. At minimum, you should have the oggenc encoder that generates Ogg Vorbis format files with the extension *.ogg*. Ogg Vorbis is an open, patent-free audio encoding and streaming technology; it is claimed to give better sound quality than MP3 for equivalent file size. (See *http://www.vorbis.com* and *http://www.xiph.org*.) The Ogg Vorbis format is fine if you are planning to keep your music within your Linux system—you can organize it, play it, and burn it to CD using the *.ogg* format. It is not a complete solution, though. For example, my iPod won't play Ogg Vorbis files (well, not unless I run Linux on it... see *http://www.ipodlinux.org*).

> I have always thought of Ogg Vorbis as one of the characters Douglas Adams would have invented if he had been into Linux and not Apple Mac. I see Ogg as the young Vogon guard that threw Arthur and Ford out of the airlock in *The Hitchhiker's Guide to the Galaxy*. If you have no idea what I'm talking about, don't panic…it is not important to the understanding of this book.

To rip a CD and encode it in Ogg Vorbis format, first select the Tracks tab of Grip and click the checkbox under the Rip column for those tracks you want to rip, or click the Rip column heading to select all the tracks. Now select the Config → Encode → Encoder tabs and select "oggenc" as the encoder in the drop-down list. Now select the Rip tab and click Rip and Encode. (If you click Rip Only, you will just get the *.wav* files). You will see progress bars showing the progress of the ripping and encoding processes, both for the current track and for all the selected tracks. When the process is complete, you will find files with the *.ogg* extension in a folder under *~/mp3*.

Figure 3-12 shows the encoder selection screen in Grip. Note the three levels of tabs!

If you want to encode your files in MP3 format, you will need to download and install an MP3 encoder—none is included with the SUSE Linux distribution. The two best known MP3 encoders are BladeEnc and LAME. A Google search on a string

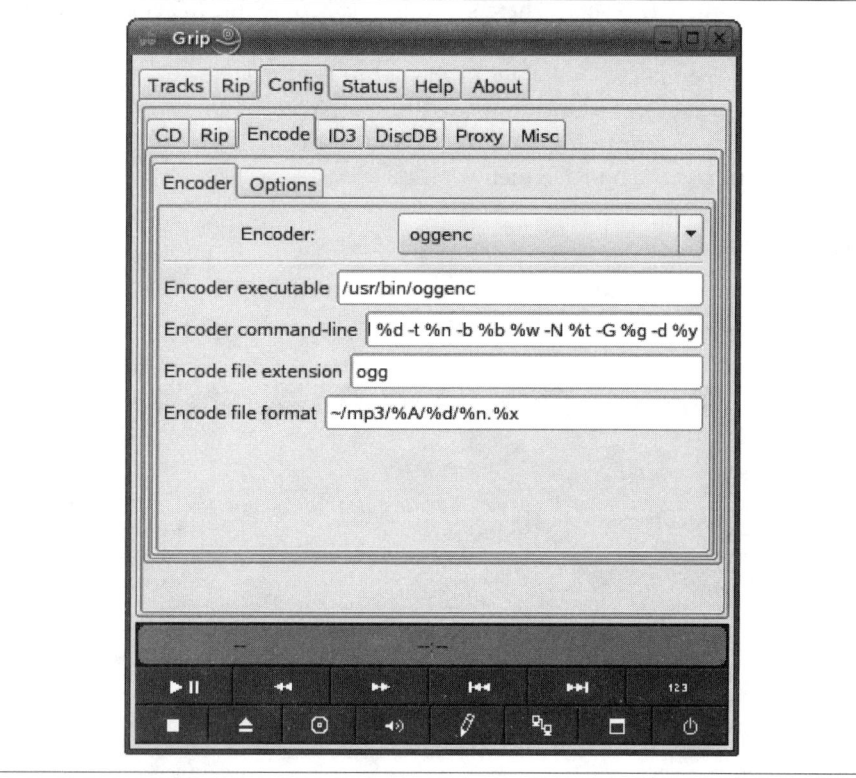

Figure 3-12. Selecting an encoder in Grip

such as "bladeenc-0.94.2-src-stable.tar.gz" might help, but you should be aware that patents on MP3 technology have been granted in some countries, and this may restrict your ability to use these encoders. If you choose to use BladeEnc, you must unpack the BladeEnc tarball, build the BladeEnc executable, and copy it into */usr/local/bin* (this is the default location assumed by Grip). The command sequence will look something like this:

```
# cd ~/build

# tar zxvf ~/downloads/bladeenc-0.94.2-src-stable.tar.gz
# cd bladeenc-0.94.2
# ./configure
# make
# cd bladeenc
# cp bladeenc /usr/local/bin
```

If you have the BladeEnc encoder installed, you can select it in Gripby selecting the Config → Encode → Encoder tabs and selecting BladeEnc as the encoder. Then, proceed to rip the tracks as before. When the process is complete, you will find files with the *.mp3* extension in a folder under *~/mp3*.

Grip is not the only CD ripper. There's another, called Sound Juicer (Multimedia → Audio Player → CD Ripper from the main KDE menu), that has a much simpler user interface. It can encode tracks as Ogg Vorbis, FLAC (a lossless compression format), or as *.wav* files, which is an uncompressed format. You might also try KAudioCreator, a very nice tool for ripping multiple CDs (select Multimedia → CD/DVD Tools → CD Ripper from the main KDE menu).

To play audio files

Several applications play audio files. My preference is amaroK, which has excellent playlist management, shown in Figure 3-13.

Figure 3-13. amaroK playlist management

SUSE Linux 10.1 ships with an audio player called Banshee, which is a Mono application (and therefore requires the Mono infrastructure to run). Banshee is also able to rip and burn audio CDs; it has great playlist management and can synchronize with an iPod.

What About...

...playing video content? The core playback engine for video content on Linux is xine, which is a library that is used by a number of video playback tools. Many of them provide a user interface that resembles a domestic video player; some are intended to be embedded into a web browser. SUSE Linux includes several players—Kaffeine (a KDE application), totem (a GNOME application), RealPlayer 10, and xine; of these, I have had greatest success with Kaffeine.

The world of digital multimedia is in its infancy and is currently plagued by a plethora or formats, patents, and digital rights management issues. SUSE Linux does not include the codecs you need to play video encoded using proprietary Microsoft formats such as WMV. (Codecs are the pieces of software that understand and decode specific multimedia formats.) It is possible to download and install the Win32 codecs.

Try downloading the package *essential-20050412.tar.bz2* (you may have to search a little to find it—go to *http://www.mplayerhq.hu* and click the Download link), putting it into any convenient directory. In this directory, unpack the tarball:

```
$ tar xjvf  essential-20050412.tar.bz2
```

then, as root, move the codecs into the folder */usr/lib/win32*:

```
# cd essential-20050412
# mv * /usr/lib/win32
```

I have also found it helpful to update to a more recent version of the xine library. If you have the development toolchain installed (gcc, make, and so on), you can download this and build it from source. Go to *http://xinehq.de* and download the latest version of xine-lib (at the time of writing, it was *xine-lib-1.1.1.tar.gz*) into any convenient directory. In this directory, unpack the tarball:

```
$ tar xzvf xine-lib-1.1.1.tar.gz
```

For some reason the build requires the Xfree86 development tools. Using YaST, install the package xorg-x11-devel from the SUSE CDs. Now you can build the library:

```
$ cd xine-lib-1.1.1
$ ./configure
$ make
```

Then, as root, from the same directory, install the library and rebuild the dynamic linker cache:

```
# make install
# ldconfig
```

You will find more detailed build instructions on the xinehq web site.

What About...

...playing DVDs? Most commercial DVDs are encrypted using CSS (Content Scrambling System). To play them on Linux, you need a library called `libdvdcss`. There are a number of sites that carry RPMs for this—for example, *libdvd-css-1.2.8-2.network.i386.rpm*. You can install this with YaST or from the command line with `rpm -i`; the library itself installs in */usr/lib/libdvdcss.so.2.0.7*. You should investigate whether it is legal to use this software in your country. Nonencrypted DVDs play fine in xine without this library.

Where to Learn More

Take a look at *Linux Multimedia Hacks* by Kyle Rankin (O'Reilly). This book covers a wide range of topics, including image manipulation and editing, playing and recording digital audio, ripping CDs and DVDs, creating VDS and DVDs, and watching broadcast TV—all on Linux.

3.8   Burn Your Own CDs and DVDs

Burning CDs and DVDs can be useful as a convenient and cheap form of backup, as a way of producing audio or video discs for home entertainment use, or even to produce your own Linux distribution. There are (of course) quite a number of CD-writing tools for Linux. Most of them are basically graphical frontends to the underlying command-line tools, which we'll discuss later in this lab. This lab looks at K3b, one of the best of these tools. K3b is available from the main KDE menu at Multimedia → CD/DVD burning → K3b.

How Do I Do That?

We'll look at five tasks: creating a data CD, creating an audio CD, burning a CD from an existing ISO image, copying a CD, and creating an ISO image from a CD.

To create a data CD

Launch K3b and select File → New Project → New Data CD Project from the menu. The Current Project window will open in the lower half of the screen. You may now navigate the filesystem and drag the files or folders that you want to include on your CD into the Current Project window. A green progress bar across the bottom of the screen shows how much space will be used on your CD. When you've completed adding files to the project, click on Burn. (If you think you're likely to want to burn the same set of files to CD again, save the project using File → Save As from the menu.) Projects are stored as XML text in zipped files with the extension *.k3b*. The Burn screen offers many configurable settings under five tabs. Most of these can be left alone. Settings you might want to consider changing are listed next.

On the Writing tab, you can:

- Select the CD writer (if you have more than one).
- Set the writing speed.
- Turn off the "on the fly" option. This tells K3b to build the disk image before starting to write it, and might be helpful on older, slower machines.
- Turn on the "Only create image" option. This tells K3b to create an ISO image of the CD rather than actually burn one. You might want to do this to put the image onto a web site, for example. Note that you can subsequently do a loop-back mount on the ISO image with a command something like:

```
# mount -o loop mycdimage.iso /mnt
```

On the Settings tab, you can create multisession CDs.

On the Volume Desc tab, you can give the volume a name. This name may be used as a mount point under */media* if Linux subsequently automounts the CD.

On the Filesystem tab, you can:

- Generate Rock Ridge extensions. This is an extension to the original ISO 9660 format that allows long filenames.
- Generate Joliet extensions. This extension to the ISO 9660 format allows Linux-style file ownership and access permissions to be stored. This is the default setting for K3b.

With all the settings made (it will probably be fine if you just leave them all at their defaults), click on Burn. Log messages and a progress bar indicate how far the process has advanced.

To create an audio CD

Launch K3b and select File → New Project → New Audio CD Project. You may then drag and drop audio files into the project area. The version of K3b shipped with SUSE Linux professional will burn from *.wav* files or from *.ogg* (Ogg Vorbis) files. Within the project area, you can drag the tracks around until you get the desired playing order. Then click Burn to create your audio CD as before.

SUSE does not include MP3 support in the version of K3b that they ship. To burn audio CDs from MP3 files, you need to install the package k3b-mad, available from the Packman site (for SUSE 10.0, the URL is *http://packman.iu-bremen.de/suse/10.0*). You'll learn about adding new packages in Chapter 5.

To burn a CD from an ISO image

If you already have an ISO image for your CD (for example, you have downloaded one from Novell's web site or from the OpenSuSE.org site), you can easily burn it to a CD. From the K3b menu select Tools → CD → Burn CD Image. Then, click on the little folder icon in the panel labeled "Image to Burn" and navigate to your ISO file. Once the ISO file is selected, you can optionally select which CD writer to use, what speed to write at, and the number of copies you want. Then click Start.

To copy a CD

From the K3b menu, select Tools → CD → Copy CD. If you have two CD-R drives, select one for reading and the other for writing. If you have only one drive, K3b will read the source disc, create an ISO image, then ask for blank media to write.

To create an ISO image from a CD

Proceed as for copying a CD but select Only Create Image in the Options panel.

How It Works

The filesystem on a CD does not use the same structure as a Linux filesystem such as *ext3*. A CD's structure is defined by the ISO9660 standard. CD images are often known simply as ISO images. The original ISO standard (level 1) specified a rather DOS-like structure, with filenames restricted to eight characters and a three-character extension, and uppercase letters only. It also restricts the depth of the directory hierarchy to eight levels. ISO 9660 level 2 allows filenames up to 31 characters with a larger character set. There are various extensions to the basic structure. Joliet extensions relax the filename restrictions in the basic ISO9660 spec. Rockridge extensions are intended for Unix/Linux systems and support even longer file names, Linux file ownerships and access permissions, symbolic links, and a deeper directory hierarchy. El Torito extensions allow CDs to be bootable.

What About...

...doing it from the command line? Underlying K3b are a number of command-line utilities that can, if you prefer, be invoked directly to create CDs. In particular, mkisofs can be used to build an ISO image, and cdrecord can be used to burn an image to CD. These are contained in the packages cdrecord and mkisofs, respectively.

Let's say I have a directory called *susebook* that I'd like to back up onto CD. A typical command to create an ISO image from this directory might be:

```
$ mkisofs -V 'Suse Book Backup' -J -R -o /tmp/book.iso \
    /home/chris/susebook
```

The -V flag assigns a volume name to the image. The -J flag adds Joliet extensions. The -R flag adds Rockridge extensions so that the file ownerships and access modes are preserved. This is useful if you're planning to restore files from the CD back onto the *same* Linux box, but is less useful if the CD is likely to be accessed from a different machine, since the ownerships will probably mean nothing. In that case, the -r flag may be better. This also adds Rockridge extensions, but sets the uid and gid of all files to be 0 (root), turns off write permissions, and a few other things. The `-o` flag specifies the name of the file where the image is to be written. Finally, any remaining arguments specify the files and folders to be included in the image.

You need to take care if there are any symbolic links amongst the files included in the image. If Rockridge extensions are in use, `mkisofs` will simply include the symbolic link as is. This is unlikely to be useful, as the file that the link points to is probably absent on the machine on which the CD is accessed. The `-f` flag tells `mkisofs` to follow the symbolic link—that is, to include the actual file on the image.

You can check the ISO image you've created using a *loopback mount*, which allows you to mount a filesystem image contained in a file (instead of on a disk partition) onto a mount point. In this case, you could do the following (as root):

```
# mount -o loop,ro /tmp/book.iso /mnt
```

Now you can explore the filesystem on */mnt* (i.e., the filesystem in the ISO image) like any other. Remember to unmount the filesystem when you're done:

```
# cd /
# umount /mnt
```

To burn your ISO image to CD, use `cdrecord`. At minimum, `cdrecord` needs the name of the device to write to and the name of the ISO image. The device name may not be obvious. You can try looking for it using the `-scanbus` option to `cdrecord`. The following is an edited extract:

```
# cdrecord   -scanbus
scsibus1:
        1,0,0    100) '        ' 'disgo         ' '4.60' Removable Disk
        1,1,0    101) *
        1,2,0    102) *
        1,3,0    103) *
scsibus2:
        2,0,0    200) 'Slimtype' 'COMBO LSC-24082K' 'JKON' Removable CD-ROM
        2,1,0    201) *
        2,2,0    202) *
        2,3,0    203) *
        2,4,0    204) *
```

Here, `disgo` is a memory stick in the first USB port, and `COMBO LSC-24082K` is a CD writer in the second USB port. To use this writer with `cdrecord`, I would specify the device `dev=2,0,0`. The machine also has an internal writer on an ATAPI interface, which doesn't show up here. To see this, I need to explicitly specify ATAPI. Again, the output is heavily edited:

```
# cdrecord dev=ATAPI -scanbus
scsibus0:
        0,0,0      0) 'SAMSUNG ' 'CDRW/DVD SN-308B' 'U003' Removable CD-ROM
        0,1,0      1) *
        0,2,0      2) *
        0,3,0      3) *
```

So, for example, you could burn the image using the Samsung CD writer with the command:

```
# cdrecord dev=ATAPI:0,0,0 -v -eject /tmp/book.iso
```

You may also find it works to simply specify dev=/dev/hdc.

The -v flag means verbose, and -eject says to eject the disc afterwards. Another useful flag is -dummy. This flag causes cdrecord to go through the entire burn process but with the laser turned off; it is useful to determine whether the system is likely to experience a buffer underrun during the burn, a condition which usually results in a useless CD. If buffer underruns do occur, try reducing the write speed and/or increasing the size of the buffer. For example:

```
# cdrecord speed=4 fs=32m dev=ATAPI:0,0,0 -v -eject /tmp/book.iso
```

will burn at 4× speed (cdrecord will normally use the maximum speed reported by the device) with a buffer size of 32 MB.

Where to Learn More

There's a good (though slightly out of date) HOWTO on burning CDs from the command line at *http://howto-pages.org/cdwriting.php*.

Chapter 15 of the SUSE Linux Professional User Guide discusses K3b in a little more detail (in the KDE help center, it's under Multimedia). There's further documentation on K3b at *http://www.k3b.org*.

3.9 Capture Screenshots

Capturing screenshots (images of what you can see on the screen) is a fairly common requirement. Those of us who write books or training materials do a lot of it, of course, but it's also not unusual to want to insert some kind of screenshot into a document, or to email an image to a friend or preserve a particularly interesting web page for posterity. This lab looks at some of the tools for capturing screenshots.

How Do I Do That?

If you're working with a KDE desktop, I recommend KSnapshot. It's available on the menus under Utilities → Desktop → KSnapshot. (This is not a very convenient location, so if you're planning to take a lot of screenshots, you might want to put a launch icon for it onto the main panel. Lab 3.3, "Configure the KDE Menus and Panel," shows how to do that.) KSnapshot also works fine on a GNOME desktop.

KSnapshot is easy to use. It offers a choice of three capture modes:

- Full screen
- Window Under Cursor (either with or without the window borders)
- Region

There is also the option to delay for a specified number of seconds before taking the picture. This gives you time, for example, to get the input focus into the right window. KSnapshot automatically hides its own window while it is taking the picture.

The Region mode allows you to drag with the mouse to select the region you want to capture. (Position the cursor at the top-left corner of the region, press and hold down the left mouse button, drag to the bottom-right corner, then release.)

Once the picture has been taken, Ksnapshot displays a thumbnail of the image. You then have the option to save the image to a file or to print it. (See Figure 3-14.) Clicking Save As brings you to the Save As dialog. If you expand the drop-down list labeled Filter, you will see the image formats supported by KSnapshot. Unless you're seriously into image processing, you will probably not be familiar with most of these. For capture of a typical screenshot, the PNG format works well and offers a good compromise between image size and quality. If the image is more naturalistic (for example, a photograph), you may find that JPEG works better.

Figure 3-14. KSnapshot

There are no hotkeys associated with KSnapshot in the default KDE desktop, but it is easy to define one if you want. See Lab 3.3, "Configure the KDE Menus and Panel," earlier in this chapter.

There are a number of other tools that will take screenshots. If you use a GNOME desktop, you may prefer the GNOME screen capture tool. This is available on the Desktop menu. The tool is even simpler to use than KSnapshot—it takes a shot of the entire screen and brings up a dialog to ask you where you want to save it. Even more convenient and flexible, the GNOME desktop binds the keys Print Screen and

Alt-Print Screen to the GNOME screen capture tool. These are the same hotkeys that Windows uses and they do basically the same job: Print Screen captures the whole screen and Alt-Print Screen captures a single window. However, instead of placing the image on the clipboard (as Windows does), you'll be prompted to save the image in a file.

You can also invoke this tool from the command line. For example:

    $ gnome-panel-screenshot

will capture the entire screen, whereas:

    $ gnome-panel-screenshot --window --delay=5

will capture just the window with the input focus after a five-second delay.

As far as I can tell, this tool will save only in PNG format.

There's also a rather ancient application called XV. (From the main menu select Graphics → Viewer → XV.) Although the look and feel of its user interface is old-fashioned (it reminds me of the Motif desktop I used to run on my Sun workstation), it is in fact a remarkably powerful and usable tool. Right-click on its splash screen to reach its main interface. From here you can not only grab screenshots, but also load and display existing images and perform a variety of traditional image transformations such as blur, sharpen, edge detection, horizontal and vertical flips, and rotation. It will also offer you control over the degree of compression to apply when saving an image, allowing you to trade off image size against quality.

Finally, there's a collection of command-line tools that are part of the ImageMagick package. Amongst these are `import`, which grabs screenshots, and `display`, which (guess what?) displays images. For example:

    $ import test.png

grabs an image and saves it in the file *test.png*. Select the area you want to grab with the mouse:

- To grab the entire screen, left-click on the desktop.
- To grab a single window, left-click in the window.
- To grab a rectangular region, drag with the left mouse button to define the rectangle.

Because the output filename is specified on the command line, there is no Save As dialog to deal with.

The `display` command is equally easy to use; for example:

    $ display test.png

launches a new window to display the image. This tool does far more than just displaying. Clicking on the image brings up the main ImageMagick menu, which offers a variety of transformations, enhancements, and effects. Another of the strengths of ImageMagick is the huge range of image formats it supports—about 100 of them!

What About...

...cropping the image? Sometimes you'd like to crop the image you've captured, to show just a part of a window. I normally use the GIMP for this. Admittedly, the GIMP is a bit over-the-top for a simple task like cropping—the old saying about saplings and chainsaws (or was it nuts and sledgehammers?) comes to mind—but it's available, so why not use it?

GIMP stands for GNU Image Manipulation Program. As its name suggests, it's from the GNU people—the Free Software Foundation. It is one of the flagship products of open source development and is, broadly, on a par with Adobe's Photoshop as an image editing and manipulation suite.

> Okay, before all you Photoshop enthusiasts out there write in to complain, it's probably true that if you need to push a commercial workflow through a professional artwork and print house, you'll probably prefer Photoshop. (In fact, you'll probably prefer a Mac.) Nonetheless, the GIMP is an astonishingly powerful application.

You will find the GIMP on the main KDE menu at Graphics → Image Editing. The first time you start it, you will be taken through some setup screens to calibrate your display. Unless you need to display images to their exact size, you don't really need to do this. Once the GIMP is up and running, to crop an image, select File → Open from the main GIMP menu, navigate to the file, and open it. The file will open in a new window. Now, from the tool palette in the main GIMP window, select the crop tool (the icon looks like a scalpel). Move the cursor to the top lefthand corner of the rectangle you want to crop to, press and hold down the left mouse button, then drag out the desired rectangle. If you get it wrong, repeat the operation. With the correct area selected, either double-click within the image to complete the crop or click Crop from the Crop and Resize dialog. If you want more precision, you can use the Crop and Resize dialog to adjust the position and size of the crop rectangle on a pixel-by-pixel basis. Finally, from the File menu of the window in which you are viewing the image (*not* the main GIMP window), select Save (or Save As if you want to save under a different name or as a different file type).

If you're cropping an image because it has a lot of whitespace around it, select Autocrop Image from the Image menu of the window in which you are viewing the image. This will automatically crop the image to exclude the surrounding whitespace.

Actually, you can use the GIMP to grab the original screenshot too. From the main GIMP menu, select File → Acquire → Screenshot. Again, you have the option of grabbing the entire screen, or a single window, with an optional delay. The GIMP will open up a new window to display the grabbed image for cropping or further processing.

Where to Learn More

Read the ImageMagick manpage for an introduction to the command-line tools such as `import` and `display`. Each of the commands also has its own manpage. Also see *http://www.imagemagick.org*.

There are several books about the GIMP, but nothing (at least, nothing in English) anywhere near recent enough to cover the current version (2.2). Take a look at *Grokking the GIMP* by Carey Bunks (*http://gimp-savvy.com/BOOK/*). However, the GIMP's web site at *http://www.gimp.org* has extensive documentation and tutorials. (Be warned, though, that the GIMP has a steep learning curve.)

3.10 Use Command-Line Tools

It may seem strange to include a lab about using the command line in a chapter about using the desktop, but the truth is, you'll benefit greatly in your use of Linux from some measure of proficiency at the command line, and you should regard the command prompt as your friend. In Chapter 2, you've already seen a number of commands for filesystem management and for creating user accounts. This lab looks at a few more useful commands and how to use them in combination. This is a very brief treatment of what is really a very extensive subject. Most books devote entire chapters to command line use. In fact, some books devote entire books to it!

How Do I Do That?

To start a terminal window, select System → Terminal → Konsole from the main KDE menu. (Konsole is just one of several terminal emulators; they all do more or less the same thing, but some of them are prettier than others.) From GNOME, select Applications → System → Terminal → Konsole.

A terminal emulator is basically an application that provides a window that behaves like an old-fashioned character terminal. It provides an environment in which command-line tools can run within a graphical environment. It does obvious things like scrolling (if the text has reached the bottom line of the screen and another line is entered, the existing text is moved up one line to make room). This sort of behavior is so obvious that we take it for granted, but it does not happen by magic...it happens because the terminal emulator is written that way. Terminal emulators designed to run in graphical environments usually provide additional cosmetic features such as the ability to change the font or the background color, and the ability to cut and paste text to or from other applications. In the introduction to Chapter 2, you also saw how to get a really authentic command-line experience by dropping out of the graphical desktop entirely and using a virtual terminal.

The terminal window will automatically start a shell. "Shell" is the Linux word for a command interpreter (like a Windows "Command Prompt," but more powerful).

There are several shells available for Linux; the one that will be started is specified in your account (it is the last field in the /etc/passwd file). Most Linux users favor the bash shell, though at the level of this lab, all the shells are much the same. In this lab, you'll use the shell as a command interpreter: it prompts you for a command, you type one in, and it runs the command, waits for it to finish, and prompts you for the next command. However, the shells also provide other features—variables, loops, branches, arithmetic, and so on—that make them into full-blown programming languages. Writing programs in shell (known as shell scripts) is a powerful way of automating system administration or other repetitive tasks, but it is beyond the scope of this lab.

This lab gives you a glimpse of the power of the command line by focusing on six simple but useful commands, shown in Table 3-3.

Table 3-3. Six useful commands

Command	Function
less	Browse text files
grep	Search for patterns in files
wc	Count characters, words, and lines in a file
head	Display the beginning of a file
tail	Display the end of a file
sort	Sort the contents of a file

You met the `less` command in Chapter 2, where we used it to browse the contents of a file. You can also use `less` to browse the output from some other command; this is very commonly used in conjunction with commands that generate a lot of output. For example:

```
$ ps ax | less
```

will show a list of all running processes, and allow you to browse the output using `less`. The | symbol (vertical bar) tells the shell to run the commands `ps` and `less` concurrently, and connects the output of `ps` to the input of `less`. This connection is called a *pipe*.

The grep command searches its input for lines that contain a match for a specified text pattern. At its simplest, it is used like this:

```
$ grep 'string' file1 file2 ...
```

For the sake of an example, imagine a file called *shopping*, with the following contents:

```
Supermarket   1    Chicken       4.55
Supermarket  50    Clothespegs   1.25
Bakers        3    Bread         2.40
DIY           1    Hosepipe     15.00
Clothes       1    Trousers     24.99
DIY           2    Doorknob      8.40
```

```
Supermarket   2    Milk         1.25
Clothes       6    Socks        9.00
DIY           2    Screwdriver  2.00
Clothes       2    Skirt       28.00
DIY          20    Sandpaper   10.00
Bakers       10    Muffin       1.95
Bakers        2    Quiche       6.50
DIY          50    Nails        0.95
```

The file represents a shopping list; each line has four fields as follows:

- The shop
- The number of items to be purchased
- The item description
- The total cost

So, to find all the Clothes items, you could use the command:

```
$ grep 'Clothes' shopping
Supermarket 50   Clothespegs  1.25
Clothes      1   Trousers    24.99
Clothes      6   Socks        9.00
Clothes      2   Skirt       28.00
```

In fact, this isn't quite right—you got a match on "Clothespegs," which you didn't really want. However, grep can be smarter than this. The string that grep searches for is called a *regular expression*, and can contain special characters that match specific patterns in the text. As a simple example, the characters ^ and $ anchor the search to the beginning and end of the line, respectively. Using ^, you can improve the previous solution by looking for "Clothes" only if it appears at the start of the line:

```
$ grep '^Clothes' shopping
Clothes      1   Trousers    24.99
Clothes      6   Socks        9.00
Clothes      2   Skirt       28.00
```

> Regular expressions are widely used in Linux, not only by programs like grep but by many other tools, including string searches and substitutions in vi, in classic text-processing programs like awk, and also in languages like Perl where they are central to the power of the language. You could fill an entire book describing the power and subtlety of regular expressions; indeed, Jeffrey Friedl did in his book *Mastering Regular Expressions* (O'Reilly)!

The command wc counts lines, words, and characters in its input files:

```
$ wc /etc/passwd shopping
 32   76 1726 /etc/passwd
 15   56  491 shopping
 47  132 2217 total
```

Options for wc include those shown in Table 3-4.

Table 3-4. Options for the wc command

Option	Meaning
-l	Show only the line count
-w	Show only the word count
-c	Show only the character count

wc is great for authors tasked to write "3,500 words about asexual reproduction in haggis":

```
$ wc -w haggis_article.txt
2120 haggis_article.txt
```

wc can also be used, for example, to count the number of lines of output from other commands. There are some examples later in this lab.

The command head displays the beginning of one or more files; for example:

```
$ head -4 shopping
Supermarket  1   Chicken       4.55
Supermarket  50  Clothespegs   1.25
Bakers       3   Bread         2.40
DIY          1   Hosepipe      15.00
```

Without the -4 option, 10 lines would be shown by default.

The command tail displays the end of a file; for example:

```
$ tail -1 /etc/passwd
isaac:x:1002:100:Isaac Newton:/home/isaac:/bin/bash
```

shows the last line of */etc/passwd*. 10 lines are shown by default. tail is often used to look at the end of log files, where the interesting stuff is.

The command sort sorts its input line by line. By default, it performs an alphanumeric sort on the entire line, but it has lots of options, including those shown in Table 3-5.

Table 3-5. Key options for the sort command

Option	Meaning
-f	Ignore upper/lower case distinction
-n	Numeric sort
-r	Reverse sort
-k 3	Sort on field 3 (first field is 1)

For example, you can do a reverse numeric sort on the fourth field of a file:

```
$ sort -n -r -k 4 shopping
Clothes   2   Skirt      28.00
Clothes   1   Trousers   24.99
DIY       1   Hosepipe   15.00
```

```
DIY           20   Sandpaper     10.00
Clothes        6   Socks          9.00
DIY            2   Doorknob       8.40
Bakers         2   Quiche         6.50
Supermarket    1   Chicken        4.55
Bakers         3   Bread          2.40
DIY            2   Screwdriver    2.00
Bakers        10   Muffin         1.95
Supermarket   50   Clothespegs    1.25
Supermarket    2   Milk           1.25
DIY           50   Nails          0.95
```

Programs such as grep, wc, head, tail, and sort are called *filters*. In addition to acting on the contents of one or more files, they can also act on the output of some other program. This example sorts the DIY (do-it-yourself) items from the shopping list according to cost:

```
$ grep '^DIY' shopping | sort -n -k 4
DIY           50   Nails          0.95
DIY            2   Screwdriver    2.00
DIY            2   Doorknob       8.40
DIY           20   Sandpaper     10.00
DIY            1   Hosepipe      15.00
```

This example counts the number of running processes on the machine:

```
$ ps ax | wc -l
140
```

Pipelines of three (or even more) stages are also used occasionally. For example, to count the number of directories in */lib*:

```
$ ls -l /lib | grep '^d' | wc -l
```

How It Works

Every program started from the command line has three standard streams:

Stream 0
: Standard input (*stdin*); comes from the keyboard by default

Stream 1
: Standard output (*stdout*); goes to the terminal by default

Stream 2
: Standard error (*stderr*); goes to the terminal by default

The "normal" output of a program is written to standard output. The shell can be told to redirect standard output to a file:

```
$ ls /lib > myfile
```

The plumbing for this command is shown in Figure 3-15. Actually, ls is not a true filter program, because it does not read its standard input. Redirecting standard output leaves standard error connected to the screen. That way, you get to see if anything went wrong. You can redirect standard error like this:

    $ ls /lib /nosuchfile 2> error_file

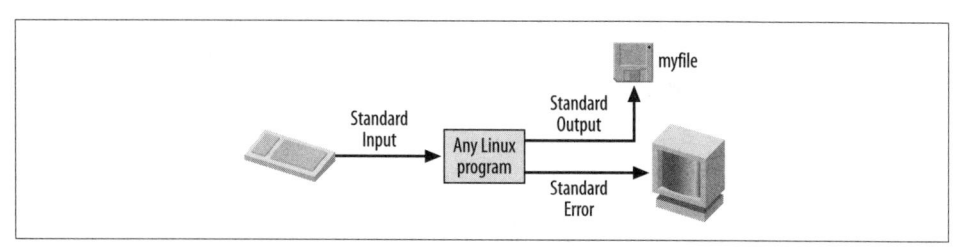

Figure 3-15. Redirecting standard output

You can also say "combine standard error with standard output," with this rather clunky notation:

    $ ls /lib/nosuchfile 2>&1 > myfile

A command such as:

    $ grep DIY shopping | sort -n -k 4

runs the programs grep and sort concurrently and creates a pipe to connect the standard output of grep to the standard input of sort. The plumbing is shown in Figure 3-16. Combining two or more general-purpose filter programs in this way to solve specific problems is at the heart of the power of the Linux command line.

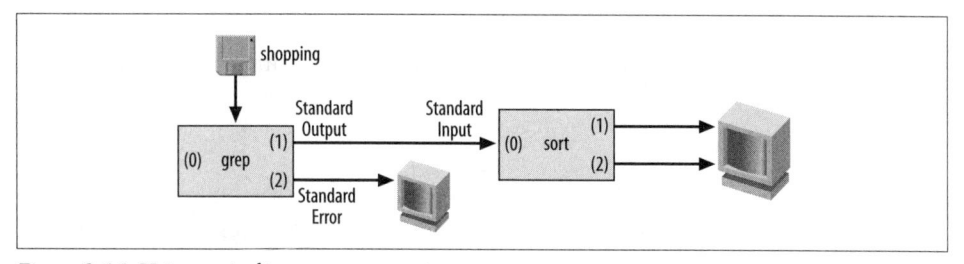

Figure 3-16. Using a pipeline

What About...

...convenience features? The shell supports a number of convenience features that will help you to be more productive. The first of these is the use of *wildcards*—special characters used to match patterns in filenames. When wildcards appear in a command line, the shell generates a list of files with matching names and substitutes this list back into the command line. The command—whatever it is—sees only the list of matching names. The process is shown in Figure 3-17.

Table 3-6 lists the wildcard characters.

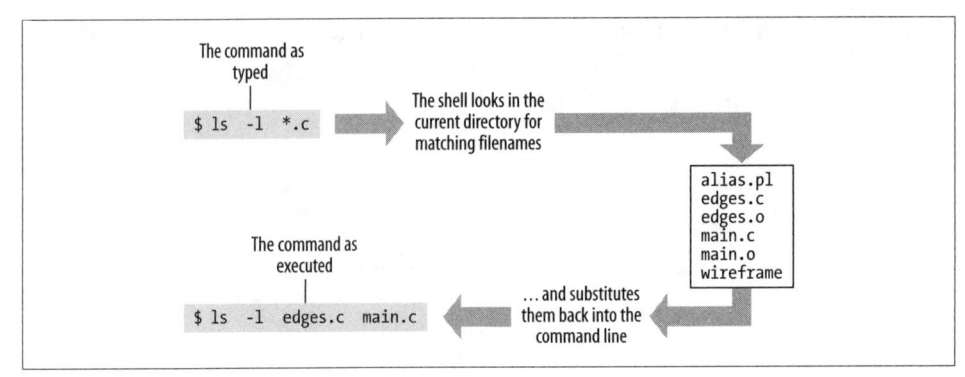

Figure 3-17. Wildcard expansion

Table 3-6. Wildcard characters

Wildcard	Meaning	Example	Example explained
*	Zero or more characters	*.txt	Matches any name ending in *.txt*
?	Exactly one character	invoice??.doc	Matches names such as *invoice23.doc* or *invoice_B.doc* but not *invoice 451.doc*
[ ]	Any one of the enclosed characters	[CcHh]at	Matches Cat or cat or Hat or hat
[x-y]	Any one character within the specified range	data[0-9][0-9]	Matches names such as data05 or data99 but not data7 or dataXY

Wildcards can be extremely powerful if used imaginatively. For example:

```
$ mv *.odt chapters
```

will move all your *.odt* files into the *chapters* folder. (It's assumed here that *chapters* is the name of an existing folder.)

Here's one more example:

```
$ grep O_RDONLY /usr/include/*/*.h
```

This command will search all the *.h* files (C program header files) in all immediate subdirectories of */usr/include* for the string O_RDONLY.

Another time-saving feature of bash is its command history. The command history will show you the most recent commands you've entered (by default, the last 1,000). A typical fragment of output is:

```
656  chmod 500 junk
657  ls -ld junk
658  less junk/SLES9-CD1
659  chmod 700 junk
660  cd junk/
661  ls -l
662  chmod 444 SLES9-CD1
663  rm SLES9-CD1
664  man getfacl
665  man mount
666  ls /tmp
```

The easiest and most intuitive thing you can do with your command history is to scroll up and down it using the up/down arrow keys. When you reach a command you want to re-execute, you can press Enter or you can edit it first. You can also recall commands by number; for example:

```
$ !660
```

will reexecute command 660 from your history. You can also recall commands using a string search; for example:

```
$ !chmod
```

will reexecute the most recent command beginning with the string chmod.

The shell uses the character ~ (tilde) as a shorthand for your home directory. Because my own home directory is */home/chris*, the example *~/downloads* is shorthand for */home/chris/downloads*. You'll see many examples of this notation throughout the book. Less commonly used, a notation such as ~simon refers to the home directory of the account simon.

Finally, the bash shell also does filename completion, using the Tab key. This feature comes in very handy to avoid typing in long, nasty filenames like *Xfree86-4.3.99.902-43.22.i586.rpm*. The idea is that you just type the leading part of the name, then press Tab, and bash will complete as much of the name as it can complete unambiguously, based on the files in the current directory. Sometimes you'll need to enter a couple more characters to disambiguate the name, then try Tab again, until you get the entire name completed. (It's easier to do than it is to explain!) If you press Tab twice in a row, bash shows you all possible completions.

Where to Learn More

This lab barely scrapes the surface of the power of the Linux command line. There are several excellent books that deal with this topic in depth. *Unix Power Tools* by Powers et al. (O'Reilly) is still one of the best books, in my view, for really giving an appreciation of the power of the Unix/Linux command line. You might also try *Classic Shell Scripting* by Arnold Robbins and Nelson Beebe (also from O'Reilly).

The bash reference manual is online at *http://www.gnu.org/software/bash/manual/bashref.html;* however, this is a reference manual, not a tutorial, and should not be attempted after a heavy meal.

3.11 Configure Multiheaded Displays

Multiheaded graphics cards (cards with two or more video outputs) from NVIDIA, ATI, Matrox, and others are now commonplace. Also, modern laptops can generally use their external video connector to drive a display that is independent of the display on the laptop's own screen. There are two rather different reasons why you might want two displays. The first, common on multiheaded desktop machines used for technical design or creative art work, is to provide a bigger working area, either by stretching one desktop over two displays or by having two independent desktops. The second, common on laptops, is to drive an external monitor or data projector for presentations or for teaching. In this case, you usually want the second display to be a clone of the first. In this lab, you'll see how to set up both types of dual-head configuration.

> It's even possible to attach a second keyboard and mouse, and let someone else use the other display with a totally separate X session. For more information, see the "Multiple local XFree users under Linux" HOWTO at *http://cambuca.ldhs.cetuc.puc-rio.br/multiuser/*.

How Do I Do That?

The screen configuration is configured by SaX2 (SUSE advanced X11 configuration). From the main KDE menu, select System → Configuration → Configure X11 System (SaX2). You can also start it from the main YaST screen by selecting Hardware → Graphics Card and Monitor. The main screen of SaX2 is shown in Figure 3-18.

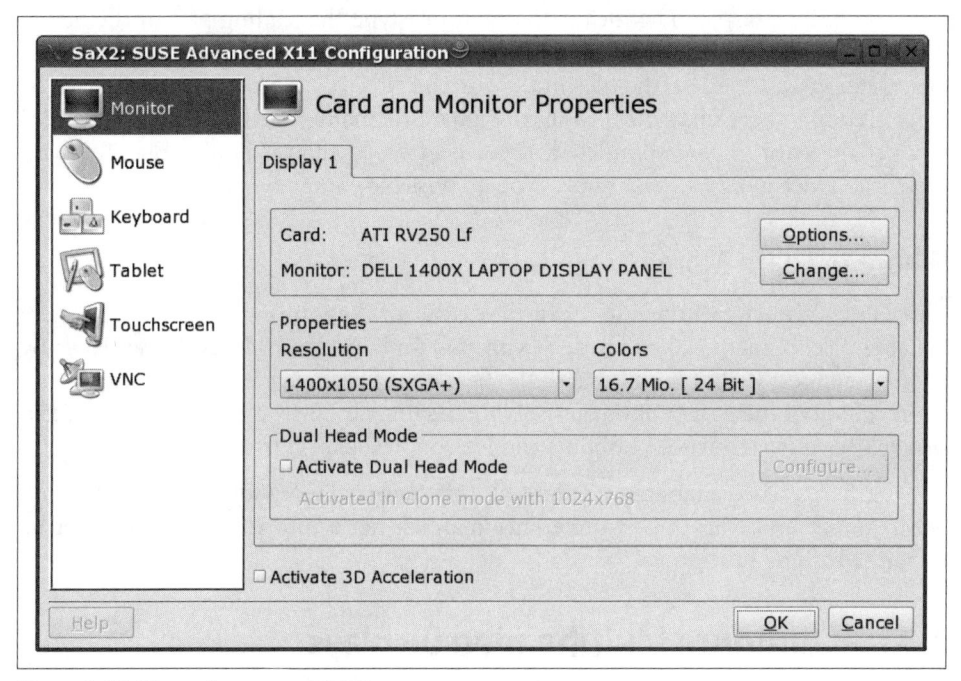

Figure 3-18. The main screen of SaX2

> If you're familiar with SUSE 9.3, you'll notice that this screen is easier to navigate than it used to be. On the downside, this version of SaX2 appears to have dropped the option to configure two displays as independent screens.

To activate the second display, check the box labeled Activate Dual Head Mode and click Configure (see Figure 3-19).

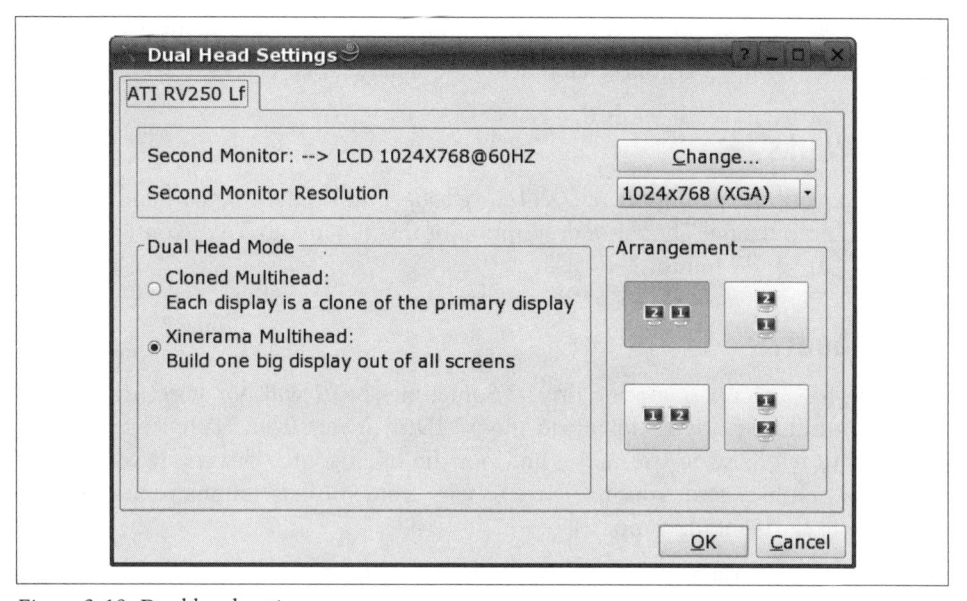

Figure 3-19. Dual head settings

Here, you can specify the manufacturer and model of your second monitor, or select one of the generic LCD settings. You can select the resolution that the second display will run at. If possible, use the same resolution for both displays. You can also choose between cloned multihead mode or Xinerama. (There's a sci-fi B movie in there somewhere—"Curse of the multihead clones," perhaps? Shot in Xinerama, of course.) Cloned is appropriate for a laptop driving a projector; Xinerama allows you to stretch one desktop over two displays. You can also specify the spatial relationship of the two displays. In Xinerama mode, the mouse will traverse off the edge of one display onto the other.

Back on the main SaX2 screen, click OK to complete the configuration. You'll be offered the opportunity to test your settings, and I strongly recommend doing so. It's possible that your monitors won't sync up at the resolution you've chosen, in which case, type Ctrl-Alt-Backspace to terminate the test or wait 30 seconds for it to time out.

Things get interesting if the resolution of the two displays don't match. In cloned mode, your external display becomes a window onto your full display size. So in the example shown in Figures 3-18 and 3-19, you would end up with a 1024×768 window that will automatically pan and scroll around inside the 1400×1280 display. In this situation, you would probably want to use the Resize and Rotate applet (in KDE, Start → System → DesktopApplet → Screen resize and rotate) or resapplet (GNOME) to drop the resolution of the primary display down to match that of the secondary display. That way, the secondary display won't be scrolling around.

In Xinerama mode, you have much the same problem. The smaller display ends up being a window onto a virtual screen that is the same size as the larger display.

How It Works

SaX2 writes out the config file */etc/X11/xorg.conf*. Editing that file by hand is possible, but is deep magic. There is a description of this file in Lab 3.1, "Configure Your Graphics Card and Monitor."

What About...

...forcing SaX2 to use a specific driver? Sometimes SaX2 will not select the correct driver. For example, if you download the NVIDIA drivers from NVIDIA's web site, you need to tell SaX2 to use those, and not the open source drivers. If you have a really new graphics card, you may have to use "frame buffer" graphics (an old standard that all cards should support).

To force SaX2 to use a specific driver, use the -m option. For example, to use the frame buffer device, you would run:

```
# sax2 -m 0=fbdev
```

To force it to use the NVIDIA binary drivers (available from the NVIDIA site), run:

```
# sax2 -m 0=nvidia
```

To use the open source built in NVIDIA drivers:

```
# sax2 -m 0=nv
```

What About...

...configuring two independent displays? If you have two displays that are of different resolution, an alternative way of using them is to configure them as independent screens. In X-Windows-speak, the first is known as :0.0 and the second as :0.1. Each screen has its own X server. If you launch an X application from the command line, you can direct it to use a specific screen with the -display option; for example:

```
$ xeyes -display 0:1
```

You can also set the DISPLAY environment variable.

In SUSE 10.0, SaX2 can't create the *xorg.conf* file needed to handle multiple independent displays. You can hand-edit the file, or take one from an earlier distribution. Here are the useful sections:

```
#two monitor sections, one for each display.
Section "Monitor"
  Option        "CalcAlgorithm" "CheckDesktopGeometry"
  DisplaySize   360 280
  HorizSync     31-64
  Identifier    "Monitor[0]"
  ModelName     "1280X1024@60HZ"
  Option        "DPMS"
  VendorName    "--> VESA"
  VertRefresh   50-60
  UseModes      "Modes[0]"
EndSection

Section "Monitor"
  Option        "CalcAlgorithm" "CheckDesktopGeometry"
  DisplaySize   280 220
  HorizSync     28-60
  Identifier    "Monitor[1]"
  ModelName     "1024X768@60HZ"
  Option        "DPMS"
  VendorName    "--> LCD"
  VertRefresh   40-60
  UseModes      "Modes[1]"
EndSection

#And the serverlayout section, to hang them all together. See the
#screen lines for How it Works.

Section "ServerLayout"
   Identifier   "Layout[all]"
   InputDevice  "Keyboard[0]" "CoreKeyboard"
   InputDevice  "Mouse[1]" "CorePointer"
   InputDevice  "Mouse[3]" "SendCoreEvents"
   Option       "Clone" "off"
   Option       "Xinerama" "off"
   Screen       "Screen[0]"
   Screen       "Screen[1]" RightOf "Screen[0]"
EndSection
```

Where to Learn More

There is a description of SaX2 in the SUSE Linux Reference Manual (section 3.11), available via the SUSE Help Center. There is a little more information on SaX2 in its manpage. There is very detailed information on the X config file in the manpage for *xorg.conf*. There are many documents available at *http://www.x.org*, including some background on the architecture, and man pages for all the X-related commands.

O'Reilly has a large number of technical books about X, for both developers and administrators.

3.12 Animate the Desktop with Xgl and Compiz

Given the rapid pace of software development in the Linux world, it is inevitable that some topics that are bleeding-edge as this book goes into production will be mainstream technology by the time you get to read it. One such is the Xgl X server and the compositing window manager `compiz`. Together with a modern graphics card, these components (which are shipped with SUSE Linux 10.1) offer some stunning visual desktop effects comparable (dare I say this?) to the best that the Mac has to offer. These effects include transparent windows, fade-in/fade-out of windows and menus, animated window minimization, and the ability to put four desktops onto four faces of a cube and spin the cube (in 3-D) to switch desktops. The overall result is to give the desktop a more fluid, organic feel.

> Of course, the command-line die-hards will consider 3-D on the desktop about as much use as a carpet in the garage. I am personally not a great fan of so-called eye-candy. But then, I don't buy decorations for my mobile phone, download polyphonic ring-tones, or wear jewelry in my navel. I think it's an age thing.

At the time of writing, this technology is running on only a limited number of platforms and you may have a rough ride working through this lab. Novell is planning to release this technology as a core part of SLED (SUSE Linux Enterprise Desktop—the new name for NLD) in Spring 2006. If you would like to see what it can do without actually installing it, there are some demo movies at *http://www.novell.com/linux/xglrelease*.

How Do I Do That?

To get Xgl working well, it is essential to harness the 3-D rendering capabilities of your graphics card. Without that, desktop animation is desperately slow. At the present time, Xgl is working well with cards based on ATI and NVIDIA chipsets; I'll use NVIDIA as my example. NVIDIA is one of the few manufacturers of graphics chips that actually supply Linux drivers. There is an open source driver called `nv` included in SUSE Linux that will drive most NVIDIA cards acceptably, but to get full 3-D performance (and to run Xgl), you should install NVIDIA's proprietary driver. This driver is not included in the SUSE distribution, because it is not open source and has its own license agreement. The driver is, however, free, and may be downloaded from NVIDIA's web site, *http://www.nvidia.com*. At the time of writing, the latest driver version is 1.0-8178 and the file you need to download is *NVIDIA-Linux-x86-1.0-8178-pkg1.run*, which is a self-extracting shell archive. (For some reason,

NVIDIA chose not to use RPM as a package format.) The first step is to unpack the archive. In the following example, I have downloaded this file into my ~/downloads directory.

```
# cd ~chris/downloads
# sh NVIDIA-Linux-x86-1.0-8178-pkg1.run -x
Creating directory NVIDIA-Linux-x86-1.0-8178-pkg1
Verifying archive integrity... OK
Uncompressing NVIDIA Accelerated Graphics Driver for Linux-x86 1.0-8178........
```

This file will unpack into the directory *NVIDIA-Linux-x86-1.0-8178-pkg1.run*. Prior to installing the driver, you should stop the existing X server by rebooting into runlevel 3 or switching to that run level with `init 3`. You should also unload any existing NVIDIA driver from the kernel:

```
# rmmod nvidia
```

Now you're ready to install the new driver. Just `cd` to the directory you just created and run the installer script:

```
# cd NVIDIA-Linux-x86-1.0-8178-pkg1
# ./nvidia-installer -q
```

If for any reason this fails because of problems with the precompiled kernel interface, you can force the installer to rebuild this with the -n option. (For this option to work, you must install the packages `kernel-source`, `make`, and `gcc`.)

```
# ./nvidia-installer -q -n
```

Finally, you need to reconfigure the X server using SaX2; note that it's the digit 0 (zero), not the letter O:

```
# sax2 -m 0=nvidia
```

If all is well, you should now be able to switch back to runlevel 5 and restart your X desktop using the proprietary NVIDIA driver. You will know if the NVIDIA driver is in use because it displays the NVIDIA splash screen for a moment each time the server is started. (You may also hear your fan slow down. Don't panic; this just means that the NVIDIA driver has enabled thermal management that the free driver didn't support.)

I have in the past managed to get myself into the situation where the new driver simply didn't work, and no amount of tweaking the X server config file or running SaX2 would produce a working X server. If this happens to you, don't panic! Just breathe into a paper bag for a bit, then back out of the installation using the --uninstall option of the NVIDIA installer. First, force a reboot (you should be able to do this with Ctrl-Alt-Delete even if you can't see anything on the screen) and boot into runlevel 3. Log in as root and `cd` into the directory you unpacked the driver files into. Then, run this command:

```
# ./nvidia-installer --uninstall
```

to uninstall the new driver.

Assuming that you have the NVIDIA driver installed and working, the next step is to install Xgl and compiz. (You should install Xgl *after* installing the NVIDIA driver, because the NVIDIA driver installer actually removes the `libglx` library, which is part of the Xgl package.) Simply use the YaST package manager and install the packages Xgl and compiz along with their dependencies. Next, edit the file */etc/sysconfig/displaymanager* and change the definition of `DISPLAYMANAGER_XSERVER` to read:

```
DISPLAYMANAGER_XSERVER="Xgl"
```

(Once you have the server working you may want to come back to this file, read the comments at the end, and adjust the options defined in `DISPLAYMANAGER_XGL_OPTS`.) Now you must propagate these changes into the system by running:

```
# SUSEconfig -module xdm
```

Now you're ready to try starting the Xgl server. Cross your fingers (or perform whatever superstitious behavior local custom dictates) and start (or restart) the desktop. If all is well, your graphical desktop should start and behave essentially the same as it did before. The next step is to start the composite window manager, compiz. This manager uses external plug-ins for all operations, even basic things such as moving a window. So, to get even basic functionality, you will need to open a terminal window and load a minimal set of plug-ins like this:

```
$ compiz --replace decoration \
    move resize place minimize &
```

A more ambitious list of plug-ins might look like this:

```
$ compiz --replace decoration wobbly fade minimize cube rotate zoom scale \
    move resize place switcher &
```

However, to get basic window decorations (title bar, borders, and so on), you should also run:

```
$ gnome-window-decorator &
```

Now try creating, moving, resizing, and minimizing some windows. If compiz and Xgl are working correctly, you should experience a substantially more fluid feel to the desktop.

> The decision to use external plugins for compiz is, of course, an excellent way to harness the efforts of open source developers around the world to extend the repertoire of effects of which compiz is capable. It is similar to the adoption of a documented module interface in Apache. Judging by the amount of activity on the Web, a subindustry of compiz plugin developers is already building.

The compiz plug-ins exist as dynamically linked libraries in the directory */usr/lib/compiz*. The plug-ins listed here ship as part of compiz; the following third-party plug-ins also exist:

Decoration
   This plug-in provides the standard window decorations, including the title bar, minimize, maximize, and close buttons, and the resizing handles.

Fade
   Adds a fade-in/fade-out effect to windows and menus as they appear and disappear.

Cube
   This plug-in gives you four desktops on the faces of a virtual cube that you can turn to use another desktop. This is perhaps the most glitzy of the plug-ins. It also needs the following Rotate plug-in to do anything useful.

Rotate
   Allows you to switch between the cube faces. The key combinations Ctrl-Alt-Left Arrow and Ctrl-Alt-Right Arrow rotate between adjacent faces. Ctrl-Alt with the left mouse button lets you drag the cube around manually in 3-D. By tweaking the configuration, it's even possible to put an image onto the top face of the cube.

Minimize
   Causes windows to shrink smoothly onto the task bar when they are minimized and to grow smoothly back to their normal size when they are reopened. This is similar to, but not quite as cool as, the "genie" effect in Mac OS X.

Move
   Allows windows to be moved from one cube face to another.

Place
   Places windows at the appropriate positions when mapped.

Resize
   Allows moving and resizing of windows. In addition to picking up a window by its title bar in the conventional way, using appropriate meta-keys allows you to pick up a window *anywhere* to resize it.

Scale
   Provides an easy way to see all your windows and select a specific window. An initial keystroke (F12 by default) makes all the windows shrink and rearrange themselves on the screen so that they do not overlap. Selecting a window with the mouse causes all windows to return to their original size and position, with the selected window on top. This is similar to the Exposé tool in Mac OS X and is, in my opinion, one of most genuinely useful plug-ins.

Switcher
   Implements Alt-Tab window switching using a film-strip metaphor.

Wobbly
   Distorts windows as they are moved or resized, giving the illusion that the window is some sort of gooey membrane rather than a rigid object. It's hard to demonstrate such an essentially dynamic effect in a book, but there is a screenshot in

Figure 3-20, where if you look carefully in the window's title bar, you can also see transparency.

Zoom

Provides the capability to zoom in and out of screen areas. Potentially this could significantly improve accessibility of the desktop to visually impaired users.

Gconf

This is a special plugin that stores settings for compiz and its plug-ins inside the gconf registry.

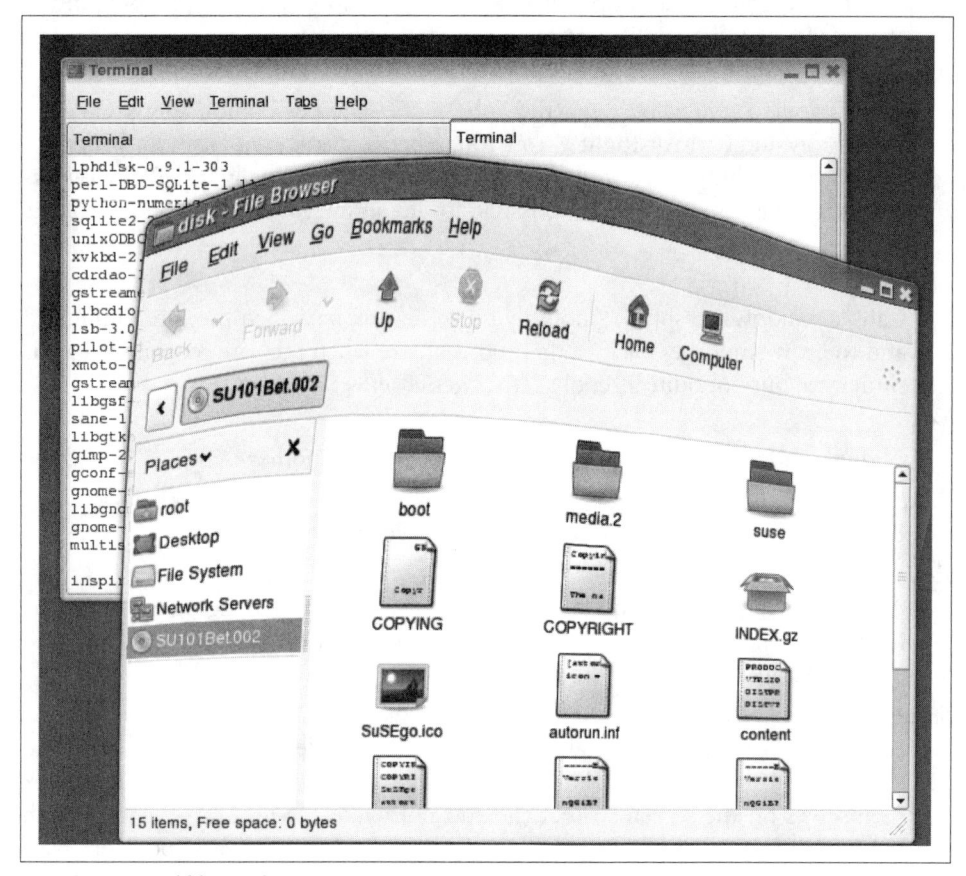

Figure 3-20. Wobbly window

How It Works

Xgl is an X server architecture layered on top of OpenGL (Open Graphics Library) via the image compositing library `glitz`. It takes advantage of modern graphics cards via their OpenGL drivers, supporting hardware acceleration of all X, OpenGL, and

XVideo applications as well as graphical effects by a compositing window manager such as compiz. When Xgl is launched, it launches the Xorg server (the normal X server used by SUSE Linux), which in turn loads NVIDIA's X driver and NVIDIA's libglx library. For a more detailed description of the interaction between Xgl, the Xorg server, and other components, see *http://principe.homelinux.net*.

OpenGL is a specification defining a language-independent API for writing applications that produce 3-D (and 2-D) graphics. The interface consists of more than 250 different function calls that can be used to draw complex three-dimensional scenes from simple primitives.

Compiz is a compositing window manager. It can replace the Gnome window manager (metacity) or the KDE window manager (Kwin). *Compositing* is a term borrowed from the movie industry and refers to the creation of complex images by combining images from different sources.

The `gconf` registry settings (discussed in the following section) are stored in a hierarchy of XML files under *~/.gconf*. The file hierarchy exactly matches the hierarchy of registry keys.

What About...

...configuring the plug-ins? Configuration data for the compiz plugins is stored in the gconf registry. Gconf is a registry system that applications can use for persistent storage of key-value pairs. It's organized in a hierarchy and is not dissimilar to the registry in Windows. Gconf was written to support the configuration of Gnome applications, although it does not require Gnome (or even an X server) to work and can be used outside of the Gnome environment. In the present context, we are interested only in the keys under the registry folder */apps/compiz*. Using the graphical tool `gconf-editor` (part of the `gconf-editor` package), you can edit these registry keys to control the function-key bindings for the various compiz operations, the speed of the effects, and much else besides. Figure 3-21 shows the key */apps/compiz/plugins/cube/screen0/options/in* open for editing. At the present time, there is relatively little documentation on these keys.

Where to Learn More

There are excellent instructions on installing the NVIDIA drivers at *http://www.suse.de/~sndirsch/nvidia-installer-HOWTO.html*. The OpenSUSE web site carries several pages describing Xgl and compiz, and how to get them working on SUSE Linux. In particular, take a look at *http://en.opensuse.org/Xgl*, *http://en.opensuse.org/Compiz*, and *http://en.opensuse.org/Using_Xgl_on_SUSE_Linux*.

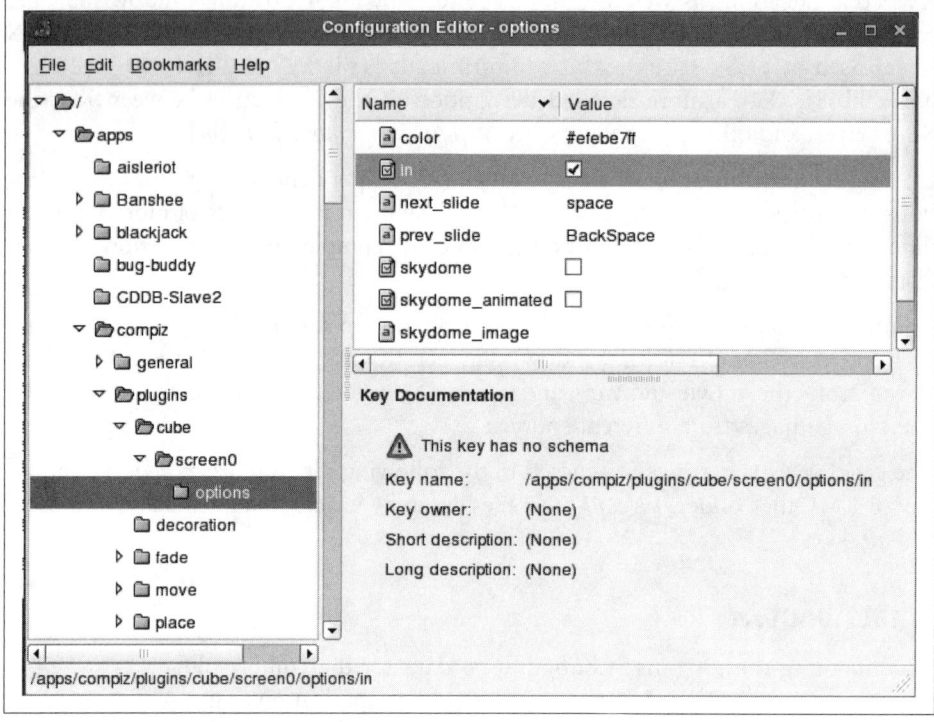

Figure 3-21. The gconf-editor tool

> In answer to the question I posed in Lab 3.2, "Configure Your Keyboard and Mouse," the computer mouse was invented in 1964 by Douglas Engelbart.

CHAPTER 4
Using Linux on Your Laptop

Laptops present special challenges, not only for Linux but for all operating systems. They often have special low-power versions of standard chipsets that have in the past presented a major obstacle to getting Linux installed and running properly. Nowadays, laptops are mainstream and hardware support in Linux is excellent. Nonetheless, there remain a few challenges, which I discuss in this short chapter—configuring power management to conserve battery life, using wireless and Bluetooth connectivity, and synchronizing the files on your laptop with those on your desktop system.

4.1 Configure Laptop Power Management

The term *power management* refers to a group of techniques that (for the most part) are designed to reduce the power consumption of a PC (particularly a laptop running on battery power). These techniques include suspend-to-disk, suspend-to-RAM, processor frequency scaling (reducing the processor clock speed), spinning down the hard disk, and thermal management (starting the fans).

Linux support for power management on laptops lagged behind Microsoft Windows support for many years. It has come a long way in the last few years; however, it is still considered experimental in the current kernel. Before playing with any of the settings here, make sure that everything is backed up.

How Do I Do That?

In theory, three *suspend* modes are supported:

Suspend-to-disk
 Saves the actual state of the machine to disk and powers it down entirely. When the machine is next booted, the previous state is restored and the computer resumes where the suspend was triggered. The ACPI term for this is *ACPI S4*. (Suspend-to-disk is the most reliable of the three modes and is considered

"mainstream." It works fine on my laptop; however, it's the slowest to suspend and resume.)

Suspend-to-RAM

The machine state is saved in RAM, most of the devices in the computer are powered down, and only the memory is powered to keep its contents. The ACPI term for this is *ACPI S3*. Suspend-to-RAM is still considered experimental. On my laptop, the suspend is very quick, but unfortunately the machine won't come back up again without forcing a power on/off cycle. Your mileage may vary.

Standby

Processes are stopped, and some hardware is deactivated. The ACPI term for standby is *ACPI S1*. On my laptop, this works and is quite quick, but the LCD screen is not powered down.

Because these features are still experimental, you need to enable them explicitly in YaST. From YaST's main screen, select System from the left pane, then Power Management from the righthand pane. On the main Power Management Settings screen, click Suspend Permissions. Here you can specify which of the three modes to allow. To exit, click OK and then Finish.

Once the modes are enabled, to enter one of the power-save modes, click on the kpowersave icon (it looks like a small electric plug when running on electric power, and a battery when on battery power, and should appear on the KDE panel).

From the KPowersave menu, shown in Figure 4-1, you can suspend the machine using any of the enabled modes. The first time you do this, take care to save any work and open files, as you may end up forcing a reboot to recover. From this menu, you can also select which power management scheme (policy) is currently in effect. I discuss these schemes later.

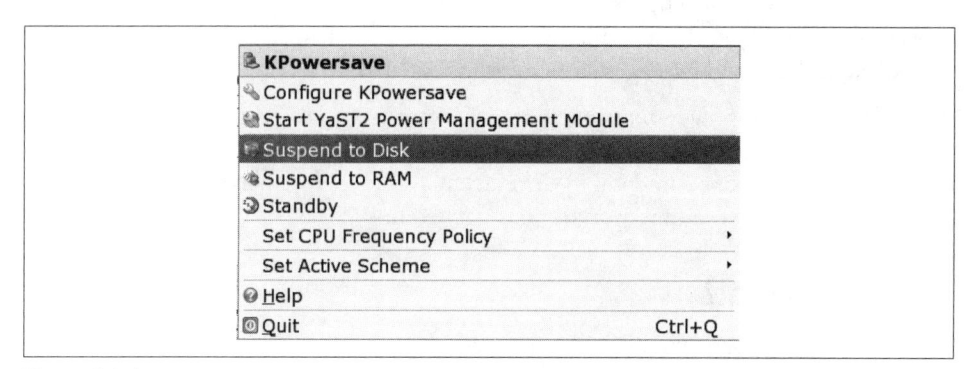

Figure 4-1. kpowersave menu

Please note that if you use suspend-to-disk on a machine that is set up to dual boot and that shares partitions between the operating systems, it is *essential* to make sure that only one operating system can edit a partition at a time. For example, if you suspend Windows to disk (called *hibernation* in Windows parlance) and then boot into Linux, you must ensure that you do not change *any* data on the Windows partition. Similarly, if you suspend Linux to disk while a FAT32 or NTFS partition is mounted, you must ensure that you do not change any data on the partition when you boot back into Windows. If you do not do this, it is almost certain that you will corrupt the filesystem and lose data.

Fortunately, the default configuration with SUSE Linux 10.0 is to try to unmount any FAT32 partitions before entering suspend-to-disk. If it fails to unmount all the FAT32 partitions, it will refuse to suspend. This will not protect you if Windows is suspended, or if you are dual-booting multiple Linux installations. You have been warned!

From the YaST Power Management Settings screen, you can also configure how the system will respond when one of the power management buttons is pressed. To do this, click the button labeled ACPI Settings. On the next screen, labeled ACPI Buttons, you'll see three drop-down lists that configure the response of the system to the power button, the sleep button, and the little switch that detects when you close the laptop lid. The default setting for the power button is to initiate a shutdown. You may find it convenient to change this to initiate a suspend-to-disk, or you may prefer to use the laptop lid button for this purpose.

How It Works

Most power management is performed by the daemon powersaved, which is started at boot time in runlevels 2, 3, and 5. A number of configuration files in the directory */etc/sysconfig/powersave* are consulted when the daemon is started. These are the files that are edited by the YaST power management module. They are plain text files and heavily commented. The easiest way to hand-edit these settings is with the sysconfig editor module in YaST (System → /etc/sysconfig Editor). The files that define the power management schemes are also in this directory:

```
# ls /etc/sysconfig/powersave/
.         common    events              scheme_powersave      thermal
..        cpufreq   scheme_acoustic     scheme_presentation
battery   disk      scheme_performance  sleep
```

Behind the scenes, the daemon relies on the use of one of two possible standards for interacting with the power management hardware of your computer: Advanced Power management (APM) and the later, more configurable Advanced Configuration and Power Interface (ACPI).

To see which one is controlling your machine, run this command as root:

```
# powersave -S
```

and it will tell you.

One of the key differences between APM and ACPI is that with APM, the BIOS is responsible for putting the machine in a state such that suspend-to-disk or suspend-to-RAM will work. With ACPI, it is the operating system that must prepare itself to be able to be suspended. Consequently, the older APM suspend modes tend to work better. However, ACPI gives much finer control of the hardware and helps to prolong battery life. Note that ACPI is not specific to Linux. It is a PC industry standard that specifies how an operating system should interact with power management features in the BIOS and PC hardware.

What About...

...configuring the power management policy? The power management software is configured using a named *scheme* or *policy*, which determines how aggressive the power saving will be, and, broadly, trades off performance against power saving. There are four predefined schemes, but you can edit them or add your own if you want. The schemes are:

Acoustic
    Scheme designed to make the machine run as quietly as possible.

Performance
    Scheme designed to let the machine run on maximum performance. This is the preferred scheme for a machine running on AC power.

Powersave
    Scheme designed to minimize power usage. This is the preferred scheme for a machine running on battery power.

Presentation
    In this scheme, display standby mode and screensaver are disabled.

From the YaST Power Management Settings screen, you can specify which scheme will be used in AC-powered mode, and which scheme will be used in battery-powered mode. To change the schemes, click on Edit Scheme, then select a scheme and click Edit. From here, a sequence of two screens allows you to specify:

- A name and text description for the scheme.
- The use of frequency scaling and throttling of the CPU (dynamic frequency scaling automatically reduces the CPU clock frequency if the system is lightly loaded).
- How aggressively the system will spin the hard disk down to conserve power. (You will notice 1- to 2-second delays if the system has to wait for the disc to spin up. Also keep in mind that spinning up a stationary disk uses significant

power, and constantly stopping and starting the disk may reduce its working life, so there's a balance to be struck here.)
- The cooling policy. There are two options; if the machine temperature rises, the active policy turns on the fans first and reduces the CPU frequency only if this isn't sufficient; the passive policy reduces the CPU frequency first and turns the fans on as a last resort.
- The action to be taken if the machine overheats.

Finally, there are even more power-save parameters that you can change using KPowersave. Click on its icon (the little plug, remember?), then select Configure KPowersave from the menu. From here, a rather confusing tabbed dialog lets you turn on auto-suspend mode (if the user remains idle for a specified time) and select sound effects that will accompany specific events such as AC power on and AC power off.

Where to Learn More

There's a good description of the powersave daemon on your system at */usr/share/doc/packages/powersave/powersave_manual.html*.

You might also read the manpages for `powersave` and `powersaved`.

You can find the ACPI specification here: *http://www.acpi.info/*.

There's a lot of work on powersave going on at the moment that should soon lead to very intelligent power management and even better battery life than in Windows. The project is hosted at *http://forge.novell.com/modules/xfmod/project/?powersave*.

4.2 Configure Wireless Networking

Wireless networks in Linux are one of those areas that generally either work perfectly straight out of the box, or don't work straight out of the box and give you hours of grief. This lab is mostly dedicated to the poor souls (like myself) whose experiences fall into the second category.

How Do I Do That?

From the YaST main screen, select Network Devices from the pane on the left, then Network Card from the pane on the right. From the command line, you can go straight to the screen you need with:

```
# yast2 lan
```

If your wireless card shows up in the list at the top (see Figure 4-2), then the odds are good that you are going to belong to the first, luckier group of people. It's not completely plug-and-play, though—most cards need firmware loaded to make them work, because most wireless LAN manufacturers don't put the intelligence into the actual driver. How you obtain and load the firmware depends on the card. Some cards will prompt, as you configure them to install the appropriate RPM, others will require a download via YOU (YaST Online Update), and some may require that you manually track down the firmware.

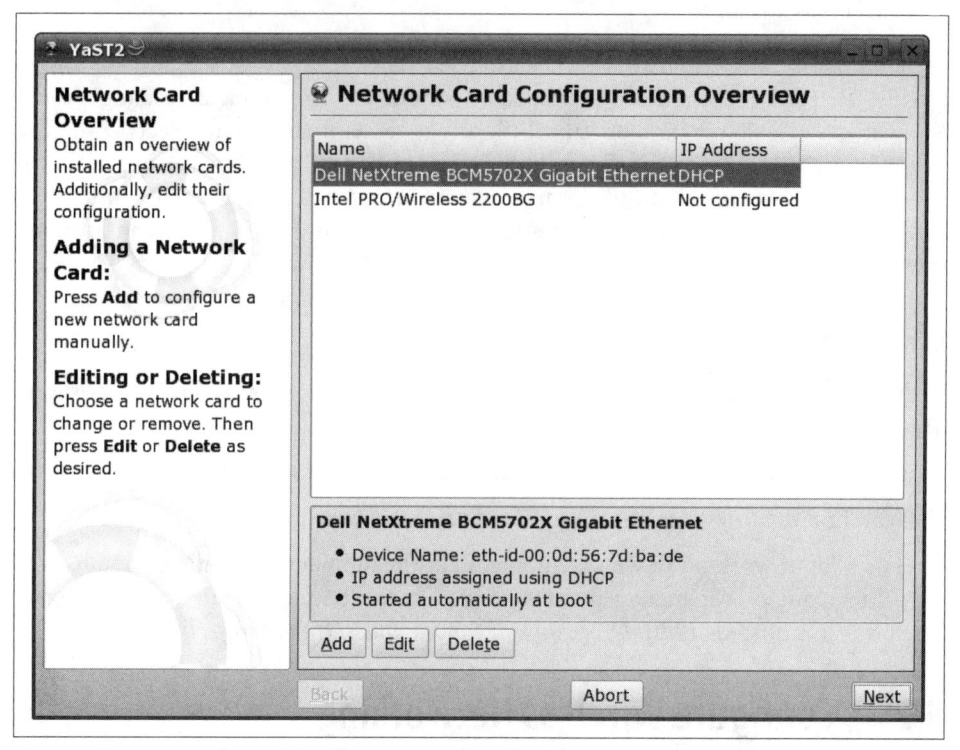

Figure 4-2. YaST wireless card configuration—main screen

To configure your card, select it from the list and click Edit. In the case of the Intel IPW2200 card shown in Figure 4-2, YaST will prompt you, if necessary, to install the RPM that contains the firmware binaries. This should be included on your installation media. An RPM containing firmware for the Atmel AT76C50X card is similarly available.

For "legal reasons" (I am left pondering the concept of an "illegal reason"), firmware for other wireless cards is not included in the distribution but is available via YaST Online Update. (See Lab 5.5, "Perform an Online Update" for information about YOU.) This includes firmware support for ACX100, ACX111, and PrismGT wireless LAN cards.

Once the firmware is downloaded, you'll see the standard YaST network configuration screen. Here you can configure your IP address settings (probably you'll want

Automatic). Clicking Next will get you to the wireless configuration screen, shown in Figure 4-3.

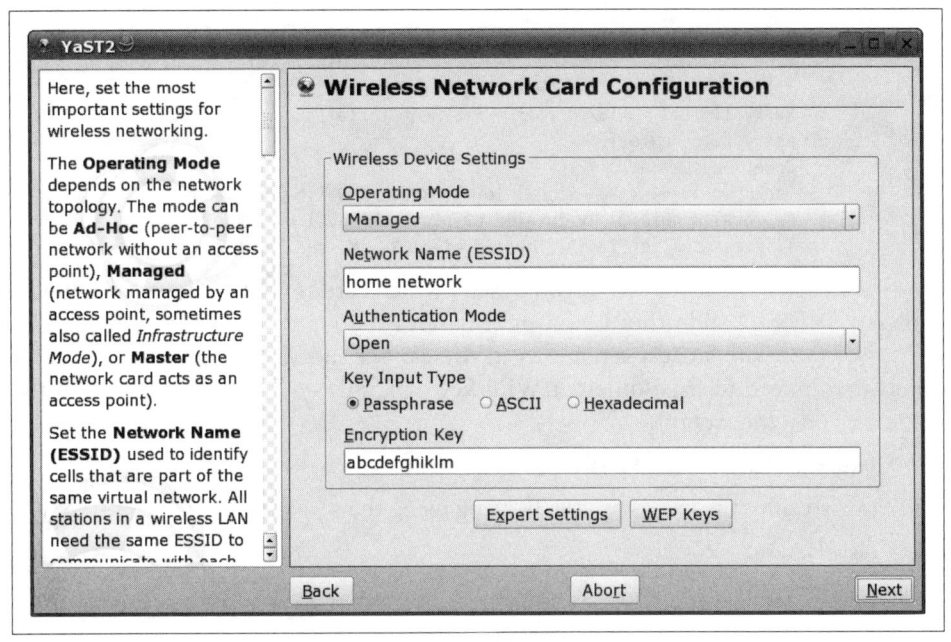

Figure 4-3. Wireless Network Card Configuration screen

Here you can set your wireless settings. If you have multiple WEP keys, click on the WEP Keys button; otherwise, just add your main key under Encryption Key. Once it's all filled in, click Next a couple more times and YaST should set everything up and close.

If you have both wired and wireless network connections, just unplugging your network card probably won't result in your wireless network automatically being selected. To swap successfully to wireless, start the network selector applet (from the main menu, select System → Desktop Applet → Network Selector Panel Applet). This applet lets you choose between your various network connections.

How It Works

Behind the scenes, iwconfig is the backend program that configures the wireless card settings. It can be very useful for differentiating between IP network problems and wireless networking problems. Just run iwconfig, and you should see something like this:

```
# iwconfig
lo        no wireless extensions.
```

4.2 Configure Wireless Networking | 161

```
sit0      no wireless extensions.

eth0      no wireless extensions.

eth2      IEEE 802.11b  ESSID:"home network"
          Mode:Managed  Frequency:2.412 GHz  Access Point: 00:60:B3:78:38:AB
          Bit Rate=11 Mb/s   Tx-Power=20 dBm
          Retry limit:7   RTS thr:off   Fragment thr:off
          Encryption key:off
          Power Management:off
          Link Quality=95/100  Signal level=-31 dBm  Noise level=-82 dBm
          Rx invalid nwid:0  Rx invalid crypt:0  Rx invalid frag:0
          Tx excessive retries:0  Invalid misc:37   Missed beacon:0
```

As you can see, the output shows you exactly which card is your wireless card. It also shows your ESSID and other useful information. If your wireless card has successfully associated with an access point, then you can see the MAC address of the access point. If you need to try a different WEP key or ESSID, you can set these from the command line; for example:

```
# iwconfig eth2 enc "abaa6533aa8d"
```

You can also enter the key as an ASCII string using the s: prefix:

```
# iwconfig eth2 enc s:keyhere
```

To set your ESSID, use

```
# iwconfig eth2 essid "home network"
```

This approach is much quicker than going in and out of YaST all the time. After changing the settings, run iwconfig again to see whether your system has now associated with an access point. If it has, then you can enter the values into YaST, and hopefully everything will work.

In SUSE 10.1, you may prefer to do all of this with NetworkManager. Using NetworkManager, it is still necessary to specify the key and ESSID of each wireless network you use the first time you connect, but thereafter NetworkManager will automatically switch to the best wireless network (the one with the strongest signal) as your laptop changes location. See Figure 4-4.

What About...

...cards that don't have Linux drivers? There is a solution to this, but it's not pleasant. Because not all wireless manufacturers produce Linux drivers, and because the interface between a Windows network driver and Windows is well documented and understood, someone decided it might be a possible to emulate that small part of Windows so the driver thinks it's running in Windows. For this purpose, NdisWrapper was born.

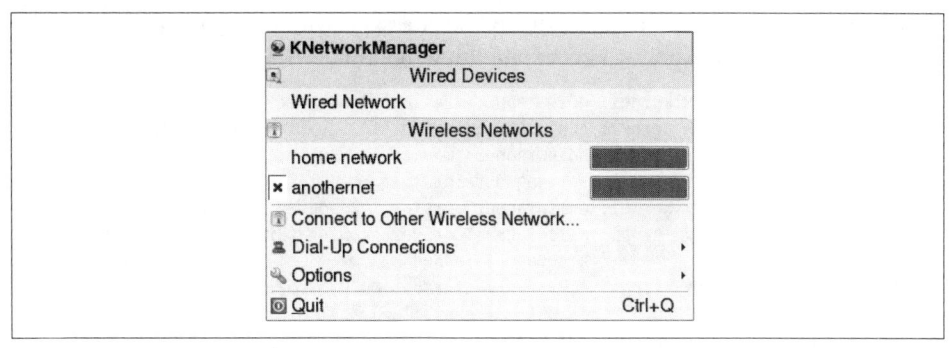

Figure 4-4. Using KNetworkManager

NdisWrapper is not an elegant solution. The word "kludge" comes to mind. (To quote the inspired Wikipedia, a kludge is similar in spirit to a workaround, only without the grace.) You end up with code written for one operating system running in the kernel address space of another. Any bugs in the Windows drivers will, in all probability, crash Linux. Of course, it also encourages wireless manufacturers to be lazy and not produce Linux drivers.

> As an example of the kind of problems you can end up with, I had a situation where NdisWrapper would work correctly if the laptop also had a Bluetooth chip on the motherboard. If the laptop didn't, then with NdisWrapper configured, the machine would cold-boot only while on AC power. It would crash every time it was powered on while running on battery.

If you really need to use NdisWrapper, read on.

First, you need to track down the Windows drivers for your card. That in itself can be a problem. Some drivers work better than others, and there are often many versions of the driver available from the manufacturer's web site. The NdisWrapper wiki has a good list of cards that work, and the best driver for them—see *http://ndiswrapper.sourceforge.net/mediawiki/index.php/List*.

Once you've located the driver files (probably a *.inf* file and a *.sys* file), download them and save them to a temporary directory. Then, open two terminal windows (as root). In one, run:

```
# tail -f /var/log/messages
```

so that you can see what's being written to the system log. In the other window, run:

```
# ndiswrapper -i foo.inf
# rmmod ndiswrapper
# modprobe ndiswrapper
```

substituting your actual driver name for ***foo.inf***.

Among the lines of detail that scroll up the message window, you should see the MAC address of the adapter. Expect something like this:

```
Nov 20 14:14:13 linux kernel: ndiswrapper: device wlan0 removed
Nov 20 14:14:13 linux kernel: ACPI: PCI interrupt for device 0000:02:03.0 disabled
Nov 20 14:14:13 linux kernel: ndiswrapper: module not supported by Novell,
                              setting U taint flag.
Nov 20 14:14:13 linux kernel: ndiswrapper version 1.2 loaded (preempt=no,smp=no)
Nov 20 14:14:13 linux kernel: ndiswrapper: driver bcmwl5a (Broadcom,04/09/2004,
                              3.40.69.0) loaded
Nov 20 14:14:13 linux kernel: ACPI: PCI Interrupt 0000:02:03.0[A] -> Link [LNKB]
                              -> GSI 5 (level, low) -> IRQ 5
Nov 20 14:14:13 linux kernel: ndiswrapper: using irq 5
Nov 20 14:14:14 linux kernel: wlan0: ndiswrapper ethernet device
                              00:90:4b:69:c1:4e using driver bcmwl5a,
                              configuration file 14E4:4324.5.conf
Nov 20 14:14:14 linux kernel: wlan0: encryption modes supported: WEP, WPA with
                              TKIP, WPA with AES/CCMP
```

The line to look for is the one showing the card's MAC address. If this is in there, then in all probability the card will work. If it's not there, then before you start trying other drivers, make sure that the card isn't disabled in the BIOS of the machine, or turn it on with the function keys (for example, you can toggle the WiFi card on and off with Fn-F2 on Dell notebooks). Each time you try to reload NdisWrapper to try a new driver, remember to unload it first.

If you have a stubborn built-in wireless chipset that just won't cooperate, consider getting a PC Card wireless adapter that is known to work with Linux. For example, Ralink makes an 802.11g chipset with GPL drivers (see *http://rt2400.sourceforge.net*). If you're feeling adventurous, you may be able to pick up a Mini-PCI version of a supported card, and replace the wireless card that came with your notebook computer.

If you do see the MAC address, you can run `iwconfig` to see whether you can find your access point (see the previous explanation). If that all works, run:

```
# ndiswrapper -m
```

which adds an alias to */etc/modprobe.d* so that NdisWrapper is loaded automatically when wlan0 is accessed. Then, go into YaST, as discussed earlier in this lab, and configure the network card permanently as follows:

1. Click Add.
2. Under the "Device type" drop-down menu, select Wireless.
3. Under Module Name, enter `ndiswrapper` and then click on Next.
4. Enter the IP address, or select Automatic if you have DHCP.
5. Click Next, and enter your wireless details (see the previous discussion), then click Next, and Next.

That's about it!

Where to Learn More

For information about firmware and the command-line wireless networking tools, see the files in */usr/share/doc/packages/wireless-tools*. Also read Chapter 22 ("Wireless Communication") of the SUSE Linux Documentation, available under SUSE Help Center.

For information about NdisWrapper, chek out *http://ndiswrapper.sourceforge.net/mediawiki/index.php/Main_Page*.

The Linux Wireless Howto is at *http://www.hpl.hp.com/personal/Jean_Tourrilhes/Linux/Wireless.html*.

For detail on Linux wireless networking, Bluetooth, and infrared, try the book *Linux Unwired*, by Weeks et al. (O'Reilly).

4.3   Configure Bluetooth Devices

Bluetooth is a short-range wireless protocol used to connect devices such as mobile phones, PDAs, and computers. It is named, so I'm told, after King Harald Bluetooth, who united Denmark and Norway. (This was back in about 950 AD, so you may be forgiven if your memory of it is hazy.) Anyway, the idea is that Bluetooth as a personal network technology can unite digital devices.

In reality, there can often be problems getting your phone working with your hardware and doing everything that the feature list says it should be able to. This is true for Windows as well as Linux. There are many features that *may* work on Bluetooth, and potentially many devices you might interact with, but in this lab we'll concentrate on interacting with a phone. That should be enough to get you going with other Bluetooth-enabled devices.

How Do I Do That?

First things first—check to see whether your laptop or PC has recognized the Bluetooth device. Many laptops now come with these as standard, but if not, you can also get USB-capable Bluetooth devices, which generally work fine. You should also make sure you have the packages `bluez-libs` and `bluez-utils` installed. (Bluez is the Bluetooth protocol stack used by SUSE.)

To configure Bluetooth using YaST, from the main YaST screen click on Hardware in the panel on the left, then Bluetooth in the panel on the right. This will bring you to the main Bluetooth screen shown in Figure 4-5.

On this screen, you can enable the Bluetooth service. You also need to enter the name your laptop will be known as. There are a couple of shorthand items that you can use here: %h stands for the hostname of the system, and %d stands for the interface number (in case you have more than one Bluetooth adapter). On this screen you

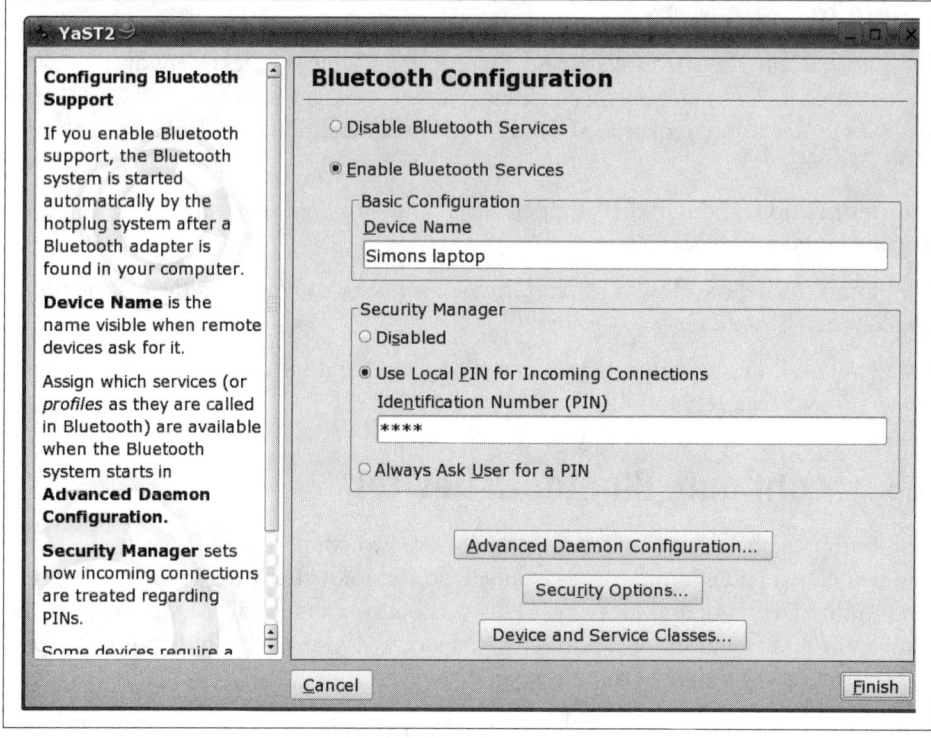

Figure 4-5. The main YaST Bluetooth Configuration screen

can also enter the PIN code that your laptop will ask for whenever a device is trying to connect with it, or you can configure it so that it always asks you for a PIN. This option allows you to use different PINs for different devices.

If you click on Advanced Daemon Configuration, you can configure the various Bluetooth services (called *profiles* in Bluetooth-speak) on your machine, as shown in Figure 4-6.

If you look at the figure, you'll see that I've enabled only the first four services. This is enough to get images and ring tones onto your phone, and to use your phone as a modem. The PAND daemon is interesting—it allows your computer to connect to Ethernet networks using Bluetooth—but is more relevant for PDAs. DUND (the Bluetooth dial-up networking daemon) isn't necessary, in my experience.

Back at the main Bluetooth configuration screen, click on Security Options. While we're getting this working, it is best to disable Authentication and Encryption on this page. Make sure Inquiry Scan and Page Scan are selected.

The Device and Service Classes page allows you to change what kind of device your laptop will announce itself as to other Bluetooth devices. Generally, Object Transfer is the useful one, although you may wish to experiment with Information and Networking at some time. You can select multiple classes.

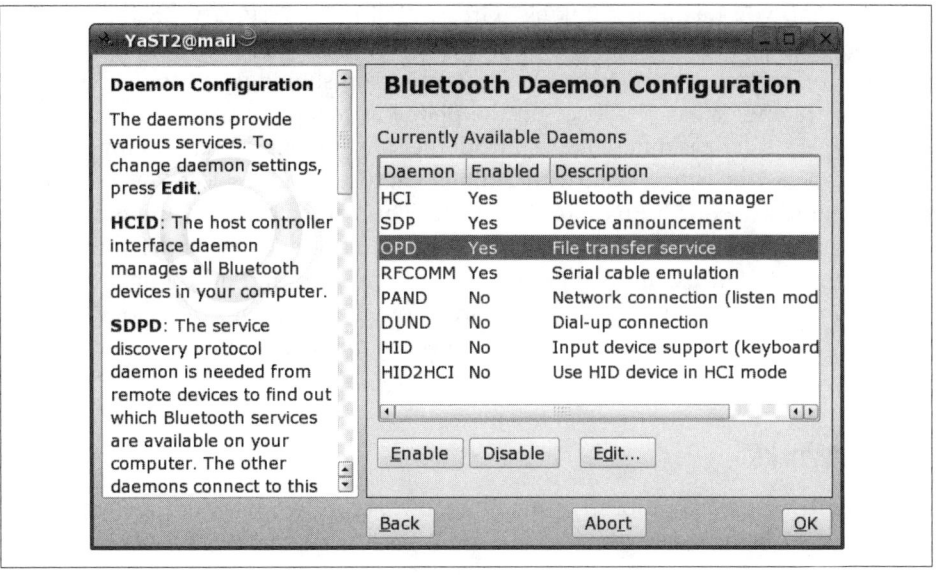

Figure 4-6. Bluetooth Daemon Configuration screen

Once the basic configuration is complete, start Konqueror and enter the URL *bluetooth:/* (or click on the Bluetooth item in the system tray, if you have one). Konqueror should show you all the Bluetooth devices in range—hopefully one of them is your phone. If not, check the Bluetooth settings on the phone and make sure that Bluetooth is enabled.

If you click on the Konqueror icon representing your phone, you should see a list of services similar to the one shown in Figure 4-7.

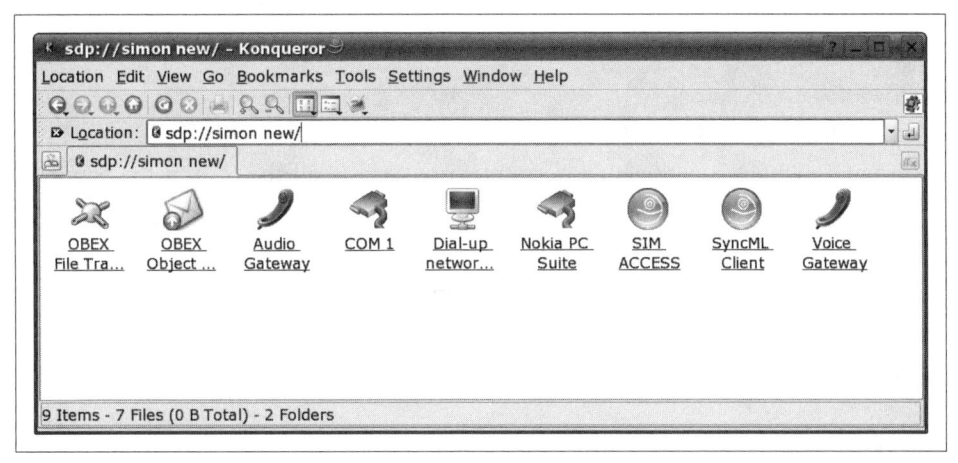

Figure 4-7. Bluetooth services

At this point, you might be thinking "Great, it all looks very easy." Sadly, it's not. Currently (as of SUSE Linux 10.1), Konqueror understands only the first object, OBEX File Transfer. If you click on that, your laptop should try to contact and pair with your phone. What you'll see on the phone at this point varies from phone to phone—every phone is different, even from the same manufacturer. On my phone, I see a message "Exchange Data with Simons Laptop?" and I select "Accept." I am then prompted to enter a PIN into the phone. This can be any PIN. On the laptop I am then prompted to enter the same PIN. Then I see a folder view of the phone's pictures, ringtones, videos, and so on. It's then easy to drag and drop things from the phone to your PC or, indeed, drag and drop content back onto the phone. On the phone, you can normally select "Auto connect without confirming" (or something similar) to simplify this process.

How It Works

The underlying configuration files for Bluetooth are in */etc/bluetooth*, together with the file */etc/sysconfig/bluetooth*.

The Konqueror plug-ins are essentially frontends for `hcitool` and `obexftp`. `hcitool` is used to configure Bluetooth connections and (to quote the manual page) "send some special command to Bluetooth devices." One of the most useful commands is:

```
# hcitool scan
```

which shows all devices in range.

ObEx is the Object Exchange protocol. The `obexftp` command allows you to send and receive files from your phone using this protocol. It is part of the `obexftp` package; this may not be installed by default. The command:

```
# obexftp -b
```

searches for Bluetooth devices that understand the Object Exchange protocol. The command:

```
# obexftp -b 00:11:22:33:44:55 -l
```

(with your phone's Bluetooth address substituted) lists all the files in the top-level directory of the phone. The command:

```
# obexftp -b 00:11:22:33:44:55 -l Images
```

lists the *Images* directory, and finally, the command:

```
# obexftp -b 00:11:22:33:44:55 -g Images/Image010.jpg
```

would grab the specified picture from your camera phone.

What About…

…accessing contacts or PIM information? There are many synchronization tools included with SUSE Linux—in fact, some days it seems hard to move around without bumping into one—but none of them seems to work with mobile phones. Multi-Sync (*http://multisync.sourceforge.net*) looks the most promising, as it has a SyncML plug-in available. However, the SyncML plug-in expects to talk to a SyncML server in one way or another, and so does the SyncML client on the phone. To add to the complications, most phones that support SyncML allow syncing to a SyncML server only over-the-air (such as via a GPRS or EDGE connection), and if your telecom provider doesn't offer a SyncML server, you'll need to either set up your own SyncML server (see *http://www.funambol.com/opensource/*) or set up an account with a third-party provider. To use SyncML, you must configure your phone and your SUSE Linux system (via MultiSync) to sync to the same SyncML server.

So, the best quick-and-dirty tool for backing up your contact information at the moment is gnokii, a text mode application that can interact with the phone over serial connections, Bluetooth, or infrared. A little configuration is required to make this work. First, run hcitool to find out the phone's Bluetooth address:

```
# hcitool scan
Scanning ...
        00:11:9f:03:1a:50       Simons phone
```

Now copy the sample gnokii configuration file to your home directory:

```
$ cp /usr/share/doc/packages/gnokii/sample/gnokiirc ~/.gnokiirc
```

then edit this file and replace the following settings to match your phone:

```
port = 00:11:9f:03:1a:50
model = 6510
connection = bluetooth
```

You may have to experiment to find a model number that works. Both 9510 and 6310i seem to work well for most Nokia phones. If nothing else works, use ATGEN.

Now run gnokii --identify to confirm that your laptop can talk to your phone. You should see something like:

```
$ gnokii --identify
GNOKII Version 0.6.8
IMEI         : 351457203296651
Manufacturer : Nokia
Model        : NPL-1
Revision     : V 5.22
```

If all's well, you should now be able, for example, to upload the phone's address book book:

```
$ gnokii --getphonebook ME 1 end -r > myphonebook
```

Here I've redirected the output to a file. The format is suitable for downloading back into the phone:

```
$ gnokii --writephonebook -o -m PE < myphonebook
```

Depending on your phone, you may have some, little, or no success in saving PIM entries, speed dial settings, to-do lists, calendar entries and so on. Read the gnokii manual page for details of other command options. There's also a graphical frontend to this, called xgnokii (installed as a separate package), which provides screens to view and edit your phone's contact list, calendar, and SMS texts. A sample screen from xgnokii is shown in Figure 4-8.

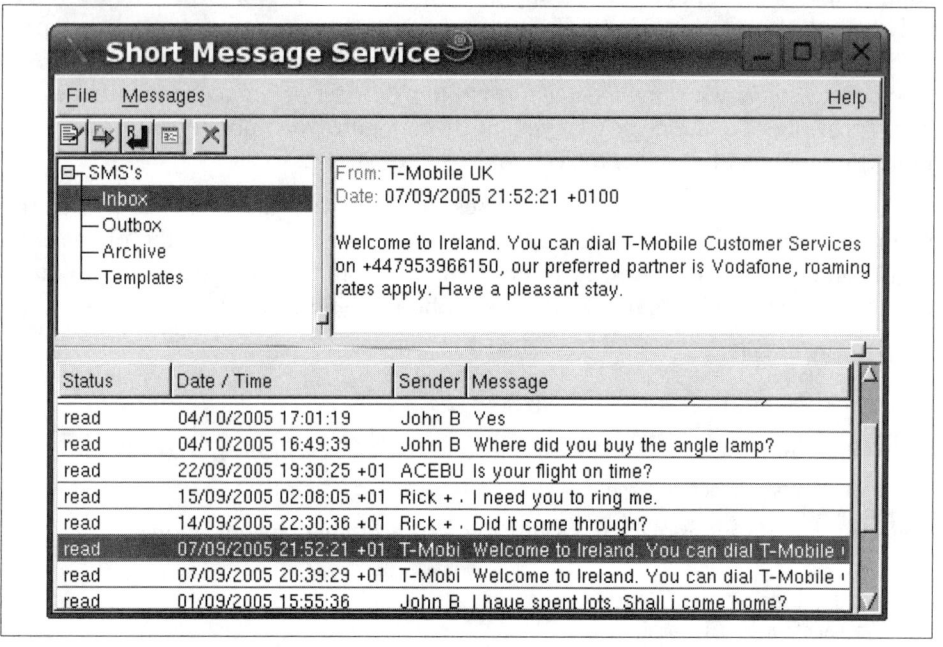

Figure 4-8. xgnokii SMS text screen

I have had reasonable success with xgnokii, but have seen some strange behavior, too.

What About...

...using your phone as a modem? This is quite simple to do. Once your phone and laptop are paired, edit the file */etc/bluetooth/rfcomm*. Make sure you have an entry that looks something like this:

```
rfcomm0 {
        # Automatically bind the device at startup
        bind yes;

        # Bluetooth address of the device
        device 00:11:9f:03:1a:50;

        # RFCOMM channel for the connection
        channel 3;

        # Description of the connection
        comment "Simons phone";
}
```

Next, ensure that `RFCOMM` is set to Yes in the advanced section of YaST's Bluetooth configuration screen (discussed earlier), and restart Bluetooth with:

```
# rcbluetooth restart
```

Test your configuration with:

```
# rfcomm release rfcomm0
# rfcomm connect rfcomm0
```

If that works, run:

```
# rfcomm bind all
```

This command associates all device names listed in /etc/bluetooth/rfcomm with their respective Bluetooth devices. There is only one in the preceding example: /dev/rfcomm0. The kernel will now automatically connect to the Bluetooth phone when the device is opened. You should then be able to use any appropriate application, such as Minicom, to open up /dev/rfcomm0 and dial out. You can also use YaST to set up the modem and associate an Internet service provider with it. Just use /dev/rfcomm0 as the modem name. (To my astonishment, this worked the first time for me!)

Although you can dial a modem with a cellular phone, you will find that it's very slow. Typically, speeds are limited to 9,600 bits per second. However, most cellular carriers offer packet data plans, sometimes for a reasonable flat rate, sometimes for a per-kilobyte charge, which can be substantial. If you use a GSM phone (as do most European carriers, and Cingular and T-Mobile in the United States), you should ask your cellular carrier about their GSM or EDGE data plans. If you use a CDMA phone (such as Sprint and Verizon in the United States), you'll need to ask about 1xRTT or 1xEV-DO data plans.

Typical speeds are about 40 kbps for GSM, 50-130 kbps for EDGE and 1xRTT, and 300 kbps and higher for 1xEV-DO (although the 1xEV-DO upstream speed is limited to 1xRTT speeds).

Make sure you get a complete explanation of the pricing structure of the data plan before you use it—it is possible to rack up thousands of dollars in charges if you are on a per-kilobyte plan. (Even on a flat rate plan, roaming charges can be very high when you are in another country.)

Although these data plans make a packet data connection to the cell tower, they still use PPP as the primary interface. The key difference is that you'll dial a pseudo phone number: usually *99# for GSM and EDGE, and #777 for 1xRTT and 1xEV-DO. For more information, including some tips on creating scripts to automate the process, see this article on O'Reilly's Linux DevCenter: *http://www.linuxdevcenter.com/pub/a/linux/2004/02/05/linux_cellular.html*.

Where to Learn More

For more detail on configuring Bluetooth, read Chapter 22 of the SUSE Linux documentation. There are manual pages for command-line tools such as `hcitool`, `gnokii`, pand, dund, and `rfcomm`. There's more information about gnokii at *http://www.gnokii.org*. There are links to a great collection of Bluetooth "howto" documents at *http://www.holtmann.org/linux/bluetooth*.

4.4   Synchronize Files with Your Desktop

I envy people who have only one computer. (Sometimes I *really* envy people who don't have a computer at all, but that's another story.) Those of use who routinely use two (or three, or four…) computers face the problem of synchronization—making sure that the most recent version of whatever document we're working with is actually on the machine we're working at. Without tools to help, it's very easy to lose track of where things are and discover you've just spent an hour editing a file that's two weeks out of date compared to the copy on your other computer.

Data synchronization between two or more machines can be tricky to manage. There's the problem of how to actually copy the data from one machine to another, and then there's the problem of deciding which files actually need to be copied. The first problem is easily solved; using tools like `scp` and `rsync`, it's quite easy to move data around. Deciding what needs to be copied is harder, and traditionally requires the discipline to update your central repository every time you update a file—otherwise, you may update a file in two places, and then you are almost bound to lose data.

How Do I Do That?

Novell sells a mature synchronization product called iFolder. Using iFolder, users keep personal data files within one or more nominated directories (which they call their iFolders) on their personal machine(s). At regular intervals (usually every few minutes), their iFolder client connects to the iFolder server (which maintains a central repository of their iFolder files) and figures out which files have been updated and need to be uploaded or downloaded. Of course, even when the personal machine is offline, the local copies of the files continue to be available. Multiple users can subscribe to the same iFolder, so that the product allows file sharing amongst user communities who are often working offline. Beyond some initial setup, the service is completely automatic and needs no intervention. This commercial product is based around a closed source server and open source clients. However, iFolder3 is an open source server implementation that runs on Mono (in case you don't know, Mono is a cross-platform implementation of Microsoft's .NET Framework). iFolder3 is still in early development, and it is significantly more limited than the commercial server from Novell, but it should do the job.

> I don't know who made up the name "iFolder," but because the implementation presumably relies on comparing the time stamps on files, I can't help but wonder if it was originally called "if older."

This lab is more bleeding edge than the others in this book. The problem isn't in the iFolder client (which ships as part of the SUSE Linux distribution); it's in the server. It's an example of an open source project at an early stage of its life cycle, before it has been built as a binary RPM and put onto the distribution media. Be warned that iFolder3 is a work in progress, so you should make sure that you have backups of your critical data before installing it. Also, the code may have changed significantly since this was written. Please check the URLs listed in this lab to see if there are any simpler or better instructions.

First, you need to get the server working. You need to do this only on one, central machine. There are some prerequisites to download. First, you'll need the latest Mono, from *http://www.mono-project.com/Downloads*. You can either download the binary installer, download the RPMs, or even use the Red Carpet Update tool, rug:

```
# rug sa http://go-mono.com/download
# rug sub mono-1.1-official
# rug in mono-complete
```

Now download the latest version of log4net. It should be here (check for later versions): *http://forgeftp.novell.com/ifolder/required/log4net/linux/*. Then, install it with a command of the form:

```
# rpm -i ~/downloads/log4net-1.2.9-1.i586.rpm
```

(By the way, there are labs on package management in Chapter 5 to help you with these commands.)

Next, you need to download the source code for iFolder3. Some projects will release snapshot versions of software that are (at least in theory) stable. The simple iFolder server isn't that mature yet, so you need to check out the source direct from the developers' code repository, which uses an open source revision control system called subversion. The command-line client for subversion is svn. You have two options here. You can grab the version of the source that is exactly the same as the version I used to write these instructions, or you can grab the latest and greatest. I'd suggest using the same version I used, and if that works, try again with the latest version. The commands you need will look something like this:

```
# cd /usr/local/src
# mkdir ifolder
# cd ifolder
# svn checkout svn+ssh://anonymous@forgesvn1.novell.com/svn/simias/trunk \
  -r "{"20051218"}"
```

The password for the svn login is "anonymous". If you want to check out the latest version, just remove the -r option from the svn command:

```
# svn checkout svn+ssh://anonymous@forgesvn1.novell.com/svn/simias/trunk
```

Normally, you would build your source as a nonroot user, and you would run the service as a nonroot user, but right now there seem to be some problems with the simple server if you do this. So, you should continue as root:

```
# cd trunk/simias
# ./autogen.sh -prefix=/opt/simias
# make
# make install
# cd other/SimpleServer
# make install-simpleserver
```

There's one other thing to do before starting the server: you need to configure the user accounts that are allowed to log into your server. Edit the file */opt/simias/etc/SimpleServer.xml*, supplying usernames and passwords as required. The format should be fairly self-explanatory. Make sure you remove the default users! I also suggest changing both the domain name and description to something relevant to your site. Here's a minimal version of the file:

```
<?xml version="1.0" encoding="utf-8" ?>
<Domain Name="SimpleServer" Description="Simon's Simple Server">
        <Member Name="simon" Password="novell" Owner="true">
                <First>Simon</First>
                <Last>Crute</Last>
        </Member>
</Domain>
```

> Yes, this is a rather primitive way of defining user accounts. The commercial iFolder server integrates with Novell's eDirectory (LDAP), so iFolder accounts are synced with LDAP/eDirectory accounts.

Now you're ready to start the iFolder server:

```
# /opt/simias/bin/simpleserver --start
```

And you can stop it with:

```
# /opt/simias/bin/simpleserver --stop
```

There's no manpage for the server, but the following command should help:

```
# /opt/simias/bin/simpleserver --help
```

Note in particular the `--datadir` option to change the location of the data store.

Now I'll turn my attention to the client. You need to install this on every machine you want to sync. There is an iFolder client shipped with SUSE Linux (package ifolder3); for other platforms, download the client straight from the iFolder site: *http://www.ifolder.com/index.php/Download*. There are clients for Linux, Windows 2000 and XP, and Mac OS X. This lab looks at only the SUSE Linux version of the client.

Start your iFolder client from the main menu at Start → Internet → Data Exchange → iFolder 3, or enter the command:

```
# /opt/novell/ifolder3/bin/ifolder
```

You should see a yellow folder with an "I" on it, on the task bar. Right-click it, and select Accounts from the pop-up menu. Here you can enter the name or IP address of the server, the port number, and your user ID and password, as shown in Figure 4-9.

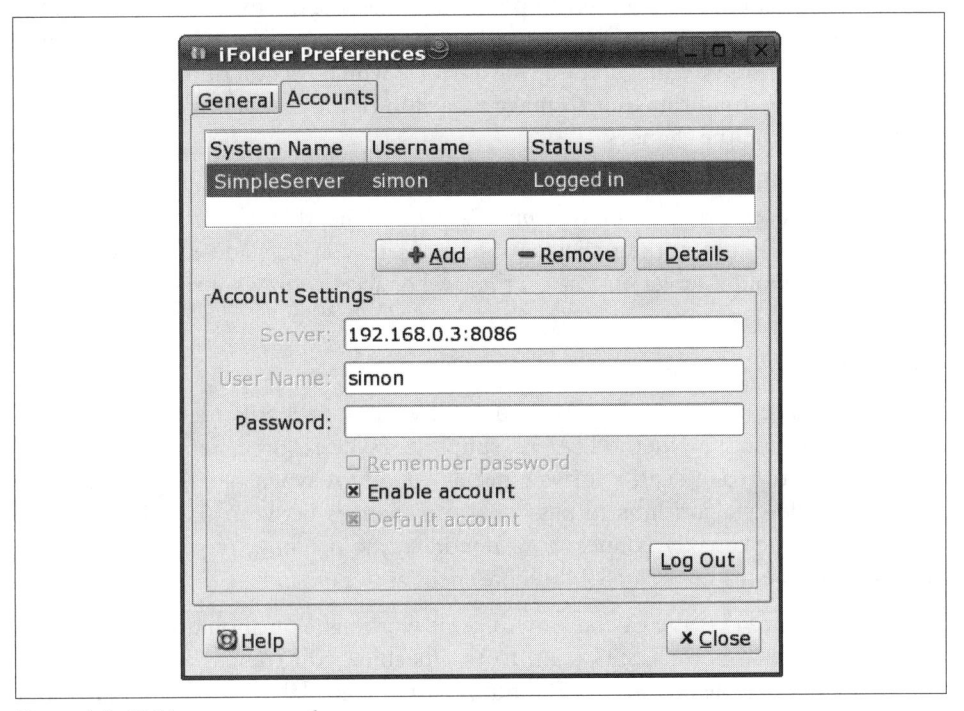

Figure 4-9. iFolder account preferences

Finally, you'll need to mark at least one of your directories as an iFolder. Right-click the iFolders icon again, and select iFolders from the pop-up menu. Click New. Type in the name of the directory you want to become an iFolder (or browse to it), and click OK. Be aware that when you initially establish a directory as an iFolder, the entire folder content will be copied onto the server; this may take some time. Subsequent synchronizations will be quicker, as only the differences are propagated. The directory then becomes an iFolder, and files you put in this directory are made available to anyone else who has shared that iFolder.

Once you're successfully logged into the iFolder server, and have defined which directories are to be your iFolder, synchronization is automatic.

How It Works

The iFolder client detects any changes to any of the files in the iFolders you are sharing. It then copies those changes (or the entire file) to the server. The server then notifies all the other iFolder clients that are subscribed to that iFolder that the file has changed, and the clients can then download the changes (or the entire file). If anyone deletes a file from the iFolder, it will be deleted from the iFolder of people who have that iFolder. If two clients update the same file, the following happens: the server accepts the update from the first client to connect to it. The second client is then notified about a conflict and is given a choice which version of the file to accept. It would be prudent at this time to make a backup of the conflicting file, so you can manually reconcile the changes.

If you want to share an iFolder between multiple users, not just multiple machines, make sure the user is defined in the *SimpleServer.xml* file, then go into the iFolder client, click on the folder, then click on Share. Here you can add any user who is defined to the iFolder server, and select the level of access you want them to have.

What About...

...other synchronization methods? If you don't want to set up iFolder, rsync is probably the next best sync method. At its simplest, rsync is just a remote copy command (similar to rcp or scp), but it is especially good for synchronizing large files, as it has some clever algorithms to pass only the changes between the files. You can either have rsync directly connect to a remote rsync daemon, typically using TCP port 873, or have it run it over SSH (secure shell) as a transport.

Running it over SSH is the easiest way to get it working. You should first verify that you can perform a normal SSH login to the machine you want to synchronize to. (SSH works out of the box on SUSE Linux, but there is a lab on SSH in Chapter 8 if you need help.)

Here's a simple rsync command to copy a single file:

```
$ rsync test.nbe happy:laptop
```

That command copies the file *test.nbe* to the (existing) directory *laptop* on the machine called happy. Here's another example:

```
$ rsync -avz EPIC happy:
```

This command recursively transfers all files from the directory *EPIC* on the local machine into your home directory on the machine happy. The files are transferred in "archive" mode (-a flag), which ensures that symbolic links, devices, attributes, permissions, ownerships, and so on are preserved in the transfer. Additionally, compression (-z flag) will be used to reduce the size of data portions of the transfer. The -v flag enables verbose mode—files are listed as they are transferred.

You can, of course, copy files the other way, from the remote machine to the local one. Here's one more example:

```
$ rsync --delete -av simon@happy:/home/simon/mydata \
    /home/simon/mydata
```

This command copies all the files from */home/simon/mydata* on machine happy, into the directory */home/simon/mydata* on the local machine. The notation `simon@` tells `rsync` to perform an SSH login on the remote machine as `simon`. The default behavior is to log in with whatever name you're logged in as on the local machine. The `--delete` flag tells `rsync` to delete files at the destination that don't exist on the sender.

Of course, for this approach to work, you need some discipline in how you use and update files. For example, if you have two machines (a laptop and a desktop) and you consider the desktop to hold the master copies of your files, at the beginning of a work session on the laptop you should `rsync` the relevant directories from the desktop, and at the end of the session you should `rsync` them back to the desktop. The `rsync` solution does not protect you against the situation where you update two copies of the same file at different locations.

There is another open source synchronization tool called Unison that's worth looking at. It's from Benjamin Pierce at the University of Pennsylvania. Unison uses the same update protocol as `rsync` (for efficient propagation of small changes to large files), but is smarter than `rsync` because it can propagate changes between two replicas of a filesystem in both directions. Whereas `rsync` is a unidirectional mirroring tool that needs to be told "this machine holds the true copy of the filesystem; please make the other replica look the same," Unison is a true synchronization tool. Like rsync, Unison can run in a simple client/server mode in which one instance of Unison listens on a socket and another instance makes a direct TCP connection to it. However, this mode is insecure, and instead it is preferable to tunnel Unison traffic over an encrypted SSH connection.

SUSE Linux ships with Unison (simply install the package `unison`), but be aware that you need to be running the same version on each of the machines you want to synchronize. For example, Unison 2.9.1 (shipped with SUSE 10.0) will not interoperate with Unison 2.13.16 (shipped with SUSE 10.1). Fortunately, upgrading the older one is easy: copy across the executable */usr/bin/unison* from the machine with the newer copy. Alternatively, you can download a prebuilt Linux executable from *http://www.cis.upenn.edu/~bcpierce/unison*. There is no installation procedure, as such; it simply needs to be uncompressed and copied into */usr/bin*.

Once you have Unison installed, try these commands on the local machine as a simple test:

```
$ unison -version
$ ssh remote_host unison -version
```

This test will confirm whether the SSH connection is working and that Unison is on the SSH search path on the remote machine. You should also verify that the version number reported by the remote host matches the version number reported locally.

Unison works by synchronizing two *replicas*. Usually one is local and one is remote. It's important to note that the synchronization is bidirectional: files that have been created or changed on the local replica will propagate to the remote replica, and files that have been created or changed on the remote replica will propagate to the local replica. Unison will detect and flag cases where the same file has been updated (differently) on the two replicas. It makes no attempt to resolve such conflicts automatically.

You can run Unison very simply from the command line. For example:

```
$ unison /home/chris ssh:/happy.example.com/
```

This command synchronizes */home/chris* (my home directory on the local machine) with my home directory on the machine `happy.example.com`, using SSH as the transport. You will be prompted for your password or SSH passphrase. The two arguments supplied here are examples of what Unison calls a *root*, which simply means the top-level directory of a replica. Instead of this simple usage, you can also build *named profiles* and specify the profile name on the command line. A profile can specify, among other things, the names of the two roots, an explicit list of files and folders to be synchronized, and a list (using wildcards) of files that should be ignored.

You can also run Unison with a graphical interface. Unison will report the updates it believes are necessary, showing new files, changed files, and conflicts, as shown in Figure 4-10. From this screen, you can manually select exactly which updates you want to propagate.

Where to Learn More

Visit the iFolder3 project page at *http://www.ifolder.com*.

For information on iFolder clients, visit *http://www.ifolder.com/index.php/Download*.

The `rsync` command is described in the `rsync` manual page.

There is an excellent, detailed manual for Unison in the folder */usr/share/doc/packages/unison*. The home page is *http://www.cis.upenn.edu/~bcpierce/unison*.

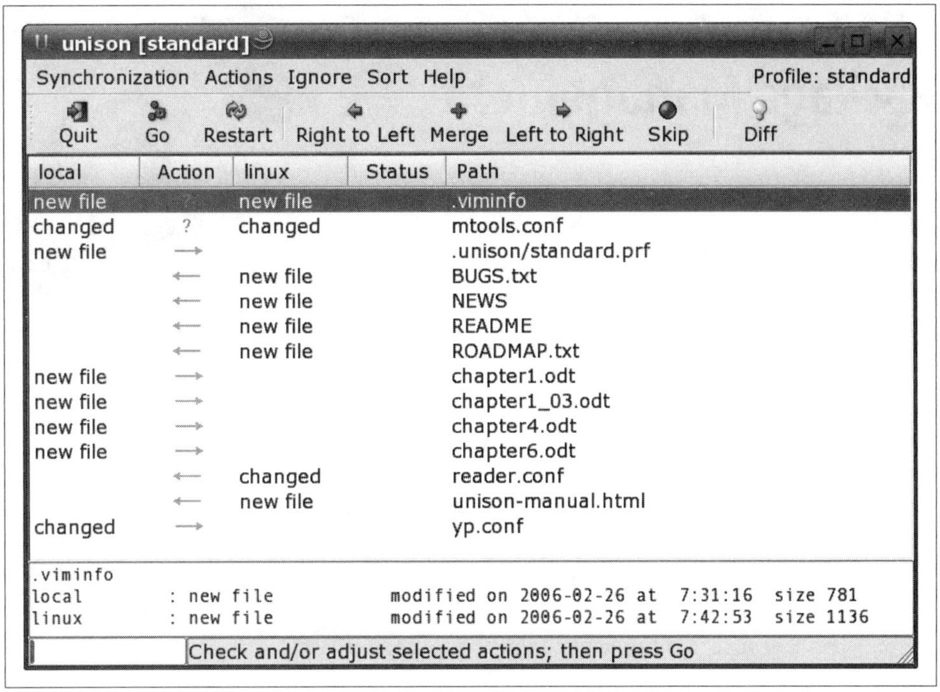

Figure 4-10. Synchronizing files with Unison

CHAPTER 5
Package Management

I am not a follower of fashion. I prefer to think that fashion is a follower of me. In reality, what happens is that fashion goes in cycles while I remain stationary. Once per cycle, roughly every 15 years, I come briefly into fashion and then pass out again, in much the same way that a clock that has stopped is right twice a day. All of which is by way of introducing the observation that Linux users tend to be followers of software fashion. They love to load the newest applications and try out the latest cool stuff simply because it is the latest cool stuff.

The labs in this chapter will show you how to find new packages, how to install them, how to find out what's already installed, and how to build applications from source. The underlying package management technology is RPM, but there are several fancy package management tools that build on top of this, as you'll discover.

5.1   Find Out What's Installed

The most common format in which software packages are made available for SUSE Linux is a package format called RPM, which originally stood for "RedHat Package Manager" because it was developed by Linux distributor RedHat, but now stands for "RPM Package Manager" because it is used by many Linux distributions. RPM is not the only package format around; another popular format is the one used by Debian Linux (usually called *.deb* packages), which has many ardent supporters. There are other formats used to distribute software—in particular, *.tar* archives ("tarballs"), which are more often used to distribute source code. (See Lab 5.8, "Compile and Install Source Code," later in this chapter.) Other versions of Unix have their own formats, such as the `pkgadd` format used by Solaris.

SUSE Linux, however, uses RPM, and in a sense a SUSE Linux distribution can be regarded simply as a large collection of RPM packages.

In addition to the actual files, an RPM package contains a number of components of metadata, including:

- A collection of files that will be installed on the system; that is, the actual contents of the package.
- A brief text description of what the package is and does.
- Information about the dependencies of the package (the components that must already be installed in order for the package to work) and the capabilities that this package provides.
- Pre-install and post-install scripts (for example, a script to add an entry for the package to the desktop menus), and also pre-uninstall and post-uninstall scripts.
- A digital signature that can be used to verify the authenticity of the package if you have the public key of the package's author. This provides a way to verify that the package has not been corrupted, either accidentally or maliciously, since the time that the author signed it.

There is a command-line utility called (unsurprisingly) rpm that allows you to query, install, upgrade, and uninstall software packages. This lab will concentrate on querying packages—both those that are already installed and those that are sitting on the distribution CDs waiting to be installed. Later labs deal with installation and removal of packages.

How Do I Do That?

I will not attempt a systematic description of all the command-line options to the rpm command—that's what the manpage is for. Suffice it to say that there are quite a lot of them, and they combine in slightly confusing ways. Let's take a look at a few examples. First, to get a list of all installed packages, use rpm -qa. Because the list is long, pipe the output into head to see just the first 10 lines:

```
$ rpm -qa | head
ghostscript-fonts-other-8.15.2rc1-8
x11-input-wacom-0.7.2-5
glibc-2.3.90-67
dosfstools-2.11-6
libdrm-2.0-6
lzo-2.02-3
popt-1.7-247
attr-2.4.28-4
libstdc++-4.1.0_20060218-2
libsidplay1-1.36.59-4
```

Note the standard form for the name of a package: a base name, such as glibc, followed by a version, such as 2.3.90, and a build number, such as 67. So, just how many packages are actually installed? That's easy—let wc count the number of lines of output from rpm:

```
$ rpm -qa | wc -l
1181
```

Yes, that's 1,181 packages! More useful perhaps is to query for specific packages. The filter grep is useful here. Let's imagine that you've heard about some Linux tools that implement the Simple Network Management protocol (SNMP). Do you have a package installed that might be it? Just use grep to search the output from rpm -qa:

```
$ rpm -qa | grep snmp
net-snmp-5.3.0.1-5
```

It's also possible to supply wildcards directly to the rpm -qa command:

```
$ rpm -qa '*snmp*'
net-snmp-5.3.0.1-5
```

That looks hopeful. You can get more information about the net-snmp package with the rpm -qi command. This queries a specific installed package:

```
$ rpm -qi net-snmp
Name        : net-snmp       Relocations: (not relocatable)
Version     : 5.3.0.1        Vendor: SUSE LINUX Products GmbH, Nuernberg, Germany
Release     : 5              Build Date: Mon 20 Feb 2006 22:49:39 GMT
Install Date: Wed 01 Mar 2006 15:56:56 GMT      Build Host: ensslin.suse.de
Group       : Productivity/Networking/Other  Source RPM: net-snmp-5.3.0.1-5.src.rpm
Size        : 6088568                        License: Other License(s), see package
Signature   : DSA/SHA1, Mon 20 Feb 2006 22:51:31 GMT, Key ID a84edae89c800aca
Packager    : http://bugs.opensuse.org
URL         : http://sourceforge.net/projects/net-snmp
Summary     : SNMP Daemon
Description :
This package was originally based on the CMU 2.1.2.1 snmp code. It has
been greatly modified, restructured, enhanced, and fixed. It hardly
looks the same as anything that CMU has ever released. It was renamed
from cmu-snmp to ucd-snmp in 1995 and later renamed from ucd-snmp to
net-snmp in November 2000.



Authors:
--------
    Wes Hardaker <hardaker@users.sourceforge.net>
Distribution: SUSE LINUX 10.0.42 (i586)
```

You can find out what files are in the package with rpm -ql. The output has been heavily edited to save trees:

```
$ rpm -ql net-snmp
/etc/init.d/snmpd
/etc/logrotate.d/net-snmp
/etc/snmpd.conf
/usr/bin/encode_keychange
/usr/bin/fixproc
/usr/bin/ipf-mod.pl
/usr/bin/net-snmp-config
/usr/bin/snmpbulkget
/usr/bin/snmpbulkwalk
/usr/bin/snmpcheck
/usr/bin/snmpconf
/usr/bin/snmpdelta
... edited ...
```

```
/usr/lib/libnetsnmp.so.5
/usr/lib/libnetsnmp.so.5.2.1
/usr/lib/libnetsnmpagent.so.5
/usr/lib/libnetsnmpagent.so.5.2.1
... edited ...
/usr/sbin/rcsnmpd
/usr/sbin/snmpd
/usr/sbin/snmptrapd
/usr/share/doc/packages/net-snmp
/usr/share/doc/packages/net-snmp/AGENT.txt
/usr/share/doc/packages/net-snmp/COPYING
/usr/share/doc/packages/net-snmp/EXAMPLE.conf
/usr/share/doc/packages/net-snmp/EXAMPLE.conf.def
/usr/share/doc/packages/net-snmp/FAQ
/usr/share/doc/packages/net-snmp/NEWS
/usr/share/doc/packages/net-snmp/README
... edited ...
/usr/share/man/man1/mib2c.1.gz
/usr/share/man/man1/snmpbulkget.1.gz
/usr/share/man/man1/snmpbulkwalk.1.gz
/usr/share/man/man1/snmpcmd.1.gz
... edited ...
/usr/share/snmp/mib2c-data/default-mfd-top.m2c
/usr/share/snmp/mib2c-data/details-enums.m2i
/usr/share/snmp/mib2c-data/details-node.m2i
/usr/share/snmp/mib2c-data/details-table.m2i
/usr/share/snmp/mib2c-data/generic-ctx-copy.m2i
/usr/share/snmp/mib2c-data/generic-ctx-get.m2i
... edited ...
```

This list, though heavily edited, shows most of the types of file that commonly make up a package:

- Configuration files (e.g., */etc/init.d/snmpd* and */etc/snmpd.conf*)
- Command-line tools (executables such as *snmpcheck* in */usr/bin*)
- Libraries (in */usr/lib*)
- A daemon or two (in */usr/sbin*)
- Some documentation for the package (in */usr/share/doc/packages*)
- Some manual pages (in */usr/share/man*)
- Some data files (in */usr/share/snmp*)

It's possible to do the query the other way round. That is, you can ask, "Which package does this file come from?":

```
$ rpm -qf /usr/bin/snmpcheck
net-snmp-5.3.0.1-5
```

The result of this tells you that the file */usr/bin/snmpcheck* comes from the package net-snmp.

There are additional options to list other aspects of the packages. For example, you can list a package's "helper" scripts that run at installation time or uninstallation time with a command such as:

```
$ rpm -q --scripts net-snmp
```

Many packages just run the command /sbin/ldconfig in their helper scripts. This command rebuilds the linker cache to make the system aware of any libraries that have been added or removed as a result of installing or uninstalling the packages.

So far, you've been running queries on packages that are already installed. With the addition of the -p flag, you can also query uninstalled packages (i.e., RPM files). If you mount any of the SUSE Linux installation CDs and go to the suse directory on the CD, you'll see directories corresponding to the various process architecture that the distribution supports. For example:

```
$ cd /media/disk/suse
$ ls
i586   i686   noarch
```

Here, noarch refers to architecture-independent packages (often documentation).

Most of the packages are in the *i586* folder. Each CD contains several hundred packages. Here are the first 10 packages on CD2:

```
$ ls -l i586 | head
total 521083
-r--r--r--  6 cbrown users  3390981 2005-08-07 15:52 abiword-2.2.9-3.i586.rpm
-r--r--r--  6 cbrown users   181684 2005-08-06 19:27 alsa-tools-1.0.9-4.i586.rpm
-r--r--r--  6 cbrown users  5977840 2005-08-07 03:53 amarok-1.3beta3-2.i586.rpm
-r--r--r--  6 cbrown users    15763 2005-08-07 03:53 amarok-xmms-1.3beta3-2.i586.rpm
-r--r--r--  5 cbrown users   974826 2005-08-06 20:03 aspell-af-0.50.0-7.i586.rpm
-r--r--r--  5 cbrown users 13486171 2005-08-06 20:03 aspell-bg-0.50.0-21.i586.rpm
-r--r--r--  5 cbrown users   379056 2005-08-06 20:03 aspell-br-0.50.2-195.i586.rpm
-r--r--r--  6 cbrown users  1956607 2005-08-06 20:03 aspell-ca-0.50.2-195.i586.rpm
-r--r--r--  6 cbrown users 20257598 2005-08-06 20:03 aspell-cs-0.51.0-5.i586.rpm
```

Now, you can run rpm queries on any of these (uninstalled) packages—for example, to find what files are contained in a package:

```
$ rpm -qlp amarok-1.3beta3-2.i586.rpm
/opt/kde3/bin/amarok
/opt/kde3/bin/amarokapp
/opt/kde3/lib/kde3/kfile_modplug.la
/opt/kde3/lib/kde3/kfile_modplug.so
/opt/kde3/lib/kde3/konqsidebar_universalamarok.la
/opt/kde3/lib/kde3/konqsidebar_universalamarok.so
/opt/kde3/lib/kde3/libamarok_kdemmengine_plugin.la
... this list goes on for a lot longer ...
```

Note that you need to specify the complete filename here (though of course you can use filename completion to avoid actually typing it all in).

The YaST package manager allows management of RPM packages from the comfort of a graphical interface. Actually, the YaST package manager is not just prettier; it is smarter than the raw `rpm` command in a number of other ways, as you'll see in the labs later in this chapter. For now, I'll show you how to use it just to query installed packages.

To launch the package manager and query the currently installed packages, start YaST, and in the main screen's left pane select Software, then Software Management in the right pane. This will bring you to the YaST package manager screen. There is a drop-down list labeled Filter in the top-left corner that lets you choose how you want to view the packages. To view all installed packages, select Installation Summary from the Filter list. Make sure all the checkboxes are checked in the panel labeled "Show packages with status" (including the checkbox labeled Keep). You should now see a list of all installed packages in the top-right pane. Click on a package name to select it. In the pane at the bottom right, you should see a description of the package. Other information is available by clicking the tabs labeled Technical Data, Dependencies, and Versions at the top of this pane. (See Figure 5-1.)

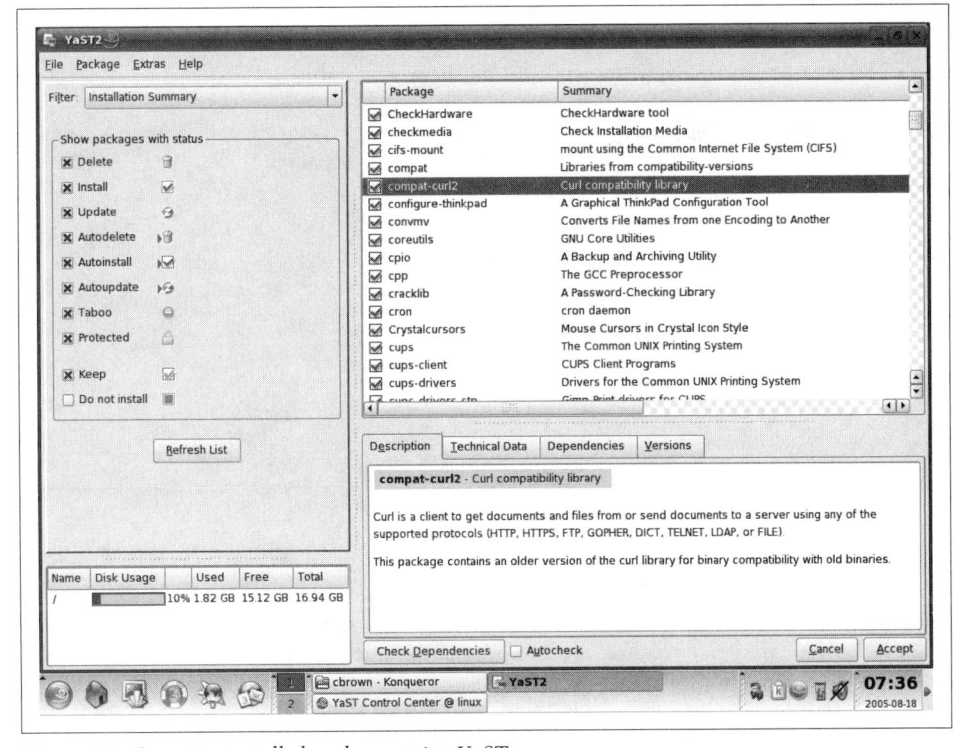

Figure 5-1. Querying installed packages using YaST

How It Works

An RPM file contains a header, followed by a `cpio` archive of the files that make up the package. The header contains meta-information about the package, pre-install and post-install scripts to be run, the digital signature of the package, and other information.

Information about the currently installed packages are held in a series of databases in the directory */var/lib/rpm*. Most of the files in this directory are in Berkeley DB format; this is a format for storing records consisting of key-value pairs with a hashed index for efficient lookup. This format has been around in Unix/Linux for many years. It's a binary format that cannot be viewed directly by programs such as `less`.

What About...

...verifying package integrity? The `--verify` option of `rpm` verifies the integrity of an installed package. This process compares information gleaned from the actual installed files in the package with information about the files taken from the package metadata stored in the rpm database. Among other things, verifying compares the size, MD5 sum, permissions, type, owner, and group of each file. Any discrepancies are displayed.

Each discrepancy shows as a single letter, as shown in Table 5-1.

Table 5-1. Discrepancies reported by rpm --verify

Code	Description
S	Wrong file size
M	Wrong mode (access permissions and file type)
5	Wrong MD5 checksum (contents have been changed)
D	Wrong major/minor device number
L	Wrong link status
U	Wrong owner
G	Wrong group
T	Wrong modification time stamp

Discrepancies in configuration files are inevitable, but discrepancies in binaries might be evidence that your system has been compromised by an attacker.

> If you are interested in a much more thorough change-detection tool, take a look at Tripwire. This utility builds an encrypted snapshot of the key parts of your filesystem and periodically checks the actual filesystem against the snapshot. Tripwire is not part of the SUSE Linux distribution and seems to have recently "gone commercial" (see *http://www.tripwire.com*). Another such tool is AIDE (Advanced Intrusion Detection Environment), available from *http://sourceforge.net/projects/aide*, but also included on the SUSE Linux distribution. You'll see how to use AIDE in Chapter 8.

Here's an example:

```
# rpm --verify tomboy
S.5....T   /usr/bin/tomboy
```

The output here indicates that the file /usr/bin/tomboy (part of the package tomboy) has evidently been tampered with: the file size, MD5 checksum, and last modification time stamp all differ from the values held in the metadata in the RPM database. (OK, officer, I confess. I edited the file on purpose to prove a point. I'd like to ask for 17 other similar offenses to be taken into consideration.)

Verifying the installed files against the package metadata makes sense only if you trust the original package. For a more thorough check, you can also verify the authenticity of the RPM file itself by checking its digital signature; for example:

```
# rpm --checksig xine-lib-1.1.0-2.i586.rpm
xine-lib-1.1.0-2.i586.rpm: sha1 md5 gpg OK
```

A digital signature is essentially an MD5 checksum of the package encrypted with its author's secret key. In recognition of the fact that your brain cells are finite in number, and that you may be reading this after a heavy meal, I will not embark on a theoretical discussion about MD5 or public and private key cryptography. However, you should understand that you can verify a digital signature only if you have the author's public key that corresponds to the secret key he signed it with. Public keys can be added to the RPM database using the `--import` option. An imported public key is carried in a package header, and management of public keys is performed exactly like package management. For example, all currently imported public keys can be displayed using:

```
$ rpm -qa 'gpg-pubkey*'
```

> Verifying the signature of a package put onto a CD by SUSE against a public key also put onto the same CD by SUSE doesn't really count for much. If you don't trust the package, why trust the key? You really need to get the signature and the public key from independent sources for the check to have any real meaning. Verifying packages downloaded from the Internet against a known good public key is a different matter, and can be a useful safeguard against installing packages that have been maliciously tampered with or simply corrupted in transit.

Where to Learn More

There is a useful comparison of Linux package formats at *http://www.kitenet.net/~joey/pkg-comp*. The definitive coverage of RPM is a book called *Maximum RPM* by Ed Bailey (printed by Sams, or available as a free download from *http://www.rpm.org*). Then, of course, there's the manpage for the `rpm` command.

If you're interested in learning a little more about public/private key cryptography, MD5 digests, and digital signatures, take a look at Bob Cromwell's little introduction entitled "Just Enough Cryptography" at *http://www.cromwell-intl.com/security*. If that doesn't interest you, try his collection of photographs of eastern European toilets, on the same site.

5.2   Finding the Packages You Need

Abbe d'Allainval once wrote a play called *An Embarrassment of Riches*. I don't know exactly when he wrote it, but it couldn't have been very recent because he died in 1753. Since then, his phrase has been widely quoted. It is sometimes translated (the original was in French) as "The more alternatives, the more difficult the choice." The vast amount of open source software available for Linux certainly represents an embarrassment of riches. Given the power of the Internet search engines, finding stuff is not hard. Finding stuff that *actually works* can be more of a challenge.

This lab looks at some of the places you can find software for SUSE Linux.

How Do I Do That?

This is not a particularly exciting or inspired thing to say, but the first place to look for additional packages is on the SUSE Linux distribution CDs. The packages you'll find there are, by definition, built for your Linux distribution and will almost certainly work. The YaST package manager offers the easiest way to query the available packages because it knows about all the packages in the distribution. (See Lab 5.3, "Install and Upgrade RPMs," later in this chapter.) Alternatively, you can browse the CDs directly. Each SUSE CD contains a file called *ls-lR.gz*, which is a compressed (gzipped) recursive directory listing of the contents of all the CDs. To make it easier to browse for packages, you can copy this file into your home directory and unzip it:

```
$ cd /media/disk
$ cp ls-lR.gz ~
$ cd ~
$ gunzip ls-lR.gz
```

Now you have a file called *ls-lR* that you can easily search (using grep, for example) to see what packages are available. For example:

```
$ grep amarok ls-lR
-rw-r--r--   3 root root   5813077 Mar 23 19:22 amarok-1.2.2-5.i586.rpm
-rw-r--r--   3 root root     15248 Mar 23 19:22 amarok-xmms-1.2.2-5.i586.rpm
-rw-r--r--   3 root root     13032 Mar 23 19:22 amarok-libvisual-1.2.2-5.i586.rpm
```

> There are other ways you could get this information. For example, you could use zgrep (a version of grep that can peek into compressed files) on the compressed file itself. Also, you could do an actual recursive directory listing of each CD and store the results in your home directory (for example `ls -lR /media`).

You can also find an archive of all the SUSE Linux RPMs at *ftp://ftp.suse.com*. For example, the URL *ftp://ftp.suse.com/pub/suse/i386/9.3/suse* gets you to the official collection of RPMs for SUSE Professional 9.3, and *ftp://ftp.suse.com/pub/suse/i386/10.1/iso* gets you to the ISO CD images for the entire SUSE Linux 10.1 The SUSE FTP site has many mirrors around the world; see *http://www.novell.com/products/suselinux/downloads/ftp/int_mirrors.html* for a list.

The site *http://rpmfind.net* indexes a very large collection of RPMs that are indexed by group (functional category), by Linux distribution, by vendor (author), by creation date, and by name. There is also a very powerful search engine. This is an excellent site, but it seems to be oriented toward RedHat/Fedora rather than SUSE Linux.

There are also many software repositories that can be directly added into YaST as installation sources (see Lab 5.3, "Install and Upgrade RPMs," later in this chapter). The article at *http://www.opensuse.org/Additional_YaST_Package_Repositories* has (at the time of this writing) a list of about 15 such repositories. The Packman repository, in particular, is known for its extensive multimedia support. Also check the article at *http://susewiki.org/index.php?title=Finding_RPMs*, which has a large list of YaST repositories.

The site *http://sourceforge.net* hosts a vast number of open source projects (more than 100,000). On the home page, click on the Software Map tab to drill down into the available projects by topic. Most of the software available here is source code in various formats, including *.zip* files and compressed *tarballs* (archives created by the tar command). Not all of it is for Linux. For $39 a year, you can subscribe to the site and get additional services.

Each of these sites offers an arrestingly large number of files for download. How do you know when you've found what you're looking for? In the case of a binary RPM, you'll be looking for a filename of the form *foobar-3.2-6.i586.rpm*. Here, *foobar* is the name of the package, *3.2* is the version number, *6* is the build number, and *i586* is the processor (meaning a Pentium or equivalent). A package built for an earlier processor architecture, such as i386, should also work fine (i386 is a sort of "lowest common denominator" that should run on all Intel processors). Sometimes you'll see a string included in the name that identifies the Linux distribution for which the package was built; for example, the "mdk" in *chkconfig-1.3.13-3mdk.i586.rpm* signifies a package built for the Mandrake (now Mandriva) distribution, but most names do not include this. A few packages, including some documentation-only packages, are inherently independent of both the architecture and the distribution and may have names ending in *.noarch.rpm*.

In the case of a source RPM, you'll be looking for a name of the form *foobar-3.2-6.src.rpm*. I talk more about installing from source RPMs in Lab 5.8, "Compile and Install Source Code," later in this chapter.

You will not always find an RPM that exactly matches the version of SUSE Linux that you're running, and you may find yourself asking, "Is the version I've found good enough?" There is no definitive, general answer to this. One thing's for sure—a binary RPM compiled for the wrong processor architecture will not work. So, for example, an RPM such as *apache-1.3.27-1.6.2.sparc.rpm* is built for the SPARC architecture and will not work on a platform based on the Intel processor family. Because most RPMs are for PCs built around Intel processors (or compatible CPUs from other manufacturers such as AMD and Transmeta), this doesn't really filter much out.

At the other end of the spectrum, a package built for, say, SUSE Linux 10.0 has a good chance of working on version 10.1, though this will be affected by the package's dependencies. There is a middle ground of compatibility questions that are harder to decide. Will a package built for RedHat Linux work on SUSE? Probably not, or at least not without some tinkering after the installation. The problem with cross-distribution compatibility lies not so much in differences in the executable code (there is a standard called the Linux Standards Base (LSB), which—if followed—should ensure that a binary compiled for RedHat will run on SUSE) as in the differences between the administrative commands used in the pre-install and post-install scripts in the package, in the placement and syntax of configuration files, and in the list of dependent packages required. For example, if you're installing a service, the install script will likely put the startup script for the service in the folder */etc/init.d*. It will then add a number of symbolic links to determine which run levels the service will start up in. I discuss the whole business of boot-time service startup in Chapter 6, but for now, the point is that the way these links are managed is quite different in the RedHat and SUSE distributions. In general, installing a RedHat RPM onto a SUSE system may well put things like binaries and libraries in the right places but is likely to mess up on the rest of the configuration. Having said that, there are some RPMs that just drop a couple of binaries, libraries, or documentation files into place and don't require further configuration. Such RPMs will probably work across different Linux platforms.

If you can't find an RPM for the package that looks like it will work on SUSE Linux, consider downloading the source code and building the program from that. It usually isn't very difficult. Lab 5.8, "Compile and Install Source Code," shows how to do it. Source code is usually distributed as a tarball and will have a name like *foobar-3.2.tar.gz* or *foobar-3.2.tar.bz2*. (The *.gz* and *.bz2* extensions denote different types of compression, discussed in the same lab later in this chapter.)

Quite a lot of the major packages have their own web sites. Examples of such sites include *http://www.gimp.org*, *http://www.apache.org*, *http://www.samba.org*, and *http://www.scribus.org.uk*. Developer sites like these are more likely to offer source code rather than binary RPMs. Another good place to go is *http://freshmeat.net*, especially for the very latest releases.

As you browse web sites that carry Linux software, pay some attention to the currency of the site. Some sites are extremely active and enthusiastically maintained; others are derelict. It is sometimes hard to tell the difference—the derelict sites do not actually have cobwebs festooned on the hyperlinks or grass growing out of the cracks in the brickwork—but you can often find the signs. Some pages announce their "last updated" time at the bottom of the page. If you're using Firefox as your browser, selecting Page Info from the Tools menu will show you the "last modified" time stamp of the page. If most of the discussion on the site concerns the relative merits of the mangonel and trebuchet, or if the most recent reference to Linux you can find is to RedHat version 6.0, or if all the discussion is about the latest and greatest of the upcoming 2.2 kernel, be afraid. Be very afraid. Well, no, don't be very afraid—that would be silly—but be aware that the site may not be actively maintained anymore. The presence of a few ancient pages on the site does not, by itself, indicate that the entire site is unmaintained, but the absence of any recent pages is cause for concern. There are some packages that haven't changed for five years or more but that are still perfectly serviceable.

Now that you've found some cool software, see Lab 5.3, "Install and Upgrade RPMs" and Lab 5.8, "Compile and Install Source Code" to find out how to install it.

What About...

...magazine cover discs? You can find huge amounts of software on the cover discs of some of the Linux magazines. The UK-published magazine *Linux Format*, for example, carries a DVD full of stuff every month.

> Whenever I'm teaching or charging money for consultancy, I'm always a little embarrassed to confess that I picked up such-and-such a piece of software from the cover disc of a magazine I bought at a newsagent. It seems so unprofessional, somehow. The truth is that I find it a really convenient source of new software.

Where to Learn More

There are countless other sites where you can learn about software for Linux. Try *http://freshmeat.net*, which features newly released packages and updates, or the Linux Software Map at *http://www.boutell.com/lsm*.

5.3 Install and Upgrade RPMs

When you initially install SUSE Linux, you get the opportunity to choose which packages you want to include. Realistically, though, if you're new to Linux, you will probably have little idea at that stage of what you want to install beyond the vague knowledge that, for example, "I want to install a KDE desktop system." Fear not...it is easy to install additional packages at a later stage. And, of course, one of the joys of using an open system like Linux is that there are literally thousands of third-party packages out there waiting to be installed and explored. This lab shows you how to install new software in the form of RPM packages.

How Do I Do That?

From the command line, the simplest thing is to use `rpm -i`. For example:

```
# cd /media/SU100_001/suse/i586
# rpm -i autotrace-0.31.1-369.i586.rpm
```

In many cases, that's all there is to it! Note that the name SU100_001 is specific to this example. Your mileage may vary.

Using the `-i` option, the `rpm` command will refuse to install a package that's already installed. There's also the `-U` (upgrade) option, which will automatically remove the previous version of the package before installing the new one. If there is no existing version of the package, `-U` behaves like `-i`. Some users prefer to use `-U` all the time and ignore `-i`. The `-v` and `-h` options are also useful in conjunction with `-i` or `-U`, as they provide a simple progress report so that you're not left wondering whether the system has crashed if you're installing a large RPM. Putting these together, you may prefer to use a command such as:

```
# rpm -Uvh autotrace-0.31.1-369.i586.rpm
```

to install a package.

The `rpm` tool will check that all the dependencies required by the package are present; if they are not, it will report the error and abandon the installation. For example:

```
$ rpm -i ImageMagick-devel-6.1.8-6.i586.rpm
error: Failed dependencies:
        libtiff-devel is needed by ImageMagick-devel-6.1.8-6
        libjpeg-devel is needed by ImageMagick-devel-6.1.8-6
        liblcms-devel is needed by ImageMagick-devel-6.1.8-6
```

It's now left up to you to locate the missing packages. In this case, it turns out to be easy because they are on the SUSE DVD in the same directory, so you can just install them all in one command like this:

```
$ rpm -i ImageMagick-devel-6.1.8-6.i586.rpm libtiff-devel-3.7.1-7.i586.rpm \
    libjpeg-devel-6.2.0-4.i586.rpm liblcms-devel-1.14-3.i586.rpm
```

From this example, you'll see that you don't need to put the dependencies first in the argument list. `rpm` is smart enough to check dependencies on the assumption that all the specified RPMs have been installed.

If you would simply like to check for dependencies without actually installing anything, add the `--test` option:

```
$ rpm -i --test ImageMagick-devel-6.1.8-6.i586.rpm
```

It is possible to turn off dependency checking with the --nodeps option. For example:

```
$ rpm -i --nodeps ImageMagick-devel-6.1.8-6.i586.rpm
```

Do not do this without a good reason, however, because it's almost certain that the package won't work without the dependencies. A couple of possible "good reasons" come to mind. First, you might be intending to download and install the other packages at a later stage; second, you might have installed the required libraries from source, so that they are not in the RPM database.

The whole business of package dependencies and the problems of resolving missing dependencies can be a tricky one (sometimes known as "dependency hell"). You can explicitly check a package's dependencies (the things that must be present for the package to work) with the --requires flag. The following example has been edited:

```
$ rpm -q --requires net-snmp
insserv
sed
devs
fillup
coreutils
/sbin/chkconfig
... edited ...
/bin/sh
/usr/bin/perl
libbz2.so.1
libc.so.6
libc.so.6(GLIBC_2.0)
... edited ...
```

You can also query dependencies of an uninstalled packages by adding the -p flag and specifying the RPM filename:

```
$ rpm -qp --requires autotrace-0.31.1-369.i586.rpm
```

However, this is where the rpm tool starts to run out of steam. The dependencies are listed as a set of named *capabilities* that must be present. Sometimes the name of the capability is the same as the name of the package that provides it. In the previous list, for example, inserv and sed are both package names. Sometimes the name of the capability is the name of a file, such as */sbin/chkconfig* in the example. Sometimes the name of the capability is a more descriptive string. Generally speaking, what you really need to know is the name of the package you must install to resolve the dependencies—that is, the package that actually provides the missing capabilities. It is possible to query the RPM database (the installed packages) to find out which package provides a specific named capability; for example:

```
$ rpm -q --whatprovides /sbin/chkconfig
aaa_base-9.3-9.2
```

However, it is not possible to scan the *uninstalled* packages in this way. Sometimes, it requires a certain amount of intelligence and guesswork on the part of the user to figure out what needs to be installed.

> As you'll see later in this chapter, there are smarter package managers (yum, for example) that address some of the shortcomings of rpm. You might take a look at APT—the Advanced Packaging Tool—which was originally written for Debian Linux but is also available for SUSE. The Debian supporters claim that APT is what RPM would like to be when it grows up.

You can do some of these same things (and more) using the YaST Package Manager. Launch the package manager from YaST's main screen by clicking Software in the left pane, then Software Management in the right pane.

In addition to providing a more comfortable user interface for installing packages, YaST offers a couple of other advantages over direct use of rpm. First, it knows which CD each package is on, so you don't have to hunt around. Second, it will (if asked) resolve missing package dependencies automatically. In contrast, the rpm tool reports dependencies but leaves you to sort them out for yourself. With YaST you can also add additional sources from the Internet, and install those as if they were on the local CD.

As discussed in Lab 5.1, "Find Out What's Installed," earlier in this chapter, the YaST package manager screen allows you to choose how you want to view and select packages through the Filter drop-down list in the top left corner of the screen. The possible filter settings are:

Selections
: This provides a list of about 25 possible software categories, such as Games, Multimedia, and Mobile Computing. This is a rather coarse-grained selection, but in reality is just the right level of detail for people who are new to Linux.

Package Groups
: This provides a hierarchical view of the available packages via a tree-view control.

Languages
: This provides a view of the language-specific packages. (By "language" here, I mean French or Spanish or German, not Java or Fortran or Python.)

Search
: This view provides a text field into which you can type a partial package name to search on. This view is useful if you have some idea what the package is called.

Installation Summary
: This view shows what will happen to each package when you click Accept—which packages will be installed, which will be deleted, which will be kept, and so on. To see just a list of what's currently installed, uncheck all the checkboxes except Keep.

Installation Sources
> This filter, new in SUSE Linux 10.1, allows you to specify explicitly which installation sources you want to view. If you select this filter, a drop-down list labeled "Secondary Filter" appears, allowing you to select one of the filters listed above in conjunction with this installation source.

Whichever filter view you select, you will get to see a list of the relevant packages in the pane at the top right of the package management screen. At the left of each listed item (see Figure 5-2) is a checkbox. An empty checkbox indicates that the package is not installed; a checkmark shows that it is. To select a package for installation, click in the checkbox. You can select as many packages as you want in this way.

When you're done selecting packages, click Accept. YaST will now perform a dependency check. Unlike rpm, however, which complains at you and gives up if there are unresolved dependencies, YaST automatically figures out which packages need to be installed to provide the missing capabilities and adds them to the list. If appropriate, it will bring up a dialog listing the extra packages that it's proposing to install. You can see an example of this in Figure 5-2, where I have searched for the package ImageMagick-devel by name and selected it for installation. You will see that YaST is reporting the same set of dependencies that rpm did (libtiff-devel, libjpeg-devel, and liblcms-devel).

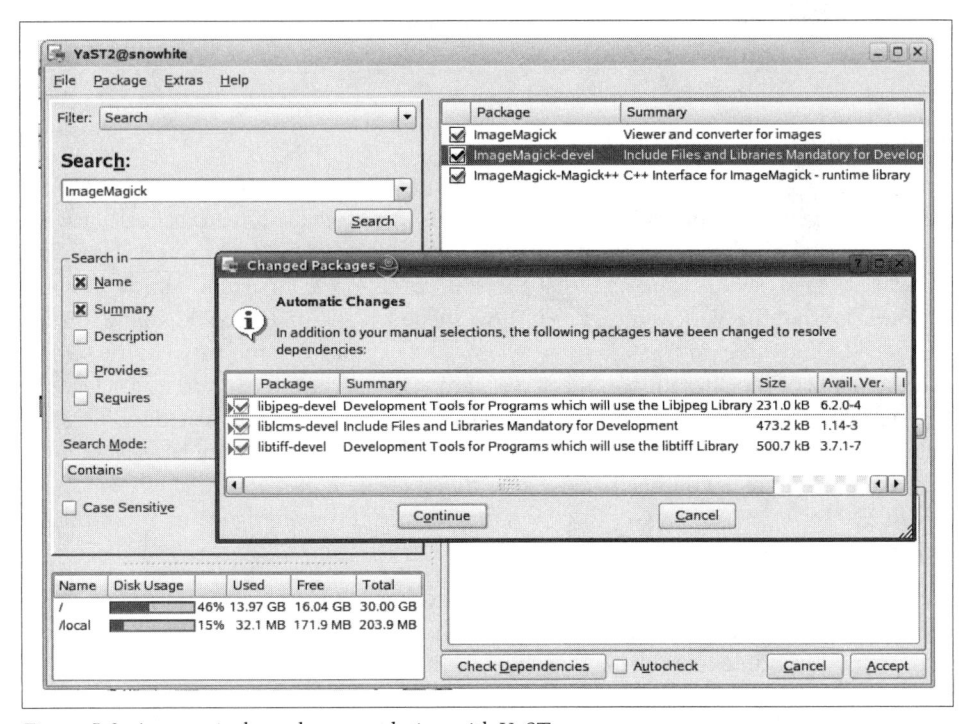

Figure 5-2. Automatic dependency resolution with YaST

Assuming that you accept YaST's judgment on the matter, click Continue. YaST prompts you for the CDs that it needs, and provides a progress bar as the installation proceeds.

Let's return briefly to the Search filter of the YaST Package Manager. Using this filter, you can perform text searches under five headings that relate to five different types of information included in the package metadata:

- Name
- Summary
- Description
- Provides
- Requires

You can see these headings in Figure 5-2. The final two searches (Provides and Requires) are based on capability names. You'll see from this that the YaST package manager is capable of searching the entire package database (not just the installed packages) for packages that provide a specific capability. This is what allows YaST to resolve dependency problems automatically, and is something that you can't do with the command-line rpm tool. (By the way, there is a tool called y2pmsh, which provides a command-line equivalent to the YaST package manager. This is intended as a debugging and development tool; there is probably little reason why the average user would want to use this.)

What About...

...installing from Internet archives? You can easily add installation sources to YaST to locate packages from Internet archives. From the YaST main screen, select Software from the panel on the left, then Installation Source from the panel on the right. The Software Source Media screen will list the sources that YaST currently knows about. Chances are that this will, at minimum, show the local CD drive. To add a new source, you need to know the protocol to use (probably FTP or HTTP), the name of the server, and the name of the directory on the server. From this screen, click Add and select the appropriate protocol from the drop-down list. Here's how to add an installation source called packman, accessible via HTTP at *packman.iu-bremen.de*. This site has several mirrors, which you are encouraged to use. See *ftp://packman.links2linux.de/pub/packman/ MIRRORS* for a list. Once you've picked a site, just fill in the fields of the form, as shown in Figure 5-3.

YaST will verify the installation source before adding it to the list. You can enable or disable the individual installation sources in the list. Be aware that YaST's Software Management module may be slow to start up if you have busy FTP servers listed in your installation sources. SUSE Linux 10.1 also supports HTTPS (secure HTTP) as a download protocol.

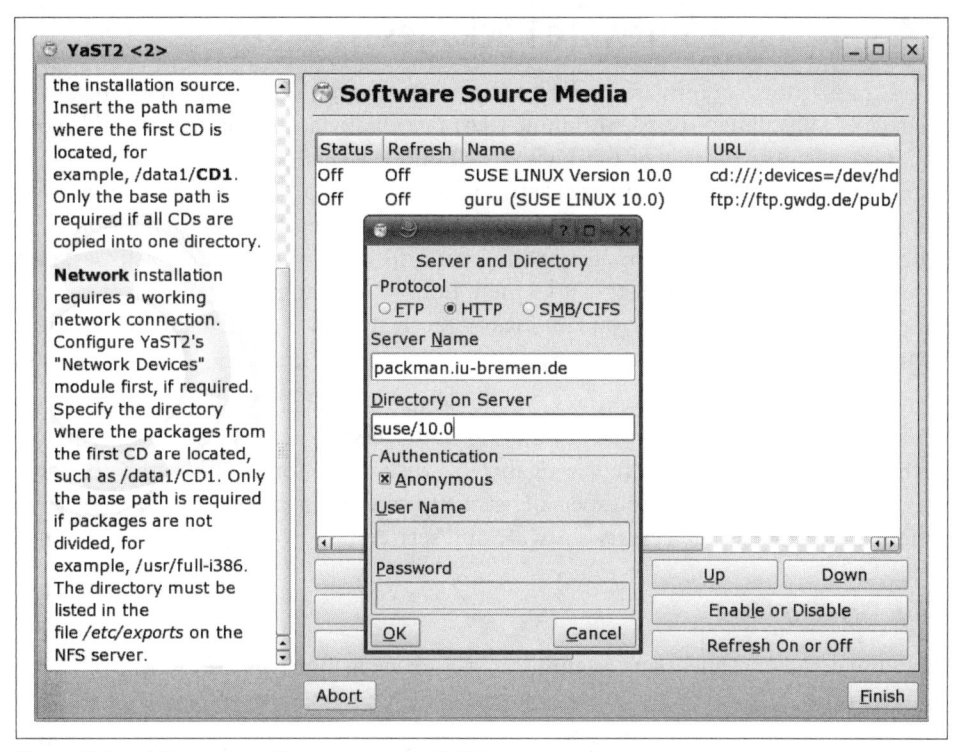

Figure 5-3. Adding an installation source to YaST

From the command line, the rpm tool can take an FTP or HTTP URL instead of a package filename and can perform as an anonymous FTP or HTTP client to download the package. For example, to download and install a package from SUSE's FTP server:

```
$ rpm -i ftp://ftp.suse.com/pub/suse/i386/9.3/suse/i586/abiword-2.2.4-3.i586.rpm
```

It's also possible to make an explicit (nonanonymous) login to an FTP server with a URL syntax such as:

```
$ rpm -i ftp://USER:PASSWORD@HOST/path/to/something.rpm
```

Where to Learn More

The book *Maximum RPM* by Ed Bailey, available from Sams or as a free download (follow the links at *http://www.rpm.org*), is rather old (1997) but still probably the most thorough and systematic treatment of RPM. There is a description of the YaST Package Manager in Chapter 2 of the SUSE Reference Manual. Then, of course, there's always the manual page for the rpm command.

5.4 Remove Software Packages

I find that removing software packages is a far less common activity than installing them. After installing, say, SUSE Linux 10.0, I gradually accumulate more and more packages installed on top of the base distribution. Usually, this process continues until I decide to upgrade to a later distribution. There is an analogy here with moving into a new house. Once you've "moved in" to one particular distribution, you proceed to make it your own: customizing your desktop, adding new packages, and so on, until the time comes to find a new house. At that point you throw all the excess baggage away so that you can make a fresh start in your new life in your new home.

I can think of two reasons why you might want to explicitly delete software from your machine. The first is if you're running out of disk space. (This is less common in these days when you can buy a gigabyte of disk space for less than the cost of a beer.) The second is if you're especially security-conscious and want to *harden* your system by removing unnecessary software and services.

How Do I Do That?

From the command line, you can uninstall a package using rpm -e. For example:

```
# rpm -e xosview
```

Dependency checking kicks in for package removal as well as for package installation. The xosview package is easy to remove, because nothing is dependent on it. It is at the end of the food chain—nothing dies of starvation if xosview is removed. In many other cases, life is not so simple. In this next example, I have chosen the m4 package, more or less at random, for removal. (Of course I'm sure that you've got more sense than to delete packages at random just for the fun of it.)

```
# rpm -e m4
error: Failed dependencies:
        m4 = 1.4.2 is needed by (installed) autoconf-2.59-80
        m4 is needed by (installed) bison-1.875-55
        /usr/bin/m4 is needed by (installed) lsb-2.0-8
```

The rpm tool refuses to remove the package because other installed packages depend on it. It's possible (but not recommended) to explicitly disable the dependency check with the --nodeps flag:

```
# rpm -e --nodeps m4
```

Of course, you can do the same things using the YaST package manager. To delete a specific named package, select the Search filter and type in the name of the package, such as m4. The YaST package manager will show you the (one and only) matching package in the top-right pane. By clicking in the checkbox to the left of the package listing, you can select the desired action to perform on the package—to keep it, to update it, or to delete it. Try marking the package for deletion. To confirm the action, click Accept. YaST will now check the dependencies and report essentially the same set of problems that rpm reported from the command line (see Figure 5-4).

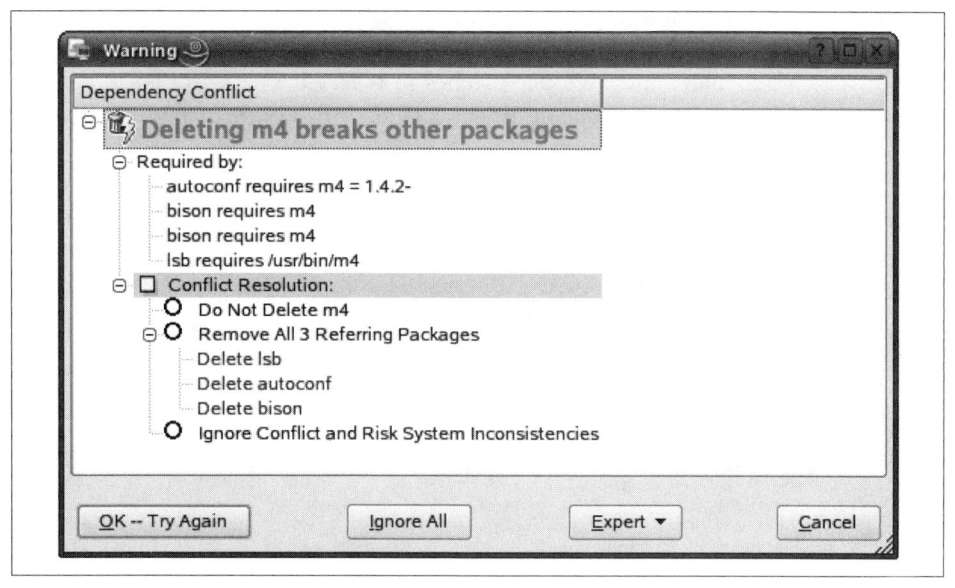

Figure 5-4. YaST dependency checks for package removal

From the figure you can see that YaST also proposes three ways forward: abandon your plans to delete the m4 package, delete m4 and all the referring packages, or just delete m4 and hope for the best.

5.5 Perform an Online Update

SUSE maintains web servers that contain patches and updates for the various SUSE Linux products. These servers are mirrored at various sites around the world, providing an effective way to obtain the latest patches and updates. In particular, it helps to ensure that you are not running versions of software that have known security vulnerabilities. The YaST module that interacts with this service is call YaST Online Update (YOU).

How Do I Do That?

From the main YaST screen, select Software from the left pane, then Online Update from the right pane. On the main Online Update screen, choose an FTP server from the drop-down list. You can also set up your own update server (perhaps on the corporate network) and add it to the list by clicking on New Server. It is also possible to supply updates on CD or DVD.

Once you've selected an update source, click Next. YaST will download a list of updates from the server and display them. In Figure 5-5, the list on the left shows the available patches and their sizes. Security-related patches are shown in red, recommended patches in blue, and optional patches in black. If you select an item from this list, a description of the patch and its purpose is shown in the pane below, and a list of the packages that make up the patch is shown in the pane on the right (a patch can include several packages—you must install all the packages in the patch). This screen is really just the YaST Package Manager screen that you have seen in other labs.

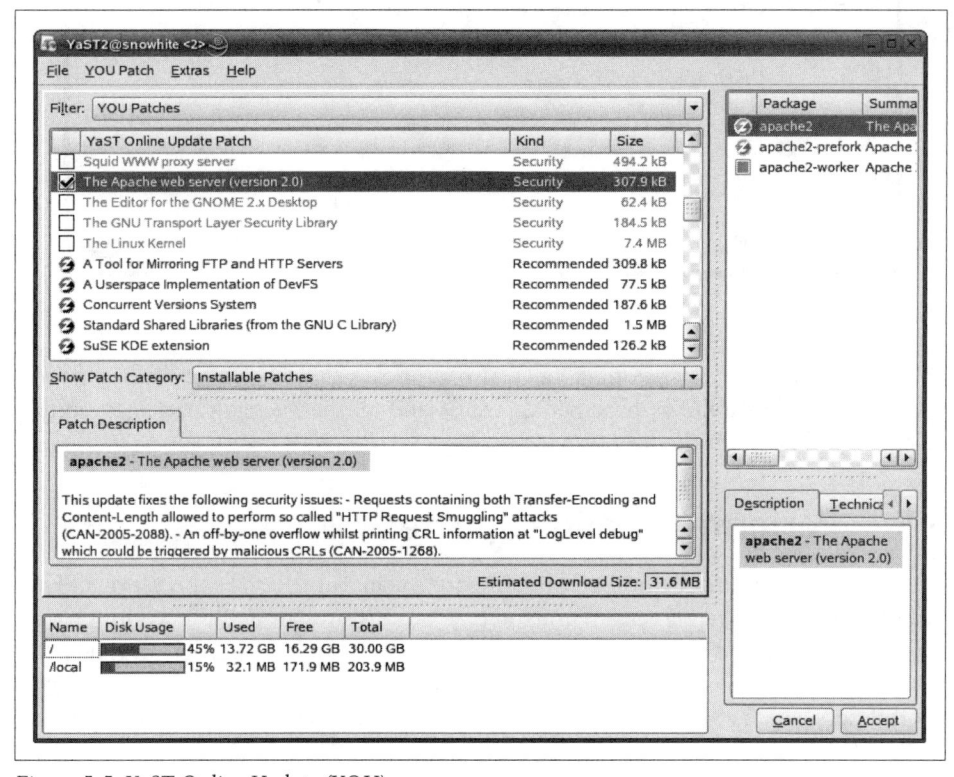

Figure 5-5. YaST Online Update (YOU)

> Use of the term *patch* has become somewhat confused within SUSE. In traditional Unix parlance, a patch is a set of *deltas* (changes from the original or prior version) or *diffs* that can be applied to a file to create a later version of the file. Patches were popular in the BB (Before Broadband) era, as they saved lots of time compared with downloading the entire file. In the current context, a patch just means a related collection of package updates. Just to make life more confusing, there are such things as patch RPMs, which are patches in the original sense, so that downloading an update to (say) the kernel sources downloads only a very small amount of data.

To select just a couple of patches for installation, go to the YOU Patch menu, select All In This List, then select Do Not Install. Now select individual patches for installation by ticking the checkbox to the left of the package. The icons used to indicate the status of the patch are not obvious (and two of them look identical to me). They are shown in Figure 5-6.

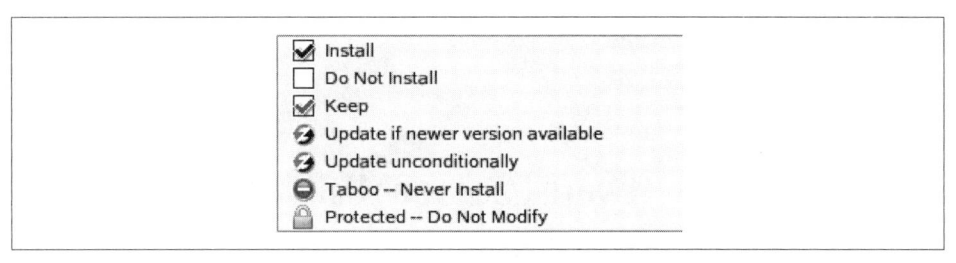

Figure 5-6. Patch status icons

With all desired patches selected, click Accept. The Patch Download and Installation screen appears. Here, a log of the actions is displayed, with progress bars for the current package and the entire upgrade. Patch download and installation can be slow. Some patches may display a message describing an action that should be taken to make the patch "kick in" (restarting a daemon, for example). Once the process is complete, the log will report the total number of patches installed. Click Finish to complete the process. YaST will run the SUSEConfig scripts to propagate any changes into the rest of the system configuration.

What About...

...doing updates automatically? An application called SUSEWatcher polls for new updates. SUSEWatcher is normally configured to start automatically when you log in and appears as a green "smiley gecko" icon in the applet tray within the main panel. SUSEWatcher can be configured to check for updates periodically, or you can initiate a manual check by clicking on the gecko icon in the applet tray and then clicking "Check for Updates" in the SUSEWatcher window. The check usually takes several minutes to complete. If there are updates available, the smiley gecko icon turns into a red, shiny circle. Both icons are shown in Figure 5-7. Clicking Start Online Update in the SUSEWatcher window launches the YaST Online Update module that you've just seen.

Figure 5-7. The smiley gecko and the red circle

You can also configure automatic updates by clicking the Configure Fully Automatic Update button on the main YaST Online Update screen. From here, you can configure a daily or weekly check for updates.

What About ...

...doing updates from the command line? The command online_update can be used as an alternative to Yast Online Update. Sadly, it doesn't seem to have a manual page, but:

```
$ online_update --help
```

might be sufficient to get you started.

5.6 Manage Software Packages Using ZENWorks

Novell has traditionally supported two solutions for package management and online package updates: there was the YaST package manager, which came from SUSE, and there was Red Carpet, which came from Ximian. Other package repository "standards" are in use, including YUM and Open Carpet. In SUSE 10.1, the YaST package manager (described elsewhere in this chapter) remains. The original Red Carpet client, which was shipped with Novell Linux Desktop, is not included in current SUSE Linux distributions. With SUSE 10.1, Novell has provided a new package manager resolver library called libzypp. The new library handles YUM metadata, YaST sources (via FTP, HTTP, NFS, or SMB), and also Zenworks, Open Carpet, and Red Carpet Enterprise (RCE) repositories. Along with libzypp comes a command-line tool called rug and three graphical tools called zen-installer, zen-updater, and zen-remover, together with the underlying zmd daemon. It is these tools that I'll be looking at in this lab.

How Do I Do That?

It takes a little time to get your head around rug due to its large number of subcommands. Most of the command names have a long form, such as file-list, and a short form, usually two letters, such as fl. Table 5-2 lists some of these commands. It is not a complete list, and you should consult the manpage for a full description.

Table 5-2. Important rug subcommands

Command	Short form	Description
catalogs	ca	List the catalogs available for the services you have added.
subscribe	sub	Subscribe to the specified catalog.
unsubscribe	unsub	Unsubscribe from a specified catalog.
packages	pa	List the packages in a specified catalog (default is all catalogs).
list-updates	lu	List updates available in a specified catalog.
install	in	Install the specified package (and any dependencies).
remove	rm	Remove the specified package.
info	if	Display full RPM info for the specified package.
file-list	fl	List the files within a package.
search	se	Search for packages matching a specified pattern.
update	up	Download and install updates for a specified catalog (default is all catalogs).
service-add	sa	Adds the specified service (you need to provide the URL of a management server).

You should begin by defining one or more services (repositories) that rug knows about. The command to do this is of the form:

```
# rug sa --type=service-type URI service-name
```

A number of service types are supported; the subcommand service-types provides a list:

```
# rug service-types

Alias     | Name     | Description
----------+----------+-------------------------------------------
yum       | YUM      | A service type for YUM servers
zypp      | ZYPP     | A service type for ZYPP installation source
nu        | NU       | A service type for Novell Update servers
rce       | RCE      | A service type for RCE servers
zenworks  | ZENworks | A service type for Novell ZENworks servers
mount     | Mount    | Mount a directory of RPMs
```

ZYPP is, apparently, the new name for a YaST repository. RCE refers to Open Carpet or Red Carpet Enterprise repositories, also sometimes referred to as ZENWorks Linux Management 6. ZENWorks refers to ZENWorks Linux Management 7, and Mount means a repository mounted directly into the filesystem. (With all this renaming, it is hard to avoid the suspicion of a deliberate plot to confuse everyone!)

Here I add the SUSE factory repository. It is rather large, and on my system it took the best part of half an hour to download and process the metadata for this repository:

```
# rug sa --type=yum http://ftp.gwdg.de/pub/opensuse/distribution/SL-OSS-factory/inst-source/suse factory
```

```
Adding YUM service http://ftp.gwdg.de/pub/opensuse/distribution/SL-OSS-factory/inst-
source/suse...
                                                                              100%

Successfully added service 'ftp://ftp.gwdg.de/pub/suse/i386/10.1/inst-source-extra/
suse'
```

The subcommand service-list lists all the services that rug currently knows about. In this example, I have added four services:

```
# rug service-list

# | Status | Type | Name      | URI
--+--------+------+-----------+-------------------------------------------------
1 | Active | YUM  | factory   | http://ftp.gwdg.de/pub/opensuse/distribution/...
2 | Active | YUM  | factory-e | ftp://ftp.gwdg.de/pub/suse/i386/10.1/inst-sou...
3 | Active | ZYPP | zypp      | ftp://ftp.gwdg.de/pub/suse/i386/10.1/SUSE-Lin...
4 | Active | YUM  | packman   | http://packman.iu-bremen.de/suse/10.0
```

Each repository publishes one or more *catalogs*. A catalog is a collection of related packages. You need to explicitly subscribe to the catalogs you want to receive software from. The subcommand catalogs lists all catalogs available for the services you have added, and shows which catalogs you are currently subscribed to:

```
# rug catalogs

Sub'd? | Name         | Service
-------+--------------+----------
Yes    | factory-e    | factory-e
Yes    | Zypp service | zypp
       | packman      | packman
Yes    | factory      | factory
```

The subscribe subcommand subscribes to one or more catalogs. Each specified catalog must be available from one of the services you have added.

```
# rug sub packman
Subscribed to 'packman'
```

Alternatively:

```
# rug sub -a
```

subscribes to all available catalogs.

Now that you have defined some services and subscribed to some catalogs, you can query and install the available packages. The packages subcommand shows all the packages in a given catalog (or, by default, in all catalogs). The following example shows only the beginning of a rather long list:

```
# rug packages

S | Bundle | Name                  | Version         | Arch
--+--------+-----------------------+-----------------+-------
i |        | 3ddiag                | 0.729-7         | i586
v |        | 3ddiag                | 0.731-2         | i586
```

```
|               | 3ddiag-debuginfo | 0.731-2 | i586
|               | 3dto3d           | 3.5-28  | i586
```

The search subcommand shows all packages that match a specified pattern:

```
# rug search yum

S | Catalog       | Bundle | Name           | Version  | Arch
--+---------------+--------+----------------+----------+-------
  | Zypp service  |        | kyum           | 0.7.5-10 | i586
  | factory       |        | kyum           | 0.7.5-11 | i586
  | factory       |        | kyum-debuginfo | 0.7.5-11 | i586
  | Zypp service  |        | yum            | 2.4.2-6  | i586
  | factory       |        | yum            | 2.4.2-7  | i586
  | Zypp service  |        | yumex          | 0.44.1-6 | noarch
  | factory       |        | yumex          | 0.44.1-7 | noarch
  | factory       |        | yum-utils      | 0.3.1-8  | noarch
  | Zypp service  |        | yum-utils      | 0.3.1-7  | noarch
```

The list-updates subcommand lists all available package updates in all the channels that you have subscribed to. Again, this example shows only the beginning of a very long list:

```
# rug list-updates

S | Catalog | Bundle | Name          | Version    | Arch
--+---------+--------+---------------+------------+-------
v | factory |        | 3ddiag        | 0.731-2    | i586
v | factory |        | 855resolution | 0.4-12     | i586
v | factory |        | a2ps          | 4.13-1068  | i586
v | factory |        | aaa_base      | 10.1-10    | i586
```

The info subcommand queries the RPM metadata for a specified package:

```
# rug info kyum
Catalog: http://ftp.gwdg.de/pub/opensuse/distribution/SL-OSS-factory/inst-source/suse
Name: kyum
Version: 0.7.5-11
Arch: i586
Installed: No
Status: up-to-date
Installed Size: 0
Summary: Graphical User Front-End (GUI) for yum
Description: KYum is a graphical user front-end (GUI) for yum. You can use it to
 modify your repository files and to control the most common operations of yum
```

At last, we get to a command that actually does something useful! The install subcommand installs one or more packages. You can simply specify the package name or use the notation *catalog:packagename* to install a package from a specific catalog. rug will automatically detect and resolve any dependencies in the package you have asked to install, using all available catalogs. Here's an example in which rug decides to install five additional dependencies:

```
# rug install yum-utils
Resolving Dependencies...
```

```
   The following packages will be installed:
     yum-utils 0.3.1-8 (http://ftp.gwdg.de/.../SL-OSS-factory/inst-source/suse)
     libxml2-python 2.6.23-9 (http://ftp.gwdg.de/.../inst-source/suse)
     libxml2-python-2.6.23-9.i586[factory] needed by yum-2.4.2-7.i586[factory]

     python-sqlite 1.1.6-11 (http://ftp.gwdg.de/.../SL-OSS-factory/inst-source/suse)
     python-sqlite-1.1.6-11.i586[factory] needed by yum-2.4.2-7.i586[factory]

     yum 2.4.2-7 (http://ftp.gwdg.de/.../SL-OSS-factory/inst-source/suse)
     yum-2.4.2-7.i586[factory] needed by yum-utils-0.3.1-8.noarch[factory]

     python-urlgrabber 2.9.7-9 (http://ftp.gwdg.de/.../SL-OSS-factory/inst-source/suse)
     python-urlgrabber-2.9.7-9.i586[factory] needed by yum-2.4.2-7.i586[factory]

     python-elementtree 1.2.6-12 (http://ftp.gwdg.de/.../suse)
     python-elementtree-1.2.6-12.i586[factory] needed by yum-2.4.2-7.i586[factory]

     rpm-python 4.4.2-31 (http://ftp.gwdg.de/.../SL-OSS-factory/inst-source/suse)
     rpm-python-4.4.2-31.i586[factory] needed by yum-2.4.2-7.i586[factory]

   Proceed with transaction? (y/N) y

   Downloading Packages...   100%, 24.0 KB/s

   Transaction...            100%

   Transaction Finished
```

What About...

...using a graphical user interface? There is, at the present time, no YaST module to provide functionality equivalent to rug. In fact, I suspect that there never will be. Novell seems to be moving towards a Mono-based implementation of these tools that would, presumably, be difficult to integrate into YaST. Currently, there are three separate graphical tools called zen-installer, zen-updater, and zen-remover. Each presents a similar user interface. Figure 5-8 shows a screenshot of zen-installer. The tool presents a list of software available for installation. Select the packages you want and click Install. Click Configure to add new services or catalogs; the screenshot shows the services that I have added. Click on Add Service to add a new service; this is equivalent to running:

```
# rug sa server_url
```

at the command line. Click on the Catalogs tab to display a list of catalogs; checkboxes allow you to subscribe or unsubscribe from each catalog.

The program zen-updater shows available package updates and presents a similar interface, shown in Figure 5-9. When the tool is started, it initially installs an icon in the system tray to indicate whether updates are available. This tool effectively replaces the SUSEWatcher tool described in Lab 5.5, "Perform an Online Update."

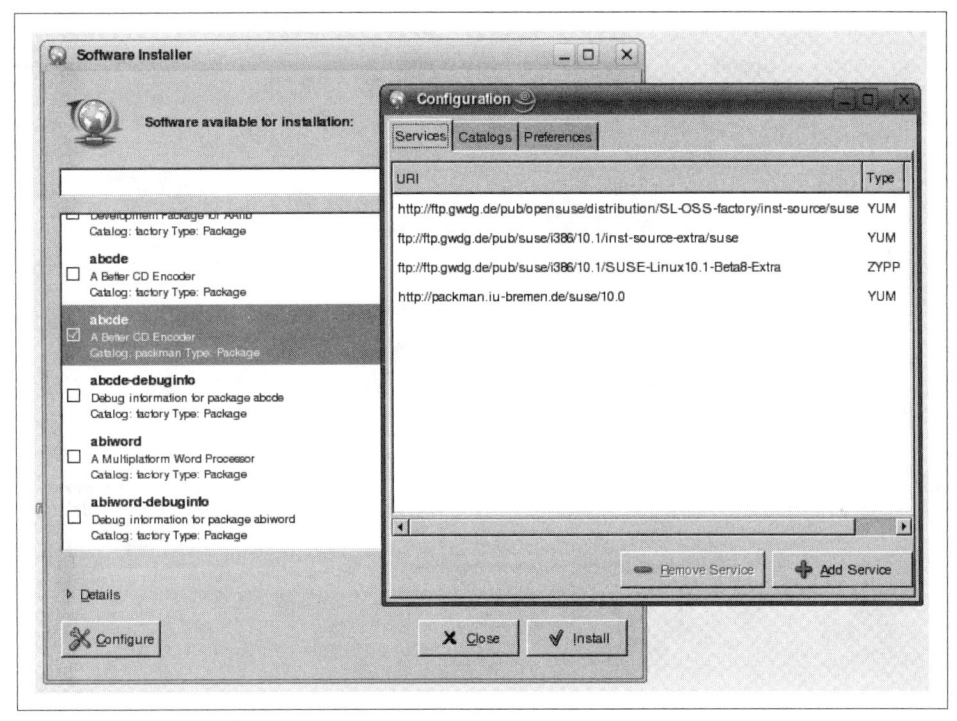

Figure 5-8. ZEN Installer

How It Works

The rug command-line tool and the graphical tools zen-installer and zen-updater talk to zmd, the ZENworks Linux management daemon. You can verify that the daemon is listening like this:

```
# rug ping
ZMD 7.1.1, Copyright (C) 2005 Novell, Inc.
Started at 03/23/2006 15:40:37 (uptime: 0 days, 2 hours, 2 minutes)
RSS size: 54948
Network Connected: Yes

OS Target: SUSE Linux 10.1 (i586)

Module Name         | Description
--------------------+----------------------------------------
NetworkManager      | NetworkManager support
Package Management  | Package Management module for Linux
ZENworks Server     | SOAP methods used by a ZENworks server
XML-RPC interface   | Export ZMD public interfaces over XML-RPC
```

You can start, stop, and restart this daemon like any other, with the commands:

```
# rczmd start
# rczmd stop
# rczmd restart
```

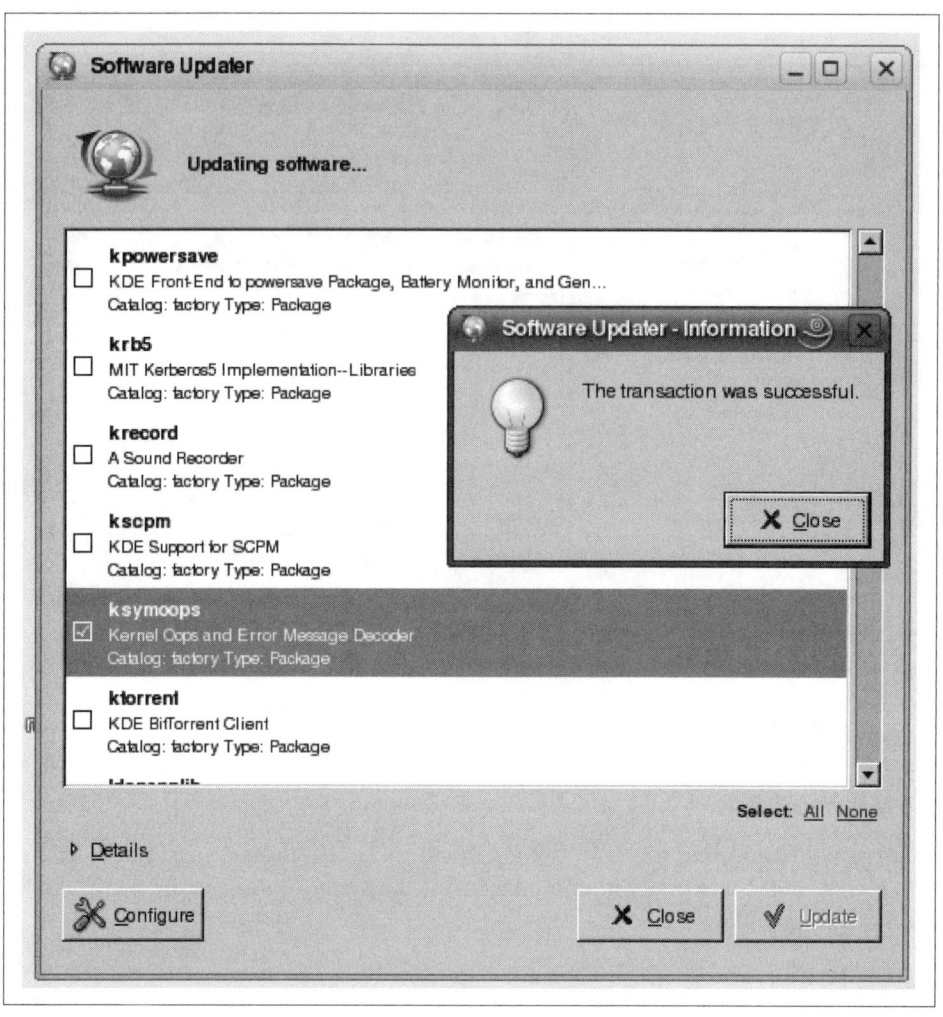

Figure 5-9. ZEN Updater

All of these tools, including rug and zmd, are CLI (Common Language Infrastructure) bytecode applications running on Mono, an open source runtime and development environment compatible with .NET.

Where to Learn More

The libzypp library and the tools that depend on it are relatively new, and currently, documentation is sparse, though there is a detailed manpage for rug. There are brief descriptions at *http://lwn.net/Articles/171841/* and *http://en.opensuse.org/Libzypp*. Hopefully by the time you read this, the documentation will have improved!

5.7 Manage Software Packages Using YUM

Yet another package management tool that is becoming increasingly popular is YUM. (Apparently, it stands, for "Yellow Dog Updater Modified." Yellow Dog is a version of Linux for the Power PC.) YUM is available for SUSE Linux and looks set to become the package management tool of choice. In this lab you'll see how to use it.

How Do I Do That?

First, you'll need to install the packages yum, kyum, and yum-utils. (No, you can't install them with yum. You'll have to make do with YaST!) As you may have guessed, yum is the command-line tool and kyum is the graphical frontend.

YUM needs a little bit of setup—it doesn't just work out the box. Its primary configuration file is */etc/yum.conf* (run **man yum.conf** for the details). In here, you need to specify the URL for at least one repository. (A *repository* is a prepared directory or web site or FTP server that contains software packages and index files.) Alternatively, you can define your repositories in separate *.repo* files in a specified directory. In the default installation of yum, the config file contains a few basic settings and the line:

    reposdir=/etc/yum.repos.d

which tells yum to read repository information from the files in */etc/yum.repos.d*; however, in the default installation, this directory is empty. I created two files in here. The first, which I called *base.repo*, defines a repository called base:

    [base]
    name=SUSE LINUX 10.0 - Base
    baseurl=ftp://ftp.gwdg.de/pub/opensuse/distribution/SL-10.0-OSS/inst-source/suse
    mirrorlist=/etc/yum.repos.d/base.mirrors
    enabled=1

The `baseurl=` line specifies the URL for this repository, and the `mirrorlist=` line names a file that contains alternative URLs that provide mirrors of this repository. When yum is downloading packages, if one of the servers isn't responding, it will automatically switch to a different mirror from the list. This is a very useful feature (and one that YaST doesn't support).

The second file *base.mirrors* is just a list of URLs, which looks something like this:

    ftp://ftp.rz.uni-wuerzburg.de/pub/linux/opensuse/distribution/SL-10.0-OSS/inst-source/suse
    ftp://ftp.uniroma2.it/Linux/opensuse/distribution/SL-10.0-OSS/inst-source/suse

With these two files in place, you can run yum from the command line; for example, to list all available packages:

    $ yum list available
    Setting up repositories
    Reading repository metadata in from local files
    Available Packages

```
3ddiag-debuginfo.i586          0.728-2           base
3dto3d.i586                    3.5-22            base
844-ksc-pcf.noarch             19990207-595      base
AtaAuto.i586                   1.5.0-176         base
... rest of a very long list deleted ...
```

Installing packages is easy. Here's how to install a KDE utility called basket (a kind of clipboard on steroids):

```
# yum install basket
Setting up Install Process
Setting up repositories
Reading repository metadata in from local files
Parsing package install arguments
Resolving Dependencies
--> Populating transaction set with selected packages. Please wait.
---> Package basket.i586 0:0.5.0-13 set to be updated
--> Running transaction check
--> Processing Dependency: libartskde.so.1 for package: basket
--> Restarting Dependency Resolution with new changes.
--> Populating transaction set with selected packages. Please wait.
---> Package kdelibs3-arts.i586 0:3.4.2-24 set to be updated
--> Running transaction check

Dependencies Resolved

=============================================================================
 Package                Arch       Version           Repository        Size
=============================================================================
Installing:
 basket                 i586       0.5.0-13          base             338 k
Installing for dependencies:
 kdelibs3-arts          i586       3.4.2-24          base             148 k

Transaction Summary
=============================================================================
Install      2 Package(s)
Update       0 Package(s)
Remove       0 Package(s)
Total download size: 486 k
Is this ok [y/N]: y
Downloading Packages:
Running Transaction Test
Finished Transaction Test
Transaction Test Succeeded
Running Transaction
  Installing: kdelibs3-arts           ######################### [1/2]
  Installing: basket                  ######################### [2/2]

Installed: basket.i586 0:0.5.0-13
Dependency Installed: kdelibs3-arts.i586 0:3.4.2-24
Complete!
```

Notice the automatic dependency check, resulting in the installation of one additional package, `kdelibs3-arts`. Also note that installation must be done as root.

Table 5-3 summarizes some of the most important yum commands. See the manpage (man yum) for details.

Table 5-3. Some yum commands

Command	Description
`yum install foo`	Install package `foo` and any dependencies
`yum remove foo`	Remove package `foo` and any dependencies
`yum info foo`	Print the summary fields from package `foo`
`yum search xxx`	Search for packages containing the string `xxx` in the package name, description, or summary fields
`yum update foo`	Update the package `foo`
`yum update`	Update every currently installed package

Now let's take a look at the graphical frontend, KYum. If you're going to use it to install packages, you'll need to run it as root, so start it with `su -c`, which prompts you for the root password and executes the specified command as root:

```
$ su -c kyum
```

The main screen of KYum is shown in Figure 5-10. In this example, I have just installed the package basket. (The package appeared in the "available" list but disappeared after I installed it.) Note the pane in the bottom-left corner that shows the underlying command-line dialog with yum. For an alternative graphical frontend to YUM, try the package yumex.

What About...

...verifying package signatures? YUM can be configured to verify the digital signatures on the packages that you ask it to install. To do this, it needs the public key of the author who signed the package. You can configure one or more locations for retrieving public keys in the repository definition files. For example, here's an extended version of the *base.repo* file you saw earlier:

```
[base]
gpgkey=ftp://ftp.gwdg.de/pub/opensuse/distribution/SL-10.0-OSS/inst-source/gpg-
pubkey-0dfb3188-41ed929b.asc
name=SUSE LINUX 10.0 - Base
baseurl=ftp://ftp.gwdg.de/pub/opensuse/distribution/SL-10.0-OSS/inst-source/suse
mirrorlist=/etc/yum.repos.d/base.mirrors
enabled=1
gpgcheck=1
```

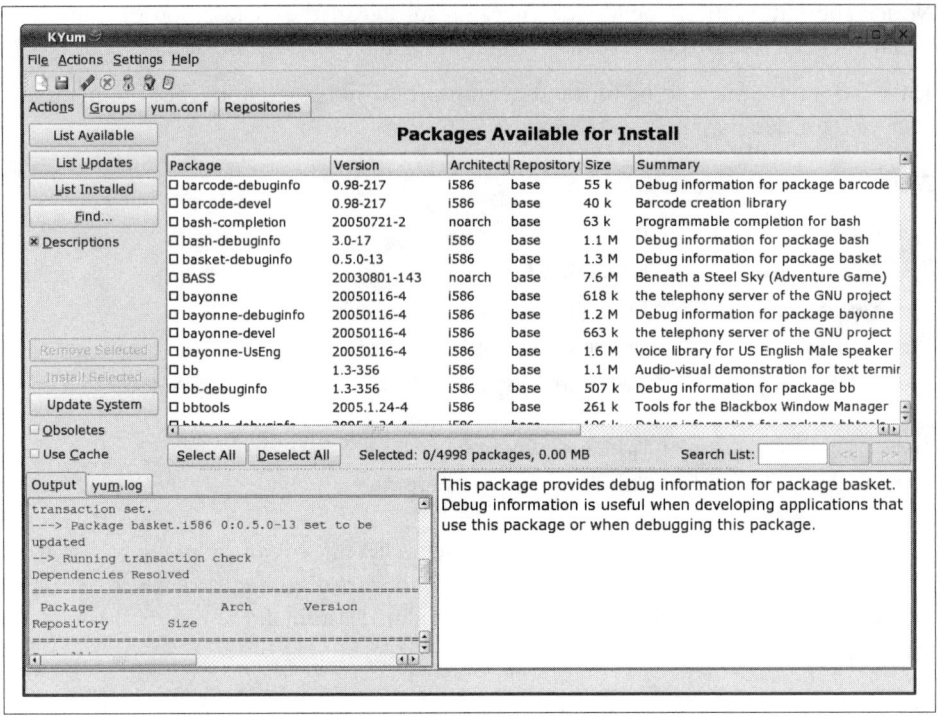

Figure 5-10. The main screen of KYum

The line beginning gpgkey= specifies a URL pointing to the GPG key file for the repository. This option is used if YUM needs a public key to verify a package and the required key hasn't been imported into the RPM database. If this option is set, YUM will automatically import the key from the specified URL. The line gpgcheck=1 specifies that YUM should perform a GPG signature check on packages downloaded from this repository.

Where to Learn More

Read the manual pages for yum and *yum.conf*. There is further information and a FAQ at *http://linux.duke.edu/projects/yum*.

5.8   Compile and Install Source Code

Installing prebuilt binary packages, as I discussed in Lab 5.3, "Install and Upgrade RPMs," is a fine way to extend your SUSE Linux distribution. However, sometimes you'll come across an application for which no binary package is available.

> The distinction between a binary (machine code) package and a source package is important. A binary package includes one or more executable binary programs—files that contain machine code for a specific processor such as a Pentium, or a SPARC, or an IBM Z-series mainframe. The machine code contained in these packages consists of instructions that can be executed by a specific processor. A binary package built for one processor architecture won't work on another. A source package, on the other hand, contains files of *source code* written in a specific programming language (often the C language in the case of Linux applications). These files cannot, as they stand, be run on any processor at all. They need to be translated (compiled) into machine code for a specific processor. To do this, you need to have the appropriate development packages installed on your machine.

Some people are put off the idea of installing from source, thinking that they will need to look at, and understand, the source code of the applications they are installing. This is hardly ever the case. There is a standard sequence of commands, discussed in this lab, that will build most source packages on your Linux platform. It is not really any more complicated than the commands needed to install a binary package. In the (unlikely) event that you start seeing incomprehensible error messages from the compiler as you try to build the package, my advice is: if you can't figure out what's wrong within 15 minutes, give up! Unless you're a seasoned developer, you have little chance of fixing it (and even if you are, you'd probably just cut and paste those error messages into a bug report anyhow). Lest you become discouraged by this, I should emphasize that most source packages will build without any difficulty on your SUSE Linux distribution.

The advantages of installing an application from source code instead of a binary are:

- A single source package can be distributed that can be built and run on multiple architectures—various versions of Linux and Unix, and even (sometimes) on Windows.
- You can get the latest and greatest versions of applications for which no-one has (yet) built a binary package for your platform. Availability of binary packages always lags a little behind the source packages. For some applications, you cannot necessarily rely on someone building a binary package for your platform at all, though this is less likely to be true for a popular distribution such as SUSE.
- If you build a package from source, you get a lot more flexibility in deciding which features of the application you want to include and exclude. You also get to decide where the various pieces will be installed—for example, the directory in which the executables themselves will go, where the config files will go, where the documentation will go, and so on. If you install a binary package, you must accept the configuration decisions made by whoever built the package.

How Do I Do That?

First, make sure that you have the development tools installed. The key packages are:

gcc
   The GNU C Compiler

cpp
   The C preprocessor

make
   A tool for controlling the build process

These are all included with the SUSE distribution. The easiest way to make sure you have them is to open the YaST package management screen, select the Selections filter, and make sure that the "C/C++ Compiler and Tools" checkbox is checked. Some packages have installation scripts written in Perl, so it wouldn't do any harm to have the `perl` package installed as well.

Next, you'll need to find and download the source code archive of the package you want to install. You can find some advice on actually locating the package in Lab 5.2, "Finding the Packages You Need."

Most source code archives are delivered as compressed tar archives, commonly known as *tarballs*. There are two types of compression in common use. One is called gzip, and usually the filename will end in *.tar.gz*, or occasionally *.tgz*. The other is bzip2, and usually the filename will end in *.tar.bz2*. Bzip2 compression is a little more effective than gzip; it gives smaller file sizes. The GNU version of tar is able to decompress both formats on the fly, provided that you supply the right flags: z for gzip decompression and j for bzip2 decompression.

> No, you're right, there is not much mnemonic value in using j for bzip2 decompression. However, tar has so many options that I think they were running out of letters.

You should adopt some sort of directory organization for downloading and building things. My own preference is for a directory *~/downloads* into which I download the archive, and a directory called *~/builds* into which I unpack the archive and do the build. Each archive unpacks and builds in its own subdirectory. There is nothing particularly special about these choices—I just find them convenient.

> The tilde (~) is shorthand, understood by the shell (and hopefully by you, the reader!) to mean the user's home directory.

As an example in this lab, you will download and install a KDE-based image viewer called `showimg`. At the time of writing, the most recent version is 0.9.5. I found the archive *showimg-0.9.5.tar.bz2* by going initially to the site *http://extragear.kde.org*, then following the link to the project's home page at *http://www.jalix.org/projects/ showimg*. The name *showimg-0.9.5.tar.bz2* is a typical example of the naming convention for a tarball; the name is comprised of three components: the package name, the version information, and an extension denoting the file type. I downloaded this file into my *~/downloads* directory.

Next, I changed to my *builds* directory and unpacked the archive:

```
$ cd ~/builds
$ tar jxf ~/downloads/showimg-0.9.5.tar.bz2
```

Don't forget to use the filename completion facility in the shell to avoid typing the whole name. You should now find that you have a directory called *showimg-0.9.5*. Change into that directory and take a look around. Most packages will provide a file called something like *README* or *INSTALL* that provides installation instructions. It's worth reading this through (twice) before you do anything else:

```
$ cd ~/builds/showimg-0.9.5
$ less README
$ less INSTALL
```

Some source packages come with their own custom scripts to handle the installation, but the majority are built using a utility called autoconf. This tool (which is run by the package developer, not by you) creates a very clever shell script called *configure* (which is run by you, not the package developer). The *configure* script probes your system to determine various features of the platform you're building on (including the libraries that are available and the characteristics of your compiler) and generates one or more *Makefiles*, which will control the actual build process. As this proceeds, you will see a large number of messages scrolling past as the script repeatedly probes the system. You do not need to read all of these, but you should check the last few lines for any evidence that the process has failed.

> There is a well-known quote from Arthur C. Clarke that "any sufficiently advanced technology is indistinguishable from magic." By this definition, the *configure* script is magic.

If the *configure* script runs successfully, you're ready to go ahead and build the application. The command sequence will look something like this:

```
$ cd ~/builds/showimg-0.9.5
$ ./configure
$ make
```

The make command actually compiles and builds the application, and can take a while to run—anywhere from a minute to an hour depending on the size of the package and the speed of your machine. During this time, even more (mostly incomprehensible) messages will scroll past. Again, you should check the last few lines for any evidence that something went wrong. A few compilation warnings are nothing to worry about, but any actual errors need to be investigated. (In fact, the `showimg` compilation produces a huge number of warnings.) Once the `make` command has completed, all the components of the application have been built, but they all remain within the folder in which you did the build. If you changed your mind at this stage and deleted this folder and the original tarball, you would remove the package without a trace.

The final step is to install the package; that is, to copy the executables, libraries, configuration files, documentation, and so on, into the correct system directories. You need to be root for this. Just `cd` to the build directory and run the command:

```
# make install
```

This step is a little harder to back out from, should you change your mind. Sometimes you'll find a `make uninstall` option for the package, but many don't provide this. In this case, you would need to manually find and delete each of the installed files. There are usually options available for the `./configure` command to specify where the pieces will get put (see the following discussion). Running ./configure --help will generally show these and tell you what the defaults are. You may wish to get into the habit of saving a listing of the install directories prior to the installation, repeating the listing after the installation, and doing a `diff` on the two. For example, because I know that the package installs into */opt/kde3* on a SUSE system, I might use this sequence of commands:

```
# ls -lR /opt/kde3 > /tmp/kde1
# make install
# ls -lR /opt/kde3 > /tmp/kde2
# diff /tmp/kde1 /tmp/kde2
```

An alternative way to tackle the same problem might be to interrogate the time stamps on the files. You can do this with the `find` command using this sequence of commands:

```
# touch /tmp/now
# make install
# find /opt/kde3 -type f -newer /tmp/now
```

Okay, so now you have the package installed. What next? Using a new package may simply be a case of running the binary. You may have to invoke it by name from a command prompt, because an installation from source is unlikely to add an entry to your desktop menus for you, though this is not hard to do manually. You can learn how to edit the KDE menus in Lab 3.3, "Configure the KDE Menus and Panel," in Chapter 3. Also, be aware that the directory you install the binaries into may not be on your search path, so you may have to specify a full pathname to the binary. Some packages have *wrapper* scripts to simplify the task of launching the applications. Other packages have nontrivial configuration files and will require further work before you can get the program to do anything useful.

What About...

...specifying build options? The configure script usually has a shedload of options for customizing the build process. The exact options depend on the package. Run the command:

```
$ ./configure --help
```

to see all available options. This example, obtained by running the configure script of the Apache server, is heavily edited:

```
$ ./configure --help
`configure' configures this package to adapt to many kinds of systems.

Usage: ./configure [OPTION]... [VAR=VALUE]...

To assign environment variables (e.g., CC, CFLAGS...), specify them as
VAR=VALUE.  See below for descriptions of some of the useful variables.

Defaults for the options are specified in brackets.

Configuration:
  -h, --help              display this help and exit
      --help=short        display options specific to this package
      --help=recursive    display the short help of all the included packages
  -V, --version           display version information and exit
  -q, --quiet, --silent   do not print `checking...' messages
      --cache-file=FILE   cache test results in FILE [disabled]
  -C, --config-cache      alias for `--cache-file=config.cache'
  -n, --no-create         do not create output files
      --srcdir=DIR        find the sources in DIR [configure dir or `..']

Installation directories:
  --prefix=PREFIX         install architecture-independent files in PREFIX
                          [/usr/local/apache2]
  --exec-prefix=EPREFIX   install architecture-dependent files in EPREFIX
                          [PREFIX]

By default, `make install' will install all the files in
`/usr/local/apache2/bin', `/usr/local/apache2/lib' etc.  You can specify
an installation prefix other than `/usr/local/apache2' using `--prefix',
for instance `--prefix=$HOME'.

For better control, use the options below.

Fine tuning of the installation directories:
  --bindir=DIR            user executables [EPREFIX/bin]
  --sbindir=DIR           system admin executables [EPREFIX/sbin]
  --libexecdir=DIR        program executables [EPREFIX/libexec]
  --datadir=DIR           read-only architecture-independent data [PREFIX/share]
  ... edited ...

System types:
  --build=BUILD     configure for building on BUILD [guessed]
```

```
      --host=HOST         cross-compile to build programs to run on HOST [BUILD]
      --target=TARGET     configure for building compilers for TARGET [HOST]

Optional Features:
  --disable-FEATURE       do not include FEATURE (same as --enable-FEATURE=no)
  --enable-FEATURE[=ARG]  include FEATURE [ARG=yes]
  --enable-layout=LAYOUT
  --enable-v4-mapped      Allow IPv6 sockets to handle IPv4 connections
  --enable-exception-hook Enable fatal exception hook
  --enable-maintainer-mode
                          Turn on debugging and compile time warnings
  --enable-modules=MODULE-LIST
                          Modules to enable
  --enable-mods-shared=MODULE-LIST
                          Shared modules to enable
  --disable-access        host-based access control
  --disable-auth          user-based access control
  --enable-info           server information
  ... edited ...

Optional Packages:
  ... edited ...
  --with-suexec-docroot   SuExec root directory
  --with-suexec-uidmin    Minimal allowed UID
  --with-suexec-gidmin    Minimal allowed GID
  --with-suexec-logfile   Set the logfile
  --with-suexec-safepath  Set the safepath
  --with-suexec-umask     umask for suexec'd process

  ... edited ...
```

The range of options that we see in this output is typical for a configure script. Usually, there are options to:

- Control the operation of the script itself (e.g., **-q** for the "quiet" option).
- Specify the directories into which the various pieces will be installed. Typically, the option **--prefix** specifies the top-level directory, and the other install directories are derived from that. Optionally, you can fine-tune the directories with options such as **--bindir**, which determines where the executables will go.
- Specify the platform for which the package will be built. Usually, the platform you're building on is the same as the platform you'll be running on, so you just let the script probe the system to determine the platform automatically.
- Enable or disable optional features of the package. Apache has quite a lot of these options, because most of its functionality is provided through the use of modules that can be either statically built into the executable or loaded dynamically. For example, the directive --enable-info specifies inclusion of a module that provides a web page of information about the server itself.

A simple example of a `configure` command for Apache, which includes the `info` module in the build and installs into */opt/apache2*, would be:

```
$ ./configure --prefix=/opt/apache2 --enable-info
```

The commands can get much longer than this.

What About...

...installing from source RPMs?

There is another format that's sometimes used for distributing source code: a source RPM. Source RPM files have names ending in *.src.rpm*. They contain an archive (usually a compressed tar archive) of the source code for a package, along with a *spec file* that specifies how to build the binary version of the package from the source. Source RPMs are what you'll find on the source code CD or DVD that comes as part of your SUSE Linux distribution. SUSE uses source RPMs to maintain a common code base for SUSE Linux and the many packages it includes, across the various hardware architectures that SUSE supports. This includes 32-bit and 64-bit Intel architectures, IBM Power PC, and IBM zSeries mainframes.

If you install a source RPM package (using the `rpm -i` command in the usual way), you will end up with the package files in the folder */usr/src/packages/SOURCES* and the spec file in */usr/src/packages/SPECS*. You can build a binary RPM from a source RPM using a command of the form `rpmbuild –bb specfile`.

How Does It Work?

The real magic behind installing from source is the *configure* script. This is a shell script generated by the utility called `autoconf`, which is run by the developer of the package. Autoconf creates the *configure* script from a template file that lists the operating system features that the package can use, in the form of `m4` macro calls. (m4 is a macro text processor that has been part of Unix/Linux for many years.) The configure script does not actually build the package; it runs a sequence of feature tests to see what features the system can support and, based on the results of these tests, generates one or more "makefiles" that control the build itself. It is this process that enables the same source package to be built on a wide range of Unix and Linux platforms.

Makefiles define a set of rules that can be used to build one or more components (called *targets*) from their constituent parts. They define the dependencies of the targets on the constituent pieces (in this case, the source modules) and are interpreted by a tool called `make`, which figures out the commands that need to be executed to build the targets. Makefiles and the `make` utility are commonly used to control the building (and rebuilding) of software projects. After source code has been edited, make compares the time stamps on the source and binary files to figure out which binaries are out of date and need to be recompiled. In the case of building a package from source code you have just downloaded, none of the binaries exist of course, so everything needs to be compiled.

A full treatment of make would require a chapter (or book) to itself, but I will present a simple example to give you an idea of how it works. The problem that make is designed to solve is that most applications are built from many source files. When one or more of those source files has been edited and the application needs to be rebuilt, only those files that were changed need to be recompiled. The make utility helps to automate the process of figuring out exactly what needs to be done to rebuild the application. Make relies on the "time of last modification" time stamp on the files, and on the notion of a "dependency graph" (discussed shortly) that shows which files depend on which others. This approach is much smarter than (for example) writing a shell script that simply recompiles everything in sight, and can save substantial time in rebuilding an application.

make can be used in any situation where files must be built that depend on other files. For example, documentation files can be built automatically from comments in program source code. Indexes can be built from collections of text files. However, it is in the building and rebuilding of applications from their source code that make finds its widest application. This is the example that I consider here. Let's take a hypothetical (and much simplified) example based on the showimg application, which is distributed across three C source files:

ui.c
    The code that creates the user interface

png.c
    The code for displaying PNG images

jpg.c
    The code for displaying JPEG images

In addition, there are two header files, *png.h* and *jpg.h*, that define the interfaces to the png and jpg modules. The build model for an application written in C is that each source file is separately compiled into an object file (for example, *ui.c* is compiled into *ui.o*), then the object files are linked together to create the application—in this case, showimg. Figure 5-11 shows the dependency graph of these pieces. This dependency graph shows that (for example) showimg is dependent upon the files *ui.o*, *png.o*, and *jpg.o*. This dependency implies that (a) all three of these .o files must exist before *showimg* can be built, and (b) if the last-modified time stamp on any of the .o files is more recent than the last-modified time stamp of *showimg*, then *showimg* is out of date and needs to be rebuilt. Similarly, working our way down the graph, *ui.o* is dependent on *ui.c* and the header files *png.h* and *jpg.h*, and so on.

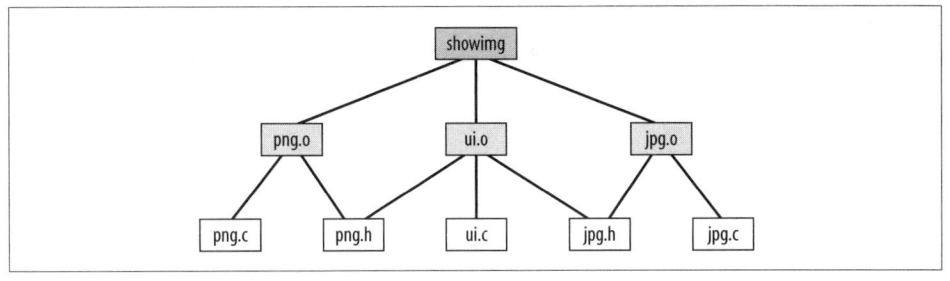

Figure 5-11. Dependency graph for make

To use make, a *Makefile* must be built that describes the dependency graph. The *Makefile* for this example might look like this:

```
showimg:     ui.o  png.o  jpg.o
             gcc ui.o png.o jpg.o -o showimg

ui.o:        ui.c  png.h  jpg.h
             gcc -c ui.c

png.o:       png.c png.h
             gcc -c png.c

jpg.o:       jpg.c jpg.h
             gcc -c jpg.c
```

Each entry in the file is of this format:

```
target:      dependencies
             rebuild commands
```

The *target* simply names a file that make knows how to rebuild. The *dependencies* list the files that must be present (and, in their turn, up to date) in order to build the target. The rebuild commands (which appear on a separate line and must be indented by a tab character) specify the commands that must be executed to bring the target up to date, assuming that up-to-date copies of the dependencies exist.

Once the *Makefile* is created, make is invoked by specifying a target name as an argument, for example:

```
$ make showimg
```

If no argument is given, make defaults to building the first target, in this case showimg. It will begin by making sure that this target's dependencies are up to date (in this case the files *ui.o*, *png.o*, and *jpg.o*) by looking them up as targets and, in turn, verifying their own dependencies. In this way, make performs a "depth-first traversal of the dependency graph" (a phrase I have found to be a wonderful conversation stopper at parties), bringing everything up to date as it works its way back up to the top of the dependency tree.

Some of the targets in a *Makefile* define administrative actions rather than the creation of a file. There is often a target named `install` that installs the application into the appropriate system directories. In this example, it might look like this:

```
install:        showimg
                mv showimg /opt/kde3/bin
```

Now I can type:

> # **make install**

to move the program into its proper place. Defining `showimg` as a dependency of the `install` target will cause `make` to ensure that `showimg` is up to date before installing it into the system directory */opt/kde3/bin*.

Another common target, conventionally named `clean`, is used to remove any intermediate files used in the build process. For example, you might add this target to the Makefile:

```
clean:
                rm ui.o png.o img.o
```

With this target in place, you can type

> $ **make clean**

to get rid of the *.o* files (thus forcing a full recompile next time).

You can also define variables in Makefiles. Variables are commonly used to centralize the specification of system-dependent commands or directories, or to give a name to a long list of files (often a list of *.o* files) to avoid repeating that list in multiple places in the file. In fact, almost 40 percent of the real Makefile for the `showimg` application consists of variable definitions. As a simple example, here's a revised version of the Makefile that uses three variables—one to define the system-specific command to run the C compiler, one to define the directory that the application should be installed into, and one to provide a shorthand for the list of object files. Notice the use of the notation $(CC), which is replaced by the value of the variable:

```
CC = gcc
INSTALLDIR = /opt/kde3/bin
OBJECTS = ui.o png.o jpg.o

install:        showimg
                mv showimg $(INSTALLDIR)

showimg:        $(OBJECTS)
                $(CC) $(OBJECTS) -o showimg

ui.o:           ui.c  png.h  jpg.h
                $(CC) -c ui.c
```

```
png.o:   png.c    png.h
                  $(CC) -c png.c

jpg.o:            jpg.c jpg.h
                  $(CC) -c jpg.c

clean:
                  rm $(OBJECTS)
```

This brief treatment barely scratches the surface of make. The automatically generated Makefiles that you'll come across if you install software from source represent much more advanced examples of the Makefile writer's art.

Where to Learn More

There is more information about autoconf at *http://www.gnu.org/software/autoconf*, and also in the book *GNU Autoconf, Automake, and Libtool* by Elliston et al. (Sams). This book is also available online at *http://sources.redhat.com/autobook*.

For information on making .SRPMs, take a look at *http://www.opensuse.org/SUSE_Build_Tutorial*. You don't (generally) need to be a seasoned developer to package software, but you do need to know your way around the system you are packaging for quite well.

For everything you always wanted to know about make, but were too embarrassed to ask, try *Managing Projects with Make* by Mecklenburg (O'Reilly).

CHAPTER 6
System Administration for Servers

Although the popularity of Linux on the desktop is growing, it is as a server platform that Linux has its most firmly established market niche. The flexibility and openness of Linux, its relatively small hardware footprint, its good reputation for security, and its extensive support for a wide variety of network services make it a popular server platform. Of course, the fact that it's free helps, too!

This chapter discusses the "infrastructure" for a Linux server. It will examine the mechanics of service startup; the management of disk space through the use of partitions and logical volumes; the importance of logging, tools for monitoring system activity, load, and performance; and some network configuration and debugging issues. Chapter 7 continues the story by discussing key application-level services in detail.

In some sense, this chapter marks a transition into a more professional view of Linux. However, I hope that the enthusiastic desktop user will also find useful information here.

6.1   Control Boot-Time Service Startup

Chapter 2 examined the early stages of the boot process, but left the story at the point where the kernel was up and running and had launched a program called init. This lab picks up the story at that point, showing how to determine which services are started by init at boot time.

How Do I Do That?

Central to the operation of init is the concept of a *runlevel*. The runlevel determines which services should be running. The basic idea is that the higher the runlevel, the higher the level of activity in the system; that is, the more services that are running. The runlevels are defined as shown in Table 6-1.

Table 6-1. System runlevels

Runlevel	Description
0	System is halted.
S	Single user. This runlevel is useful for filesystem maintenance because no processes (except a command-line shell) are running, so the filesystem is quiescent.
1	Single user.
2	Local multiuser mode without networking. "Local multiuser" really makes sense only in the context of a machine with multiple terminals attached (via serial lines for example), which is rare these days. This runlevel brings up login prompts on these terminals as well as the main console.
3	Full multiuser mode with network services running, but no graphical login manager. This is the runlevel typically used by a "headless" Linux server (one that you're running without a graphical desktop).
4	Not used (though you could in theory define your own).
5	Full multiuser with network services running and an X display manager such as KDM, XDM, or GDM. This runlevel is appropriate for a single-user machine intended for use with a graphical desktop.
6	Switching to this runlevel forces a reboot.

You can control which services will be started at each runlevel using the YaST runlevel editor. From the main YaST screen, select System from the pane on the left, then System Services (Runlevel) from the pane on the right. This brings you to the main runlevel editor screen. In its "simple mode," which is displayed by default, you can enable or disable the startup behavior for each service. So, for example, if you scroll down the list, select sshd, and click Disable, YaST will immediately shut down the sshd daemon. If you click Finish, YaST will also modify the system configuration so that sshd will not be started at boot time. Conversely, if you click Enable, YaST will immediately start the daemon and arrange for it to be started automatically at boot time. In this "simple" mode you cannot control the behavior of each runlevel individually. You have to accept the default behavior for each service. In the case of sshd, for example, enabling it causes it to start in runlevels 3 and 5.

Switching to Expert Mode brings up the screen shown in Figure 6-1.

On the screen you'll see a drop-down list allowing you to set the default runlevel (the one that the system will boot into) to 2, 3, or 5. You can also configure the behavior of each service at each individual runlevel, rather than accepting the defaults like you had to in Simple mode. Just select the service from the list and click the checkboxes for the runlevels you want it to start at. YaST will automatically check for any service dependencies and will complain if we try to configure a service to start at a runlevel at which other, required services are not running. For example, if you try to start sshd at runlevel 1, YaST will report that sshd needs the network up and running and that the network isn't started at runlevel 1.

In case you were wondering, the checkbox labeled "B" is used for scripts that are run at an early stage in the boot process—before Linux starts to think about entering a runlevel. Most of these scripts simply perform some boot-time initialization; they

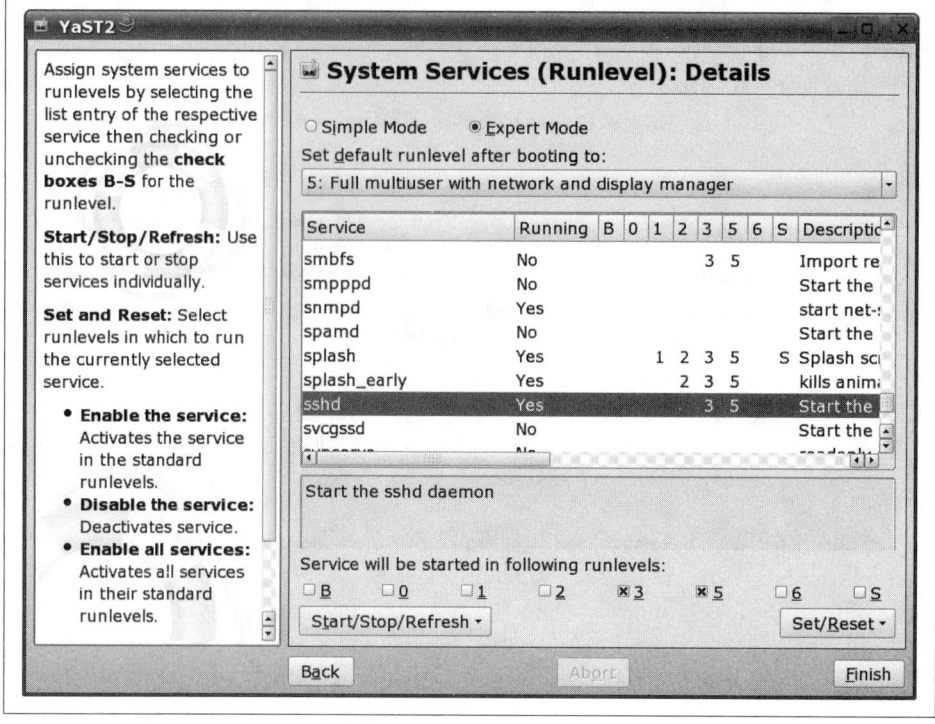

Figure 6-1. YaST runlevel editor in Expert Mode

don't start a service in the usual sense of launching a long-lived background process. You're unlikely to need to change any of these.

The button labeled Start/Stop/Refresh can be used to perform an immediate startup or shutdown of the service, or to report whether it's currently running. Don't forget that actual configuration updates aren't made until you click Finish.

How Does It Work?

The hierarchy of configuration files and scripts that control boot-time behavior is fairly complex. There are several layers to disentangle before the entire picture emerges, so be patient! The top-level control file, read by init, is */etc/inittab*. This file tells init what to run at each runlevel. Here's a slightly modified version of the file. The line numbers are for reference; they are not part of the file:

```
1  # The default runlevel is defined here
2  id:5:initdefault:
3
4  # First script to be executed, if not booting in emergency (-b) mode
5  si::bootwait:/etc/init.d/boot
6
7  # /etc/init.d/rc takes care of runlevel handling
8
```

```
9   l0:0:wait:/etc/init.d/rc 0
10  l1:1:wait:/etc/init.d/rc 1
11  l2:2:wait:/etc/init.d/rc 2
12  l3:3:wait:/etc/init.d/rc 3
13  #l4:4:wait:/etc/init.d/rc 4
14  l5:5:wait:/etc/init.d/rc 5
15  l6:6:wait:/etc/init.d/rc 6
16
17  # what to do in single-user mode
18  ls:S:wait:/etc/init.d/rc S
19  ~~:S:respawn:/sbin/sulogin
20
21  # what to do when CTRL-ALT-DEL is pressed
22  ca::ctrlaltdel:/sbin/shutdown -r -t 4 now
23
24  # getty-programs for the normal runlevels
25  # <id>:<runlevels>:<action>:<process>
26  # The "id" field MUST be the same as the last
27  # characters of the device (after "tty").
28  1:2345:respawn:/sbin/mingetty --noclear tty1
29  2:2345:respawn:/sbin/mingetty tty2
30  3:2345:respawn:/sbin/mingetty tty3
31  4:2345:respawn:/sbin/mingetty tty4
32  5:2345:respawn:/sbin/mingetty tty5
33  6:2345:respawn:/sbin/mingetty tty6
```

Line 2 defines the default runlevel. You can hand-edit this entry if you wish. Line 5 runs the script */etc/init.d/boot*. In turn, this script runs all the scripts in the directory */etc/init.d/boot.d*. These all perform low-level initialization and correspond to the "B" checkbox in the YaST runlevel editor. Lines 9–15 are the heart of the file. For each runlevel that init is asked to enter, these lines tell init to run the script */etc/init.d/rc* with the runlevel as an argument. This is where the real business of starting up the services takes place; I discuss this script in a moment. Lines 28–33 control the startup of the six virtual consoles that Linux provides by default. These are the console screens you reach with the shortcut keys Ctrl-Alt-F1 through Ctrl-Alt-F6.

Next, take a look at the directory */etc/init.d*:

```
# ls /etc/init.d
.                     boot.localnet             irda           rc6.d
..                    boot.md                   isdn           rcS.d
.depend.boot          boot.preload              joystick       reboot
.depend.start         boot.preload_early        kbd            resmgr
.depend.stop          boot.proc                 ksysguardd     rpasswdd
Makefile              boot.restore_permissions  lm_sensors     rpmconfigcheck
README                boot.rootfsck             mdadmd         rsyncd
SuSEfirewall2_init    boot.sched                mdnsd          sane-dev
SuSEfirewall2_setup   boot.scpm                 microcode      saslauthd
acpid                 boot.scsidev              network        setserial
alsasound             boot.shm                  nfs            single
apache2               boot.swap                 nfsboot        skeleton
atd                   boot.sysctl               nfsserver      slpd
autofs                boot.udev                 nmb            smb
```

```
autoyast              cron              nscd         smbfs
bluetooth             cups              ntp          smpppd
boot                  cupsrenice        openct       snmpd
boot.cleanup          dbus              pcscd        spamd
boot.clock            earlykbd          portmap      splash
boot.coldplug         earlykdm          postfix      splash_early
boot.crypto           earlysyslog       powerfail    sshd
boot.d                esound            powersaved   svcgssd
boot.device-mapper    fam               random       svnserve
boot.idedma           fbset             raw          syslog
boot.ipconfig         gpm               rc           xdm
boot.isapnp           gssd              rc0.d        xfs
boot.klog             haldaemon         rc1.d        xinetd
boot.ldconfig         halt              rc2.d        ypbind
boot.loadmodules      halt.local        rc3.d
boot.local            hplip             rc4.d
boot.localfs          idmapd            rc5.d
```

The files in here are mostly shell scripts; these are actually responsible for starting and stopping the daemons. I'll refer to these as the *master scripts*. Each of these scripts takes an argument to specify its action; the arguments shown in Table 6-2 are supported by most scripts.

Table 6-2. Startup script arguments

Argument	Meaning
start	Start the daemon.
stop	Stop the daemon.
restart	Equivalent to stop followed by start.
reload	Signal the daemon to reload its configuration file.
status	Report status (at minimum, reports whether the daemon is running).

So, for example, you can use these scripts to manually start, query, and stop the sshd daemon as shown in this sequence:

```
# cd /etc/init.d
# ./sshd start
Starting SSH daemon                                    done
# ./sshd status
Checking for service sshd                              running
# ./sshd stop
Shutting down SSH daemon                               done
# ./sshd status
Checking for service sshd                              unused
```

Looking back at the listing of */etc/init.d*, you'll also notice a series of directories with names of the form *rcN.d* where *N* corresponds to a runlevel. For example, the directory */etc/init.d/rc3.d* corresponds to runlevel 3. Let's look at its contents:

```
# ls -l /etc/init.d/rc3.d

... list edited ...
```

```
lrwxrwxrwx  1 root root   7 Oct 21 09:45 K10sshd -> ../sshd
lrwxrwxrwx  1 root root   6 Oct 11 09:35 K12nfs -> ../nfs
lrwxrwxrwx  1 root root   9 Oct 11 09:33 K16syslog -> ../syslog
lrwxrwxrwx  1 root root  10 Oct 11 10:44 K17network -> ../network

... list edited ...

lrwxrwxrwx  1 root root  10 Oct 11 10:44 S05network -> ../network
lrwxrwxrwx  1 root root   9 Oct 11 09:33 S06syslog -> ../syslog
lrwxrwxrwx  1 root root   6 Oct 11 09:35 S10nfs -> ../nfs
lrwxrwxrwx  1 root root   7 Oct 21 09:45 S12sshd -> ../sshd
```

This output has been heavily edited to retain the entries for just four services. You'll see that each of these entries is a symbolic link to one of the master scripts in /etc/init.d. You'll also see that each link name begins with either a K or an S followed by two digits. I'll call these the *K links* and *S links*. The S links are there to start the services when Linux enters this runlevel, and the K links are there to kill (stop) the services when Linux leaves this runlevel.

Okay, now it's time to drop the final piece of this puzzle into place by looking at the script /etc/init.d/rc. Remember, init calls this script with the runlevel as argument each time it enters a runlevel. The script looks at the S and K links both in the *rcN.d* directory for the current runlevel and for the runlevel Linux is moving into. (If you're booting from scratch, there is no current runlevel.) The logic goes like this: for each service, if there's a K link in the current runlevel but no S link in the target runlevel, the K script is run with the argument stop. This causes termination of any service which was running in the current level but should not be running in the target level. Conversely, for each service that has no S link in the current runlevel but does have an S link in the target level, the S script is run with the argument start. This launches any service that was not running in the current level but should be running in the target level.

This logic prevents stopping then immediately restarting a service when making a transition between two runlevels in which both of the service should be active. The bottom line of all this is that control of which services start at which runlevel is determined entirely by the presence of K links and S links for the service in the *rcN.d* directory for that runlevel. Note that a service intended to run in (say) level 3 will have both an S link *and* a K link in that directory.

You can see this arrangement for sshd with a carefully crafted wildcard:

```
# ls -l /etc/init.d/rc?.d/*sshd
lrwxrwxrwx 1 root root 7 Oct 21 09:45 /etc/init.d/rc3.d/K10sshd -> ../sshd
lrwxrwxrwx 1 root root 7 Oct 21 09:45 /etc/init.d/rc3.d/S12sshd -> ../sshd
lrwxrwxrwx 1 root root 7 Oct 21 09:45 /etc/init.d/rc5.d/K10sshd -> ../sshd
lrwxrwxrwx 1 root root 7 Oct 21 09:45 /etc/init.d/rc5.d/S12sshd -> ../sshd
```

If you're familiar with RedHat Linux or Fedora, note that the behavior is different. In RedHat, a service has either an S link or a K link for each runlevel, not both.

The two digit numbers in the link names are used to control the order in which the scripts are executed. This can be important, because if service A depends on service B, SUSE Linux must ensure that B starts before A, and A is stopped before B. In the listing shown earlier, you'll notice that the K links for the four services shown appear in exactly the reverse order of the S links.

Finally we get to tie this discussion back to the runlevel editor by asking "How do the Slinks and Klinks get there?" Well, the runlevel editor puts them there. In expert mode, you specify explicitly which runlevels to use. But there is a bit more to it than that. The author of each master script places within the script a set of comment lines that specify which runlevels this service is "supposed" to run at, and what services it depends on. For example, in the master script for `sshd` you see these lines:

```
### BEGIN INIT INFO
# Provides: sshd
# Required-Start: $network $remote_fs
# Required-Stop: $network $remote_fs
# Default-Start: 3 5
# Default-Stop: 0 1 2 6
# Description: Start the sshd daemon
### END INIT INFO
```

If you use the runlevel editor in simple mode to enable the service, it will look inside the master script for the `Default-Start` line to decide which runlevels to enable the service in. It will also look at the `Required-Start` and `Required-Stop` lines to figure out whereabouts in the startup and shutdown order the S links and K links should be placed (in other words, to figure out what two-digit value to include in the link name).

What About...

...starting and stopping services manually? As you've seen, you can start and stop a service manually (as root) by running the master script in /etc/init.d with the argument start or stop. For example:

```
# /etc/init.d/sshd start
```

However, /etc/init.d isn't on root's search path and the full pathname is tedious to type. For convenience, SUSE Linux places symbolic links to these scripts in usr/sbin. The symbolic links begin with rc. For example:

```
# ls -l /usr/sbin/rcsshd
lrwxrwxrwx   1 root root 16 Oct 11 09:37 /usr/sbin/rcsshd -> /etc/init.d/sshd
```

Using this, you can start or stop `sshd` a little more easily with:

```
# rcsshd start
Starting SSH daemon                                         done
# rcsshd stop
Shutting down SSH daemon                                    done
```

This is something you might find yourself doing quite a lot of if you're debugging the configuration for a network service.

What About...

...editing the runlevels from the command line? The unimaginatively named utility chkconfig can be used to manipulate and interrogate the Slinks and Klinks from the command line. Table 6-3 shows some examples.

Table 6-3. Working with chkconfig

Command	Description
chkconfig --list	Display the settings for all services at all runlevels
chkconfig --list sshd	Display the settings for the sshd service
chkconfig sshd on	Enable sshd at its default runlevels
chkconfig sshd 5	Enable sshd to start at level 5 only
chkconfig sshd off	Disable sshd

Here's a sample of dialog that illustrates chkconfig in action:

```
# chkconfig -l sshd
sshd            0:off  1:off  2:off  3:off  4:off  5:off  6:off
# chkconfig sshd 235
# chkconfig -l sshd
sshd            0:off  1:off  2:on   3:on   4:off  5:on   6:off
# chkconfig sshd off
# chkconfig -l sshd
sshd            0:off  1:off  2:off  3:off  4:off  5:off  6:off
```

If you add a service with chkconfig, behind the scenes it invokes a further program called insserv, which is responsible for actually inserting the links. insserv looks at all the service dependencies and figures out what order the K-links and S-links need to run in. You should not normally need to invoke insserv directly. Finally, note that turning a service on or off with chkconfig affects the behavior only when you change runlevel (usually, this means when the system boots). It does not actually start or stop the daemon there and then.

What About...

...changing runlevels on the fly? You can do this using the command telinit. For example:

```
# telinit 1
```

will switch to runlevel 1 (for maintenance, perhaps) without rebooting. This works by signalling init, telling it which runlevel to change to.

Where to Learn More

Look at the manpages for init, inittab, and chkconfig.

6.2 Start Services on Demand

The traditional way of providing a network service is to start the service at boot time (as discussed in Lab 6.1, "Control Boot-Time Service Startup"), and leave it running the whole time. The server creates a socket, binds its *well-known port number* (such as port 80 for WWW servers) to that socket, then waits for a connection request. The server process *blocks* (sits around waiting for something to do) at that point and may well remain blocked for a very long time, until a client comes along. The daemon xinetd provides an alternative approach by listening for connection requests on behalf of other services, and only starting the services up on demand. This approach has a number of advantages:

- It prevents having many idle processes hanging around in the machine. Idle daemon processes aren't consuming CPU time but they are consuming memory (or swap space, if they're swapped out) and they are taking up a slot in the kernel's process table.
- It makes life slightly simpler for the actual daemon. Instead of creating a socket and accepting a connection on it, the daemon simply inherits the network connection on its standard input and standard output.
- It provides a level of access control to the services.
- It supports uniform logging of service access.

xinetd replaces an earlier daemon called inetd, which was used in some earlier versions of SUSE Linux such as SLES8, but which is now effectively obsolete. In this lab you'll see how to configure xinetd.

How Do I Do That?

First of all, if you're going to use xinetd, make sure that it is configured to start at boot time, for example using the YaST runlevel editor described in Lab 6.1, "Control Boot-Time Service Startup." Note that if xinetd starts up and discovers that it has no services enabled at all, it will shut down again. This is likely to be the case for a default installation of SUSE Linux, so you'll need to enable at least one service before xinetd will start up properly.

To access YaST's xinetd configuration module, from YaST's main screen select Network Services from the panel on the left, then Network Services (xinetd) from the panel on the right. This will bring you to the main xinetd configuration screen, shown in Figure 6-2.

You'll notice that there's an overall on/off switch for xinetd, in the form of two radio buttons labeled Enable and Disable. You must click Enable before the rest of the user interface becomes active. Now you can scroll down the list, select a service, and click on Toggle Status to turn it on or off. In the figure, I have just enabled the service swat (swat is a web-based configuration service for Samba). Some of the really simple

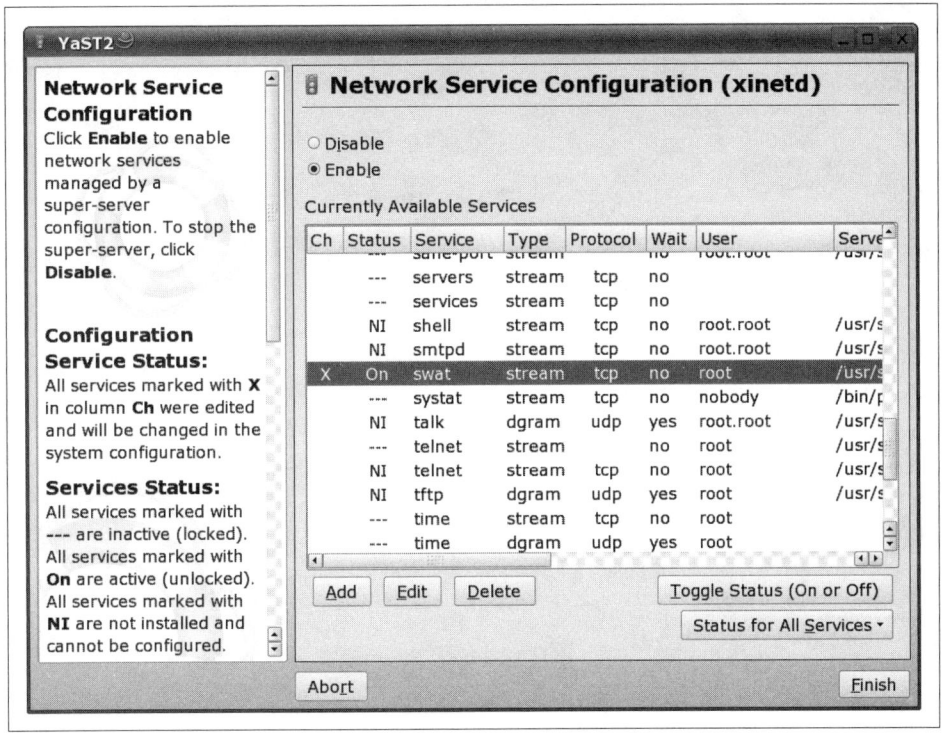

Figure 6-2. Main screen of YaST's xinetd module

TCP-based services such as chargen, daytime, and echo (which are really only useful for testing and demonstration) are provided internally by xinetd, but are usually disabled. The remaining services are provided by external programs that xinetd starts as required.

In most cases, turning a service on or off is all you'll need to do. It is, however, possible to edit the service settings in more detail by selecting the service and clicking Edit. This will bring you to the Edit Service Entry screen shown in Figure 6-3. On this screen, you can edit a number of fields. Chances are you'll not need to change anything here, unless you're creating a new entry from scratch.

The fields are:

Service
> This is the name of the service. Usually, xinetd looks this up in */etc/services* to figure out what port number to listen on, though it is also possible to define unlisted services for which the port number is specified explicitly.

RPC version
> Relevant only for RPC (Remote Procedure Call) services.

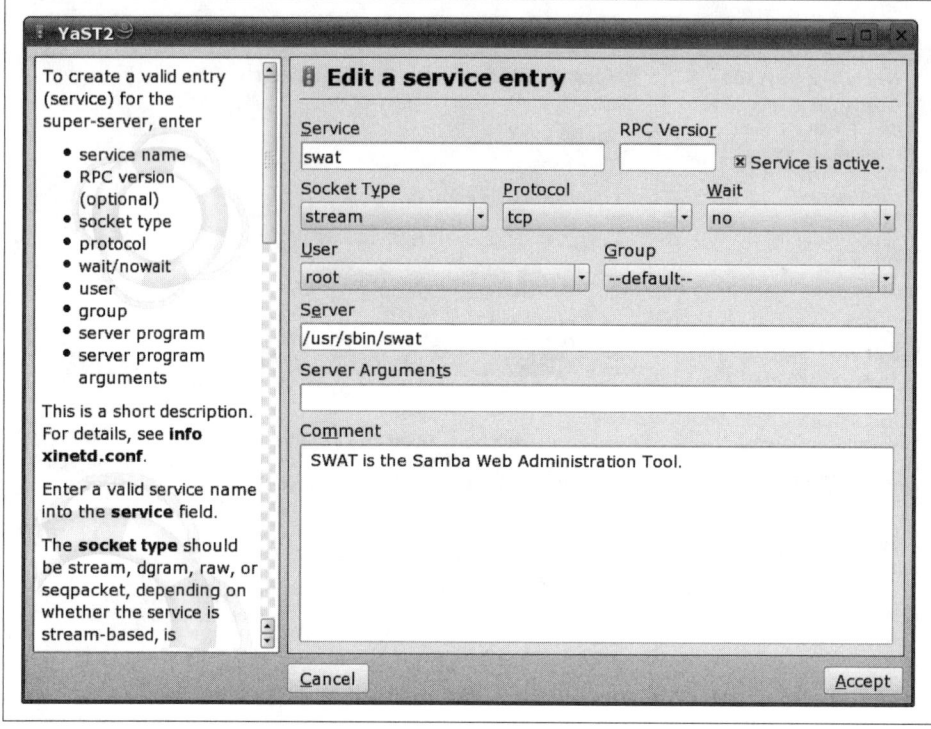

Figure 6-3. Editing xinetd service settings

Socket Type

    Usually *stream* for a connection-oriented service such as swat, *dgram* for a connectionless service such as tftp.

Protocol

    The transport protocol to use. This is usually *tcp* for connection-oriented services, *udp* for connectionless services.

Wait

    This setting (yes or no) controls whether xinetd will wait for a service to terminate, before accepting further connection requests and spawning further instances of the program. It is usually set to yes for udp services and no for tcp services.

User

    The user ID (either a name or a numeric ID) under whose identity the service will run. This is most commonly root, but standard security practice recommends running it as the least privileged user you can get away with.

Group

    The group ID under whose identity the service will run.

Server
    This is the full pathname of the program that xinetd should execute when a connection for this service is received.

Server arguments
    This contains any command-line arguments that should be passed to the server. These are sometimes used, for example, to pass options or numeric parameters to a server, or to specify a location for the configuration file.

Comment
    This is a human-readable comment.

Note that there are considerably more options available within xinetd that can be set or edited on this screen. I discuss a few of these shortly.

How Does It Work?

xinetd works by establishing multiple sockets, one for each of the services it is configured to listen for. For TCP services, xinetd waits for a connection request. For UDP services, it waits for a datagram to arrive. xinetd then forks a child process. In this child, the file descriptors referencing the network connection are copied onto the standard input and standard output. The child process then executes the program specified by the Server field in the configuration, passing the arguments specified by the Server arguments field.

xinetd reads the configuration file */etc/xinetd.conf*. In principle, it is possible to place all the service definitions in here, but normal practice is to use this file merely to define a few default settings, and to define each service in a separate file in the directory */etc/xinetd.d*. It is these files that are edited by the YaST xinetd module. On my system, */etc/xinetd.conf* looks like this. The line numbers are for reference; they are not part of the file.

```
1   defaults
2   {
3           log_type        = FILE /var/log/xinetd.log
4           log_on_success  = HOST EXIT DURATION
5           log_on_failure  = HOST ATTEMPT
6           instances       = 30
7           cps             = 50 10
8   }

9   includedir /etc/xinetd.d
```

Lines 3–5 control the default logging behavior; I discuss this later. Lines 6 and 7 provide some defense against runaway activity or denial-of-service attacks. Line 6 limits the number of simultaneously active instances of each service. Line 7 limits the rate of acceptance of incoming connections. If the rate is higher than 50 per second, the service will be temporarily disabled for 10 seconds. Line 9 tells xinetd to read all the files in */etc/xinetd.d*. It is here that the actual service definitions appear.

Here's the file */etc/xinetd.d/swat*, which shows the service definitions for the SWAT service discussed earlier in the lab:

```
# SWAT is the Samba Web Administration Tool.
service swat
{
        socket_type     = stream
        protocol        = tcp
        wait            = no
        user            = root
        server          = /usr/sbin/swat
        only_from       = 127.0.0.1
        log_on_failure  += USERID
        disable         = no
}
```

You should be able to tie most of these attributes into the fields you saw in the YaST module. If you choose to hand-edit the file, the line you're most likely to change is the setting of the `disable` attribute. Note the negative logic here; `disable = no` enables the service. You can also use the `chkconfig` command to enable and disable xinetd-based services. For example, the command:

> # **chkconfig swat off**

adds the line `disable = yes` to the file */etc/xinetd.d/swat*.

There are a number of other attributes that are not visible in the YaST module and can be set only by hand-editing the file. Table 6-4 shows some of these.

Table 6-4. Examples of xinetd.conf attributes

Attribute	Description
only_from = 192.168.0.0	Allow access only from the 192.168 network.
only_from = 127.0.0.1	Allow access only from the loopback address (127.0.0.1 always loops back to your own machine).
only_from = novell.com	Allow access only from the novell.com domain.
access_times = 0:00-7:30	Allow access only between the hours of midnight and 7:30 a.m.
log_type = FILE /var/log/xinetd.log	Log all service access to this file.
log_type = SYSLOG auth warning	Log all service access via *syslog* at priority *auth.warning*.
type = UNLISTED	The service is not listed in */etc/services*.
port = 5901	Port to listen on (used by UNLISTED services).
log_on_failure += USERID	Add the user ID to the list of items that will be logged when a connection request is rejected. (The base list of items is established in */etc/xinetd.conf*; this example adds to it).
instances = 30	Limits the number of simultaneous instances of any one service that can be active.
cps = 50 10	Limits the rate of incoming connections. If the rate of new connections exceeds 50 per second, the service will be disabled for 10 seconds.

Note that specifying access controls based on the domain name of the client (as in the third row of the table) forces xinetd to do a reverse DNS lookup to map the client's IP address onto a hostname. Not only is this likely to slow things up significantly, it is also of limited value, as most clients are masqueraded anyway and may well appear to come from an ISP's IP address, which is of little help in identifying the actual client. Note also that the USERID (in the last row of the table) is the identity of the user at the other end of the connection as established by the identd service. Because this service is virtually never run, this information is unlikely to be available (and if it is available, it's unlikely to have a meaningful value).

If you hand-edit any of these files, you will need to force xinetd to re-read them. You can do this by sending it a HUP (hangup) signal. Something like this should do the trick:

```
# killall -HUP xinetd
```

What About...

...the logfiles? xinetd logs to a file, or via syslogd, depending on the log_type attribute. Of course, you can specify a separate logfile for each service if you want. Here a fragment of the log showing one failed access and one successful access to the swat service. Each entry starts with a date and time stamp.

```
05/10/20@17:36:12: FAIL: swat address from=192.168.0.17
05/10/20@17:36:12: START: swat from=192.168.0.17
05/10/20@17:36:12: EXIT: swat status=0 duration=0(sec)
05/10/20@17:37:08: START: swat from=127.0.0.1
05/10/20@17:37:08: EXIT: swat status=0 duration=0(sec)
```

The failed access was from 192.168.0.17, which failed because my definition of the swat service allows access only from the local host.

What About...

...performance implications? Starting a service up via xinetd imposes the overhead of a process creation (fork) and program execution (exec) every time. These are relatively expensive operations. For a service that receives a hit only every few seconds this is fine, but for a service that is likely to receive hundreds of hits a second, the overhead is likely to be unacceptable. Services like apache and samba are not started this way.

Where to Learn More

Look at the manpages for xinetd and xinetd.conf.

6.3 Create and Mount Disk Partitions

When SUSE Linux is initially installed, it normally creates at least two partitions on the hard drive—one for the filesystem (the root partition) and one for swap space.

More complex partitioning schemes are discussed in Chapter 9. The time may arise, however, when you wish to create additional partitions, perhaps to put disk space that was left free at install time into use, perhaps because you've added a second drive to your machine, or maybe—just maybe—because you've decided it's time to get rid of that Windows partition you've left lying around and put it to better use.

The system used in this lab was originally installed with a 10 GB partition (*/dev/hda1*) as the root partition, and a 1 GB swap partition (*/dev/hda2*). The total disk capacity was 38 GB. It was decided to create another 5 GB partition to use as the */home* partition for the users' home directories. There were already some user accounts, with content under */home*; initially, of course this content was on the root partition.

How Do I Do That?

Partitions are most easily created using YaST.

In the main YaST screen, click System in the panel on the left, then Partitioner in the panel on the right. This will bring you to the Expert Partitioner screen which will show your existing partition structure. From this screen, click Create. Depending on how many partitions currently exist, you may be asked whether you want to create a primary partition or an extended partition. (As discussed later in this lab, you can create a maximum of four primary partitions or three primary and one extended.) As there are currently only two partitions defined, you'd create a third primary partition.

Now you'll see the partition creation screen shown in Figure 6-4.

Linux supports several filesystem formats. (The filesystem format refers to the underlying data structures kept on the disk. All these formats present themselves to the user in the same way, as a hierarchy of folders and files.) Click the Format radio button and select the filesystem type you want to create from the drop-down list labeled File System. The choices are:

ext2
    This is one of the "original" Linux filesystems (there was also plain old "ext" before then). It is a perfectly serviceable filesystem, but it does not support journaling.

ext3
    This filesystem adds journaling capability to an ext2 filesystem. Journaling is the process of writing out a log of updates of the filesystem's metadata. The presence of a journal makes the process of recovering a damaged filesystem (e.g., after a power outage) much faster. The journal does, however, consume a small amount of space. The ext3 format is upward-compatible from ext2. You can mount an ext3 filesystem as ext2 and ignore the journal.

Reiser
    This filesystem, designed by Hans Reiser, is a total redesign of the filesystem structure. Unlike ext2/ext3, it does not use a fixed-size inode table. It is claimed

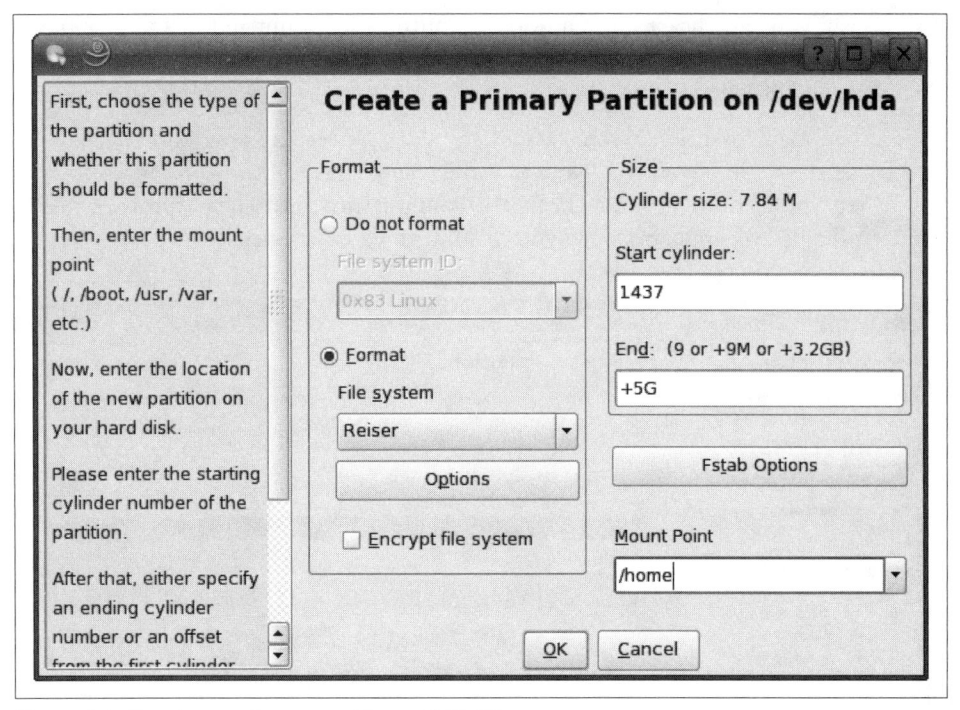

Figure 6-4. Creating a primary partition with YaST

to give significantly better performance for small files, but benchmarks suggest that there is little difference in speed between Reiser and ext2 for large files. It's also possible (apparently—I haven't actually tried it) to resize a Reiser filesystem without losing the data. Reiser is the preferred filesystem type for SUSE Linux.

FAT
   This is the old DOS-compatible filesystem. You're only likely to want to choose this if you need the filesystem to be accessible by a DOS/Windows operating system.

XFS
   XFS is another journaling filesystem, from SGI.

swap
   This isn't a filesystem format at all—it's the partition type you define for use as swap space.

For this lab, select Reiser. In the field labeled "Start Cylinder," you'll be shown the lowest available cylinder number. Unless you want to do something funny like deliberately leave a gap on the disk, just accept this default. In the field labeled "End," you can either type in the ending cylinder number or (much easier) type in the size, such as +5G. In the field labeled "Mount Point," type in the desired mount point; in this case, it is */home*. (Actually, */home* is one of the choices available in the drop-down list so you can just select it from there.)

If you wish, you can click Fstab Options to control the mount settings for the partition in more detail. I'll take a look at that in a minute, but the defaults are usually OK. Click on OK when you're done.

Back at the main partitioner screen, you should now see the new partition you've created, as shown in Figure 6-5. Note that the change hasn't been committed to disk yet. When you're done, double-check the configuration and click Apply. A rather dramatic dialog box appears asking you to confirm your actions.

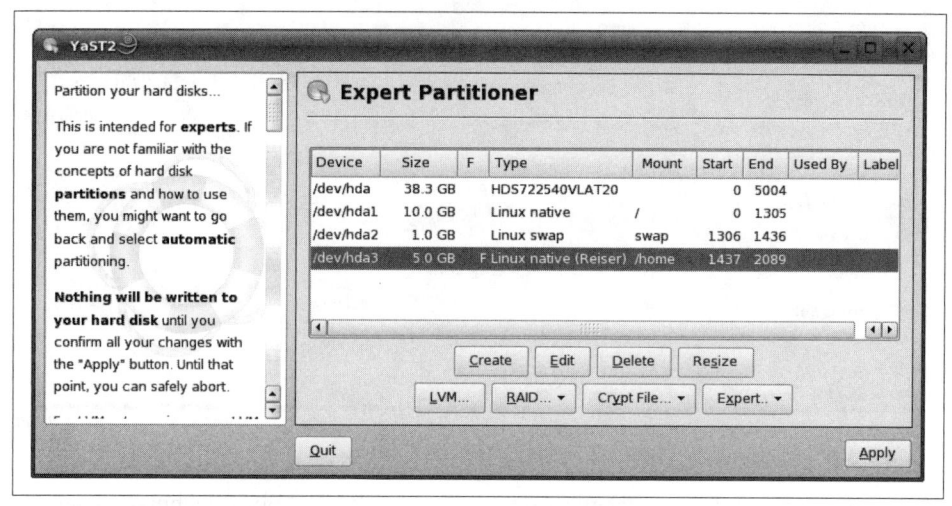

Figure 6-5. YaST Expert Partitioner screen

The Fstab Options screen is shown in Figure 6-6.

A partition can be identified in several ways. The first is by the Linux device name, such as */dev/hda2*. The second is by its volume label, which is a string recorded within the partition itself. In the *fstab* file, which I'll get to later, partitions are associated with mount points. You can use either the device name or the label to identify the partition. Labels have the advantage of staying constant if you move the disks around within the machine, whereas the device names may change. On this screen, you can specify whether *fstab* will use device names or volume labels, and actually assign a label to the partition. (You can also set a volume label from the command line using e2label.) A partition can also be identified using a UUID (Universally Unique Identifier) which is one of those giant numbers that looks like this: 70b0d8db-adad-49e0-bfc1-a55c0bfcd98e. UUIDs serve a similar purpose to volume labels.

The read-only mount option is self-explanatory. It is good security practice to mount partitions read-only if you can. If */usr* is on a separate partition, it is often mounted read-only to make it harder for intruders to replace system binaries. You might do the same with a partition containing a large, static archive of stock images, for example. However, it's probably not useful to mount a brand-new empty partition read-only!

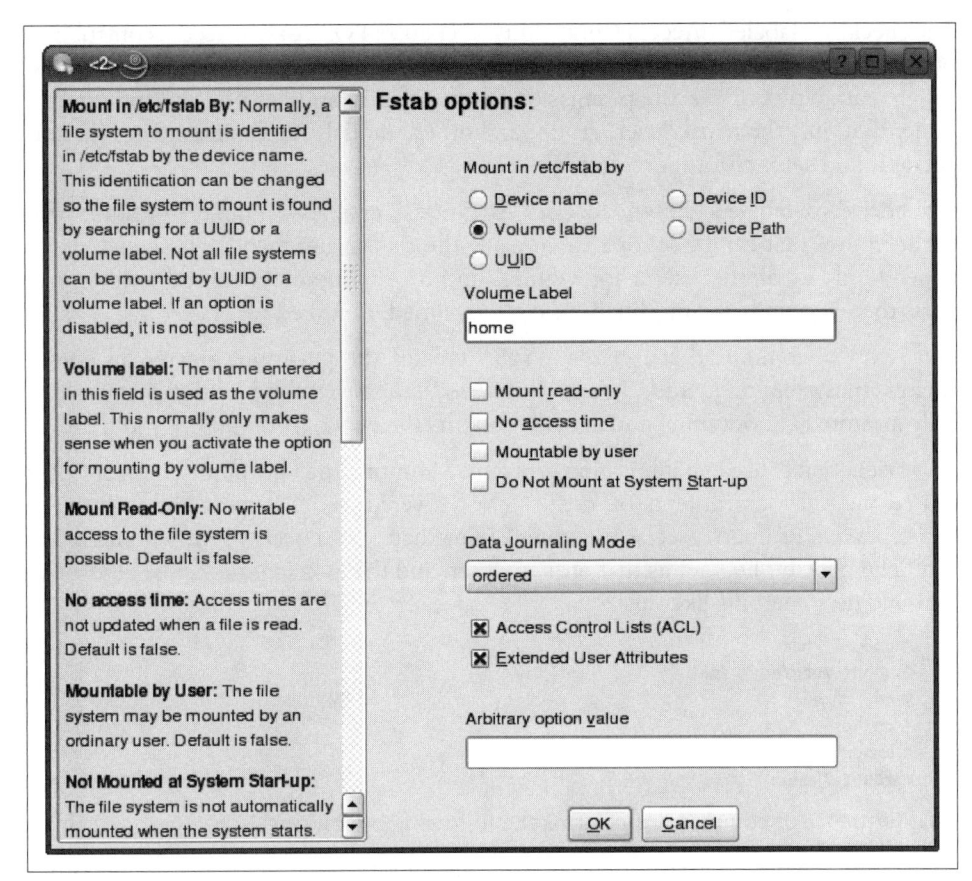

Figure 6-6. Setting mount options in YaST

The checkbox labeled "No Access Time," if checked, stops Linux from updating the *last access timestamp* on each file every time it is accessed. If you don't care about knowing when the files were last accessed, you might speed things up slightly by selecting this option. You might choose to do this, for example, on a partition that contains static web content.

The checkbox labeled "Do Not Mount at System Startup," if checked, stops this mount from being put in place automatically when the system boots.

The checkbox labeled "Mountable By User," if checked, allows nonroot users to mount and unmount the device. Typically this option is used for removable media but not for partitions on hard drives.

The drop-down list labeled "Data Journaling Mode" allows the selection of three modes: journal, ordered, and writeback. These modes control the way in which an ext3 filesystem writes its journal. The ordered mode offers a good balance of speed and safety and is recommended for most purposes.

The checkbox labeled "Access Control Lists" enables POSIX-style access control lists on the filesystem. ACLs allow you to extend the traditional Linux security model to assign read, write, or execute permission to an arbitrary number of users and groups, rather than just the usual "user, group, and other" model. See the manpages for `acl`, `getfacl`, and `setfacl` for more details.

The checkbox labeled "Extended User Attributes" enables a number of additional file attributes that can be set or cleared using the `chattr` command. These include an append-only attribute, useful for logfiles, and an immutable attribute, which prevents the file from being modified, deleted, renamed, or linked to.

Once you've committed the change, YaST creates the partition, creates an empty (Reiser) filesystem on it, adds an entry into */etc/fstab* so that the partition is automatically mounted at boot time, and actually mounts the new partition there and then.

This last action caused an interesting problem. Mounting the new partition onto */home* caused the previous contents of */home* to be "covered up." As I was logged into the desktop as an ordinary user at the time, I immediately lost access to my home directory. The remedy? Log out as that ordinary user, and then log in on a virtual console as root and do something like this:

```
# umount /home
# mount /dev/hda3 /mnt
# cd /home
# cp -pr . /mnt
# umount /mnt
# mount /home
```

That sequence of commands performs the following operations:

1. Unmounts the new partition that YaST just mounted, so that I can see the original */home* directory "underneath" it.
2. Mounts the new partition onto */mnt*, so that I can access it.
3. Copies the contents of the original */home* directory onto the new partition, preserving the timestamps, ownerships, and permissions.
4. Unmounts the new partition from */mnt* and mounts it back onto */home*.

> Those are the kind of moments when I feel grateful for having enough traditional Linux command-line experience to dig myself out of trouble. However, I was left wondering how a Linux newcomer might react to discovering that YaST had, apparently, emptied his home directory.

How It Works

When you create a partition with YaST, it does four things:

1. It modifies the partition table on the hard drive, and tells the kernel to re-read it.
2. It creates an empty filesystem structure on the partition.

3. It creates an entry in /etc/fstab (yes, we'll get to that in a minute) so that the partition will be mounted automatically at boot time.

4. It mounts the partition onto the designated mount point.

A partition is a fixed-sized part of a hard drive. It could be the whole drive, but even if it isn't, think of it as a separate hardware device. The beginning and end of a partition are defined in terms of cylinder numbers. Originally, a cylinder was that set of tracks on a multiplatter disk that can be accessed for any given radial position of the disk read/write heads. Modern drives often hide their true physical geometry behind the disk controller. However, the concept of cylinders remains, and a partition must be a whole number of cylinders. This is why the partition size you get may be slightly different from the size you ask for.

Historically, a PC could have only four partitions on a disk. This limitation arose from the BIOS of early PCs. The concept of extended and logical partitions was introduced to overcome this limitation.

> This discussion applies specifically to PCs derived from the original Intel architecture. If you're running SUSE Linux on other hardware, your mileage (to quote the famous disclaimer in the car ads) may vary.

You can put up to three *primary* partitions on a drive, and one *extended* partition. Within the extended partition, you can place a relatively large number of *logical* partitions. YaST takes note of this scheme, and if you choose to create four primary partitions it will refuse to create any more. If you already have three primary partitions, the next one you create should be an extended partition, which will normally encompass all the remaining space on the disk. Thereafter, YaST will automatically assume that any further partitions you ask to create should be logical partitions within the extended partition. Figure 6-7 shows a typical scenario with three primary partitions (hda1, hda2, hda3), one extended partition (hda4), and two logical partitions (hda5, hda6) within the extended partition. Note that you can't put a filesystem on hda4. Because hda4 is an extended partition, it's simply a container for the logical partitions.

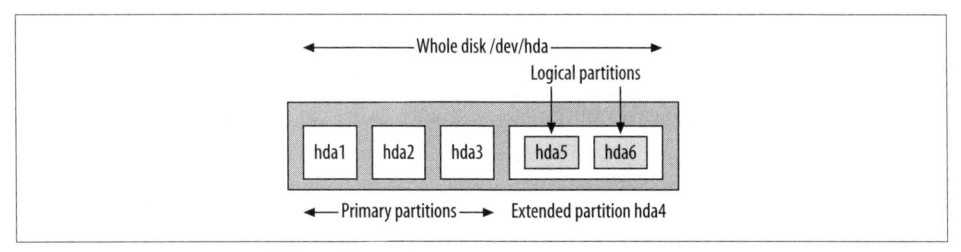

Figure 6-7. Primary, extended, and logical partitions

The /etc/fstab file is a key system configuration file that specifies which partitions should be mounted. An error in this file can cause real problems, and may even prevent the system from booting. An entry in *fstab* associates a partition (identified by a

device name or a volume label) with a mount point, a filesystem type, and a set of
mount options that controls the behavior of the filesystem within this partition.

Here's the entry that YaST created in *fstab* for the partition that we created in this
lab:

```
/dev/hda3       /home           reiserfs   acl,user_xattr     1 2
```

You will notice that the entries made in the YaST partitioner screens correspond
directly to fields in this file. The fields are:

/dev/hda3/
> Identifies the partition. It is most commonly the device name, such as /dev/hda3,
> but may also be an entry of the form LABEL=*home* (where *home* is the label), or
> UUID=70b0d8db-adad-49e0-bfc1-a55c0bfcd98e, or (if this is a filesystem on an NFS
> file server) an entry of the form *hostname:directoryname*. The use of labels and
> UUIDs to identify partitions has the benefit that if the drive is physically reas-
> signed within the machine (so that, for example, hda3 becomes hdb3), the label
> and UUID remain constant.

/home
> The mount point for this partition. Normally this is an empty directory created
> solely for the purpose of being a mount point. If the directory is not empty, any
> content will be "covered up" when the mount is in place.

reiserfs
> The filesystem type of this partition. The keyword auto in this field tells mount
> to figure out the filesystem format for itself by examining the partition.

acl,user_xattr
> The mount options for this partition. This is a comma-separated list of options,
> and this is where the going gets tough; some details are listed in Table 6-5.

1
> The fifth field is used by the dump command (a utility for performing incremental
> backups of a partition). A 1 in this field indicates that the filesystem should be
> included by dump. This tool has largely fallen out of use and the field has little
> meaning these days.

2
> The sixth field is used by the file consistency check program fsck to determine
> the order in which filesystem checks are done at boot time. The root filesystem
> should have a value of 1; other filesystems will normally have a value of 2.

There are, potentially, many options that can be specified in the fourth field. Some of
them apply to all filesystem types and some are specific to the filesystem. Table 6-5
shows some of the most useful options.

Table 6-5. Mount options

Option	Opposite	Description
atime	noatime	Updates the last-access timestamp for each access.
auto	noauto	Mounts this partition at boot time (more specifically, in response to a mount -a command).
dev	nodev	Allows "device special files" on this filesystem.
exec	noexec	Allows files on this filesystem to be executed.
rw	ro	Mounts the filesystem with read/write access.
suid	nosuid	Honors the "set user id" bit on files in this filesystem.
dev	nodev	Allows device special files to be recognized on this filesystem.
user	nouser	Allows ordinary users to mount this filesystem. By default, only root is allowed to mount filesystems.

There are some significant security implications in allowing ordinary users to mount filesystems, especially those on removable media that might have been prepared on some other system to which the user has root access. Several of the options listed in the table are designed to address these issues. For example, a potential intruder wishing to gain root access to the machine might create a copy of the bash shell on a CD, which is owned by root and has the setuid bit on. If the intruder is able to mount the CD, he or she can now run a root shell on the machine. Setting the nosuid mount option stops the setuid bit from taking effect and defeats this attack. Similarly, the intruder might choose to create an entry for a special device file such as */dev/hda1* on the removable medium, and to give himself read and write access to that device. The intruder can then (with a bit of effort) write a program to open the device directly and examine the files on it, bypassing the filesystem entirely. The nodev mount option prevents device files from being recognized and defeats this attack. There is a third, similar option called noexec, that prevents the system from executing any program stored on the mounted filesystem. The user option, which allows ordinary users to mount the filesystem, implies the nosuid, nodev, and noexec options; however it is possible, if you really want to, to override this. For example, you can specify the options user, exec to allow ordinary users to mount the filesystem and still allow executable programs.

What About...

...doing it from the command line? The program cfdisk provides a character-based tool for partition management. It is an ncurses based program that provides a nice screen layout, as shown in Figure 6-8.

Use the up/down arrow keys to select an existing partition, or (as shown in the figure) the unpartitioned free space. Use the left/right arrow keys to select a command

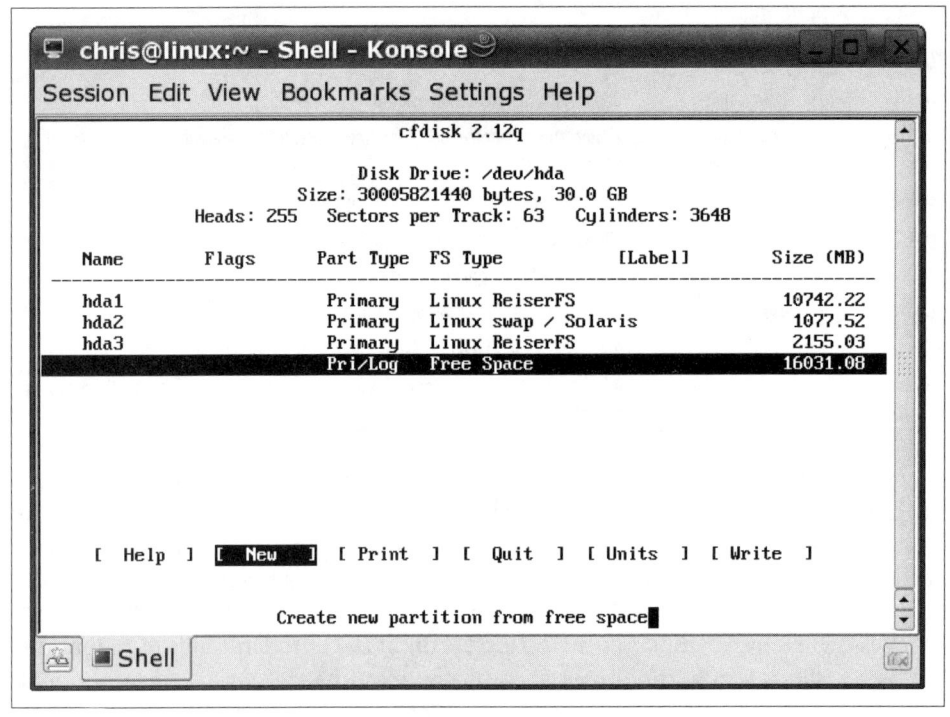

Figure 6-8. Partition management with cfdisk

(shown across the bottom of the screen) appropriate to the partition you've selected. For example, to create a new partition select New and press Enter. You'll be asked if you want to create a primary or logical partition. (The extended partition, hda4, is created automatically when required, as with YaST. It is not shown in the list.) You'll be prompted for a partition size, and whether you want to create the partition at the beginning or the end of the free space. To write out the new partition table, select Write. For a full command summary, select Help.

For an even more old-fashioned partition management tool, try fdisk. This does not use ncurses; it is a tool you could even use on a teletype (though you may need to visit your local computer museum to find one). It is driven by a menu of single-letter commands. From the fdisk prompt, type m to see these. fdisk is unlikely to be your tool of choice for creating partitions, but it is occasionally useful to run it in a noninteractive mode to display the current partition table:

```
# fdisk -l /dev/hda

Disk /dev/hda: 30.0 GB, 30005821440 bytes
255 heads, 63 sectors/track, 3648 cylinders
Units = cylinders of 16065 * 512 = 8225280 bytes

   Device Boot      Start         End      Blocks   Id  System
/dev/hda1               1        1306    10490413+  83  Linux
/dev/hda2            1307        1437     1052257+  82  Linux swap / Solaris
```

```
/dev/hda3         1438      1699    2104515   83  Linux
/dev/hda4         1700      1723     192780    5  Extended
/dev/hda5         1700      1723     192748+  83  Linux
```

All that `cfdisk` and `fdisk` do is modify the partition table. Unlike YaST, they do not create a filesystem on the partition, they do not create entries in *fstab*, and they do not mount the partition. For these operations, you need additional commands.

After quitting from `cfdisk` or `fdisk`, you should run `partprobe`, which forces the kernel to read the new partition table. Alternatively, you can reboot, but that takes longer. Now that the kernel knows about the partition, you can create an empty filesystem on it. To create an ext3 filesystem, use a command of the form:

```
# mke2fs -j /dev/hda5
```

The `-j` flag tells mke2fs to create a journal; that is, to create an ext3 filesystem, not ext2.

To create a Reiser filesystem on the partition, use a command of the form:

```
# mkreiserfs /dev/hda5
```

> Be very careful with these commands, especially with the device name. Making a new filesystem on a partition will destroy any existing content. Both mke2fs and mkreiserfs will refuse to create new filesystems on partitions which are already mounted, which provides some measure of protection. Nevertheless, a careless typo here can easily lose a lot of data. Above all, make sure you've replaced *hda5* with the correct partition name!

Now you can create a mount point and attach the new filesystem to it:

```
# mkdir /mymountpoint
# mount /dev/hda5 -o acl,user_xattr /mymountpoint
```

However, if you want this mount to be permanent—that is, to be put in place automatically at boot time—it is better to add a line to */etc/fstab*. For example:

```
/dev/hda5         /mymountpoint        reiserfs   acl,user_xattr 1 2
```

With this line in place, you can mount the partition more easily:

```
# mount /mymountpoint
```

The `mount` command will consult `fstab` to discover the partition device name and the mount options that it should use.

Once you've mounted the filesystem, run the `df` command to verify that the filesystem is now mounted:

```
# df -hT
Filesystem      Type     Size  Used Avail Use% Mounted on
/dev/hda1       reiserfs  11G  6.9G  3.2G  69% /
tmpfs           tmpfs    252M   12K  252M   1% /dev/shm
/dev/hda3       reiserfs 2.1G   33M  2.0G   2% /local
/dev/hda5       reiserfs 189M   33M  157M  18% /mymountpoint
```

Where to Learn More

Well, to be honest, this is a pretty complete treatment of the topic! You might want to read the manpages for `fstab`, `cfdisk`, or `fdisk`. The manpage for `mount` documents the mount options in detail.

6.4 Create Logical Volumes

The problem with fixed-size disk partitions, discussed in Lab 6.3, "Create and Mount Disk Partitions," is just that: they are of fixed size. If your system usage outgrows a particular disk partition, you will need to save the partition's contents somewhere (perhaps by copying a `tar` archive across the network to another machine), create a larger partition, then restore the tar archive onto it. Even creating a larger partition can be tricky—you can't just grow a partition, unless it happens to be followed by free space on the disk, in which case you can delete the existing partition and create a bigger one.

Logical volumes provide a more flexible way of managing and allocating disk space. Using logical volumes, you create one or more physical disk partitions (they don't all need to be on the same drive) and allocate them to a *volume group*. The volume group represents a "pool" of disk space out of which you can carve some *logical volumes*. Then you create filesystems on the logical volumes and mount them into the directory hierarchy. At a later date, if part of the filesystem outgrows its logical volume, you can simply pump some more space into the logical volume from the free space available in your volume group. In other words, you can defer the decision about how much space is allocated to each part of your filesystem hierarchy, and extend the logical volumes as required. The relationship between physical partitions, volume groups, and logical volumes is illustrated in Figure 6-9.

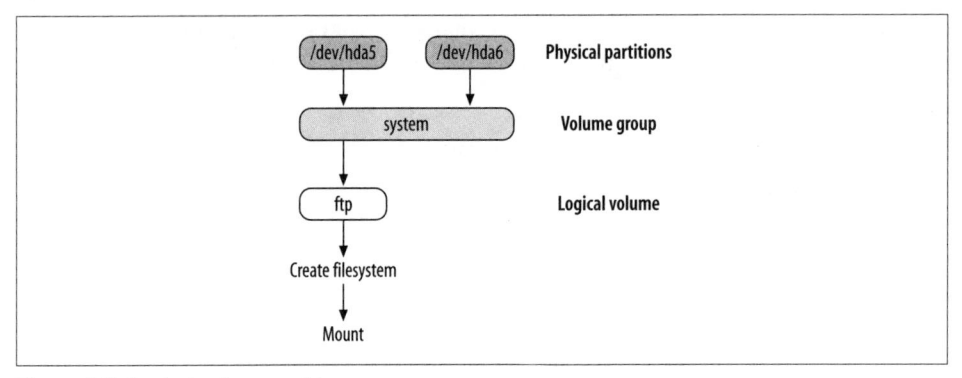

Figure 6-9. Logical volume architecture

Let's be quite clear about how logical volumes do and don't help. They do provide greater flexibility in allocation of disk space to filesystems. They don't provide improved reliability; indeed, if a logical volume spans multiple partitions, a problem on any of the partitions is probably going to lose you the entire volume. Also, logical volumes do not (primarily) improve performance, although a logical volume striped across multiple hard drives may show improvement in I/O bandwidth.

How Do I Do That?

The logical volume management tools are contained in package lvm2, which you'll need to install, because it's not installed automatically.

To create a logical volume using YaST, you'll first need to create one or more physical partitions to provide raw space for your volume groups. The lab "Create and Mount Disk Partitions" shows how to do this. In this case, however, the partitions must have a *type code* (YaST calls it the *file system ID*) of 8e (the partition type code reserved for partitions that are intended for use in a volume group). You do not specify a mount point, as you will not place a filesystem directly onto this partition. In this lab, you'll create two partitions (hda5 and hda6) for this purpose.

In reality, there is little benefit in splitting a volume group amongst two or more physical partitions if they are all on the same drive. You'd be better just creating a single, large partition. However, I've chosen to do this in the lab to illustrate the multipartition scenario on a machine that happens to have only one drive. If you have more that one hard drive, of course, you'll necessarily have more than one physical partition.

Once your physical partitions are defined, go to the Expert Partitioner screen in YaST and click LVM to proceed to the Logical Volume Management screen. If this is the first time you've done this, there will be no volume groups, and YaST will pop up a dialog named "Create a Volume Group" so that you can create one. You need to specify two things: first, a name for the volume group (YaST proposes the name "system," and there is no real reason to change this); and second, a size for the physical extent of the volume group. The physical extent determines the granularity with which space can be allocated from the volume group— that is, the size of a logical partition must be a multiple of the physical extent of the volume group it's created from. The default is 4 MB and this is probably fine. The only reason to increase it is to allow for extremely large volume groups. With a 4 MB physical extent, the maximum size of the volume group is 256 GB. Increasing the physical extent to (for example) 16 MB would increase the maximum size of the volume group to 1,024 GB. You cannot change the physical extent of a volume group at a later stage.

After dismissing this dialog, the next screen you'll see is labeled "Logical Volume Manager: Physical Volume Setup." See Figure 6-10.

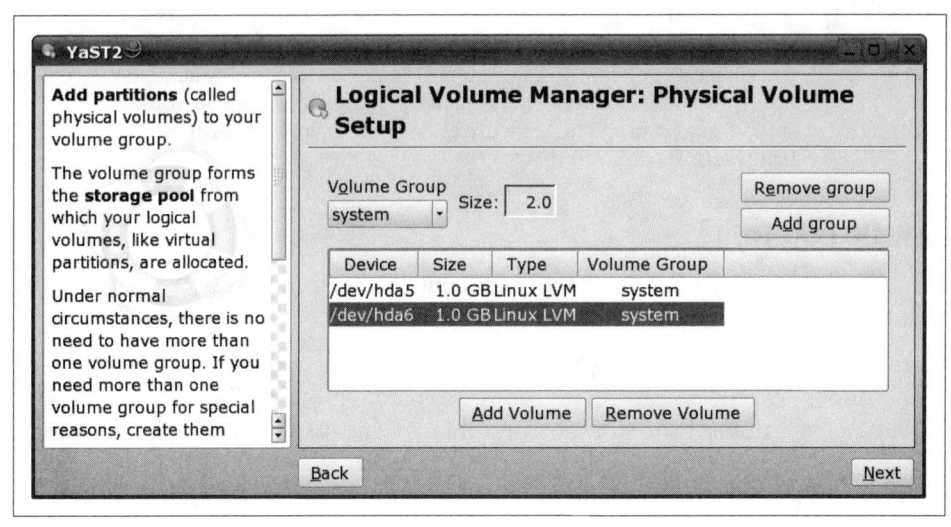

Figure 6-10. Assigning physical partitions to a volume group

Here, you're able to assign physical partitions to the volume group. In this example, I have added both hda5 and hda6 to the volume group called system. To do this, just select each partition in turn and click Add Volume. (I think "Add Partition" would be a better label for this button.) Notice that this screen only shows you partitions of type 8e. Also the tool is smart enough to prevent you from assigning the same physical partition to more than one volume group.

Having assigned some physical partitions to our volume group, click Next. The next screen, labeled "Logical Volume Manager: Logical Volumes" is shown in Figure 6-11.

This screen is analogous to the main Expert Partitioner screen in YaST, except that here you're creating logical partitions using space on a volume group, rather than creating physical partitions using space on a hard drive. To create a new logical partition, click Add. You'll see a dialog labeled "Create Logical Volume," shown in Figure 6-12.

You'll need to specify a filesystem type (I chose Reiser), a size for the logical partition, and a mount point. Unlike creating physical partitions, you also get to give the logical volume a name. There are two mysterious fields in this dialog, labeled "Stripes" and "Stripe size." Striping of a logical volume means distributing the data in the volume amongst the partitions "turn and turn about." Striping can improve performance, but only if:

- The physical partitions are all on different drives
- The physical partitions are all the same size
- The number of stripes is equal to the number of physical partitions

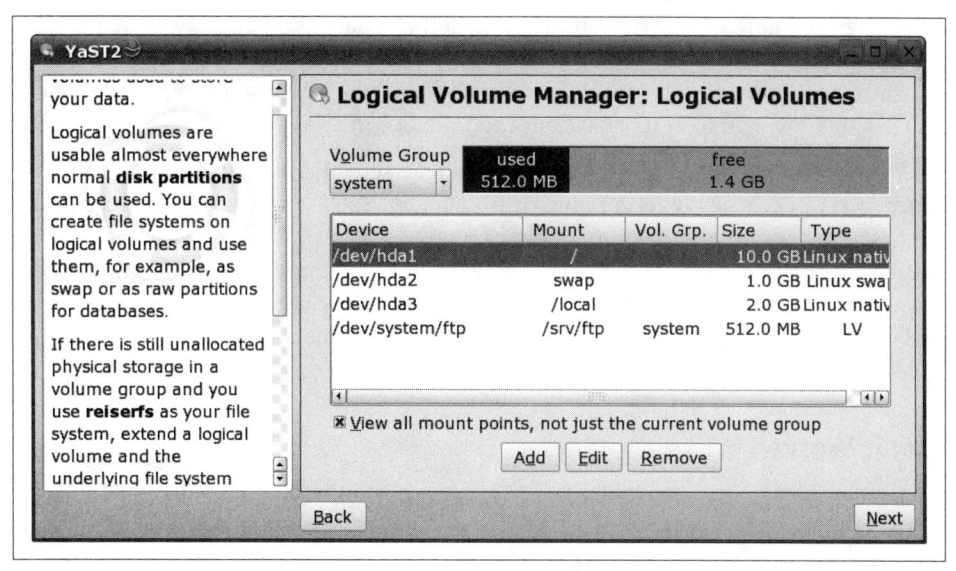

Figure 6-11. Managing logical volumes

Figure 6-12. Creating a logical volume

In this case, with two physical partitions on the same drive, striping across these two partitions is not a good idea.

Returning to Figure 6-11: you'll notice a little bar chart showing how much of the volume group is allocated. It is not necessary to allocate the entire volume group straight away; indeed, that would in a sense defeat the purpose of logical volumes, which is to allow you to defer space allocation decisions.

Click Next to exit the Logical Volume Manager screen. Back at the Expert Partitioner screen, click Apply to commit your changes. YaST displays a scary green dialog box with a summary of what it's planning to do. Check this over carefully before confirming that you want to go ahead. Remember, deleting or reformatting a partition that's in use is going to lose you a lot of data. Now you have a new filesystem ready for use. It's formatted, it's mounted on your specified mount point (*/srv/ftp* in this example), and there's an entry for it in *fstab*.

How It Works

Behind the scenes, a collection of command-line tools (contained in the package `lvm2`) are used to perform the real work. These include the commands shown in Table 6-6.

Table 6-6. LVM command-line tools

Command	Description
`pvcreate`	Initializes a physical volume (partition) for later use by the logical volume manager.
`vgcreate`	Creates a named volume group containing one or more physical volumes. The physical volumes must have been initialized by `pvcreate`.
`vgextend`	Extends a volume group by adding more physical volumes to it.
`vgreduce`	Removes physical volumes from a volume group.
`lcvreate`	Creates a logical volume of a specified size within an existing volume group.
`lvextend`	Increases the size of an existing logical volume.
`lvreduce`	Reduces the size of an existing logical volume.
`resize_reiserfs`	Changes the size of an (unmounted) Reiser filesystem. (This tool is part of the `reiserfs` package, not the `lvm2` package, but is relevant here if you need to change the size of a logical volume with a Reiser filesystem on it.)

To see these commands in action, here's how you would use them to perform the same logical volume management tasks you performed using YaST.

You need to create physical partitions of type 8e first using any of the partitioning tools (YaST, `cfdisk`, `fdisk`) described earlier. Be sure to verify that these partitions exist before you proceed:

```
# fdisk -l

Disk /dev/hda: 30.0 GB, 30005821440 bytes
255 heads, 63 sectors/track, 3648 cylinders
Units = cylinders of 16065 * 512 = 8225280 bytes
```

```
Device Boot     Start       End      Blocks   Id  System
/dev/hda1           1      1306   10490413+   83  Linux
/dev/hda2        1307      1437    1052257+   82  Linux swap / Solaris
/dev/hda3        1438      1699    2104515    83  Linux
/dev/hda4        1700      1961    2104515     f  W95 Ext'd (LBA)
/dev/hda5        1700      1830    1052226    8e  Linux LVM
/dev/hda6        1831      1961    1052226    8e  Linux LVM
```

Next, you must prepare the physical volumes hda5 and hda6 for use by the logical volume manager:

```
# pvcreate /dev/hda5 /dev/hda6
  Physical volume "/dev/hda5" successfully created
  Physical volume "/dev/hda6" successfully created
```

Next, you should create a volume group called system, comprising these two physical volumes:

```
# vgcreate system /dev/hda5 /dev/hda6
  Volume group "system" successfully created
```

Next, create a logical volume called ftp by allocating 512 MB of space from the volume group system:

```
# lvcreate -n ftp -L 512 system
  Logical volume "ftp" created
```

You can verify the device name of the new logical volume using lvscan:

```
# lvscan
  ACTIVE            '/dev/system/ftp' [512.00 MB] inherit
```

The next task is to create a filesystem on this partition:

```
# mkreiserfs /dev/system/ftp
mkreiserfs 3.6.18 (2003 www.namesys.com)

... some messages edited out here ...

ALL DATA WILL BE LOST ON '/dev/system/ftp'!
Continue (y/n):y
Initializing journal - 0%....20%....40%....60%....80%....100%
Syncing..ok
ReiserFS is successfully created on /dev/system/ftp.
```

Next, add an entry to /etc/fstab. For example:

```
/dev/system/ftp        /srv/ftp        reiserfs   acl,user_xattr 1 2
```

Finally, you can create the directory for the mount point, and, if you wish, mount the partition here:

```
# mkdir -p /srv/ftp
# mount /srv/ftp
```

The underlying kernel technology that supports logical volumes is the *device mapper*, which is a part of the Linux 2.6 kernel. It provides a generic way to create virtual layers of block devices that can do different things on top of real block devices;

this includes things like striping, concatenation, mirroring, snapshotting, and the provision of encrypted filesystems.

What About...

...extending a logical volume? The whole point of logical volumes is that you can grow them as needed. For example, suppose that the /srv/ftp filesystem is getting rather full:

```
# df -h /srv/ftp
Filesystem            Size  Used Avail Use% Mounted on
/dev/mapper/system-ftp
                      512M  428M   85M  84% /srv/ftp
```

To increase the size of this logical volume, you can use the main Logical Volume Management screen. In the first part of this lab, YaST guided you so carefully through the appropriate series of screens that you never actually saw this screen! You reach it from the top-level YaST screen by selecting System from the panel on the left, then LVM from the panel on the right. This screen, shown in Figure 6-13, allows the creation of new volume groups and the management of existing ones.

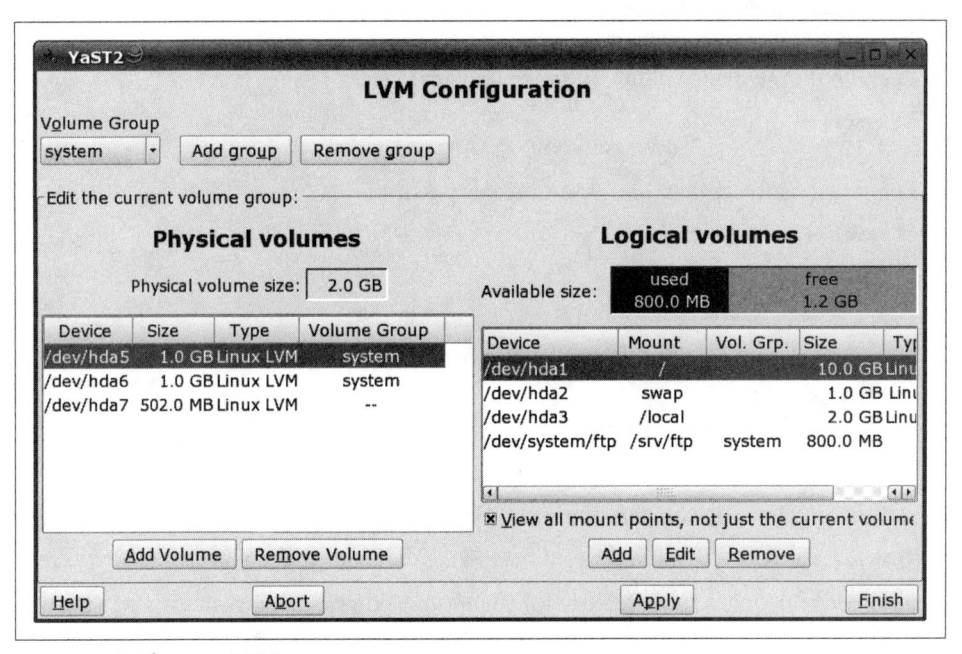

Figure 6-13. The main LVM management screen

To enlarge a logical volume, select the volume from the panel on the right (labeled Logical Volumes), click Edit, then enter the new size in the Edit Logical Volume dialog. Click OK to dismiss the dialog, then Finish to commit the change. Immediately, you'll see the extra space showing up in the filesystem:

```
# df -h /srv/ftp
Filesystem            Size  Used Avail Use% Mounted on
/dev/mapper/system-ftp
                      800M  428M  373M  54% /srv/ftp
```

Notice that the filesystem was actually mounted while you did this. This is quite an impressive feat, and so much easier than trying to resize a physical partition.

Of course, you may have no free space within the volume group to allocate. If this is the case, you need to create another physical partition of type 8e. Then, within the main LVM management screen, select this partition from the panel on the left (labeled Physical volumes) and click Add Volume. The additional space immediately shows up in the volume group. Note that I have created only one volume group. If you have more than one, the drop-down list labeled "Volume Group" in the top-left corner of this screen lets you choose which one to operate on.

> Of course, you may reach the point when you have no free space on your hard drive to create another partition. In this case, YaST will automatically send out begging letters, via email, to raise the necessary cash, then contact the web site of your local hardware supplier to order a new drive. Well, maybe in the next release.

Where to Learn More

Read Chapter 2 (especially section 2.2) of the online SUSE Linux reference manual, available within the SUSE Help Center. For more background and detail, try the LVM HOWTO at *http://tldp.org/HOWTO/LVM-HOWTO*. Also read the manpages for commands such as pvcreate, vgcreate, lvcreate, vgextend, and lvextend.

6.5   Monitor and Manage Processes

Every running program in a Linux system runs within the context of a *process*. It's important to understand the distinction between a program and a process. A program is a comparatively concrete thing—it's a sequence of instructions telling the computer what to do. A process is more abstract—it's the thing that holds together the context needed to execute the program. The context includes the memory regions that hold the program's code and data; open file descriptors such as standard input and standard output; a list of variables known as the environment; a priority that determines how favored it will be by the scheduler; a user ID and a group ID that define the identity with which the process is running; a current directory; and a few more technical things like the signal-handling settings. Indeed, in a sense, this collection of items *is* the process.

From a user's perspective, processes get started in several ways (from the kernel's perspective there is only one way—through the execution of a fork( ) system call). Some processes are started at boot time to run the daemons that provide network services. Others are started by users by selecting an item from a menu or typing a command in a shell. Some applications create multiple processes of their own, often for performance reasons. When a new process is created, the process that did the creating is called the *parent*, and the new process is called the *child*.

Processes are the lifeblood of Linux. As you work on the computer, they come and they go. As I write this, my laptop is running 93 processes, and it isn't really *doing* anything! For the most part, you don't need to be aware of process activity, but when things aren't behaving, it helps to know your way around. In this lab, you'll see how to examine process activity and how to manage processes. As with the other labs, I show both the graphical utilities and the command-line tools.

How Do I Do That?

KDE provides a nice graphical tool called KDE System Guard. (I have no idea why it's called that—by no stretch of the imagination does it guard the system.) From the main menu select System → Monitor → Performance Monitor. Alternatively, you can start it by typing ksysguard in a terminal. The main screen of KDE System Guard has two tabs labeled System Load and Process Table. For now, I focus on the Process Table tab, shown in Figure 6-14.

On this screen, you can see a one-line entry for each process. The columns are:

Name
    The name of the program that this process is running.

PID
    The numeric ID of this process. These are allocated sequentially starting when the system boots. (The init process discussed earlier in the chapter is always process ID 1.)

User%
    The percentage of CPU time that this process is executing in user mode; that is, executing instructions that are part of the program itself.

System%
    The percentage of CPU time that this process is executing in system mode; that is, executing instructions within the kernel on behalf of this process (processing system calls). In the screenshot, you can see that the only process consuming significant CPU resources is running the program md5sum, and this process is consuming 21.5% of the CPU time in total (16% user, 5.5% system).

    The nice value indirectly controls the scheduling priority of the process. Values range from –20 to +19. Negative nice values cause the process to be scheduled more aggressively. Only root can decrease the nice value of a process. Positive nice values lower the priority of the process. The default is 0.

VmSize
    This is the total memory size of the process in kilobytes.

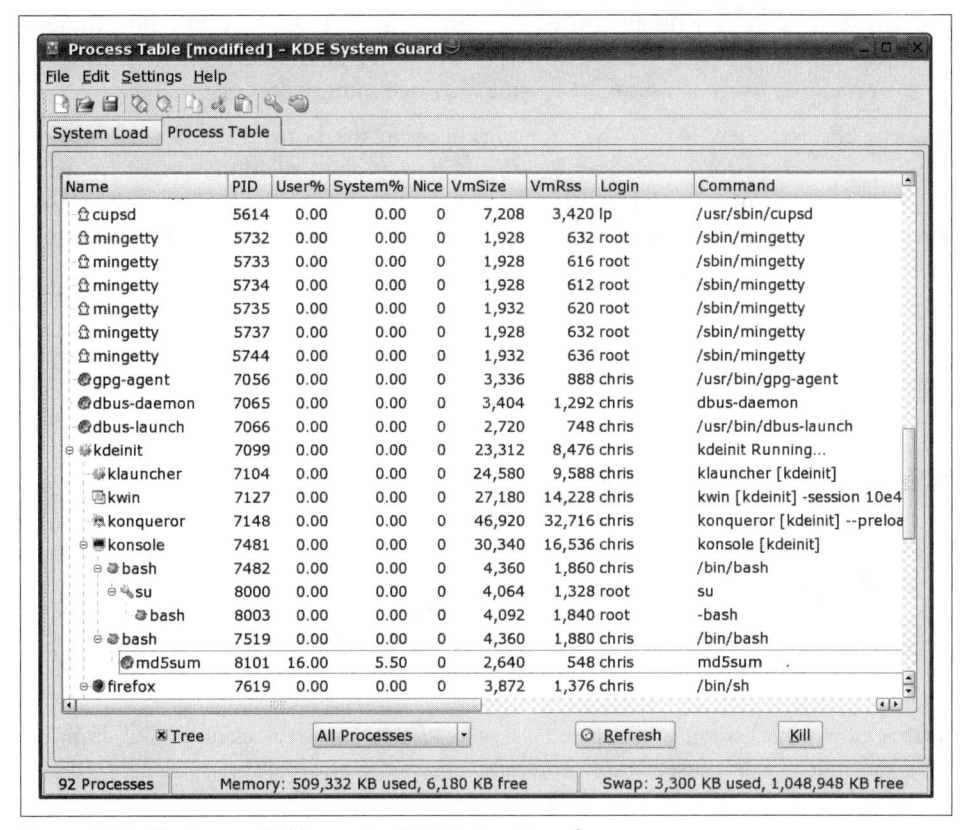

Figure 6-14. The Process Table view in KDE System Guard

VmRss
> This is the amount of actual physical memory that the process is using. (RSS stands for Resident Set Size.)

Login
> This is the user identity with which the process is running.

Command
> This is the command line used to start the process. (This doesn't imply that the process was actually started by typing a command into a shell—very few of the processes in this list were started this way. All processes received "command-line" arguments from their parents, not just ones started from a shell.)

There are several ways in which this display can be customized. For a start, there are additional columns that can be added to the display. These include the numeric user ID of the process, the parent process ID, and the process status (sleeping or running). To add a column, right-click anywhere within the display area and select Show Column. To delete a column, right-click the column (not the column heading) and select Hide Column.

You can sort the display on any of the columns—just left-click the column heading. Click the column heading again to reverse the order of the sort. Sorting on CPU usage or memory usage is useful for finding resource-hungry processes.

Selecting the tree view (using the Tree checkbox in the bottom left corner) as I've done in the screenshot allows you to see the parent/child relationships of the processes and to expand or collapse branches of the process ancestry. There is a drop-down list to select which processes you want to see: all processes, system processes, user processes, or just the processes you own. The Refresh button forces a refresh of the display; by default, it refreshes every two seconds anyway.

Let's interpret some of the entries in the screenshot. Near the top, you can see six processes running `mingetty`. These are the processes that print the login prompts on the six virtual consoles (Ctrl-Alt-F1, Ctrl-Alt-F2, and so on). These processes are spawned directly by `init`. You saw the entries for this in *inittab* in Lab 6.1, "Control Boot-Time Service Startup," earlier in the chapter.

> `mingetty` is short for *minimal getty*. In turn, getty was the program traditionally used to issue login prompts on terminals connected via serial lines. Going back even further in time, tty stood for teletype (an old mechanical terminal device); any character terminal connected via a serial line was known as a *tty device*.

Further down the listing, you can see a few KDE support services and KDE applications running. All of these, you'll note, are descendants of `kdeinit` (process 7099). Evidently I am running `konqueror`, `konsole`, and `firefox`. The `konsole` process provides me with a terminal window. Within this window, running as children of `konsole`, are two bash shells. Notice that these are all running as me (`chris`). In one of my shells I have run the command `su` (to become `root`) and the `su` command in turn has spawned a child process to run a further instance of `bash` (process 8003), this time running as `root`. In my other bash shell, I'm running `md5sum` to compute the checksum of a (very large) file. This process is taking a significant amount of CPU time.

KDE System Guard allows you to perform one rather basic action on a process—it allows you to kill it. Just select the process from the listing and click Kill. You can select multiple processes from the list and kill all of them with a single click. Be aware, however, that this is a rather brutal way of terminating a process—it doesn't get any opportunity to clean up—so you should regard it as a last resort.

From the command line the nearest equivalent to KDE System Guard is `top`. Figure 6-15 shows `top` in action.

At the top of the display, we see some overall performance measurements—CPU usage, memory usage, and so on. The main part of the display contains a list of processes; the columns are similar (but not identical) to the columns you saw in KDE

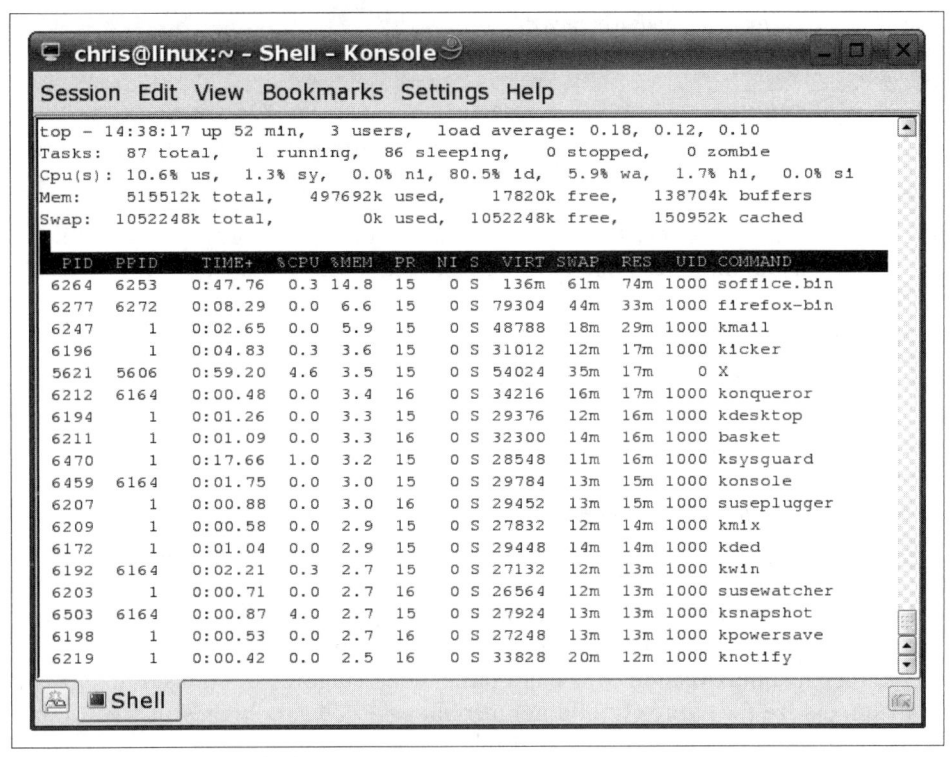

Figure 6-15. Using top to display processes

System Guard and shouldn't need further explanation. By default, the display refreshes every three seconds.

The display is configurable through a series of one-letter commands. Some of the commands are shown in Table 6-7.

Table 6-7. Selected top commands

Command	Description	Example	Description
q	Quit from program	(no arguments)	
h	Display help screen	(no arguments)	
f	Toggle fields (columns) on/off	f *a*	Turn PID field on/off
		f *b*	Turn %CPU field on/off
F	Select field for sorting	F *a*	Sort on PID field
		F *k*	Sort on %CPU field
R	Toggle normal/reverse sort		
u	Show processes for user	u *chris*	Show processes for user chris
d	Set update interval	d *1*	Set interval to 1 second
n	Set number of processes in list	n *10*	10 processes in list

Table 6-7. Selected top commands (continued)

Command	Description	Example	Description
k	Kill process	k 1499 15	Kill process 1499 by sending it signal type 15
r	"Renice" a process	r 1510 5	Set nice value of process 1510 to 5 (you cannot reduce the niceness unless you're root)

The greatest benefit of top, of course, is that it runs in an ordinary terminal. It doesn't need a graphical desktop. The interface feels a little clunky until you get used to it. There are help screens along the way—for example, to show you the field names. It's best just to try it out.

For a true (noninteractive) command line experience, use the ps command. By default, ps selects all processes owned by the current user and associated with the same terminal the command was invoked on. It displays the process ID (PID), the terminal associated with the process (TTY), the cumulative CPU time (TIME), and the executable name (CMD). The command has more options than you can shake a stick at. Most of the options either select which processes will be listed, or select what information is shown for each process. Historically in Unix, a number of variants of the ps command emerged, each with subtly different options. In an heroic (but possibly misguided) attempt to be backward-compatible with as many versions as possible, the Linux version of ps has a rather confusing set of options. Rather than try to summarize the entire (1,100-line) manual page, I'll simply present four examples which I've found useful, shown in Table 6-8.

Table 6-8. Selected ps command options

Command	Description
ps -e	Show brief information on all processes (PID, associated TTY, CPU time, and command)
ps -ef	Show fuller information on all processes (adds UID, Parent PID, start time fields)
ps -u chris	Show all processes owned by chris
ps -e --forest	Show all processes with parent/child relationships in a tree view

Here's a (heavily edited) example of running ps:

```
> ps -u chris -f
UID        PID  PPID  C STIME TTY        TIME CMD
chris     6429  5117  0 20:21 ?      00:00:00 /bin/sh /usr/X11R6/bin/kde
chris     6477     1  0 20:21 ?      00:00:00 /usr/bin/gpg-agent --sh --daemon
... lots edited out here ...
chris     7913  6521  2 20:30 ?      00:00:00 konsole [kdeinit]
chris     7914  7913  0 20:30 pts/3  00:00:00 /bin/bash
chris     7933  7914  0 20:31 pts/3  00:00:00 ps -u chris -f
```

You can use the kill command to send a signal to a process. I discuss signals in more detail in the next section. There are two common reasons for sending a signal to a process. The first is to force it to terminate, the second is to force it to reread its configuration file. Many applications respond to a *TERM* signal by terminating gracefully. Many daemons respond to a *HUP* signal by rereading their config file.

How Does It Work?

Commands like top and KDE System Guard that display process information obtain most of their raw data from the */proc* filesystem. The files in this directory, which are entirely a figment of the kernel's imagination, provide a way to see inside running processes and other kernel tables.

> You could argue that *all* files are a figment of the kernel's imagination, on the basis that the entire filesystem is an illusion created by the kernel. If you looked directly at the hard disk, all you'd see are zeros and ones. But at least the contents of an ordinary file do correspond to data stored on a hard drive. The contents of the files under */proc* are just "made up" by the kernel on the fly.

It's possible (and quite interesting, in a nerdy sort of way) to examine the files in */proc* directly with traditional commands like ls and less, but you'll find that much of the information is very low-level and hard to interpret. It is generally better to examine processes using commands such as top and ps. As a quick example of the kind of thing you'll find in */proc*, here's the current contents of */proc/meminfo* on my machine:

```
MemTotal:         515512 kB
MemFree:           15804 kB
Buffers:           26148 kB
Cached:           124932 kB
SwapCached:         6404 kB
Active:           418048 kB
Inactive:          32448 kB
HighTotal:             0 kB
HighFree:              0 kB
LowTotal:         515512 kB
LowFree:           15804 kB
SwapTotal:       1052248 kB
SwapFree:        1005548 kB
Dirty:                 8 kB
Writeback:             0 kB
Mapped:           396640 kB
Slab:              38088 kB
CommitLimit:     1310004 kB
Committed_AS:     592628 kB
PageTables:         3104 kB
VmallocTotal:     507896 kB
VmallocUsed:        9616 kB
VmallocChunk:     497776 kB
HugePages_Total:       0
HugePages_Free:        0
Hugepagesize:       4096 kB
```

Here, you'll see more detail about the current state of the virtual memory system than you probably wanted to know.

It may help in interpreting the output of programs such as KDE System Guard and top to understand a little about the mechanics of process creation and the normal life cycle of a process. Figure 6-16 shows the typical sequence of events.

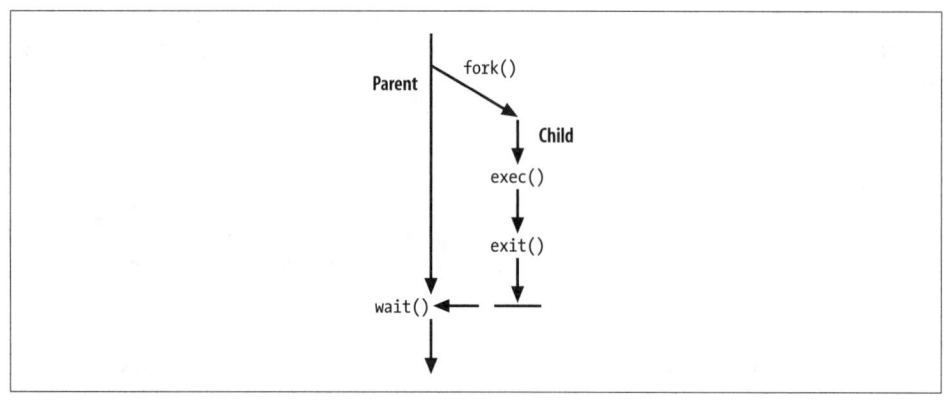

Figure 6-16. Normal process life cycle

Some process (the *parent*) creates a new process (the *child*) by making a fork( ) system call. The two processes proceed to run concurrently. Initially, the child is running the same program as the parent, but usually the child makes an exec( ) system call that causes the memory image of the process to be replaced by that of some other program. At some later time, the program running in the child completes its tasks and makes an exit( ) system call which terminates the process. Meanwhile, back in the parent, a wait( ) system call has been made. This causes the parent to wait until the child exits. At that point, the child passes its exit status back to the parent and the parent continues. In the Linux world, it is common for parents to outlive their children in this way.

There are several variations on this theme. The parent does not always wait for the child. Sometimes the two really do continue to execute in parallel. This happens, for example, if you start a background program in the shell (by putting an & at the end of the command line). Sometimes the child does not execute a different program but continues to execute the same program as the parent. This happens, for example, when the Apache web server *preforks* a number of child processes to allow it to handle multiple simultaneous connections.

What About...

...orphans and zombies? There are a couple of special cases of process life cycles worth mentioning. If a process exits while it has children still running, the children become *orphans*. Happily, the kernel arranges for them to be inherited by init (process ID 1). The init process, which stays running throughout, always has a wait( ) system call outstanding and will collect (and ignore) the exit status of any orphaned process when it terminates. Occasionally, a process creates a child and then gets stuck for some reason. It may be in a compute-bound loop, or (more likely) it may be waiting to read from a network connection. In this case, when the child process exits, it discovers that no one is waiting for it, so it has nowhere to return its exit status to. In this case, the child enters a *zombie* (also called *defunct*) state. It is not running, but it is not completely laid to rest either.

Under normal circumstances, zombies should not occur. They generally represent a design or coding error in the parent. However, it is easy to create zombies on purpose. Consider the following C program:

```
/* file zom.c */

#include <stdlib.h>

main( )
{
    int i;
    for (i=0; i<3; i++)
        if (fork( ) == 0) exit(0);
    pause( );
}
```

The program loops around three times, creating three child processes, each of which immediately exits. Then, the parent calls pause( ), which causes it to block indefinitely. If you compile and run this program, it will block indefinitely, as expected:

```
$ cc zom.c -o zom
$ ./zom
```

Now open a second terminal and have a look at what processes were created:

```
$ ps -ef | grep zom
chris     8473  7738  0 17:27 pts/1    00:00:00 ./zom
chris     8474  8473  0 17:27 pts/1    00:00:00 [zom] <defunct>
chris     8475  8473  0 17:27 pts/1    00:00:00 [zom] <defunct>
chris     8476  8473  0 17:27 pts/1    00:00:00 [zom] <defunct>
chris     8504  8431  0 17:27 pts/3    00:00:00 grep zom
```

Notice the three zombie processes (marked "defunct" in the listing), which have a common parent (process ID 8473). You cannot kill these zombies; even if you send the unignorable KILL signal, they remain:

```
$ kill -KILL 8474
$ ps -ef | grep zom
chris     8473  7738  0 17:27 pts/1    00:00:00 ./zom
chris     8474  8473  0 17:27 pts/1    00:00:00 [zom] <defunct>
chris     8475  8473  0 17:27 pts/1    00:00:00 [zom] <defunct>
chris     8476  8473  0 17:27 pts/1    00:00:00 [zom] <defunct>
chris     8529  8431  0 17:30 pts/3    00:00:00 grep zom
```

The way to kill a zombie is to terminate its parent. Then, the zombie will be inherited by `init`, which will lay the process finally to rest. Here we see that if you kill the parent, all the zombies go away:

```
$ kill 8473
$ ps -ef | grep zom
chris     8560  8431  0 17:36 pts/3    00:00:00 grep zom
```

Where to Learn More

Look at the manual pages for `top` and `ps`. A superb reference on the "systems programming" aspects of processes (and all else to do with Unix and Linux) is *Advanced Programming in the UNIX Environment* by Stephens and Rago (Addison-Wesley). (Not for the casual reader.)

6.6   Examine and Manage Logfiles

Many Linux utilities, especially the network services, write information about their activities to various logfiles. In conformance with the FHS (Filesystem Hierarchy Standard), the logfiles are in */var/log* or in subdirectories thereof. Some logfiles are overwritten each time the service starts; others simply grow without limit unless steps are taken to manage them. If the system is misbehaving, logfiles can provide vital clues to the cause. They can also provide evidence of attempts to breach system security.

In my experience, there are a couple of problems with logfiles. First, they contain a great deal of "noise" (messages of no importance), which makes it hard to find the few significant entries that are present. Second, there seems to be a particular brand of obfuscation that application developers reserve for the messages they write to logfiles—in other words, they are hard to understand.

This lab looks at some key logfiles, mentions some tools that can help analyze and manage the logs, and shows how to configure the logging behavior.

How Do I Do That?

Table 6-9 shows some of the key logfiles you'll find in */var/log*.

Table 6-9. Selected logfiles

Logfile	Content
boot.msg	Contains boot-time messages from the kernel and (towards the end) reports of service startup. It is overwritten each time the system is booted. Most of this is low-level rumbling inside the kernel, which won't make much sense to most of us.
faillog	Contains failed login attempts. This is a binary database and should be examined with the `faillog` command.

Table 6-9. Selected logfiles (continued)

Logfile	Content
firewall	This file contains messages from the packet filtering code in the kernel. How much you'll see in here depends entirely on how firewall logging is configured. See Lab 8.3, "Set Up a Firewall" for details. Typically, it might contain details of suspicious packets that were dropped.
lastlog	This file is a database containing the time and date of the last login of each user. It is a binary file and should be examined with the `lastlog` command.
mail	Contains all messages from the mail facility (i.e., from the postfix mail delivery agent). Messages with priorities information, warn, and err are also broken out into the files *mail.info*, *mail.warn*, and *mail.err*.
messages	This is the main logfile. All messages logged through `syslog` are written here (and often to other files as well), except those from `iptables` and from the mail and news facilities.
warn	All messages logged through `syslog` at priorities of warn, level, or crit are logged here. This is a good place to look to see if the system is having any significant problems.
Xorg.0.log	The start-up log of the X server. The "0" in the name refers to the display number; in the unlikely event that you have two displays, the startup log for the second display would be written to *X.org.1.log*. This file is overwritten each time the server starts. It's a very detailed, low-level report; look at it only if your X server won't start properly.

Depending on what other packages you have installed, you may have other logfiles. For example, the Apache web server writes its logs to files in the subdirectory */var/log/apache2*, and Samba logs to files in the subdirectory */var/log/samba*. (Both of these locations are configurable, of course.)

A property of logfiles is that the interesting entries are usually the recent ones near the end. For this reason, the `tail` command is often used for examining logs. For example, the command:

```
# tail -20 /var/log/warn
```

shows the final 20 lines of the file. Also useful is `tail -f`, which shows the final 10 lines of the file but then hangs around, displaying any additional lines as they are written to the file. A useful technique to debug startup of a network service is to run `tail -f` on its logfile in one terminal window, and start up the service in another. If you want to do longer term monitoring of logfile growth, you might prefer to use `tailf`. This command works much like `tail -f` except that it doesn't access the file while it isn't growing. `tailf` is especially useful for monitoring logfiles on a laptop when logging is infrequent and you want the hard disk to spin down to conserve battery life.

If you'd prefer a graphical tool for viewing logfiles, try `kwatch` (not installed by default—just install the `kwatch` package). `kwatch` lets you do the equivalent of a `tail -f` on multiple logfiles in a single window. Whenever new content appears in any of the logfiles, `kwatch` displays it. If the content is from a different file than the previous line that was shown, it is prefixed by a header giving the filename. It is easy to set up the list of files you want `kwatch` to monitor; it does not come with a predefined list. Note that because some of the logfiles are readable only by root, you may wish to run kwatch as root. From a command prompt, you can do this easily with a command such as:

```
$ su -c kwatch
```

Of course, you'll be prompted for the root password.

How It Works

Some services, such as Samba and Apache, write their own logfiles directly. Many others log via a special system logging daemon called `syslog`.

> There is an old joke from the *Goon Show* that goes something like this: "Don't throw your old jam-jars away; send them to Madge Quigly, and let her throw them away for you." I thought it was quite funny at the time. (In defense, I was only nine years old.) Anyway, it reminds me of the Linux system logging daemon, `syslogd`, of which it might be said, "Don't write your log messages to a file; send them to `syslogd`, and let it write them to a file for you."

The logging daemon traditionally used in the Linux world was called `syslogd`, which read a configuration file called */etc/syslog.conf*. Applications that sent messages to `syslogd` assigned to each message a facility (that said where the message came from) and a priority (that said how important the message was).

The `syslogd` daemon recognized a fixed list of facilities as follows: `auth`, `authpriv`, `cron`, `daemon`, `kern`, `lpr`, `mail`, `news`, `syslog`, `user`, and `uucp`, in addition to eight "user-defined" facilities named `local0` through `local7`. Some of these names, especially `uucp`, give a hint to how long ago all this was designed—uucp was a utility for copying files over dial-up connections, and its widespread use predates even that of TCP/IP! Similarly, there was a recognized list of priorities, ranging from the totally benign to the totally catastrophic: `debug`, `info`, `notice`, `warning`, `err`, `crit`, `alert`, and `emerg`.

The *syslog.conf* file contained a series of rules that determined how `syslog` would dispose of a message based on its facility and its priority. A rule might have looked like this:

```
mail.*          /var/log/mail
```

which says that messages from the mail facility at all priorities (note the use of "*" as a wild card) should be appended to the file */var/log/mail*.

I have written the last few paragraphs in the past tense, because recent versions of SUSE Linux have replaced `syslog` with a newer version called `syslog-ng` (I assume that "ng" is a Star-Trekian abbreviation for "next generation"). The `syslog-ng` daemon is backward-compatible with `syslog` (it retains the concepts of facilities and priorities) but supports a much more fine-grained approach to controlling where messages will be received from and where they will be sent to. The configuration file is */etc/syslog-ng/syslog-ng.conf*. Compared to the original `syslog`, this file allows far greater control over how messages will be logged, at the expense of a substantially more complicated syntax. Entries in *syslog-ng.conf* define one of four things, shown in Table 6-10.

Table 6-10. syslog-ng configuration file entries

Keyword	Description
source	A source entry defines a named set of places where syslog-ng will read messages from. Sources can include files, a TCP or UDP socket (i.e., a network connection), or a Unix domain socket. (Unix domain sockets are named entries in the filesystem. They work rather like network sockets, except that they are accessible only from processes running on that machine.) There's a special source called internal that relates to messages generated directly by syslog-ng. Having syslog-ng listen on a network connection is useful to collect logs forwarded by syslog daemons on other machines onto a central logging host on the network. Normally, UDP port 514 is used. There is a commented-out entry for this in the default syslog-ng.conf.
destination	A destination entry defines a named set of places where syslog-ng will write messages to. As for a source, the list can include files (probably the most important destination), network sockets, and Unix domain sockets. In addition, there are destination drivers that will write messages to the terminal of a logged-in user, or will write messages to the standard input of any named program (which is run as a child of syslog-ng). Writing messages to a network connection (usually UDP port 514) is useful to forward the logs to a central logging host.
filter	A filter defines a set of matching rules that will be applied to messages. Messages can be matched based on their facility and priority (the old syslog behavior) and also by performing a regular expression match on various pieces of the message itself.
log	A log entry defines a message path through syslog-ng. This is really where the whole thing comes together. A message path consists of one or more sources, one or more filtering rules, and one or more destinations. If a message enters syslog-ng through one of the specified sources, and if that message matches the filtering rules, it goes out using the specified destinations.

You need at least one each of a source, destination, filter, and log to make a working file. Here is a minimal example, to give you some idea of the syntax. The line numbers are for reference, they are not part of the file.

```
1  source src { internal(); unix-dgram("/dev/log"); };
2  destination firewall { file("/var/log/firewall"); };
3  filter f_iptables   { facility(kern) and match("IN=") and match("OUT="); };
4  log { source(src); filter(f_iptables); destination(firewall); };
```

Line 1 defines a source called src that refers to the Unix domain datagram socket */dev/log* in addition to internally generated messages. */dev/log* is the traditional endpoint to which applications log messages. Line 2 defines a destination called firewall that refers to the file */var/log/firewall*. Line 3 defines a filter rule called f_iptables that will match messages coming from the kern facility that contain the strings "IN=" and "OUT=". Note that this level of filtering is beyond the capabilities of the old syslog. Finally, line 4 defines a message path, saying that messages from the source src that match the filter f_iptables should be sent to the destination firewall.

A useful feature of syslog-ng is its ability to forward messages to the syslog-ng daemon on a second machine. Using this technique you can consolidate the logs for all your machines on a single "logging host." You might do this just for convenience, or, by keeping the logging host secure, you might do it for security, to prevent an intruder from covering his tracks by doctoring the logfiles. To do this, you might define a destination like this:

```
destination forward { udp(ip("192.168.0.42") port(514)) };
```

Then, on the logging host, modify the source to include a UDP socket:

```
source src { internal(); unix-dgram("/dev/log"); udp(ip("0.0.0.0") port(514)};
```

If you want to change syslog-ng's configuration, you should not edit the file *syslog-ng.conf* directly. Instead, you should edit *syslog-ng.conf.in* (in the same directory) which is used as a template by the `SuSEconfig` utility to generate the actual *syslog-ng.conf* file. (YaST runs this program pretty well every time you commit a change, but if you want to force *syslog-ng.conf* to be regenerated you can run `SuSEconfig` from the command line as root.)

What About…

…managing the logfiles? There are a number of tools that will help pull the significant entries out from amongst the background noise in the logfiles. These include swatch (a Perl script available at *http://swatch.sourceforge.net*) and logcheck (a shell script that uses grep to do the regular expression matching, available at *http://www.palmcoder.net/files/suse-rpms/9.1*). These tools work by matching regular expressions (read from one or more configuration files) against the lines in the logfiles to determine which lines are and aren't of interest. Other tools include `logrep` (*http://sourceforge.net/projects/logrep*), which is a tool for collection and presentation of information from various logfiles including Snort, Squid, Postfix, Apache, Sendmail, and iptables. It can generate HTML reports, graphs, and multidimensional analysis. None of these tools ships with SUSE Linux, and to the best of my knowledge none is specifically tuned to work with SUSE.

For analyzing access logs from the apache web server there are many tools available, some free and some commercial. Some of these are mentioned in Lab 7.6, "Configure a Web Server with Apache," in Chapter 7.

Without intervention, many logfiles will simply grow without bound. Of course, much of the data in the file is too old to be useful. A tool that is included with the SUSE Linux distribution is `logrotate`. This tool rotates the logfiles; that is, it periodically divides them into manageable pieces and keeps only the most recent. Typically, logrotate is run daily as a `cron` job. It has its own configuration file (of course) specifying which logs to manage. Logs can be rotated after a set period of time (daily, weekly, or monthly), or when they exceed a specified size. The old logs can be compressed, and files can be mailed to specified users.

The top-level configuration file for `logrotate` is */etc/logrotate.conf*. This file defines some default settings for `logrotate`, and uses an include directive to include config files for individual services from the directory /etc/logrotate.d. It is quite possible to put the entire configuration for logrotate into a single file, but splitting it up into individual service-specific files in this way allows each service to drop its own config file into /etc/logrotate.d as it is installed. Excluding the comment lines, *logrotate.conf* looks like this:

```
1  weekly
2  rotate 4
3  create
4  include /etc/logrotate.d
```

The line numbers in this listing are for reference only; they are not part of the file. Line 1 says that files should be rotated every week. Other directives appropriate at this point are `daily` and `monthly`. Line 2 says that the last 4 logfiles should be kept; in the context of this example, this means the logfiles for the last 4 weeks. As logfiles are rotated, the current logfile (for example */var/log/warn*) is renamed as *warn-1*; the file *warn-1* is renamed as *warn-2*, and so on. Line 3 says that after each log has been rotated, a new logfile will be created. Finally, line 4 says that `logrotate` should read all the config files in the directory */etc/logrotate.d*.

As an example of a service-specific file, let's take a look at */etc/logrotate.d/syslog*. This file controls the rotation of all the logfiles generated by `syslog`. The line numbers are for reference only; they are not part of the file.

```
1   /var/log/warn /var/log/messages /var/log/allmessages \
2   /var/log/localmessages /var/log/firewall {
3       compress
4       dateext
5       maxage 365
6       rotate 99
7       missingok
8       notifempty
9       size +4096k
10      create 640 root root
11      sharedscripts
12      postrotate
13          /etc/init.d/syslog reload
14      endscript
15  }
16
17  /var/log/mail /var/log/mail.info /var/log/mail.warn /var/log/mail.err {
18      compress
19      dateext
20      maxage 365
21      rotate 99
22      missingok
23      notifempty
24      size +4096k
25      create 640 root root
26      sharedscripts
27      postrotate
28          /etc/init.d/syslog reload
29      endscript
30  }
```

Lines 1 and 2 list the logfiles to which the following entries relate. Line 3 says that the old (rotated) logfiles are to be compressed using the `gzip` utility. Line 4 says that the names of the rotated files should be formed by adding a date (in the form YYYYMMDD), rather than simply a number. For example, the file */var/log/warn* might be rotated as */var/log/warn-20051206*. Line 5 says to remove any rotated logfiles older than a year. Line 6 says to retain 99 generations of the log (note that this overrides the default set in *logrotate.conf*). Line 7 tells `logrotate` not to complain if the file was missing and line 8 says to ignore the file if it's empty. Line 9 forces a rotation if the file is bigger that 4 MB. Line 10 (overriding the setting in *logrotate.conf*) says that after rotating, the logfile should be recreated with the specified mode, ownership, and group. Lines 12–14 define a series of shell commands that should be run after the logfile has been rotated; typically, these commands are used to force the daemon to start a new logfile.

Where to Learn More

For `syslog`, read the manpages for `syslog-ng` and `syslog-ng.conf`. There is also a well-written reference manual for `syslog-ng` included in the distribution, in the file */usr/share/doc/packages/syslog-ng/syslog-ng.txt*, and an online version at *http://www.balabit.com/products/syslog_ng/reference-1.6/syslog-ng.html/intro.html*.

The manpage for `logrotate` describes both the command itself and the directives recognized in its configuration file.

6.7   Monitor System Load and Performance

Linux makes available an enormous amount of performance and system load information, through the */proc* filesystem and in other ways. This includes data on CPU utilization, memory and swap space usage, network traffic, and disk I/O activity. A careful analysis of this data, obtained under conditions of typical or heavy system load, can help find performance bottlenecks and identify how a redistribution of load, or a well-chosen hardware upgrade, can improve system performance.

Most of the raw statistics are low-level, detailed, and difficult to interpret. This lab looks at a number of the tools that are available to present the data in a more readily digested form.

How Do I Do That?

You have already met KDE System Guard, in Lab 6.5, "Monitor and Manage Processes," earlier in this chapter. There you saw how to use its process table display as a way of monitoring and killing processes. Here, you'll get familiar with its role as a system load monitoring tool.

Launch KDE System Guard from the main menu via System → Monitor → Performance Monitor. The program displays system load information via a "worksheet"—a collection of displays arranged in rows and columns, as shown in Figure 6-17. The program uses the metaphor of a *sensor*, analogous to a thermometer or an oscilloscope probe monitoring a signal on a circuit board. A wide range of sensors, covering CPU load, memory use, and load average, is available.

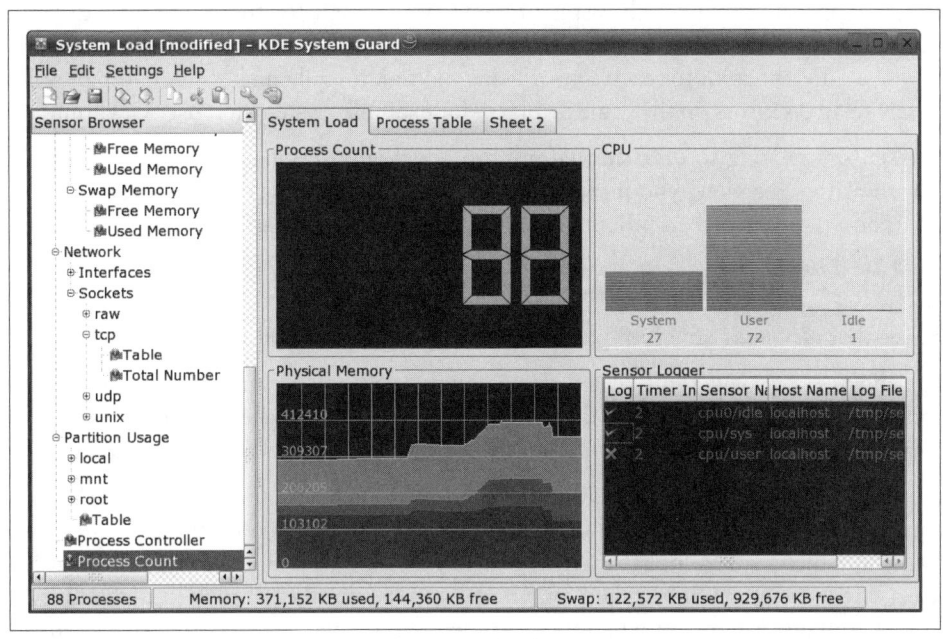

Figure 6-17. KDE System Guard displaying system load

Several display formats are available:

Scrolling signal plotter
　This is probably the most useful format, because it provides an historical record.

Digital multimeter display
　The sensor value is simply displayed as a number.

Bar chart
　The sensor value is represented by the height of the bar.

Sensor logger
　The sensor values are written to a file. Each line of the file contains a date and time, the host name, the sensor name, and the sensor value.

All of the display types appear in Figure 6-17. Each display updates at regular intervals. You can set the update interval separately for each display, but by default the entire worksheet updates every two seconds.

Bar charts have a useful "alarm" facility. You can define minimum and maximum limits for the sensor reading. If the reading falls outside that range, the bar changes color. By default you get a blue bar for in-range readings and a red bar for out-of-range readings, but the colors are user-definable.

The available sensors are shown in a tree view in the panel on the left. To add a sensor, drag it to the desired display. If this is the first sensor that's been added to this display, a menu appears asking which display type to use. Except for the multimeter display type, you can add several sensors to a display. The signal plotter will automatically choose a different color for each sensor being plotted. It really makes sense to plot only closely related sensors on the same display—for example, system and user CPU time.

The sensors relating to disk throughput are a little mysterious. If you open up that branch of the tree view, you'll see strange names like 1:0 and 3:1. These refer to the major and minor device numbers of the block devices. On my machine, for example:

```
# ls -l /dev/hda1
brw-r-----  1 root disk 3, 1 Nov  7 19:27 /dev/hda1
```

we see that */dev/hda1* (my root partition) is accessible as sensor 3:1.

To configure a display, right-click it. Here you can pause or resume the update, set the update interval, set the title for the display, set the colors of the various parts of the display, remove individual sensors from the display, or remove the display altogether.

Worksheets can be saved to disk and loaded back using the File menu, much as a document can be saved to disk or opened in an editor. (It's only the design of the worksheet that's saved, not the actual sensor readings.) To create a new worksheet, select File → New; you'll be asked for a name and the number of rows and columns it should contain. A new tab will appear in the main display area. To remove a worksheet, select its tab, then select File → Close. To save a worksheet, select its tab, then select File → Save As.

Some of the sensors provide an entire table of data rather than just a single reading. Examples are the table of active TCP endpoints and the table showing disk partition usage. These work best on worksheets consisting of only one row and one column.

Turning your attention away from KDE System Guard and back to the command line, there are a number of tools that provide system load and performance data. Many of these overlap significantly in terms of the data they provide. Some of them are summarized in Table 6-11.

Table 6-11. Performance tools

Tool	Description
vmstat	A tool that has been around in Unix and Linux for many years; displays a number of CPU, memory, and disk activity measures. It can repeat the display at regular intervals (such as every 5 seconds).
iostat	Displays statistics for CPU usage and I/O to devices and partitions. To quote the manpage: "The iostat command generates reports that can be used to change system configuration to better balance the input/output load between physical disks." Part of the sysstat package—not installed by default.

Table 6-11. Performance tools (continued)

Tool	Description
sar	System activity reporting tool. A large number of command line flags determine what is displayed. Part of the sysstat package.
mpstat	Displays CPU usage information. Particularly intended for use on multiprocessor systems. Part of the sysstat package
top	Shows a useful summary of CPU and memory usage along with a list of the "top" (most resource-hungry) processes. This tool is discussed in Lab 6.5, "Monitor and Manage Processes."

A thorough discussion of all these tools would fill several (very boring) pages, so I'll just look briefly at one of them: vmstat. Here, I invoke vmstat to print a summary every five seconds, and to repeat four times. This was done on an idle system:

```
# vmstat 5 4
procs -----------memory---------- ---swap-- -----io---- --system-- ----cpu----
 r  b   swpd   free   buff  cache   si   so    bi    bo   in    cs us sy id wa
 2  0 112708  11452 157588 139764    6   11   109    55  490   566 10  2 81  7
 0  0 112708  11452 157588 139764    0    0     0    13  460   435  1  1 88 10
 0  0 112708  11468 157588 139764    0    0     0     0  462   353  0  1 99  0
 0  0 112708  11452 157588 139764    0    0     0     0  459   349  0  2 98  0
```

The first line of output shows average figures since the system was booted. Subsequent lines show figures for each five-second period. The fields in this output are as follows:

procs

    r: The number of processes waiting for run time

    b: The number of processes in "uninterruptible sleep"

memory

    swpd: the amount of swap space in use (the figures are in kilobytes)

    free: the amount of unused memory

    buff: the amount of memory used as buffers

    cache: the amount of memory used as cache

swap

    si: Amount of memory swapped in from disk (kilobytes per second)

    so: Amount of memory swapped out to disk

    (Strictly, this is paging activity, not swapping.)

io

    bi: Blocks read from disk (blocks per second)

    bo: Blocks written to disk

system

    in: The number of interrupts per second, including the clock

    cs: The number of context switches per second

cpu

    us: Time spent running nonkernel code (user time)

    sy: Time spent running kernel code (system time)

    id: Time spent idle

    wa: Time spent waiting for IO

    (These figures are percentages of total CPU time.)

In the preceding example, notice that the CPU is almost completely idle, and there is no disk I/O.

This next example was done while running a long `find` command:

```
# vmstat 5 4
procs -----------memory---------- ---swap-- -----io---- --system-- ----cpu----
 r  b   swpd   free   buff  cache   si   so    bi    bo   in    cs us sy id wa
 3  1 112708  11524 154864 138312    6   11   109    55  490   567 10  2 81  7
 0  1 112708   9044 157140 138312    0    0   422   610  613   577  0  2  0 98
 0  1 112708   6064 160144 138312    0    0   601    13  596   566  2  3  0 95
 0  1 112708   5880 160640 138300    0    0   295   402  571   509  0  3  0 97
```

Notice that the amount of free memory is steadily falling (though there is no swapping activity), and there is heavy disk I/O. The CPU idle time has dropped to 0%, though it turns out that it is spending almost all its time waiting for I/O (the very last column). Clearly, this task is entirely disk I/O bound.

> By the way, seeing a low figure in the "free memory" column, or even seeing some swap space in use, does not necessarily mean that the system is short of memory. Linux is aggressive in commandeering unused memory for buffer space and cache. A clearer sign that you're short of memory is seeing nonzero values in the "swap out" column.

How It Works

Most of these tools read their raw data from the */proc* filesystem.

What About…

…monitoring load on remote systems? KDE System Guard is able to display load information from a remote system that is running the `ksysguardd` daemon. There are two ways you can connect. The first is by using `ssh`, which connects to `sshd` on the target and requests it to run `ksysguardd`. The second way is to connect to `ksysguardd` directly.

To connect using `ssh`, you must have previously stored the target machine's public host key on the local machine (Lab 8.2, "Provide Secure Remote Login with SSH," provides detail on this). As a useful check, from a command prompt on the local machine, try:

```
# ssh snowhite ksysguardd
Password:
ksysguardd 1.2.0
(c) 1999, 2000, 2001, 2002 Chris Schlaeger <cs@kde.org> and
(c) 2001 Tobias Koenig <tokoe@kde.org>
This program is part of the KDE Project and licensed under
the GNU GPL version 2. See http://www.kde.org for details.
ksysguardd> quit
ksysguardd> #
```

If you see a prompt from ksysguardd, as shown in the example, all is well.

To connect directly to ksysguardd, on the target machine you must verify that the daemon is running (try `rcksysguardd status` to check, or `rcksysguardd start` to start it). You should also make sure that the ksysguardd port (3112) is open in the target's firewall. Keep in mind that the traffic will be encrypted if you use ssh, but not if you connect to ksysguardd directly.

One interesting way of using the remote sensor capability of KDE system guard is to graphically monitor the load on a server farm. The idea is to set up a worksheet with, for instance, 25 displays, and use each display to show a bar graph of the same key sensor (perhaps the percentage of CPU utilization or the load average) from each of the servers. This technique works well in conjunction with the "alarm" facility, described earlier in this lab, which changes the color of the bar if the sensor reading goes outside the prescribed range. This lets you easily see which of your servers are in trouble.

Where to Learn More

The KDE System Guard handbook (accessible via SUSE Help Center or on the KDE web site) describes the use of the tool in more detail. Read the manpages for tools like vmstat and top.

To learn a lot more, buy Phillip Ezolt's book *Optimizing Linux Performance* (Prentice Hall).

There was a brief article on vmstat in the December 2005 edition of *Linux Journal*.

6.8 Backup and Restore Filesystems

It has been said that system administrators fall into one of two categories—those that perform regular backups, and those that wish they had.

I have lost files for a number of reasons. I have hard disks fail catastrophically. I have accidentally deleted the original copy of a directory full of user files, instead of the (very old) backup copy. Most spectacularly, I once caught my foot in a network cable plugged into my laptop and pulled the whole thing onto an (uncarpeted) floor. When I was a product manager for a large training company, my authors would regularly report data loss due to all sorts of reasons ranging from lightning strikes to a toddler dropping a loose hard drive into the toilet. Interestingly, the probability of such events peaked sharply a week or two prior to a deadline.

How Do I Do That?

There are several options for creating backups of your SUSE Linux system, including:

- You can manually create (and optionally compress) a `tar` archive of any desired set of files and directories. The archive can then be copied onto another machine, (using `scp` for example) or burned to a CD. It's also possible to perform incremental backups using `tar`.
- You can burn a part of the filesystem directly to CD.
- You can use the YaST backup tool.

Let's look at each of these in turn.

Creating a compressed tar archive is a simple but effective option. You will need either enough free space in the filesystem to hold the archive, or access to free space on a file server, using NFS for example. (To learn how to burn files to CD, see Lab 3.8, "Burn Your Own CDs and DVDs." To learn how to export and mount filesystems using NFS, see Lab 7.3, "Share Files Using NFS.") In any event, you must end up with the archive residing somewhere other than the machine you're backing up. Leaving the archive on the same hard drive as the files you're backing up is just silly.

For example, to back up the home directory of user `simon`:

```
# cd ~simon
# tar cjpf /tmp/simon.tar.bz2 .
```

When using tar it is, in general, best to `cd` to the directory you want to archive and specify . as the directory to archive, as in the example just shown. This makes it easy to restore the archive to a different directory, should you wish. The meaning of the flags on tar are shown in Table 6-12.

Table 6-12. Some tar options

Option	Description
c	Create archive.
j	Apply bzip2 compression. You can alternatively use z to apply gzip compression, but bzip2 generally generates smaller files. For example, on one test, gzip reduced the archive size to 22% of the uncompressed size, whereas bzip2 reduced it to 18%.

Table 6-12. *Some tar options (continued)*

Option	Description
p	Preserve the access permissions and ownership of the files.
f *name*	Write the archive to the file named in the *name* argument.

When extracting files from the archive, there are a couple of things to remember. First, make sure you cd to the right directory before you extract the archive. Otherwise you'll end up sprinkling files into whatever directory you happen to be in at the time. (Rather like spilling confetti in the vestry—it takes ages to clear up.) Second, if you are extracting specific files, use names of the form ./something; otherwise, the files won't be found. For example, to extract simon's directory foo into the directory */usr/local*:

```
# cd /usr/local
# tar xjvf /tmp/simon.tar.bz2 ./foo
```

The second backup option, burning a copy of the filesystem to CD, is really easy. You can do it from K3b if you want a graphical tool, or from the command line. You'll need to create an ISO image first, then burn it. The commands will look something like this:

```
# mkisofs -V simon_backup -J -R -o /tmp/simon.iso /home/simon
# cdrecord dev=/dev/hdc -v -eject /tmp/simon.iso
```

This is an easy option, and has the benefit that you can mount the CD back into the filesystem and access the archive directly; however, you don't get the benefits of any compression, and you can run into problems with very long filenames on the CD image.

The final method of performing backups is to use the YaST backup module. This tool is intended to provide an efficient system-wide backup (as opposed to archiving specific pieces of the filesystem). It is relatively intelligent about what needs to be included on the backup. In particular, it excludes any files that are included in the RPMs present on the installation media, and which are unchanged from those original versions.

To use the YaST backup module, go to the main YaST screen and select System from the pane on the left, then System Backup from the pane on the right. If you haven't used it before, you'll have to begin by creating a profile. The main System Backup screen shows a list of available profiles (none is provided by default) and the drop-down menu accessible from the Profile Management button allows you to add, duplicate, edit, rename, or delete a profile.

To get started, select Add. You'll be taken through a series of dialogs to define the profile.

On the first dialog, choose a name for the profile. For this lab, the intent is to define a profile that will back up the system areas (excluding the users' home directories) on a machine called shrek, so I called the profile "Shrek System Backup."

On the Archive Settings dialog, shown in Figure 6-18, you define where, and in what format the backup will be created.

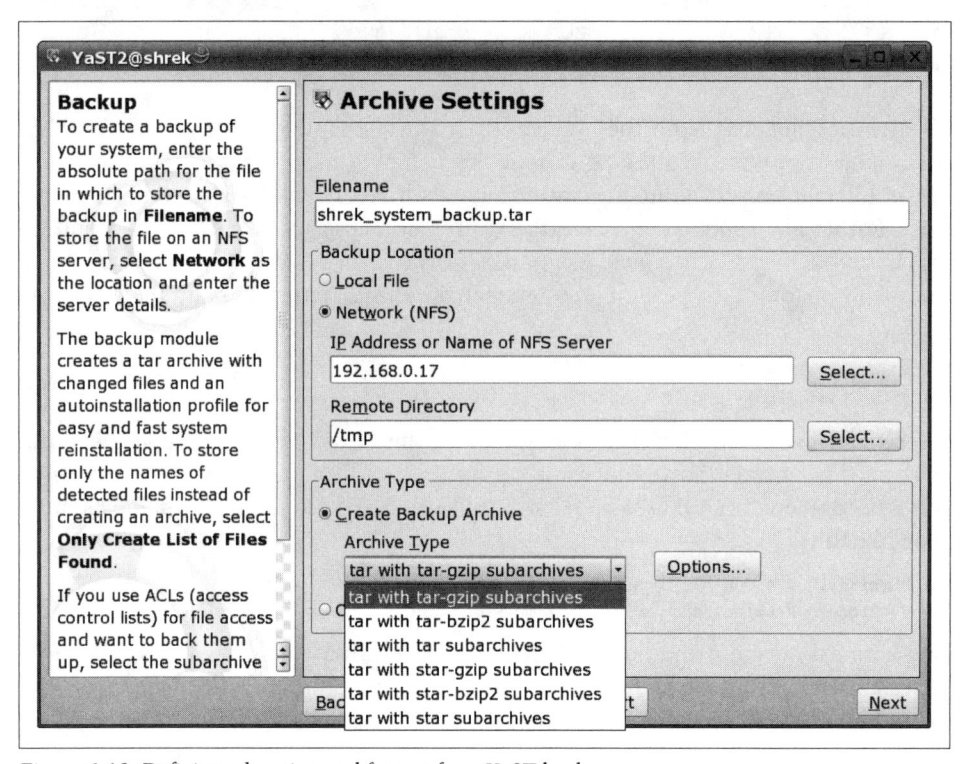

Figure 6-18. Defining a location and format for a YaST backup

You can specify a local filename (as long as you're planning to copy the backup somewhere else afterward), or you can write it to an NFS filesystem (which will be mounted for you automatically), in which case you'll need to supply the hostname or IP address of the NFS server and the name of the exported directory on that server. You can also specify the format for the archive. Basically, it's a tar archive of tar archives, but there are several variations on the theme, as shown in the drop-down list visible in the figure. Each subarchive contains the files corresponding to one installed RPM package; then there's a subarchive for the files that aren't contained in any package. The smallest archive will probably be the "tar with tar-bzip2 subarchives" format. The help panel advises using a "star" subarchive (star is a POSIX-compliant version of tar) if you are using POSIX-style access control lists on your filesystem, and wish to preserve the ACLs in the backup. Finally on this screen, the Options button lets you create a multivolume archive; helpful, for example, if you wish to write the archive to CDs. (There's even the option to split it into floppy-disk-sized pieces—good luck with that one!)

On the next dialog, labeled "Backup Options," you begin to specify how YaST will select the files that will be backed up. The basic idea is to identify those files that originated as part of an RPM file but that have changed since installation. (Service configuration files are obvious examples.) You can also choose to back up any files that don't belong to any package—for example, applications installed from source, or user data under /home, or user-installed content for a web site. The checkbox labeled "Display List of Files Before Creating Archive" does exactly what it says—and gives you the opportunity to manually exclude files from the backup if you wish. The check box labeled "Check MD5 Sum instead of Time or Size" tells YaST to use the MD5 checksum of each file as a basis for determining whether the file is different from the originally installed version. This is a marginally more reliable way of detecting changed files but takes substantially longer to build the archive list. (In one test, using MD5 increased the time to build the archive list from 9 minutes to 30.) You can also provide a text description of the archive, if you want.

On the next dialog, labeled "Search Constraints," you can exclude specific files, directories, or filesystem types from the backup. The list is prepopulated with likely candidates for exclusion, such as the pseudo-filesystems proc and sysfs, and also such directories as /var. You can add to this list as you wish. Because this is intended as a system backup, I chose to exclude /srv and /home. You can also exclude files based on a regular expression match on the filename. For example, to exclude .bak files, add the regular expression \.bak$ to the list.

This completes the definition of the profile. Returning to the main System Backup screen, click Create Backup to start the process. YaST will now spend some considerable time building the list of files to be included in the archive.

Once the backup is complete, a summary is displayed, as shown in Figure 6-19.

In addition to the tar archive itself, an auto-installation profile (.*xml* file) is also generated. This file can be used to reinstall the system from scratch.

> My personal view of this tool is that while it might have seemed like a good idea at the time, it has a certain more-trouble-than-it's-worth feel to it. Also, it doesn't effectively address the backup of user data areas (yes, it will back them up, but there is no support for incremental backup). On a mature system, the user data is much bulkier, and more valuable, than the system areas.

Let's suppose you have a catastrophic failure that destroys your root (/) and /usr partitions. To restore your system from the archive, you would first need to reinstall the system (using the auto installation profile generated by the YaST backup tool to ensure that you get the same set of packages as you originally installed) from the installation media, then run the YaST restore module once your system is up and running. This module can be directed to read the archive from a local file, from an NFS server, or from removable media. You may then view the files in the archive;

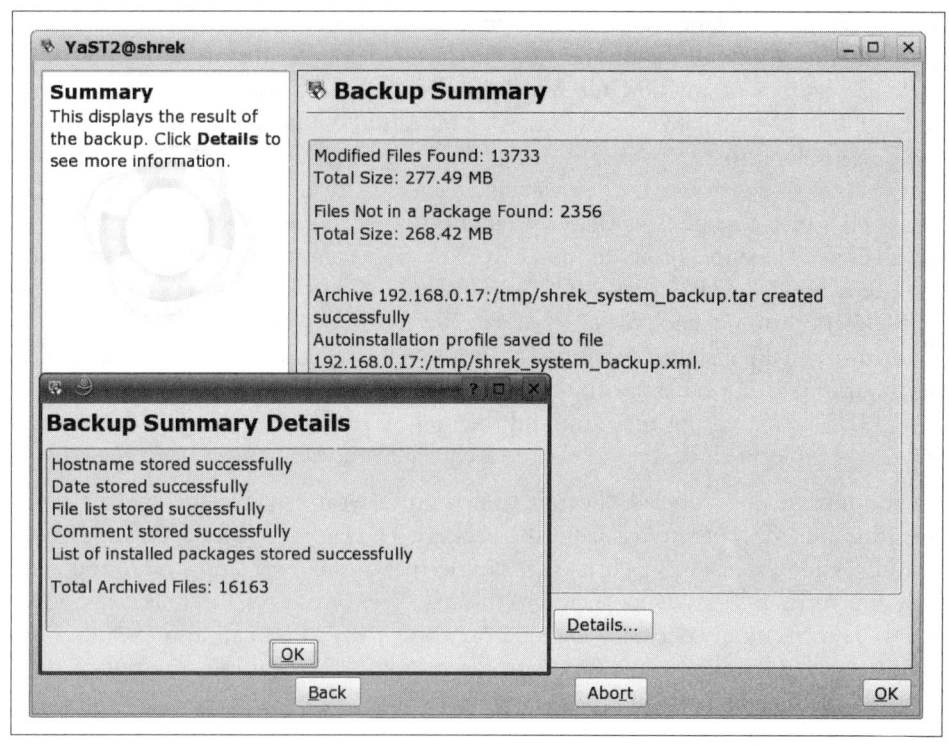

Figure 6-19. YaST Backup Summary

however, there doesn't seem to be any way of manually selecting which files you want to restore, so you'll have to go ahead and do a complete restore.

What About . . .

...backing up live filesystems? In the days when the programs `dump` and `restore` were the preferred backup solution, many system administrators would take the filesystems offline (that is, unmount them) before backing up. There was a risk that dump would fail if a live filesystem were updated during the dump. This technique was possible because dump opened the raw device (such as */dev/hda1*), and decoded the filesystem structure directly, rather than going through the usual system-call interface to access the directories and files. This technique won't work for tools like `tar`, which (like any other normal application) require a filesystem to be mounted before its contents can be accessed. There is a small risk that a file will end up corrupt on a tar archive if it happens to get updated while `tar` is in the middle of reading it. If this risk is not acceptable, one option is to bring the system down to single-user mode, so that the filesystems are quiescent.

If your filesystem is on a logical volume, another option is to take a snapshot of the volume, then archive the snapshot. In Lab 6.4, "Create Logical Volumes," earlier in this chapter, you saw how to create a logical volume called */dev/system/ftp*. It was part of a volume group called system. You can create a new logical volume that contains a snapshot of this filesystem with the commands:

```
# modprobe dm-snapshot
# lvcreate -L 512M -s -n ftpsnap /dev/system/ftp
```

Here, the modprobe command was necessary to load the device mapper snapshot module into the kernel (one of the few times I've found it necessary to load a module explicitly). The -s flag to lvcreate says to create a snapshot. The -n flag gives the snapshot logical volume a name (it will be created within the system volume group) and the final argument names the existing logical volume you want to take the snapshot of. After this, you have two logical volumes, like this:

```
# lvscan
  ACTIVE    Original '/dev/system/ftp' [512.00 MB] inherit
  ACTIVE    Snapshot '/dev/system/ftpsnap' [512.00 MB] inherit
```

Now you can mount the snapshot:

```
# mount /dev/system/ftpsnapshot /mnt
```

and use tar, for example, to safely archive the files from it.

Creating a snapshot logical volume does not just blindly copy the whole of the original volume into the snapshot—it's more intelligent than that. A snapshot contains only those blocks that differ from the original. As the original or the snapshot is written to, obviously the number of different blocks will grow.

What About...

...doing incremental backups? If you want to be able to restore the state of a filesystem after a total disk failure so that it is no more than (say) 24 hours out of date, you obviously need to create a backup at least every 24 hours. However, for most filesystems, most of the contents won't have changed from one backup to the next. Consequently, doing a full backup every day is wasteful of time, bandwidth, and backup media. Incremental backups allow you to begin by creating a full backup (with all files on it), then subsequently create (much smaller) backups that contain only the files that are new or that have changed.

The ancient programs dump and restore were designed to work in exactly this way; however, they work only with ext2/ext3 filesystems, not reiser. These programs can also run into difficulties dumping "live" filesystems, and their use seems to be firmly deprecated these days.

However, the GNU version of tar has an incremental archive facility, though it is not well documented either in the manpage or the info page. It works like this: consider the scenario of backing up Simon's home directory. To begin, on day 1 you make a "level 1" archive (all files) like this:

```
# cd /home/simon
# tar czvf /tmp/simon1.tar.gz -g /tmp/simon-snapshot .
```

This assumes that the snapshot file /tmp/simon-snapshot does not exist prior to executing this command. In response to the -g option, tar uses the specified file to record what's in the archive.

The following day, you might do:

```
# tar czvf /tmp/simon2.tar.gz -g /tmp/simon-snapshot .
```

This gets you a level 2 archive containing only the stuff that is new or modified since the previous day. The snapshot file is updated accordingly. You could continue like this, creating a level 3 archive the next day, level 4 the next, and so on. After a week (for example), delete the snapshot file to force a new level 1 archive, and start over. (I'm creating the archives in /tmp for simplicity; of course in reality they should be copied off the machine somewhere.)

Now suppose that on day 4, a catastrophe causes Simon to lose the entire contents of his home directory. Starting with an empty directory, he can restore the archives in turn (at that point he will have level 1, 2, and 3 archives):

```
# tar xzvf /tmp/simon1.tar.gz -g /dev/null
# tar xzvf /tmp/simon2.tar.gz -g /dev/null
# tar xzvf /tmp/simon3.tar.gz -g /dev/null
```

Note that the -g option must be supplied when restoring from these incremental backups to get the correct behavior, but the actual snapshot file is not used; here you'd supply the name /dev/null as a placeholder. Specifically, when extracting an archive, the -g option causes tar to delete files that have been removed from one level of the archive to the next.

> These incremental archives use a nonstandard format and are not readable by non-GNU versions of tar.

The incremental scheme described here is a little inconvenient, in that there are potentially a lot of archives to keep and restore from. An alternative scheme is to create a level 1 archive to begin with, then create level 2 archives on each successive day of the week. This requires a bit of copying of the snapshot file to get the right behavior. Then, at any one time, you need to keep (and restore from) only your level 1 archive and your most recent level 2.

It's also possible to construct efficient, multigeneration backup solutions using rsync. For a good discussion of this, and some working scripts, see *http://www.mikerubel.org/computers/rsync_snapshots*.

Where to Learn More

The full manual on GNU tar is at *http://www.gnu.org/software/tar/manual*; see Chapter 5 of the manual for a discussion of incremental backups. For backing up to CD, look at the manpages for mkisofs and cdrecord, or see Lab 3.8, "Burn Your Own

CDs and DVDs." For a fuller discussion of snapshots of logical volumes, see *http://www.tldp.org/HOWTO/LVM-HOWTO/snapshotintro.html*.

6.9 Configure and Debug Network Interfaces

In Lab 1.4, "Configure a Network Card," you saw how to use YaST to perform basic network card configuration—setting its IP address, and so on. This lab examines the command-line tools for doing these things, and also some tools for diagnosing network-related problems.

How Do I Do That?

You can configure a network card "just for now" with the `ifconfig` command. (By "just for now," I mean that settings you establish in this way won't survive a reboot. Indeed, they won't even survive if you restart the networking.) Table 6-13 shows some sample commands.

Table 6-13. Sample ifconfig commands

Command	Description
`# ifconfig eth0 down`	Disable the interface
`# ifconfig eth0 up`	Enable the interface
`# ifconfig eth0 192.168.1.44`	Set the IP address
`# ifconfig eth0 netmask 255.255.255.0`	Set the subnet mask

Running `ifconfig` with no arguments will show you your current configuration. Note that you don't have to be root to do this:

```
$ /sbin/ifconfig
eth0      Link encap:Ethernet  HWaddr 00:0D:56:78:CD:BF
          inet addr:192.168.0.3  Bcast:192.168.0.255  Mask:255.255.255.0
          UP BROADCAST NOTRAILERS RUNNING MULTICAST  MTU:1500  Metric:1
          RX packets:7 errors:0 dropped:0 overruns:0 frame:0
          TX packets:17 errors:0 dropped:0 overruns:0 carrier:0
          collisions:0 txqueuelen:1000
          RX bytes:777 (777.0 b)  TX bytes:1712 (1.6 Kb)
          Interrupt:11

lo        Link encap:Local Loopback
          inet addr:127.0.0.1  Mask:255.0.0.0
          UP LOOPBACK RUNNING  MTU:16436  Metric:1
          RX packets:729 errors:0 dropped:0 overruns:0 frame:0
          TX packets:729 errors:0 dropped:0 overruns:0 carrier:0
          collisions:0 txqueuelen:0
          RX bytes:89323 (87.2 Kb)  TX bytes:89323 (87.2 Kb)
```

You can define IP aliases (that is, assign additional IP addresses to a single card) with a command syntax like this:

```
# ifconfig eth0:1 192.168.2.44 netmask 255.255.255.0
```

This trick is sometimes used if your machine is hosting multiple virtual sites. It's also handy if you're trying to familiarize yourself with routing behavior on a machine with only one network interface.

The first time that a machine wishes to send an IP datagram to some other machine (on the same network), it will broadcast an ARP (Address Resolution Protocol) request to discover the MAC address of that machine. To avoid doing this prior to every single datagram transmission, the kernel maintains an *ARP cache* (a list of IP-to-MAC address bindings) for machines with which it has communicated recently. For the most part, this cache is maintained automatically. Entries are added as they're discovered, and are removed after a timeout period of approximately 10 minutes.

You can examine the ARP cache with arp -a:

```
# arp -a
? (192.168.0.4) at 00:60:97:5E:B9:E2 [ether] on eth0
? (192.168.0.33) at 00:60:97:1A:37:BF [ether] on eth0
? (192.168.0.1) at 00:50:BA:99:C1:A9 [ether] on eth0
```

You can obtain the same information (in a different format) by examining the file */proc/net/arp*.

You can manually add entries to the ARP cache (though you shouldn't really need to) with arp -s:

```
# arp -s 192.168.0.33 00:60:97:1A:37:BF -i eth0 temp
```

You can delete entries from the arp cache with arp -d:

```
# arp -d 192.168.0.33
```

> I recall an interesting episode some years ago when I was investigating a network problem on a Sun workstation. In the time-honored tradition of fault-finding, I swapped the network cards on two workstations (let's call them A and B), and rebooted them. Several interesting minutes ensued, during which all other machines on the network sent A's datagrams to B and B's datagrams to A, until the ARP caches timed out. If I had known about arp -d at the time, it would have helped.

Add static routes to the routing table with route add:

```
# route add -net 192.168.4.0/24 gw 192.168.0.254 dev eth0
```

Examine the routing table with route (the command netstat -r is similar):

```
# route
Kernel IP routing table
Destination     Gateway         Genmask         Flags Metric Ref    Use Iface
192.168.4.0     192.168.0.254   255.255.255.0   UG    0      0        0 eth0
192.168.0.0     *               255.255.255.0   U     0      0        0 eth0
link-local      *               255.255.0.0     U     0      0        0 eth0
loopback        *               255.0.0.0       U     0      0        0 lo
default         192.168.0.1     0.0.0.0         UG    0      0        0 eth0
```

SUSE Linux also provides the package `iproute2`. This package includes, among others, the tools `ip` and `tc`. `ip` is an all-embracing tool for managing network interfaces and the IP stack. It effectively replaces tools like `ifconfig`, `route`, and `arp`. `tc` manipulates traffic control settings in the kernel. It's a TCP/IP performance-tuning tool. These are advanced tools designed to manage the policy routing features in the kernel; here, I'll simply look at some of the more straightforward uses of the `ip` command.

> I keep hearing rumors that commands like `ifconfig` and `route` are going to go away. However, I feel they may have some sympathy with Mark Twain who famously wrote, "The report of my death was an exaggeration."

Because of its wide scope, the `ip` command has a rather complex syntax. It operates on one of eight types of "objects," as shown in Table 6-14.

Table 6-14. ip command objects

Object	Description
link	A network device
address	An IP address associated with a device
neighbour	An entry in the ARP cache
route	An entry in the routing table
rule	A rule in the routing policy database
maddress	A multicast address
mroute	A multicast routing cache entry
tunnel	A tunnel over IP

The first two of these objects are the ones you're most likely to use. For each object type, there are various actions that `ip` can perform. Each object supports a different set of actions, but they all support the action `help`, which provides a summary of the command syntax for that object. For example:

```
$ ip link help
Usage: ip link set DEVICE { up | down |
                           arp { on | off } |
                           dynamic { on | off } |
                           multicast { on | off } |
                           allmulticast { on | off } |
                           promisc { on | off } |
                           trailers { on | off } |
                           txqueuelen PACKETS |
                           name NEWNAME |
                           address LLADDR | broadcast LLADDR |
                           mtu MTU }
       ip link show [ DEVICE ]
```

All object types also support the actions show or list (they are equivalent), which list the current settings or status of the object. For example, to see the status of the network devices:

```
$ ip link show
1: lo: <LOOPBACK,UP> mtu 16436 qdisc noqueue
    link/loopback 00:00:00:00:00:00 brd 00:00:00:00:00:00
2: eth0: <BROADCAST,MULTICAST,NOTRAILERS,UP> mtu 1500 qdisc pfifo_fast qlen 1000
    link/ether 00:0d:56:78:cd:bf brd ff:ff:ff:ff:ff:ff
```

Adding the -s flag shows a summary of the traffic through each interface:

```
# ip -s link show
1: lo: <LOOPBACK,UP> mtu 16436 qdisc noqueue
    link/loopback 00:00:00:00:00:00 brd 00:00:00:00:00:00
    RX: bytes  packets  errors  dropped overrun mcast
    83983      659      0       0       0       0
    TX: bytes  packets  errors  dropped carrier collsns
    83983      659      0       0       0       0
2: eth0: <BROADCAST,MULTICAST,NOTRAILERS,UP> mtu 1500 qdisc pfifo_fast qlen 1000
    link/ether 00:0d:56:78:cd:bf brd ff:ff:ff:ff:ff:ff
    RX: bytes  packets  errors  dropped overrun mcast
    20704993   17062    0       0       0       0
    TX: bytes  packets  errors  dropped carrier collsns
    1914345    14564    0       0       0       0
```

As another example, to see the routing table entries (not very exciting on this machine):

```
# ip route show
192.168.0.0/24 dev eth0  proto kernel  scope link  src 192.168.0.3
169.254.0.0/16 dev eth0  scope link
127.0.0.0/8 dev lo  scope link
default via 192.168.0.1 dev eth0
```

To see IP address assignments, use the address object:

```
# ip addr show
1: lo: <LOOPBACK,UP> mtu 16436 qdisc noqueue
    link/loopback 00:00:00:00:00:00 brd 00:00:00:00:00:00
    inet 127.0.0.1/8 scope host lo
2: eth0: <BROADCAST,MULTICAST,NOTRAILERS,UP> mtu 1500 qdisc pfifo_fast qlen 1000
    link/ether 00:0d:56:78:cd:bf brd ff:ff:ff:ff:ff:ff
    inet 192.168.0.3/24 brd 192.168.0.255 scope global eth0
```

Use the dev keyword to make the command refer to a specific device:

```
# ip addr show dev eth0
2: eth0: <BROADCAST,MULTICAST,NOTRAILERS,UP> mtu 1500 qdisc pfifo_fast qlen 1000
    link/ether 00:0d:56:78:cd:bf brd ff:ff:ff:ff:ff:ff
    inet 192.168.0.3/24 brd 192.168.0.255 scope global eth0
```

It's time to get a bit more proactive and use ip to actually change something! The link object supports the action set to change the device's characteristics. For example:

```
# ip link set dev eth0 promisc on
```

turns on promiscuous mode for eth0. Promiscuous mode tells the interface to capture all packets that it sees on the wire, not just those that are addressed to its own MAC address. This mode is commonly used by packet sniffer software such as tcpdump or ethereal.

As another example, you can turn an interface off completely:

```
# ip link set dev eth0 down
```

To assign an IP address to an interface, use the address object:

```
# ip address add dev eth0 192.168.0.42/24
```

Notice that this command doesn't replace any existing address that's assigned to the interface, it adds a new one (sometimes referred to as an *IP alias*), as you can see by listing the address object for eth0:

```
# ip address list dev eth0
2: eth0: <BROADCAST,MULTICAST,NOTRAILERS,UP> mtu 1500 qdisc pfifo_fast qlen 1000
    link/ether 00:0d:56:78:cd:bf brd ff:ff:ff:ff:ff:ff
    inet 192.168.0.3/24 brd 192.168.0.255 scope global eth0
    inet 192.168.0.42/24 scope global secondary eth0
```

You could delete this address from the interface like this:

```
# ip address del dev eth0 192.168.0.42/24
```

You could manually add an entry to the ARP table like this:

```
# ip neighbour add to 192.168.0.56 lladdr 1:2:3:4:5:6 dev eth0
```

Then you could examine the ARP cache like this:

```
# ip neighbour show
192.168.0.4 dev eth0 lladdr 00:60:97:5e:b9:e2 REACHABLE
192.168.0.56 dev eth0 lladdr 01:02:03:04:05:06 PERMANENT
192.168.0.2 dev eth0   FAILED
192.168.0.1 dev eth0 lladdr 00:50:ba:99:c1:a9 STALE
```

Be aware that as for `ifconfig`, any changes you establish with `ip` are only temporary (even the one described by the manpage as "permanent in the arp cache"), in the sense that they will not survive a reboot.

How It Works

There's all sorts of background information relevant here, but rather than present a complete TCP/IP primer, I'll just explain how to interpret the routing table.

Consider the simple network shown in Figure 6-20. Here we see two small networks (192.168.0 and 192.168.1) connected by the machine S which acts as a router. Machines D and S are said to be *multihomed*—that is, they have connections to more than one network. Machine D has an external facing interface that is the only one with a non-private IP address. (The 192.168 IP address space is designated as private space and addresses within this space cannot be used for routing on the Internet.)

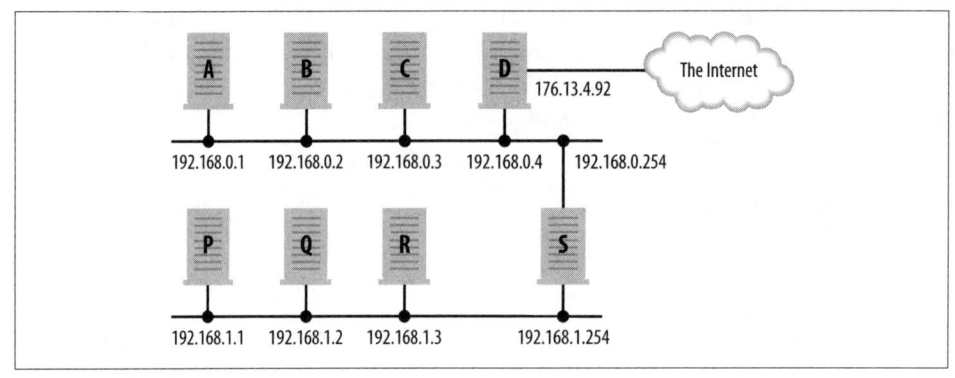

Figure 6-20. A typical small network

Consider machines P, Q, and R. They know that they can reach the 192.168.1 network directly, and they know that to get anywhere else, they need to forward the traffic via 192.168.1.254. This is known as their *default gateway*. The routing table for these machines will look something like this:

```
# route -n
Kernel IP routing table
Destination     Gateway         Genmask         Flags Metric Ref    Use Iface
192.168.1.0     0.0.0.0         255.255.255.0   U     0      0        0 eth0
127.0.0.0       0.0.0.0         255.0.0.0       U     0      0        0 lo
0.0.0.0         192.168.1.254   0.0.0.0         UG    0      0        0 eth0
```

The first line effectively defines the local network. It says "to reach the network 192.168.1, you don't need to use a gateway. Just send the packet out on the interface eth0." This entry is added automatically by the kernel when the IP address is assigned to the interface.

The second line defines the loopback address (so called because it loops back to the same machine). It says "to reach the network 127. send the packet out on the interface lo (the loopback device)."

The third line defines the default gateway. It says "If you don't have any more specific information on where to send the packet, send it to 192.168.1.254 via the interface eth0." This entry was either taken from the file */etc/sysconfig/network/routes*, or added by the `dhcpcd` daemon.

The routing table for machines A, B, and C is slightly more interesting, because it requires an additional entry to explain how to reach the 192.168.1 network. This route might be added dynamically with the command:

```
# route add -net 192.168.1.0/24 gw 192.168.0.254
```

or (as a permanent measure) via a line in */etc/sysconfig/network/routes*:

```
# Destination   Gateway         Netmask         Device
192.168.1.0     192.168.0.254   255.255.255.0   eth0
```

The routing table for machine A looks like this:

```
# route -n
Kernel IP routing table
Destination     Gateway         Genmask         Flags Metric Ref    Use Iface
192.168.1.0     192.168.0.254   255.255.255.0   UG    0      0        0 eth0
192.168.0.0     0.0.0.0         255.255.255.0   U     0      0        0 eth0
127.0.0.0       0.0.0.0         255.0.0.0       U     0      0        0 lo
0.0.0.0         192.168.0.4     0.0.0.0         UG    0      0        0 eth0
```

How is this table interpreted? When the kernel is trying to decide where to send a packet, it scans this table looking for an entry that matches the packet. The entry is considered to match if the destination IP address of the packet, bitwise anded with the value in the Genmask column, is equal to the value in the Destination column. If there is more than one match, the one with the longest genmask (i.e., the most specific route) is chosen. The last line in the routing table always matches (anything bitwise anded with 0 gives 0), but it is always the last resort, as it contains the shortest possible genmask.

What About...

...turning off IPV6? This is one very specific configuration task that I've come up against. SUSE Linux ships with IPV6 enabled by default but it's easy to turn it off. Edit the file */etc/modprobe.conf* and find the line:

```
alias net-pf-10         ipv6
```

Replace this line with:

```
install net-pf-10   /bin/true
```

To make the change take immediate effect, run:

```
# depmod -a
# modprobe -r ipv6
```

If `modprobe` refuses to remove the module, reboot.

What About...

...fault-finding network connectivity? I am not a great believer in laying out prescriptive fault-finding recipes, but the following sequence represents a "bottom-up" approach to debugging network connectivity that I have found helpful in practice.

1. Does your network interface have an IP address and netmask assigned?

    Use a command such as `ifconfig eth0` to verify this.

    If no IP address is assigned, and you have a static IP configuration, check the config file for the interface. Its name will be in the form: */etc/sysconfig/network/ifcfg-eth**. Try restarting the network with `rcnetwork restart`.

    If you are using DHCP, confirm that a DHCP server is accessible. For example, are there any other machines on the network able to get an IP address via DHCP?

2. Can you reach a machine on your local network?

    Use a command such as `ping -c 1 192.168.0.22` to verify this. Choose a target for the ping that you know is up!

    A reply of "Network is unreachable" suggests a problem with the routing table. The kernel simply doesn't know how to get packets out onto that network. This probably indicates that the interface didn't come up properly. Try `route -n` and see whether there's a route out to the local network.

    A timeout followed by a reply of "Destination Host Unreachable" usually means that an ARP request was sent to the target machine but no reply was received. Suspect an unplugged network cable, or a faulty hub or network card.

3. Can you reach your default gateway?

    Again, use `ping` to verify this. For a small home network with an ADSL connection, your default gateway will be the "inward-facing" IP address of your ADSL modem/router.

4. Can you ping a known good machine beyond your default gateway by IP address?

    For a known good machine, you might try DNS root nameserver A, which is at 198.41.0.4. (But don't overdo it—this machine has better things to do!)

    A "Network Unreachable" reply suggests that you have no default route defined. (Try `route -n` and check for a line with a destination of 0.0.0.0.) This is probably either a DHCP server error or a problem in your */etc/sysconfig/network/ifcfg-** file.

    A timeout followed by a report of 100% packet loss is indicative of a fault on the "outside" of your default gateway. It could be a problem with your ADSL modem (do the lights look normal?) or it could be Somebody Else's Problem.

5. Can you ping a known good machine beyond your default gateway by name?

    This is where name resolution needs to be working. Try something like `ping -c 1 www.oreilly.com`. If this works, you're more or less home and dry. If it fails, try to distinguish the case where your machine can find its DNS server but the DNS server can't resolve the name, from the case where your machine can't find its DNS servers. In the former case, you'll fairly quickly see the message "unknown host." In the latter case, there'll be a fairly long timeout before you see the message.

If you think you have DNS problems, try the following:

1. Look in */etc/resolv.conf* to find out where your machine thinks your DNS servers are. Try to ping them by IP address.

    If this fails, you may have the wrong IP addresses, or the server(s) may be down (it does happen occasionally).

2. Try looking up a name using `dig`.

A typical command might be dig *www.oreilly.com*. The output from dig makes it very easy to distinguish the case where your machine can find its DNS server but the DNS server can't resolve the name from the case where your machine can't find its DNS servers.

3. Make sure you're not trapped at a hotspot.

   Wireless hotspots often use a *captive portal*, a special web page that you need to log into before any other networking will function. Typically, the captive portal works by automatically redirecting any web requests to a special page, which goes away once you've provided a password, a credit card number, or maybe just agreed to some terms of service. The problem with a captive portal is that pings will usually go through, as will DNS lookups. But nothing will work quite right until you've gone through the captive portal, because the network you're on is purposely misconfigured (and sometimes called a *wounded subnet*).

Any problems beyond this point are likely to be at the application level. If you're using an application that can be configured to use a proxy server (such as a web browser), make sure that it's correctly configured. If you're on a network that requires a proxy server and you haven't configured it properly, the Web won't work. Conversely, if you've configured your web browser to use a proxy server, but you're on a different network (such as when taking a computer from work to home), you probably won't be able to reach that proxy server.

Just a couple of final thoughts: first, are your problems caused by your own machine's firewall blocking access? You can turn the firewall off (temporarily) with:

```
# rcSuSEfirewall2 stop
```

but don't forget to turn it on again once you've proved the point. Second, a packet monitoring tool such as ethereal is invaluable in those cases where you really can't figure out what's going on. It's best to run on a "third-party" machine; I have an aging laptop that I sometimes plug in for this purpose.

Where to Learn More

Look at the manpages for ifconfig, route, and arp. The manpage for ip is a bit terse (as manpages should be), but there's an excellent manual at */usr/share/doc/packages/iproute2/ip-cref.pdf*. There's also an article about some of the more advanced uses of ip at *http://www.deepspace6.net/docs/iproute2tunnel-en.html*.

There's a good discussion of the older commands (ifconfig, route, arp, netstat, and so on) in Chapter 4 of the *Linux Network Administrator's Guide*, 3rd Edition, by Bautts et al. (O'Reilly).

6.10 Configure Name Resolution

When you enter a URL such as *www.oreilly.com* into your browser, the browser converts this name to an IP address. When you use a command such as:

```
# chown chris foo
```

the chown command looks up the username chris to get the corresponding UID. These are examples of *name resolution*. Linux uses a number of "maps" that support such lookups (including those shown in Table 6-15).

Table 6-15. Linux resolver maps

Map	Principal use
passwd	Maps user names to UIDs. The map is also used (in reverse) by programs such as ls -l to map from the owner's numeric UID (found in the file's inode) to the username.
group	Maps group names to GIDs.
hosts	Maps host names (such as "www.novell.com") to IP addresses (such as "130.57.4.27").
services	Maps service names (such as "smtp") to port numbers (such as 25). For example xinetd consults this to find out what port numbers to listen on for each service.
protocols	Maps protocol names (such as "UDP") to protocol numbers (like 17). This relates to what we might call "infrastructure" protocols, not application-level protocols.
networks	Maps network names to IP addresses.

> I'm using the word "map" here for want of anything better. (It's the term used by NIS, one of the possible lookup services.) You might prefer the term "database," provided you don't think of a full-blown relational database. Or you might prefer the term "service," provided you don't think of a network service like HTTP or FTP.

Some of the maps (for example, services, protocols, and networks) are fairly small and static (how often a new Internet protocol gets invented for instance). However, the information held in the first three maps listed earlier is typically more extensive and more volatile. Linux makes provision to store this information in a variety of places. In this lab, you'll see how to tell it where to look.

How Do I Do That?

Map information can be stored in several places, depending on the map:

- Local files such as */etc/hosts* and */etc/passwd*
- An NIS server (useful for consolidating maps across a number of machines that are under common administrative control)
- An LDAP directory server (used only for user accounts)
- A DNS server (used only for hostname lookups)

The file /etc/nsswitch.conf (the so-called *name service switch file*) specifies where to do the lookups. It is a simple text file that contains one line for each map and is easy to edit by hand. Here's a sample:

```
passwd:         files ldap
shadow:         files ldap
group:          files ldap

hosts:          files nis dns
networks:       files dns

services:       files
protocols:      files
```

Here, lookups in the `passwd` map start by consulting the local file (/etc/passwd), and if the name is not found there, an LDAP directory server will be consulted. Similarly, host name lookups will begin by consulting the local /etc/hosts file, then will consult NIS, and finally DNS. Lookups in the services and protocols map use only the local files.

> You should always include "files" in the list for the passwd map. Without it, if your LDAP server fails, you won't be able to log in as a local user—not even as root.

If you're using DNS for host name resolution, there's one more step: you need to make your machine aware of the IP address of at least one DNS server (and preferably—to avoid a single point of failure—two or three). You can do this using YaST. Go to the main YaST screen and select Network Services from the pane on the left, then DNS and Hostname from the pane on the right. This brings you to the Host Name and Name Server configuration screen, where you can enter the IP addresses of your DNS servers. I covered this in detail in Lab 1.4, "Configure a Network Card."

It may be convenient to implement name resolution for the machines on your local network (provided they don't change too often) using a local file (/etc/hosts). This is another plain text file with a simple format; for example:

```
127.0.0.1       loopback
192.168.0.1     sneezy    sneezy.example.com
192.168.0.2     happy     happy.example.com
192.168.0.254   snowhite  snowhite.example.com
```

Note the use of aliases, allowing a machine to be referenced by more than one name. This file is trivial to hand-edit, but if you prefer you can do it with YaST—select Network Services from the pane on the left then Hostnames from the pane on the right.

How It Works

Down in the depths of the standard C library (`glibc`) is a collection of functions known as *resolvers*, because they resolve queries, with names like `gethostbyname( )`

and getpwuid( ). The resolvers read the *nsswitch.conf* file, and it's really the behavior of these resolvers that you're configuring here. The entries in *nsswitch.conf* map directly onto the names of the shared libraries that the resolvers will invoke to do the lookup. For example, the line:

```
hosts:          files nis dns
```

tells the resolver to first try the lookup using the library *libnss_files.so.x*, then the library *libnss_nis.so.x*, and finally *libnss_dns.so.x* (*x* is the library version number).

In the name service switch file, for the passwd and group maps you may come across a curious entry called `compat`—short for compatibility. This refers to an earlier scheme (introduced by Sun Microsystems in the days before `nsswitch` was invented) in which you put a plus sign at the end of the *passwd* and *group* files to tell the resolver "now go and look in NIS." I have had limited success in making this work on Linux.

In the case of DNS (only), the resolvers also consult the file */etc/resolv.conf,* which says where the DNS servers are and specifies any default domains to search. Here's an example:

```
nameserver 192.168.0.1
nameserver 213.253.16.72
search novell.com
```

The name servers are tried in the order specified. Obviously, this is the file that the YaST configuration screen is editing.

What About...

...testing? There are a couple of command-line tools that can help verify that your name resolution is working. First, getent is basically just a wrapper around the resolvers. Usage is simply:

```
# getent map_name key
```

where ***map_name*** is one of the maps discussed in this lab, and ***key*** is what you're looking for. For example:

```
# getent passwd chris
chris:x:1000:100:Chris Brown:/home/chris:/bin/bash
# getent group users
users:x:100:
# getent hosts www.oreilly.com
208.201.239.36   www.oreilly.com
208.201.239.37   www.oreilly.com
```

Then there's dig, a command-line tool for performing DNS lookups. dig provides a wealth of information to help debug DNS. Here's an example:

```
# dig www.bbc.co.uk

; <<>> DiG 9.3.1 <<>> www.bbc.co.uk
;; global options:  printcmd
```

```
;; Got answer:
;; ->>HEADER<<- opcode: QUERY, status: NOERROR, id: 3256
;; flags: qr rd ra; QUERY: 1, ANSWER: 2, AUTHORITY: 2, ADDITIONAL: 2

;; QUESTION SECTION:
;www.bbc.co.uk.                 IN      A

;; ANSWER SECTION:
www.bbc.co.uk.          738     IN      CNAME   www.bbc.net.uk.
www.bbc.net.uk.         246     IN      A       212.58.224.121

;; AUTHORITY SECTION:
bbc.net.uk.             155216  IN      NS      ns0.thdo.bbc.co.uk.
bbc.net.uk.             155216  IN      NS      ns0.thny.bbc.co.uk.

;; ADDITIONAL SECTION:
ns0.thdo.bbc.co.uk.     68833   IN      A       212.58.224.20
ns0.thny.bbc.co.uk.     68833   IN      A       212.58.240.20

;; Query time: 30 msec
;; SERVER: 192.168.0.1#53(192.168.0.1)
;; WHEN: Tue Nov 15 16:56:11 2005
;; MSG SIZE  rcvd: 151
```

Here, dig tells you more than you really asked for. Not only do you get to know the IP address for *www.bbc.co.uk*, you also get to know where the authoritative servers are for that domain, and what their IP addresses are. I revisit dig in Lab 7.2, "Configure a DNS Server," where I hope that this output will make more sense!

What About…

…improving efficiency? SUSE Linux runs the daemon nscd—the name service caching daemon—that speeds lookups in three of the most used maps (passwd, group, and hosts) by caching results in memory. It's normally started at boot time, reads the configuration file */etc/ncsd.conf*, and listens on the Unix-domain socket */var/run/nscd/socket*. This file enables and disables the cache for each of the maps and controls the length of time that items will stay in the cache, among other things. Here's part of it—the entries for the group and host maps are similar:

```
            logfile                 /var/log/nscd.log
            debug-level             1
            paranoia                no
            restart-interval        3600

            enable-cache            passwd          yes
            positive-time-to-live   passwd          600
            negative-time-to-live   passwd          20
            suggested-size          passwd          211
            check-files             passwd          yes
            persistent              passwd          yes
            shared                  passwd          yes
```

Chances are good that you will never need to change this file or interact with nscd in any way. However, it's best to be aware that it's there. For example, if you're busy updating your DNS configuration or your NIS maps, and you seem to be getting stale results, try stopping the daemon for a while:

```
# rcnscd stop
```

Where to Learn More

Look at the manpages for nsswitch.conf, resolv.conf, hosts, getent, dig, nscd, and nscd.conf.

CHAPTER 7
Network Services

In the previous chapter, I discussed what I called the "infrastructure" of a Linux server. This chapter continues the server theme by discussing some key network services in detail. In the first lab, I'll show how to set up disk quotas to limit the disk space an individual can use. Later labs show how to provide DHCP and DNS services—in many ways the "glue" of the Internet. You'll also learn how to provide file sharing services using both the native Unix protocol (NFS) and the native Windows protocol (SMB/CIFS). I'll describe how to share out printers, using CUPS (Common Unix Print System). The final labs show how to set up your own web servers to host multiple sites on a single machine, and how to build a mail server.

Keep in mind that all of these services are available out of the box in a SUSE Linux distribution. In my view, it is the range and quality of these open source network solutions that really establish Linux's credentials as a world-class operating system.

7.1   Set Up Disk Quotas

Question: what does this command do?

```
$ cp /dev/zero foo
```

Answer: it will fill up all the free space on whatever partition your home directory is on. Linux does not, by default, limit the amount of disk space that a single user can use. If /home is on its own partition, a single user can starve all other users of disk space. If /home is not on a separate partition, a single user can probably bring the system to its knees by filling up the root partition.

However, Linux supports a disk quota mechanism, which limits both the number of files and the number of disk blocks that a given user (or group) can use. Separate limits can be applied to each partition, although typically only the partition carrying the user's home directory have quotas applied. The mechanism allows for both a soft limit, which can be exceeded for a specified grace period (a day, perhaps), and a hard limit, which can never be exceeded. In this lab, you'll see how to manage the quota system.

How Do I Do That?

For this lab, I used YaST to create a 100 MB partition /dev/hda6 with a Reiser filesystem, mounted on /home2. I also created a user called robin, whose home directory is /home2/robin.

Without quotas, *robin* can fill the entire partition:

```
$ cp /dev/zero foo
cp: writing `foo': No space left on device
$ df -h /home2
Filesystem            Size  Used Avail Use% Mounted on
/dev/hda6             102M  102M     0 100% /home2
$ rm foo
```

To enable quotas, edit /etc/fstab and add the mount option usrquota for the partition hda6, so that the line looks like this:

```
/dev/hda6      /home2      reiserfs   acl,user_xattr,usrquota   1 2
```

Now remount the partition so that the new mount option kicks in:

```
# mount -o remount /home2
```

Next, initialize the quota system on the partition. You need to do this only once:

```
# quotacheck -u /home2
```

Next, you must turn on the quota mechanism:

```
# quotaon -u /home2
```

Note that you must turn on the quota mechanism every time the system is booted. The best way to do this is to add the command:

```
quotaon -u -a
```

to the script /etc/init.d/rc.local. This script is run at boot time, after the filesystems are mounted but before run-level processing is started. The -a flag tells quotaon to enable quotas on all filesystems listed in /etc/fstab that have the usrquota mount option set.

Now the quota system is enabled, you need to establish quotas for your users. Here's how to set quotas for *robin*:

```
# edquota robin

Disk quotas for user robin (uid 1003):
  Filesystem         blocks       soft       hard     inodes     soft     hard
  /dev/hda6            1460       5000      10000         31        0        0
```

What isn't obvious from the way this looks on the printed page is that edquota has dropped me into the vi editor to allow me to edit *robin*'s quotas. The fields you see here are:

Filesystem
   The partition to which this entry relates (there can be more than one partition).

blocks
: The number of 1 KB blocks this user is currently using.

soft
: The soft limit on block count. This can be exceeded for a specified grace period (I get to that in a minute), but the user will receive a warning.

hard
: The hard limit on the block count. This cannot be exceeded and the user receives an error (as if the disk was full) if he tries to exceed it.

inodes
: The number of inodes that this user is currently using. This equates to the number of files the user has, more or less.

soft
: The soft limit on the number of inodes.

hard
: The hard limit on the number of inodes.

Note that a value of zero for any of the limits means that no limit is enforced. For a Reiser filesystem, limiting the number of inodes is a bit pointless, because a Reiser filesystem doesn't have a fixed-size inode table like ext2 does. You use edquota by actually editing the soft and hard-limit fields then saving the "file" and quitting the editor. In the preceding example, I set a soft limit of 5,000 blocks (5 MB) and a hard limit of twice that.

By default, edquota will invoke vi for you to edit the quotas, but if you have a strong aversion to vi, you can change this by setting the environment variable EDITOR to your editor of choice. From the command prompt, and easy way to do this is:

```
# EDITOR=kwrite edquota robin
```

> This way of working—dropping you into an editor—must have seemed like a good idea to someone at the time, but it's a strange arrangement and out of keeping with conventional command-line style.

The command setquota provides an alternative, noninteractive way of setting quotas. For example:

```
# setquota -u robin 5000 10000 0 0 /home2
```

is equivalent to our previous example. Quotas need to be set only once; they do not need to be reestablished each time the machine is booted.

With quotas enabled, and *robin*'s quota set, his attempt to fill up the partition is thwarted:

```
$ cp /dev/zero foo
hda6: warning, user block quota exceeded.
```

```
hda6: write failed, user block limit reached.
cp: writing `foo': No space left on device
$ ls -l foo
-rw-r--r-- 1 robin users 10227712 2005-11-17 19:07 foo
```

Notice the separate warning (when the soft limit is exceeded) and error (when the hard limit is exceeded).

There are a couple of utilities for reporting quotas and actual utilization. First, quota reports quotas for a specified user:

```
# quota robin
Disk quotas for user robin (uid 1003):
     Filesystem  blocks   quota   limit   grace   files   quota   limit   grace
     /dev/hda6    3425    5000   10000             135       0       0
```

Second, repquota reports quotas for all users on a given partition:

```
# repquota /home2
*** Report for user quotas on device /dev/hda6
Block grace time: 7days; Inode grace time: 7days
                        Block limits                File limits
User            used    soft    hard  grace    used  soft  hard  grace
----------------------------------------------------------------------
root         --    1       0       0              1    0     0
robin        --  3425    5000   10000            135    0     0
tuck         +-  7654    5000   10000  4 days   117    0     0
marion       --   638    5000   10000             29    0     0
```

The -- displayed after each user is a quick way to see whether the block or inode limits have been exceeded. If either soft limit is exceeded, a + will appear in place of the - (the first character represents the block limit and the second represents the inode limit). Notice that *tuck* has exceeded his block soft limit, and has four days of his grace period remaining. If *tuck* does not reduce his space usage below the soft limit, after four days he will not be allowed to consume additional disk space.

Anyone can view their own quotas, but only root can view everyone's quotas.

How It Works

Quota information is held in two files in the top-level directory of the partition it relates to. The files are aquota.user for the user quotas and aquota.group for the group quotas (discussed later). Quotas are enforced by the kernel. When a filesystem is mounted with quotas enabled, every write operation to a file is checked in order to ensure that quota settings are not exceeded.

What About…

…setting the grace period? The grace period, which determines the length of time that a user is allowed to exceed his soft limits, is also set using the curious edquota command:

```
# edquota -u -t
```
```
Grace period before enforcing soft limits for users:
Time units may be: days, hours, minutes, or seconds
  Filesystem              Block grace period     Inode grace period
  /dev/hda6                      7days                  7days
```

Again, you'll be placed in an editor to make the changes. Notice that you can set a different grace period for the block limit and the inode limit, and you can set a different grace period for each partition. Time units of seconds, minutes, hours, and days are understood.

What About . . .

...group quotas? You can specify quotas for groups as well as for individual users. It works much the same. The filesystem must be mounted with the grpquota option; quotas are initialized with `quotacheck -g` and enabled with `quotaon -g`. Quotas are edited with `edquota -g groupname`.

Where to Learn More

Look at the manpages for `quotacheck`, `quotaon`, `quotaoff`, `edquota`, `setquota`, `quota`, and `repquota`.

7.2   Configure a DNS Server

One of the most fundamental pieces of the infrastructure that makes the Internet work is *name resolution*—the process of converting a fully qualified domain name like *www.oreilly.com* to an IP address like 208.201.239.36. On small local networks, that task is sometimes fulfilled using NIS, or even by doing local lookups in */etc/hosts*. But to cope with Internet-wide name resolution, you must use DNS (Domain Name Service). DNS is one of the best examples we have of a distributed system—the knowledge of the IP addresses of all the machines visible on the Internet is spread across many thousands of servers.

> ### Getting the Names Straight
>
> "DNS" refers to the architecture; this name is not specific to Linux or Unix or any particular implementation. "BIND" is the name of a very popular implementation of DNS from the Internet Services Consortium, which is universally used on Linux. BIND stands for Berkeley Internet Name Domain (depending on who you ask). Finally, named is the name of the actual daemon that is part of the BIND distribution. It's pronounced "name-dee." Do not pronounce it any other way—at least, not in earshot of an expert.

In this lab, you'll see how to configure a DNS server using BIND.

How Do I Do That?

Although there is a YaST module for configuring BIND, which absolves you from the need to deal with the (rather picky) syntax of its configuration files, it will make no sense unless you understand a little about the DNS architecture. So here are the basics.

Within DNS, each machine is identified by a *fully qualified domain name* (FQDN), such as www.dcs.shef.ac.uk. This name identifies a machine within a hierarchical namespace.

> DNS names are rather like absolute pathnames in the filesystem, in that they identify a point within a tree-structured naming hierarchy. The big difference is that path names are written "big endian," with the most significant component first, as in /home/chris/book/chapter7, whereas DNS names are written little-endian.

DNS is a distributed system, and any one DNS server contains information only about machines in a part of the DNS namespace called a *zone* (or *zone of authority*). Usually, a zone corresponds to a subtree of the namespace such as "all names ending in example.com." (Technically, what I've just described is a *domain*, not a zone, but you can ignore the difference for now.) Each zone has a master DNS server. On this machine, the administrator maintains *zone files*—real text-based files on disk that hold the raw data of DNS. For improved performance, and to avoid a single point of failure, each zone has one or more slave servers. The slave servers periodically copy information about the zone from the master; this copy operation is called a *zone transfer*. It's also possible to run a *caching* DNS server. These are neither masters nor slaves—they need to forward all lookups to a more authoritative server—but they cache the results to provide faster lookups next time. It is easy (and worthwhile) to run a caching DNS server on even a modest network.

Most users think of DNS as providing translation between a FQDN and an IP address. The DNS records that provide this information are called A records. However, DNS also provides for other kinds of records, as shown in Table 7-1.

Table 7-1. Types of DNS records

Record	Description
SOA	"Start of Authority." Every zone file must have one of these. Contains (among other things) timing parameters that control the transfer of zone information from masters to slaves.
A	A records support forward lookups—mapping from a FQDN to an IP address.
PTR	Pointer records support reverse lookups—mapping from an IP address to a FQDN.
NS	Name server records specify the FQDN of the name server for a domain. (Usually there are at least two.)

Table 7-1. Types of DNS records (continued)

Record	Description
CNAME	CNAME records are like aliases. They provide a mapping from a name to another name. They are used when several sites have the same IP address; for example, when using Apache to host multiple virtual sites on a single machine.
MX	Mail exchanger records specify the mail server for a given domain.

Okay, that's enough background. Now I'll explain how to use YaST to configure a DNS server. From the main YaST screen, select Network Services from the panel on the left, then DNS Server from the panel on the right. The YaST DNS wizard provides four screens:

Start-Up
On this screen, you can specify whether to start DNS at boot time or start it manually. You can also open the DNS port in the firewall, and manually start and stop the server. (The first time you run this YaST module, the startup screen appears last in the sequence.)

Forwarders
Forwarders are the DNS servers to which your server will send queries that it cannot answer by itself. If your machine connects to the Internet via a dial-up connection, the PPP daemon will probably set this up for you, so you should click the button labeled PPP Daemon Sets Forwarders. If you connect to the Internet via an ADSL router, your router probably fulfills this function. Otherwise, specify the IP address of a DNS server provided by your ISP.

Logging
On this screen, you can specify whether DNS will log via syslog or log directly to a file. In the latter case, you can specify the maximum size of the log file, and the number of previous versions to be kept as the log files are rotated.

DNS Zones
This is the screen with all the action. Here, you can add new domains that this server will serve, specifying in each case whether it will be the master or a slave for that domain. (It's possible for a DNS server to be a master for some domains and a slave for others.) To add records to the zone file for a domain, select the domain in the list of Configured DNS Zones and click on Edit. This will bring you to the Zone Editor screen shown in Figure 7-1.

This screen has multiple tabs, as follows:

Basics
Control which machines are allowed to do a zone transfer of this zone from your server. If this is a master server for the domain, you should allow only your designated slave servers to do zone transfers. If this is a slave server for the domain, you should disallow zone transfers entirely. YaST provides limited flexibility here; for example, you cannot specify a list of specific IP addresses for your slaves. To do this, you need to hand-edit the zone file.

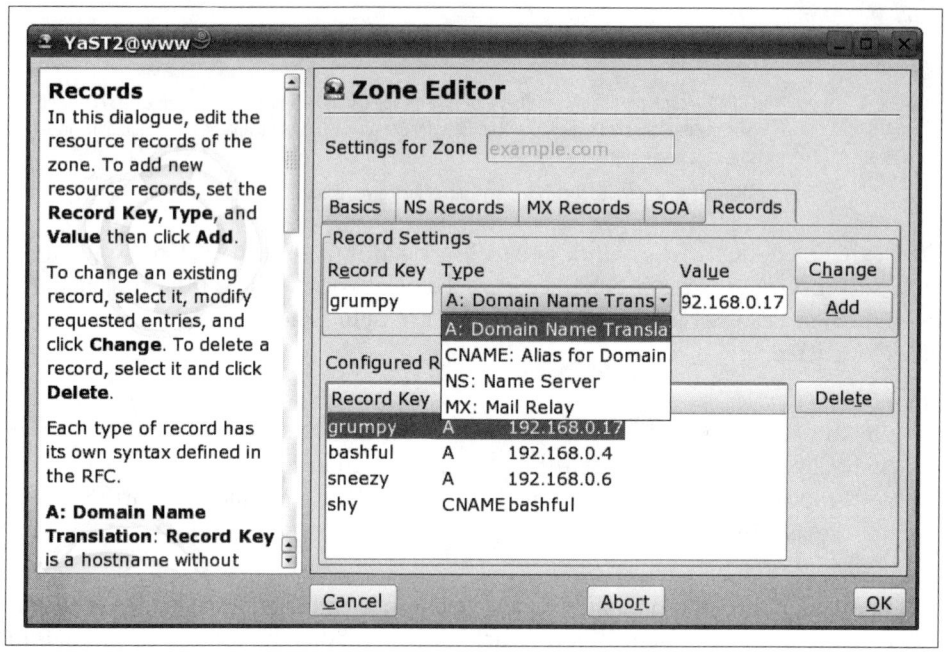

Figure 7-1. Editing DNS zone data with YaST

NS Records

Specify the name servers for this domain. You should specify both the master and the slaves. You can enter IP addresses or FQDNs here.

MX Records

Specify the mail servers that handle mail for this domain. Mail transfer agents query DNS for MX records to figure out where to send mail to a recipient in a given domain. For example, if you're configuring the domain example.com and you specify shrekmail.example.com as a mail server, mail addressed to *chris@example.com* will be sent to this server for delivery. The priority value that you can specify here is essentially a preference order in the case where a domain has more than one mail server. The server with the lowest priority is tried first.

SOA record

Enter the parameters for the Start of Authority (SOA) record for this zone. There must be exactly one SOA record for each zone. The zone editor screen for the SOA record is shown in Figure 7-2.

Records

This is the tab shown in Figure 7-1 earlier. Here you can enter, for example, A records and CNAME records for the zone. For example, if you have a machine called *grumpy* in the domain example.com with IP address 192.168.0.17, enter *grumpy* in the Record Key field, select an A record type from the drop-down list, and enter the IP address into the Value field.

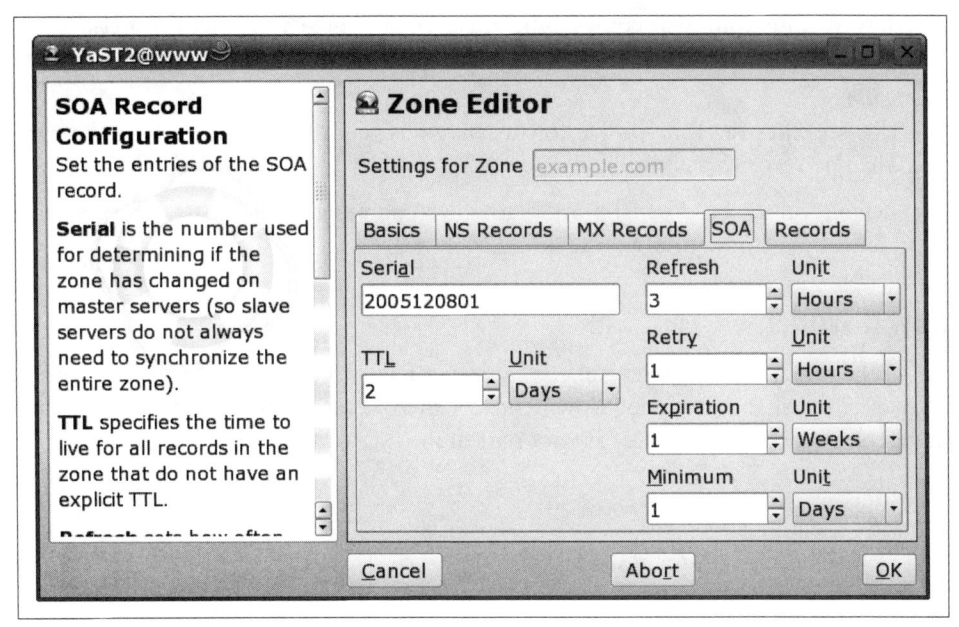

Figure 7-2. Editing a DNS SOA record with YaST

Let's look in more detail at the SOA record configuration screen shown in Figure 7-2. On this screen, the fields are:

Serial
> The serial number is used by slave servers to decide whether they need to do a zone transfer. A slave will transfer the zone only if the serial number on the master is greater than the last one it transferred. Normal practice is to use YYYYM-MDDNN (year, month, day, plus two digits). You must increment the serial number if you update the zone file. YaST does this for you.

TTL
> This is the default time-to-live for all records in the zone. After this time, any client that has cached the record should discard it and repeat the query.

Refresh
> This specifies how frequently a slave server should check back with the master to see whether the zone file has been updated (i.e., to decide whether a zone transfer is needed).

Retry
> If a slave tries to check the master's serial number but the master does not respond, this parameter specifies how often the slave should retry.

Expiration
> If a master server is down for a long time, slaves will try many times to refresh their data. The expiration parameter specifies how long the slaves will continue

to serve data from their copies in the absence of the master. After this period, the slave considers it better to supply no data than to supply stale data.

Minimum

This specifies the time-to-live for negative answers that are cached (in the case when no record was found).

The default values proposed by YaST for these parameters are reasonable. Tweak them only if you know what you're doing.

How It Works

Under the hood, DNS uses several configuration files. The top-level file is */etc/named.conf*. Here's a slightly stripped-down copy of the file that YaST generated. The line numbers are for reference; they are not part of the file.

```
 1  options {
 2          directory "/var/lib/named";
 3          notify no;
 4          forwarders { 192.168.0.1; };
 5  };
 6
 7  zone "." in {
 8          type hint;
 9          file "root.hint";
10  };
11
12  zone "localhost" in {
13          type master;
14          file "localhost.zone";
15  };
16
17  zone "0.0.127.in-addr.arpa" in {
18          type master;
19          file "127.0.0.zone";
20  };
21
22  zone "example.com" in {
23          allow-transfer { any; };
24          file "master/example.comX";
25          type master;
26  };
```

If you choose to hand-edit this file, take great care with the curly brackets and semicolons. BIND is very picky about the syntax. After hand-editing the file, run `tail -f` on */var/log/messages* the next time you start named to see if any errors are reported.

Line 2 specifies the directory that the zone files will be found in. Lines 22–26 say that the server is a master server for the example.com zone and that the zone file is *master/example.comX* (in the directory */var/lib/named*). Lines 7–10 specify a *root hints* file, which gives the names and addresses of the 13 name servers at the very top of the DNS hierarchy.

The zone files themselves live in */var/lib/named*. SUSE Linux puts the zone files in subdirectories called *master* and *slave*, but there is no requirement to do this. Here's the zone file for the example.com domain. You should be able to tie it back to the information entered in the YaST screens shown earlier.

```
$TTL 2d
@       IN SOA    www.example.com.         root.www.example.com. (
                  2005120800      ; serial
                  3h              ; refresh
                  1h              ; retry
                  1w              ; expiry
                  1d )            ; minimum

example.com.      IN MX           0 shrekmail.example.com.
example.com.      IN NS           shrek.example.com.
grumpy            IN A            192.168.0.17
bashful           IN A            192.168.0.4
```

What About…

…diagnostic tools? There are a couple of diagnostic tools that you should be aware of. First, dig is a general-purpose query tool for DNS. If you believe the manual page, dig stands for "domain information groper." The general form of the command is:

$ **dig @***server name type*

where ***server*** is the name or IP address of the DNS server to be queried, ***name*** is the name of the resource record you're looking for, and ***type*** is the type of record you want (typically, one of A, NS, MX, and so on) By default, dig looks for A records. This example queries the DNS server on the local machine for an A record for grumpy.example.com:

```
# dig @127.0.0.1 grumpy.example.com

; <<>> DiG 9.3.1 <<>> @127.0.0.1 grumpy.example.com
; (1 server found)
;; global options:  printcmd
;; Got answer:
;; ->>HEADER<<- opcode: QUERY, status: NOERROR, id: 58345
;; flags: qr aa rd ra; QUERY: 1, ANSWER: 1, AUTHORITY: 1, ADDITIONAL: 0

;; QUESTION SECTION:
;grumpy.example.com.            IN      A

;; ANSWER SECTION:
grumpy.example.com.     172800  IN      A       192.168.0.17

;; AUTHORITY SECTION:
example.com.            172800  IN      NS      shrek.example.com.

;; Query time: 3 msec
;; SERVER: 127.0.0.1#53(127.0.0.1)
```

```
;; WHEN: Thu Dec  8 15:47:01 2005
;; MSG SIZE  rcvd: 72
```

The QUESTION section just echoes the query. The ANSWER section shows the requested A record, and the authority section shows the NS record for the server that provided the result. The large number (172,800) accompanying these records is the time to live (2 days) in seconds.

The command rndc provides for some runtime interaction with the DNS server; for example, rndc status will report on the server's current status; rndc reload will force the server to reload the config file and zone file.

Where to Learn More

I was silently bemoaning the lack of documentation about BIND included with SUSE Linux, until I discovered that I didn't have the bind-doc package loaded. With this installed you'll find lots of documentation including a collection of relevant RFCs; note especially the Administrators' Reference Manual at */usr/share/doc/packages/bind/arm/Bv9ARM.html*. You'll also find extensive documentation on the Web at *http://www.bind9.net*.

The definitive book on BIND is *DNS and BIND*, Fourth Edition, by Albitz and Liu (O'Reilly). There's also an extensive chapter on DNS in the *Linux Administration Handbook* by Nemeth et al. (Prentice Hall).

7.3 Share Files Using NFS

NFS, the Network File System, is a file-sharing technology pioneered by Sun Microsystems. It has been widely implemented for many years across many versions of Unix and Linux and can rightly be considered the "native" file-sharing protocol for Linux. This lab explains how to export filesystems from an NFS server and how to mount exported filesystems into the filesystem of a client.

How Do I Do That?

To configure an NFS server, you must first define one or more *exports*. An export simply means a piece of the server's filesystem that it is willing to make available to clients. You must make sure that the relevant daemons are running. For reasons that I discuss later, there are three daemons: nfsd, mountd, and the portmapper. And of course, you must ensure that access to these daemons is not blocked by your firewall.

You can configure the server using YaST. From YaST's main screen, select Network Services from the panel on the left, then NFS Server from the panel on the right. On the first screen you can choose whether to run the NFS server, and whether to open up the relevant ports in the firewall. To enable NFS, select both of these options and proceed to the next screen.

This is where the real configuration happens. Here, you can add one or more directories that you want to export. (Click on Add Directory.) For each directory you add, you supply the full pathname of the directory (for example, */home*). You must also supply an access control entry, which consists of a client specifier (YaST calls this field "Host Wild Card") and a set of export options. I will get into the details of these in a moment; as a simple example, setting the client specifier to * and the options to ro makes the export available read-only to all clients. As you add more directories in this way, the list of exported directories appears in the upper panel.

Each exported directory can have more than one access control entry. If you select a directory from the upper panel, its access control entries are shown in the lower panel. To add a new access control entry, click on Add Host. A typical screen is shown in Figure 7-3.

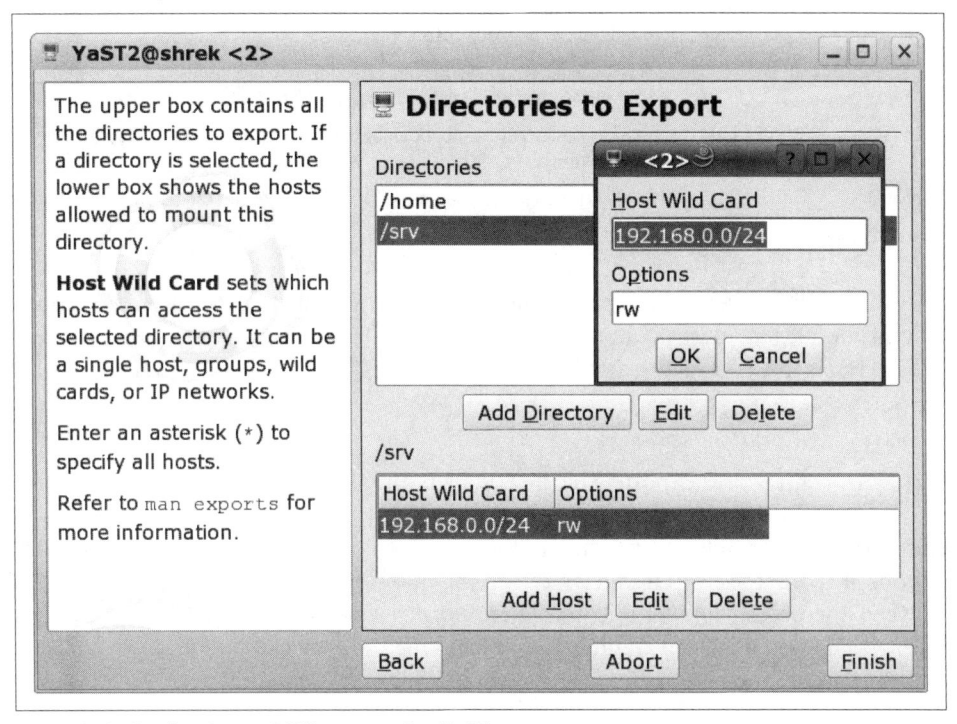

Figure 7-3. Configuring an NFS server using YaST

Within an access control entry, the client specifier can take several forms. It can be the DNS name of a single machine, such as marvin.example.com. It can include * and ? wildcards, so that *.example.com matches anything within the example.com domain. It can be a full IP address, such as 192.168.4.56, or it can include a netmask, such as 192.168.0.0/24.

There are a number of export options—some commonly used, some rather obscure. The ones you're most likely to need are listed in Table 7-2.

Table 7-2. *NFS export options*

Option	Description
ro	Read-only (this is the default).
rw	Read-write.
sync	Forces synchronous operation. An NFS server must ensure that any file updates have been committed to stable storage (i.e., written to the disk) before acknowledging completion of a write request to a client. This is the default, and is "safest"; that is, least likely to result in data loss in the event of a server crash.
async	The opposite of sync. Use of async may yield some improvement in performance on writing, but is less safe.
root_squash	This option prevents super-user identity from propagating from an NFS client to an NFS server. Specifically, when a process running as root on a client requests file access on the server, his effective ID on the server (i.e., the ID that file permission checks will be made against) is mapped to the so-called *anonymous user*. The user name is usually nobody and the numeric UID is 65534. The group identity is also mapped and becomes nogroup on the server.
root_no_squash	The opposite of root_squash. Using root_no_squash, root on the client remains as root on the server. Use this option with caution, and offer it only to trusted clients.
all_squash	Causes all users to be squashed down to nobody/nogroup. You might use this if you're providing a "communal" export to many users.
anonuid=N	Specifies the user ID of the anonymous account. The default, as mentioned earlier, is nobody.
anonguid=N	Specifies the group ID of the anonymous account.

The YaST NFS server configuration module is just a (rather half-hearted) wrapper around the file */etc/exports*, and it is just as easy to hand-edit this file as it is to use YaST. Here's the exports file that YaST generated:

```
/home    *(ro) trusty(rw,no_root_squash)
/srv     192.168.0.0/24(rw)
```

Each line defines one export. The first field is the exported directory. Remaining fields represent access control entries. The entries are separated by spaces. Each entry consists of a client specifier followed by a comma-separated list of export options in parentheses. The file is rather picky on syntax. There *must* be a space between the access control entries. There *must not* be a space between the client specifier and the opening parenthesis that introduces the option list.

After you've edited */etc/exports*, you must run:

```
# exportfs -a
```

to make the mountd daemon aware of the change. Alternatively, you can run:

```
# rcnfsserver restart
```

You don't need to do this if you use YaST—it will handle this for you.

> To compare NFS with Windows file sharing for a moment, Windows has the notion of a *share point*, which maps onto some underlying directory in the server. Shares are accessed using UNC names of the form \\SERVERNAME\SHARENAME. The share itself has a name, which doesn't need to be the same as the name of the underlying directory. In NFS, there is no such intermediate name. The name of the exported resource as seen by the client is the name of the directory on the server.

On the client side of things, you can also use YaST to mount an exported filesystem. From the main YaST screen, select Network Services from the panel on the left, then NFS Client from the panel on the right. To add an NFS mount, click Add and fill in the form as shown in Figure 7-4.

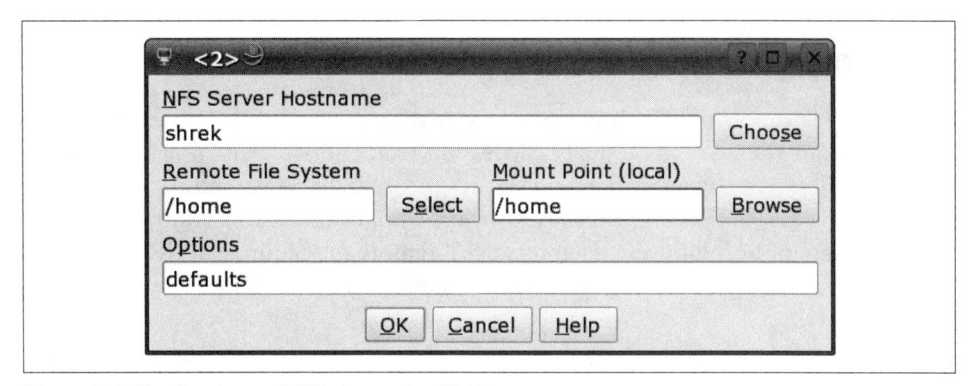

Figure 7-4. Configuring an NFS client using YaST

Notice there is no need for the directory name on the remote filesystem and the directory name of the mount point on the local filesystem to be the same, although they often are. YaST will do two things—it will mount the remote filesystem "for the here and now," and it will put an entry into */etc/fstab* so that the mount will automatically be put into place when the client boots.

You can, of course, do these things manually. The mount command equivalent to the mount shown in the YaST screen above would be:

```
# mount shrek:/home /home
```

The entry in *fstab* needed to make the mount kick in at boot time looks like this:

```
shrek:/home     /home    nfs    defaults    0 0
```

Once the mount is in place, you can access the contents of the server's */home* directory on the client just as if it were part of the client's filesystem, as shown in Figure 7-5.

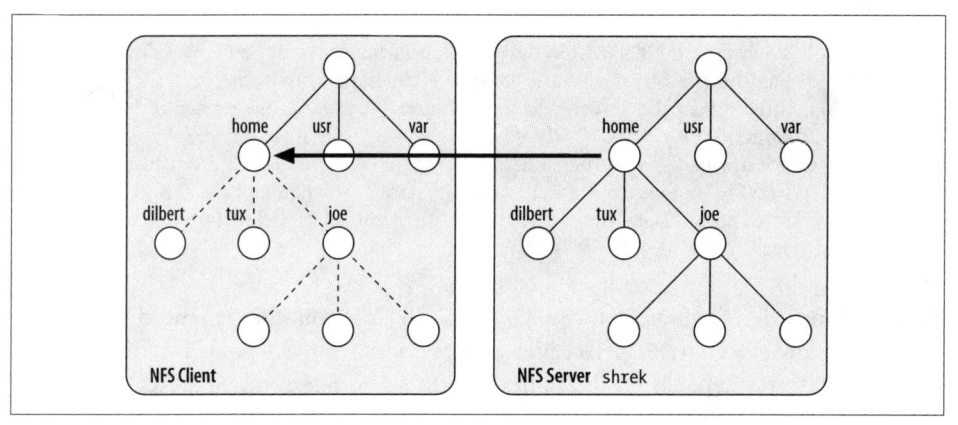

Figure 7-5. Mounting an NFS export

How It Works

NFS service is supported by three daemons: `nfsd`, `mountd`, and the `portmapper`. The `nfsd` daemon is the one that actually carries out read and write operations on NFS-mounted files. The `mountd` daemon is responsible for responding to mount requests; it is `mountd` that reads */etc/exports* and applies the access controls that are specified therein. Both of these daemons use a remote procedure call (RPC) mechanism that was devised by Sun Microsystems and used to implement services such as NFS and NIS.

A discussion of how RPC works is not necessary here; however, one relevant aspect of Sun's RPC scheme is that the servers are identified not by port number in the traditional way, but by a program number and a version number. When an RPC server starts up, it registers with the `portmapper` on its local machine, giving the program number(s) and version number(s) that it supports, and the port(s) that it's listening on. This is shown in steps 1 and 2 in Figure 7-6. The `portmapper` records these in a table. If you're interested, the program numbers are defined in */etc/rpc*.

When an NFS client needs to access `mountd` or `nfsd`, it must first query the `portmapper` on the server to discover what ports to use. It asks for the service by program number and version number. This is shown in steps 3 and 4 in Figure 7-6. Once it knows the ports, it can request a mount operation. The `mountd` daemon makes the relevant access control checks against that client, and if successful, it passes back a *handle* that can be used in subsequent calls to the `nfsd` daemon to access files in that export. The `portmapper` itself always listens on port 111.

This behind-the-scenes stuff is important to you only if it stops working. In particular, if the `portmapper` isn't running, or if the `nfsd` and `mountd` services aren't registered with it, NFS will not work.

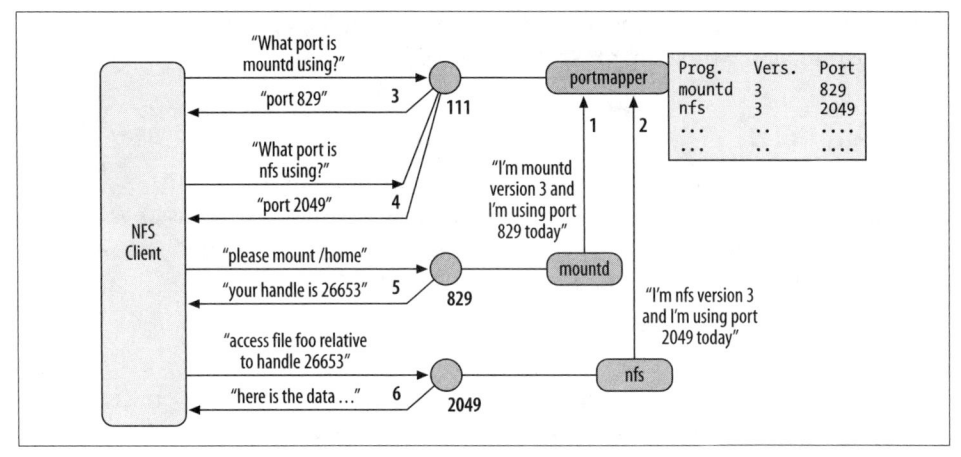

Figure 7-6. The portmapper

You can query the `portmapper` on the NFS server to see what services are registered. If NFS isn't working, this is a good first diagnostic step:

```
# rpcinfo -p shrek
   program vers proto   port
    100000    2   tcp    111  portmapper
    100000    2   udp    111  portmapper
    100003    2   udp   2049  nfs
    100003    3   udp   2049  nfs
    100003    4   udp   2049  nfs
    100003    2   tcp   2049  nfs
    100003    3   tcp   2049  nfs
    100003    4   tcp   2049  nfs
    100024    1   udp   1031  status
    100021    1   udp   1031  nlockmgr
    100021    3   udp   1031  nlockmgr
    100021    4   udp   1031  nlockmgr
    100024    1   tcp   1050  status
    100021    1   tcp   1050  nlockmgr
    100021    3   tcp   1050  nlockmgr
    100021    4   tcp   1050  nlockmgr
    100005    1   udp    828  mountd
    100005    1   tcp    829  mountd
    100005    2   udp    828  mountd
    100005    2   tcp    829  mountd
    100005    3   udp    828  mountd
    100005    3   tcp    829  mountd
```

Notice that most servers register more than one version of the service.

You can also query the `mountd` daemon directly to ask for its export list; for example:

```
# showmount -e shrek
Export list for shrek:
/home *
/srv  192.168.0.0/24
```

If this works, then the `portmapper` and `mountd` must both be up and running. For performance tuning, the program `nfsstat` may provide useful statistics.

What About…

…access control and security? NFS is not especially secure. It is really intended for use only across trusted local networks. In particular, any files read or written via NFS are transmitted in clear text across the network and are easily sniffed. There are ways of making NFS secure—it can be tunneled over an SSH connection, or it can be run over *secure RPC*.

Access controls within NFS are applied at two levels. First, the */etc/exports* file controls which clients can mount which exports. Second, the usual file permissions on the server are applied against the client user's identity. Neither of these is secure, as client machine identity and user identity are both easily forged in an NFS request.

In a "traditional" NFS setup, filesystems (typically users' home directories) are made available from a central server to many clients. The idea is that the users all have an account on each machine and can log in to any of the machines and see the same environment. When a request is made to an NFS server, it is the user's numeric UID that is propagated to the server and used to make file permission checks. This goes seriously wrong if the user IDs aren't consistent across the machines. For example, if `chris` has UID 1005 on the client and `simon` has UID 1005 on the server, `chris` will appear to own `simon`'s files on the server. In a traditional system, consistency of UIDs is usually guaranteed by serving all user accounts from a NIS server, or latterly perhaps, from an LDAP server.

Where to Learn More

Read the manual pages for `exports`, `mountd`, `nfsd`, and `showmount`. For a complete reference, try *Managing NFS and NIS* by Hal Stern (O'Reilly).

7.4 Serve Filesystems to Windows with Samba

Linux systems rarely live on Linux-only networks. Most of them find themselves within existing infrastructures that contain large numbers of Windows machines. The Samba suite of programs allows a Linux system to integrate with Windows networks by providing file, print, and authentication services to Windows clients using the native Windows file-sharing protocols. Other components of Samba allow Linux to act as a client, accessing file and print resources on Windows servers. Using Samba as a server provides an easy, cost-effective, and relatively low-risk way for Linux to "get a foot in the corporate door," so to speak. As such, Samba is strategically an important suite of programs.

In this lab, you'll see how to serve filesystems to Windows clients, and how to authenticate users. Keep in mind that Samba is a large topic that has given rise to some fairly thick books all by itself. As a result, the treatment in this lab is necessarily brief.

How Do I Do That?

First, make sure you have the relevant packages installed. You need `kdebase3-samba`, `libsmbclient`, `samba`, `samba-client`, `samba-doc`, `samba-vscan`, `yast2-samba-client`, and `yast2-samba-server`.

Most services can be configured in two ways (one using YaST and one using the command line), but in the case of Samba there are actually three, because there's also a browser-based graphical configuration tool called SWAT, which comes as part of the Samba suite. SWAT is my preferred tool and is the one I'll cover here. SWAT is started via `xinetd` and must be enabled. Edit the file */etc/xinetd.d/swat* and change the line:

```
disable = yes
```

to read:

```
disable = no
```

Then tell `xinetd` to reread the file:

```
# rcxinetd restart
```

Now enter the URL *http://localhost:901* into your browser. You'll be prompted to log in—enter root and your root password. (Be warned that if you choose to configure Samba from a browser on a remote machine, this login will pass root's password over the network in plain text.) You should see the SWAT home page shown in Figure 7-7.

From this screen you can access the online documentation, which is extensive. Note that there seems to be a disagreement between where SWAT expects the online documentation to live and where it is actually installed. This is easily fixed with a well-placed symbolic link:

```
# cd /usr/share
# ln -s doc/packages/samba/htmldocs/manpages-3  samba/swat/help/manpages
```

The buttons along the top of SWAT's home page give you access to the main configuration screens. Let's set Samba up to serve out users' home directories. Start with the wizard page. Here you can specify the role that your Samba server will play—as a standalone server, as a member of a domain, or as a domain controller. I strongly recommend that you start with a standalone server. Under Expose Home Directories, click Yes. Now click the Edit Parameter Values button and fill in the form shown in Figure 7-8.

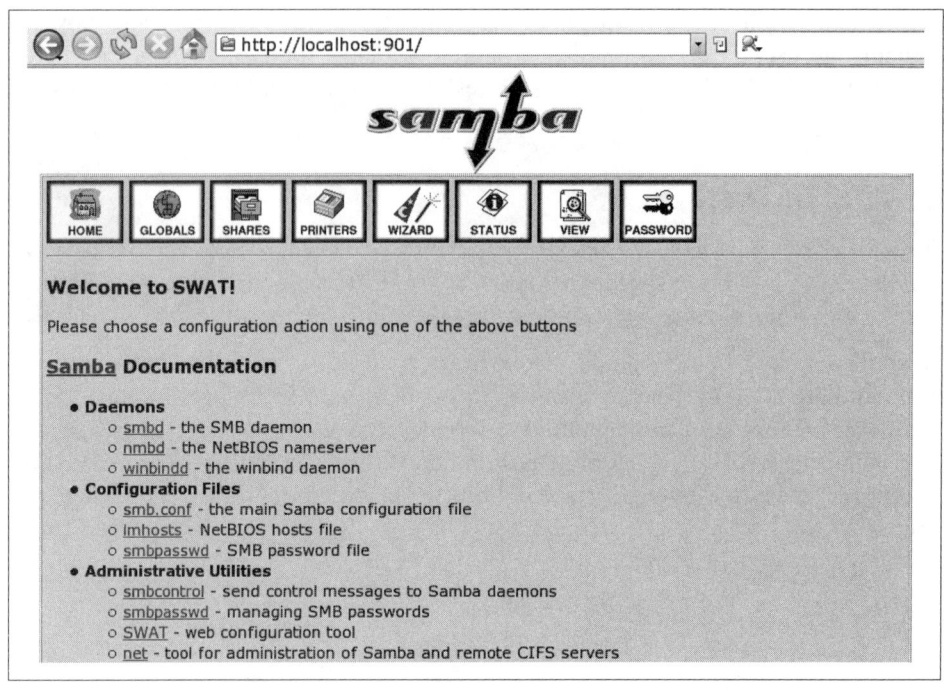

Figure 7-7. SWAT home page

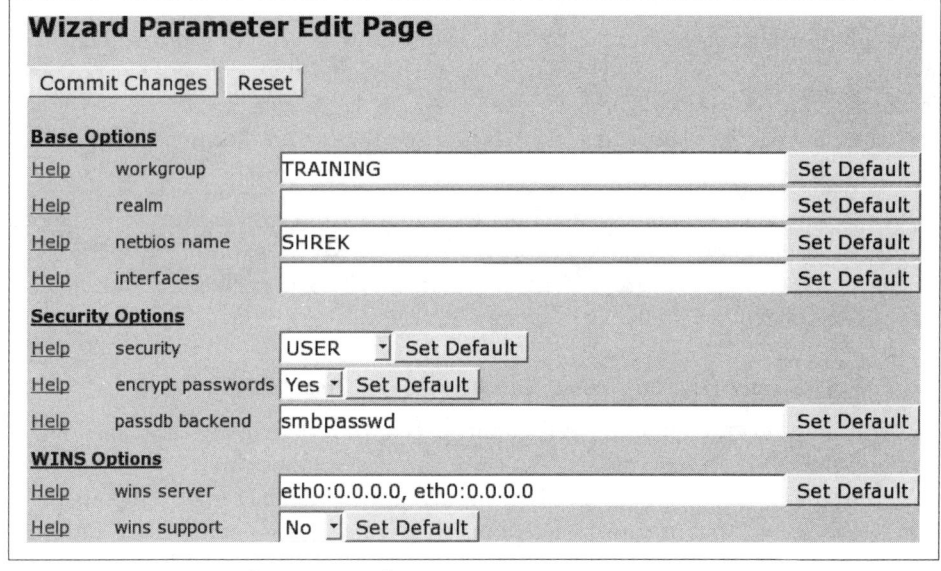

Figure 7-8. SWAT Wizard Parameter Edit Page

You will probably want to enter a name for your workgroup, and a NetBIOS name (which Windows machines will use to specify your Linux server) for the machine. Click Commit Changes.

Now go to the status page. If the daemons `smbd` and `nmbd` are not running, click their Start buttons. You can also start the daemons from the command line with:

```
# rcnmb start
# rcsmb start
```

There is one final step needed to make home directory shares work. You need to provide a way to allow Samba to authenticate the users. The simplest way to do this is to use a flat file as the *account database*. This file is managed from the command line. Suppose you want to serve the home directories for user `simon`. To add a Samba account for this user, run the command:

```
# smbpasswd -a simon
New SMB password:
Retype new SMB password:
Added user simon.
```

The password you set here should match the password set for `simon`'s account on the Windows client. Also, `simon` must already have a regular Linux account on the server.

With all these pieces in place, `simon` should be able to log in on the Windows client and browse via "My Network Places" to the workgroup and NetBIOS name defined for your Samba server. There, `simon` should see a Samba share (try saying that after a large gin!) corresponding to his home directory on the server.

Let's take this example one step further by using SWAT to define a share called `doc` that provides access to the */usr/share/doc* hierarchy. (Okay, I guess that the average Windows user is probably not interested in reading Linux documentation.) Go back to the SWAT home page and click the Shares button. Type in the name for the new share, then click Create Share (yes, you really do have to do it in that order). You'll see the screen shown in Figure 7-9.

Here you can see some of the settings for the share. (I say "some" because this is only the basic view. There are many more settings in the advanced view.) Most settings take sensible defaults and can be left blank, but note in particular the `path` definition, the `read only` and `guest only` settings, and the `hosts allow` setting that will restrict access to the local network. Click Commit Changes to write the settings out. Notice the Help hyperlinks on the left; these take you to the relevant entry describing that setting in the manual pages.

How It Works

The underlying configuration file is */etc/samba/smb.conf*. The example shown here is simpler than the one generated by SWAT, but is sufficient to meet the aim of

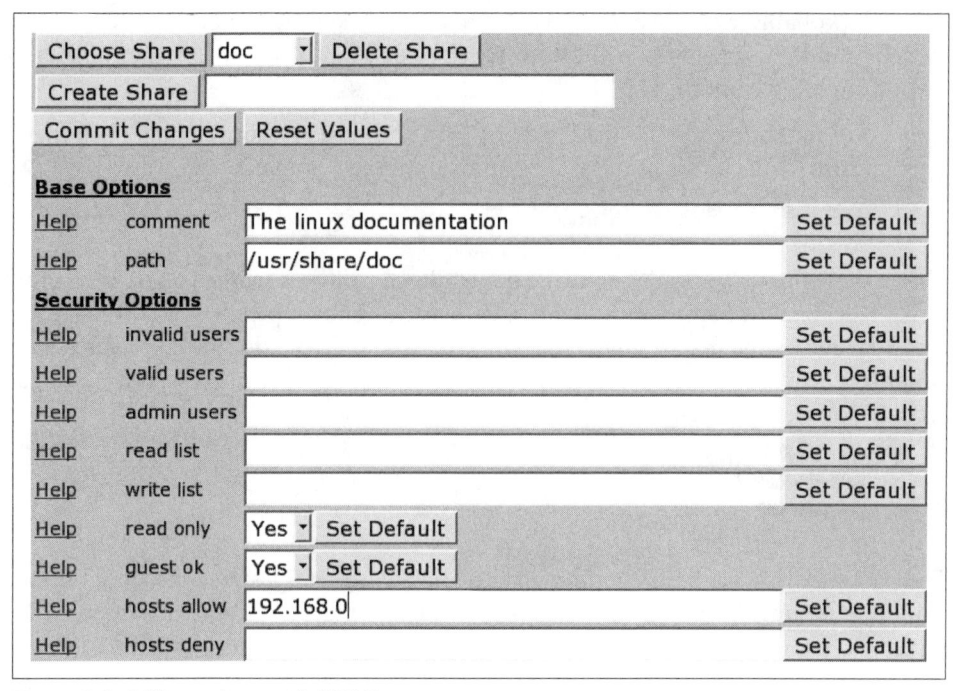

Figure 7-9. Adding a share with SWAT

sharing out home directories. The line numbers are for reference; they are not part of the file.

```
1  [global]
2          workgroup = TRAINING
3          netbios name = SHREK
4          map to guest = Bad User
5
6  [homes]
7          comment = Home Directories
8          valid users = %S
9          read only = No
10         inherit acls = Yes
11         browseable = No
12
13 [doc]
14         read only = yes
15         guest ok = yes
16         path = /usr/share/doc
17         hosts allow = 192.168.0
```

Line 1 introduces the global section. This contains directives that apply to the operation of the server as a whole. Lines 2 and 3 set the workgroup name and NetBIOS name of the server. Line 4 says that users that do not have an account will be allowed to connect, but will be treated as a guest user (the default identity of this user on the samba server is nobody).

Line 6 defines the homes share. This is a special share that tells Samba to create a share on the fly depending on the identity of the user that connects. If simon connects, a share corresponding to simon's home directory will be created. If chris connects, a share corresponding to chris's home directory will be created, and so on. Line 8 says that the only user allowed to connect to the share is the one for whom it was created. Line 11 prevents the homes share itself from showing up in the browse list.

Lines 13–16 define a read-only share called doc that provides access to the documentation on the Samba server.

As you can see, it is not hard to hand-edit the config file.

The actual samba servers are nmbd and smbd. The daemon nmbd provides NetBIOS name resolution services. It also participates in the browsing protocols that make up the Windows "Network Neighborhood" view. The daemon smbd provides the actual file- and print-sharing services. There is a third daemon called winbindd that allows users whose account information is stored in a Windows domain to authenticate on the Linux system, and to resolve their names to a Linux UID. This removes the need for client users of a Samba server to have accounts on the Linux box. It is not used in the simple scenario used in this lab.

What About...

...the client side of Samba? First, there are a number of command-line tools that are mainly diagnostic in nature. For example, to list all the SMB servers, use findsmb:

```
# findsmb
                            *=DMB
                            +=LMB
IP ADDR        NETBIOS NAME     WORKGROUP/OS/VERSION
---------------------------------------------------------------------
192.168.0.3    SHREK            [TRAINING] [Unix] [Samba 3.0.20-4-SUSE]
192.168.0.4    BASHFUL          +[WESTWICK] [Windows 5.0] [Windows 2000 LAN Manager]
```

To list the shares on a specific server, use smbclient:

```
# smbclient -U chris -L bashful
Password:
Domain=[BASHFUL] OS=[Windows 5.0] Server=[Windows 2000 LAN Manager]

        Sharename       Type      Comment
        ---------       ----      -------
        chris           Disk
        IPC$            IPC       Remote IPC
        print$          Disk      Printer Drivers
        hpoffice        Printer   hp officejet 6100 series
        transfer        Disk
        ADMIN$          Disk      Remote Admin
        C$              Disk      Default share
Domain=[BASHFUL] OS=[Windows 5.0] Server=[Windows 2000 LAN Manager]
```

You can also use `smbclient` to connect to a share and to copy files to or from it. It works rather like a command-line `ftp` client. Here, it connects to the share //bashful/chris, lists its contents, and retrieves one file from it:

```
# smbclient -U chris //bashful/chris
Password:
Domain=[BASHFUL] OS=[Windows 5.0] Server=[Windows 2000 LAN Manager]
smb: \> dir
  .                                   D        0  Thu Mar 24 07:23:59 2005
  ..                                  D        0  Thu Mar 24 07:23:59 2005
  Application Data                   DH        0  Tue Dec 21 08:58:48 2004
  camtasiaf.exe                       A 25380456  Tue Dec 21 08:14:24 2004
  coda-ch02.ppt                       A   731136  Fri Nov 28 13:33:45 2003
  Cookies                            DS        0  Sat Aug 27 06:56:54 2005
  Desktop                             D        0  Sat Aug 27 06:56:46 2005
  dotnetfx.exe                        A 24265736  Sat Dec 18 15:35:32 2004
  ... lots of files edited out ...
  SNMP-Ch01.ppt                       A   630784  Thu Jan  1 20:32:57 2004
  SNMP-Ch02.ppt                       A   824832  Fri Jan  2 10:59:54 2004

            40005 blocks of size 524288. 12299 blocks available
smb: \> get SNMP-Ch01.ppt
getting file \SNMP-Ch01.ppt of size 630784 as SNMP-Ch01.ppt (3850.0 kb/s)
                              (average 3850.0 kb/s)
smb: \> quit
```

It's also possible, and more useful, to mount an SMB share into the Linux filesystem, using the `smbfs` filesystem.

```
# mount -t smbfs -o username=chris,uid=chris,gid=users //bashful/chris /mnt
Password:
```

Now you can list the files in the share as if they are local:

```
# ls -l /mnt
total 161422
drwxr-xr-x   1 chris users    4096 Dec  5 19:18 .
drwxr-xr-x  27 root  root      648 Dec  4 07:42 ..
drwxr-xr-x   1 chris users    4096 Dec 21  2004 Application Data
drwxr-xr-x   1 chris users    4096 Aug 27 07:56 Cookies
drwxr-xr-x   1 chris users    4096 Aug 27 07:56 Desktop
... lots of files edited out ...
-rwxr-xr-x   1 chris users  630784 Jan  1  2004 SNMP-Ch01.ppt
-rwxr-xr-x   1 chris users  824832 Jan  2  2004 SNMP-Ch02.ppt
```

Notice that the files appear to be owned by `chris` with group `users`. They aren't really, of course—the Windows server knows nothing of Linux users and groups—but the filesystem is pretending they are, as a result of the `uid=chris,gid=users` options on the `mount` command.

Finally, you can browse and access SMB shares within Konqueror. You can start by clicking on the Network Browsing icon on your desktop, then select SMB Shares, then drill down through the workgroup, server name, and share name to see the files. Alternatively you can just enter a URL such as `smb://shrek/docs/packages` directly into Konqueror's location bar.

Where to Learn More

This has been a lightning tour through a rather complex service. I have skirted around a number of difficulties caused by incompatibilities of the Linux and Windows filesystems—different handling of case sensitivity, different limits on filename length, different notions of ownership and access control, and so on. I have not discussed any of Samba's more advanced capabilities, such as the support for roaming profiles and logon scripts (*.bat* files), or Samba's interaction with CUPS to provide print services, or its role as a Primary Domain Controller, and several other things.

For a thorough introduction to Samba, try *Using Samba* by Ts et al. (O'Reilly). If you'd prefer something slightly more up to date, try *The Official Samba 3 HOWTO and Reference Guide* by Vernooij and Terpstra (Prentice Hall). (Make sure you get the latest edition, as Samba is evolving quickly.) This is a detailed and authoritative book, but not an easy read. A companion to this is *Samba 3 by Example: Practical Exercises to Successful Deployment* by Terpstra (Prentice Hall). You should be aware, however, that all these books are included in PDF format as part of the distribution, in the directory */usr/share/doc/packages/samba*—though if you're like me, you may prefer to read such extensive documents on paper rather than on the screen.

Of course, you should also look at the manual pages for `smbd`, `nmbd`, `smb.conf`, `smbmount`, `smbclient`, and so on. The manpage for `samba` provides a short list of the various programs that make up the suite.

7.5 Configure a DHCP Server

DHCP servers provide network configuration parameters to machines when they boot (or to be more accurate, when they start their network interfaces). DHCP stands for Dynamic Host Configuration Protocol. Most users think of DHCP as providing IP addresses for its clients to use, but it is able to supply many other pieces of configuration information, including the subnet mask, the broadcast address, the IP address of the default gateway, the IP address of one or more DNS servers, time servers, print servers, and so on. It can even supply a domain name for the client. This information (in particular the IP address) is not assigned to a client in perpetuity, but is leased to it for a specified time, which will typically be a few hours or days. The client can request a lease time when it makes the DHCP request. The server is configured with a maximum lease time (which will override the client if it asks for too long a lease) and a default lease time (which will be used if the client doesn't request a specific duration). Clients are expected to request renewal of their leases if they wish to keep using their assigned IP address, or to stop using the IP address if they allow the lease to expire.

DHCP offers a number of conveniences. First, it allows large-scale deployment of desktop systems by allowing each system to be imaged with an identical configuration. There is no need to go around and "tweak" each system to set its IP address and other settings. Second, it allows those of us who regularly move our laptops between networks to automatically pick up appropriate settings for that network, without tedious manual reconfiguration. Third, it allows reuse of IP addresses through the reclamation and reissue of expired leases.

How Do I Do That?

You can configure a simple DHCP server with YaST. Select Network Services from the pane on the left of the main YaST screen, then choose DHCP Server from the pane on the right. The DHCP configuration module provides four screens on which you can specify settings as follows:

Start-Up screen
Specify whether dhcpd (the DHCP server) will be started at boot time, and start and stop it manually. (The first time you run this YaST module, the start-up screen appears last in the sequence.)

Card Selection
Specify which of your network interfaces the DHCP server will listen on. You can also specify that the DHCP port (UDP port 67) be opened in the firewall.

Global Settings
As shown in Figure 7-10, specify global settings (settings that will apply to all subnets that this server services). These settings include the domain name, primary and secondary DNS servers, the default gateway, an NTP time server (you're less likely to need this), a print server, and a default lease time.

Dynamic DHCP
As shown in Figure 7-11, specify the available IP address range for the subnet that you're serving. You can also specify the default and maximum lease time that will be offered for this subnet.

Once you've completed setup of these four screens, click Finish to commit the changes. At this point, you should have a working DHCP server.

How It Works

The YaST DHCP configuration module creates the file */etc/dhcpd.conf*. This is a plain text file; it is well documented and easy to edit by hand if you prefer. Here's an example corresponding to the configuration established using YaST and shown in the preceding figures. The line numbers are for reference; they are not part of the file.

```
1  option broadcast-address 192.168.0.255;
2  option domain-name "example.org";
3  option domain-name-servers 192.168.0.1, 213.253.16.72;
4  option routers 192.168.0.1;
5  default-lease-time 14400;
6  # this statement is needed by dhcpd-3
7  ddns-update-style none;
```

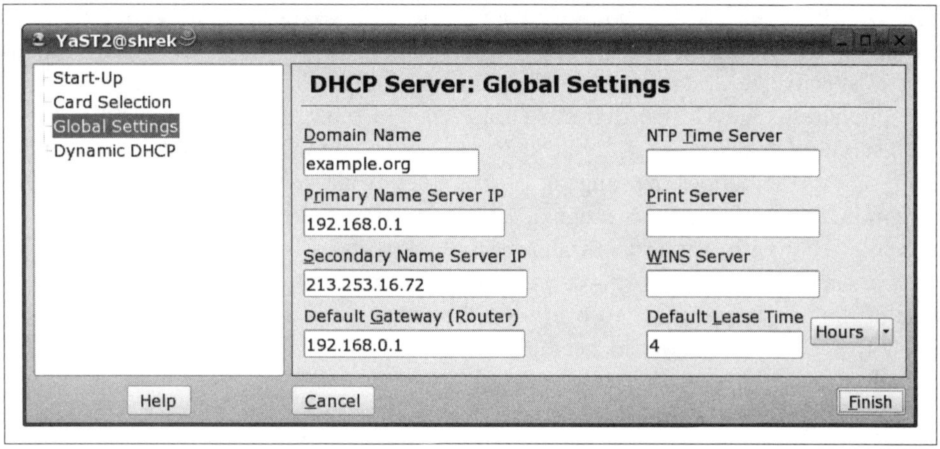

Figure 7-10. DHCP global settings

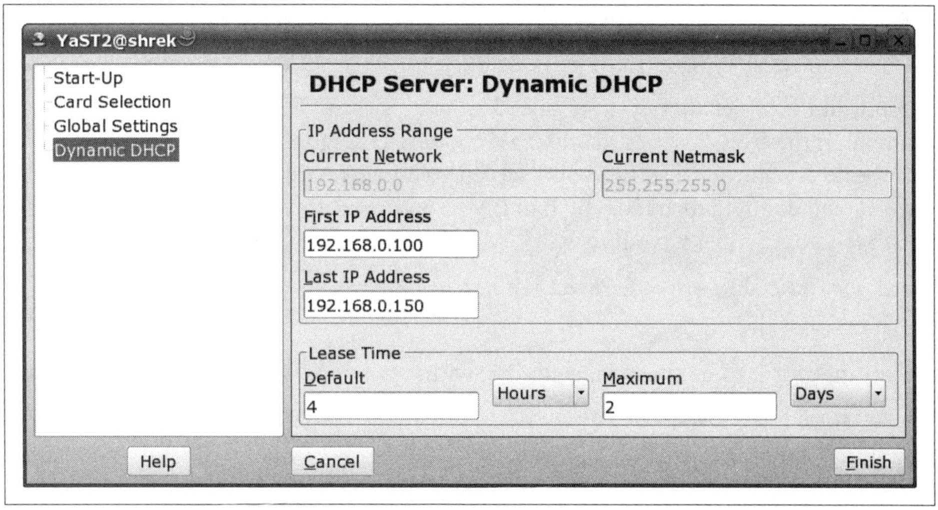

Figure 7-11. DHCP dynamic settings

```
 8  ddns-updates off;
 9  authoritative ;
10  # Define the facility at which dhcpd will log via syslog
11  log-facility local7;
12  subnet 192.168.0.0 netmask 255.255.255.0 {
13    range 192.168.0.100 192.168.0.150;
14    default-lease-time 14400;
15    max-lease-time 172800;
16  }
```

Lines 1–5 define "global" settings—that is, settings that will apply to all subnets. The names of these parameters are self-explanatory. The lease times are in seconds.

7.5 Configure a DHCP Server | 323

The DHCP server has the ability to dynamically update the Domain Name System, assuming that your DNS server supports dynamic updates. The dhcpd server requires you to specify the update scheme you want to use; lines 7 and 8 disable dynamic DNS updates. Lines 12–16 define a subnet. There must be a subnet definition for each subnet that the server is connected to. The key line within the subnet definition is line 13, which defines the range of IP addresses available to this DHCP server. It is important to ensure that this range doesn't overlap with any other DHCP servers on this subnet, or with any statically allocated IP addresses. Lines 14 and 15 define lease time parameters specific to this subnet; they override any settings in the global section of the file. It's possible to override other settings in this way; for example, it's likely that each subnet would need a different option routers setting to specify its default gateway.

If you choose to configure your DHCP server by hand (without using YaST), there are a couple of other things to be done. First, you also need to edit the file */etc/sysconfig/dhcpd* and find the line beginning DHCPD_INTERFACE. Edit it to specify the name of the interface you want your DHCP server to listen on; for example:

```
DHCPD_INTERFACE="eth-id-00:0d:56:78:cd:bf"
```

Second, don't forget that you may need to open up the DHCP port on the firewall running on the DHCP server. If you used YaST to configure your DHCP server, there is a checkbox on the Card Selection screen offering the option to do this automatically. If you configured DHCP by hand, you will need to explicitly open the DHCP port. See Lab 8.3, "Set Up a Firewall," for details on how to do this.

Third, you'll need to start the server with:

```
# rcdhcpd start
```

and arrange for it to be started at run time with:

```
# chkconfig --add dhcpd
```

The DHCP server records the leases it has assigned in the file */var/lib/dhcp/db/dhcpd.leases*. A sample entry in this file looks like this:

```
lease 192.168.0.150 {
  starts 5 2005/11/18 11:52:57;
  ends 0 2005/11/20 11:52:57;
  tstp 0 2005/11/20 11:52:57;
  binding state active;
  next binding state free;
  hardware ethernet 00:06:5b:ba:6e:fb;
  uid "\001\000\006[\272n\373";
  client-hostname "snowhite";
}
```

Leases are appended to this file as they are granted, and it's not an error to see the same IP address appear more than once in the file. The daemon uses this file to recover its list of leases when it restarts.

As a security measure, dhcpd runs in a so-called *chroot jail*—that is, it changes its notion of the root directory (to */var/lib/dhcp*), which prevents it from accessing any files above that point in the filesystem tree. To allow dhcpd to operate in this jail, a number of files are copied into the jail by the startup script, including *dhcpd.conf*.

What About...

...assigning static IP addresses with DCHP? This is something you might want to do for the servers on your network, which need to be at known addresses. It's possible to put host-specific settings, such as IP addresses, into a DHCP config file. The entry typically looks like this:

```
host bambi {
   hardware ethernet 00:00:45:12:EE:F4;
   fixed-address 192.168.0.9;
}
```

This entry effectively binds the IP address to the specified MAC address. (When a DHCP client sends a request, its MAC address is really the only unique value available to identify it.)

What About...

...diagnostic tools? The package dhcp-tools contains a couple of diagnostic tools called dhcping and dhcpdump. The former is intended to provide a simple "are you listening?" check for DHCP servers—I haven't had much success with it, but your mileage may vary. The latter is intended to give a human-readable display of DHCP traffic from a packet capture generated by tcpdump or ethereal. Here is an example of piping the output from tcpdump directly into dhcpdump; some of the fields have been edited out for brevity, but you can clearly see the parameters that were requested and the parameters that were returned:

```
# tcpdump -lenx -s 1500 port bootps or port bootpc | dhcpdump
tcpdump: verbose output suppressed, use -v or -vv for full protocol decode
listening on eth0, link-type EN10MB (Ethernet), capture size 1500 bytes
   TIME: 20:18:09.779804
     IP: > (00:06:5b:ba:6e:fb) > BOOTP/DHCP (ff:ff:ff:ff:ff:ff)
     OP: 1 (BOOTPREQUEST)
  HTYPE: 1 (Ethernet)
   HLEN: 6
 CHADDR: 00:06:5b:ba:6e:fb:00:00:00:00:00:00:00:00:00:00
  SNAME: .
  FNAME: .
 OPTION:  53 (  1) DHCP message type         3 (DHCPREQUEST)
 OPTION:  57 (  2) Maximum DHCP message size 548
 OPTION:  50 (  4) Request IP address        192.168.0.17
 OPTION:  51 (  4) IP address leasetime      -1 ()
 OPTION:  55 ( 20) Parameter Request List    1 (Subnet mask)
                                             3 (Routers)
                                             6 (DNS server)
```

```
                               12 (Host name)
                               15 (Domainname)
                               17 (Root path)
                               23 (Default IP TTL)
                               28 (Broadcast address)
                               29 (Perform mask discovery)
                               31 (Perform router discovery)
                               33 (Static route)
                               40 (NIS domain)
                               41 (NIS servers)
                               42 (NTP servers)
                                9 (LPR server)
                                7 (Log server)
                               44 (NetBIOS name server)
                               45 (NetBIOS datagram
                                   distribution server)
                               46 (NetBIOS node type)
                               47 (NetBIOS scope)
OPTION:  12 (  9) Host name                 snowhite
OPTION:  60 ( 32) Vendor class identifier   Linux 2.6.11.4-21.8-default i686
OPTION:  61 (  7) Client-identifier         01:00:06:5b:ba:6e:fb
---------------------------------------------------------------------------
  TIME: 20:18:09.785853
    IP: > (00:50:ba:99:c1:a9) > BOOTP/DHCP (ff:ff:ff:ff:ff:ff)
    OP: 2 (BOOTPREPLY)
 HTYPE: 1 (Ethernet)
  HLEN: 6
CHADDR: 00:06:5b:ba:6e:fb:00:00:00:00:00:00:00:00:00:00
 SNAME: .
 FNAME: .
OPTION:  53 (  1) DHCP message type         5 (DHCPACK)
OPTION:  54 (  4) Server identifier         192.168.0.1
OPTION:  51 (  4) IP address leasetime      259200 (3d)
OPTION:   1 (  4) Subnet mask               255.255.255.0
OPTION:   3 (  4) Routers                   192.168.0.1
OPTION:   6 (  8) DNS server                192.168.0.1,213.253.16.72
OPTION:  15 (  1) Domainname
OPTION:  44 (  8) NetBIOS name server       0.0.0.0,0.0.0.0
```

Where to Learn More

Look at the manpages for dhcpd and dhcpd.conf. The manpage for dhcp-options lists all the options that can be returned by DHCP. There is extensive documentation in the directories dhcp, dhcp-server, dhcp-tools, and dhcpd under the directory */usr/share/doc/packages*, including the official RFCs defining the protocol, and a HOWTO document about dynamic DNS updates.

You might want to take a look at the file */etc/sysconfig/dhcpd*, which contains some low-level configuration for how dhcpd is started.

There's an entire book about DHCP: *The DHCP Handbook* by Droms and Lemon (Sams).

7.6 Configure a Web Server with Apache

The Apache web server is one of the flagship successes of the open source community. According to recent Netcraft (*http://www.netcraft.com*) surveys, Apache is running about 70% of the world's active web sites. In this lab, you'll see how to set up a simple site.

How Do I Do That?

Hosting a web site with Apache on SUSE Linux involves four steps:

Install the relevant RPMs
> If you did a default installation of SUSE Linux, Apache is probably not installed. In the YaST software management module, select the Selections filter, then check the box labeled Simple Web Server with Apache 2. This should install all necessary packages.

Create a configuration for the server
> The server configuration files are the main focus of this lab.

Put some content (.html files and so on) into the Server Root directory
> Actual content generation (HTML, CSS, and so forth) needs a whole book to itself. We'll content ourselves with some very simple pages, just to prove that it's working.

Start the server
> To arrange for the server to start at boot time, use the YaST runlevel editor (see Lab 6.1, "Control Boot-Time Service Startup") or enter the command:
>
> ```
> # chkconfig apache2 on
> ```
>
> To start and stop the server manually (for testing perhaps), use:
>
> ```
> # rcapache2 start
> # rcapache2 stop
> ```

Apache comes preconfigured and works out of the box, so even if you only do the first and last steps listed, you should be able to point your browser at *http://localhost* and see the placeholder home page that comes with the Apache distribution. On that page is a link to the documentation (also included as part of the distribution), which is very complete and very good.

Once the novelty of seeing the default home page has worn off, you will want to start providing your own content. The default configuration of apache sets a *document root* directory of */var/www/htdocs*. The document root is the top-level directory of the filesystem that corresponds to this site's contents. For example, entering the URL *http://localhost/images/logo.png* in the browser would cause the server to look for the file */var/www/htdocs/images/logo.png*. This placement of the document root is consistent with the guidelines of the Filesystem Hierarchy Standard (FHS).

If you look inside */var/www/htdocs* you will see a number of files with names of the form *index.html.xx*, where *xx* is a two-letter language code. As you may know, *index.html* is the default file that will be served if none is specified by the browser (in other words, if the browser submits a URL like *http://somesite.com* that contains only the site name). The multiple versions of this file are there to support Apache's language negotiation feature, which allows the browser to specify the user's language preference (such as English) and associates specified file extensions with specified languages to deliver, if possible, content in the user's language of choice.

A very simple way to start serving your own site is to rename the original htdocs out of the way and create a new one:

```
# cd /var/www
# mv htdocs htdocs.original
# mkdir htdocs
```

Now, you can create your own */var/www/htdocs/index.html*. This lab is not about HTML (that's an entirely separate can of worms), so I'll keep this very simple:

```
<HTML>
<HEAD>
    <TITLE> The Linux Limericks Site </TITLE>
</HEAD>
<BODY>
There was a young lady from Leek <BR>
Who was horribly bored by a geek <BR>
Said she: "This is awful<BR>
It shouldn't be lawful<BR>
I'd rather be gored by a beak!"
</BODY>
</HTML>
```

Of course, you can include hyperlinks in your document, and add content in a directory structure under */var/www/htdocs*.

To go further, you'll need to work with the configuration files. The main configuration file is */etc/apache2/httpd.conf*. It looks scarier than it is. For a start, most of it is comments, and most of the rest consists of *Include statements* that pull in configuration from a dozen or more other files. The idea is to give each of the various aspects of the configuration its own file—error handling directives in one file, server tuning directives in another, and so on. It doesn't have to be like this: there's no reason not to put the entire configuration into one file. If you're comfortable with the structure of the include files supplied by default, fine. If you're confused by them, I recommend that you throw them all away and start from scratch.

Apache supplies sensible defaults for most settings, and you can actually get the server working with a very simple config file like this. The line numbers are for reference; they are not part of the file.

```
1  User wwwrun
2  Group www
```

```
3  Listen 80
4  DocumentRoot /srv/www/htdocs
5  LoadModule mime_module /usr/lib/apache2-prefork/mod_mime.so
```

Lines 1 and 2 define the user and group identity that the server will run under. (The server starts running as root so that it can bind the privileged port to listen on, but then reverts to the identity specified by these two directives.) In a simple case, where Apache is serving a single site, the files making up the site's contents should have owner wwwrun and group www. This user and group are predefined in SUSE Linux.

Line 3 specifies which port to listen on. If the server has more than one network interface, you can also specify the IP address of the interface you want it to listen on.

Line 4 defines the top-level directory containing the site contents, as discussed previously.

Line 5 tells apache to load the module mime_module. Much of the functionality of apache is provided by modules that are usually loaded at startup time by LoadModule directives, and in a production server you will probably find yourself loading 10 or 20 modules. This particular module is the one that figures out the mime type of the data being returned to the browser. Without it, the server will return a mime type of text/plain, which will likely cause the browser to misinterpret the data (HTML files should have a mime type of text/html).

This configuration file is sufficient to get a basic server up and running.

SUSE Linux includes a YaST module for editing the Apache configuration. After working with it for a while, I'm of the opinion that you're better off to ignore it and hand-edit the config file. The YaST module does not remove the need to understand what most of the directives do, and it does not offer support for many of Apache's advanced features.

As an example of taking things a little further, I'll extend the configuration to include Apache's status module, which delivers an HTML page showing the status of each of Apache's worker processes. Add the following lines (without the line numbers!) to *httpd.conf*:

```
1  LoadModule status_module /usr/lib/apache2-prefork/mod_status.so
2  <Location /status>
3  SetHandler server-status
4  </Location>
5  ExtendedStatus On
```

Line 1 loads the relevant module. Lines 2 and 4 together form a *container directive*. They say that the directives in between only apply if the resource being requested is within the status namespace; that is, if the URL is something like *http://www.mysite.com/status*. Line 3 says "refer any requests for this location to the server-status handler, which is provided by the status_module." Line 5 requests a more detailed status report.

With these directives in place, entering the URL *http://localhost/status* into the browser will produce a screen similar to Figure 7-12.

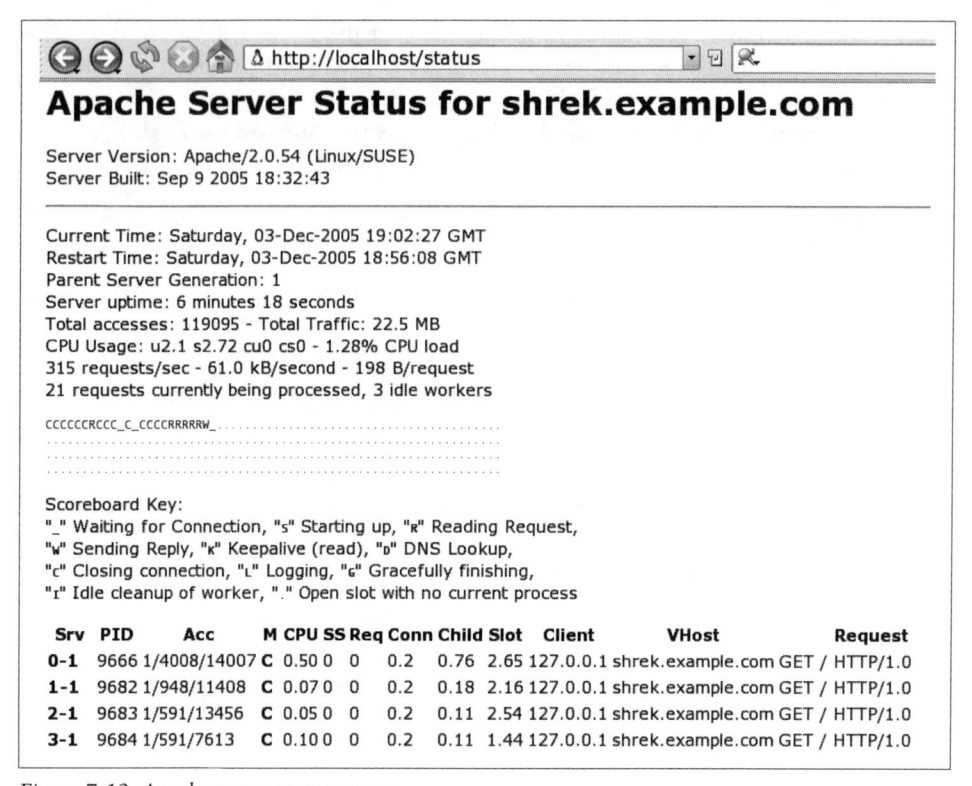

Figure 7-12. Apache server status screen

This screen gives a little insight into the multiprocessing behavior of Apache. This is the "prefork" version of the server, which means that it achieves concurrency by spawning additional processes, and that to improve performance it preforks (forks ahead of time) a number of children that simply wait for connections. At the time that the report was made, there were 24 processes running (see the character map in the center of the screen). Some are busy closing connections, some are reading from connections, three are idle, and one (the one sending us this screen, of course!) is writing a reply.

Let's take the example one step further. You might prefer not to make this status information available to all and sundry, but to restrict it to, say, a browser running on the same machine (i.e., a browser connecting to the loopback address). There are access control directives to do this. Here's the extended config file:

```
1  User wwwrun
2  Group www
3  Listen 80
4  ServerName shrek.example.com
```

```
 5  DocumentRoot /srv/www/htdocs
 6  LoadModule mime_module /usr/lib/apache2-prefork/mod_mime.so
 7  LoadModule access_module /usr/lib/apache2-prefork/mod_access.so
 8  LoadModule status_module /usr/lib/apache2-prefork/mod_status.so
 9  <Location /status>
10  SetHandler server-status
11  Order deny,allow
12  deny from all
13  allow from localhost
14  </Location>
15  ExtendedStatus On
```

I have added line 7 to load the module that does access control. And inside the Location container, at lines 11–13, I have established an access control policy that denies access to this location to all client machines except localhost. You can still see the status page from the local browser, but access from a browser on any other machine will be forbidden.

How It Works

A web browser and a web server communicate using the HTTP protocol. This is a text-based protocol, and the communication can be readily observed using a packet sniffer such as Ethereal. Here's the HTTP request sent by the browser when it visits the URL *http://shrek.example.com/index.html*:

```
 1  GET /index.html HTTP/1.1
 2  Host: shrek.example.com
 3  User-Agent: Mozilla/5.0 (X11; U; Linux i686; en-US; rv:1.7.12) \
                Gecko/20050920 Firefox/1.0.7 SUSE/1.0.7-0.1
 4  Accept: text/xml,application/xml,application/xhtml+xml,text/html;q=0.9, \
                text/plain;q=0.8,image/png,*/*;q=0.5
 5  Accept-Language: en-gb,en;q=0.5
 6  Accept-Encoding: gzip,deflate
 7  Accept-Charset: ISO-8859-1,utf-8;q=0.7,*;q=0.7
 8  Keep-Alive: 300
 9  Connection: keep-alive
10  Pragma: no-cache
11  Cache-Control: no-cache
12
```

Line 1 defines the HTTP operation. It is a GET request, naming the resource being requested, and the HTTP protocol version in use. Line 2 tells the server which site the resource is being accessed from; this is important if the server is hosting multiple sites (discussed later in the lab). Line 3 identifies the browser (it is actually Firefox). Lines 4–7 specify the types of acceptable response, in terms of its MIME type, language, and so on. Line 12 is a blank line. This line is important; it marks the end of the HTTP header. If there were a body to the request (for example if it was a POST request), it would follow the blank line.

In this simple case of requesting static HTML content, Apache looks up the resource in the server root directory, appends an HTTP response header to it, and sends the whole thing back to the browser. Here's the entire reply:

```
1   HTTP/1.1 200 OK
2   Date: Sat, 03 Dec 2005 20:12:17 GMT
3   Server: Apache/2.0.54 (Linux/SUSE)
4   Last-Modified: Sat, 03 Dec 2005 09:52:33 GMT
5   ETag: "4c179-119-a517ba40"
6   Accept-Ranges: bytes
7   Content-Length: 281
8   Keep-Alive: timeout=15, max=100
9   Connection: Keep-Alive
10  Content-Type: text/html
11
12  <HTML>
13  <HEAD>
14      <TITLE> The Linux Limericks Site </TITLE>
15  </HEAD>
16  <BODY>
17  There was a young lady from leek <BR>
18  Who was horribly bored by a geek <BR>
19  Said she: "This is awful<BR>
20  It shouldn't be lawful"<BR>
21  I'd rather be gored by a beak!"
22  </BODY>
23  </HTML>
```

Line 1 shows the status of the reply. About 40 three-digit status codes are defined by the HTTP protocol; common codes include 200 (OK), 403 (Forbidden), and 404 (Not Found). Line 2 is a timestamp on the message, line 3 announces what the server is, and line 4 says when the resource being delivered was last modified. Line 10 is important; it tells the browser what MIME type is contained in the message body, so that the browser knows how to interpret it. In this case, it's HTML, but it could be a plain text, a JPEG image, a PDF document, or one of many other types (see *http://www.iana.org/assignments/media-types/* for a complete list). Line 11 is a blank line. This line terminates the response header. The rest of the message at lines 12–23 is the message body, containing the HTML content of our web page.

What About...

...serving multiple sites from a single server? Many service providers serve multiple web sites from a single Apache server. This is called *virtual hosting*. There are two ways to do this.

The first way, called IP-based virtual hosting, uses a different IP address for each site. The server figures out which site is being accessed by which IP address the request was received on. This does not imply that the server must have multiple physical network connections: Linux supports *IP aliasing*, which allows multiple IP addresses to be associated with a single card. This method is rarely used, as it eats up dwindling IP address space.

The second way is called name-based virtual hosting. Each of the sites being hosted has a DNS entry pointing to the same IP address. The server figures out which site is being accessed using the Host: header in the HTTP request (see the earlier example). Let's see how to set this up. Suppose we want to host sites for the Pregnant Ladies Leapfrog team and the Sumo Wrestlers' quilting bee. They have registered the domains mumsleapfrog.org and sumobee.com, respectively, and they have entries in DNS for www.mumsleapfrog.org and www.sumobee.com pointing to an IP address which is (for this example) 172.66.47.2.

Here are the lines you need to add to *httpd.conf*:

```
1  NameVirtualHost 172.66.47.2

2  <VirtualHost 172.66.47.2>
3      ServerName www.mumsleapfrog.org
4      DocumentRoot /srv/www/htdocs/leapfrog
5  </VirtualHost>

6  <VirtualHost 172.66.47.2>
7      ServerName www.sumobee.com
8      DocumentRoot /srv/www/htdocs/sumobee
9  </VirtualHost>
```

Line 1 says "for requests we receive on this IP address, use name-based virtual hosting; that is, look at the server name in the request header to decide which site to serve." Lines 2 and 5 define a virtual host container. Within the container, lines 3 and 4 say that the document root for site www.mumsleapfrog.org is the directory */srv/www/htdocs/leapfrog*. Similarly, lines 6–9 define a second virtual host, associating the document root */srv/www/htdocs/sumobee* with the site www.sumobee.com.

All that remains is to put content in the directories. So come on, wrestlers—keep those trapunto photos rolling in!

Where to Learn More

Apache can do far more that I touched on in this lab. Just to list a few of its other capabilities:

Logging
    Log errors and accesses using standard and custom formats.

Secure sockets layer
    Conduct encrypted communication and verification of site identity.

Language negotiation
    Deliver language-specific content depending on browser preferences.

Proxying
    Act as either a reverse or forward proxy.

Authentication
   Authenticate users against user database held in a flat file or a database.

CGI scripting
   Run external CGI scripts to generate content.

Server-side scripting
   Embed server-side code within HTML pages, using PHP or Perl. This is a very popular technique for constructing commercial web sites, using MySQL as a back-end relational database.

To learn more, read *Apache: The Definitive Guide* by Laurie and Laurie (O'Reilly) and *Apache Security* by Ivan Ristic (also from O'Reilly).

For an excellent treatment of the HTTP protocol, see *HTTP: The Definitive Guide* by Gourley and Totty (also from O'Reilly).

Before you spend money on more books, though, there is extensive documentation (both reference and tutorial) shipped with the distribution. This is accessible via the default home page. It is also on online at *http://httpd.apache.org/docs/2.0*.

7.7 Configure a Mail Server

I sometimes wonder why folks pay good money for software to build a mail server when they can do a perfectly good job using free, open source applications. I'll show you how to do that in this lab.

Before I get down and dirty with the details of configuring a mail server, I'll take a look at the big picture of how mail is delivered. Figure 7-13 shows the overall architecture.

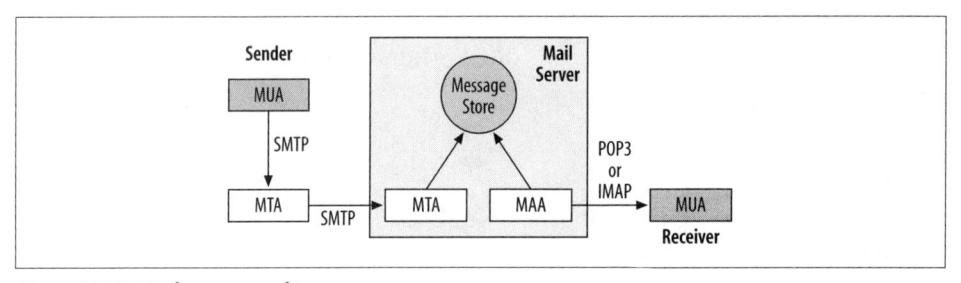

Figure 7-13. Mail system architecture

A *mail user agent* (MUA) is the program that an end user interacts with in order to compose or read email. Behind the scenes, the two roles of an MUA (sending and receiving) are largely separate. The MUA integrates the two by providing a unified system of folders for storing the messages it has received and the messages it has sent. It also provides ways for users to reply to or forward mail messages. There are many mail user agents. On SUSE Linux, KMail and Evolution are popular choices, but there is also the stalwart command-line tool simply called `mail`, which is useful if you need to send email from within a script. An MUA needs to be configured to tell it how to send outbound mail, and how to retrieve inbound mail. I discussed this in Lab 1.3, "Get Started with Email." Generally, the MUA hands off outbound messages to a *mail transfer agent* (MTA) for delivery.

The MTA is the piece of the system responsible for the "long haul" of email delivery. Mail is sent and received using a protocol called SMTP—Simple Mail Transfer Protocol. This is a text-based protocol and it's quite easy to conduct an SMTP conversation "by hand" using telnet. At first sight, pushing email around sounds like a pretty simple job, but it turns out to be surprisingly complex—determining whether the recipient is local or remote, queuing mail that can't be delivered immediately, bouncing messages that can't be delivered at all, filtering spam, and so on. The preferred MTA in SUSE Linux is `postfix`. This is the one we'll use in the lab, but there are others, including Exim, QMail, and the venerable but incomprehensible sendmail.

Returning to Figure 7-13: if `postfix` receives mail for a user in a domain that it is configured to serve, it will save the message in a system message store (sometimes known as a `maildrop`), which is a set of files or directories on that machine. The message will remain there until somebody comes along to read it. If `postfix` receives a message for a user in some other domain, it will consult DNS for an MX record for that domain, and attempt to forward the message to the MTA identified by that record.

In the early days of Internet email, the MTA (sendmail) delivered my mail right to the machine that sat on my desktop. It was a Sun workstation and it was called `eddie`. When I was away from work, I would log in directly into `eddie` using `telnet`, and pick my mail up straight from the maildrop using the command-line `mail` program.

> The first set of names we chose for our machines at Sheffield was inspired by the Marx Brothers. This turned out to be a bit short-sighted because we only knew three of them (there were in fact five—chico, harpo, groucho, gummo, and zeppo), so we soon outgrew this namespace and moved on to *The Hitchhikers' Guide to the Galaxy*. This gave us a rather richer vein to mine—arthur, ford, trillian, zaphod, benjie, frankie, and so on, though no one wanted slartibartfast. My own machine, eddie, was the ship-board computer on the *Heart of Gold*. Aficionados will remember; no one else will care.

Nowadays, it would be unusual for end users to telnet into the mail servers to read their mail. Instead, mail is retrieved from the message store and delivered to the user's desktop using a Mail Access Agent (MAA). There are two protocols in common use for retrieving mail via a MUA: POP3 and IMAP. Most ISPs use POP3. Using POP3, the receiving user's MUA connects to the mail server, downloads any messages waiting in the message store, then disconnects. Usually, the MUA asks the MAA to delete the messages from the mail server once they're downloaded. Using POP3, the responsibility for long term filing and storage of email rests with the end user's machine. When using IMAP, on the other hand, the email archive remains on the server. An end user's MUA stays connected to the IMAP server for as long as the user wishes to read, search or manage email. IMAP is a better solution for corporate mail servers providing email access to mobile employees.

In this lab, you'll learn how to set up qpopper—a POP3 mail access agent. Overall, the mail server you'll learn how to build corresponds to the box labeled "Mail Server" in the figure.

How Do I Do That?

You're going to set up a mail server for the hypothetical domain example.com. This mail server will be called mail.example.com. For the sake of this exercise, assume that the necessary entries exist in DNS—specifically, there must be an A record for mail.example.com pointing to our IP address, and there must be an MX (mail exchanger) record for example.com pointing to mail.example.com. There should also be a PTR record in DNS to support a reverse lookup of your mail server's IP address. You can check these things by running the following commands:

```
# dig mail.example.com
# dig example.com mx
# dig -x <IP address of your mail server>
```

Let's do the postfix configuration first. First, check that you have the postfix package installed with the command

```
# rpm -q postfix
```

(Refer to Lab 5.3, "Install and Upgrade RPMs" if you need help installing the package.)

Next, make sure that postfix is configured to start at boot time. To do this, use the YaST runlevel editor or run the command:

```
# chkconfig --add postfix
```

(Lab 6.1, "Control Boot-Time Service Startup" provides more detail.)

For testing, you can start and stop postfix manually with the commands:

```
# rcpostfix start
# rcpostfix stop
```

Postfix almost works out of the box, but there are two things you will need to tweak in the configuration file */etc/postfix/main.cf*. First, find the line:

```
inet_interfaces = 127.0.0.1
```

and change it to:

```
inet_interfaces = all
```

This change tells postfix to listen for SMTP connections on all of this machine's network interfaces, not just the loopback interface.

You should also find the line that begins:

```
mydestination = ...
```

and append $mydomain to the end of the line. The mydestination parameter specifies the list of domains that this machine considers itself the final destination for. The $mydomain variable holds the domain name of this machine. By default, this will be derived from the hostname, so in this case the machine mail.example.com will have a default domain name of example.com.

You should run the command:

```
# rcpostfix restart
```

after making these changes to the configuration file.

You should now be able to send mail to any user who has an account on the mail server (for example, mail to the user *tom@example.com*), and have it show up in their message store. I discuss the format of the message store in the "How It Works" section later in this lab.

Now let's turn our attention to the mail access agent. There are at least five POP3 servers included in the SUSE Linux distribution, in the packages cyrus-imapd, courier-imap, dovecot, imap, and qpopper. We'll use qpopper, because it works right out of the box and no setup is required to manage the interaction between postfix and qpopper. Note, however, that qpopper requires every user who wishes to receive mail to have a Linux account. This is probably not what you want on a system that does nothing but serve many thousands of mail accounts, and in this situation you may prefer the Cyrus IMAP server.

All we need to do to make qpopper work is enable it. Because it's started via xinetd, we need to edit */etc/xinetd.d/qpopper*, and change:

```
disable = yes
```

to:

```
disable = no
```

then restart xinetd with:

```
# rcxinetd restart
```

That's it! You should have a working POP3 server.

How It Works

The MTA listens on port 25 for TCP connections. The protocol used by MTAs is a text-based protocol called SMTP (Simple Mail Transfer Protocol) or ESMTP (Extended Simple Mail Transfer Protocol). Here's a sample of an ESMTP conversation in which *chris@idlearn.com* sends mail to *tom@example.com*:

```
220 mail.example.com ESMTP Postfix
EHLO [192.168.0.2]
250-mail.example.com
```

```
250-PIPELINING
250-SIZE 10240000
250-VRFY
250-ETRN
250 8BITMIME
MAIL FROM:<chris@idlearn.com>
250 Ok
RCPT TO:<tom@example.com>
250 Ok
DATA
354 End data with <CR><LF>.<CR><LF>
Subject: Meeting with JPF tomorrow
From: Chris Brown <chris@idlearn.com>
To: tom@example.com
Content-Type: text/plain
Organization: Interactive Digital Learning
Message-Id: <1134576128.3269.13.camel@localhost.localdomain>
Mime-Version: 1.0
X-Mailer: Ximian Evolution 1.4.6 (1.4.6-2)
Date: Wed, 14 Dec 2005 16:02:08 +0000
Content-Transfer-Encoding: 7bit

Hi Tom,

JPF has asked if we can bring tomorrow's meeting forward to 10 am as he
has just remembered he's supposed to be at the dentist for 11.30.

Best Regards,

Chris

.
250 Ok: queued as 9CE8B49CF6
RSET
250 Ok
QUIT
221 Bye
```

The lines beginning with a three-digit number are the responses from the receiving MTA. All the other lines are commands and data from the sending MTA. It is fairly easy to trace through the dialog. An important (though undramatic) feature of the protocol is the line consisting of a .; this marks the end of the body of the mail message.

It is easy to hand-craft an SMTP conversation by using telnet to connect to port 25 on the mail server; the conversation would start like this:

```
# telnet mail.example.com 25
Trying 11.22.33.44...
Connected to mail.example.com.
Escape character is '^]'.
220 mail.example.com ESMTP Postfix
... Now you can enter the SMTP commands ...
```

The traditional format for the message store on a Linux system is the *mbox* format. Using this format, each user's incoming mail is stored in a single file; for user tom, this file is */var/spool/mail/tom*. This is a plain text file; messages are simply appended to the file as they arrive. The beginning of each message is marked by a line beginning with "From" followed by a space. (Don't confuse this with the line you'll usually see in a mail header that begins with "From" followed by a colon.) Here are the contents of tom's mbox message store after two messages have been delivered:

```
From chris@idlearn.com  Wed Dec 14 15:59:11 2005
Return-Path: <chris@idlearn.com>
X-Original-To: tom@example.com
Delivered-To: tom@example.com
Received: from [192.168.0.2] (unknown [192.168.0.2])
        by mail.example.com (Postfix) with ESMTP id 9CE8B49CF6
        for <tom@example.com>; Wed, 14 Dec 2005 15:59:11 +0000 (GMT)
Subject: Meeting with JPF tomorrow
From: Chris Brown <chris@idlearn.com>
To: tom@example.com
Content-Type: text/plain
... further header lines edited out ...

Hi Tom,

JPF has asked if we can bring tomorrow's meeting forward to 10 am as he
has just remembered he's supposed to be at the dentist for 11.30.

Best Regards,

Chris

From isaac@trinity.cam.ac.uk  Wed Dec 14 16:28:08 2005
Return-Path: <isaac@trinity.cam.ac.uk>
X-Original-To: tom@example.com
Delivered-To: tom@example.com
Received: from [192.168.0.2] (unknown [192.168.0.2])
        by mail.example.com (Postfix) with ESMTP id 1A5864DB58
        for <tom@example.com>; Wed, 14 Dec 2005 16:28:08 +0000 (GMT)
Subject: I think I've just discovered gravity
From: Isaac Newton <isaac@trinity.cam.ac.uk>
To: tom@example.com
Content-Type: text/plain
... further header lines edited out ...

Tom,

When you have a minute, could you stop by my office? I had an
interesting experience yesterday I'd like to discuss with you.
An apple fell on my head.

Isaac
```

Mail access agents such as qpopper usually know about the mbox format and look in these files by default.

You may also come across the *maildir* format for the message store. A maildir message store has three directories: tmp, new, and cur. These directories are usually below a mail directory in the user's home directory. Each mail message is stored in a separate file. There are no "From" lines to separate the messages. Files in the new directory contain messages that have been delivered but not yet read. Once a message has been viewed it is moved to the cur directory. postfix is able to deliver messages in *mbox* or *maildir* formats.

What About…

…serving multiple domains? The configuration you created in this lab barely hints at the power of postfix. It can also be set up to host multiple domains. The simplest form of virtual hosting provides a common namespace across all the domains and requires all recipients to have Linux accounts. Suppose that you'd also like to host the domain example.net. First, you need to create an additional MX record in DNS for the example.net domain, pointing to mail.example.com. Lab 7.2, "Configure a DNS Server," shows how to do this. The record in the zone file will look something like:

```
example.net.    IN MX    0 mail.example.com.
```

Add the new domain name to the mydestination parameter in *main.cf*, like this:

```
mydestination = $myhostname, localhost.$mydomain $mydomain example.net
```

Now, mail to *tom@example.com* or *tom@example.net* will arrive in tom's maildrop on mail.example.com.

You can also define aliases. An alias says, in effect, that mail addressed to user A should actually be delivered to user B. For example, suppose you would like mail addressed to *sales@example.com*, *orders@example.com,* and *info@examples.com* to arrive in tom's maildrop. postfix uses the file */etc/aliases* to define these aliases; this choice is deliberately backward-compatible with the way sendmail does it, to make it easier to migrate from sendmail to postfix. The entries you would need to put into */etc/aliases* are:

```
sales:   tom
orders:  tom
info:    tom
```

Now you must run the command:

```
# postalias /etc/aliases
```

to (re)create the alias database. There is no need to restart postfix.

Aliases can also be used to build simple distribution lists. For example, this line in */etc/aliases*:

```
support:    tom, chris
```

will cause mail addressed to *support@example.com* to arrive in the maildrops of both tom and chris.

`postfix` also provides an address re-writing engine that rewrites mail addresses at various points in the message processing chain under control of a so-called *canonical map*. Once such map is */etc/postfix/canonical*. The map starts life as a plain text file; a typical entry in a map might be:

```
cbrown@example.com      chris_brown@example.com
```

The map must be converted into a simple indexed database before it can be used. Do this with the command:

```
# postmap /etc/postfix/canonical
```

There must also be an entry in *main.cf* to tell `postfix` to use this map:

```
canonical_maps = hash:/etc/postfix/canonical
```

This entry should be present already.

There are two other canonical maps, `sender_canonical` and `receiver_canonical`, that work the same way but only rewrite sender or receiver addresses, respectively.

As an example, suppose that *tom@example.com* hides behind the alias guru. In other words, outsiders send mail to *guru@example.com*; they don't know his real name is Tom. If a user hides his identity behind an alias for incoming mail, he may wish to hide it for outgoing mail, too. The following line in */etc/postfix/sender_canonical* should do the job:

```
tom@example.com         guru@example.com
```

Where to Learn More

There's a good tutorial on setting up postfix at *http://www.metaconsultancy.com/whitepapers*.

There is extensive, well-written documentation included with the distribution. Start by browsing */usr/share/doc/packages/postfix/html/index.html*. The same documentation is also available at *http://www.postfix.org/documentation.html*. There's also a book, *Postfix: The Definitive Guide* by Kyle Dent (O'Reilly). There are lots of helper and utility programs that make up the `postfix` suite. Each of these has a manual page. Start with `man postfix` and look at the SEE ALSO section for a list of all the others.

qpopper has its own user guide in */usr/share/doc/packages/qpopper/GUIDE.pdf*.

CHAPTER 8
Security

This chapter is about keeping your system secure. It is, I think, a terrible indictment of human nature that such a chapter should be necessary at all. If people didn't try to attack computer systems, there would be no need to defend them. Sadly, we need to take security seriously.

Securing your system is a kind of risk management strategy, and there is usually a trade-off between security and convenience of use. You might try to quantify the cost of a security breach of your system like this:

```
Expected cost = (probability of an attack's success) * (cost of that attack)
```

Reducing the probability of an attack's success is generally known as *hardening* the system. A lot of this is common sense—educate users to choose strong passwords, disable or delete services you don't need, tighten up permissions on files as far as possible, establish a firewall, keep abreast of newly discovered vulnerabilities and keep software up to date, don't give out the root password, and so on. Reducing your cost of an attack is equally important. For example, detecting intrusion quickly is much better than allowing a breach to go unnoticed for days. Maintaining regular backups will limit any potential loss of data. Splitting your services across multiple machines (also known as not putting all your eggs into one basket) can help prevent a single breach from bringing your entire organization down.

The chapter is about defense rather than attack. You'll see how to thwart some of the more obvious ways of gaining root access to your machine by setting a grub password. You'll discover how to use the secure shell to access systems remotely without the risk of your activities and passwords being intercepted on the network. You'll learn how to set up a firewall and tighten file access permissions. You'll see how to break out from the all-or-nothing super-user model in Linux by implementing role-based access control. You'll meet vulnerability assessment tools that can help find insecurities and filesystem integrity tools that can help detect intrusion. The lab on AppArmor is of particular interest. It represents a novel way to profile the "normal" behavior of an application and prevent it from operating outside of that profile.

Although it is convenient to group this material into a single chapter, it would be a mistake to think of security as something that you do as an afterthought, or in isolation from everything else. To be a responsible system administrator, security should be in your thoughts in everything you do.

8.1 Set a Boot-Time Password

Most SUSE Linux systems use grub as their boot loader. grub offers a lot of flexibility, including the option to intercept the boot process and edit the commands used to boot the system (or even to type new commands in from scratch). One particularly interesting trick is to append the parameter `init=/bin/sh` to the end of the kernel command used to load the Linux kernel. This tells the kernel to run a shell instead of the usual `init` program, and gives you root access to the filesystem without requiring the root password. There are obvious security implications here.

In this lab, you'll see how to password-protect grub to disable its interactive options unless a password is entered. Note that the password is not required to boot the system using the predefined entries in the grub config file, but only to edit them or enter other interactive commands.

> Intercepting grub's boot process requires physical access to the machine, and there are other ways an unauthorized user can get at the machine's filesystem if he or she has physical access. For example, the intruder can boot from rescue media, or—if all else fails—physically remove the hard drive and take it somewhere else.

How Do I Do That?

Setting a grub password is easy. Just hand-edit the grub config file (by default, it's */boot/grub/menu.lst*) and add a line to the global settings near the top of the file that looks something like this:

```
password --md5 $1$H06141$PTIpTGW7fNKspluqd1Mdk.
```

The long string beginning with a $ is the md5-encrypted password. To generate this, run grub from a shell command prompt (this will take you to grub's interactive prompt) and enter the command `md5crypt`. You be asked to enter the desired password, and then it will display the encrypted version. The procedure looks like this:

```
# grub
    GNU GRUB  version 0.95  (640K lower / 3072K upper memory)

 [ Minimal BASH-like line editing is supported.  For the first word, TAB
   lists possible command completions.  Anywhere else TAB lists the possible
   completions of a device/filename. ]

grub> md5crypt
```

```
Password: *********
Encrypted: $1$HO6141$PTIpTGW7fNKspluqd1Mdk.
```

grub> **quit**

Now you can cut and paste the encrypted password into the *menu.lst* file.

If you boot the system with this line in place, grub will not present its graphical menu screen but will instead use a text-based menu. You can still use the up and down arrow keys to select which operating system to boot, but any other action requires you to type **p** and then enter the password to unlock the interactive feature set.

What About...

...restricting the choice of bootable systems? There are a couple of ways that you can exercise control over which operating systems a user is allowed to boot by password-protecting individual selections from the grub menu. The first is to use the command lock. For example, to prevent booting into the Xen virtualization layer (see Lab 9.4, "Run Multiple Operating Systems with Xen") without a password, add a line to the appropriate stanza of the file *menu.lst*, something like this:

```
title XEN
    lock
    kernel (hd0,1)/boot/xen.gz
    ... and so on ...
```

With this line in place, an attempt to boot Xen fails unless the user enters a password.

You can set a different password for each bootable selection by using the password command instead of lock. For example:

```
title XEN
    password --md5 $1$HO6141$PTIpTGW7fNKspluqd1Mdk.
    kernel (hd0,1)/boot/xen.gz
    ... and so on ...
```

With this line in place, you'll be prompted for the appropriate password if you attempt to boot from this selection.

Where to Learn More

The full grub manual is available at *http://www.gnu.org/software/grub/manual/grub.pdf*.

8.2 Provide Secure Remote Login with SSH

> In those days the stakes were high, men were real men, women were real women and small furry creatures from Alpha Centauri were real small furry creatures from Alpha Centauri. Spirits were brave, men boldly logged in to remote computers to which no man had remotely logged in before.
>
> *(With apologies to Douglas Adams)*

Although they didn't realize it at the time, this was a daring, dangerous thing to do. They used a remote login service called *telnet*, which required them to supply a user name and a password to the server, both of which were passed over the network in clear text—that is, without encryption. Moreover, once they were logged in, their entire command-line dialog was carried over the network in clear text. FTP (File Transfer Protocol), another of the early work-horses of the Internet, suffered from similar problems. It remains popular to this day, though mainly in the form of *anonymous ftp*, in which no password is required and the files being transferred are publicly accessible anyway, so the lack of encryption is less of an issue. Of course, those were gentler times. Many of those early networks were local area networks with no direct connection to the Internet, and a (relatively) trustworthy user community. Even the people with access to the Internet were nice people and wouldn't dream of stealing passwords or eavesdropping on our digital conversations.

> As an academic, for years I used to do a telnet login to my desktop machine at the university to read my email if I was working away from home. It never occurred to me that it might be insecure, and I never had the slightest problem with it. Spam was a brand of tinned ham, nothing more.
>
> Nowadays, as a trainer, I sometimes set up in-class demonstrations in which I invite an attendee to perform a telnet login to my machine using a secretly supplied user name and password. I run an Ethereal (*http://www.ethereal.com*) packet capture session and show how to pull the login credentials "off the wire." Many attendees already understand the reality of how easy this is, but there are still some who are genuinely shocked by the ease of sniffing passwords from the network in this way.

A few years later (in geological timescales, not very long at all—I should probably draw some analogy here comparing the diameters of a human hair and Shea Stadium) some folks at UCB (University of California at Berkeley) came up with a suite of programs that became known as the *r-star utilities* (because their names all began with "r"), which provided "remote" versions of a few key Unix commands. Thus we had `rlogin` (the remote version of `login`), `rsh` (the remote version of `sh`), and `rcp` (the remote version of `cp`). These tools were Unix-specific (unlike `telnet`, which was designed to work on any operating system) and supported a more convenient log-in mechanism through the concept of *trusted hosts*. This mechanism allowed a server to define a number of trusted or *equivalent* client machines from which logins would be accepted without requiring the user to reauthenticate. By regarding a machine as trusted, the server was effectively saying "If this client says that it's user `joe` logging in, that's good enough for me. I believe it." The r-star commands were really convenient to use, and perhaps marginally more secure than `telnet`, because (using the trusted hosts mechanism) they could avoid sending passwords over the network.

However, they still didn't encrypt any of the actual dialog, and in any case, it was rather easy to spoof the identity of a trusted host.

In 1995, Tatu Ylönen from Helsinki University of Technology in Finland developed a secure remote login protocol called SSH-1 (Secure Shell), which is able to do strong authentication (using public/private key technologies to avoid revealing the password over the network) and also derives a shared key that is used to encrypt all subsequent traffic. Tatu set up a company called SSH Communications Security (*http://www.ssh.com*) to commercialize and support this product.

More recently, a new development under the auspices of the OpenBSD project has provided users with an open-source implementation of the same technologies called OpenSSH (*http://www.openssh.org*). This is the version used in SUSE Linux. The OpenSSH suite includes the ssh program, which replaces rlogin and telnet; scp, which replaces rcp; and sftp, which replaces ftp. Also included is sshd, which is the server side of the package. In this lab, you'll learn how to use and configure OpenSSH.

How Do I Do That?

Before I get into too much detail about configuring OpenSSH, here are some examples of it in use. At its simplest, a remote login using ssh will look something like this:

```
$ ssh bashful
Password: ********
Last login: Tue Sep 13 08:38:44 2005 from 192.168.0.17
Have a lot of fun...
$
```

Here, bashful is the name of the host I'm logging in to. If you want, you can supply an IP address here instead. After logging in, I see a command prompt from a shell on bashful, and any commands I enter will be executed on that machine. To log out and return to a command prompt on the local machine, just log out as you normally would from a shell—enter exit or logout or Ctrl-D.

The default behavior of ssh is to log in on the remote machine with the username that you're currently logged in under on the local machine. If you would like to log in with a different identity, use the syntax user@host, something like this:

```
$ ssh root@bashful
Password: ********
Last login: Tue Sep 13 08:33:30 2005
Have a lot of fun...
#
```

It's also possible to use ssh to execute a single command rather than logging into an interactive shell. For example, to eject the CD on bashful:

```
$ ssh bashful eject
Password: ********
$
```

Note that in this case, you're returned to a command prompt on the *local* machine.

When you use ssh in this way, there is an authentication step occurring that is not immediately obvious. The local (client) machine makes sure it is connecting to the machine it thinks it is connecting to using a *challenge/response authentication* against the remote (server) machine. To do this, it needs the server machine's public host key (more detail on this later). Now, the server actually sends this key to the client as part of the handshake that occurs on an ssh connection, and the client keeps a record, in a local file, of which public keys are considered valid for which hosts. However, the first time that a client connects to any given server, it has no way to verify that server's public key. It therefore throws the onus back onto the user, essentially asking him to confirm that he's sure he's connecting to the right machine. The dialog looks something like this:

```
cbrown@linux:~>
$ ssh bashful
The authenticity of host 'bashful (192.168.0.4)' can't be established.
RSA key fingerprint is e8:18:8e:b6:fa:25:5b:f4:78:c5:6b:d7:95:6d:01:e2.
Are you sure you want to continue connecting (yes/no)? yes
Warning: Permanently added 'bashful' (RSA) to the list of known hosts.
Password: ********
Last login: Tue Sep 13 08:35:02 2005 from 192.168.0.17
Have a lot of fun...
$
```

Once you've answered "yes" here, the client adds the server's key to the list of known hosts. Next time you connect, you won't see this message.

A potentially more serious warning will be issued if the host key offered by the server actually disagrees with the one already known to the client, like this:

```
$ ssh bashful
@@@@@@@@@@@@@@@@@@@@@@@@@@@@@@@@@@@@@@@@@@@@@@@@@@@@
@       WARNING: POSSIBLE DNS SPOOFING DETECTED!        @
@@@@@@@@@@@@@@@@@@@@@@@@@@@@@@@@@@@@@@@@@@@@@@@@@@@@
The RSA host key for bashful has changed,
and the key for the according IP address 192.168.0.4
is unknown. This could either mean that
DNS SPOOFING is happening or the IP address for the host
and its host key have changed at the same time.
@@@@@@@@@@@@@@@@@@@@@@@@@@@@@@@@@@@@@@@@@@@@@@@@@@@@
@    WARNING: REMOTE HOST IDENTIFICATION HAS CHANGED!     @
@@@@@@@@@@@@@@@@@@@@@@@@@@@@@@@@@@@@@@@@@@@@@@@@@@@@
IT IS POSSIBLE THAT SOMEONE IS DOING SOMETHING NASTY!
Someone could be eavesdropping on you right now (man-in-the-middle attack)!
It is also possible that the RSA host key has just been changed.
The fingerprint for the RSA key sent by the remote host is
e8:18:8e:b6:fa:25:5b:f4:78:c5:6b:d7:95:6d:01:e2.
Please contact your system administrator.
Add correct host key in /home/cbrown/.ssh/known_hosts to get rid of this message.
Offending key in /home/cbrown/.ssh/known_hosts:3
RSA host key for bashful has changed and you have requested strict checking.
Host key verification failed.
```

As the message says, it's possible that the target machine is being spoofed, although in my experience the most common explanation is that the server's host keys have changed because I've just reinstalled Linux on it. (Generation of SSH host keys is an install-time operation.) You'll also see this error message (a lot) if the machines on your network have constantly changing IP addresses that are assigned by a DHCP server. To fix this, you just need to delete the entry for that host from *~/.ssh/known_hosts* and try again.

Okay, let's turn our attention to scp, the secure file copy program. It uses the same techniques as ssh to perform secure authentication and to derive a session key with which the file transfer will be encrypted. It's syntax is based on the syntax of rcp (one of the r-star commands), which is in turn an extension of the good ol' cp command. Essentially, the extension is simply to allow the syntax hostname:filename for either the source or destination file. Here's a typical example:

```
$ scp httpd-2.0.54.tar.bz2 bashful:/tmp/httpd_copy
Password: ********
httpd-2.0.54.tar.bz2                      100% 5437KB    5.3MB/s    00:01
$
```

As you can see, you get a report of the file size and transfer time. You can use a relative pathname on the remote machine, in which case it will be interpreted relative to your home directory on that machine. This example copies the file *navpage.html* from your home directory on bashful into the current directory (named as .) on the local machine:

```
$ scp bashful:navpage.html .
Password: ********
navpage.html                              100%   345    0.3KB/s    00:00
```

How It Works

The simplicity of the end-user's experience of ssh belies the complexity of the cryptographic technology that lies behind it. There is a classical underlying client/server architecture, with ssh and scp as the clients and sshd as the server. But to understand how ssh and sshd work, you need to soil your hands with a little cryptographic theory. I promise you this won't hurt (a line I learned from my dentist), but a little theory and notation are unavoidable.

Let's deal with the basics. Figure 8-1 shows the flow of data through an encrypted channel.

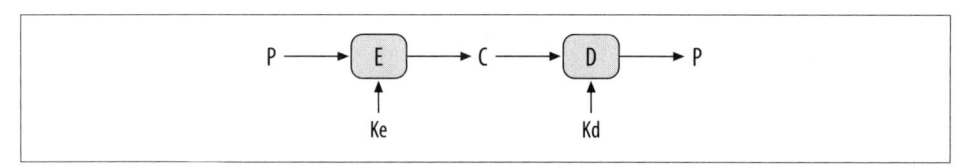

Figure 8-1. Basic cryptographic terminology

The sender of a plain text message (P) passes the message through an encryption algorithm (E), which turns it into cipher text (C), which is transmitted to the recipient. The recipient passes the cipher text through a decryption algorithm (D) to recover the original plaintext (P). The idea is that a "bad guy," who intercepts the cipher text, cannot easily figure out what the original plain text was. The security of encryption does not rely on the obscurity and secrecy of the encryption process itself, but on the secrecy of encryption and decryption keys which control the operation of the encryption and decryption algorithms in some way. In Figure 8-1, the key Ke controls the encryption algorithm and the key Kd controls the decryption algorithm. Okay so far?

Let's consider a simple example: the "Caesar cipher," which (according to the historians) was invented by Julius Caesar as a way of communicating with the commanders in his army.

> Whether he came up with this before or after the salad is open to debate—but you have to admire someone who can invent a cipher *and* get his name onto the restaurant menu.

Caesar's encryption algorithm was: "Rotate each letter of the plain text N positions to the right" where N is the encryption key (Ke in Figure 8-1). So, for example, if N is 5, the message "attack at dawn" becomes "fyyfhp fy ifbs". The decryption algorithm, obviously, is "rotate each letter of the plain text N positions to the left" (Kd in Figure 8-1. Notice that Ke and Kd are identical here. This will become more significant in a moment.)

By modern standards, Julius Caesar's cipher is rather easy to break. For a start, there are only 25 possible values for the key, so it really wouldn't take very long to try all the possible key values to see which resulted in meaningful text. Cryptographers nowadays would say that "the key space is too small." Modern encryption algorithms are much more sophisticated (and our computers are faster than Caesar's), but the concept of relating the difficulty of breaking a cipher to the size of the key space remains.

> There is a program called caesar (shipped with SUSE Linux) that will try to break a Caesar cipher based on known letter frequencies in the English language. A specific form of this cipher lives on in a form called "rot13." This is a Caesar cipher with a shift of 13 characters. Because the English alphabet has 26 characters, rot13 has the benefit of being its own inverse. It's sometimes used in Usenet news articles and other postings to protect the punchlines of jokes, movie spoilers, or potentially offensive content from a casual glance. It's the digital equivalent of the puzzle magazine's strategy of printing the solution upside down.

Now it gets slightly more complicated. There are two major categories of encryption algorithm, known as *symmetric* and *asymmetric*. Symmetric algorithms (like the Caesar cipher) use the same key for encryption and decryption. In other words, Ke and Kd are equal. For asymmetric algorithms, Ke and Kd are different.

Historically, asymmetric algorithms are much more recent; in fact, asymmetric algorithms have only been known for 30 years or so. The idea is to generate a pair of keys, K1 and K2, using some fancy mathematics. The key pair has the property that (a) you cannot derive one key from the other, and (b) plain text encrypted with either of the keys can be decrypted with the other key (see Figure 8-2).

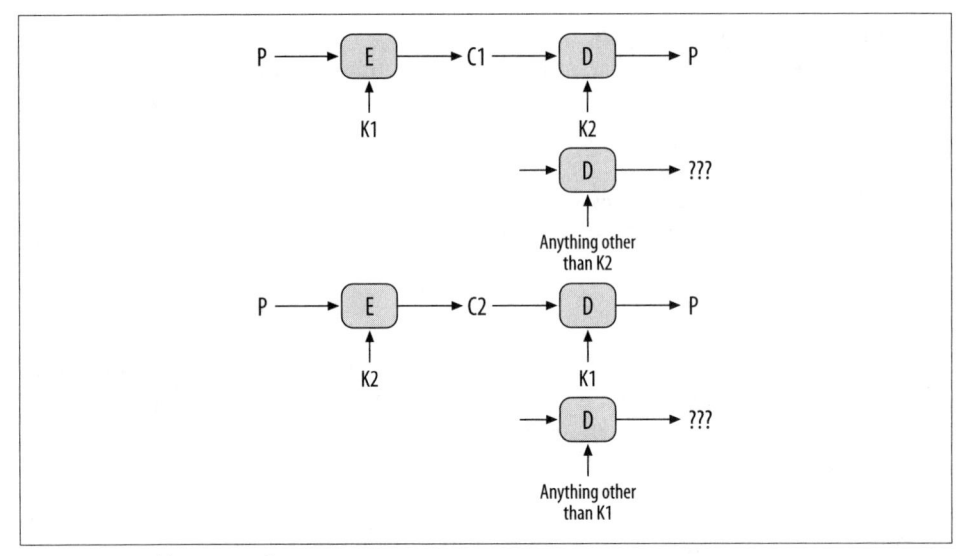

Figure 8-2. Public/private key encryption

If I knew of a simple, intuitive example of asymmetric cryptography similar to the Caesar cipher, I would share it with you. But I don't. I don't think there is one. Asymmetric encryption is much more computationally intensive than symmetric encryption (and needs much longer keys for equivalent security), so it is not usually used for encryption of "bulk data," but instead is used for secure authentication, and to provide a way to securely exchange the "shared secret" key required by a symmetric encryption technology.

To use asymmetric encryption, an entity (typically a computer or a user) generates a pair of keys. One of the keys—called the private or secret key—is closely guarded. It is usually stored in a file accessible only to its owner, and for extra security the key itself is often encrypted with a *passphrase*, which the user must supply each time she wants to use the key. The other key—called the public key—is made widely known, perhaps by publishing it on its owner's web site or on a public key server.

Using public/private key encryption for authentication essentially involves a person or a computer proving that he, she, or it knows their private key without actually exposing it onto the network. Let's suppose I'm talking via some network connection to an individual claiming to be Michelle. I make up some random data, called the *challenge*, and send it to Michelle. Michelle encrypts it with her private key, sending the result, called the *response*, back to me. I decrypt this with Michelle's public key, and compare the result with the original challenge. If they match, the person at the other end of the line must be Michelle, because the stuff that Michelle sent back to me decrypts with Michelle's public key, so it must have been encrypted with Michelle's private key, which only Michelle knows. This challenge-response authentication protocol is used in ssh both by the client (to verify the identity of the server) and by the server, to verify the identity of the user who is logging in.

> You'll sometimes hear this kind of authentication called a Challenge/Handshake Authentication Protocol (CHAP). A more accurate description would be the Challenge-Response Authentication Protocol, but I'm guessing the lawyers were having a problem with the acronym.

Although the theory behind all this public/private key stuff is a touch cerebral, the practical applications are widespread. It's the technology that underpins not only ssh, but the whole "public key infrastructure" (PKI) that supports secure web transactions.

With this theory in mind, let's examine the authentication steps followed during a ssh/sshd login. Figure 8-3 shows the big picture.

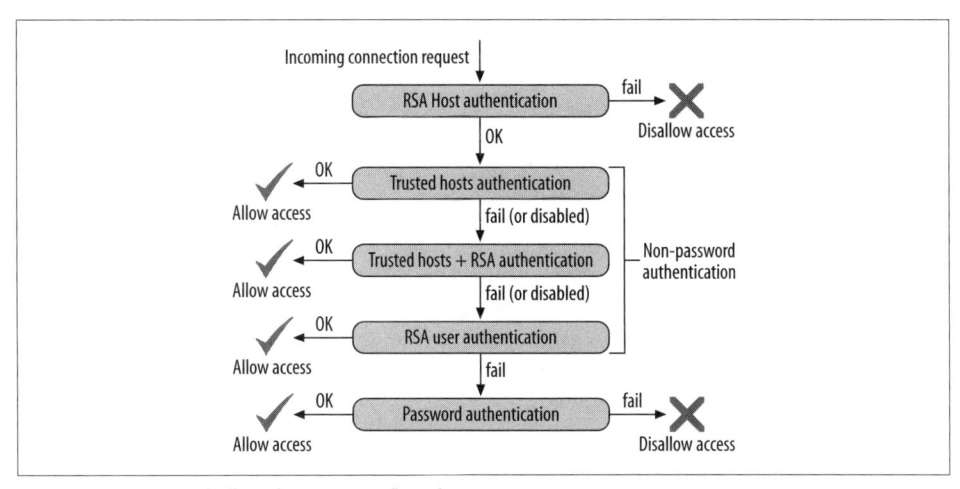

Figure 8-3. Secure shell authentication flowchart

First, the client (ssh) verifies the authenticity of the server machine with a challenge-response authentication based upon the public and private keys of the server machine. This key pair is generated the very first time `sshd` is started; effectively, this means at the time that the system was installed. The private key is stored in */etc/ssh/ssh_host_key* and the public key in */etc/ssh/ssh_host_key.pub*. For this authentication to work, the client needs to know the server's public key. How does it get this? That's a good question! In fact, the server passes its public key to the client at the beginning of the host authentication dialog. If the client has never seen this key before, it will ask you to verify that (on this occasion at least) you are confident you are connected to the right server, and not an impostor. (You saw the dialog for this earlier in the lab.) Assuming that you answer "yes" to the question "Are you sure you want to continue connecting?", the authentication process will complete and the client machine will capture the server's public host key into the file *~/.ssh/known_hosts* so that the next time you connect, authentication of the server can complete without user intervention. (Because this file lives within a user's home directory, it applies only to that user. To make a server's public host key visible to all users, copy it to the system-wide file */etc/ssh/ssh_known_hosts*.) As an important by-product of this authentication dialog, the client and server securely exchange a *session key*, which is used to encrypt all subsequent traffic between them for this session, using a symmetric algorithm.

> While we're on the subject of authenticating the server, I may as well voice my opinions about the current fashion of using "chip and pin" as a way of authenticating debit card transactions at point-of-sale terminals such as supermarket checkouts. Under this system, you're asked to enter a four-digit Personal Identification Number (the only thing that stands between you and financial oblivion) into a small box connected by a piece of wire to a computer which—for all I know—has been installed by the supermarket for the express purpose of capturing PINs. Ostensibly, you're authenticating yourself to your bank. How much effort does the bank put in to authenticate itself to you? Zero. This worries me. What worries me even more is that 99% of the paying public don't seem to worry about it.
>
> There is an important point here that goes beyond the crazed rantings of a demented debit card holder. When you're accessing a service, sometimes it is just as important for the service to authenticate itself to you as it is for you to authenticate yourself to the service.
>
> I think this was the motivation behind the concept of reserved ports in Unix and Linux. (A program can only use a port number less than 1024 if it's running with super-user privilege.) The idea was that a normal (nonroot) user couldn't run a program that impersonated (say) the telnet server because telnet used a reserved port (23) and the user wouldn't be able to assign it. This feature has become rather meaningless because a lot of ordinary users know their root passwords, and anyway the reserved port rule doesn't apply to DOS or Windows. But it seemed like a good idea at the time, no doubt.

Assuming that the server authentication step was successful, the server (sshd) will proceed to authenticate the user. There are several ways it can do this. First, it can use the old rlogin "trusted hosts" scheme, but this is not considered terribly secure and it usually disabled in the sshd configuration file, so you can ignore it. One way to authenticate the user is to prompt for a password and verify it against the password set for the user on the server. This sounds pretty much like the way telnet does authentication, except that this time, there is an encrypted channel already in place between the client and the server so that the plain text password is not exposed on the network. This is the default authentication method used by ssh and the one that's assumed by the ssh command examples that you saw earlier in the lab.

The second way that sshd authenticates its users uses a challenge-response authentication of the user based on the user's public and private keys. For this to work, a couple of setup steps are needed. First, the user needs to generate his or her own key pair. No, you don't have to scribble 15 pages of dense mathematics to do this; you just run the command ssh-keygen. The public key is stored (on your local machine) in *~/.ssh/id_rsa.pub* and the private key is stored in *~/.ssh/id_rsa*. When you run ssh-keygen, you'll be asked to supply a passphrase, which is used to encrypt your private key before storing it on disk. This means, of course, that you'll have to supply your passphrase to unlock your private key each time it's required. The second step is to append your public key to the file *~/.ssh/authorized_keys* on the server so that it can perform its half of the user authentication handshake. To generate the key pair, the dialog will look something like this:

```
$ ssh-keygen -t rsa
Generating public/private rsa key pair.
Enter file in which to save the key (/home/cbrown/.ssh/id_rsa):
Enter passphrase (empty for no passphrase): ********
Enter same passphrase again: ********
Your identification has been saved in /home/cbrown/.ssh/id_rsa.
Your public key has been saved in /home/cbrown/.ssh/id_rsa.pub.
The key fingerprint is:
ae:8e:23:86:19:15:e3:1c:79:f6:d1:b3:48:26:d9:ee cbrown@snowhite
$
```

To append the public key to the *authorized_keys* file on the server, the dialog will look something like this:

```
$ ssh bashful mkdir .ssh
Password: ********

$ ssh bashful "cat >> ~/.ssh/authorized_keys" < ~/.ssh/id_rsa.pub
Password: ********
id_rsa.pub                          100%   225     0.2KB/s   00:00
$
```

> At risk of getting sidetracked from the main plot, it's interesting to contemplate the plumbing of the central command here. The < character is interpreted by the local shell; it redirects the standard input of the ssh client from the file ~/.ssh/id_rsa.pub. Also note that this ~ is expanded to be the pathname of your home directory on the local machine. In contrast, the >> notation is enclosed in quotes, protecting it from interpretation by the local shell. Instead, it's the shell on bashful that interprets this and appends the standard output of cat to the file ~/.ssh/authorized_keys on the remote machine. Similarly, this ~ is expanded to the pathname of your home directory on the remote machine.
>
> So, what happens is, the contents of ~/.ssh/id_rsa.pub on the local machine is presented to the standard input of ssh which sends it (via the encrypted channel) to sshd on bashful which in turn presents it as the standard input to cat, which then appends it to ~/.ssh/authorized_keys.
>
> Okay, back to the plot....

Once you've done this, the remote login dialog looks slightly different:

```
$ ssh bashful
Enter passphrase for key '/home/cbrown/.ssh/id_rsa': ********
Last login: Tue Sep 13 10:31:59 2005 from 192.168.0.17
Have a lot of fun...
$
```

This time, ssh used RSA user authentication, using the user's private key to encrypt a reply to a challenge sent by the server. The password was not used. Of course, from the end user's point of view, supplying a passphrase to unlock his or her secret key is just as inconvenient as entering a password. To avoid this inconvenience, the program ssh-agent can be used to hold a user's passphrase for the duration of a login session, and supply it as required. ssh-agent should be started like this:

```
$ eval $(ssh-agent)
Agent pid 24809
```

Now, you can add your private key(s) to the list that ssh-agent is holding:

```
$ ssh-add
Enter passphrase for /home/cbrown/.ssh/id_rsa: ********
Identity added: /home/cbrown/.ssh/id_rsa (/home/cbrown/.ssh/id_rsa)
```

Now you can verify that ssh-agent is holding the key for you:

```
$ ssh-add -l
1024 b6:ac:b5:9f:09:c8:48:43:5e:71:10:5c:2f:9c:5f:b2 /home/cbrown/.ssh/id_rsa (RSA)
```

Finally, you can perform a secure remote login without supplying either a password or a passphrase:

```
$ ssh bashful
Last login: Wed Sep 14 08:21:56 2005 from 192.168.0.17
Have a lot of fun...
cbrown@linux:~>
```

This instance of `ssh-agent` will be known only to the shell in which you ran the `eval` command, or to any child of that shell.

What About . . .

...running remote graphical applications securely? So far, you've seen how to use `ssh` to obtain a command prompt on a remote machine in a secure way. What if you want to run a graphical application remotely, and have it display on the local screen? You have seen elsewhere in this book that this is possible, due to the client/server architecture of the window system—a graphical application running remotely can connect to the X server on the local machine and talk to it using the X11 protocol. This protocol, however, is not encrypted, so potentially this traffic is also subject to eavesdropping.

To remedy this, the secure shell supports X forwarding; that is, it can tunnel X11 traffic through its encrypted connection. As well as thwarting eavesdroppers, this technique can get X11 packets through a firewall that is configured to block regular X11 traffic.

X forwarding is very easy to set up; use the `-X` flag when starting `ssh`. The `sshd` will create a connection to listen for X11 connections and will set the `DISPLAY` environment variable to point to it. Any connections will then be accepted and the traffic relayed to the `ssh` client which in turn will pass the (clear text) X11 traffic to the real, local X server. This example shows the use of this technique to run the graphical version of YaST on the remote machine:

```
$ ssh -X bashful
Enter passphrase for key '/home/cbrown/.ssh/id_rsa': ********
Last login: Wed Sep 14 08:41:06 2005 from 192.168.0.17
Have a lot of fun...
/usr/X11R6/bin/xauth:  creating new authority file /home/cbrown/.Xauthority
$ su -c /sbin/yast2
Password: ********
```

> If this doesn't work, it may be that the remote machine is not configured to support this feature. To enable it, you'll need to edit */etc/ssh/sshd_config* on the remote machine, and make sure that `X11Forwarding` is set to yes, and then restart the OpenSSH server on that machine.

Actually, X forwarding is a special case of *port forwarding*—a feature of `ssh` that allows TCP/IP traffic from arbitrary ports to be tunneled through the encrypted connection. For more information on port forwarding, read up on the `-L` and `-R` options in the ssh manpage.

Where to Learn More

There's quite a lot more to `ssh` and `sshd` than I covered in this lab. Look at the manpages for `ssh`, `scp`, and `sshd`. Both programs also have their own config files. Look at the manpages for `ssh_config` and `sshd_config`. For a much more complete reference, see the O'Reilly book *SSH: The Secure Shell* by Barrett and Silverman, sometimes known as the "snail book" because of its front cover illustration. The book *Linux System Security* by Mann et al. (Pearson) also has a long chapter on `ssh`.

8.3 Set Up a Firewall

Down in the bowels of the Linux kernel lurks a piece of code known as *netfilter*. The netfilter code performs filtering of IP packets. It examines every packet that flows into, out of, or through the machine and decides the fate of the packet based on things such as the source and destination IP addresses, the source and destination port numbers, the flags present in the TCP header, and other stuff besides. The two basic actions that netfilter can perform on a packet are to accept it or to discard it. It can also log packet traffic via the *syslogd* service. Using netfilter, it is possible to set up a Linux system as a packet-filtering firewall. The traditional role of a firewall is as a machine that stands between an internal company network and the big bad Internet, protecting the former from the latter. In this case, filtering is applied to packets being forwarded between the machine's inward-facing network interface(s) and its outward-facing interface. It is also possible to filter packets flowing into or out of the firewall itself, allowing netfilter to be used to construct a sort of "personal firewall" that is useful even in the simplest case of a single home machine connected via an ADSL line or dial-up connection to the Internet.

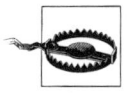

> Indeed, the Internet has become a sufficiently threatening environment that you would be well advised never to connect a machine to it directly without a personal firewall in place.

Netfilter is configured by a number of filtering *rulesets*. From the command line, rules are managed using the `iptables` command. The syntax of `iptables` represents a complete packet-filtering "language" in its own right. A typical rule includes components that identify which packets the rule matches, and ends with a statement of whether to accept or drop packets that match the rule. To give the merest hint of how it looks, here's an example:

```
iptables -A INPUT -i eth0 -p udp \
     -s $NAMESERVER --sport 53 \
     -d 140.116.5.1 --dport 53 -J ACCEPT
```

It is possible, in theory, to build a complete firewall ruleset by hand-crafting a series of `iptables` commands such as the one just shown. In brief, you start with a security policy that states which services should be accessible, figure out what IP traffic you'd expect that to generate, and put rules in place that will allow that traffic while denying everything else. This approach requires extensive knowledge of TCP/IP and enormous attention to detail. Rulesets can run to several hundred lines. There are books that teach how to do this and I am sure that there are security specialists who build their firewall rulesets at this level.

For the more cerebrally challenged amongst us, SUSE Linux provides a YaST firewall configuration module (the subject of this lab) that lets you configure your firewall at about the same level that you would define your security policy (as opposed to all the tedious mucking about with `iptables` commands that would be required if you built your firewall ruleset manually). It is reasonably successful in achieving this; nonetheless, it can be a confusing module to use. The design of this module has changed significantly from earlier versions of SuSE Linux.

How Do I Do That?

Start the module by selecting Security and Users from the panel on the left of the main YaST screen, then Firewall from the panel on the right. Within the firewall module, the panel on the left serves a dual purpose. First, it can display brief help messages relating to the configuration screen you're viewing. Second, it lets you select any one of seven screens on which you can specify firewall settings. Use the button labeled Help to switch to the Help view (the button label will change to Tree, which brings you back to the default view).

The first time you use this module, it's probably best to work through the seven screens in the order they are shown. Thereafter you can just go to the screen that you need to change. The screens are:

Start-Up
> On this screen you can specify whether the firewall rules will be established automatically at boot time. This screen is a bit of a no-brainer. Just select Service Start When Booting and be done with it.

>> There are also options on this screen to start and stop the firewall whenever you want. These are useful options if you are trying to get a network service to work, and you suspect that the packet filtering rulesets might be defeating it. I am a little embarrassed to own up to the amount of time I have wasted trying to get some service or other to function, only to discover that it was blocked by the firewall. Using this screen to turn the firewall off (briefly!) makes it easy to prove the point one way or the other.

Interfaces
> On this screen you can define the network topology for your firewall. Each of your network interfaces can be assigned to one of three zones: External, Internal,

or Demilitarized. If you are a security expert, these terms will be familiar to you, but if you're not, they can be hard to understand. Figure 8-4 explains.

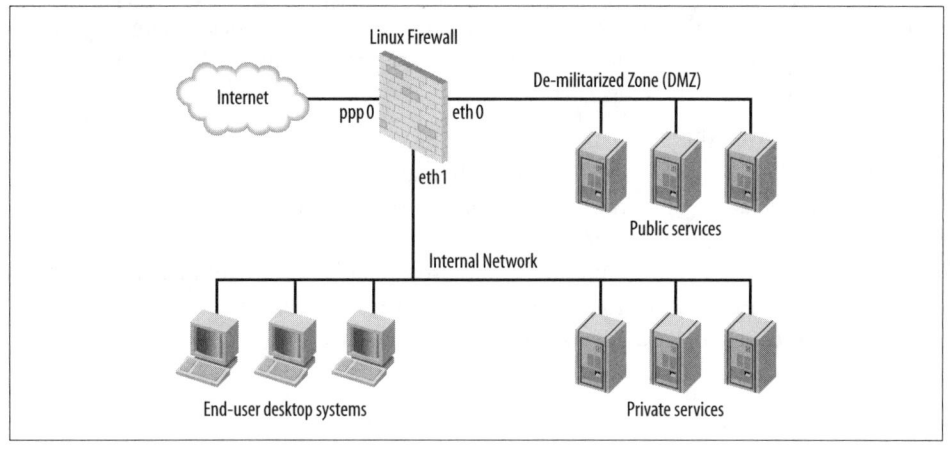

Figure 8-4. Typical firewall topology

Your external interfaces are those that connect to the big bad world of the Internet. If you have a typical home setup, this is the interface that connects to your ISP via a dial-up or ADSL connection. If you have just one machine with an Internet connection and nothing else, this is your only interface.

Your internal interfaces are those that connect to your trusted internal networks. In a small office setup, if you're using a SUSE Linux box to act as a gateway between the Internet and an internal network, these are the interfaces (or interface—it's unlikely that there is more than one) that connect to this internal network.

The *demilitarized zone* (DMZ) is a network on which you'll place the machines that host the services that you want to be visible from the Internet, such as web, FTP, or mail services. To be brutally honest, if you're configuring a firewall for use in a corporate environment that has a DMZ, you'll want to read a more specialized Linux security text than this. Also, this YaST module does not have the flexibility needed to configure the forwarding of packets between (say) the internal network and the DMZ; it is primarily concerned with simply defining rules to limit access to *this* machine from each of the three zones.

If you have only one interface on the machine, it really doesn't matter whether you consider it to be in the internal or external zone. Just pick one, and then define the allowed services for that zone, as I'll explain next.

Allowed Services
On this screen you can define the services (running on this machine) that are accessible from each of the three zones. You select which zone you're configuring using the drop-down list labeled Allowed Services for Selected Zone. For

each zone, a second drop-down list labeled Service to Allow lets you choose from a predefined list of services—DNS, HTTP, SSH, and so on. To allow a service, select it from this list and click Add. To disallow a service, select it from the Allowed Service list and click Remove. For services not on the list, you'll need to specify the service port number explicitly. For example, to enable telnet logins (you would probably only want to do this from your trusted internal network, if at all) click Advanced and enter the telnet port number (23) into the field labeled TCP Ports.

The Internal Zone requires slightly different handling. At the bottom of the screen is a checkbox labeled Protect Firewall from Internal Zone. Unless this is checked, no packet filtering will be applied to traffic coming from your internal network.

Masquerading

On this screen you can enable or disable masquerading. I discuss this in more detail in the "How It Works" section later in this lab.

Broadcast

On this screen you can specify which broadcast UDP packets will be accepted from each of the three zones (internal, external, and DMZ). You can also specify whether rejected broadcast packets will be logged. Unless you know what you're doing, it's probably best not to change these settings.

IPsec Support

On this screen you can enable and disable support for "secure IP." This is the underlying technology that supports the construction of a Virtual Private Network (VPN). The basic idea of a VPN goes like this: a real private network consists of a physically enclosed, trusted LAN, probably contained entirely within your company's premises. Because of its physical isolation, the Bad Guys can't eavesdrop on traffic sent over this LAN or obtain unauthorized access to services on it by spoofing the identity of legitimate clients. A virtual private network uses cryptographic technologies to establish encrypted tunnels that extend the privacy of a secure LAN connection out across the Big Bad Internet. VPNs are commonly used to connect corporate branch offices in different cities. They are also used to allow an individual carrying his laptop to a conference in San Jose to connect securely to his internal company network in Manhattan to pick up his email or interrogate his company's databases. In this context, the ability of Linux to allow a machine to act as its own VPN gateway is especially valuable.

By clicking on the Details button on this screen, you can also specify how you want the system to treat packets received via an IPsec connection. A likely setting here is to trust packets received using IPsec as if they were coming from the internal zone, so that a user connecting via a VPN has the same access as a user sitting at a machine which is physically on the internal network.

Logging Level

On this screen you can control the amount of logging that will be performed by the netfilter code in the kernel as packets are processed by the rulesets and are then either accepted or rejected. For each case (accepted or rejected) you can:

- log all packets
- log only "critical" packets
- log nothing

It is not entirely clear what a "critical packet" is. The documentation states (somewhat vaguely) that for accepted packets, "critical" includes TCP connection requests, RPC connection requests, access to high UDP/TCP ports and forwarded packets. For rejected packets, "critical" includes spoofed packets, TCP connection requests and certain ICMP types.

Logging dropped packets helps you determine whether legitimate traffic is being inadvertently dropped by the firewall due to misconfiguration (though your users will also let you know about this!) or if there is evidence of having your doorknobs rattled by would-be intruders. Logging critical accepted packets might help you log legitimate service usage (though there are better ways to do this). Logging all accepted packets on a production machine is probably a bad idea. It will slow the system down and fill up the disk with huge log files.

> If you choose to hand-edit the SuSEfirewall2 config file (discussed later in this lab), it is possible to set a parameter called `FW_LOG_LIMIT` to rate-limit the number of log entries that will be generated; for example you could limit to 10 entries per hour. The default is 3 per minute. The YaST firewall configuration module does not offer the capability to set this parameter.

The log is written using the standard syslogd logging facility. With the default syslog configuration, these messages will reach the file */var/log/firewall*.

The top-level workflow within the YaST firewall configuration module is a little confusing. After specifying the settings on each individual screen, clicking the Next button will present you with a Firewall Configuration Summary screen (see Figure 8-5). This screen has three buttons: Back, Abort, and Accept. Click Back if you want to select one of the other screens to change settings there. Click Abort if you want to quit the entire session (and abandon any changes you've made). Click Accept if you're done making changes and want to commit them.

How It Works

The YaST firewall module edits the file */etc/sysconfig/SuSEfirewall2*. I'd strongly recommend you take a look at this file. It is heavily commented and will give you a better understanding of what the YaST module is doing, as well as providing you with

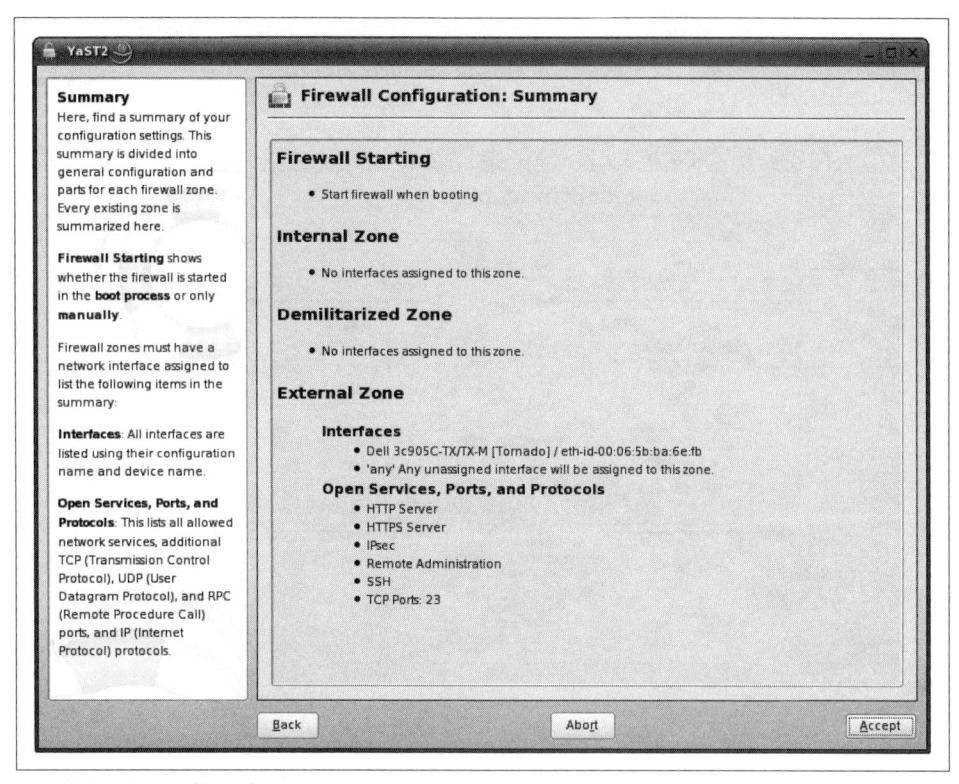

Figure 8-5. Firewall configuration summary

examples of the syntax you should use in some of the more advanced options within the YaST module.

The firewall itself is normally set up at boot time via two scripts in the directory */etc/rc.d*, called *SuSEfirewall2_init* and *SuSEfirewall2_setup*. The *init* script runs early in the boot process and closes the firewall completely except for *bootp* and *ping* traffic. The *setup* script runs later in the boot process and is responsible for establishing the firewall rulesets when the firewall is started and removing them when the firewall is stopped. These scripts are run through the standard boot script hierarchy. Both scripts call */sbin/SuSEfirewall2* to do the real work. This is another shell script and is the real "engine room" of the SuSEfirewall2 mechanism. It is here that the actual `iptables` commands are generated based on the security settings defined in */etc/sysconfig/SuSEfirewall2*. I wouldn't especially recommend that you examine */sbin/SuSEfirewall2* (especially after a heavy meal) unless you'd like to see an example of a relatively complex shell script.

Masquerading, which can easily be enabled or disabled from within the YaST firewall module, is a Cunning Trick that can be performed by a firewall that sits between your internal network and the Internet. It is implemented as part of the netfilter code in the Linux kernel. Masquerading is a specific form of a more general technique called *Network Address Translation* (NAT) which essentially means fiddling around with the IP addresses and/or port numbers in the headers of packets that pass through the gateway. Masquerading allows outbound traffic from machines on your internal network to appear to be coming from the gateway machine. Figure 8-6 shows an example of masquerading in action.

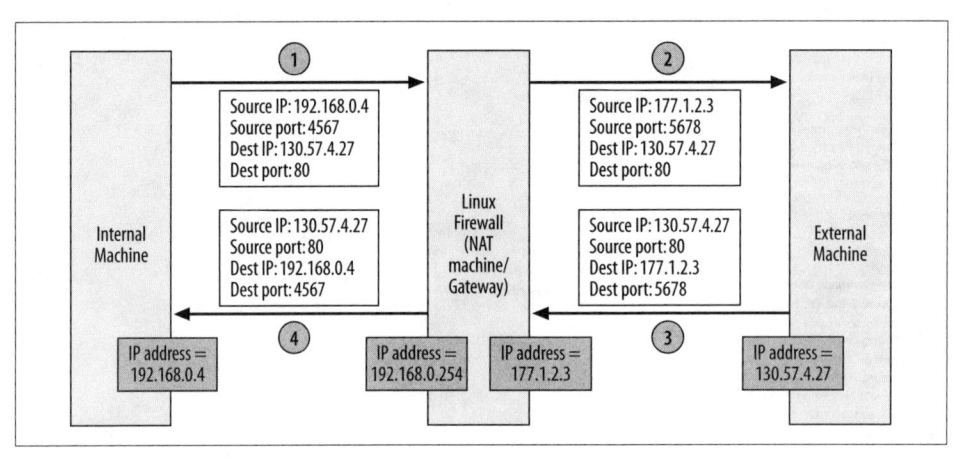

Figure 8-6. Masquerading

At step 1 in the figure, a machine on the internal network with IP address 192.168.0.4 sends a packet to Novell's web server (port 80 at IP address 130.57.4.27). Because of the default route in the internal machine's routing table, it actually sends the packet to the inward facing interface of the Linux firewall/gateway machine, at 192.168.0.254. The gateway machine, which has an external-facing interface at 177.1.2.3, picks a new source port (5678) for the packet and rewrites the source IP address and port number of the packet so that it appears to come from the gateway machine. At step 2, it forwards the packet to the original destination IP address and port number. At step 3, the web server sends a reply packet. The gateway, recognizing this as an inbound packet on a masqueraded connection, replaces the destination IP address and port number in the packet with those of the originating machine, and forwards the packet (step 4) onto the internal network.

Masquerading has two significant benefits. First, it allows your site to use private IP address space (for example the 192.168.0.0/16 space) and consume only a single, real, routable IP address (the address assigned to the external-facing interface of your gateway). By allowing the private address spaces to be re-used over and over on countless internal networks, this technique has significantly slowed the exhaustion of IP address space, which ten years ago was beginning to be a worry. The second benefit of masquerading is that it improves security by effectively hiding your internal network from the Internet. It is simply not possible for an external client to reach through the NAT machine to connect to a server running on the internal network.

However, it remains possible for your internal machines to establish outbound connections to external Internet servers. If you have a broadband (such as ADSL or cable) router in your network, it will perform masquerading for you automatically.

What About...

...testing the firewall configuration? SUSE Linux includes a port-scanning tool called nmap (part of the nmap package—not installed by default), which will tell you which ports are actually open on your firewall. By running it from machines on the local network, from the DMZ, and from the external network, you can get a picture of what's accessible from each of these networks.

Where to Learn More

The definitive text on Linux firewalls is *Linux Firewalls* by Robert Ziegler, now in its third edition—and its third publisher (Novell Press)! This is an authoritative book about Linux firewalls and how to build them at the iptables level; it does not discuss the use of SuSEfirewall2 or the SUSE YaST firewall configuration module, or anything specific to SUSE Linux. There is a published description of the *SuSEfirewall2* config file at *http://susefaq.sourceforge.net/guides/fw_manual.html*; it is a little out of date but I don't know of anything more recent. You might also try looking at the files in */usr/share/doc/packages/SuSEfirewall2*.

8.4   Define a Security Level

An initial default installation of Linux will inevitably establish a certain level of security, as defined by the overall file permissions, the range of enabled network services, the firewall rules, and so on. Early distributions of Unix and Linux were relatively open in their settings "out of the box," with practically every available network service enabled by default. Over the years, default installations have become more closed and secure, requiring the user to explicitly open the system up and enable just those services they want to run. However, there is no "one size fits all" answer to the question of what the default security settings should be. Settings that would work fine for an isolated, single-user home machine would certainly not be appropriate for a so-called *bastion host* on a company's DMZ network. With this in mind, SUSE Linux includes a sort of security wizard that allows you to specify a number of security related settings that, overall, define the security level of the system.

How Do I Do That?

To run the security wizard, start YaST. From the main YaST screen, select Security and Users from the panel on the left, followed by Local Security from the panel on the right. From the screen titled "Local Security Configuration," you can select one of three predefined sets of security settings, in order of increasing security:

- Home workstation
- Networked workstation
- Network server

If you wish, you can simply select one of these levels, click Finish, and be done with it. This might feel like a rather dumb way of configuring your system's security, but it's a lot better than doing nothing at all. To configure your security in more detail, select Custom Settings and click on Next. (Though you really need to sit down and write down a security policy first.) This will take you to the first of five screens on which you can specify a variety of security settings:

Password Settings

On this screen you can enable or disable password strength checking. This is a check applied at the time that a user chooses a new password that helps ensure that the password cannot be easily guessed by a program like crack. It ensures that passwords are not simple words found in the dictionary and that they contain a sufficiently complex mix of characters.

Also on this screen you can specify the password encryption method. (Technically, the passwords stored on a Linux system are not encrypted, they are *hashed*. The key difference, in this context, is that encryption is reversible, if you know the key; hashing is not.) DES (Data Encryption Standard) is the hash traditionally used on UNIX and Linux systems. MD5 and Blowfish are more modern (and more secure) hashes. Except in the unlikely event that you need to maintain backward compatibility with hashed passwords inherited from some other system, I recommend using Blowfish here.

Also on this screen you can specify the minimum password length. I suggest a minimum of eight characters. (If you can't remember an eight-character password, you probably shouldn't be using Linux!)

Finally, on this screen you can also specify the password aging parameters. These control the maximum number of days for which a password remains valid and the amount of warning you will receive of password expiry. Some companies have specific policies about this. Personally I have never been a great believer in password aging. It seems to me that if your account has been compromised, it is little consolation to know that you'll be changing your password within the next 60 days. Also there's a danger that too-frequent password changes will lead to a weak choice of passwords.

Boot Settings

On this screen you can control whether Ctrl-Alt-Delete will initiate a reboot, and who can shut the system down from the KDM login manager. These settings have a negligible effect on security if users have physical access to the machine, as they can always press the reset button or the on/off switch.

Login Settings

On this screen you can control the delay after an incorrect login attempt. Increasing this delay will certainly slow down an intruder making repeated manual login attempts, but it would be an unsophisticated villain indeed who tried to compromise your system in this way! You can also control whether successful login attempts will be recorded. (Unsuccessful attempts are always recorded.)

User Addition

On this screen you can control the minimum and maximum numeric user IDs and group IDs that will be used for account creation. The convention on SUSE Linux is to reserve UIDs below 1000 for "system" accounts. The only reason I can think of for changing these values would be to accommodate a merger of user accounts from some other system, to prevent UID or GID clashes within a specific range.

Miscellaneous Settings

On this final screen you can control how tightly the system file permissions will be locked down. There are three settings: Easy, Secure, and Paranoid. The exact policies enforced by each of these settings are discussed later in the "How It Works" section.

There are a couple of other settings on this screen that are quite subtle in their implications. First, there's the setting that controls who runs the program `updatedb`. This program is part of the package `findutils-locate` (not installed by default). If installed, it is run once per day (via cron) and builds a database (usually in the file */var/lib/locatedb*) of all the filenames present in the filesystem. This database can be queried using the `locate` command, which gives a much faster way of searching the filesystem than `find` does (because it simply has to query the database rather than performing an exhaustive search). However, if `updatedb` is run a root, it may include filenames in the database that an ordinary user should not normally be able to see. For example, I'll be able to see the names of files in other users' `Documents` directories, which I do not normally have permission to list. Running `updatedb` as "nobody" will only allow it to index files in directories that are world-readable.

Second, there are settings on this screen that control whether . (the current directory) should be included in the search path for root, and for ordinary users. Here's the scoop on this. Suppose that you're logged in at a command prompt and you use the `cp` command to copy a file. Which program will you actually run? The answer is: you will run whichever executable file called `cp` the shell finds first as it traverses your search path looking for the command. Hopefully it will be the "real" `cp` command in the */bin* directory. However, if you include . in your search path (especially if you include it before */bin*), there's a real danger that the `cp` command you actually run will be one installed by the Bad Guy in whatever happens to be your current directory. In this way, Bad Guys can arrange to run any program of their choice under your identity. If your identity happens to be root, the consequences can be especially serious. For this reason, it is generally advisable not to include . in search paths, either for root or for ordinary users. The downside to this is that if you do actually want to run an executable from your current directory, you will have to do so explicitly, by entering (for example) `./myprog` rather than just `myprog`.

How It Works

The settings established by this sequence of screens are stored in a variety of system configuration files.

The password length and strength checking is performed by the PAM module pam_pwcheck and its configuration is stored in */etc/security/pam_pwcheck.conf*. The encryption method is specified by a line of the form:

```
CRYPT_FILES=blowfish
```

in the file */etc/default/passwd*.

The password aging parameters are stored in the file */etc/login.defs*, something like this:

```
PASS_MAX_DAYS   60
PASS_MIN_DAYS   1
PASS_WARN_AGE   14
```

These values simply provide defaults when a new account is created; the actual password aging parameters for each user are stored in */etc/shadow*. The file */etc/login.defs* also controls other aspects of login behavior, such as the delay after a failed login attempt, and the minimum and maximum values for UIDs and GIDs.

The File Permissions setting on the final screen of the sequence is rather more interesting. SUSE Linux includes a utility called chkstat (not the most imaginative name) that checks, and optionally corrects, the ownerships and permissions of key files in the filesystem. As such, it can be used as a low-grade system hardening tool or perhaps for intrusion detection, if an intruder has left permissions deliberately lax. chkstat reads one or more permissions files to find out what files to check, and what the ownership and permissions are supposed to be. The system ships with several permissions files, described in Table 8-1.

Table 8-1. Permission files for use with chkstat

File in /etc	Description
permissions	A really basic set of permissions. File modes that differ from the settings in this file should be considered broken, not merely insecure.
permissions.easy	A fairly lax set of permissions for use on standalone single-user systems.
permissions.secure	A more secure set of permissions for use on multiuser or networked systems. To quote from the comments in the file itself: "The primary target of this configuration is to make the basic things such as changing passwords, the basic networking programs as well as some of the all-day work programs properly function for the unprivileged user."

Table 8-1. *Permission files for use with chkstat (continued)*

File in /etc	Description
permissions.paranoid	A very secure set of permissions. This file is similar to *permissions.secure* but has all the set-user-id and set-group-id bits cleared. These settings will prove inconvenient for ordinary users and are probably best reserved for servers or firewalls which do not support ordinary user log-ins.
permissions.local	This file provides a place for administrators to add entries for locally installed programs; for example those in */opt* or */usr/local*.

Entries in these files have the syntax:

```
filename  owner:group  mode
```

For example, here are a few lines from */etc/permissions.secure*:

```
/usr/bin/passwd              root:shadow      4755
/usr/bin/crontab             root:trusted     4750
/etc/fstab                   root:root        644
/var/spool/fax/archive       fax:uucp         700
```

The file permissions (mode) are written in octal. The 4000 bit is the set-user-id bit; the bottom three digits correspond to the usual `rwxrwxrwx` permissions on the file.

Comparing *permissions.secure* with *permissions.paranoid*, you can see that (for example) in the paranoid settings the `passwd` command does not run set-uid to root:

```
/usr/bin/passwd                          root:shadow        0755
```

This means that nonroot users would not be able to change their passwords.

To run `chkstat` against the *permissions.secure* file (for example), just supply the file name as an argument. On my test system, the command:

```
# chkstat /etc/permissions.secure
```

produces no output—the system passes with flying colors (whatever that means). Running chkstat against permissions.paranoid, however, produces a long list of warnings, mostly about config files that are readable by nonroot users, or about programs that have the set-user-id bit on.

Running chkstat with the `--set` option tells it to fix the problem automatically. Let's try making one of the permissions deliberately too lax, and re-run the program. The line numbers in this listing are for reference; they are not part of the input or output.

```
1   # chmod 666 /etc/fstab
2   # chkstat /etc/permissions.secure
3   Checking permissions and ownerships - using the permissions files
4          /etc/permissions.secure
5   /etc/fstab should be root:root 0644. (wrong permissions 0666)
6   # chkstat --set /etc/permissions.secure
7   Checking permissions and ownerships - using the permissions files
8          /etc/permissions.secure
9   setting /etc/fstab to root:root 0644. (wrong permissions 0666)
10  # ls -l /etc/fstab
11  -rw-r--r--  1 root root 670 Oct 11 09:35 /etc/fstab
```

At line 1, I deliberately changed the permissions on */etc/fstab*. At lines 2–5, I ran chkstat and it duly reported the problem. At lines 6–9, I ran chkstat again with the --set flag and at lines 10 and 11 verified that chkstat had indeed corrected the permissions problem.

It's time to tie all this up with the File Permissions setting in the YaST security module you've seen in this lab. The setting made within YaST sets a line in the file */etc/sysconfig/security*; for example if I set the file permissions to "Easy," I will see a line in */etc/sysconfig/security* like this:

    PERMISSION_SECURITY="easy local"

This line says to run chkstat with the files permissions.easy and permissions.local as parameters.

The chkstat program is run by SuSEconfig, the script that YaST runs whenever it commits a configuration change. This means that the file permissions are checked pretty well every time you change something in YaST.

Where to Learn More

Take a look at the manpage for login.defs and also at the file itself (*/etc/login.defs*). Look at the manpage for chkstat.

8.5 Provide Role-Based Access Control with sudo

The security model in Linux goes back a long way—to the early days of Unix, in fact, round about 1969. To set this into context, that was the year that man first landed on the moon, Woodstock happened, and the Foundations had a hit with "Build Me Up Buttercup." However, the original IBM PC wouldn't be invented for another 12 years. If you're too young to know what I'm talking about, what I mean is that "it was a long time ago…."

Surprisingly, the security model hasn't evolved much since then. We still have read, write, and execute permissions on files for user, group, and others. There have been a few additions, such as POSIX *capabilities*, "immutable" files, and *access control lists* (not much used in my experience), and recently we've seen the introduction of SELinux (Security Enhanced Linux) from the National Security Agency in the United States, which brings mandatory access controls to Linux at the expense of rather complex configuration. But the basic model remains.

One of the things most obviously missing from Linux is the lack of a role-based access control model (such as is found in Solaris, for example). The idea of role-based access control (RBAC) is that you can define roles such as "Printer Administrator" or "Network Administrator" and define privileges for these roles. For example, a printer administrator might be allowed to purge all jobs from the print queues, a network administrator might be allowed to change a machine's IP address, and a user manager might be able to add user accounts. Then you assign roles to users. So, Joe might have the roles "Network Administrator" and "User Manager" and Mary might have the role "Printer Administrator."

Under the basic Linux model, there is really only one special role—the super-user—which is associated with the root login. As you know, this is a rather all-or-nothing approach to granting privilege, as the super-user can do anything.

The subject of this lab is a utility called sudo, which allows something approximating a role-based access control model on Linux. sudo allows specified (nonroot) users to execute specified commands as root, under control of a configuration file.

How Do I Do That?

sudo is configured using the file */etc/sudoers*. Mastering sudo is largely a matter of mastering the syntax of this file. Unfortunately, the manpage for sudoers describes the syntax in a very formal way using *Extended Backus-Naur Form*, a notation for formally describing grammars that is great if you have recently completed a degree in computer science and almost completely unintelligible otherwise.

As a simple example, suppose that you want to grant a user called cbrown the ability to set the time and date from the command line, using the date command. Now, the date command will allow ordinary users to invoke it with no arguments, just to report the current time and date, like this:

```
$ date
Thu Sep 15 07:56:52 BST 2005
```

However, any attempt to change the date will be rejected unless you're root:

```
$ date 09150755
date: cannot set date: Operation not permitted
Thu Sep 15 07:55:00 BST 2005
```

There are quite a few commands in Linux that show this behavior; that is, they will allow an ordinary user to invoke them simply to report current settings, but to actually change the settings, they insist on being run as root. The ifconfig command, used to view and change settings of network interfaces, is another example.

To allow cbrown to change the date, you need to configure sudo to allow cbrown to run the date command as root. You do this by putting a line in */etc/sudoers*, like this:

```
cbrown   snowhite=(root)   /bin/date
```

In sudo terminology, this line is called a *privilege specification*. Let's look at the fields in turn:

cbrown
> The first field is the Linux user account name to which the privilege is being granted.

snowhite
>The second field in the hostname of the machine to which the entry relates. Specifying a specific host here allows you to share a single *sudoers* file across many machine (using NFS for example) but still make per-host customizations. It's common to see the keyword ALL in this field.

=(root)
>This notation specifies the target user identity that the command can be run as.

/bin/date
>The final field is the name of the command that the user can run. Note that you need to specify a full pathname here.

You need to be root to edit the sudoers file, and you should use the visudo command (rather than editing it directly). visudo will lock the file against simultaneous updates and it will check the file for syntax errors before saving it.

With this line in place, cbrown is able to change the date by telling sudo to run the date command, like this:

```
$ sudo date 09150755

We trust you have received the usual lecture from the local System
Administrator. It usually boils down to these three things:

    #1) Respect the privacy of others.
    #2) Think before you type.
    #3) With great power comes great responsibility.

Password: *******
Thu Sep 15 07:55:00 BST 2005
```

The rather pompous warning is displayed only the first time you run sudo. Recent versions of SUSE Linux include, by default, a line in */etc/sudoers* like this:

```
Defaults targetpw
```

With this line in place, the user will be required to enter not his or her own password but the password of the "target" user—that is, the user whose identity the command will be run under, which is usually root. You should delete this line when you configure sudo, so that the user is prompted for his own password, not root's. Otherwise, the whole point of providing a more fine-grained privilege escalation is lost. You should also delete the line:

```
ALL ALL=(ALL) ALL
```

Once you have used sudo and entered your password, sudo will allow you to execute further commands without supplying your password again for a specific period of time. The default timeout is five minutes; you can change this in the sudoers file by adding a line such as:

```
Defaults timestamp_timeout=0
```

which will force sudo to ask for a password every time.

It's time to look at some more features of the sudoers file. First, the keyword ALL is heavily used in several contexts of the file. For example, the line:

```
isaac   ALL=(ALL) ALL
```

says that user `isaac` can run any command under any user identity on any machine. (Of course, he'll need to supply either his own or the target user's password.)

You can also define *aliases*. Aliases are just named shortcuts for lists of users, lists of hosts, or lists of commands. By themselves, aliases don't really do anything, but they make the privilege rules much easier to write, and in reality contribute a great deal to the power and usability of sudo. Let's see an example.

Suppose that you want to grant a user the privilege to manage user accounts. There are several command-line tools used for this—useradd, groupadd, and so on. In the sudoers file, you could define a command alias (let's call it USERMGMT) like this:

```
Cmnd_Alias USERMGMT=/usr/sbin/useradd,/usr/sbin/usermod,\
           /usr/sbin/groupadd,/usr/sbin/groupmod,\
           /usr/sbin/userdel,/usr/sbin/groupdel
```

Notice the use of \ to signal line continuation. With this alias defined, you can grant user `isaac` permission to run any of these commands as root with a privilege specification like this:

```
isaac   ALL=(root) USERMGMT
```

You can think of USERMGMT as a *rôle* (though the sudo documentation doesn't use that term) defined in terms of the commands that someone with this role would need to execute.

You can also define a user alias (a named list of users), then assign privileges to all users in that list:

```
User_Alias ADMINS tom,joe,sue
ADMINS     ALL=(root) USERMGMT
```

Effectively, we are saying that `tom`, `sue`, and `joe` can assume the USERMGMT role.

As an alternative, you can use Linux groups as a way of granting privileges to a group of users. For example, the line:

```
%powerusers    ALL=(root) /bin/mount,/bin/umount
```

allows members of the `powerusers` group to execute the mount and umount commands. Note the use of % to prefix a group name.

You can also define a host alias (a named list of hosts) in terms of their IP address range, or their hostnames. For example:

```
Host_Alias LOCALNET 192.168.0.0/255.255.255.0
Host_Alias TRUSTEES snowhite,happy,sneezy
```

Now we can grant privileges that apply only to specific groups of machines; for example:

```
ADMINS    TRUSTEES=(root) USERMGMT
```

How It Works

Operation of sudo relies on a clever feature in Linux called the *set user ID bit*. Look at the ownership and permissions on the sudo command:

```
$ ls -l /usr/bin/sudo
-rwsr-xr-x  1 root root 97676 2005-06-23 10:31 /usr/bin/sudo
```

First, note that it's owned by root. Second, notice the s in the permission string (where the "user execute permission" bit would normally be). This flags this executable file as "set user ID," and means that when the sudo command is run, it runs with the effective identity of whoever owns it; in this case, root. The program is said to run "setuid to root."

> It's fairly widely known (so forgive me for reporting it here) that a patent application for the setuid mechanism was filed by Dennis Ritchie in 1973 (U.S. patent number 4135240). It's interesting because the patent describes the implementation in terms of hardware (logic gates and so on) because at the time it wasn't thought that software-implemented inventions could be patented. You can find the patent at *http://patft.uspto.gov*. It's worth a glance, if only as an example of the patent lawyers' exquisite skills of obfuscation. In a relatively lucid moment, they describe the central idea thus: "…whereby said current user selectively may be given access by said computer system to files owned by said file owner during the execution of said program instructions." Enough said.

So, when sudo starts running, it starts running as root. A program running as root is able to switch its effective user identity to anything it likes. (See the manpages for the setuid and seteuid system calls if you're really interested.) Thus, the sudo process can assume the identity of the target user specified in the sudo command (root, by default), then execute the specified program.

What About…

…the difference between sudo and su? Well, sudo and su both let you run commands as root. The difference is that using su requires you to know the root password, but sudo (depending on how it's configured) doesn't. The whole point of sudo is to dole out administrative privileges in a more fine-grained way than the all-or-nothing tell-'em-the-root-password approach required by su. On a single-user machine, such as a personal laptop, where you probably did the installation yourself and set your own root password, sudo doesn't really buy you much. On a larger multiuser system such as you might find in a corporate or university environment, sudo can be very useful.

There's another important feature of sudo that su doesn't have—logging. The sudo command will log all the commands it's asked to execute, which can be valuable as an audit trail. You can configure sudo to log to a specified file with a line in the *sudoers* file something like this:

```
Defaults    logfile=/var/log/sudo
```

With this line in place, sudo will append an entry to */var/log/sudo* for each command that it executes (otherwise, it will log to */var/log/messages*). The entry includes the date and time, the user that ran the command, the user's current directory at the time, the user that the command was run as, and the command itself. Be aware, however, that the -s option gives the user a root shell, in this case only the call to sudo -s itself is logged; any commands executed by that root shell will not be tracked in the log:

```
$ sudo rm /some/random/file
$ sudo -s
# rm /top/secret/file
# tail -2 /var/log/messages
Mar 30 14:30:32 snowhite sudo:   cbrown : TTY=pts/3 ; PWD=/home/cbrown ; USER=root ;
COMMAND=/bin/rm /some/random/file
Mar 30 14:30:35 snowhite sudo:   cbrown : TTY=pts/3 ; PWD=/home/cbrown ; USER=root ;
COMMAND=/bin/bash
```

If a user not listed in the sudoers file tries to use sudo, mail will be sent to "the proper authorities" (that means root). The user himself receives a report of the form:

```
isaac is not in the sudoers file.  This incident will be reported.
```

which suggests that you should hide in the basement in expectation that the sudo police will turn up with a search warrant and handcuffs, but really it just means that email will be sent to root, who will be much too busy browsing slashdot.org to take any notice.

The whole sudo thing is really intended to control access to command-line tools. It doesn't really afford fine-grained privileges to tools such as YaST. Either you run YaST as root (in which case you can do anything), or you don't (in which case you can do almost nothing.) You can't set sudo up so that a nonroot user is able (for example) to use YaST to add a user account but not to add a partition to your hard drive.

Where to Learn More

You can try looking at the manpages for sudo and sudoers, though, as noted earlier, they are heavy going. The book Linux System Security by Mann et al. (Pearson) has a good chapter on sudo with a more complex example of a sudoers file.

8.6 Assess Vulnerabilities Using Nessus

Okay, so you've taken all the usual advice about creating a secure system. You've enabled only the services you actually need. You're running SuSeFirewall2. You've downloaded all the security-related updates from YaST Online Update. You've tightened down the file permissions as far as you can. Can you be sure that your system is secure? Well, it will certainly be more secure than if you hadn't done those things, but to answer the question with more confidence, consider running a security assessment tool. In this lab, you'll see how to use Nessus, a network vulnerability scanner included in the SUSE Linux distribution, to remotely scan the systems on your network for potential security problems.

How Do I Do That?

First, make sure you have the packages nessus-core, libnasl and nessus-libraries installed. (I am disappointed to note that these packages are not on the SUSE Linux 10.1 beta CDs from the OpenSUSE site; however, you should be able to download them from *ftp://ftp.gwdg.de/pub/opensuse/distribution/SL-10.0-OSS/inst-source/suse/i586*.) Nessus has a client and server component. The server, called nessusd, is the piece that performs the actual tests, and the client, nessus, is a graphical application that allows you to log in to the server, specify the tests you want to perform, and view the test results. For the client to connect to the server, the server must present a known SSL certificate to the client, and the client must present a valid username and password to the server. So, on the machine on which you plan to run the server, there are a couple of things you need to do. First you need to create a Nessus user account. These are used only to control login to the Nessus server and aren't related to regular Linux accounts. The account creation tool, nessus-adduser, is quite chatty and the dialog is fairly self-explanatory. Here's an example:

```
# nessus-adduser
Using /var/tmp as a temporary file holder

Add a new nessusd user
----------------------

Login : joe
Authentication (pass/cert) [pass] :
Login password :
Login password (again) :

User rules
----------
nessusd has a rules system which allows you to restrict the hosts
that joe has the right to test. For instance, you may want
him to be able to scan his own host only.

Please see the nessus-adduser(8) man page for the rules syntax

Enter the rules for this user, and hit ctrl-D once you are done :
(the user can have an empty rules set)
accept 192.168.0.0/24
default deny
```

```
Login              : joe
Password           : **********
DN                 :
Rules              :
accept 192.168.0.0/24
default deny

Is that ok ? (y/n) [y]
user added.
```

Each user has an associated set of rules, which restricts the systems that the user can scan. The simple two-rule set established in the preceding transcript allows joe to scan systems on the 192.168.0.0/24 network, and nothing else.

The second thing you must do is to create an SSL certificate for the server. This is easy:

```
# nessus-mkcert
/var/lib/nessus/CA created
-------------------------------------------------------------------
                  Creation of the Nessus SSL Certificate
-------------------------------------------------------------------

This script will now ask you the relevant information to create the SSL
certificate of Nessus. Note that this information will *NOT* be sent to
anybody (everything stays local), but anyone with the ability to connect to your
Nessus daemon will be able to retrieve this information.


CA certificate life time in days [1460]: 365
Server certificate life time in days [365]:
Your country (two letter code) [FR]: UK
Your state or province name [none]:
Your location (e.g. town) [Paris]: Sheffield
Your organization [Nessus Users United]: Little ol' me


-------------------------------------------------------------------
                  Creation of the Nessus SSL Certificate
-------------------------------------------------------------------

Congratulations. Your server certificate was properly created.

/etc/nessus/nessusd.conf updated

The following files were created :

. Certification authority :
   Certificate = /var/lib/nessus/CA/cacert.pem
   Private key = /var/lib/nessus/CA/cakey.pem

. Nessus Server :
    Certificate = /var/lib/nessus/CA/servercert.pem
    Private key = /var/lib/nessus/CA/serverkey.pem

Press [ENTER] to exit
```

Now you're ready to start the Nessus daemon. You can arrange for the daemon to start automatically at boot time with the command:

```
# chkconfig --add nessusd
```

or you can start it manually like this:

```
# rcnessusd start
Starting nessusd Loading the Nessus plugins...                          done
Loading the plugins... 918 (out of 2301)
-------------------------------------------------------------------------------
You are running a version of Nessus which is not configured to receive
a full plugin feed. As a result, your security audits might produce incomplete
results.

To obtain a full plugin feed, you need to register your Nessus scanner
at the following URL :

            http://www.nessus.org/register/

-------------------------------------------------------------------------------

All plugins loaded
```

Now you're ready to perform a security scan. Start the client:

```
$ nessus
```

Because of the client/server architecture of Nessus, the client does not need to run on the same machine as the server. Servers can be placed at various strategic points on a network allowing tests to be conducted from various points of view. You can manage multiple Nessus servers from a single machine (the one on your desktop). The Nessus window has multiple tabs; on the first one (Nessusd host), you specify where the nessusd server is running, give a valid nessusd username (joe, in this case) and password, then click Login. The first time you connect, the server's SSL certificate will be presented to you. You'll need to manually verify this and accept it.

Once you're connected, proceed to the Plugins tab of the Nessus screen. Here, you can specify which vulnerability tests you want to perform. This is where the going gets tough in terms of detail. Nessus uses *plugins* to perform the actual vulnerability tests, and on my system, there are almost 10,000 Nessus plugins loaded. The Nessus screen shown in Figure 8-7 provides a two-level view of the available plugins with the top-level categories shown in the top pane and the individual plugins listed in the bottom pane. Under the category SUSE Local Security Checks, for example, about 170 plugins are listed. Click on an individual plugin to obtain a description of the vulnerability tested by that plugin. One of these is shown in Figure 8-7.

You will also want to visit the Target tab of the Nessus screen. Here you can specify (by name or by IP address) the target machines you wish to scan. There are other

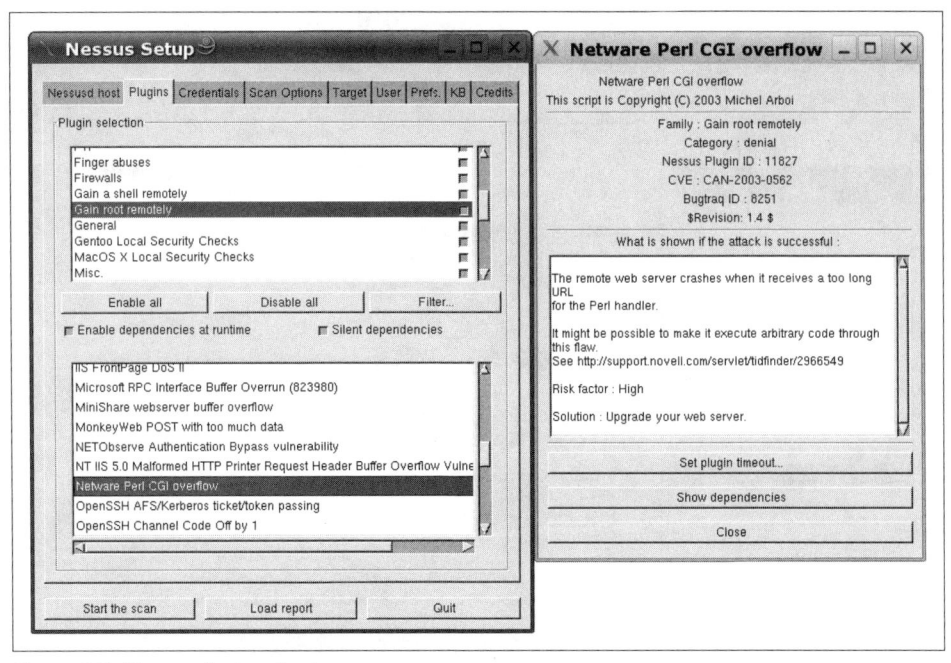

Figure 8-7. Nessus plugin selection

tabs you may wish to visit. On the Credentials tab, for example, you can specify credentials for SMB and SSH logins on the target. (Allowing Nessus to perform SSH logins on the target means that it can perform more thorough testing and use additional techniques to perform vulnerability scanning "from the inside.") On the Scan Options tab, you can specify the port scanning techniques to use. All in all, you'll need to spend some time exploring these screens to get the most out of Nessus.

When the scan is configured to your liking, click "Start the scan." Nessus will show you progress bars for each of the machines being targeted. When the scan is complete the Nessus report screen shown in Figure 8-8 will open automatically. The various panels on this screen allow you to drill down into the details of the report. Select a subnet, then a specific host. You'll see a list of the open ports on that host. Against each one, you'll see an icon indicating the severity of the security issue (if any) associated with that port. Select a specific port to see the associated severity warnings. Select a specific warning to see a detailed description of the security issue and suggested fix. The amount of information available in these reports is substantial. (I should 'fess up that the report shown in Figure 8-8 was a sample downloaded from the Nessus web site. My own test results, which I ran on a SUSE Linux system, a Windows 2000 box, and my ADSL router, didn't show up too many issues.)

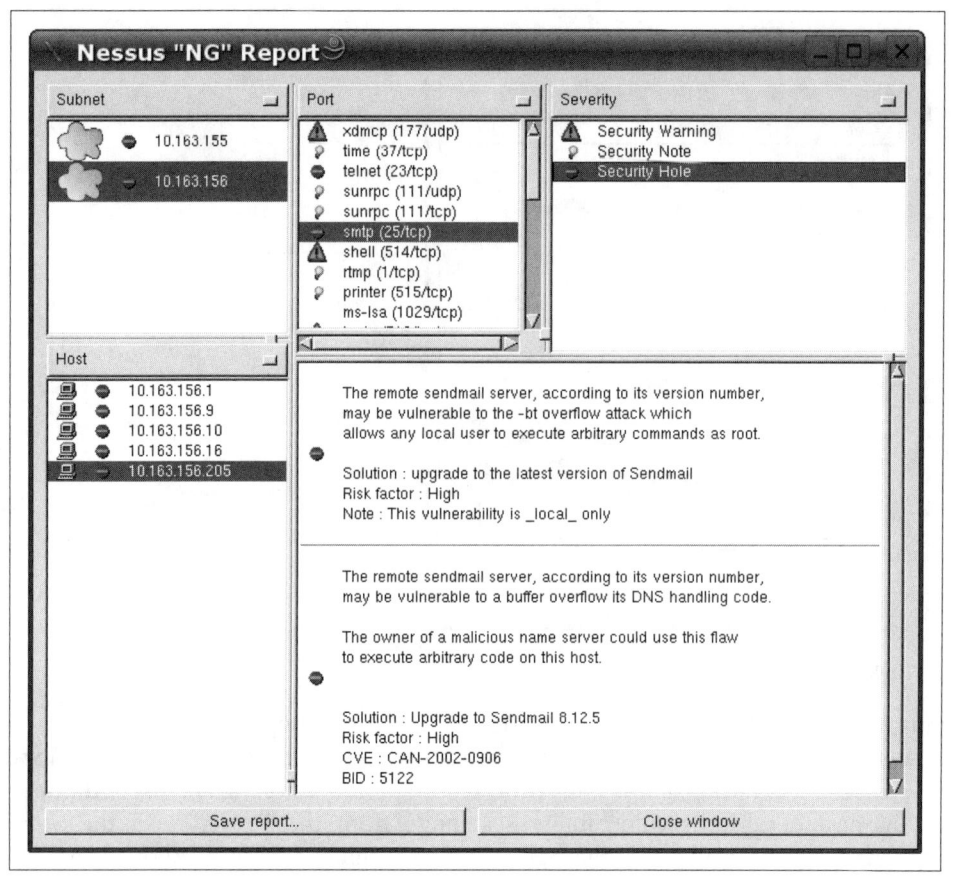

Figure 8-8. Nessus report screen

> You should take care when scanning production servers with Nessus. If you're in a corporate environment, don't scan your servers without your manager's permission. Some of the scans perform denial of service attacks and may well bring the server down. These scans are disabled by default; nonetheless I managed to scan my ADSL router to death and had to cycle the power to revive it. The best time to perform a vulnerability scan is before a server goes into production service. If you need to scan them at a later time, choose a time when temporary loss of service will have minimal impact.

How It Works

The real business of Nessus is carried out using plugins. A plugin is a script written in a purpose-designed language called NASL (Nessus Attack Scripting Language). NASL plugins run in a contained environment on top of a virtual machine. The plugins are stored in the directory */usr/lib/nessus/plugins*; there are a lot of them!

Nessus scans for open ports on the target machine in a variety of ways, including the external scanner `nmap`, by running `snmpwalk`, by connecting to the `netstat` service or by running the `netstat` command on the target if it has `ssh` access, or by using an internal plugin. For each open port, the `find_service` plugin tries to identify what runs behind it; first by trying SSL connections (TLSv1, SSLv3, SSLv2), then plain connections, then by sending miscellaneous sequences to the service and looking at the answers. The `find_service` plugin stores its finding as keys in a knowledge base (KB).

Nessus then tries miscellaneous attacks on every open port. For example, if an open port is found with an HTTP or HTTPS server behind it, all plugin scripts that target web servers will be launched. Nessus probes remote services using plugins that attempt to exploit known vulnerabilities such as input validation, buffer-overflows, improper configuration, and so on.

What About…

…keeping up to date with security vulnerabilities? New software vulnerabilities are discovered daily and announced by organizations such as CERT/CC. The producers of Nessus, Tenable Network Security, provide scanner updates in the form of new plugins to check for new vulnerabilities as they are discovered. You will need to sign up for a registered feed subscription (it's free—but they capture your email address) in order to receive this. Go to *http://www.nessus.org* and click on Register. There's a long license agreement to read and a short form to fill in. An activation code is then emailed to you. Once you have this, from the command line, run:

```
# nessus-fetch --register <your activation code>
```

which will register your activation code and download all the latest plugins. (When I did this, about 7,000 new plugins were downloaded). Subsequently you should run `nessus-update-plugins` on a regular basis (perhaps as a daily `cron` job) to keep up to date.

Where to Learn More

The distribution includes manpages for the Nessus command-line tools, including `nessusd` (the actual daemon), `nessus-adduser`, `nessus-mkcert`, `nessus-fetch`, `nessus-update-plugins`, and so on. There is a limited amount of documentation in */usr/share/doc/packages/nessus-core* and */usr/share/doc/packages/nessus-libraries*, but it is mostly in the form of README-style text files. You should definitely read *usr/share/doc/packages/nessus-core/WARNING.En*. As far as I can tell, there is no user guide as such; however there is a book *Nessus Network Auditing* by Renaud Deraison et al. (Syngress).

8.7 Detect Intrusion

There are a number of tools available for Linux that can help alert you to unwanted intrusion into your system by detecting unexpected changes to the filesystem. Such tools support a reactive, as opposed to proactive, attitude to security and should not be considered a substitute for the system hardening techniques discussed elsewhere in this chapter. The idiom "closing the stable door after the horse has bolted" comes to mind here. Nonetheless, if your system has been hacked, it is much better to know than to not know. The idiom "hiding your head in the sand" also comes to mind here, and I suppose that if you were a horse-owning ostrich you could do both. But I digress.

In this lab, I'll look at an intrusion detection tool called AIDE (Advanced Intrusion Detection Environment), which is included with the SUSE Linux distribution. AIDE works by first taking an initial "snapshot" of the state of the filesystem. Subsequently, AIDE can be run to compare the current filesystem status against the snapshot, and report any discrepancies.

How Do I Do That?

Assuming that AIDE is already installed on your system (it is part of the SUSE Linux distribution; use `rpm -q aide` to check, and install it using YaST if it is not), you should begin by taking an initial snapshot of the filesystem. To do this, log in as root and run the command

```
# aide --init
```

You should do this at a time when you are confident that the system is in an uncompromised state (for example, after installing it from trusted media and performing the initial configuration, but before connecting it to a network). Because this command scans the entire filesystem it will likely take several minutes to complete.

By default, the snapshot is written to */var/lib/aide/aide.db.new*. This is a plain text file. A "snapshot" of the filesystem is not a complete binary copy, but a summary of file attributes and file contents designed to allow detection of changes. A snapshot of a file includes its name, access permissions, user and group ownership, size, time of last modification, time of last status change, inode number, link count, and one or more *digests* (cryptographic hashes) of its contents.

There is no mechanism built into AIDE itself to protect this database (using encryption for example, or by storing a digital signature offline). So the developers of AIDE recommend that you keep the snapshot on read-only media (such as a CD) along with the AIDE configuration file, which I'll discuss presently, and the AIDE executable itself. If you simply keep the snapshot in the local filesystem, a knowledgeable intruder could easily cover their tracks by rebuilding the snapshot after installing their rootkit or making other changes to the filesystem.

If you would just like to see AIDE in action, you will at minimum need to rename the snapshot from *aide.db.new* to *aide.db* because that's where the --check option of aide expects it. (Yes, that's configurable—you'll get there shortly!) Once you've done this you can run aide again in checking mode. The session might look something like this:

```
# aide --check -V
Dead symlink detected at /etc/hotplug.d/ttyUSB1/50-visor.hotplug
Dead symlink detected at /lib/modules/2.6.11.4-21.8-xen/build
Dead symlink detected at /opt/kde3/share/doc/HTML/da/k3b/common
... lots of lines edited out ...
AIDE found differences between database and filesystem!!
Start timestamp: 2005-09-15 21:29:58
Summary:
Total number of files=226210,added files=1,removed files=0,changed files=14

Added files:
added:/var/lib/aide/aide.db
Changed files:
changed:/var/log/YaST2/y2log
changed:/var/log/YaST2/y2log-1
changed:/var/log/YaST2/y2log-2
changed:/var/log/YaST2/y2log-3
changed:/var/log/YaST2/y2log-4
changed:/var/log/YaST2/y2log-5
changed:/var/log/YaST2/y2log-6
changed:/var/log/YaST2/y2log-7
changed:/var/log/YaST2/y2log-8
changed:/var/log/YaST2/y2log-9
changed:/etc
changed:/etc/cups/certs
changed:/etc/cups/certs/0
changed:/etc/passwd
Detailed information about changes:

File: /var/log/YaST2/y2log
  Inode    : 180841                              , 187369

File: /var/log/YaST2/y2log-1
  Inode    : 109851                              , 180841

File: /var/log/YaST2/y2log-2
  Inode    : 109749                              , 109851

File: /var/log/YaST2/y2log-3
  Inode    : 50698                               , 109749

File: /var/log/YaST2/y2log-4
  Inode    : 108401                              , 50698

File: /var/log/YaST2/y2log-5
  Inode    : 201921                              , 108401
```

```
File: /var/log/YaST2/y2log-6
  Inode    : 201047                        , 201921

File: /var/log/YaST2/y2log-7
  Inode    : 71618                         , 201047

File: /var/log/YaST2/y2log-8
  Inode    : 71742                         , 71618

File: /var/log/YaST2/y2log-9
  Inode    : 72581                         , 71742

Directory: /etc
  Mtime    : 2005-09-15 13:56:43           , 2005-09-15 20:51:37
  Ctime    : 2005-09-15 13:56:43           , 2005-09-15 20:51:37

Directory: /etc/cups/certs
  Mtime    : 2005-09-15 17:55:48           , 2005-09-15 21:26:32
  Ctime    : 2005-09-15 17:55:48           , 2005-09-15 21:26:32

File: /etc/cups/certs/0
  Mtime    : 2005-09-15 17:55:48           , 2005-09-15 21:26:32
  Ctime    : 2005-09-15 17:55:48           , 2005-09-15 21:26:32
  Inode    : 187219                        , 187668
  MD5      : Hkbdds5p9A/OC1NyDeJAhw==      , xAy49xSXJ42MkBG8aGPlbQ==
  SHA1     : ZojOw5ZZU32a9VpQ+WlmyhRb/Xw=  , QnBQBjEA94BeRhRlcKXFKJHg3Qc=

File: /etc/passwd
  Size     : 1779                          , 1781
  Mtime    : 2005-08-30 14:47:11           , 2005-09-15 20:51:37
  Ctime    : 2005-08-30 14:47:11           , 2005-09-15 20:51:37
  Inode    : 48258                         , 187658
  MD5      : PnKFC2HwMHvZ5ni/ZySC9w==      , r1uMTWBw/2f58oNBxguMMw==
  SHA1     : r5EvUXv9/jtf+2+WtrnWuK1t9qI=  , Jdok56xkiXjs+7eiyxAook9FrU4=
```

Most of the changes in this report relate to YaST's rotation of its log files. One new file was detected (*/var/lib/aide/aide.db*) which was to be expected. The only real changes that were detected were to the files */etc/cups/certs/0* and */etc/passwd*. (I edited the latter on purpose to force it to appear in the report.)

Now that you've seen the basic operation of AIDE, let's take a look at its configuration file, */etc/aide.conf*. The main purpose of this file is to specify which directories and files AIDE should include in its check, and for each of those directories, specify what file properties it should monitor. There are predefined symbols for each of these properties, as shown in Table 8-2.

Table 8-2. AIDE properties

Property name	Meaning
p	permissions
i	inode number
n	number of links

Table 8-2. AIDE properties (continued)

Property name	Meaning
u	user (owner)
g	group
s	size
b	block count
m	time of last modification
a	time of last access
c	time of last status change
S	check for growing size
md5	md5 checksum
sha1	sha1 checksum
R	p+i+n+u+g+s+m+c+md5
L	p+i+n+u+g
E	empty group

You can also define your own property sets with lines in the config file, like this:

```
Binlib      = p+i+n+u+g+s+b+m+c+md5+sha1
Logs        = p+i+n+u+g+S
```

This defines two property sets. The first is called `Binlib` and comprises essentially every file property, including its md5 and sha1 digests. The only property missing from this list is a, the time of last access. This property set is appropriate for system executables and libraries, which shouldn't change at all. The property set `Logs` is more relaxed; this is for files that are allowed to grow in size. (Note the difference between the properties s and S—the former is for files whose size should not change, the latter is for files that are allowed to grow.) This property set is appropriate for log files.

> I assume that the a property (time of last access) is just there for sake of completeness, but I can't see when you'd want to use it. It seems to me that if you want AIDE to report when a file was merely *accessed*, you might be better advised to encrypt the file or move it somewhere secure.

Okay, now we get to the hard part—the rules that actually determine which pieces of the filesystem AIDE will check, and what checks it will make. Most rules are fairly simple. For example, the rule:

```
/lib     Binlib
```

means that AIDE will check the entire filesystem under */lib*, using the `Binlib` property set defined earlier. In other words, I want AIDE to report any changes to any file under */lib*.

When AIDE is checking the filesystem, the left-hand side of the rule (*/lib* in the example) is matched against the file names as a regular expression that is implicitly anchored to the beginning of the name. Thus, a left-hand side such as */lib* will match */lib/libc.so.6* and */lib/security/pam_unix.so*, but it won't match */var/lib/locatedb*. You can anchor a match to the end of the name using $; so, for example a left-hand side such as `/tmp$` will match only `/tmp` and nothing else. You can exclude matching names by prefixing the rule with !, so for example the rule

    !/.*/BACKUP

will exclude any *BACKUP* directories wherever they appear in the filesystem.

There is a sample AIDE configuration file included with SUSE Linux that provides "reasonable" rules. It is certainly far preferable to run AIDE with this default rule set than not to run it at all. But it's better still to give some thought to your own circumstances and come up with your own security policy and your own rule sets. To quote the developers:

> It is generally a good idea to ignore directories that frequently change, unless you want to read long reports. It is good practice to exclude tmp directories, mail spools, log directories, proc filesystems, users' home directories, web content directories, anything that changes regularly. It is good practice to include all system binaries, libraries, include files, and system source files.

The problem with being over-cautious (i.e., making too many or too stringent checks) is that you get a lot of false positives, resulting in a long report from AIDE in which any real problems may be hard to spot, or, worse, make the report so daunting that you don't read it at all.

There are a few other directives that can go into the config file that control the behavior of the program as a whole. Some of them are shown in Table 8-3.

Table 8-3. AIDE config file directives

Parameter	Meaning
database	The filename from which the database is read; for example, when doing a --check. Filenames are specified using a URL-like syntax; for example, *file:/var/lib/aide/aide.db*.
database_out	The file name that the new database is written to.
verbose	Controls the level of detail of the messages written by aide. Value in range 1–255. Can be overridden by -V command line flag.
report_url	The filename that the report is written to. The default is stdout.
warn_dead_symlinks	Boolean parameter that controls whether AIDE will report broken symbolic links.

Here's the entire sample config file provided with the AIDE distribution, minus a few commented-out lines:

```
# Configuration parameters
#
database=file:/var/lib/aide/aide.db
database_out=file:/var/lib/aide/aide.db.new
```

```
verbose=1
report_url=stdout
warn_dead_symlinks=yes
#
# Custom rules
#
Binlib          = p+i+n+u+g+s+b+m+c+md5+sha1
ConfFiles       = p+i+n+u+g+s+b+m+c+md5+sha1
Logs            = p+i+n+u+g+S
Devices         = p+i+n+u+g+s+b+c+md5+sha1
Databases       = p+n+u+g
StaticDir       = p+i+n+u+g
ManPages        = p+i+n+u+g+s+b+m+c+md5+sha1

#
# Directories and files
#
# Kernel, system map, etc.
/boot                           Binlib

# watch config files, but exclude, what changes at boot time, ...
!/etc/mtab
!/etc/lvm*
/etc                            ConfFiles

# Binaries
/bin                            Binlib
/sbin                           Binlib

# Libraries
/lib                            Binlib

# Complete /usr and /opt
/usr                            Binlib
/opt                            Binlib

# Log files
/var/log$                       StaticDir
/var/log                        Logs

# Devices
!/dev/pts
/dev                            Devices

# Other miscellaneous files
/var/run$                       StaticDir
!/var/run
/var/lib                        Databases

# Test only the directory when dealing with /proc
/proc$                          StaticDir
!/proc
```

At the risk of stating the obvious, as an intrusion detection technique, AIDE is effective only if it is run on a regular basis (such as once a day, perhaps as a cron job) and if someone actually looks at the output. Judicious use of `grep` can help remove some irrelevancies from the report, but ultimately it needs to be examined on a daily basis by a real person.

What About...

...other intrusion detection products? Probably the best established tool for filesystem scanning and intrusion detection is tripwire. Tripwire began life at Purdue University in 1992 and was originally released under a license that allowed free redistribution. Since then the tool has moved into the commercial domain (see *http://www.tripwire.org*). Free binaries for Linux have in the past been available and were included, for example, in some RedHat distributions, but these no longer seem to be available and Tripwire is certainly not included in the SUSE Linux distribution. There is an open-source version of tripwire hosted at *http://sourceforge.net/projects/tripwire*, although the latest release there appears to be in 2001. Anyway, Tripwire works in a very similar way to AIDE. It has a policy file with a syntax not dissimilar to AIDE's configuration file. One important feature of Tripwire is the ability to encrypt the policy file and the database, to prevent unauthorized tampering with these by an intruder with root access trying to cover his tracks.

Other intrusion detection tools for Linux include `viperdb` and `integrit`.

Where to Learn More

There is relatively little coverage of AIDE in the current security text books. There is a manual of sorts at *http://www.cs.tut.fi/~rammer/aide/manual.html*. The project is currently hosted by SourceForge at *http://sourceforge.net/projects/aide*. You can of course read the manpages for `aide` and `aide.conf`, though the description of the file name matching rules seems to contradict itself in places.

8.8 Protect Your Applications with AppArmor

AppArmor is a product that Novell acquired when they bought the company Immunix in May 2005. It provides an interesting alternative to traditional security measures. AppArmor works by *profiling* the applications that it is protecting. A profile records the files that an application needs to access, and the capabilities it needs to exercise, during normal, "good" operation. Subsequently, a profile can be "enforced"; that is, attempts by the application to access resources not explicitly permitted by the profile are denied. Properly configured, AppArmor ensures that each profiled application is allowed to do what it is supposed to do, and nothing else.

The documentation uses the metaphor of "immunizing" the applications, but the product does not actually prevent an application from being infected or compromised. Rather, it limits the damage that an application can do if this should happen.

If we must have a medical metaphor, "quarantine" might be better, or you might think of it as offering the program a large white handkerchief to sneeze into to prevent it from spreading germs.

AppArmor was originally a closed-source product, but became open source in January 2006. It is included with SUSE Linux 10.1 and with SLES9 SP3. It was also included with SUSE Linux 10.0, but the profiling tool was deliberately restricted in scope and required the purchase of a license file to become fully functional.

How Do I Do That?

To give you a feel for how AppArmor works, in this lab I'll use it to profile and contain a very simple C program. Whilst this example is undeniably simplistic, it does help to show how AppArmor actually works.

Here's the program that you will profile. It's called `scribble`, because it scribbles on files:

```
#include <stdio.h>

int main(int argc, char *argv[])
{
    int i;
    FILE *fd;
    for (i=1; i<argc; i++) {
        fd = fopen(argv[i], "w");
        if (fd == NULL) {
            fprintf(stderr, "fopen failed for %s\n", argv[i]);
            return 1;
        }
        fprintf(fd, "scribbled on file %s\n", argv[i]);
        fclose(fd);
    }
}
```

If you can't read C, don't worry, it doesn't really matter. The program loops over its command-line arguments, treating each as a filename. For each one, it tries to open the file for writing, writes a line of text to it, then closes the file. If it can't open the file, it prints an error message. I created the source file *scribble.c* in my home directory and compiled it with:

```
$ cc scribble.c -o scribble
```

Before proceeding further, you must ensure that the `apparmor` module is loaded into the kernel. To do this, run the following command as root:

```
# rcapparmor start
```

To build a profile for this application, you can use YaST. From YaST's main screen, select Novell AppArmor from the panel on the left, then Add Profile Wizard from the panel on the right. On the wizard's first screen, you're invited to enter the name of the application you want to profile. Since I built scribble in my home directory, I entered the name /home/chris/scribble then clicked Create. On the next screen, you're invited to "start the application to be profiled in another window and exercise its functionality now". The idea is to run the program and make it do the full range of things that it is "supposed to do". In this case, I simply ran my little program with the command:

```
$ ./scribble apple orange /tmp/banana
```

causing it to open and write to three files. As the program runs, AppArmor records each resource that is accessed in the system log, /var/log/messages. You can run the program as many times as you want to get a complete, representative profile. When you're done profiling, click the button labeled "Scan system log for AppArmor events." Now we're taken one by one through the events that AppArmor logged. For each one, AppArmor makes suggestions about what should be added to the profile. An example is shown in Figure 8-9.

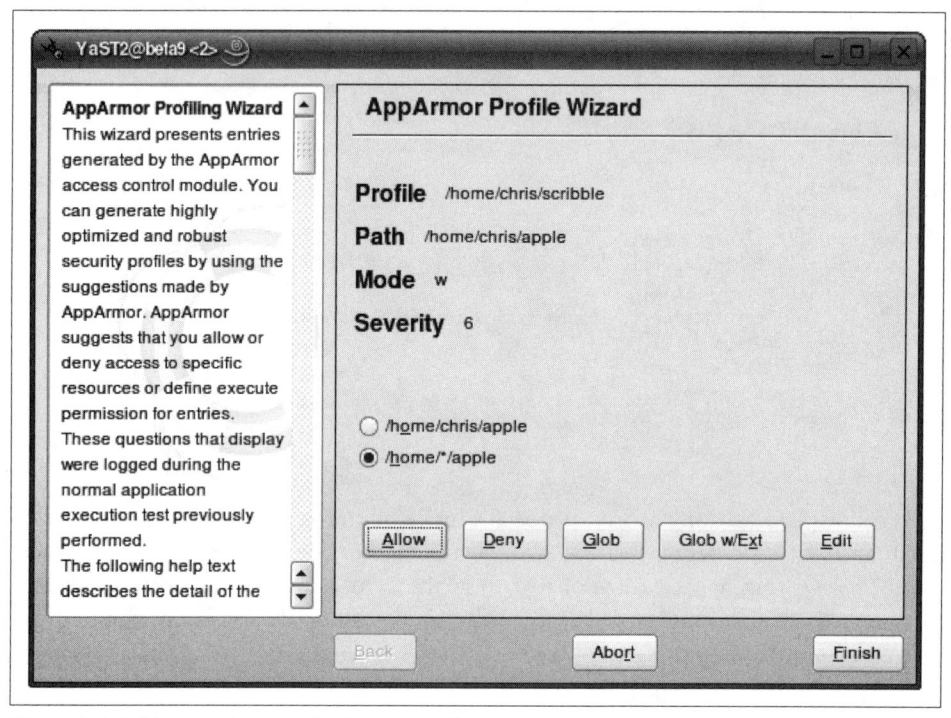

Figure 8-9. Adding a rule to an AppArmor profile

In this figure, the program's action of writing to the file /home/chris/apple has been noted and you're offered a number of choices of what should be added to the profile to allow this. This is where you need to put your thinking cap on. One of the options is to allow access just to that one file: /home/chris/apple. Another option proposed by AppArmor is a generalization—namely, to allow writing to a file called *apple* in any user's home directory (/home/*/apple). Clicking the Glob but-

ton will suggest a still broader rule to add to the profile; in this case */home/*/**.
("Glob" is short for "globbing," a slang Unix expression relating to the use of filename wildcards.) The button labeled "Glob w/Ext" will broaden the pattern using a * wildcard, but retain the filename extension. For example, */home/chris/testimage.png* would be broadened to */home/chris/*.png*. Obviously, you need to make your own judgment here about what makes sense for the application. Having selected an appropriate rule, click Allow to add it to the profile, or click Deny if you don't want it added to the profile. You'll need to proceed event by event through the activities that AppArmor has logged in order to complete the profile.

Once the profile is built, AppArmor will automatically begin to enforce it. If I now try to use `scribble` to write to a file that's within the profile, all is well, but if I try to access a file that's not in the profile, it fails:

```
$ ./scribble apple
$ ./scribble mango
fopen failed for mango
```

The restrictions imposed by AppArmor are, of course, in addition to those imposed by the underlying filesystem. For example,

```
$ ./scribble /etc/passwd
```

will fail regardless of AppArmor, because I don't have write permission on the file.

Profiling needs to be done with care. Too tight a profile means that the application can't do its job. For example, one version of AppArmor I tested shipped with a profile for the PDF viewer acroread, which, if enforced, prevented Adobe Acrobat Reader from viewing the AppArmor documentation!

How It Works

AppArmor installs a module into the Linux kernel that monitors resource usage of programs according to their profiles. A profile can be interpreted in one of two modes: enforce mode, and complain (or learning) mode. In complain mode (used by the create profile wizard), AppArmor logs a line to */var/log/audit/audit.log* through the kernel logging daemon `klogd` for each resource that the application accesses. Here's a typical entry:

```
type=APPARMOR msg=audit(1144091465.305:6): PERMITTING w access to /home/chris/apple
(scribble(26781) profile /home/chris/scribble active /home/chris/scribble)
```

In the second stage of profile generation, the profile wizard works its way through these lines, prompting you for the rules to be added. Behind the scenes, the utility `logprof` does the work here. (`logprof` can also be used to build the profile from the command line instead of using the YaST wizard.)

In enforce mode, system calls made by the process for resources not explicitly allowed by the profile will fail (and a message will be logged to */var/log/messages*).

The profiles are stored in the directory /etc/apparmor.d. They are loaded into the kernel by the program `apparmor_parser`. The profile for my little /home/chris/scribble application is written to the file home.chris.scribble. The profile I generated looks like this. The line numbers are for reference; they are not part of the file.

```
1  # Last Modified: Wed Dec  7 15:13:39 2005
2  /home/chris/scribble {
3    #include <abstractions/base>
4
5    /home/chris/orange w,
6    /home/chris/scribble r,
7    /tmp/banana w,
8  }
```

Line 2 (along with the matching bracket on line 8) defines the application that this profile applies to. Line 3 includes the contents of the file /etc/apparmor.d/abstractions/base. AppArmor uses a lot of #include files to factor out common sets of access requirements into separate files. For example there are #include files for access to audio devices, for authentication, and for access to name servers. The *abstractions/base* file referenced here is largely to do with allowing access to shared libraries. Lines 5–7 are the rules for this specific application.

To profile an application in complain mode, add the notation `flags=(complain)` to line 2 of the profile, so that it reads:

```
/home/chris/scribble flags=(complain) {
```

You can also do this from the command line using:

```
# complain /etc/subdomain.d/home.chris.scribble
```

and you can set the profile back to enforce mode with:

```
# enforce /etc/subdomain.d/home.chris.scribble
```

Using `complain` and `enforce` also loads the new profile into the kernel.

AppArmor refers to the type of profiling I just performed as *standalone* profiling. It also supports *systemic* profiling, which puts all the profiles into complain mode and allows you to run them over many hours or days (even across reboots) to collect as complete a profile as possible.

The range of resource requests that AppArmor can allow or deny is broader than the simple file access checks used in this example. For example, it's also capable of restricting program execution (via the exec system call). Table 8-4 shows some example of profile rules to give you some idea of what's possible.

Table 8-4. Example profile rules

Example	Description
/etc/ld.so.cache r,	The file can be read.
/var/run/myprog.pid rw,	The file can be read and written.

Table 8-4. Example profile rules (continued)

Example	Description
/etc/apache2/* r,	All files in /etc/apache2 can be read.
/srv/www/htdocs/** r,	All files in (and below) htdocs can be read.
/tmp/myprog.* l,	The program can create and remove links with this name.
/bin/mount ux	The program can execute /bin/mount which will run unconstrained; that is, without an AppArmor profile.
/usr/bin/procmail px	The program can execute procmail, which will run under constraint of its own profile.
/usr/bin/sendmail ix	The program can execute sendmail, which will inherit the profile of the current program.

Earlier versions of AppArmor included rules that restricted the establishment of UDP and TCP connections. These rules have been removed from the current version of the product, but may be restored in a future version.

What About...

...deciding what to profile? AppArmor is not intended to provide protection against execution of ordinary tools run by ordinary users. You already have the classic Linux security model in place to constrain the activities of such programs. AppArmor is intended for use on servers which typically have few or no regular user accounts. Indeed, there is no way to define user-specific profiles in AppArmor, and there is no concept of a role.

AppArmor should be used to constrain programs that (quoting the user guide) "mediate privilege"; that is, programs that have access to resources that the person using the program does not have. Examples of such programs include:

- Programs that run setuid or setgid (i.e., which run with the identity of the program's owner or group). You can find programs that run setuid to root with the command:

    # find / -user root -perm -4000

- Programs run as cron jobs. You can find these by ferreting around in the crontab files in directories such as /etc/cron.d, /etc/cron.daily, /etc/cron.weekly, and so on.
- Web applications; for example, CGI scripts or PHP pages invoked by a web server.
- Network applications that have open ports. AppArmor provides a little utility called unconfined that uses the output from netstat -nlp to identify programs that are currently running with open network ports, but which currently have no profile.

Where to Learn More

For a brief but more technical overview, read the `apparmor` manpage. For full details of the syntax of the profile files, read the `apparmor.d` manpage.

There's an interesting comparison of containment technologies such as chroot, Xen, selinux, and AppArmor at *http://crispincowan.com/~crispin/TUT304_final.sxi*.

In SUSE Linux 10.0, there is a detailed user guide at */usr/share/doc/packages/subdomain-docs/ug_apparmor.pdf*. Although it's thorough, it is rather labored and has a decidedly non-open-source feel; it even contains the immortal line "contact your sales representative for more information." This guide has been removed in SUSE Linux 10.1, but documentation is available by following the links from *http://en.opensuse.org/Documentation*.

CHAPTER 9

Alternative Installations

In Chapter 1, I discussed how to install SUSE Linux in some detail. At one end of the scale, you can do the job with almost no thought whatsoever by booting off the installation DVD and repeatedly clicking Next until you end up with a working system. At the other end of the scale, there are a number of more complex scenarios you may need to deal with, and it is these that I discuss in this chapter.

You'll see how to configure a dual-boot system to retain the option of booting into Windows. You'll learn how to set up an installation server to facilitate installation over the network instead of from local disk media. You'll discover how to automate installations entirely by preparing a control file that captures the decisions that you would normally make manually during an installation. Finally, I'll show you how to use Xen (a "paravirtualization" technology) to install and run multiple operating systems—simultaneously—on one machine.

9.1 Configure a Dual-Boot System

Some of us Linux enthusiasts would like to imagine that users migrating to a Linux desktop actually throw their Windows installations away, with looks of rapture like someone newly converted to The Faith turning away from their erstwhile sinful existence. In reality, few of us can leave our Windows systems behind completely. You probably still need some applications that run only on Windows—that program your friend gave you for doing your VAT returns, and the cross-stitch design program your wife uses, not to mention that flight simulator you're rather partial to. There are several ways that you can retain the ability to run Windows applications after migrating to Linux. In some cases, you can install and run the apps over Linux using Crossover Office (a product based on the wine library). Or, you may decide to install Windows inside a VMware virtual machine hosted on Linux. (This is actually my preferred solution, but it needs plenty of memory and doesn't support graphics-intensive applications such as games.) But the most common solution is probably to create a dual-boot installation in which Windows and Linux exist side-by-side on the hard drive, each in its own partition, so that you can choose which to boot when you power on.

In this lab, you'll see how to create a typical dual-boot system using Windows XP and SUSE Linux.

How Do I Do That?

The most important piece of advice I have is: put the Windows installation on first. The Linux installer will recognize existing Windows partitions and take them into account. It will automatically put an entry into the grub configuration file to allow you the option of booting into Windows, and it will put entries into */etc/fstab* so that the Windows partitions are automatically mounted into the Linux filesystem at boot time. Doing it the other way around is more problematic.

There are two scenarios to consider. The first is when you're starting from scratch installing both operating systems onto an empty machine. When you do the install of Windows XP, you should explicitly set the size of the partition it will install into. Its default behavior is to use all the free space on the drive. It's up to you to determine how best to split the disk space between Windows and Linux. Another point to consider is that Linux supports read/write access to FAT filesystems, but only read access to NTFS filesystems. If you are intending to share your main user file area between Windows and Linux, you may prefer to specify a FAT filesystem.

Once the Windows installation is complete, insert your SUSE Linux installation media and reboot to install it. During its probe of the disk, the installer will notice the existing Windows partitions and propose a partition scheme that takes this into account. See Figure 9-1.

Notice that the installer has chosen to leave the Windows partition hda1 alone, and to use hda2 and hda3 for Linux. It has also proposed the creation of mount points for the Windows partition (and a USB memory stick, sda1, which I left in by accident). Once the installation is complete, you should find that when you reboot, the option to boot Windows is included on the boot menu and that the windows partition ("drive C," in Windows-speak) has been mounted on */windows/C*.

> If you have an old PC with a BIOS that can't read beyond cylinder 1023 on the drive, you may run into trouble if your Windows partition pushes the files in */boot* beyond that boundary, because the boot loader relies on the BIOS to read the kernel image and the initial ram disk image at boot time.

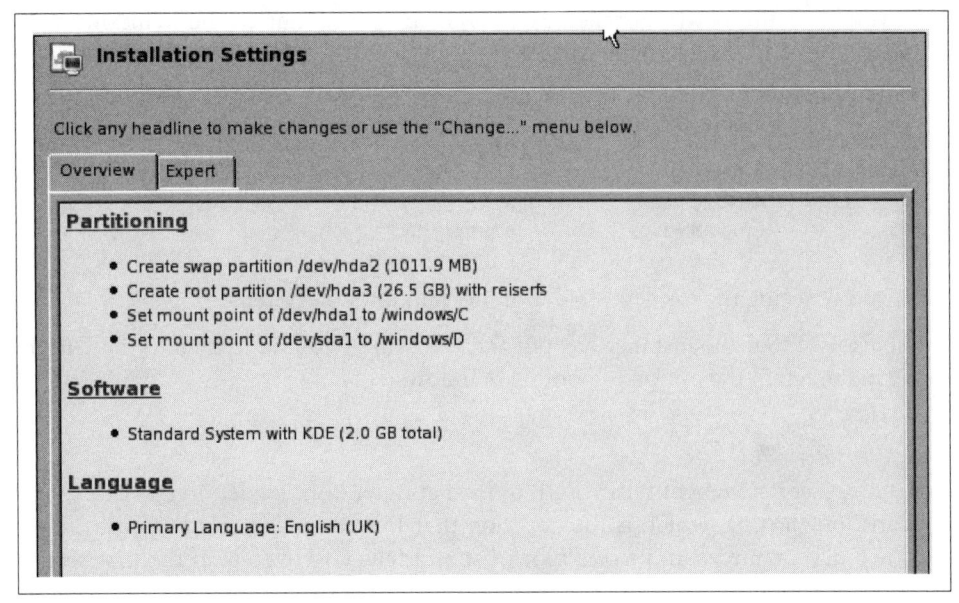

Figure 9-1. Partitioning proposal for dual-boot installation

How It Works

SUSE uses the *etc/fstab* file to control how the Windows partitions are mounted while you're running Linux, and the grub configuration file (*/boot/grub/menu.lst*) to make your Windows partition available on the boot menu.

Let's look at the entries that the installer put into */etc/fstab*:

```
/dev/hda1    /windows/C    ntfs    ro,users,gid=users,umask=0002,nls=utf8 0 0
/dev/sda1    /windows/D    vfat    users,gid=users,umask=0002,utf8=true 0 0
```

The mount options on the first command are as follows:

ro
> Mount read-only (Linux cannot safely write to NTFS filesystems).

users
> Allow (nonroot) users to mount this filesystem.

gid=users
> Pretend that the files are owned by the group *users*. (Remember, these are files in an NTFS filesystem which knows nothing of Linux users and groups.)

umask=0002
> Controls the access permission bits that the files appear to have. The value is a bitmask in octal and works "upside down"; that is, bits set in umask will be cleared in the file's permission set. In this case, the umask is suppressing "world write" permission on the files.

After you boot the newly installed SUSE system, the mount of the Windows filesystem is indeed in place, as you can see:

```
# ls /windows/C
.              Documents and Settings  System Volume Information
..             IO.SYS                   WINDOWS
AUTOEXEC.BAT   MSDOS.SYS                boot.ini
CONFIG.SYS     NTDETECT.COM             ntldr
DELL           Program Files            pagefile.sys
```

Here, you're seeing the top-level folder of the Windows filesystem.

You'll also see that the installer has put the following two-line entry into the GRUB config file to retain the option of booting Windows:

```
title Windows
    chainloader (hd0,0)+1
```

The `chainloader` statement tells GRUB to load another boot loader, in this case from the partition (hd0,0), which is the partition that Linux would refer to as hda1. The "+1" is a degenerate example of a block list and tells GRUB to load the first sector from that partition.

What About...

...the case where Windows is already installed on your computer? This is the most likely scenario. If your existing Windows installation has left sufficient unpartitioned space on the disk to create the Linux partitions, then it's easy—you can proceed as shown in this lab. But this is unlikely to be the case—most Windows installations use the entire disk. This is where the going gets tougher. It is not possible to install SUSE Linux into free space within a Windows filesystem. You need free *unpartitioned* space on the hard drive to create your Linux partitions (at minimum, a root partition and a swap partition). It is, however, possible to resize the Windows partition (assuming that there is free space, of course) to make room for Linux. Before you embark on this process you *must* back up the important files on your Windows system. I have seen Windows filesystems entirely destroyed by attempts to resize them.

Opinions differ on whether it is necessary to compact (defragment) the Windows filesystem prior to resizing it. The documentation for the latest version of the resizer used by YaST claims this is not necessary, but I have generally done so. For example, to do this in Windows XP, open Windows Explorer, right-click the hard drive (C:) and select Properties. Select the Tools tab and click Defragment Now. Click Analyze to examine the current disk fragmentation, followed by Defragment to compact the filesystem towards the beginning of the partition. I have had mixed success with this. Defragmentation of a large partition that has seen a lot of action (and is therefore badly fragmented) can take well over an hour, and I have in the past found it necessary to carry out the process two or three times to get good compaction.

> You may have better success if you first disable the paging file in Windows, as Windows won't defragment it, and also disable hibernation to delete the hibernation file, too. Then, you can do the defragmentation and resize the partition (making sure you leave enough space for the two files to be recreated of course). You can reenable the page file and hibernation the next time you boot into Windows.

Assuming you've been able to successfully compact your Windows filesystem, you're ready to install SUSE Linux. The installer, noticing that you have a Windows partition filling the disk, will offer to resize it for you. (See Figure 9-2.)

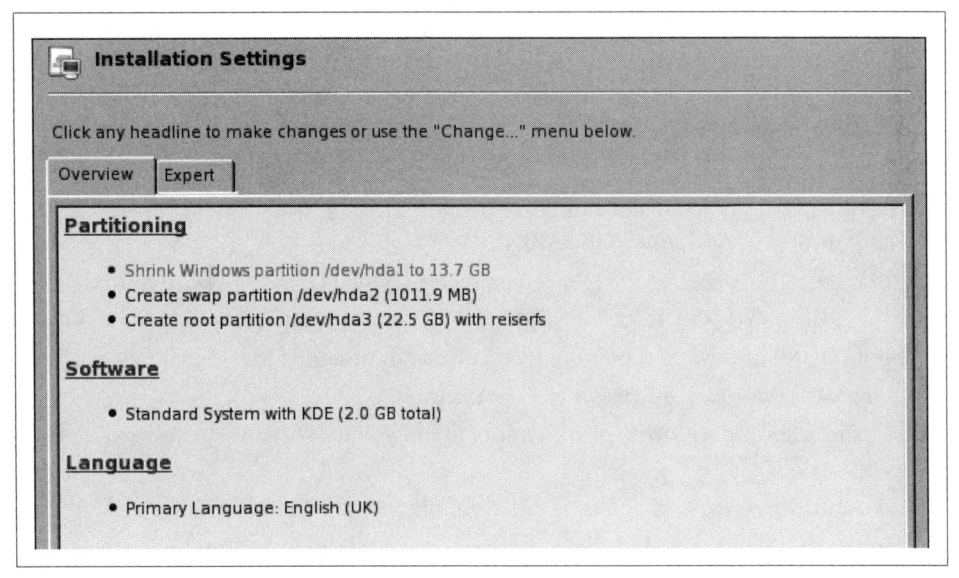

Figure 9-2. Shrinking a Windows partition

In the figure, the installer has offered to shrink the Windows partition to 13.7 GB. (It's not clear where it got this figure from, and you can't edit it, though you can, as usual, edit the sizes of any new Linux partitions the installer is proposing to create.) Once the partition has been resized, creation of the remaining partitions and installation should proceed as normal. Be aware that a standard SUSE Linux installation will replace the master boot record (MBR) of the hard drive.

To resize the NTFS partition, YaST uses a tool called `ntfsresize`, which is part of the `ntfsprogs` packages, included with the SUSE Linux distribution. This tool is also available as part of the SUSE Linux "rescue boot" image, in case you need to run it standalone. To do this, perform a rescue boot from CD1 then enter a command such as:

```
# ntfsresize -if /dev/hda1
```

This command will report a recommended minimum size to which the filesystem can be resized. Then you can resize the filesystem; in this example to 5 GB:

```
# ntfsresize -s 5000M /dev/hda1
```

> ntfsresize resizes only the filesystem, it doesn't resize the partition. You would need to use fdisk or an equivalent tool to do that. Delete the partition, then recreate it with the same partition type (usually 7) and the same starting cylinder and with the new, reduced size. Don't make it smaller than you resized your NTFS filesystem to.

It's also possible to retain the Windows boot loader in the master boot record and use that to boot into Linux or Windows, but this way is a good deal messier to set up. Some writers have reported problems booting Windows with anything other than the Windows boot loader in the master boot record. Although I used to have this problem with Windows NT, I have not had trouble booting Windows XP with GRUB in the MBR. If you really need to do this, proceed as follows:

1. Make sure that you install Linux with the first stage boot loader written to the Linux root partition, *not* to the MBR.
2. Boot your Linux system using a rescue CD (SUSE CD1 should work fine).
3. Peel off the first 512 bytes of your Linux partition (this contains the partition boot record) and write them to a file. The dd command is ideal for this:

   ```
   # dd if=/dev/hda2 of=linux.bin bs=512 count=1
   ```

4. Put this file onto a floppy or a memory stick—somewhere you can read it from Windows.
5. Boot into windows and copy the *linux.bin* file into the Windows partition.
6. Modify the Windows file *boot.ini* to add a new boot option. You'll need to add a line something like this:

   ```
   C:\linux.bin="Linux"
   ```

Other dual-boot scenarios are possible; for example SUSE and RedHat, or SUSE and FreeBSD, or just two versions of SUSE. Just remember to leave unpartitioned space when you do the first installation. Also, you might want to save a copy of the GRUB config file from the first installation, and if necessary copy the appropriate stanza into the config file of the new installation so that you can boot them both. You should be able to share a single swap partition between multiple Linux installations, because you can boot only one at a time, but beware that since "suspend to disk" writes the memory image into the swap space you won't be able to suspend system A, boot system B, then resume system A. You may also find it appropriate to put */home* onto a separate partition and share it amongst the installations, although you may find some conflict amongst the desktop configuration files.

Where to Learn More

For information on the ntfsprogs suite of programs, read the ntfsprogs manual page and the manpages for the individual programs. There are a couple of HOWTO documents about dual booting (neither very recent) available at *http://www.tldp.org/ HOWTO*. There's an article that focuses on the use of GRUB in dual-boot scenarios at *http://geodsoft.com/howto/dualboot/grub.htm*.

9.2 Install from an Installation Server

If you have many machines to install, and if they're all on your network, you may find it convenient to configure a machine as an installation server and pull the installation from the server, rather than using local DVDs or CDs. This is especially helpful for machines that have no DVD drive (or won't boot from DVD) because it saves shuffling the CDs around during the installation. Once you have initiated an installation, you can walk away from it. This lab first examines how to configure the installation server, then shows how to launch a network installation.

You can set up an installation server on any machine able to support NFS, FTP, or HTTP—it doesn't have to be a Linux machine. But as this book's interest lies in SUSE Linux, I use that as the basis of the installation server.

How Do I Do That?

You can configure an installation server using YaST. To do this, you'll need to have the package yast2-instserver installed. You can check this using:

```
$ rpm -q yast2-instserver
```

If it isn't installed, install it now using YaST → Software → Software Management (Lab 5.3, "Install and Upgrade RPMs" in Chapter 5 shows how to do this). Once the package is installed, quit and restart YaST, then go to YaST → Miscellaneous → Installation Server.

At the Installation Server screen, click Server Configuration. As you will see from the "Initial Setup—Servers" screen, you can build your server to use NFS, FTP, or HTTP. Whichever you choose, YaST will try to configure the relevant service to make the installation images available (unless you check the box labeled "Do not configure any network services"). Also on this screen, specify the directory where you want to put the CD images. This is entirely up to you—but choose a directory on a partition with plenty of free space. In this lab, I configure the server as an HTTP source and put the CD images into the directory */installroot*.

On the next screen, provide the name of an *alias* that will be used by the HTTP server to reference the installation root directory. This name will form part of the URL that you'll specify when you launch the installation on the target machine. In this lab, I use the name suse.

Now click on Add. Enter a source name that describes the version of SUSE Linux you're loading the installation images for; for example "suse93". The installation images will be created in a subdirectory of this name under the installation root. In this example, this directory will be */installroot/suse93*.

> The idea behind this naming scheme is that you can carry installation images for several different SUSE Linux versions; for example, you could put SUSE Professional in */installroot/suse93* and SLES9 in `/installroot/sles9`.

Checking the box labeled "Announce as installation server with SLP" will make it easier to find the server, as it will automatically announce itself on the network. The target systems are just booted using the SLP boot option and should find the network installation source without any further configuration.

At the Source Configuration screen, you now have two choices: you can copy the data from the installation CDs or DVD, or you can use the ISO CD images, if you have them. (You can download the ISO images from *http://download.novell.com* or from *http://www.opensuse.org*, but keep in mind that there are five of them and each is about 670 MB). In this lab, I show how to install from CDs. On the next screen, you'll be prompted to insert the CDs in order. It's not absolutely necessary to load all the CDs—it depends on how full an installation you're going to be doing on your target machines—but the only way I know of figuring this out is to do a real installation from CD and record which disks it asks for. If you don't want to load all the CDs, click Cancel.

With all the CDs loaded, back at the Installation Server screen, you should see your new installation source listed in the lower panel. Click Finish to complete the job.

Now take a look at the contents of */installroot/suse93*:

```
$ ls /installroot/suse93/
ARCHIVES.gz   COPYRIGHT                        INDEX.gz        media.4
autorun.inf   COPYRIGHT.de                     LICENSE.TXT     media.5
boot          directory.yast                   LIESMICH        pubring.gpg
ChangeLog     docu                             LIESMICH.DOS    README
content       dosutils                         ls-lR.gz        README.DOS
control.xml   gpg-pubkey-0dfb3188-41ed929b.asc media.1         suse
COPYING       gpg-pubkey-3d25d3d9-36e12d04.asc media.2         SuSEgo.ico
COPYING.de    gpg-pubkey-9c800aca-40d8063e.asc media.3
```

YaST will also have configured the Apache web server to serve this directory. Take a look at */etc/apache2/conf.d/inst_server.conf*; it will be something like this:

```
# httpd configuration for Installation Server included by httpd.conf
<IfDefine inst_server>
    Alias /suse /installroot
    <Directory /installroot>
```

400 | Chapter 9: Alternative Installations

```
        Options +Indexes +FollowSymLinks
        IndexOptions +NameWidth=*

        Order allow,deny
        Allow from all

    </Directory>
</IfDefine>
```

The key line here is:

```
Alias /suse /installroot
```

which tells Apache that a URL such as `http://this_server/suse` should refer to the *installroot* directory on the server.

You will, of course, need to ensure that Apache is actually running. You can start it manually (as root) with the command rcapache2 start. Also, unless you are already running Apache on your installation server, chances are that you will need to open up the firewall on the server to allow the HTTP traffic through. (See Lab 8.3, "Set Up a Firewall," for details on how to do this.)

So much for building the server. How do you actually do a network installation on a target machine? The first thing you'll need is a network boot CD. You can download a suitable ISO image from, for example, *ftp://ftp.suse.com/pub/suse/i386/9.3/boot/boot.iso*. This is a 58 MB download. Then, burn it to CD using K3b. (See Lab 3.8, "Burn Your Own CDs and DVDs," for details on how to do this.)

You can avoid the need to download the CD image by making your own, using the installation image you just created. Proceed as follows:

```
$ cd ~
$ cp -a /installroot/suse93/boot/loader ~
$ chmod -R u+w loader
$ cd loader
$ mkisofs -o ../install.iso -b isolinux.bin -c boot.cat \
    -no-emul-boot -boot-load-size 4 -boot-info-table .
```

Note the presence of the . (meaning "the current directory") at the end of the mkisofs command, and the use of ~ to refer to your home directory. Now you should have an ISO image called *install.iso* in your home directory, which you can burn to CD as before.

Now boot the target machine from the CD you just created. At the initial menu screen, press F3, then select HTTP. (SUSE Linux 10.1 adds an extra layer to the menus. You need to press F3, then F4.) At the HTTP Installation screen, enter the IP address of your installation server and the name of the directory that you loaded the images into. In our case, this is suse/suse93 (remember, "suse" is an alias for */installroot* in the Apache web server). Press Enter to start the installation. The installation will proceed as normal, except that of course you won't have to insert the CDs.

If you have many machines to install from your boot CD, you can change the actual boot menu to do a network install. Before building the ISO image, edit the file *isolinux.cfg* in your *~/loader* directory and add something like `install=http://192.168.0.17/suse/suse93` to the end of the "append" line in the section with the label "linux." (Here, 192.168.0.17 is the IP address of the installation server.)

What About...

...installing from ISO images? You have two options here. You can copy content from the ISO images into the */installroot* directory using YaST → Misc → Installation Server, much as you did for the CDs. Alternatively, you can ignore YaST and simply perform a loopback mount of the ISO image onto some suitable directory. If you have access to an ISO image of the DVD, it's rather easy. In the following example, I mount the image *SUSE-10.1-DVD-GM-DVD1.iso* onto */mnt/suse101*:

```
# mkdir /mnt/suse101
# mount -o loop ~/isos/SUSE-10.1-DVD-GM-DVD1.iso /mnt/suse101
```

Then create a file in the directory */etc/apache2/conf.d* to make this available. The file will need to look something like this:

```
<Directory /mnt/suse101>
  Options +Indexes +FollowSymLinks
  IndexOptions +NameWidth=*
  Order allow,deny
  Allow from all
</Directory>
```

If you have only the CD ISOs, you need to add some extra files and symlinks. Here are the commands you'll need:

```
# mkdir /mnt/suse10.1
# mkdir /mnt/suse10.1/{cd1,cd2,cd3,cd4,cd5}
# mount -o loop ~/isos/suse10.1-i386-cd1.iso /mnt/suse10.1/cd1
# mount -o loop ~/isos/suse10.1-i386-cd2.iso /mnt/suse10.1/cd2
# mount -o loop ~/isos/suse10.1-i386-cd3.iso /mnt/suse10.1/cd3
# mount -o loop ~/isos/suse10.1-i386-cd4.iso /mnt/suse10.1/cd4
# mount -o loop ~/isos/suse10.1-i386-cd5.iso /mnt/suse10.1/cd5
# cd /mnt/suse10.1
# ln -s cd1/boot boot
# ln -s cd1/content content
# ln -s cd1/control.xml control
# ln -s media.1 cd1/media.1
# mkdir yast
# cd yast
# echo cd/cd1 > instorder
# echo cd/cd1 cd/cd1 > order
```

Then, on the target system, you should specify an install point of */mnt/suse10.1/cd1*.

What About...

...using a non-Linux system as the installation server? You can use any system capable of supporting file access via HTTP, FTP, NFS, or CIFS (also known as "SMB"). For example, I have successfully installed SUSE Linux from CD images obtained using an FTP login on an Apple Mac. If you have a Windows machine, it's most likely that you'll want to install from a CIFS share. You should copy the entire contents of the DVD to a directory on your Windows machine, ensure that Windows file sharing is enabled, and share the directory as (for example) *suse93*. Make sure you know the name and password of an account that can access the share. Then, on the target machine, press F3 at the initial menu screen and select SMB/CIFS as the installation source. (Again, on SUSE Linux 10.1, hit F3 then F4.) At the next screen, enter the NetBIOS name of the server, the share name, domain name, and an account name and password.

9.3   Automate Installations with AutoYaST

Working manually through the SUSE Linux installation screens once (or even twice) is quite interesting; perhaps even enjoyable. Doing it 200 times is tedious. AutoYaST enables you to prepare the answers that the installer asks you ahead of time and put them into a *control file*. This saves a huge amount of time if you're installing many machines. If all the machines are the same, it's very easy. If the machines are broadly similar, then it's still quite easy. Even if there are quite drastic differences between the machines, it's still possible to prepare a control file so that different machines get different configurations. AutoYaST is SUSE's answer to RedHat's Kickstart; indeed, it is even possible to import a Kickstart file into YaST as a starting point. AutoYaST works well in combination with installing from a network server to provide an almost completely "hands-off" installation process.

How Do I Do That?

First, make sure you have the packages `autoyast2`, `autoyast2-utils`, and `autoyast2-installation` installed.

AutoYaST needs two things—a network installation server (see Lab 9.2, "Install from an Installation Server") and a control file. It's also possible to do an AutoYaST installation from CDs or DVD, but because the whole point is to minimize the amount of manual intervention, I'll not consider that case.

The control file can be created in several ways; it's an XML file and can be created manually (preferably using an XML editor such as KXML Editor), but the easiest way is to use YaST, which will create a control file based on your currently installed system. From the YaST main screen, select Miscellaneous from the panel on the left, then Autoinstallation from the panel on the right. From the Tools menu of the next screen, select Create Reference Profile. On the next screen, you can select which components (beyond the default) of the configuration of this machine will be copied into the control file. See Figure 9-3.

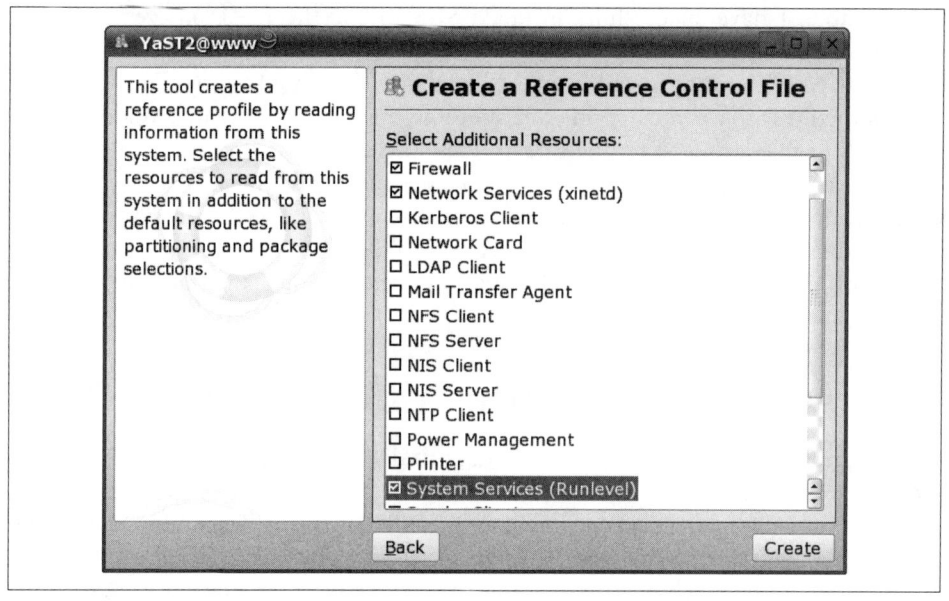

Figure 9-3. Creating an AutoYaST control file with YaST

Typically, you would select the following:

- Firewall
- Network Services (xinetd)
- System Services (Runlevel)
- Sound
- Graphics Card and Monitor

Now click Create to create the control file. (This may take a while.) Back at the main AutoYaST screen, you can now edit the settings by navigating through the tree view in the panel on the left, as shown in Figure 9-4. To edit an item, select it from the tree view and click Configure. The screens you'll see here are similar or identical to the screens you'd see during a normal installation.

When you're happy with the configuration, select Save As from the File menu. I called my file *d600* because it was created for a Dell D600 laptop.

By default, the control file is saved in */var/lib/autoinstall/repository*. Next, you need to decide how you're going to make the file available to the target system. You can copy it onto a floppy (your local computer museum may have some!), you can add it to your boot CD, or you can put it onto the installation server. This is simply a mat-

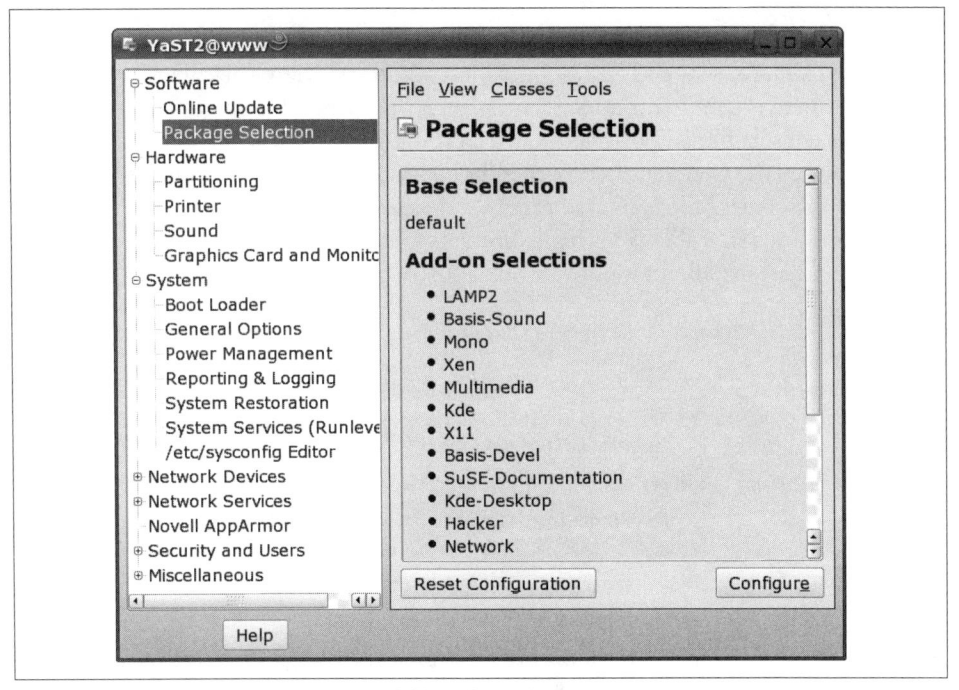

Figure 9-4. Editing an AutoYaST control file with YaST

ter of copying it into the installation server tree. Assuming you're using the same installation server structure as in "Install from an Installation Server," just copy the file like this:

```
# mkdir /installroot/suse93/autoyast
# cp /var/lib/autoinstall/repository/d600 /installroot/suse93/autoyast
```

Assuming that your web server is configured to export the *installroot* directory as in "Install from an Installation Server," you should now be able to see the control file with your web browser, through the URL *http://localhost/suse/suse93/autoyast/d600*.

Now you're all set to perform an automated installation. All you should need to do is to boot your target machine from SUSE Linux CD1 (or you can use the boot CD you created in Lab 9.2, "Install from an Installation Server"), select Installation from the main boot menu, and add something like this to the boot options line (on some versions of SUSE Linux you must press F3 to display the boot options field):

```
install=http://192.168.0.44/suse/suse93
autoyast=http://192.168.0.44/suse/suse93/autoyast/d600
```

Of course, you should substitute the IP address of your install server. The installer will analyze the control file and present you with a screen letting you make changes, or accept the proposal read from the control file. Once you click OK, the rest of the installation should proceed automagically.

How It Works

The key to AutoYaST is the XML control file. You can view this file directly from YaST's AutoYaST configuration screen by selecting View → Source from the main menu. The control file is too long (500–1,000 lines) to show in its entirety here, so I'll simply show the overall structure then home in on one specific example. The root element of the control file is named profile. Beneath this, a number of resources are defined, as shown in Table 9-1 (this is not a complete list). Some of these resources control the actual installation; other control post-installation configuration.

Table 9-1. Top-level resources in the AutoYaST control file

Element Name	Description
<bootloader>	Specifies the modules to be included in the initrd (initial ramdisk) image and the choices to be included in the GRUB boot menu.
<firewall>	Specifies the system's firewall configuration.
<general>	Specifies settings related to the installation process and environment of the installed system. This includes settings for the clock, time zone, language, keyboard, and mouse.
<inetd>	Specifies the configuration of the xinetd super-server.
<partitioning>	Specifies the physical drives, partition types, and sizes.
<report>	Specifies the behavior of four types of pop-ups that may appear during installation: messages, warnings, errors, and yes-no messages.
<runlevel>	Specifies the default runlevel.
<software>	Specifies the software categories and individual packages that are to be installed.
<sound>	Specifies configuration of the sound hardware.
<x11>	Specifies the configuration of the X server.

Here is a detailed extract from the file under the <partitioning> resource. The line numbers are for reference; they are not part of the file.

```
1     <partitioning config:type="list">
2       <drive>
3         <device>/dev/hda</device>
4         <partitions config:type="list">
5           <partition>
6             <filesystem config:type="symbol">reiser</filesystem>
7             <format config:type="boolean">true</format>
8             <mount>/</mount>
9             <partition_id config:type="integer">131</partition_id>
10            <partition_nr config:type="integer">1</partition_nr>
11            <region config:type="list">
12              <region_entry config:type="integer">0</region_entry>
13              <region_entry config:type="integer">1306</region_entry>
14            </region>
15            <size>10742182912</size>
16          </partition>
17          ... more partitions defined here ...
18      </drive>
19    </partitioning>
```

Lines 2–18 define a single drive, /dev/hda. Within that drive, lines 5–16 define a partition (additional partitions defined for the drive have been edited out). The partition ID specified at line 9 is 131, which is 83 hex—the ID for a Linux partition. (You also see these IDs if you create a partition using fdisk.) Lines 12–13 specify the partition cylinder boundaries, and line 15 specifies the size in bytes.

As you can see, the control file is not simply a recipe for how to drive the graphical install screens. It is a specification that is parsed by the installer to obtain configuration options instead of showing the graphical screens.

The DTD (Document Type Definition) files that define the structure of the control file are in the directory /usr/share/autoinstall/dtd.

What About...

...changing the control file? If you need to edit the control file, you can load it back in to the YaST AutoYaST module (select Open from the File menu), navigate around it using the tree view on the left, and make any changes. For example, suppose that you need to modify the installation for machines in your Paris office. As part of this, you want to add the French OpenOffice packages. In the tree view, navigate to Software → Package Selection and click Configure. You'll be presented with the same software selection screens that you'd see during a normal installation. Click Detailed Selection. Then, search for and add the package exactly as you would if you were installing it on *this* system.

Another area that often needs changing is the graphics section. In fact, it is often best leaving this as the default so that it is auto-detected at install time. If you have followed the suggestions in this lab, you will have included the graphics configuration of the current system in the control file. If you want to remove this, navigate to the graphics section (Hardware → Graphics Card and Monitor) and click Reset Configuration.

Another area that you may want to change is Miscellaneous → Complete configuration files. Here, you can add complete configuration file to be added to the control file. This is useful for things like SSH configuration files.

What About...

...custom scripts? You can create your own custom scripts in shell, Perl, or Python to be run at various stages during the installation, and add them to the control file (Miscellaneous → Custom Scripts).

The output of these scripts is written to /var/adm/autoinstall/logs. The scripts themselves, after completing installation of the target system, will be found in /var/adm/autoinstall/scripts. Scripts can run at various stages in the installation:

Pre-installation scripts
These run after the control file is parsed but before anything has actually been installed. There is a useful (undocumented) feature you can exploit here—you

can use the pre-install script to tweak the installation profile itself, prior to installation. After YaST has looked through the profile and applied any rules (discussed shortly), the control file it will use for the installation is put into */tmp/profile/autoinst.xml*. After the pre-installation scripts have run, YaST will look for a file called */tmp/profile/modified.xml*. If it finds this, it will use it in preference to *autoinst.xml* for the install. You can use this to substitute variables in the profile with items entered at the initial boot command line, and to automatically change the profile to accommodate SCSI or IDE disks, whichever the system has.

Post-install scripts

The behavior of post-install scripts depends on the setting of a boolean option set in the control file. If the option `network needed` is set to `TRUE`, the script will run while the installation network is still up, before YaST has performed the post-install configuration. This is a good place to run any custom install scripts to install any custom applications from the installation server that are not part of the distribution. A post-install script run with the option `network needed` set to `FALSE` (the default) will run after YaST has completed the installation and the system has rebooted. The network will not be available unless the script explicitly starts it, for example by running `rcnetwork start`.

Chroot scripts

The behavior of post-install scripts depends on the setting of a boolean option set in the control file. If the option `chrooted` is set to `FALSE` (the default) the script will run after all the packages have been installed but before the reboot and before the boot loader is installed. The root filesystem of the installed system will be available mounted onto */mnt*. If the `chrooted` option is set to `TRUE`, the script runs in a chroot environment so that the root of the installed filesystem appears as */* rather than as */mnt*.

Init scripts

Init scripts are run after the reboot. At this stage, YaST has finished all configuration and the */etc/init.d* scripts have run (so the network is probably up). Init scripts are effectively */etc/init.d* scripts that are run only once, on the first boot.

What About...

...adapting the profile to the machine? One of the more powerful features of Auto-YaST is its ability to merge different control file fragments according to a set of rules. This allows you to adapt the profile depending on the hardware characteristics of the target machine. To do this, you have to construct a *rules.xml* file by hand (well, with an editor) that describes the rules and the files.

The *rules.xml* file should live in a subdirectory rules of your profile location on the installation server; for example */installroot/suse93/autoyast/rules*.

Here's an example of a rules file:

```
<?xml version="1.0"?>
<!DOCTYPE autoinstall SYSTEM "/usr/share/autoinstall/dtd/rules.dtd">
<autoinstall xmlns="http://www.suse.com/1.0/yast2ns" xmlns:config="http://www.suse.
com/1.0/configns">
  <rules config:type="list">
    <rule>
      <disksize>
          <match>/dev/hdc 1000</match>
          <match_type>greater</match_type>
      </disksize>
      <result>
          <profile>machine1.xml</profile>
          <continue config:type="boolean">false</continue>
       </result>
    </rule>
    <rule>
      <disksize>
          <match>/dev/hda 1000</match>
          <match_type>greater</match_type>
      </disksize>
      <result>
          <profile>machine2.xml</profile>
          <continue config:type="boolean">false</continue>
       </result>
    </rule>
  </rules>
</autoinstall>
```

These rules say: if the size of */dev/hdc* on the target machine is greater than 1,000 MB, include the contents of *machine1.xml* in the profile. If the size of */dev/hda* on the target machine is greater than 1,000 MB, include the contents of *machine2.xml* in the profile.

> I have to say that it would be hard to find a worse syntax for a rule-based language that the XML document shown here. Am I alone in my belief that while XML might be great for computers, it is barely fit for human consumption?

The disksize attribute is one of many you can use in a rules file. Table 9-2 shows a list of them.

Table 9-2. Rules file attributes

Attribute	Description
hostaddress	The IP address of the host
hostname	The name of the host
domain	The domain name of the host
installed_product	The name of the product being installed; for example, "SUSE LINUX"
installed_product_version	The version of the product being installed; for example, "9.3"
network	The network address of the host
mac	The MAC address of the host

Table 9-2. Rules file attributes (continued)

Attribute	Description
linux	The number of installed Linux partitions on the system
others	The number of installed non-Linux partitions on the system
xserver	X server needed for graphic adapter
memsize	Memory available on host in MB
totaldisk	Total disk space available on the host in MB
haspcmcia	System has PCMCIA (laptops)
hostid	Hex representation of IP address
arch	Architecture of host
karch	Kernel architecture of host
disksize	Drive device and size in megabytes
product	The hardware product name as specified in SMBIOS
product_vendor	The hardware vendor as specified in SMBIOS
board	The system board name as specified in SMBIOS
board_vendor	The system board vendor as specified in SMBIOS

Here's an example using the board rule to use a different profile, depending on the system model. The "board" is the information returned from the BIOS about what model the system is. Some manufacturers are better than others at this. Dell can have many board numbers for each type of machine (e.g., 0X2034, 0T9369, and 0G5152 are all D600 machines), whereas IBM seems more consistent (for example, the board number is always 2673M4G for an IBM X32).

The board info is returned by the `hwinfo` command

```
# hwinfo --bios |grep -A 5 -i "board info"
  Board Info: #512
    Manufacturer: "Dell Computer Corporation"
    Product: "0X2034"
    Serial: ".31Z301J.CN486433CS4838."
  Chassis Info: #768
    Manufacturer: "Dell Computer Corporation"
```

The board name shows as the "Product" information here—0X2034. Here's a rule that includes the profile information in the file *rule-d600.xml* for this board type:

```
<rule>
    <board>
        <match>0X2034</match>
    </board>
    <result>
        <profile>rule-d600.xml</profile>
        <continue config:type="boolean">true</continue>
    </result>
</rule>
```

To match on multiple board names, as you'd need to do for the Dell D600 laptops, just add multiple <rule> entries all for the same XML file.

Where to Learn More

There is extensive documentation included with the distribution. The full manual is available at */usr/share/doc/packages/autoyast2/html/index.html* or in PDF form at */usr/share/doc/packages/autoyast2/autoyast.pdf*.

9.4 Run Multiple Operating Systems with Xen

Virtualization is a hot topic, despite the lack of any well-articulated explanation of what it actually means. At risk of contradiction, let's attempt a definition:

> Virtualization is a software technique that provides the illusion of a real machine environment but which in reality is layered on top of a (possibly quite different) hardware platform.

Some so-called virtualization products are properly called *emulators*, since they emulate one processor architecture on top of another. Microsoft's Virtual PC 7, for example, emulates an Intel processor on top of a Power PC, allowing you to run many x86 operating systems, including Microsoft Windows, Linux, BSD, and Solaris on a G3, G4, or G5 Mac. Such techniques, which must emulate one processor's instruction set on another, are usually slow.

Additionally, virtualization and emulation products are designed to support multiple virtual machines concurrently, allowing several (possibly different) operating systems to execute on the same hardware at the same time. These operating systems are called *guests* of the virtual machine environment, which runs on top of the *host* operating system.

True virtualization products create a controlled environment under which applications run directly on the host CPU. Linux running in Virtual PC on a PowerPC Mac thinks it is running on a Pentium II class CPU, because that is what Virtual PC emulates. Linux running in VMware (perhaps the best known virtualization product) on an Athlon 64 is in fact running directly on that Athlon 64, but under controlled conditions. (Virtual PC for Windows uses true CPU virtualization as well.)

This lab looks at an open source virtualization package called Xen and shows how you can create virtual machines (Xen calls them *domains*) and boot Linux inside them. Unlike VMware, Xen is a *hypervisor*; it runs directly on the bare hardware, not on top of a host operating system. When you boot a system that has been Xen-enabled, the Xen hypervisor is started up alongside your primary operating system.

How Do I Do That?

You will need to install the packages `bridge-utils`, `libreiserfs`, `multipath-tools`, `kernel-xen`, `xen`, `xen-tools`, `python`, `xen-doc-pdf` (there are also HTML and PostScript versions of the documentation), and optionally `yast2-vm`.

To use xen, you must first reboot so that the Xen hypervisor is running. If you chose to include Xen when you installed SUSE Linux, the installer should have included a suitable stanza in the grub config file */boot/grub/menu.lst*. If necessary, add the stanza manually. On my system, it looks like this:

```
title XEN
  root (hd0,0)
  kernel /boot/xen.gz dom0_mem=458752
  module /boot/vmlinuz-xen root=/dev/hda1 vga=0x314 selinux=0 splash=silent showopts
  module /boot/initrd-xen
```

This entry tells grub to uncompress, load and execute the Xen hypervisor image (*xen.gz*) and also to load into memory a modified copy of the Linux kernel (*vmlinux-xen*) and a modified ramdisk image (*initrd-xen*). Xen will create an initial virtual machine image (called Domain 0) and launch the Linux kernel. The setting for dom0_mem limits the amount of memory that will be seen by this domain. The setting is optional; if omitted, Xen will give the maximum possible memory to Domain 0. As you boot Xen, you will see—if you're quick—a few messages from Xen scroll by, followed by the kernel's usual stream of consciousness as it boots. You should end up with a running Linux system that behaves more or less the same as it did without Xen. To verify that Xen is indeed active, run the command:

```
# xm list
```

which will list the current Xen domains. You should see a single domain called Domain-0.

Next, try creating an additional domain and booting a different version of Linux in it. The first step is to create a root filesystem image for the system that you want to boot. This can be done, for example, by creating an empty partition and installing Linux into it from standard distribution media. For this lab I'm going for a real grassroots experience by using a tiny text-only Linux distribution called ttylinux. This is available from *http://sf.net/projects/xen* (click the Files link, and look for a link called "ttylinux example image"). From this site, I downloaded the file *tty-linux-xen.bz2* and put it in the directory */home/chris/xen/ttylinux-xen.bz2*. (If you can't find this file, the sites *http://www.jailtime.org* and *http://www.xen-get.org* both carry a range of xen-ported images.) The next step is to uncompress the file:

```
$ cd ~/xen
$ bunzip2 ttylinux-xen.bz2
```

Now you will have the uncompressed file *ttylinux-xen*. This file is an ext2 filesystem image and can be loopback mounted, for example:

```
# mount -o loop ~chris/xen/ttylinux-xen /mnt
```

Now you can explore this small root filesystem under */mnt*. What you're looking at here is the root filesystem of a minimal Linux system.

Next I created a disk partition (hda3), put an ext2 filesystem on it, and copied the ttylinux root filesystem onto it. The actual creation of the partition can be done using YaST, cfdisk, or fdisk; it is not shown here. Be sure to replace hda3 with the actual partition, as `mke2fs` will destroy all data on the partition you specify.

```
# mke2fs /dev/hda3
# mkdir /local
# mount /dev/hda3 /local
# cp -a /mnt/* /local
# umount /local
# umount /mnt
```

Next I created a Xen configuration file, */home/chris/xen/ttylinux-xen.conf*. This file defines a new domain called ttylinux. The details of this file are discussed later in the lab.

```
kernel  = "/boot/vmlinuz-xen"
ramdisk = "/boot/initrd-xen"
memory  = 64
name    = "ttylinux"
vif     = [ 'ip=192.168.0.90' ]
disk    = [ 'phy:hda3,sda1,w' ]
root    = "/dev/sda1 ro"
```

By passing this configuration file to `xm` (the Xen domain administration tool) I am able to start a new domain, boot the SUSE Linux Xen kernel, and pass it the `ttylinux` filesystem as its root filesystem:

```
# xm mem-set Domain-0 360
# xm create ~chris/xen/ttylinux-xen.conf -c
```

The first command reduces the amount of memory available to domain 0 (the SUSE instance that you booted into) to 360 MB to free up some memory for the second domain. The `-c` flag passed to `xm create` tells it to make this terminal the controlling console for the domain. You'll see lots of boot-time messages, followed by a login prompt from the `ttylinux` system. Notice that the kernel running here is not one that came with the `ttylinux` distribution, it's the Xen-ported kernel that came with my Linux distribution (the same kernel that's running in domain 0).

```
shrek:~ # xm create ~chris/xen/ttylinux-xen.conf -c
Using config file "/home/chris/xen/ttylinux-xen.conf".
Started domain ttylinux

... lots of messages as the system boots ...

ttylinux 4.2
Linux 2.6.13-15-xen on i686 arch

tiny.local login:
```

Login as root, with password root. Now you should see a shell prompt from the running system, and be able to enter commands:

```
root@tiny ~ # ls /
bin         etc         lost+found  root        tmp
boot        home        mnt         sbin        usr
dev         lib         proc        sys         var
```

You can detach the console from the domain with Ctrl-]. In the two lines shown next, the first prompt is from the root login in the ttylinux domain. After entering Ctrl-], the second prompt shows that we've returned to the host system in Domain 0:

```
root@tiny ~ # Ctrl-]
shrek:~ #
```

You can list the existing domains with xm list, and reconnect the terminal to a domain with xm console; for example:

```
shrek:~ # xm list
Name                  Id   Mem(MB)  CPU VCPU(s)  State  Time(s)
Domain-0              0    360      0   1        r----  253.8
ttylinux              10   64       0   1        -b---  0.6
shrek:~ # xm console ttylinux

root@tiny ~ #
```

The last line is the prompt from the ttylinux system, to which I have now reconnected.

> You can shut down a domain with xm shutdown *domain* (for example, xm shutdown ttylinux).

Instead of creating a new physical disk partition for the root filesystem of your Xen domain, you can use a file within the Domain-0 filesystem for this purpose. This will not give good performance if you wish to run I/O-intensive applications within the domain, but is an easy way to get started if you don't happen to have spare disk space for a new partition. In the following dialog, I began by creating an (empty) file. Then, I created a filesystem on it, and copied to it the contents of the ttylinux-xen filesystem:

```
# dd if=/dev/zero of=/home/chris/xen/ttylinux-root bs=1k seek=2048k count=1
# mke2fs /home/chris/xen/ttylinux-root
# mount -o loop /home/chris/xen/ttylinux-root /local
# mount -o loop /home/chris/xen/ttylinux-xen /mnt
# cp -a /mnt/* /local
# umount /local
# umount /mnt
```

To use this file instead of the hda3 partition I used earlier in the lab, I edited the configuration file, */home/chris/xen/ttylinux-xen.conf* to change the disk parameter:

```
disk    = [ 'file:/home/chris/xen/ttylinux-root,sda1,w' ]
root    = "/dev/sda1 rw"
```

The ttylinux image can now be booted as before.

There are other ways that you can create a root filesystem image for a Xen domain. For example, you can simply install an additional copy of SUSE Linux into a separate partition from regular installation media, or (of course) use an already installed image.

You can also create a root filesystem image within a regular file by using the rescue image on your installation media. This is a quick way to get started if you don't want to download the ttylinux image. The rescue image is in the file *boot/rescue* on CD1 (or the DVD). There is a shell script named *mk-xen-rescue-img.sh* in the directory */usr/share/doc/packages/xen* that will prepare the root filesystem image for you automatically. In the following dialog, it's assumed that SUSE Linux CD1 is mounted on */media/disk*.

```
# mkdir /opt/xen
# cd /usr/share/doc/packages/xen
# ./mk-xen-rescue-img.sh /media/disk/boot/i386/rescue /opt/xen/demo
Creating disk image within '/opt/xen/demo'...
Updating kernel within '/opt/xen/demo'...
'/opt/xen/demo' has been prepared successfully
Config file '/etc/xen/vm/demo' has been created.  Please review!
You may also want to add an IP address to the config file ...
Start the domain with 'xm create -c /etc/xen/vm/demo vmid=N'
```

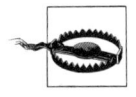

> Some versions of this script have a bug (or at least, a disagreement with reality) regarding the location of the file *xmexample.rescue*. You may need to copy this file into the correct directory using `cp /etc/xen/examples/xmexample.rescue /etc/xen` before running the script.

As you'll note from the dialog, the script has created a domain config file in */etc/xen/vm/demo*, and a filesystem image in */opt/xen/demo*. (There is nothing special about the decision to put the image into */opt/xen*, but it is considered good practice to install optional software in */opt*.) You can now boot an instance of this with the command:

```
# xm create -c /etc/xen/vm/demo vmid=4
```

How It Works

Xen is described by its developers at Cambridge University as a *hypervisor*—a relatively thin layer of software that runs underneath the operating system. The architecture is shown in Figure 9-5. Unlike VMware, Xen is not layered on top of a host operating system. Using Xen, all operating systems are guests. However, there is one guest—the one that is initially booted—that is privileged. It can access the hardware directly and has the power to create and control other virtual machines. This privileged operating system runs in domain 0. Other domains have no access to the hardware; instead they use virtual interfaces that are provided by Xen (with the help of the domain 0 kernel).

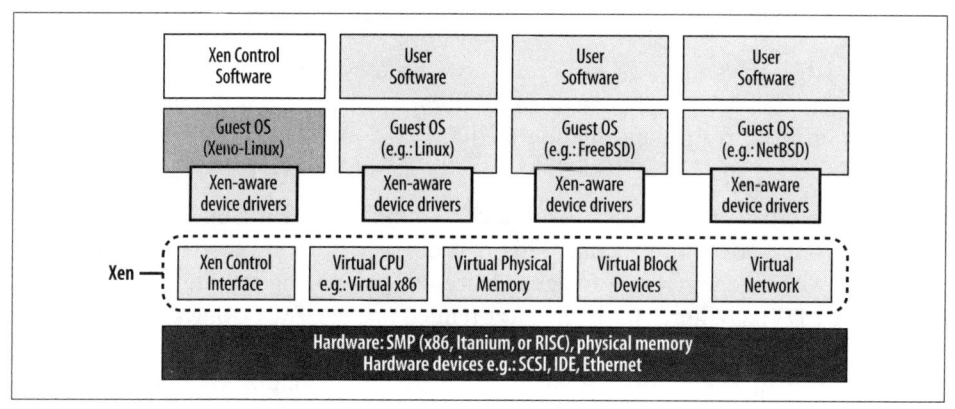

Figure 9-5. Xen architecture

Xen supports *paravirtualization*. Without getting too technical, this means that the virtual machine environment provided by Xen is not identical to the underlying hardware. Xen effectively defines a new machine architecture. Consequently, an operating system needs to be "ported" to Xen before it will run. This is relatively easy for an open-source operating system like Linux. SUSE include a suitable Linux kernel, along with its associated ramdisk image. On the SUSE Linux 10.1 distribution, these are the files */boot/vmlinuz-2.6.16-8-xen* and */boot/initrd-2.6.16-8-xen*. In addition, the Linux 2.4, NetBSD, FreeBSD, and Plan 9 kernels have been ported to Xen. (A port of Windows was also done, but cannot be distributed because of licensing restrictions.) The kernel used for domains other than domain 0 can be cut down, because no real device drivers are needed. In reality, most device drivers are implemented as loadable modules anyway, so there is little penalty, in terms of memory use, to using the same kernel for both domain 0 and for other domains.

The modified kernel is aware of its existence as a guest running in a virtualized environment, and routes any privileged instructions through the Xen hypervisor.

The big benefit of paravirtualization is that the guest OS and its applications run very close to the speed with which they would run "natively." In the future, virtualization support within the CPU itself (including Intel's VT technology amd AMD's Pacifica technology) will allow the guest OS to run on Xen without modification.

Each domain is defined in a domain configuration file. There are a couple of heavily commented sample files in */etc/xen/xmexample1* and */etc/xen/xmexample2*. Here's the one I used earlier in the lab, with line numbers added for reference:

```
1  kernel   = "/boot/vmlinuz-2.6.13-15-xen"
2  ramdisk  = "/boot/initrd-2.6.13-15-xen"
3  memory   = 64
4  name     = "ttylinux"
5  vif      = [ 'ip=192.168.0.90' ]
6  disk     = [ 'phy:hda3,sda1,w' ]
7  root     = "/dev/sda1 ro"
```

Fans of Python (the language, not Monty) may notice a little Pythonesque syntax creeping in here—particularly the lists in square brackets. This is not coincidence; the Xen control scripts are written in Python.

Line 1 specifies the path name of the Xen-ported Linux kernel to be booted, and line 2 specifies its associated ramdisk image. Line 3 specifies the amount of memory (in megabytes) to be allocated to this domain, and line 4 gives it a name. Line 5 says that one virtual network interface should be allocated to this domain, and sets its IP address. (If you want the virtual network interface to get its IP address using DHCP, put dhcp = "dhcp" here instead.)

Line 6 is more interesting. It allocates one of the domain 0 partitions (hda3) to the new domain, and makes it available as device sda1 (i.e., the guest OS in this domain will see it as a SCSI device). The "w" at the end of this list means that the partition is to be made available read/write. Finally, line 7 tells the kernel which device to use as its root filesystem. By the way, it's important that the partition that you export to the domain (hda3 in the example) doesn't remain mounted in domain 0. Having two live operating systems writing to the same filesystem is certain to corrupt it. For the same reason, don't export the same partition to more than one domain, unless, for example, you exported a partition read-only to use as the */usr* partition.

The command-line tool for domain management is xm; underlying this is a daemon called xend. The command xm help --long will give you a summary of the main commands:

```
# xm help --long
Usage: xm <subcommand> [args]
    Control, list, and manipulate Xen guest instances

xm common subcommands:
    console <DomId>          attach to console of DomId
    create <CfgFile>         create a domain based on Config File
    destroy <DomId>          terminate a domain immediately
    help                     display this message
    list [DomId, ...]        list information about domains
    mem-max <DomId> <Mem>    set the maximum memory reservation for a domain
    mem-set <DomId> <Mem>    adjust the current memory usage for a domain
    migrate <DomId> <Host>   migrate a domain to another machine
    pause <DomId>            pause execution of a domain
    reboot <DomId>           reboot a domain
    restore <File>           create a domain from a saved state file
    save <DomId> <File>      save domain state (and config) to file
    shutdown <DomId>         shutdown a domain
    top                      monitor system and domains in real-time
    unpause <DomId>          unpause a paused domain
```

There's also the command xentop, which is similar to the regular top command, except that it shows resource usage of Xen domains rather than Linux processes.

What About...

...using logical volumes with Xen? This makes for an interesting and appealing arrangement, due to the snapshot facility of logical volumes and their extensibility. Basically the idea is to create a logical volume that contains a "pristine" copy of the guest operating system you want to run. Then, you create a number of read/write snapshots of this, and use the snapshots to provide root filesystems for your virtual machines. This step requires a fairly recent Linux kernel (2.6.8 or later) that supports writable snapshots. Suppose that you have a volume group called system. (Learn how to create volume groups in the lab "Creating Logical Volumes" in Chapter 6.) You'd begin by making a logical volume within that volume group, big enough to hold the entire "pristine" root filesystem. Here, I make it 4 GB:

```
# lvcreate -L 4096M -n pristine system
```

Now, create a filesystem on the logical volume, mount it, and copy the desired root filesystem onto it somehow. For example:

```
# mke2fs /dev/system/pristine
# mount /dev/system/pristine /mnt
# cp -ax / /mnt
# umount /mnt
```

Now you can create some snapshots of this logical volume for use in your domains:

```
# lvcreate -L 512M -s -n dom1 /dev/system/pristine
# lvcreate -L 512M -s -n dom2 /dev/system/pristine
```

Notice that the snapshots can (probably) be much smaller than the original volume because they need to store only the differences from the pristine copy. However, LVM will react badly if the differences overflow the snapshot's capacity.

Now you can create a Xen config file for your domain 1, containing the lines:

```
name = "dom1"
disk = [ 'phy:system/dom1,sda1,w' ]
```

and, for domain 2, the lines:

```
name = "dom2"
disk = [ 'phy:system/dom2,sda1,w' ]
```

Not only does this avoid storing multiple copies of the common parts of the root filesystems, it provides an easy rollback capability—just destroy the snapshot and recreate it from the pristine copy.

> Although this method sounds wonderful in principal, I have had some difficulty in implementing it on SUSE Linux 10.0; I've also encountered other difficulties in, for example, getting the virtual network interface to work, and several other things. My impression is that Xen is a technology with tremendous potential, but that the packages as shipped with SUSE Linux aren't ready for prime time yet.

Where to Learn More

There are quite a number of user guides, white papers, and research papers about Xen. First, there's a user guide at */usr/share/doc/packages/xen/pdf/user.pdf*; this is excellent. For research papers and presentations, see *http://www.cl.cam.ac.uk/Research/SRG/netos/xen*.

The June 2005 edition of *Linux Format* magazine carried an extended article about Xen, and there's an interesting comparison of VM architectures at *http://en.wikipedia.org/wiki/Comparison_of_virtual_machines*.

At *http://www.xensource.com/xen/downloads,* you'll find an ISO image of a live demo CD that boots direct from the CD. This provides Xen, a Xen-aware 2.6.12.6 Linux kernel, and root filesystem images for Debian Etch and Centos 4.1. You can run either in Domain 0, then create additional domains running either image. The whole thing is very easy to use; for example, when you log in as root (password xensource), you're automatically presented with instructions on how to start additional domains. Networking is preconfigured, allowing all domains to talk to one another. Of course, like all live CDs, it runs a little slowly, but it's a great way to play with Xen and see examples of working configurations.

Finally, there are manual pages for `xm`, `xmdomain.cfg` (which describes the domain configuration file syntax), and `xentop` (which displays real-time information about a Xen system and its domains).

Index

Symbols
* (asterisk), 48
/ (forward slash), 40
%h and %d (percent h and percent d), 165
| (pipe), 137
~ (tilde), 34, 214

Numbers
3-D rendering, 148–153

A
access control, 368–373
    commands requiring root access, 369
    sudo, using, 369
access control lists, 57
ACPI S1, ACPI S3, and ACPI S4, 155, 156
AIDE (Advanced Intrusion Detection Environment), 186, 380–386
    config file directives, 384
    configuration file, 382
    installing, 380
    properties, 382
    system snapshot, 380
    testing, 381
aide.conf file, 382
aliases, 371
Alt-F7 command, 33
anonymous ftp, 345
Apache, 327–334
    configuration files, 328
    documentation, 327, 333
        document root directory, 327
    HTTP protocol, 331
    httpd.conf file, 328
    index.html, 328
    language negotiation, 328
    needed packages, installing, 327
    status module configuration, 329
    virtual hosting, 332
AppArmor, 386–392
    intended use, 391
    profile rules, 390
    standalone and systemic profiling, 390
    YaST, application profiles, creating with, 387
apropos command, 29
aquota.user and aquota.group files, 300
ARP (Address Resolution Protocol), 284
arp command, 284
asterisk (*), 48
ATI, 148
    multiheaded graphics cards, 143
audio, 123–126
authentication, 56, 347
authorization, 56
autoconf, 215, 219
AutoYaST, 403–411
    control files, 403, 406–407
    custom scripts, adding, 407
    machine profiles, 408
    required packages, 403
    system cloning profile, 12
    (see also YaST)

B

backups, 275–283
    incremental backups, 281
    live filesystems, 280
    restores from, 279
    snapshots, 280
    tar archives, 276
    to CDs, 277
    YaST, using, 277–279
Banshee audio player, 126
basket, 210
Beagle, 77
binary files, viewing, 39
binary packages compared to source packages, 213
BIND, 301
    (see also DNS; name resolution)
BIOS, 69
Bluetooth, 165–172
    configuration files, 168
    gnokii, 169
    hcitool, 169
    mobile phone synchronization, 168
    OBEX protocol, 168
    rfcomm, 170
    xgnokii, 170
BlueZ, 165
booting
    boot process, 69
    bootstrap loaders, 70
    dual-booting (see dual-boot systems)
    GRUB boot options, setting, 66
    rescuing an unbootable system, 66–72
    servers (see servers)
browsers
    Konqueror (see Konqueror)
    Nautilus (see Nautilus)
bzip2, 214

C

Caesar cipher, 349
capturing screenshots, 132–135
cd command, 43
CD installations, 2
CDs, backups to, 277
CDs, burning, 128–132
cfdisk, 245
    YaST, compared to, 247
challenge and response, 351
challenge/response authentication, 347
chkconfig utility, 231
chkstat utility, 366–368
    permission files used with, 366
chroot jail, 325
code examples, xii
command-line interface, 33
compiz window manager, 148
compositing, 153
configure script, 215
cp command, 48
CUPS (Common Unix Print System), 14, 15–16
    accessing remote printers, 57
    remote printers, accessing via, 58–59

D

data synchronization between computers, 172–179
.deb packages, 180
default gateways, 288
deltas, 201
dependencies, 198
devices, hot-pluggable, naming of, 26
/etc/dhcpd.conf, 322
DHCP (Dynamic Host Configuration Protocol), 321–326
    chroot jail, 325
    dhcpd.conf file, 322
    dhcp-tools package, 325
    DNS updates, 324
    documentation, 326
    static IP address assignment, 325
    YaST, configuration with, 322–325
diffs, 201
dig command, 294
digital signatures, 187
directories, 40
    permissions, 56
directory structure, 44–46
disk quotas, 297–301
    aquota.user and aquota.group files, 300
    edquota command, setting with, 298
    grace periods, 300
    group quotas, setting, 301
    quota command, monitoring with, 300
    repquota, monitoring with, 300
    setquota command, setting with, 299
displays, multiheaded, 143–148
DNS (Domain Name Service), 301
    dig tool, 307
    record types, 302

troubleshooting, 290
zones, 302
(see also name resolution)
DNS servers, 301–308
   caching servers, 302
   YaST, configuring with, 303–307
domains, 302
dos2unix, 39
DPMS (Display Power Management Signaling), 93
dual-boot systems
   Linux on Windows installation, 393–399
   power management and, 157
   suspend-to-disk and partitioning issues, 157
dump, 281
DVD installations, 2

E

edquota command, 298
   grace periods, setting with, 300
email, 16–21
   email storage, migration between applications, 20
   Evolution, 18–20
   Kmail, 16–18
emulators, 411
encryption, 348
   asymmetric algorithms, 350
ESC/P printers, 15
ESMTP (Extended Simple Mail Transfer Protocol), 337
/etc/aide.conf, 382
/etc/apache2/httpd.conf, 328
/etc/dhcpd.conf, 322
/etc/fstab, 243
/etc/init.d/rc, 229
/etc/inittab, 226
/etc/sudoers, 369–371
/etc/sysconfig/SuSEfirewall2, 360
Evolution, 18–20
exec( ) system call, 262
ext3 filesystem, 5
   creating, 247
   (see also filesystems)
extended partitions, 243

F

fdisk, 246
FHS (Filesystem Hierarchy Standard), 47
file command, 39

file compression types, 214
file synchronization between computers, 172–179
files, 50
   attributes, 50, 54
   attributes, viewing or changing, 52–55
   Beagle, finding with, 77
   binary files, viewing, 39
   file synchronization, 172–179
   finding, 72–78
      locate command, 76
   links, 50
   ownership, 54
   permissions, 52
   sharing over networks (see NFS)
   symlinks, 51
   text files, viewing, 34
Filesystem Hierarchy Standard (FHS), 47
filesystems, 5
   authentication and access control, 83
   backups and restores, 275–283
   ext3 filesystems, creating, 247
   file system IDs, 249
   hierarchical filesystems, 40
   Linux directory structure, 44–46
   live backups, 280
   mount options, 245
   mount permissions and security, 245
   mounting, 78–84
   navigation from the command-line, 43
   Reiser filesystems, creating, 247
   Windows clients, serving to (see Samba)
   Windows, compared to, 78
   Windows filesystem, access via Linux, 46
filters, 140
find command, 73–77
   search criteria, 74
   wildcards, 75
firewalls, 356–363
   allowed services, 358
   External, Internal, and Demilitarized zones, 357
   IPsec support, 359
   iptables command, 356
   logging level, 360
   logging of dropped packets, 360
   masquerading, 359, 361
   netfilters, 356
   nmap, testing with, 363
   SuSEfirewall2 file, 360
   YaST, configuration with, 357–363
fork( ) system call, 262
forward slash (/), 40

FQDN (fully qualified domain name), 302
fstab file, 243
FTP (File Transfer Protocol), 345
fully qualified domain names (FQDN), 302

G

gconf, 153
GDI printers, 15
gnokii, 169
GNOME, 2
    desktop configuration, 119–123
    gedit text editor, 35
    keyboard preferences, setting, 99
    Nautilus (see Nautilus)
graphics cards, configuring, 90
grep command, 137
    package lists, filtering with, 181
GRUB (GRand Unified Bootloader), 8, 66–72
    boot-time kernel options, adding, 67
    interactive options, disabling with password protection, 343–344
    lock command, 344
    md5crypt command, 343
    online manual, 72
    password command, 344
gzip, 214

H

hardening, 342
hardware compatibility database, 15
hcitool, 169
hierarchical filesystems, 40
home directory, 34
HOWTO documents, 31
HPLIP (HP Linux Imaging and Printing) driver project, 14
HTTP protocol, 331
httpd.conf file (Apache), 328
hypervisors, 411, 415

I

ifconfig, 283–284
iFolder and iFolder3, 172–176
iFolder3, 172
IMAP servers, 20
Immunix, 386
incremental backups, 281
index.html, 328
inetd, 232
info command, 29

init, 224
    /etc/inittab file, 226
    wait( ) system call and, 263
/init.d/rc script, 229
init.d/rc script, 229
initial ramdisk, 71
/inittab file, 226
inittab file, 226
inode numbers, 50
inodes, 50
installing SUSE, 1–12
    email, 16–21
    from DVD or CD distributions, 2
    installation screen, 3
    network card configuration, 21–25
    network configuration, 9
    partitioning, 4–6
    printer setup, 12–14
    software, selecting, 6
    super-user account, 9
    user accounts, adding, 10
    User Authentication Methods, 10
integrit, 386
intrusion detection, 380
    tripwire, 386
    (see also AIDE)
iostat, 272
ip command, 285–287
    command objects, 285
iproute2 package, 285
iptables command, 356
IPV6, turning off, 289
iwconfig, 161

J

Joy, Bill, 37

K

K links and S links, 229
    SUSE compared to RedHat, 229
KDE, 2
    desktop configuration, 104–119
    files, finding with kfind, 72
    Kate text editor, 35
    KDE control center, 98
        keyboard preferences, 98
        mouse configuration, 100
    KDE System Guard, 256
    KDEPrint handbook, 16
    Konqueror (see Konqueror)
    kwrite text editor, 35

keyboards, 97–99
    national differences in standards, 97
keys, 350
kill command, 260
killing processes, 258
Kmail, 16–18
Konqueror, 41–42
    file attributes, viewing or changing, 52–55
    file contents, viewing, 34
    manpages, accessing with, 29
    view modes, 41
ksysguard, 256
    ksysguardd daemon, 274
kwatch, 265

L

laptops, 155
    Bluetooth, 165–172
    desktop synchronization, 172–179
    power management, 155–159
        dual-booting and, 157
    suspend modes, 155
    wireless networking, 159–165
        card configuration via YaST, 160
        iwconfig, 161
less, 34
    browsing command output, 137
libzypp, 202
links, 50
Linux documentation, 27
Linux Documentation Project, 31
Linux Standards Base (LSB), 190
locate command, 76
lock command, 344
log files, 264–270
    kwatch, examining with, 265
    managing, 268
    selected files, 264
    syslog daemon, 266
    syslog-ng daemon, 266–268
    tail, examining with, 265
logcheck, 268
logging, xinetd, 237
logical partitions, 243
logical volumes, 248
    extending, 254
logins
    remote logins, 346
    root versus user, 11

logrep, 268
logrotate, 268
loopback address, 288
ls command, 34, 43
LSB (Linux Standards Base), 190
lvcreate, 281
lvm2, 249
    command-line tools, 252
lvscan, 253

M

magazine cover discs, 191
mail service, 334–341
    MAAs (Mail Access Agents), 335
    maildir format message store, 340
    mbox format message store, 339
    MTAs (mail transfer agents), 335
    MUAs (mail user agents), 334
    POP3 servers, 337
    qpopper, 336
    setting up a server, 336
    SMTP, 337
make command, 215, 219–223
Makefiles, 215, 221
manpages, 28
masquerading, 361
Master Boot Record (MBR), 70
master scripts, 228
MBR (Master Boot Record), 70
md5crypt command, 343
mice, 100–103
mingetty, 258
mobile phones, using as modems, 170
modal editors, 37
modems, using mobile phones as, 170
modprobe command, 281
    IPv6, turning off, 289
monitors
    configuring, 90
        damage, avoiding, 93
    manufacturers, models, and settings, 92
    multiheaded display configuration, 143–148
Mono, x, 172
    Banshee audio player, 126
    downloads, 173
more, 34
mount command, 46
    mount options for filesystems, 245
    mount points, 45, 80
        Windows mount points, 46
    mountd daemon, 312

mount command (*continued*)
    mounting filesystems, 78–84
        authentication and access control, 83
    permanent mounts, 81
mpstat, 273
multiheaded displays, 143–148
MultiSync, 169
mv command, 48

N

name resolution, 292–296, 301
    dig, 294
    DNS and BIND, 301
    named, 301
    nsswitch.conf file, 294
    resolvers, 293
    YaST, configuring with, 293
NAT (Network Address Translation), 362
Nautilus, 42–43
    file contents, viewing, 34
Nessus, 373–379
    client and server, 374
    client, performing scans with, 376
    NASL, 378
    plugins, 376
    required packages, 374
    scanner updates for new
        vulnerabilities, 379
    specifying target machines, 376
    SSL certificate, creating, 375
    starting the server, 376
    user accounts, 374
netapplet, 24
netfilters, 356
    rulesets, 356
Network Address Translation (NAT), 362
network cards, configuring, 21–25, 283–291
network configuration, 9
Network Manager, 9
networking (see DHCP)
NetworkManager, 24
NFS (Network File System), 308–314
    export options, 310
    exports, 308
    nfsd, mountd, and portmapper
        daemons, 312
    security issues, 314
    YaST, configuring with, 308
nfsd daemon, 312
nmap tool, 363
noarch, 184
nsswitch.conf file, 294

ntfsresize tool, 397
NVIDIA, 148
    multiheaded graphics cards, 143

O

OBEX (Object Exchange protocol), 168
od command, 40
online_update command, 202
open relays, 17
OpenGL, 153
OpenSSH, 346
    authentication, 347
    DNS spoofing warning, 347
    remote logins, 346
    (see also SSH)
orphans, 262

P

package management
    automatic updates, 201
    binary compared to source packages, 213
    command-line updates, 202
    dependencies, 193
    digital signatures, verifying, 211
    finding and choosing packages, 188–191
    installation from source code, 212–223
    installing from Internet archives, 196
    installing or updating RPMs, 191–197
    listing installed packages, 181
        filtering output, 181
    online updates, 199
    package file types, 183
    package formats, 180
        comparison, 187
    querying uninstalled packages, 184
    removing packages, 198–199
    rpm, 180–187
    structure of RPM files, 185
    verifying package integrity, 186
    y2pmsh command-line tool, 196
    YUM, 209–212
    ZENWorks, 202–208
paravirtualization, 416
partitions and partitioning, 4–6, 237–248
    creating from the command line, 245
    issues with power management on
        dual-boot machines, 157
    primary, extended, and logical
        partitions, 243
    root partition, 46
    type codes, 249

partprobe, 247
passphrase, 350
password command, 344
patches, 201
pathnames, 40
permissions, 368
PID, 256
Pierce, Benjamin, 177
pipe (|), 137
policies, 158
port forwarding, 355
port numbers, 232
portmapper daemon, 312
postfix, 334–341
    configuration, 336, 337
    defining aliases, 340
    service of multiple domains, 340
    (see also mail service)
power management, 155–159
    dual-boot machines and, 157
    powersaved, 157
    schemes and policies, 158
    suspend modes, 155
primary partitions, 243
Printer Type screen, 58
printers
    ESC/P printers, 15
    GDI printers, 15
    PCL printers, 15
    PostScript, 15
    remote printers, accessing, 57
    setting up, 12–14
    shared Windows printers, 59
private keys, 350
privilege specification, 369
processes, 255
    killing processes, 258
    monitoring, 256–262
        KDE System Guard, using, 256
        top, using, 258
        orphans and zombies, 262
        parent and child processes, 256, 262
prompt, 33
ps command, 260
public keys, 350

Q

Quinion, Michael, 98
quota command, 300
    (see also disk quotas)

R

RBAC (role-based access control), 368
rcp, 345
regular expressions, 138
Reiser filesystem, 5
    creating, 247
    (see also filesystems)
remote access (see VNC)
repquota command, 300
rescue media, 68
resolvers, 293
restore, 281
rfcomm, 170
rlogin, 345
rm command, 48
    -i and -r options, 48
role-based access control (RBAC), 368
root, 9
root partition, 46
root versus user logins, 11
rot13, 349
route and route add commands, 284
routing tables, 287
    examining, 284
rpm, 180–187
    importing public keys, 187
    installing or updating packages, 191–197
    listing installed packages, 181
        filtering output, 181
    package dependencies, 193
    querying uninstalled packages, 184
    removing packages, 198–199
    structure of RPM files, 185
    verifying package integrity, 186
RSA user authentication, 354
rsh, 345
r-star utilities, 345
rsync, 176
rug, 202–206
runlevels, 224
    services, matching to, 225

S

S links and K links, 229
    SUSE compared to RedHat, 229
Samba, 314–321
    client-side use, 319
    packages necessary for service, 315
    SWAT, configuration using, 315–319

sar, 273
sax2, 91–95
    configuration file, 94
schemes, 158
screenshots, capturing, 132–135
security
    access control (see access control)
    applications profiling (see AppArmor)
    boot-time password, setting, 343–344
    firewalls, 356–363
        testing, 363
        YaST, configuring with, 357–363
    hardening, 342
    intrusion detection (see AIDE)
    mount permissions and, 245
    remote logins (see SSH)
    root versus user logins, 11
    security level definition, 363–368
        chkstat utility, 366–368
        YaST, using, 363–366
    telnet, 345
    vulnerability assessment (see Nessus)
server authentication, 352
servers, 224
    boot-time services startup, 224–230
    monitoring, 270–275
    partitions, creating and
        mounting, 237–248
services
    boot-time startup, 224–230
    runlevels, matching to, 225
    starting and stopping manually, 230
    starting on demand (see xinetd)
session keys, 352
set user id flag, 83
setquota command, 299
share points, 311
shell, 33
SHMConfig, 102
SLED (SUSE Linux Enterprise Desktop), 148
smbmount, 84
SMTP servers, 17
SMTP (Simple Mail Transfer Protocol), 337
snapshot, 380
software packages, selecting, 6
sort command, 139
source code, 213
    packages, installing from, 212–223
        advantages, 213
        autoconf, 215
        build options specifying, 217–219

        builds, 215
        downloading, 214
        required development tools, 214
        source RPMs, 219–223
SSH, 344–356
    authentication, 347
    DNS spoofing warning, 347
    encryption process, 348–355
    OpenSSH, 346
    origins, 346
    public and private keys, 350
    remote logins, 346
    RSA user authentication, 354
    server authentication, 352
    session keys, 352
    ssh-keygen command, 353
    X forwarding, 355
standard input, standard output, and
    standard error, 140
startup scripts, 228
strings command, 39
su command, 372
submount, 84
sudo utility, 369–373
    aliases, 371
    privilege specification, 369
    set user ID bit, 372
    su contrasted with, 372
    sudoers file, 369–371
        defaults requiring deletion, 370
Sun Microsystems, 37
superblock, 82
super-user account, 9
SUSE installation
    automated installs with
        AutoYaST, 403–411
        control files, 403, 406–407
        custom scripts, adding, 407
        machine profiles, 408
        required packages, 403
    dual-boot system configuration (see
        Windows, dual-boot installation
        with Linux)
    over a network, 399–403
        Apache configuration for, 400
        CDs versus ISO images, 400
        installation server configuration, 399
        installs from a non-Linux server, 403
        installs from CDs, 400
        installs from ISO images, 402
SUSE Version 10.1, x
SuSEfirewall2 file, 360

SUSEWatcher, 201
swap space, 4
SWAT, 315–319
swatch, 268
symlinks (symbolic links), 51
synclient, 103
SyncML plugin, 169
syslog, 266
    syslogd service, 356
syslog-ng, 266–268
system administration, servers (see servers)
system cloning profile, 12
system load monitoring, 270–274
    remote systems, 274
system runlevels (see runlevels)

T

tail command, 139, 265
tar command, 214, 276
    incremental backups with, 281
    options, 276
    .tar archives (tarballs), 180, 214
targets, 219
telinit command, 231
telnet, 345
terminal emulation, 136
terminal windows, 33
text editors, 35
    modal editors, 37
tilde (~), 34, 214
top, 258–260, 273
touchpads, 102
Tripwire, 186, 386
trusted hosts, 345
ttylinux, 412

U

UNC (Universal Naming Convention), 80
Unison, 177
Unix, 33
unix2dos, 39
user accounts, 60–66
    management with YaST, 60
User Authentication Methods, 10
user versus root logins, 11
users, setting disk quotas for, 298
/usr directories, 46
usrquota mount option, 298

V

vi text editor, 35–39
video, 127
video acceleration support in Xgl, 152
viperdb, 386
virtual hosting, 332
virtual terminals, 33
virtualization, 411
    guests and hosts, 411
    hypervisors, 411
    (see also Xen)
vmstat, 272–274
VNC (Virtual Network Computing), 84–88
volume groups, 248
vulnerability assessment (see Nessus)

W

wait( ) system call, 262, 263
wc command, 138
web services (see Apache)
wildcards, 48, 141
Windows
    dual-boot installation with
            Linux, 393–399
        disk space allocation, 394
        /etc/fstab file, 395
        MBR (Master Boot Record), 397
        NTFS versus FAT filesystems, 394
        partitioning, 397
        retaining the Windows MBR, 398
        Windows installation, 394
        with pre-existing Windows
            installation, 396–398
    filesystem, access via Linux, 46
    Linux integration via Samba (see Samba)
wireless networking, 159–165
    cards without Linux drivers, 162
    iwconfig, 161
    YaST, configuration using, 159–163
wrapper scripts, 216

X

X servers, 89
    configuration files, 94
    configuration via sax2, 91–95
    service termination, 95
    X forwarding using SSH, 355
    Xgl (see Xgl)

Index | 429

Xen, 411–419
    booting up, 412
    configuration file, 413
    domains, 411
        domain configuration files, 416
    grub config file, editing of, 412
    hypervisor, 415
    logical volumes and, 418
    paravirtualization, 416
    required packages, 412
    root filesystem location, 414
    xentop utility, 419
    xm, 413
Xgl, 148–153
    ATI and, 148
    NVIDIA chipsets and, 148
xgnokii, 170
xinetd, 232–237
    configuration using YaST, 232–235
    inetd and, 232
    log files, 237
    xinetd.conf, 235
        examples of attributes, 236

Y

y2pmsh, 196
YaST
    Apache packages, installing, 327
    application profiles, creating with, 387
    AutoYaST system cloning profile, 12
    backups using, 277–279
        restores, 279
    Bluetooth, configuring, 165–168
    DHCP configuration using, 322–325
    DNS servers, configuring with, 303–307
    exported filesystems, mounting on a client, 311
    firewall configuration using, 357–363
    keyboard layout, choosing, 99
    Linux installation servers, configuring, 399
    logical volumes, creating with, 249
    name resolution, configuring with, 293
    network card configuration, 22
    NFS configuration, 308
    package manager, 184, 194–196
        online updates, 199–201
        packages, installing from Internet archives, 196
        removing packages, 198
    partitioning, 238–245
    remote printers, configuring, 58
    security configuration using, 363–366
    services and runlevels, matching, 225
    wireless network configuration, 159–163
    xinetd configuration, 232–235
Ylönen, Tatu, 346
YUM, 209–212

Z

ZENWorks, 202–208
    rug, 202–206
    zen-installer, zen-updater, and zen-remover, 206
    zmd, 207
zombies, 262

About the Author

Chris Brown has been using UNIX for more than 25 years, initially in his role as a Research Fellow at Sheffield University in the UK, where he carried out research into the use of tightly coupled multiprocessor systems for real-time processing of machine vision data. He has been a Linux enthusiast, user, and advocate for the last eight years and holds RedHat RHCE and Novell CLP certifications, in addition to B.A. and M.A. degrees from Cambridge University, and a Ph.D. in particle physics, which he hopes won't put you off reading his book.

Colophon

The cover image is from the *Dover Pictorial Archive*. The cover font is Adobe ITC Garamond. The text font is Linotype Birka; the heading font is Adobe Myriad Condensed; and the code font is LucasFont's TheSans Mono Condensed.

Better than e-books

Buy *SUSE Linux* and access the digital edition FREE on Safari for 45 days.

Go to www.oreilly.com/go/safarienabled
and type in coupon code LLMY-G64M-P1SN-23MH-F6AE

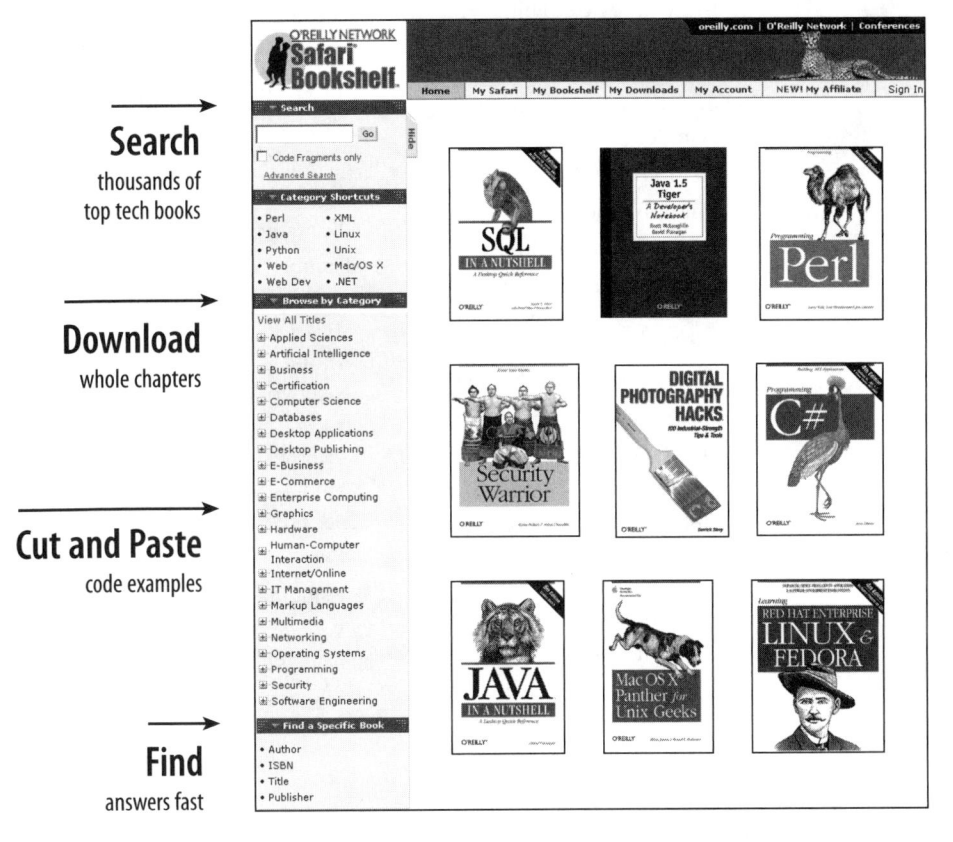

Search thousands of top tech books

Download whole chapters

Cut and Paste code examples

Find answers fast

Search Safari! The premier electronic reference library for programmers and IT professionals.

Related Titles from O'Reilly

Linux

Building Embedded Linux Systems

Building Secure Servers with Linux

The Complete FreeBSD, *4th Edition*

Even Grues Get Full

Exploring the JDS Linux Desktop

Extreme Programming Pocket Guide

GDB Pocket Reference

Knoppix Hacks

Knoppix Pocket Guide

Learning Red Hat Enterprise Linux and Fedora, *4th Edition*

Linux Annoyances for Geeks

Linux Cookbook

Linux Desktop Hacks

Linux Desktop Pocket Guide

Linux Device Drivers, *3rd Edition*

Linux in a Nutshell, *5th Edition*

Linux in a Windows World

Linux iptables Pocket Reference

Linux Multimedia Hacks

Linux Network Administrator's Guide, *3rd Edition*

Linux Pocket Guide

Linux Security Cookbook

Linux Server Hacks, *Volume 2*

Linux Unwired

Linux Web Server CD Bookshelf, *Version 2.0*

LPI Linux Certification in a Nutshell

Managing RAID on Linux

More Linux Server Hacks

OpenOffice.org Writer

Producing Open Source Software

Programming with Qt, *2nd Edition*

Root of all Evil

Running Linux, *5th Edition*

Samba Pocket Reference, *2nd Edition*

Test Driving Linux

Understanding Linux Network Intervals

Understanding the Linux Kernel, *3rd Edition*

Understanding Open Source & Free Software Licensing

User Friendly

Using Samba, *2nd Edition*

Version Control with Subversion

O'REILLY®

Our books are available at most retail and online bookstores.
To order direct: 1-800-998-9938 • *order@oreilly.com* • *www.oreilly.com*
Online editions of most O'Reilly titles are available by subscription at *safari.oreilly.com*